D1611586

A NEW HISTORY
OF THE UNITED STATES
An Inquiry Approach

Carnegie-Mellon Social Studies Curriculum
GENERAL EDITOR   EDWIN FENTON

A NEW HISTORY OF THE UNITED STATES
An Inquiry Approach

IRVING BARTLETT
Professor of History
Carnegie-Mellon University
Pittsburgh, Pennsylvania

EDWIN FENTON
Professor of History
Director, Social Studies Curriculum Center
Carnegie-Mellon University
Pittsburgh, Pennsylvania

DAVID FOWLER
Professor of History
Carnegie-Mellon University
Pittsburgh, Pennsylvania

SEYMOUR MANDELBAUM
Associate Professor of Urban History
University of Pennsylvania
Philadelphia, Pennsylvania

HOLT, RINEHART AND WINSTON, INC.
New York / Toronto / London / Sydney

ISBN: 0-03-091167-2
45678   071   987654321

Cover design: Marvin Goldman and Marilyn Bass
Text illustrations: maps by Danmark and Michaels, Incorporated;
charts by June and Stephen Negrycz

Photo research by Ellen W. McBride

CONTENTS

Chapter 3 The Maturing Colonies, 1700-1763

Chapter 4 The American Revolution

Chapter 5 The New Government

Chapter 9   The Spirit of Reform

Chapter 10   Slavery in the South

Chapter 11   National Growth and Its Effect on the Environment

Chapter 12   Civil War and Reconstruction, 1850-1877

Chapter 13   The Growth of Industry

Chapter 14   The Transformation of Agriculture and Rural Society

Chapter 15   Blacks and Whites in the Southern States

Chapter 22   The 1920's: Values and Behavior

Chapter 23   The New Deal

Chapter 24   Years of Peace and War, 1921-1945

Chapter 25   The Cold War, 1945-1974

Chapter 26   Equal Opportunity in a Democratic Society

Chapter 27 The Present and the Future

Maps

Charts and Graphs

TO THE STUDENT

This book is a new kind of textbook. Most social studies textbooks you have used in the past probably contained information about one subject, such as civics or geography. The textbooks were usually written by one or two authors who organized material into chapters, each with an important theme. The authors illustrated these books with pictures, graphs, and charts, each with a caption beneath it to explain what the illustration showed. You read or examined this material to learn the facts and generalizations it contained.

Instead of twenty or thirty chapters written by one or two authors, this textbook has 106 readings arranged in twenty-seven chapters. Each reading contains at least one piece of source material taken from a newspaper, a magazine, a book, government document, or other publication, or an article written especially for this course. Each chapter has at least one historical essay. The essays link the historical periods and summarize information contained in the readings.

An introduction which connects one reading to another, and study questions which will help guide your search for information, precede most selections. A question for thought follows each reading. It is intended to make you reflect on the connections among the readings. In addition, most readings contain two or more valuing questions, identified by the mark ▶. These questions are designed to help you consider how changes or new developments cause value dilemmas for individuals. They may also cause value dilemmas for you.

Numerous illustrations designed, like the written materials, to provoke careful thought appear throughout the book. In addition, the *Classroom Support Unit* which accompanies the course contains silent and sound filmstrips, recordings, picture cards, transparencies, tests, and dittoed hand-outs. Your teacher will use these materials from time to time. He or she will also probably encourage you to work individually or as a member of a small group on special materials designed for individual and group activities.

All these materials have been chosen or written with great care. Instead of merely memorizing facts or generalizations, you will be asked to use them to identify problems, develop hypotheses or tentative answers to questions, gather information and come to your own conclusions. Throughout this course, you will be challenged to think for yourself and to make up your own mind.

Most teachers assign one reading from this book for each night's homework. Because most classes meet about 180 times a year and there are only 106 readings in the book, there will be days when no readings from the book are assigned. There are many ways to use the extra days. Some teachers prefer to move quickly through the readings. They then develop separate activities for the remaining weeks. Others prefer to build a variety of related activities into each chapter. They assign supplementary readings, study current events, develop research projects, give tests, or hold individual conferences with students. Some teachers also devote considerable time to individual and group activities.

Today the United States ranks as the most influential nation in the world. For many years, the ideals of the American Revolution inspired imitators in lands far removed from North America. But admiration and envy are mixed with hatred and scorn. Many people in developing nations believe that the United States has turned its back on the great revolutionary tradition in which it was born. Many of its own citizens feel that the United States has abandoned its ideals. Unless people know the long history of their nation, they cannot hope to understand its place in the modern world. Nor can they understand themselves if they are cut off from the past which shaped them.

Instead of trying to pack this volume with factual information, the authors have chosen to select vital elements of the American tradition and to explore them in depth. The historical essays and time lines link the readings together and provide coherence for the American story. We welcome you to an exciting exploration of the American past, confident that it is worth studying, both for its own sake and for the insights it will provide for life in the second half of the twentieth century.

Edwin Fenton
General Editor
Carnegie-Mellon Social Studies Curriculum

HOW TO USE THIS BOOK

The textbook for *A New History of the United States* consists of 106 readings which have been edited from published works or written especially for this course. Each reading follows a common pattern:

1. *The introduction.* Each introduction relates a reading to other readings in the course and supplies the essential background information.
2. *Study questions.* A few study questions call your attention to the most important points of the reading so that you can think about them in preparation for class discussion.
3. *The article or source material.* Each reading contains one or more documents, newspaper accounts, articles from magazines, or other forms of written material.
4. *A thought question.* One question designed to provoke thought about the meaning of a reading appears at the end of each lesson.

You are expected to read each day's lesson and to take notes on it before you come to class. Since your teacher will distribute dittoed material from time to time, you ought to get a three-ring looseleaf notebook which can hold both the material to be distributed and your homework and classroom notes.

Note-taking is a vital skill. We suggest that you read and take notes (using ink so that notes will be legible at final examination time) on the readings in the following manner:

1. *Write the reading number and title at the top of a piece of notebook paper.*
2. *Skim the entire reading.* Read the first sentence in each paragraph of the introduction. Next, read the study questions and get them fixed in your mind. Finally, read the first sentence in each paragraph of the article or source material. When you have finished, try to state in your own words what the lesson for the day is all about. Skimming such as this should never take longer than a few minutes.
3. *Read the introduction and take running notes.* Do *not* read first and then read again for notes. Do *not* underline or mark the textbook in any way. Write down the major ideas from the introduction and any supporting evidence that seems particularly important. You need not use complete sentences, but remember that you may wish to study from the notes later, so take down enough information to make notes meaningful.

4. *Read the article or source material carefully and take running notes.* Do *not* read first and then read again for notes. Do *not* underline or mark the textbook in any way. Take the same sort of notes you took for the introduction. Put any conclusions you draw in parentheses to show that they are your own ideas.
5. *Go over your notes, underlining key ideas or words.* This procedure is the best way to begin learning the information in the lesson.
6. *Try to answer the question found at the end of the reading.* When you have finished studying your notes, try to answer the question that follows the reading. This question will always require you to think independently about the subject you have been studying. Do not write out the answers to this thought question. Think it through so that you will be prepared to discuss it in class.

Two additional study techniques will be useful. First, keep a vocabulary list in which to enter all new words and their definitions. In many cases, vocabulary words have been defined in the textbook in marginal notes. Second, keep your class notes and your reading notes on a lesson together in your notebook so that you can review for tests without flipping through a mass of paper to find material on the same subject.

Your teacher will help you if you have trouble with this note-taking technique. He or she may occasionally spend time in class to demonstrate good note-taking techniques and will criticize your notes in an individual conference if you request one. Do not hesitate to ask for help.

INDIVIDUAL AND
GROUP ACTIVITIES

On the next several pages, you will find descriptions of forty-five activities designed for individual or group work. They are divided into three groups: family history, community history, and ethnic history. Each activity has been planned to help you explore an aspect of your personal or community history and to report about it in some creative way. Many of the activities require you to interview people or to obtain information from local resources. If your school has purchased the *Classroom Support Unit* for *A New History of the United States*, your teacher will find an *Individual and Group Activity Component* inside it. This component may also be purchased as a separate item. Your teacher will tell you how to find detailed instructions for each activity in the *Student Book of Activities and Readings* contained in the *Individual and Group Activity Component*. He or she will also explain procedures for using this material. From time to time, teachers may also make supplementary assignments of their own, independent of the *Individual and Group Activity Component*.

FAMILY HISTORY

Before doing any of the activities in this section, listen to the recording concerned with family history. You will find it with the materials for individual and group activities. It will help you to understand what people investigate when they study family history.

Activity 1: Dating Behavior in Three Generations First describe your own dating behavior—where you go, what you do, what you wear, and so forth. Then ask your parents and your grandparents to describe dating behavior when they were your age. Report your findings by means of a recording in which you compare dating behavior and speculate about why it changed, or by means of a chart laid out in columns to make comparisons easy.

Describe in detail an actual weekday and a Sunday as you spend them during a typical week. Then ask your parents and grandparents to describe a parallel weekday and Sunday when they were your age. Report about how everyday life has changed and indicate why.

Investigate the effect of technology on everyday life in the United States by describing how people in your family do such chores as dishes, shopping, laundry, heating the house, keeping food cold, and so forth. Then find out how your parents' and your grandparents' families did these chores. Report in some creative way.

Using dittoed copies of the study guide found with the materials for individual and group activities, take or mail a list of the twentieth-century Presidential and Vice-Presidential candidates to all of the relatives you can contact. Ask them to check the candidates they voted for in each election and to tell you why they voted as they did. Then make a family voting profile to present in a creative way.

Compile an occupational history of your family for as many generations as you can obtain information. Many people have had a large number of jobs in several farm areas, towns, cities, or countries. Try to compile a full list of jobs from both the men and women in your family and present it in an interesting way.

Develop a family tree for as many generations as you can gather information. Enter the names of people, where they came from, and any other interesting information you can gather.

Write descriptions of your two best friends and tell why you like them so much. Then ask your parents, grandparents, and other members of your family to describe their best friends when they were sixteen and tell why they liked them. Report about whether the people in your family from different generations looked for the same characteristics in friends.

Find out from parents, grandparents, and other relatives what they read for pleasure when they were your age. What were their favorite books and magazines? What did they read that they did not tell their parents about? Use this information and knowledge of your own reading habits to describe family reading patterns over generations.

Most families have special family occasions and ceremonies—special ways to celebrate religious holidays, birthdays, weddings. funerals, national holidays, and so forth. Trace some of these ceremonies through three generations of your family. You might make a scrapbook to present your findings since many families will often have pictures of several generations.

Family photograph albums often contain pictures of several generations of people. They show a wide variety of dress, hairstyles, and other elements of personal appearance. Put together a family photograph album which demonstrates changing personal appearance for several generations.

First, write a description of your most memorable vacation whether or not you took it with your family. Then ask your parents and grandparents to tell you about their favorite vacation when they were adolescents. Present this information, with pictures if possible, as an account of continuity and change in leisure time activities in your family.

Many families have family artifacts—objects which have been passed down through generations. Organize a group of students all of whom have family artifacts. Bring the artifacts to class and show them to your classmates. Comment about their significance to your family's history.

Interview your parents and grandparents about their religious beliefs and the religious practices they remember when they were your age. Then write a history of religion in your family. Comment on how beliefs and practices today are similar to or different from what they used to be.

Interview your parents, grandparents, and other relatives. Find out about their ethnic ties and feelings and trace them in your family through the generations. Report, in some creative way, how you are tied to ethnic origins.

Find out what issues your parents agreed or disagreed with your grandparents about, and how your grandparents got along with your great-grandparents. What did each generation think of its parents? An account of the information you gather can become a miniature history of the relationships of parents and adolescents in recent American history.

COMMUNITY HISTORY

With the materials for individual and group activities, you will find a recording on community history. Listen to it before doing any of the activities in this section.

Before beginning a historical study of your community, familiarize yourself with available sources of information about it. Then select one information source. Use the study guide for this activity to determine the type and extent of data collected there and the availability of the information. Report your findings to the class. Exchange information about sources of community history with other members of your class.

Make or obtain two copies of an outline map of your community. Label one map 1910 and the other for the present year. Indicate the placement of major residential, manufacturing, and commercial centers on each map. Also sketch in transportation routes which connect major areas. Try a similar map of your community for 1870 if you can acquire the necessary information. If you work on this activity as a group, let each person develop one of the two or three maps. Then meet together to write a brief explanation, hypothesizing about the reasons for the changes illustrated by your maps.

Arrange to visit a local historical site individually, as a small group, or with the whole class. While on your field trip, find out what you can about the history of the preservation and maintenance of this site. Take pictures and pick up any pamphlets describing the site and its history. Compile your information into a scrapbook, bulletin board display, or collage.

When Europeans came to America, they encountered the native Indian population. Relations between the Europeans and Indians usually changed Indian life. In most areas, whites eventually took Indian land and dominated Indian life and culture. Using available community resources, write a report which traces the history of the Indians who lived in your region.

The Women's Liberation Movement has increased interest in the role of women in American life. Find out about the economic role of women in your community. Investigate the records of your school system, the local government, or a large business for the years 1900, 1935, and the latest available year to find out how many women were employed and at what jobs. With the information you have gathered, make a chart or diagram to demonstrate how the economic role of women has changed in your community or in one business.

What was school like for students who lived in your community twenty or forty years ago? Interview a teacher who started teaching twenty years ago and one who began his or her career forty years ago. Ask them what their classrooms were like then. Have them compare past conditions to the present. Either tape your interviews and write a study guide for others to use while listening to your tape or summarize your findings in the form of a chart which shows how education has changed in your community.

Activity 22: Housing in Your Community	Basic housing styles in an area vary over time due to changing lifestyles and conditions. The pictures in the *Student Book of Activities and Readings* illustrate some of these differences. Photograph single family houses and apartment buildings in your locale which were built at different times including the present. Find out what you can about each of the dwellings you have photographed. Compile your information in a photo essay in which you discuss the differences in construction, size, amount of surrounding land, out-buildings, and the like.
Activity 23: Local Government Income and Expenditures	One way to look at the role of local government is to examine its sources of income and the manner in which it spent its money. Select three years 1900, 1935, and the latest year for which information is available—to investigate. Then collect data on government income and expenditures for these years. Display your information in a series of charts like the examples in the *Student Book of Activities and Readings* or in a colorful display which clearly illustrates the changing role of government in your community.
Activity 24: Business Changes in Your Community	Interview the owner of a well-established business in your community, such as a drug store, clothing shop, or factory. Find out how the business has changed over the past ten, twenty, or fifty years. Collect as much data about the business as you can. You may even be able to obtain some old photographs of the physical operation and some old newspaper advertisements for the store's goods. Either tape your interview and write a study guide for others to use as they listen to your tape or make a display using the photographs and advertisements you have found.
Activity 25: Civil Rights Action in Your Community	Nationally, the period after World War II brought about many changes for members of American minority groups. Protests, new laws, court decisions, and violence all played a part in the expansion of civil rights for minority groups. The study guide which accompanies this activity lists key civil rights events occurring nationally since 1945. Interview someone in your community who took part in one of these national events or was active in extending civil rights for local minorities. Find out how your community has been affected by national civil rights events.
Activity 26: Settlement of Your Community	What originally caused people to settle in your community? Find out who the first settlers in your area were and why they came. What kinds of businesses did they establish? How were political decisions made then? What influences of these early settlers still exist in your community? Write an essay in which you report on the early settlement of your community.
Activity 27: A Main Street in Your Community	A community's large commercial streets are a vital reflection if its character. Collect and analyze photographs like the ones accompanying this activity in the *Student Book of Activities and Readings*. The photographs should show a main street of your town at different times in its history. Assemble

the photographs for a display with your commentary hypothesizing about the changes and developments they illustrate.

A history of your local church or synagogue reflects a great deal about the development of the community. Talk to clergy, other officials, and older members of the church or synagogue. Investigate any available records. Find out how and why the church or synagogue was founded, whether or not it has moved, how the membership has varied, how the group has been supported, and what important services it has provided for its members. Summarize your findings in a written report.

Arrange an interview with an official of juvenile court to obtain information about teen-age crime and law enforcement in your area. Find out about the rate of teen-age crime, the most commonly committed crimes, and their usual punishments. Also ask about how the rights and trial procedures for juvenile offenders have changed during your community's history. Summarize your findings in a chart or a report or play the tape of your interview for your class.

Interesting events such as strikes and famous murders have occurred in all towns. Choose one such happening from your community's past. Gather information from newspapers, eyewitness accounts, town records, and other sources. Sort and organize your information and then write a history of this famous local event.

ETHNIC HISTORY

Ethnic history is the subject of the third recording that you will find among the materials for individual and group activities. Listen to it before doing any of the activities in this section.

Find someone who knows how to do ethnic dances. Then recruit classmates and friends for an evening or two in which they will learn how to do one or two dances.

Study the dress of different ethnic groups. You can present your findings in one of several ways: by organizing a fashion show, making a portfolio of drawings, or making a slide show by using a copy camera and pictures in books.

Activity 33:
Ethnic Music

Develop a report about ethnic music. You can report in one or more of four ways: by playing and/or singing yourself, by finding someone else to play the music, by bringing in records for the class to hear, or by interviewing people who listen to programs of ethnic music over the radio.

Activity 34:
Ethnic Celebrations

Report on an ethnic picnic, dance, festival, parade, or other community celebration by taking pictures and/or making a recording. Present your report by making a slide show, a sound·slide show, a bulletin board display, scrapbook, or collage.

Activity 35:
An Ethnic Banquet

With a group of your classmates, plan, cook, and enjoy a banquet of ethnic foods. Hand out recipes so that everyone who takes part can learn how to cook the dishes they eat at the banquet.

Activity 36:
A Picture Essay
About an Ethnic
Neighborhood

Find a guide to take you through an ethnic neighborhood and help you to plan a visual display about it. Then take pictures or make sketches and present them to the class in a creative way.

Activity 37:
Making an Ethnic
Map of the Class

Determine the ethnic origins of the four grandparents of all the members of the class. Then place a symbol for each grandparent on a map of the world.

Activity 38:
Producing a Skit
About Emigration

Find other students who enjoy dramatics. Write a one-act play about the decision to emigrate. Then present the play, complete with settings and. costumes if you wish, to the class.

Activity 39:
What Was It Like
Where They Came
From?

Find out what town or section of a foreign country your ancestors came from. Then do some research at home or in the library about the area. Write a report about it. This report can become the beginning of a family history.

Activity 40:
Reporting About an
Ethnic Educational
Institution

Find a private school or after-school classes run by an ethnic organization. Interview students, parents, and school officials to find out what this educational institution contributes to their lives.

Activity 41:
Reporting About
Fraternal Associations

Find a fraternal association whose members all belong to one ethnic group. Interview several older members to find out why they joined the organization and what it means to them. Either prepare tape recordings of your interviews or write a report.

Activity 42:
Before and After
Pictures

Try to find pictures of your ancestors before they emigrated and after they had settled for a number of years in the United States. Arrange a display of the pictures to accompany an essay or poem about what it must have been like to change from one way of living to another.

xxviii

Find someone who has letters from relatives in their homeland. Get them to translate the letters if you cannot read the language. Then write a short essay about what these letters mean to the people who write and receive them.

Find an ethnic newspaper and someone to translate parts of it to you if you do not read the language yourself. Concentrate on news of the ethnic community. Develop a bulletin board or poster display to show what you have learned.

Find the customary greetings exchanged by people from all over the world, preferably from the countries from which your ancestors and those of your classmates came. Then present them on a poster or in some other creative way.

Americans and Europeans

STATING THE ISSUE

Americans today are the product of the mingling of many peoples over many centuries. The first inhabitants of what is now the United States arrived thousands of years ago. They had emigrated from Asia across the Bering Straits. Less than five hundred years ago, these peoples lived in hundreds of tribal groups scattered across the continent.

Then new peoples—Europeans—arrived to join them in occupying the land. These newcomers came to dominate the native Americans—whom they called Indians—and to occupy the entire continent. They recruited large numbers of Africans as laborers, bringing them to America as captives and keeping most of them in slavery until 1865. Millions of other European emigrants were followed by emigrants from Asia, Central America, and the Caribbean area. Where perhaps fewer than 1 million Indians lived in the late fifteenth century, more than 200 million Americans live today. Only a small proportion of these Americans claim either full or part-Indian ancestry, however.

Chapter 1 examines the first contacts between Indians and Europeans. These contacts worked to oust or exterminate most of the Indians. But why was that the outcome? Why did not the two groups usually amalgamate by intermarrying? Or why did they not usually assimilate, with one group adopting the culture of the other, or each group taking on some of the other's way of life? Or why, even, did they not accommodate to each other's presence by living separate lives in separate cultures? Readings 1 through 3 examine these questions. The chapter ends with an essay summing up the era of exploration and colonization by the Europeans.

1

1400 1500 1600 1700 1800 1900 2000

1416 Prince Henry the Navigator establishes school of navigation
1487-88 Bartholomeu Dias is first European to round the Cape of Good Hope
1492 Christopher Columbus lands on island of San Salvador
1498 Vasco da Gama is first European to reach India by sea
1500 Pedro Cabral discovers Brazilian coast
1513 Juan Ponce de León claims Florida for Spain

1542 Alvar Nuñez Cabeza da Vaca publishes memoirs of explorations of Gulf Coast
1585 Sir Walter Raleigh sends first group of settlers to Roanoke Island
1603 Samuel de Champlain explores St. Lawrence River
1609 Henry Hudson explores Hudson River
1675-76 King Philip's War is fought

1 THE INDIANS MEET THE EUROPEANS

These readings about cultural contacts focus first on the Indians' meetings with the Spanish and English. These two European groups eventually took possession of most of North America.

The English and Spanish ways of life differed somewhat. For example, the English were mainly Protestant and the Spanish were mainly Catholic. Indian ways of life differed too. The Abnaki tribe of northern New England lived mainly by hunting, fishing, and gathering fruits, nuts, and berries. But most tribes farther south along the Atlantic coast got most of their food through agriculture, usually by growing corn. The biggest differences, however, were between the cultures of the Europeans and those of the Indians. Here are five of these differences.

First, while both Spain and England were Christian, the Indians were not. Religious systems in both Spain and England were highly organized. They shared a large body of formal beliefs as well as the conviction that non-believers should be brought into Christianity. The Indians did not share one religious system. Different groups and different individuals had differing ideas about the world of the spirit. And Indians were not interested in making converts.

Second, Spain and England had governments which were much more centralized and powerful than those of the Indian groups they encountered in North America. European governments tried to enforce their rule and systems of justice over wide areas, and to demand primary loyalty to the king or queen. Indian governments were generally organized on a smaller scale.

Third, Europeans held land privately while the Indians did not. Although the king or queen ruled in England and Spain, he or she governed territory which belonged mainly to private persons. Such property was often passed along from father to son. But more and more of it could be bought and sold freely by individuals. Among the Indians, hunting and fishing tribes held their territory in common. Agricultural tribes often granted the temporary right to farm a small plot of land to a family. But if the land became unused it could be farmed by someone else.

Fourth, Europeans traded more than the Indians did. Although the economies of England and Spain were still mainly agricultural, both peoples—especially the English—had begun to turn their energies toward trade and manufacturing. Trade and manufacturing, like farming, flourished best with peace and safe roads, as well as a stable government.

Finally, the Europeans had more advanced technologies than the Indians. They used metals to make guns, other weapons, armor, and tools. They developed new sailing ships and navigational instruments which enabled them to brave unknown seas. And they spread their knowledge quickly by common languages reproduced on printing presses. The Indians, however, still used tools made of stone and wood.

These cultural differences between Europeans and Indians were important. But none of the differences meant that the contacts of these groups would necessarily have a given result, such as extermination or amalgamation. It is necessary to look carefully at the historical evidence to see how significant the cultural differences were, and to learn what resulted from them. The two documents which follow provide some of this evidence. As you read, keep the following questions in mind:

1. In what important ways did Cabeza de Vaca and Heriot find Indians different from Europeans?
2. According to these two accounts, in what ways were people from these two cultures similar to each other?

ARX CAROLINA.

1

2

The four pictures on these two pages show an Indian, a Spaniard, an Indian village in North Carolina, and an English settlement there. Would contact between the people and cultures pictured here be likely to lead to amalgamation, accommodation, assimilation, or extermination? Why?

FERDINANDO CORTES
CAVATO DA VN ORIGINALE FATTO INAZI
CHEI SI PORTASSI ALLA CONQVISTA DEL MESSICO

3

Their rype corne

Their greene corne

Corne newly sprong

Their sitting at meate

The place of solemne prayer

The house wherein the Tombe of their Herounds standeth

SECOTON

A Ceremony in their prayers w
strange restures and songs dansing
abowt postes carued on the topps
lyke mens faces.

4

5

A Spaniard in Texas

In April 1528, a Spanish expedition landed near Tampa Bay to take possession of Florida and to explore the mainland. The expedition met with difficulties and finally disaster. Some of its members sailed along the Gulf coast towards what is now Texas. There, their boats capsized on an island near the coast. Four remarkable men lived to tell the story. Three were Spaniards and one was a black from Arabia named Estevanico. They lived with the Indians of the coastal region for nearly six years. Then they began an eighteen-month journey through Texas into western Mexico, where they found Spanish settlements. The following observations about Indians in Texas are from the narrative published by one of the Spanish survivors, Alvar Nunez Cabeza de Vaca, in 1582, after his return to Spain.

The Narrative of Alvar Nunez Cabeza de Vaca, in Spanish Explorers in the Southern United States, Frederick W. Hodge, ed. (New York: Charles Scribner's Sons, 1907), pp. 50-52, 83-85. Language simplified and modernized.

Malhado means misfortune in Spanish.

The roots Cabeza de Vaca spoke of probably had to be dried, and perhaps cooked, before they could be eaten.

▶ Most doctors try to keep old, sick people alive as long as possible. Sometimes old men and women live for months or even years in comas before dying. Should society encourage this practice? Or should society adopt the attitudes of these Indians toward death?

To this island we gave the name Malhado. The people we found there are large and well formed. They have no other arms than bows and arrows. In the use of these they are very skilled. The men have one of the nipples on their chests bored from side to side. And some have both. They wear a piece of cane about a foot long and the thickness of two fingers in each nipple. They have the lower lip also bored. They wear in it a piece of cane the thickness of half a finger. Their women are used to great toil. They stay on the island from October to the end of January. Their food then is the root I have spoken of, got from under the water in November and December. They have traps of cane and take fish only in this season. Afterwards they live on the roots. At the end of February, they go elsewhere to seek food. Then the root is beginning to grow and is not good to eat.

Those people love their children the most of any in the world. They treat them with the greatest mildness. When a son dies, everyone weeps with the parents and relatives. The wailing continues for a whole year. They begin before dawn every day. The parents mourn first and after them the whole town. They do the same at noon and at sunset. After a year of mourning has passed, the rites of the dead are performed. Then they wash and purify themselves. They lament all the dead in this manner, except the aged, for whom they show no regret. They say that their time has passed, that they would no longer enjoy life if they lived, and that if they lived they would take food from the young. Their custom is to bury the dead, unless they have been medicine men. These they burn. While the fire kindles, they dance and celebrate until the bones become powder. At the end of a year the funeral honors are celebrated. Everyone takes part in them. They present the powdered ashes of the dead in water for the relatives to drink.

Every man has a recognized wife. The medicine men, however, may have two or three wives. Among these wives exist the greatest friendship and harmony.

From the time a daughter marries, all that her husband kills in hunting or catches in fishing, the woman brings to the house of her father, without daring to eat or take any part of it. From there food is taken to the husband. From that time neither her father nor mother may enter her husband's house. He cannot enter theirs, nor the houses of their children. Nor may the husband and his wife's family look at each other, or speak to each other. But the wife has liberty to speak to the parents and relatives of her husband.

Nearly all societies have some taboos against marriage or sexual relations between close relatives. In some, such as this one, the taboo was extended to prevent social contact between a man and his wife's family.

If any one falls sick in the desert, and cannot keep up with the rest, the Indians leave him to perish, unless it be a son or a brother. Him they will assist, even to carrying him on their back. Men who are childless leave their wives when they have important disagreements. And immediately they connect themselves with whom they please. Those who have children, however, remain with their wives and never abandon them. When they dispute and quarrel in their towns, they strike each other with their fists. They fight until exhausted. And then they separate. Sometimes they are parted by the women going between them. The men never interfere.

While I was among the Aguenes, their enemies came suddenly at midnight. The enemies fell upon them, killed three and wounded many, so that they ran from their houses to the fields. As soon as they found that their assailants had gone, they returned to pick up all the arrows the others had shot. Following after them in the most stealthy manner possible, they came that night to their dwellings without their presence being suspected. At four o'clock in the morning the Aguenes attacked them. They killed five, and wounded numerous others. And they made them flee from their houses, leaving their bows with all they possessed. In a little while, the wives of the Quevenes came to them and formed a treaty whereby the parties became friends. The women, however, are sometimes the cause of war. People who are enemies assassinate at night and treat each other cruelly unless they are related.

The Aguenes, or Doguenes, were a tribe of the Texas coastal region.

The Quevenes, or Guevenes, were another coastal tribe.

An Englishman in Virginia

Sir Walter Raleigh was an official at the court of Queen Elizabeth. He made two determined attempts to establish English settlements in the region he named Virginia. Both were on Roanoke Island, off North Carolina. And both failed. Thomas Heriot, a member of the first colony and an employee of Raleigh, wrote an account of the colony, the local Indians, and the new land. He tried to assure prospective settlers that they had no reason to fear the Indians. Excerpts of his account follow.

Thomas Heriot, **A brief and true report of the new found land of Virginia . . .,** in **The Principal Navigations, Voyages, Traffiques & Discoveries of the English Nation . . .,** Richard Hakluyt, comp. (Glasgow: James MacLehose and Sons, 1904), VIII, pp. 374, 375-376, 377, 378, 382-383. Language simplified and modernized.

Copper was the only metal possessed by the Indians. They used it chiefly for ornaments.

Witch hazel is a shrub which grew along the eastern seacoast of North America.

Wiroans, sometimes spelled werowance, was the name for chief in the local Indian language.

▶ In a story of creation, such as this one or such as that of Adam and Eve, does the fact that one sex was created first mean that it is superior to the other?

The native inhabitants are clothed with loose mantles made of deer skins. They wear aprons of the same around their middles. And all else is naked. They are about as tall as most Englishmen. They have no edged tools or weapons of iron or steel to threaten us. Nor do they know how to make any. Those weapons that they have are only bows made of witch hazel, arrows of reeds, and flat edged clubs of wood about a yard long. They have nothing to defend themselves but shields made of bark, and some armor made of sticks held together with thread.

In some places in the country, only one town belongs to the government of a Wiroans or chief lord. In some others, chiefs own two or three towns. Still others own many more. The greatest Wiroans that we had dealings with had only eighteen towns in his government. And he was able to command no more than seven or eight hundred fighting men. The language of every government is different from any other. The farther apart they are, the greater is the difference.

Compared to us they are poor people. Because they do not know how to use our things, they often value trinkets more than useful articles. Nevertheless, in their own way they seem very ingenious. For although they have no such tools, nor any such crafts, sciences, or arts as we do, the things they make are of high quality. The more they come to admire our knowledge and crafts, the more probable it is that they will desire our friendship and love. Thus it may be hoped, if good government is used, that they may soon be brought to civilization and true religion.

They believe there are many gods, which they call Mantoac. But they believe that they are of different kinds and importance. They believe there is only one chief and great God, who has existed throughout eternity. First, they say, were made waters. Out of these the gods made all kinds of creatures both visible or invisible.

For mankind, they say woman was made first. By the working of one of the gods she conceived and brought forth children. And thus they say have their beginning. But how many years or ages have passed since, they cannot tell. They have no letters or other such means as we have to keep records of the happenings of times past. They have only tradition from father to son.

Many of our things, such as sea compasses, the power of the magnet to attract iron, guns, hooks, writing and reading, and spring-clocks that seemed to go by themselves, were strange to them. They thought these were the works of gods rather than of men. This made many of them think that they could learn the truth of God and religion from us, whom God so specially loved.

FOR THOUGHT:

How easy or difficult would it be for the Indians and Europeans described in these two passages to amalgamate? Why?

2 WAR AND
THE MEETING
OF CULTURES

Warfare between Indians and Europeans broke out sooner or later in nearly every area where both groups lived. The stronger the Europeans had become in an area, the more probable it was that the Indians would suffer disastrous losses of life and political control. However, the reasons for such wars, and the results of those wars, were often complicated rather than simple.

King Philip's War in southern New England offers valuable evidence about the relationship between war and the meeting of cultures. Fighting broke out in June 1675, between outlying settlements of Plymouth Colony and the neighboring Wampanoag tribe. Other Indian tribes and other English colonies soon became involved. Both sides suffered heavy losses. But within a year the English crushed forever the power of their opponents.

Plymouth Colony and the Wampanoags had been allies for more than forty years. Plymouth wanted peace, and the chance to buy land and furs from the Indians. The Wampanoags wanted Plymouth's tiny army, with its firearms, to help protect them against the hostile Narragansett tribe. They also wanted or needed firearms, cloth, tools, liquor, and other goods from the English.

By 1675 conditions had changed. The old Wampanoag chief, Massasoit, was long dead. His son Metacomet, called Philip by the English, was restless. Strong evidence suggests that Philip was trying to draw the Narragansetts and other nearby tribes into a conspiracy to attack Plymouth and probably other English settlements. Warnings came to Plymouth from several directions. One warning came from an Indian who had been converted to Christianity and educated by the English, and who served both Philip as an interpreter and the English as an informant. When this man was found dead, apparently the victim of violence, Plymouth officials arrested, tried, and executed three Wampanoag braves on the testimony of another Indian who said that he had witnessed the crime. Philip did not attempt to intervene.

Blood flowed two weeks later. The first person killed may have been an Indian. Amid rumors of war and glimpses of apparently hostile groups of Indians, some outlying settlers abandoned their homes. One English writer reported that an Indian caught looting a deserted house in the little settlement of Swansea was shot and killed on June 23. Whether or not this happened, bands of Indians killed nine Englishmen at or near Swansea the next day. And the war was on.

Three excerpts dealing with King Philip's War follow. One offers some contemporary evidence about the causes of the war. The others

9

give the opinions of two modern historians about the causes and meaning of the war. Consider these questions as you read:

1. Does John Easton's account reveal a principal reason why the Wampanoags were angry at the Plymouth settlers?
2. In the modern accounts by Leach and Vaughan, how important was land as a cause of war? Do the two authors differ?

Wampanoag Indians State Their Grievances

The Rhode Island Colony adjoined both Plymouth and the Wampanoag tribal territory. About a week before fighting broke out in 1675 Rhode Island's leaders tried in vain to persuade the Indians to halt their preparations for war. John Easton, deputy governor of Rhode Island, and four other men arranged to meet Philip in his own territory. The chief was unarmed. However, he was accompanied by forty armed braves. Easton's account of the Wampanoags' complaints against the Plymouth colonists follows.

A Relacion of the Indyan Warre, by Mr. Easton, of Roade Isld., 1675, in Narratives of the Indian Wars, 1675-1699, Charles H. Lincoln, ed. (New York: Charles Scribner's Sons, 1913), pp. 10-11. Language simplified and modernized.

The first paragraph in Easton's narrative here refers to complaints by Indians in Rhode Island. The reader may infer that Easton was suggesting that the Wampanoags had the same complaints.

▶Indians who had been converted to Christianity were sometimes disloyal to their chiefs. Was it wrong of the English to convert these Indians?

Philip's older brother, Alexander, had died suddenly after a visit to Plymouth Colony in 1662. There is no known evidence that he was poisoned.

We knew what their complaints would be. In Rhode Island we had satisfied some of their complaints by sending for Indian rulers to be present whenever there was a trial for a crime involving an Indian's life. This the Indians accepted. They agreed with us as to the execution of criminals. And they said that they were able to satisfy their subjects when they knew an Indian was punished justly. But they said that outside the townships that we had purchased, they did not want us to prosecute any of their people. They also said that they greatly disliked having any of their Indians persuaded or forced to be Christian Indians. They said that such persons were in every way more troublesome, and were only liars, and that the English made them rebellious toward their own kings.

They said that their king's brother, when he was king, came to die miserably by being forced to appear in court, and, they believed, poisoned. Another grievance was that if twenty of their honest Indians testified that an Englishman had done them wrong, they were not believed. But if one of their worst Indians testified against any Indian or their king, these Indians were believed.

Another grievance was that when their kings sold land, the English would say that the amount of land was greater than the amount the Indians had agreed to. They said that some of their kings had been wrong to sell so much land, leaving their own people none. They said that the English got some kings drunk and then cheated them in bargains.

Another grievance was that the English cattle and horses had increased so much that even when Indians moved twenty miles from the English they still could not keep their corn from being spoiled, since they had never been used to fencing their land. Another grievance was that the English sold so much liquor to the Indians that many became drunk and then plundered the sober Indians.

Douglas Leach:
The Problem of Land

Douglas Leach, a modern historian, has written the best account of King Philip's War. He blames the war on a variety of factors. In the following passage, he considers the importance of the seizing of Indian lands by the Puritans as a cause of war.

Friction of various sorts between English and Indians was almost constant . . . . On both sides there were cases of trespass, assault, theft, and even murder, all of which served as a continual irritant. The Indians, moreover, felt a gnawing concern over the mounting indications that their own culture and way of life was being slowly but surely undermined by the white men.

Douglas Edward Leach, **Flintlock and Tomahawk: New England in King Philip's War** (New York: W.W. Norton & Company, 1958), pp. 14, 15-16. Copyright © 1958 by Douglas Edward Leach.

Basic to the whole problem of interracial friction, of course, was the fact that the English were gaining control over more and more land which had formerly belonged to the various tribes, thereby pushing the Indians into an ever-decreasing extent of territory. . . .

The way in which friction was produced as a result of land transactions is well demonstrated by the following case. The domain of the Wampanoag sachem [chief] Philip had formerly included an area known as Wollomonuppoag, in what is now Wrentham, Massachusetts. This land having been purchased by some Dedham people who intended to begin a settlement there, the town of Dedham now claimed jurisdiction in the area. In the early spring of 1668 the owners of the property, still living some fifteen miles away in Dedham, were disturbed by reports that the Indians were occupying their land at Wollomonuppoag, cutting wood there, and preparing to plant crops. Accordingly, the selectmen of the town sent a message to the intruders, demanding that they remove themselves, but the Indians only sneered at the message, and announced that they intended to proceed with their planting. Outraged at this defiance, the English owners appealed to Philip through Captain Thomas Willett of Rehoboth. Philip apparently questioned the title to the property, claiming that the land at Wollomonuppoag still belonged to him, but in August, 1669, he offered to grant a clear title to the property, in exchange for a down payment of £5. This offer seemed acceptable to the Dedham people,

In some sales of land to the English, the Indians reserved the legal right to hunt and fish on the land in the future.

The engravings on this page show European versions of Indian attacks. What characteristics of Indians do these engravings stress? If you were a new settler, how would these engravings make you feel about the possibility of amalgamation or assimilation?

who resolved to comply with Philip's demand. In November further negotiations were carried on with a view to purchasing all land still claimed by Philip within Dedham bounds. Over a year later the Dedham records still described the situation as a "problem," and as late as 1672 some Indians were still making use of English land at Wollomonuppoag. The hard feelings engendered by this long-drawn-out land controversy were not likely to be soon forgotten.

It would appear that Indians often did not fully grasp the meaning of landownership as understood by the English. To the Indians, the mere signing of paper did not transfer exclusive right to a piece of uncultivated land. If the English owners failed to occupy the land and use it, the natives saw no reason why they should not continue their usual activities there. Even after the English had arrived on a piece of property and constructed houses upon it, the Indians often clung to their old rights of fishing and hunting. In short, the natives of New England seemed to believe that, generally speaking, the forest belonged to him who was able to make use of it.

Alden Vaughan:
The Problem of Land

Alden Vaughan, a modern historian, has written the most thorough account of English-Indian relations in New England. He also blames King Philip's War on a variety of factors. Here he considers the Puritans' taking of land as a cause of war.

There is no substantial evidence that resentment over land transactions spurred any tribe . . . into violent reprisal. Throughout the seventeenth century, Puritan institutions and Puritan officials kept most frontier dealings [fair] as well as peaceful.

The Puritan did not push the New England Indian off his land. The myth of the early colonist as a land-grabber is one of the most persistent, for on the surface it has an immediate aura of validity. The red man once owned all the land, now he owns little or none: hence, the Puritan must have tricked, cajoled, or forced the Indian out of his birthright.

But does this . . . evidence accord with the . . . facts? The Indian did not hold that the entire continent belonged to him. It was rather the white man who introduced the idea that it was a red man's continent that purchase alone could transform into the domain of the white. The Indian . . . did not object to the occupation of . . . territory by European settlers, so long as the immigrants came as friends rather than as foes. Hence the Wampanoags did not contest the Pilgrim settlement at Plymouth and Massachusetts did not object to the establishment of English towns around Boston Harbor . . . .

Alden T. Vaughan, **New England Frontier: Puritans and Indians, 1620-1675** (Boston: Little, Brown and Company, 1965), pp. 312-313, 326-327. Some material transposed.

At bottom, Philip seems to have been moved to violence by a combination of growing Puritan influence and gradual realization of his own declining power. His father had sought out the Pilgrims as a counterforce against Narragansett attacks. The counterforce now far outweighed the ancient Indian enemy and was therefore no longer welcome. It was not so much that the Plymouth Puritans now had title to more land than the Wampanoag tribe or that they had maltreated the Indians, but that they increasingly dominated the political, economic, and social life of Philip's section of New England. . . . Most inhabitants of the territory—red and white together—now practiced the Englishman's religion, most now settled their disputes in the white man's courts, most wore English clothes, and most made their living, in part at least, in accordance with the white man's economic pattern. When disputes were to be settled between the governments of New Plymouth and the Wampanoag tribe, it was the Indian chief who traveled to the Pilgrim capital.

FOR THOUGHT:

Did King Philip's War break out because of specific differences between Indian and English cultures? Or would war probably have occurred if both sides had been Indians or both sides English?

3 WAR, RELIGION, AND THE MEETING OF CULTURES

The fate of the Indian way of life, in competition with the European, depended partly on which group became the largest. Immigration and natural increase swelled the European population. War and disease reduced that of the Indians.

The impact of the two cultures on each other also played a large part in the outcome. The attractive goods of the English—blankets, tools, liquor, clothing, firearms—quickly changed the ways of life of Indians in New England. The English systems of landholding, justice, and political authority also tended to replace those of the Indians.

King Philip's War in New England provided a year-long crisis. It tested the powers of survival of the two cultures. The first document in this reading offers the reaction of an Englishwoman to Indian life while she was a captive of war for a few months. The second document offers evidence about the impact of the Puritan version of Christianity on some New England Indians. As you read, consider these questions:

1. What evidence does Mrs. Rowlandson's narrative provide about the impact of Indian and English ways of life on each other?
2. What is the meaning of the rules of conduct adopted by the Indian village at Concord?

An Englishwoman Becomes a Captive of Indians

Mrs. Mary Rowlandson was married to the minister of Lancaster, Massachusetts. She was captured by Narragansett Indians who attacked and burned her garrison house. The raiders killed fifteen or more of the defenders and carried off twenty-seven captives. Mrs. Rowlandson was ransomed three months later after undergoing many forced marches, bitter cold, and hunger. Her three children were also taken as captives. One died from a wound suffered in the attack. But the other two were later freed.

Mrs. Rowlandson's story of her experiences was published six years after her release. It is one of the most dramatic narratives of Indian captives. It is also perhaps the best known piece of writing by a woman in the English colonies in America. While she was obviously not seeing Indian life under ideal conditions—her captors were often on the move to escape pursuit and were also often hungry—she provides a good deal of evidence about Indian ways of life, including their values. Excerpts from her narrative follow.

Narrative of the Captivity of Mrs. Mary Rowlandson, 1682, in Narratives of the Indian Wars, 1675-1699, Charles H. Lincoln, ed. (New York: Charles Scribner's Sons, 1913), pp. 125-129, 134, 135, 143, 144-145, 151,152,154. Language simplified and modernized.

In the morning, when they found out that my child was dead, they sent me home to my master's wigwam. My master was Quinnapin. He was a sagamore, and married to King Philip's wife's sister.

A sagamore, or sachem, was the chief of a group of Indians.

Soon after I came, I went to take up my dead child in my arms to carry it with me. The Indians, however, ordered me to leave it. Later I asked them what they had done with it. They showed me where it was, where I saw the ground was freshly dug. They told me that they had buried it there. God having taken away this child, I went to see my daughter Mary at a wigwam not far away. However, we had little freedom to see each other. She had been taken at first by a praying Indian and afterwards sold for a gun. When I came in sight she would begin weeping. This would provoke the Indians. And they would not let me come near her.

Those Indians converted to Christianity were called praying Indians.

As I was going up and down mourning and lamenting my condition, my son came to me and asked me how I was. I had not seen him since the destruction of the town. And I had not known where he was.

When a raiding party came back from Medfield, Oh! the outrageous roaring and whooping there was. They began their noisemaking about

Medfield was a village in eastern Massachusetts. The Indians' dawn attack on it caused the burning of many houses and barns and some loss of English life.

15

a mile before they reached us. By this noise and whooping they signified how many people they had killed, which was twenty-three. There was insulting and triumphing over some Englishmen's scalps that they had taken (as their manner is) and brought with them. One of the Indians that came from the Medfield fight had brought back some plunder. He asked me if I would like to have a Bible, as he had one in his basket. I was glad of it. And I asked him whether he thought the Indians would let me read. He answered yes. So I took the Bible, and found great comfort in it.

There were now besides myself nine English captives in this place. All were children except one woman. The woman, Goodwife Joslin, was very big with child, whose birth was expected in a week. She had another child two years old in her arms. Being so near her time, she would often ask the Indians to let her go home. They were not willing to do that. And, annoyed with her pleading, they gathered a large crowd around her, stripped her naked, and set her in the midst of them. When they had sung and danced about her as long as they pleased, they knocked her on the head, and the child in her arms with her. When they had done that, they made a fire and put them both into it. They told the other children who were with them that if they tried to go home they would treat them in the same way. The children said that she did not shed one tear, but prayed all the while.

[After traveling further the Indians and their captives reached the Connecticut River.]

In the morning we went over the river to Philip's crew. When I was in the canoe I could not help but be amazed at the numerous crew of pagans on the other side. When I came ashore, they gathered all about me, I sitting alone in the middle. They asked one another questions, and laughed, and rejoiced over their gains and victories. Then my heart began to fail. And I fell weeping, which was the first time I remember weeping before them. One of the Indians asked me why I wept. I could hardly tell what to say. Yet I answered that they would kill me. No, said he, none will hurt you. Then came one of them and gave me two spoonfuls of meal to comfort me. Another gave me a half a pint of peas.

During my stay in this place, King Philip asked me to make a cap for his boy. After this, he invited me to dinner. I went, and he gave me a pancake, about as big as two fingers. It was made of dried wheat, beaten, and fried in bear grease. I thought I had never tasted pleasanter food in my life. There was a squaw who asked me to make a shirt for her husband. She gave me a piece of bear meat for it. Another squaw asked me to knit a pair of stockings. For them she gave me a quart of peas. I boiled my peas and bear together. And

When retreating, the Indians usually killed those captives who could not travel. Those who could travel were kept as slaves or ransomed. Both Indians and English occasionally tortured male prisoners.

Christians referred to unbelievers as pagans or heathen.

Mrs. Rowlandson seems to have been treated harshly at times and kindly at others. She may have been treated kindly because the Indians knew she was the wife of a minister. This meant that she might be worth a good ransom. The Indians also respected and feared their own medicine men. And they might have feared the possible magical powers of an English religious man.

16

This picture shows an anthropologist in the midst of a primitive tribe in Africa. Suppose you had to live your life—as Mrs. Rowlandson did or this anthropologist might do—with only the company of primitive people. How would you feel? What would you miss most? In what ways, if any, might you lose your feelings of identity?

I invited my master and mistress to dinner. However, the proud woman, because I served them both in one dish, would eat almost nothing.

After going some distance further I went to see an English youth in this place, one John Gilbert. I found him lying out of doors on the ground. I asked him how he was. He told me he was very sick with diarrhea. The Indians had turned him out of the wigwam. With him was an Indian papoose, almost dead, whose parents had been killed. It was a bitter cold day. The young man himself had nothing

▶As far as can be told from the narrative, the papoose, which had no family to care for it, was left to die by both the Indians and Mrs. Rowlandson. Under the circumstances, was either wrong in doing so?

17

on but his shirt and jacket. This sight was enough to melt a heart of stone. There they lay quivering in the cold. The papoose was stretched out, with his eyes and nose and mouth full of dirt, and yet alive and groaning. I advised John to go and get some fire. He told me that he could not stand, but I urged him to do it lest he should lie there and die. With much effort I got him to a fire and then went home.

Two nights later the Indians ordered me to go out of the wigwam again. My mistress's papoose was sick. It died that night. There was one benefit in it, that there was more room in the wigwam. I went to another wigwam. And they told me to come in. They gave me a skin to lie on, and some venison and nuts, which was a choice dish among them. The next day they buried the papoose. Afterward, both morning and evening, there came a company to mourn and howl with her. But I confess I could not much sympathize with them.

[The English began a correspondence with the Indians to try to ransom the captives. One letter was brought to the Indians where Mrs. Rowlandson was staying by two Indians who lived at a Christian Indian village near her home in Lancaster.]

Then came Tom and Peter, with the second letter about the captives. Though they were Indians, I got them by the hand and burst out into tears. My heart was so full that I could not speak to them, but recovering myself, I asked them how my husband was, and all my friends and acquaintances. They said, they are all very well but sad.

There was a praying Indian, who when he had done all the mischief that he could, betrayed his own father into the English hands, in order to save his own life. Another praying Indian was at the fight at Sudbury, though, as he deserved, he was afterward hanged for it. There was another praying Indian, so wicked and cruel, as to wear a string about his neck, strung with Christians' fingers.

About this time there came an Indian to me and told me to come to his wigwam, at night, and he would give me some port and nuts. I did this. And as I was eating, another Indian said to me, he seems to be your good friend, but he killed two Englishmen at the fight at Sudbury. There lie their clothes behind you. I looked behind me. And there I saw bloody clothes, with bullet holes in them. And yet the Lord did not permit this wretch to do me any harm. Instead of that, he refreshed me many times. Five or six times he and his squaw refreshed my feeble body. If I went to their wigwam at any time, they would always give me something. And yet they were strangers that I never saw before.

[Mrs. Rowlandson was ransomed shortly afterwards by the English for twenty pounds worth of goods.]

Venison is deer meat.

Sudbury, in eastern Massachusetts, had been attacked by a large force of Indians. They killed about 30 of the English there.

Christian Indians Accept
Rules for Their Community

By 1675 English missionaries in Massachusetts Bay and Plymouth colonies had successfully converted Indians to Christianity. Most of these converts were in the Massachusetts Bay Colony, where John Eliot, the greatest missionary, was active. Among his other deeds, Eliot succeeded in translating the Bible into the Algonquian language used by most Indians in New England.

The historian Alden Vaughan estimates that about one fifth of an estimated fifteen thousand Indians in New England had become Christians by 1675. Probably a large majority of Indians in eastern Massachusetts, the heart of English power, belonged to that number. During King Philip's War, a number of these Indians served as spies, guides, and fighting allies of the English. The following rules of conduct are among those agreed to by some Christian Indians who were about to establish a town in Concord, Massachusetts, under the protection of the English in 1647.

Massachusetts Historical Society Collections, 3 Series IV, 39-40, reprinted in Alden T. Vaughan, **New England Frontier: Puritans and Indians, 1620-1675** (Boston: Little, Brown and Company, 1965), pp. 346-347. Language simplified and modernized.

1. That every one who abuses himself with wine or strong liquor shall pay twenty shillings for each time.
2. That there shall be no more powwowing among the Indians. And if any one shall hereafter powwow, both he that shall powwow, and he that persuades him to powwow, shall pay twenty shillings apiece.

A powwow was a medicine man, or priest. To powwow meant to take part in the magical or religious rites of the Indians.

3. They do desire that they may be inspired to seek after God.
5. That they may find better ways to spend their time.
6. That they may come to understand the sin of lying, and whoever shall be found guilty of lying shall pay five shillings for the first offence, 10 shillings for the second, twenty shillings for the third.
8. They desire that no Indian hereafter shall have any more than one wife.
12. That they pay their debts to the English.
13. That they do observe the Lord's Day, and whoever shall violate it shall pay twenty shillings.
15. They will wear their hair properly, as the English do, and whoever offends shall pay five shillings.
16. They intend to reform themselves, in their former greasing of themselves, under the penalty of five shillings for each default.
17. They do all resolve to set up prayer in their wigwams, and to pray to God both before and after meals.

Indians often rubbed themselves with animal fat or grease as protection against the cold.

21. Whoever commits adultery shall be put to death.
22. Intentional murder shall be punished with death.
23. They shall not put on disguises when they are mourning, as formerly, nor shall they make a great noise by howling.

19

25. No Indian shall take an Englishman's canoe without permission, under the penalty of five shillings.
26. No Indian shall come into any Englishman's house unless he knocks first. And this they shall also expect from the English.
27. Whoever beats his wife shall pay twenty shillings.
28. If any Indian has a quarrel with another Indian and beats him, he shall pay twenty shillings.

FOR THOUGHT:

Which of the following terms best fits what was happening to Indian and English cultures in New England: amalgamation, assimilation, accommodation, or extermination?

4 COLONIZING THE NEW WORLD

HISTORICAL ESSAY

The discovery and settlement of America did not grow from a single cause. They resulted from four closely related movements. Together they triggered the expansion of Europe and filled the oceans of the world with European ships.

The first of these developments was an economic revival. In the centuries following the collapse of the Roman Empire, most people in Europe lived on isolated, self-sufficient manors. Then the Italian cities began to increase their trade with the Near East and the Far East. Merchants pushed in to India and China, and Europeans began to demand their goods. A vigorous trade soon developed between the Mediterranean countries and northern Europe. Cities grew as trading and manufacturing centers. And stories of new lands, often circulated by Crusaders who fought to oust Moslems from the Holy Land, stirred interest in travel and trade.

The economic revival led to voyages of discovery and colonization for a number of reasons. It stirred people's desires for products from the Far East. Hence it encouraged them to look for new routes around Africa or across the Atlantic. It displaced many people from their traditional roles in the economy. These extra workers could be turned into colonists. Industry began to develop and with it came an increased demand for raw material which colonies could satisfy.

European merchants formed companies to carry on trade with the Near East, Russia, and the Far East. They developed ways to raise large sums of money to finance colonies. And they worked out methods of governing new colonies while they were being established.

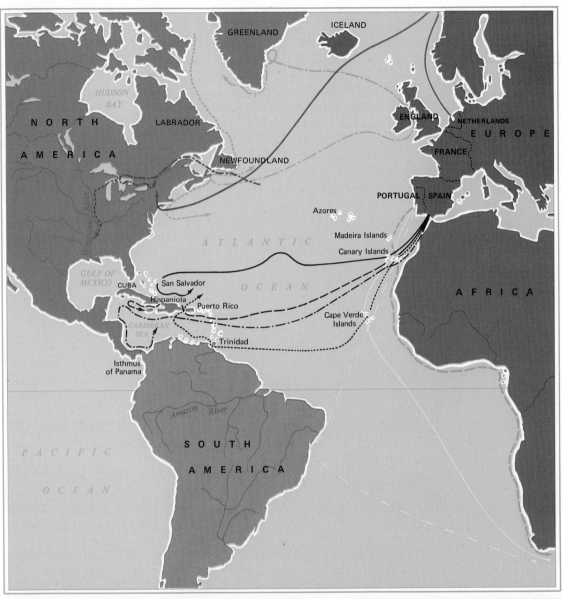

GREENLAND

ICELAND

HUDSON
BAY

NORTH

AMERICA

LABRADOR

ENGLAND

NETHERLANDS

EUROPE

FRANCE

NEWFOUNDLAND

PORTUGAL SPAIN

Azores

ATLANTIC

Madeira Islands

Canary Islands

Mississippi River

GULF OF
MEXICO

CUBA

San Salvador

Hispaniola

OCEAN

AFRICA

Puerto Rico

CARIBBEAN
SEA

Cape Verde
Islands

Trinidad

Isthmus
of Panama

Amazon River

SOUTH

AMERICA

PACIFIC

OCEAN

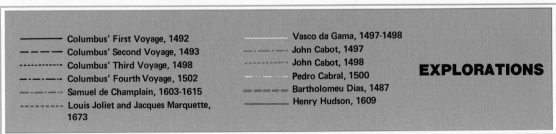

——— Columbus' First Voyage, 1492
– – – Columbus' Second Voyage, 1493
········ Columbus' Third Voyage, 1498
–·–·– Columbus' Fourth Voyage, 1502
–··–··– Samuel de Champlain, 1603-1615
········ Louis Joliet and Jacques Marquette,
1673

——— Vasco da Gama, 1497-1498
–·–·– John Cabot, 1497
········ John Cabot, 1498
–·–·– Pedro Cabral, 1500
– – – Bartholomeu Dias, 1487
——— Henry Hudson, 1609

EXPLORATIONS

The Renaissance also played an important role. Beginning in the fourteenth century, people turned their attention from thoughts of religion, which dominated the lives of medieval people, to concerns of the world around them. Some people developed new maps and charts and navigational instruments essential to later voyages of discovery. They also perfected fast new ships capable of sailing in the direction from which the wind was blowing.

A further development helped to prepare Europe for its American adventures. This was the growth in unity and power of each of the five nation-states which did most of the exploring and settling: Portugal, Spain, England, France, and the Netherlands. Stretched along the coast of the Atlantic, these states sought new routes to the Indies. They even provided government funds to finance voyages. A spirit of national rivalry grew up among them and spurred explorers and colonists to greater efforts. Nearly every promoter of colonies mentioned the need to strengthen his or her nation as one of the main reasons for colonization.

▶Should a government help finance enterprises that will bring huge profits to private groups or individuals? Why or why not?

Finally, the development of the Protestant and Catholic Reformations helped to contribute to the settlement of the Americas. Early in the sixteenth century, a movement to reform the Catholic Church began. The movement, which was led by such people as Martin Luther and John Calvin, resulted in the establishment of many Protestant churches. Religious wars and religious persecution followed. Many Europeans left their homes to escape these ills and to seek religious freedom elsewhere. Thousands of these people came to the Americas. There they settled largely in New England and the Middle Colonies. Catholic explorers and missionaries also came to the New World. They played key roles in the exploration and settlement of both Canada and South America.

Settlers Come to the Americas

Portugal Portugal, the most westerly of the five nations, was first to begin explorations. Its long coastline beckoned its people to the sea. For centuries foreign sailors had crowded its ports.

During the fifteenth century, Prince Henry the Navigator (1391-1460) rallied the resources of the Portuguese crown to push exploration. Prince Henry was anxious to find the legendary Christian kingdom of Prester John. It was supposedly located somewhere in the middle of the African continent. Prince Henry was also an ardent student of science. He wanted to develop new navigational instruments and to extend the boundaries of the knowledge of geography. Finally, Prince Henry was a practical businessman interested in trade. All these interests and motives helped to whet his appetite for voyages of exploration down the coast of Africa.

Year after year, his sailors pushed back the boundary of the unknown seas. In 1487, Bartholomeu Dias rounded the Cape of Good Hope in search of the kingdom of Prester John. However, he was turned back by his rebellious crew. Ten years later, Vasco da Gama rounded the Cape and sailed all the way to Calcutta in India. He returned to Portugal with a rich cargo of spice and precious stones.

At this time, Portugal was a tiny nation with a small population. Most of its people were farmers, fishermen, and sailors. One of its captains, Pedro Cabral, stumbled upon Brazil in 1500 when his fleet was driven westward before a storm. But Portugal lacked the resources to expand its quest for American colonies. Its influences in the New World never extended beyond Brazil. The people of this nation still speak the language of the Portuguese captains who landed on its shores.

Spain The Spanish had a larger role in colonizing the Americas. Before 1450, five kingdoms, including Portugal, existed on the Iberian peninsula. In the next sixty years, however, four of the five kingdoms were united under the joint monarchy of Ferdinand of Aragon and Isabella of Castile. Together these two monarchs broke the strength of the nobles and organized a powerful central government. They took over the military organizations, a step which filled the royal coffers with money. They established Catholicism as the state religion. And they set up the Inquisition to see that all Jews and Moslems had either become genuine converts to Catholicism or had left the country. For more than a century thereafter, Spain was the most powerful state in Europe.

Spain also dominated the Americas. Starting in 1492 with the first of the four voyages of Columbus, its soldiers and sailors explored all the Americas from Florida to Cape Horn. The Spanish subjugated the Indians and sent vast fortunes back to the homeland. But the Spanish colonies turned out to be very different from the English settlements that appeared later to the north. The motives of their settlers and the resources of the home country account for some of these differences.

Like Portugal, Spain was thinly populated. Moreover, many of its best merchants and artisans were driven out of the country after 1492 because they were Jews or Moslems. But the countryside was filled with thousands of restless men. They were the sons of petty nobles, without estates and with slim hopes for the future. Spain obtained its soldiers and settlers from among these men. Captains recruited them and formed them into armies. They conquered not only parts of Europe but also most of the Americas. However, the Spanish could spread only a thin population over the lands they conquered. They emigrated as conquerors in small numbers, and also women stayed at home.

Along with the soldiers went a host of priests. They intended to Christianize the natives and bring them within the fold of the Catholic Church. All over the Americas, Catholic priests from Spain explored the country. They ministered to others and converted the natives.

But the priests came mainly as missionaries and members of religious orders who could not marry. They did not build settlements of people of European origin like those which Protestant ministers and their congregations built in English-speaking colonies farther north.

France France entered the race for colonies in the seventeenth century. By mid-century it was developing into the most powerful nation in Europe. It was united under a powerful ruler, Louis XIV, and had a growing economy. The voyages to North America were sponsored by the king and by trading companies. They were undertaken to find a Northwest Passage through the Americas to the Far East. When the French discovered the wealth of the fur trade, a few adventurous people settled in Canada. They established trading posts chiefly along the banks of the St. Lawrence River.

But no hosts of dispossessed people, ready and able to settle, populated France. French farmers remained secure on their lands. And artisans could find plenty of work in crafts and industries. French Protestants called Huguenots were the one group which might have formed the basis for settlements. But they were forbidden by Catholic monarchs to live in France's colonies. Hence, the French colonies, like the Spanish, were lightly settled. Moreover, the settlers were largely single men who married Indian women and made their living in the fur trade.

The Netherlands The Dutch became Protestants in the sixteenth century. They fought long and costly wars against the Spanish Catholics who ruled them. Eventually, they drove out the Spanish and established a republic.

Holland's small population was occupied mainly with fishing and with far-flung manufacturing and trade enterprises. A developing industry absorbed the labor supply. And there was complete religious toleration at home. As a result, few Dutch families wanted to emigrate to the New World. After Henry Hudson sailed up the Hudson River early in the seventeenth century, a few Dutch traders established posts from Manhattan Island to Albany. But only a few thousand settlers followed. In the 1660's, England and the Netherlands went to war. The Dutch colonies were conquered by the English and Dutch colonizing ended in North America.

England Seventeenth-century England was in the midst of economic and social changes. These had a marked effect upon the American colonies. The manorial system had broken down as free labor and cash payments, combined with low prices for crops, produced a new agricultural system. Uprooted from the soil of their ancestors, farmers flocked to the cities. These footloose people flooded the labor market. Cast adrift in society, thousands of them looked across the wide Atlantic for opportunity.

So did many of the wealthy. Some wanted grants of land to establish themselves in the New World as gentry. Others wanted to trade. They

The gentry was a class of people who had wealth but no titles of nobility.

24

EDGING TOWARD MIDEAST PEACE: NEW SUCCESS FOR KISSINGER

ALL SIGNS in early March pointed toward yet another diplomatic coup for Henry Kissinger in the Middle East.

In a whirlwind tour of the region, his fourth in four months, the U. S. Secretary of State achieved what some experts had predicted would be virtually impossible:

He moved Israel and Syria closer toward separation of their military forces on the volatile Golan Heights and so improved chances of full-scale Arab-Israeli peace talks at Geneva. Also improved were chances of an end to the Arab embargo on oil shipments to the U. S.

Skirmishes between Syrian and Israeli troops almost daily had threatened to explode into full-scale fighting and to drag Egypt and Israel back into renewed war despite a mid-January agreement—also engineered by Mr. Kissinger—to disengage their military forces along the Suez Canal front.

Traveling between Damascus and Tel Aviv, the U. S. Secretary persuaded the Syrians on February 27 to disclose the names of Israeli soldiers taken prisoner during the October war, as demanded by Israel. In return, Israeli leaders agreed to open disengagement talks with the Syrians.

Mr. Kissinger's success in helping ease bitter enmity between Syria and Israel obviously pleased President Anwar Sadat of Egypt, who seems determined to ignore opposition from more-militant Arab leaders and to establish closer ties with both the U. S. and Israel.

"My friend." Greeting Mr. Kissinger in Cairo, Sadat called the American official "my friend" and said: "As long as Dr. Kissinger is handling the whole thing, everything is O.K."

President Sadat also announced on February 28 the resumption of full diplomatic relations with the U. S.—broken since the 1967 Arab-Israeli war—and invited President Nixon to visit Egypt at some future date.

The Egyptian President pointed out, however, that the turn for the better in the Mideast did not necessarily mean the Arab oil embargo would be lifted soon. "It is not my decision," he said. "It is the decision of all the Arabs."

From Damascus, John Law of the International Staff of "U. S. News & World Report" cabled this dispatch:

Despite the initial break in the stalemate between Syria and Israel, some

"THE BIG APPLE"

Mideast authorities are convinced that a final agreement on disengagement of their two forces might be impervious to even Mr. Kissinger's diplomatic skills.

Israel, these experts caution, is less willing to give up territory on the Golan Heights than it was to make concessions to Egypt in the Sinai desert. And Syria is more reluctant than Cairo was to make a deal which does not insure Israeli withdrawal from all occupied Arab territory or guarantee an independent homeland for the Palestinians.

Here in Damascus, virtually every Syrian says he wants peace—provided the Israelis get out of Arab territory they seized in the 1967 and 1973 wars.

According to a salesman in the capital: "We could do so much to build up this country if we could just stop fighting Israel. But how can Israel expect us not to fight if she stays on even one inch of our land?"

Heart of "Arabism." A fundamental problem is that Syria, with 6.5 million people, looks upon itself as bearing a historical responsibility for the entire Arab world of more than 100 million. To the Syrians, their nation is and always has been the heart of "Arabism."

A professor in Damascus says: "The Syrian thinks of himself as an Arab first and a Syrian second. Most Egyptians regard themselves as Egyp-

tians first and only secondarily as Arabs." There is another difference.

"We Syrians eat and breathe politics," says a Syrian businessman. "The Egyptians just eat and breathe."

The result is that though Syria's President Hafez Assad is a military dictator, he governs a people who are known among other Arabs for their stubborn independence. There have been a score of coups since Syria gained its independence from France in 1944. One was against Egypt's late President Gamal Abdel Nasser and broke up Syria's short-lived union with Egypt.

Shrewd, suspicious. Syrian leaders, including President Assad, are shrewd, hard, suspicious men and can be counted on to be tough in any negotiations with the Israelis. What gives observers some grounds for optimism is that present rulers are, nevertheless, more moderate than any Syria has had in years.

Assad and his top advisers, who took over power in November, 1970, have moved away from the strong Marxist dogma of their immediate predecessors. Instead, they have stressed Syria's independence from the Soviet Union and have encouraged investments from Western nations.

Last October, Assad reversed a seven-year-old Syrian policy of rejecting any form of political settlement with Israel by accepting a United Nations resolution which called for Arab-Israeli negotiations. Recently, he defused a potentially dangerous situation by ordering the withdrawal of all Palestinian guerrilla forces posted near Syria's border with Israel.

There are many Syrians, some living in exile, who are unhappy with Assad's drift to the "right" and have never ceased plotting to topple him from power. To disarm his enemies, Mideast analysts say, he needs an agreement with Israel that not only will involve a substantial Israeli withdrawal from the Golan Heights, but also will include a promise of future rollbacks.

Anything less than that, experts warn, would find little public favor and could lead to the President's replacement by leaders who favor a new round of war with Israel. According to one knowledgeable Syrian:

"There's no one on the horizon in Syria —no one at all—who would be more ready to work with the Americans than Assad is. They better hope he stays around." [END]

What does this newspaper story imply about causation?

---

had learned to form joint-stock companies. In these, a number of investors bought shares of stock. As a result, they obtained a vote in company decisions. The New World seemed to offer a fertile ground for profit for these companies. Even the Pilgrims were financed by a joint-stock company. It expected them to produce profits through fishing, lumbering, trading for furs, and farming.

In the seventeenth century, England was racked with religious dissension. As persecution of one group by another mounted, some groups decided to move to the colonies. Protestant groups like the Puritans and Pilgrims decided to settle in New England. The Catholics and the Quakers moved to the Middle Colonies.

All these changes affected the people of seventeenth-century England at once. As a result, people had mixed motives for emigrating to the New World. The Puritans' main motive was to form a Bible Commonwealth. Yet they too were urged toward the New World by the economic, political, and social changes which were sweeping their homeland.

The Quakers, or the Society of Friends, founded a religious group in England in the seventeenth century. Quakers believed that ministers and ritual were unnecessary in religious services. They were pacifists who would not bear arms. Although Quakers tolerated other persons' beliefs, they were persecuted in seventeenth-century England.

It is a general rule that major developments in history arise from a number of complex causes rather than from a single cause or from the influence of a single person. This rule is illustrated by the entire movement leading to the discovery, exploration, and settlement of America.

More than any other country in Europe, England had developed a representative government that could check the power of the king or queen. The English believed that their monarch, like anyone else, was subject to the law. English monarchs had learned to share authority with Parliament. Hereditary nobles and bishops sat in the upper chamber of Parliament, the House of Lords. Commoners from counties and towns elected their representatives, usually aristocrats, to the House of Commons. The king or queen could not tax without the consent of Parliament. They could not imprison people at their own whims. Nor could they violate legal customs established in the common law. Local government rested firmly in the hands of the influential men of the locality.

The English people who emigrated to America took with them their belief in the supremacy of law, their devotion to political institutions in which they were represented, their adherence to the common law, and their assumption that the rich and powerful should influence political affairs the most.

Africa   As the Portuguese sailed down the coast of Africa in the mid-fifteenth century, they began to buy slaves and to send them back to Portugal. Soon all the major colonizing countries entered the slave trade. It focused mainly on the southern coast of West Africa. There the population was concentrated in the tropical rain forests and in the grasslands farther inland toward the Sahara. These people fell easy prey to the advanced technology of the Europeans.

A few centuries earlier, great kingdoms had grown up in this part of Africa. Slowly, under the attacks of Arabs from the north, they decayed. By the fifteenth century, the kingdoms along the coast had broken up into small communities. They were unable to offer much resistance to European invaders.

The Portuguese, along with other Europeans who followed, began to trade with the Africans. They exchanged goods which the Africans could not obtain for slaves who were needed to work in the New World. The men and women who were bought and shipped to America became the ancestors of today's black Americans.

The American Environment Challenges the Newcomers

Three features of the New World assumed important roles in the development of the colonies. The first was the physical environment and what could be grown there. Northern Canada was cold and inhospitable. It attracted only the fur traders and trappers who exploited its animals. In southern Canada and throughout New England

and the Middle Colonies, winters were harsh and the land often rocky. But soil, rainfall, and growing season were suited to agriculture. Here, any hardworking farmer could make a good living. Most of the land was covered with trees. They could provide masts, lumber, pitch, and tar for sale in England. The forest-product industries encouraged shipbuilding and trade. The rich fishing and whaling waters off the coast furnished the basis for another industry. These resources provided the foundation for a diversified economy in which farming, manufacturing, and trade all played their parts. Such an economy demanded skilled workers who could turn their hands to many tasks.

The southern part of what is now the United States, Central America and the islands of the Caribbean, and much of the northern half of South America were warm or hot throughout the year. Much of this area had rich soil and plentiful rainfall. These conditions encouraged the production of staple crops like sugar, tobacco, indigo, or cotton. All these crops required large numbers of laborers. But their cultivation did not demand the variety of skills essential to success in the north. Hence, the natural environment of the southern areas encouraged the use of slaves. They did not have to be trained in a variety of skills new to them.

The presence of Indians was a second feature of the social environment. It played an important role in the development of the colonies. Since their emigration across the Bering Straits, the cultures of the North American Indians had changed little. Their weapons were simple. And their tribal organization allowed the whites to play one tribe off against another. They were no match for the highly organized Europeans armed with muskets. If the Indians of the north got in the way of colonists, the Europeans could either push them farther west or kill them.

A third feature of the American environment is more difficult to define. In one sense, that feature was space. Land was free for the taking. A vast wilderness waited for the plow. In another sense, it was distance. Thousands of miles separated the colonists from the source of authority and from the hand of custom in Europe. Extensive lands meant that a son need not obey his father from fear of disinheritance. He could obtain land of his own. It meant too that monarchs could reward their servants with generous grants of land. Both long distances and slow communications forced colonial rulers to make decisions without consulting the home government. And colonists who grew up in the sight of the forest and never saw the homeland became more and more inclined to make their own decisions. In addition, the harsh conditions of the new land required new types of decisions about new issues. Taken together, the rich natural resources, the presence of Indians, and the stretch of free land an ocean removed from Europe played key roles in the process of Americanizing the Europeans.

▶ The technology of the North American Indians was simpler than that of the Europeans. Did this give the Europeans the right to conquer and displace the Indians? Why or why not?

Africans and English in America, 1607-1713

STATING THE ISSUE

Between 1607 and 1713 English settlers tightened their grip on the Atlantic seaboard of North America, from Maine to South Carolina. Chapter 1 has shown how the English settlers multiplied and displaced the native Americans in one region. Similar events took place up and down the Atlantic coast. By 1713 the native Americans had been forced to yield possession of most of the long coastal strip.

In one way the English experience with the Indians resembled that of the Spanish, French, Dutch, and Portuguese. Each succeeded in taking control of territory away from the native Americans. In another way the colonial powers had different experiences. The English and the Dutch tended to displace the Indians and exclude them from their societies. The Spanish, French, and Portuguese, on the other hand, often looked upon the Indians as members of their societies. They married Indians more frequently and exploited them as laborers more successfully.

As the European nations tried to make economic successes of their colonial ventures, they were faced with labor shortages. All took the same step to remedy this problem. They imported captive Africans in large numbers to do most of the hard work in the colonies. The Africans became vital parts of the societies they joined. In most cases, they were a more important part of colonial societies than the Indians. This chapter begins with readings that examine the steps by which the captive Africans became a vital part of English colonial society.

The use of slave labor helped to make the English colonies strong and profitable. However, there were other reasons why the English succeeded in creating a secure way of life in North America. Their system of colonization gave them more human resources than both the native Americans and their European rivals. Their sea power, aided by colonial ships and crews, helped them protect their shores, ports, and maritime trade. And their colonial societies developed a remarkable degree of self-government. The essay which concludes this chapter will deal with these and other issues.

1607 London Company expedition settles in Jamestown

1608 Samuel de Champlain establishes a settlement in Quebec

1619 House of Burgesses, legislative assembly in Virginia, holds its first meeting

1619 Twenty blacks arrive in Virginia

1620 Pilgrims sign Mayflower Compact

1624 British make Virginia a royal colony

1650–51 Parliament passes first Navigation Acts to limit colonial trade

1664 English seize New Netherlands from Dutch

1676 Nathanial Bacon leads rebellion against Jamestown to gain Indian territory

1688 Glorious Revolution in England sparks uprisings in colonies

1688 German Mennonites write the first formal anti-slavery protest

1691 New English government reestablishes royal power in colonies

1693 Cotton Mather sponsors "Society of Negroes"

1700 Samuel Sewall publishes anti-slavery pamphlet "The Selling of Joseph"

1713 French cede colonial province of Acadia to English

5 THE SLAVE TRADE

The use of slaves brought to the New World by the slave trade began in the early sixteenth century. People and ships from many different nations took part in the brutal trade. The Portuguese took the lead and other Europeans followed, first the English and the French, and a little later the Dutch. A Dutch ship brought the first captive Africans to the English colonies. Twenty African men and women arrived at Jamestown, Virginia, in 1619. By the time of the American Revolution in 1775, there were half a million Africans in the English colonies, about 20 percent of the colonial population.

Most of the Indians of North America made their living by hunting and fishing. But most of the Africans who were brought to the colonies were farmers. They came from highly organized and specialized agricultural societies. The following readings describe the societies that captured West Africans came from and the slave trade that brought the Africans to North America. They may suggest some reasons why African membership in colonial society became a problem. As you read, keep these questions in mind:

1. In what ways did African societies resemble or differ from those of the native Americans or the English?
2. What impact might the slave trade have on the Africans' way of life? Why?

The pictures on these two pages show scenes from African life in the seventeenth century. To what degree did their life in Africa prepare future slaves for their lives on plantations?

From Africa to America

The following selection contains excerpts from a history by Benjamin Quarles, a modern black American historian.

Benjamin Quarles, **The Negro in the Making of America** (New York: The Macmillan Company, 1969), pp. 15-17. Copyright © 1964, 1969 by Macmillan Publishing Co., Inc.

Of the varied Old World peoples that entered America, none came from as wide a geographical area as the blacks. The vast majority came from the West Coast of Africa, a 3,000-mile stretch extending from the Senegal River, downward around the huge coastal bulge, to the southern limit of present-day Portuguese Angola. A small percentage came from the Sudanese grasslands that border the Sahara.

These groups shared no common language. . . . Indeed, there are more than 200 distinct languages in present-day Nigeria alone. There was no such thing as "the African personality," since the varied groups

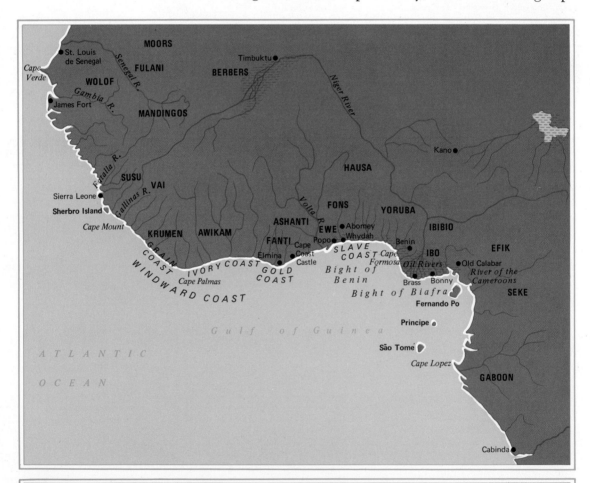

WEST AFRICA IN THE EIGHTEENTH CENTURY

differed as much in their ways of life as in the physical characteristics they exhibited and the languages they spoke. . . .

Although there were different types of societies and states, the most fundamental group politically, as in other ways, was the family. This was not one man's family; rather it was a kinship group numbering in the hundreds, but called a family because it was made up of all the living descendants of a common ancestor. . . .

Filling a definite place in the religious life of the Africans were their art forms, particularly the statuettes and masks of bronze, wood, or ivory that were produced for use in the performance of religious and magical rites. . . .

Music, too, was an important part of the Africans' way of life. Among its forms were complex melodies, rhythms, and the use of a wide variety of instruments, including the drum, harp, xylophone, violin, guitar, zither, and flute. Like music, dance was highly valued, being performed for any number of observances and purposes. Any event worthy of notice was celebrated by rhythmic movement—births, marriages, or death. Each dance served its own specific purpose; the fertility dance, for example, was a prayer that seed might take good root in the soil and grow well.

The literature produced by the Africans was primarily oral rather than written. . . . Knowledge about the history, customs, and traditions of the group was transmitted by men who made a profession of memorizing. The popular literature included tales, proverbs, and riddles passed down from one generation to another, occasionally by trained narrators, but most commonly by storytellers.

In summary, the Negroes who came to the New World varied widely in physical appearance and ways of life, but there were many common patterns of culture. Whatever the type of society, the different groups of Africans all operated under orderly governments, with established legal codes, and under well-organized social systems. . . . African societies before the coming of the Europeans were not backward and changeless. . . .

▶ Africans felt that the family was a more important group than the nation or the state. Do you value your family more than your nation, state, or community?

Two African Songs

Benjamin Quarles has maintained that music, dance, and oral and written literature were important parts of African culture. Following are two examples of African songs or poems. One would be sung by a warrior, the other by a mother to her child.

A WARRIOR'S SONG

I go in front. I fear not death. I am not afraid. If I die, I will take my blood to bathe my head.

George W. Williams, **History of the Negro Race in America, 1619-1880** (New York: Arno Press and the New York Times, 1968), pp. 78, 83. Copyright © 1968.

33

The man who fears nothing marches always in front, and is never hit by the murderous ball. The coward hides himself behind a bush and is killed.

Go to the battle. It is not lead that kills. It is Fate which strikes us and which makes us die.

A MOTHER'S SONG

▶ Do you think that the personal qualities revealed in these poems should be developed by all members of a community?

Why do you weep, my child?
The sky is bright: the sun is shining: why do you weep?
Go to your father: he loves you: go, tell him why you weep.
What! You are still weeping! Your father loves you; I caress you,
    but still you are sad.
Tell me then, my child, why do you weep?

Slave Trading and the "Middle Passage"

In the following selection Benjamin Quarles describes the process by which European traders obtained captive Africans and transported them to the New World where they would be sold as slaves. The journey from Africa to the New World was known as the "Middle Passage."

Benjamin Quarles, **The Negro in the Making of America,** pp. 20-21, 22-23.

Whatever the nation, the actual operation of the slave trade was much the same. Usually the sovereign in Europe would grant a trade monopoly to a group of favored merchants. . . . This protected the merchant company from competition, at least from others of their own nationality, and they could proceed to stock ships with the goods necessary for the exchange. Such goods consisted of textiles—woolens, linens, cottons, silks—knives and daggers; firearms, powder and shot; and iron, copper, brass, and lead in bars for local craftsmen. A staple of the trade was intoxicating drink—rum, brandy, gin, or wine. Ships also made it a point to carry a supply of trinkets—baubles, bells, mirrors, bracelets, and glass beads—which were inexpensive and had a fascination for native chiefs.

Upon landing for the first time, the trading company made arrangements to establish a fort and trading station. One of the first buildings that would be built was a warehouse where the captives could be kept until the voyage across the Atlantic. Thus, having goods to trade and storage space to accommodate the expected human cargo, the trader was ready to do business with the native chief. The whites did not go into the interior to get slaves; this task they left to the Africans themselves. Encouraged by the desire for European goods, one tribe raided another, seized whatever captives it could, and

▶ Why do you think the Africans wanted the goods Europeans brought to trade for captives? In a similar situation, what goods would you want?

marched them off in chains, with leather straps around their necks, to the coastal trading centers.

Undoubtedly, the full meaning of what they were doing did not dawn on the African chiefs. Neither intertribal warfare nor human bondage was uncommon. Indeed, traditionally, men in Africa had become slaves by being captured in warfare, or as punishment for crime, or because of failure to pay debts. There was, however, no label of inferiority attached to being a slave; no rigid class distinctions prevented a former slave from becoming free and rising to a great place. Moreover, the demand for slaves had been limited. But when the Europeans arrived, there was a great upsurge in the market for slaves, and the native chiefs were unwilling to resist the temptations of the trade. Later, when the entire West Coast had been turned into a huge slave corral, the chiefs were no longer able to stop the process. . . .

When enough Negroes had been acquired to make a full cargo, the next step was to get them to the West Indies with the greatest possible speed. Food was stocked for crew and slaves—yams, coarse bananas, potatoes, kidney beans, and coconuts. Then, after having been branded for identification, the blacks came aboard, climbing up the swaying rope ladders, prodded by whips. Men and women were placed in different compartments, with the men in leg irons. The ship then hoisted anchor and started toward the West Indies, a voyage fifty days in length, if all went well. This was the "Middle Passage," so called because it was the second leg in the ship's triangular route—home base to Africa, Africa to the West Indies, and finally back to the point of original departure.

The Middle Passage has come to have a bad name, and in truth the voyage was incredibly difficult. When in 1679 the frigate *Sun of Africa* made a trip from the Gold Coast to Martinique, there were only seven deaths out of a cargo of 250 slaves. But such a light loss was exceptional. On an average, the Atlantic voyage brought death to one out of every eight black passengers. A slave ship was usually trailed by a school of man-eating sharks.

A few captains were "loose packers," but the great majority were "tight packers," believing that the greater loss in life would be more than offset by the larger cargo. On their ships, the space allowed a slave was confined to the amount of deck in which he could lie down, and the decks were so narrow as to permit just enough height for a slave to crawl out to the upper deck at feeding time. . . .

The hazards of nature were not as troublesome as the behavior of the slaves. Some committed suicide by managing to jump through netting that had been rigged around the ship to prevent such action. Others seemed to have lost the will to live. To guard against such depression, a ceremony known as "dancing the slaves" was practiced. They were forced to jump up and down to the tune of the fiddle,

► How do you feel about the ways in which Africans tried to resist slavery?

harp, or bagpipes. A slave who tried to go on a hunger strike was forcibly fed, by means of a "mouth-opener" containing burning coals.

The most serious danger by far was that of slave mutiny, and elaborate precautions were taken to prevent uprisings. Daily searches of the slave quarters were made, and guards were posted at the gun room day and night. But the captain and his small crew were not always able to control their cargo of blacks. So numerous were the slave insurrections on the high seas that few shipowners failed to take out "revolt insurance."

But despite all risks and dangers, the slave trade flourished. The profits were great. After taking out all expenses, including insurance payments and sales commissions, a slaving voyage was expected to make a profit of thirty cents on the dollar.

FOR THOUGHT:

How might the experiences of the slave trade have affected the relationships between African captives and Europeans in the New World?

6 SLAVERY AND SERVITUDE

Why did the English find slavery an acceptable system of labor? Unlike the Spanish and Portuguese, they did not have a tradition of bringing captive Africans to their homeland as laborers. In England laborers were no longer bound to the land as serfs as they were in many parts of Europe. However, the English did use several systems of unfree labor at home and in their colonies.

The first was the system of indentured labor. A person voluntarily signed a contract, or indenture, in which he or she agreed to work for a master for a specified number of years. In return for the labor, the master agreed to feed, clothe, and house the servant and to give her or him something, usually clothes or money, at the end of the period of indenture. (Often an indentured servant was looked upon as a member of a master's household.) If a servant had been treated well and had worked satisfactorily, the contract might be renewed for another term. Such voluntary contracts were common in England, especially during hard times.

Apprenticeship was the second widely used system of unfree labor. Parents, legal guardians, or local courts assigned, or apprenticed, a boy or girl to a master until he or she reached a certain age, usually twenty-one. Society used this system to take care of orphans. Poor parents often used it to provide a better environment for their children. Other parents used the system to teach their children trades.

Under the third system of unfree labor, criminals were allowed to serve a period of indentured labor instead of being imprisoned or put to death. The courts usually sent these criminals to the colonies where their labor was sold to the highest bidder.

The English colonists were also familiar with the European custom of holding prisoners of war in servitude. Settlers followed this custom when they enslaved Indians captured in battles. Under the English law, all captive Africans were looked upon as prisoners of war, even though the "wars" were usually raids encouraged by the slave traders.

During the first part of the seventeenth century, slave traders delivered only a small number of Africans to the plantation colonies of Maryland and Virginia. Of these, some were treated as indentured servants and were granted their freedom at the end of a specified period of time. Some of these blacks owned land and eventually held slaves of their own.

Toward the end of the century, however, the nature of black servitude in the English colonies changed. White indentured servants became more expensive to use—they insisted on shorter terms and better working conditions—so owners turned to the captive blacks. They used them as gang laborers and forced them to work as long as they lived. During this period the number of Africans arriving in the English colonies grew. As more blacks joined colonial communities, prejudice against them grew among the white colonists. This prejudice may have contributed to the owners' gradual decision to keep the Africans and their children as slaves rather than servants. And, in 1671, the English government gave official support to the slave trade. It awarded a charter to the Royal African Company, which took goods to Africa and slaves to America.

By the early eighteenth century, the English had become deeply involved in the slave trade. In 1713, the peace treaty which ended a war between major European powers gave England the right to deliver African slaves to the Spanish colonies. The ships, captains, and crews of the English colonies quickly joined in this profitable but brutal business.

The documents in Reading 6 describe slavery in the colonies during the seventeenth century. As you read the following documents, consider these questions:

1. Why did black slavery gradually replace other forms of servitude in the English colonies?
2. Did Christianity encourage or hinder the growth and acceptance of black slavery in the English colonies?

Jamestown in 1619

In 1619, John Pory came to Virginia as secretary of state. On September 30, 1619, he wrote a letter to the English ambassador to the Netherlands giving his impressions of the colony. Portions of the letter follow.

Narratives of Early Virginia, 1606-1625, Lyon G. Tyler, ed. (New York: Charles Scribner's Sons, 1907), pp. 284-285.

All our riches at present consist of tobacco. One man by his own labor in one year raised tobacco valued at two hundred pounds. Another with the help of six servants cleared a thousand pounds from one crop. These to be sure are rare examples, yet it is possible for others to do as well. Our principal wealth, I should have said, consists of servants. But they must be furnished with arms, clothing, and bedding, as well as their transportation and other expenses paid while at sea and for their first year in the colony. But if they escape serious illness or death, they prove very hardy and able men.

Massachusetts Puritans Discuss Slavery

In 1645 when the Massachusetts Bay Colony was about to go to war with the Narragansett Indians, Emanuel Dowing wrote a letter to his brother-in-law, Governor John Winthrop. In it he mentioned the possibility of bringing African slaves to the colony.

Documents Illustrative of the History of the Slave Trade to America, Elizabeth Donnan, ed. (Washington, D.C.: Carnegie Institution, 1930), pp. 1, 8. Language simplified and modernized.

If we have a just war and the Lord should deliver captives into our hands, we might easily have men, women, and children enough to exchange for Africans. This would be more profitable loot for us than we can imagine, for I do not see how we can thrive until we get a stock of slaves big enough to do all our work. Our childen's children will hardly see this great continent filled with people, so that our servants will always want freedom to farm for themselves, and will not stay except for very high wages. And I suppose you know very well that it costs less to support twenty Africans than one English servant.

Virginia Laws on Slavery

In the seventeenth century the government of Virginia passed laws establishing slavery. Excerpts from those laws follow.

W. W. Hening, comp., The Statutes at Large, Being a Collection of all the Laws of Virginia (Philadelphia: Thomas DeSilver, 1823), pp. 11, 26, 170, 260, 270, 283. Language simplified and modernized.

If any English servant runs away with any Negroes, who are already servants for life, the English servant shall serve additional time not only for his absence, but for the Negroes' absence as well. (1661)

Some doubts have arisen as to whether a child is slave or free who has an Englishman for a father and a Negro slave woman for a mother. Be it enacted that all children born in this country shall be slave or free according to the condition of the mother. (1662)

Some doubts have arisen as to whether children that are slaves by birth should by virtue of their baptism be made free. It is enacted that baptism does not change the person's condition. (1667)

Some disputes have arisen as to whether Indians taken in war by another nation, and sold to the English, are servants for life or for a term of years. It is enacted that all servants who are not Christians and who are brought into this colony by shipping shall be slaves for their lives. But slaves that come by land shall serve, if they are boys or girls, until they are thirty years old, or if they are men or women, twelve years and no longer. (1670)

▶ Should a person's religion be used to determine whether he or she may join a community?

The First Protest
Against Slavery

As the slave trade grew, African slaves spread throughout the English colonies. The Africans' presence in the new colony of Pennsylvania provoked the first known protest against slavery in the English colonies. The protest was written by a group of German Mennonites living near Philadelphia and sent to the Quakers in 1688. The Quakers, who founded Pennsylvania, guaranteed toleration of religious differences in their colony.

We hear that most of such Negroes are brought here against their will, and that many of them are stolen. Now, though they are black, we cannot believe that there is any more power to make them slaves than to make slaves of whites. There is a saying, that we should do to all men as we would have them do to us, making no difference what ancestry or color they are. And those who steal or rob men, and those who buy or purchase them, are they not alike? In Pennsylvania we have freedom of thought, which is right and reasonable; here ought also to be freedom of the body.

Ah! do you consider well this thing, you who do it, if you would have it done to you the same way—and if it is done according to Christianity! This makes a bad impression in all those countries of Europe, where they hear it, that the Quakers here handle men as the Europeans handle cattle.

If once these slaves should join and fight for their freedom, will these masters and mistresses take sword in hand and war against these poor slaves? Or have these poor Negroes not as much right to fight for their freedom, as you have to keep them slaves?

▶ The Quakers did not define *slavery* and *community* the way other English colonists did. How do you define these words?

These Indians occupied the town of Wounded Knee, South Dakota

These two pictures show contemporary native Americans and black Americans involved in movements to demand their rights. In what sense, if any, are these people the heirs of a tradition reaching back to early colonial days?

Slavery and Servitude in Virginia

Robert Beverley, **The History of Virginia, in Four Parts.** Book IV. (London, 1722), pp. 235-236.

An overseer directed the work of the servants and slaves. The overseer had usually served as an indentured servant. During his term of servitude, he had acquired skill in managing a plantation. The term *freeman* referred to an adult male who was neither a servant nor a slave.

Robert Beverley, a prominent Virginian and a plantation owner, published in London in 1705 a long and favorable description of the colony and its people. Here he talks about systems of servitude in the colony.

Male servants and slaves of both sexes work together tilling the soil and sowing and planting the crops. Some distinction is made between them in their clothes and food, but the work of servants and slaves is the same as what the overseers, freemen, and the planters themselves do.

40

A distinction is made between female servants and slaves. A white woman is rarely or never put to work in the fields. To discourage all planters from using any white women as field hands, the law imposes the heaviest taxes upon the masters of female servants who are made to work the soil. The masters of all other white women do not have to pay the tax. On the other hand, it is a common thing to work a woman slave out of doors. The law does not make any distinction in her taxes, whether she works in the fields or at home.

I have heard how strangely cruel and severe some people in England believe the labor system of this country is. But I can't resist saying that the work of the servants and slaves is no different from what every common freeman does. No servant is required to do more in a day than his overseer does. And I can assure you that generally the slaves are not worked nearly so hard nor so many hours a day as the farmers and day-laborers in England.

FOR THOUGHT:

If there had been no supply of black slaves, how might the colonists have dealt with their shortage of labor?

7 BLACKS AND WHITES IN THE ENGLISH COLONIES

The growth of slavery in the English colonies brought thousands of Africans into daily contact with white Europeans. But, because the English had no tradition of black slavery, they had no established rules defining the slaves' position in the community. This situation created confusion and tension in the colonies and posed some complicated problems for the English settlers. For example, while the settlers realized that the labor of black slaves helped make the colonies profitable, they also feared the consequences of large numbers of blacks living in their midst. Greater numbers of slaves increased the chances of slave revolts and runaways.

During the seventeenth and early eighteenth centuries, the English tried different methods of solving these problems. At first, they relied upon individual owners and the church to look after the welfare of slaves and regulate relations between blacks and whites in the community. But reliance upon a few individuals and some moral teachings did not ease daily living and working relationships between the two groups. Eventually, laws were enacted within the colonies regulating the rights, privileges, and behavior of the slaves.

Nearly every individual and group in colonial society had opinions about how slaves should and should not be treated. The following documents illustrate a few of these opinions. They also provide some insight into the way in which slavery expanded from a labor system to a social institution in the English colonies. As you read the documents, consider these questions:

1. Under what conditions, if any, might blacks have been allowed limited membership in colonial society?
2. Were laws regulating relations between blacks and whites easily enforced in colonial society? How can you tell?

Court Cases and Laws in Virginia

The following selections are taken from seventeenth-century Virginia laws regulating relations between blacks and whites.

June Purcell Guild, L.L.M., **Black Laws of Virginia** (New York: Negro Universities Press, 1969), pp. 21, 37, 39, 44. Copyright © 1969.

▶ Should a society have the power to deny the right of self-protection to anyone living within it?

▶ What kinds of symbols does our society use to distinguish the rights and privileges of different groups?

All persons except Negroes must provide themselves with arms and ammunition or be fined at the pleasure of the governor and council. (1639)

The master of every runaway shall cut the hair of all such runaways close above the ears, whereby they may be more easily discovered and captured. (1658)

Negroes or Indians, though baptised and enjoying their own freedom, shall not be allowed to purchase Christians, yet they shall be permitted to buy those of their own color. (1670)

A Puritan Judge Explains an Objection to Slavery

Judge Samuel Sewall of Boston wrote the first pamphlet against slavery in the English colonies. It appeared in 1700 and was titled The Selling of Joseph. *In this pamphlet Sewall gave many reasons why the English colonists should abolish slavery.*

Massachusetts Historical Society Collections, 5th ser., pp. 17-18. Language simplified and modernized.

There is such a difference in their conditions, color, and hair that they can never become part of our society, and grow up into orderly families, so that the land can be populated. But instead they will remain in our society as a kind of foreign element. As many Negro men as there are among us, so many empty places there are among our soldiers, and they take the places of men that might make husbands for our daughters.

Rules for a Black Cultural Society

In 1693 Cotton Mather, a Puritan minister, sponsored the formation of a cultural society by and for black slaves. The constitution drawn up by this group shows the rules which blacks had to accept in order to exist in a white society.

We, the miserable children of Adam and Noah, thankfully admiring and accepting the free grace of God that offers to save us from our miseries, by the Lord Jesus Christ, freely resolve with His help, to become the servants of that glorious Lord.

Benjamin G. Brawley, **A Social History of the American Negro** (New York: The Macmillan Company, 1921), pp. 37-39.

And that we may be assisted in the service of our heavenly master, we now join together in a society in which the following rules are to be observed.

1. It shall be our plan to meet in the evening after the Sabbath and pray together by turns, one to begin and another to end the meeting. Between the two prayers, a psalm shall be sung and a sermon preached.
2. We will never come to the meeting without the permission of our masters. And we will be careful that our meeting shall begin and end between the hours of seven and nine so that we may not be absent too long from the families to whom we belong.
3. We will, as often as we can, obtain some wise and good English man in the neighborhood, especially one of the officers of the church, to look in on us and by his presence and counsel to do what he thinks fitting for us.
4. If any member of the society falls in to the sin of drunkenness, swearing, cursing, lying, stealing, or repeated disobedience or unfaithfulness to his masters, we will charge him with his wrongdoings and forbid him to come to the meeting for at least two weeks. And if he does not come then with signs of his regret and repentance, we will completely exclude him from the society, blotting his name out of our list.

▶ Should any person have to give up his or her personal beliefs to join a society? Why or why not?

Blacks and Whites in Connecticut

In 1704 Madam Sarah Kemble Knight, a schoolteacher and businesswoman, traveled from Boston to New York and kept a diary of her trip. Here she describes the relations between whites and blacks in Connecticut.

43

This photograph shows the congregation of a black church. Why do some black people prefer to meet in all-black congregations rather than in integrated ones? To what degree may the history of the treatment of black people in the United States explain this preference?

The Journal of Madame Knight, Theodore Dwight, ed. (New York, 1825). Language simplified and modernized.

Connecticut people lived very well and comfortably in their families. But they were too permissive (especially the farmers) to their slaves, allowing too great familiarity from them, permitting them to sit at the table and eat with them (as they say, to save time).

They told me that there was a farmer who lived near the town where I lodged who had some quarrel with a slave. It concerned something the master had promised him and did not punctually perform. This caused some harsh words between them. But at length they put the matter to arbitration and agreed to stand by whatever decision was reached. The arbitrators, having heard the claims of both parties, ordered the master to pay forty shillings to the slave and acknowledge his fault. And so the matter ended, the poor master very honestly abiding by the decision.

FOR THOUGHT:

Why did the English settlers gradually begin to refer to themselves as "masters" and "whites" rather than as "Christians"?

8 GROWTH AND CHANGE IN ENGLAND'S COLONIES

HISTORICAL ESSAY

The English succeeded in creating a permanent settlement at Jamestown, Virginia, in 1607. During the seventeenth century, English settlers covered a widening strip of the Atlantic coast of North America as well as islands east and south. By 1700, English settlements were the fastest growing and strongest European colonies in the New World. More than 200,000 people lived in twenty English colonies.

You have seen how the English acted toward the Indians and the growing numbers of African slaves in the colonies. You will now look at other aspects of their community-building.

European Competitors in North America

In the early seventeenth century, England, France, and the Netherlands challenged Spain's leadership in the race to dominate the New World. The map on page 48 shows each nation's claims at mid-century.

In 1608, the year after Jamestown was settled, Samuel de Champlain established a French trading post at Quebec. Between 1610 and 1613, French traders and missionaries founded outposts in the region they called Acadia (the coasts of present-day Nova Scotia, New Brunswick, and Maine). The French had little difficulty in gaining control over the St. Lawrence Valley and the area north of the Great Lakes.

The Dutch operated farther south. Parties sent out by the Dutch West Indian Company in 1722 established trading posts on the site of Albany, New York, and on the Delaware River south of Philadelphia. In 1626, the company founded New Amsterdam, later to become New York City. The Swedes, in 1638, opened rival trading posts on the Delaware River. The Dutch protested and eventually captured the Swedish settlements. Yet New Netherland remained small, solitary, and weak. It eventually fell into English hands.

England and Holland fought several times for commercial superiority in the 1650's and 1660's. The war fought from 1664 to 1667 ended with the Treaty of Breda, which gave New Netherland to England and Surinam, located on the northeast coast of South America, to Holland.

The English success in obtaining so much of North America depended partly on seapower. In the seventeenth century, England's navy and merchant marine (including colonial crews and ships) became the world's most powerful. English ships usually dominated the Atlantic, protected settlements, and made expansion possible.

Human resources and geographical position also helped to make the English colonies strong and secure. Their inhabitants—thousands of English, and a scattering of Irish, Scots, Dutch, Germans, Africans, Spanish and Portuguese Jews, and French Protestants—made up the largest source of military power in the New World. Once these settlers took control of the country inland from the coast, they could not be dislodged unless an enemy could muster greater strength. Only the Indians could occasionally do this.

Self-Government in the Colonies

Settlers in the English colonies lived under governments that gave them a remarkable amount of participation and power. This near-independence from England came partly from the failure of the English government to exercise much control over colonization.

The first colonizing expeditions to the New World were organized by commercial trading companies. Settlers arrived in North America under the auspices of these companies, not those of the English government. The Virginia Company of London organized the expedition that founded Jamestown. It hoped for quick profits in gold or other forms of wealth. Failure to find riches, epidemics of disease, and Indian attacks nearly ruined the colony. It was saved when John Rolfe introduced the colonists to tobacco growing, which he had learned from the Indians. This crop gave the colony a sound economic base because smoking had become popular in Europe.

At first, a company-appointed council ruled Virginia like a military base. The colony received more political responsibility in 1619 when the company ordered that a representative assembly be created. The assembly, known later as the House of Burgesses, was the first of many legislative bodies in the colonies.

In 1624 Virginia became a royal colony and a model for later royal colonies. The king appointed the governor who named a council to advise him. Governors almost always picked the wealthiest and most influential plantation owners to serve on the council, which became a sort of upper house of the legislature. But money to run the government came from taxes voted by the Burgesses. They could influence the governor's actions by threatening to withhold his salary and expenses or by voting him a bonus for his personal use. This relationship resulted in a pattern of uneasy cooperation and frequent conflict. Often squabbles between the governor and the legislators ended with the governor dismissing the legislators, as he had the right to do. He would then run the government with funds out of his own pocket and such other funds as he could scrape up. This pattern became common in all the royal colonies.

Governments with even greater independence developed in New England. The motivation of the colonists played a large part in this development. Most of the original settlers of this area were religious dissenters. In other words they disagreed with the policies of the Church of England, the official church of that nation. They had migrated to the New World, hoping to establish a colony in which they could practice their religion freely.

The Pilgrims were the first group of religious dissenters to arrive in what became known as New England. They arrived in Plymouth, Massachusetts, in 1620 on the ship *Mayflower*. Their expedition was sponsored by a private trading company. Before they landed, the adult males of the group signed the Mayflower Compact, an agreement which set up a government and pledged the signers to frame "just and equal laws." The simple government the Pilgrims set up consisted of a governor and an assistant. Later, the colonists set up a representative assembly. They remained virtually independent of English control in local matters until 1681. In that year England ordered Plymouth combined with the colony of Massachusetts Bay.

The Puritans, another group of religious dissenters, came to New England in 1630. They had created a private trading company to organize the expedition and intended to use the company to encourage other members of their group to migrate to the New World. The

THE ESTABLISHMENT OF AMERICAN COLONIES

Colony	Founder/Proprietor	Date	Reasons for Settlement
Virginia (Jamestown)	London Company	1607	Trade, profit, gold. Conversion of Indians.
Plymouth	Pilgrims	1620	Religious freedom for Separatists. Economic opportunity.
New Hampshire and Maine	John Mason and Ferdinando Gorges	1622–1631	More economic opportunity and religious freedom than in Massachusetts.
Massachusetts	Puritans (Winthrop)	1630	Religious freedom for Puritans. Civil and economic opportunity.
Connecticut (Hartford)	Thomas Hooker Massachusetts colonists	1636	Economic opportunity.
Rhode Island	Roger Williams and Anne Hutchinson	1636–1644	Achieve complete religious freedom.
Maryland	George Calvert, Lord Baltimore	1634	Trade and profits. Refuge for Catholics.
Delaware (Ft. Christina)	Swedish	1638	Trade and profit.
North Carolina (Albemarle)	Virginians	1653	Trade and profit.
(New Netherland) New York	Dutch Duke of York	1624 1664	Trade and profit.
New Jersey	George Carteret and John Berkeley	1664	Trade and profit.
South Carolina	Eight proprietors	1670	Trade and profit.
Pennsylvania	William Penn	1681	Religious freedom for Quakers. Economic opportunity.
Georgia	James Oglethorpe	1733	Refuge for debtors. Economic opportunity. Buffer state against Spanish.

company's royal charter gave the Puritans authority over most of Massachusetts. But instead of leaving the charter and the company's headquarters in England, the Puritans took the charter to Massachusetts and used it as the basis of their colony's constitution.

The few men who invested money in the company were called freemen. They had the right to elect its officers and to approve its rules. However, Governor John Winthrop and other leaders of the company were wise enough to see that other members of the Puritan community would need some share in the government if they were to remain loyal to it. So the leaders allowed most of the adult males to vote for officials of the colony. They granted each voter the title of "freeman." But they also took steps to insure continued Puritan

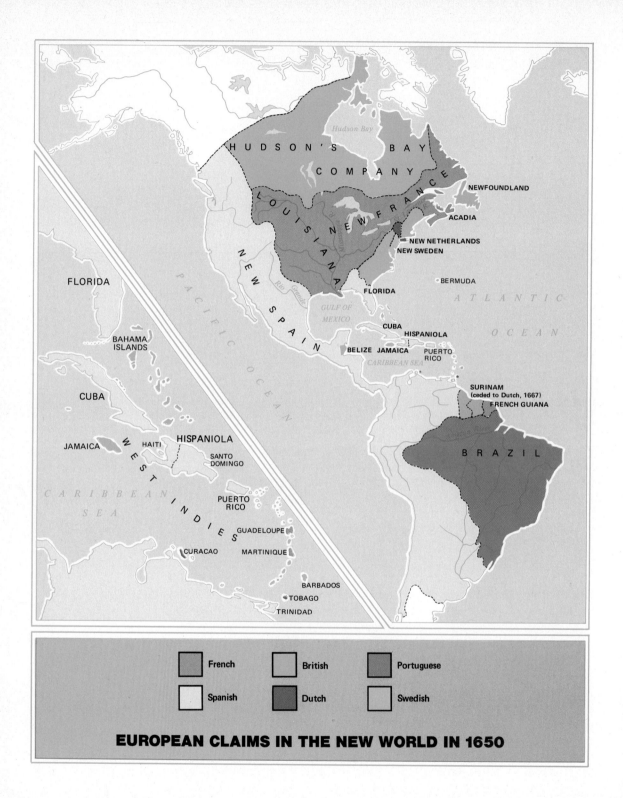

HUDSON'S BAY COMPANY

LOUISIANA

NEW FRANCE

NEWFOUNDLAND

ACADIA

NEW NETHERLANDS

NEW SWEDEN

NEW SPAIN

FLORIDA

BERMUDA

Hudson Bay

ATLANTIC

OCEAN

FLORIDA

CUBA

HISPANIOLA

BELIZE

JAMAICA

PUERTO RICO

PACIFIC OCEAN

Rio Grande

GULF OF MEXICO

CARIBBEAN SEA

BAHAMA ISLANDS

CUBA

JAMAICA

HAITI

HISPANIOLA

SANTO DOMINGO

WEST INDIES

PUERTO RICO

CARIBBEAN SEA

GUADELOUPE

CURACAO

MARTINIQUE

BARBADOS

TOBAGO

TRINIDAD

SURINAM
(ceded to Dutch, 1667)

FRENCH GUIANA

BRAZIL

French

British

Portuguese

Spanish

Dutch

Swedish

EUROPEAN CLAIMS IN THE NEW WORLD IN 1650

control. They provided that no one could thereafter become a freeman-voter unless he belonged to an approved Puritan church.

At first the Puritan officials made the colony's laws. Soon, however, freemen demanded a share in this power. Each of the colony's towns gained the right to send representatives to the General Court to join in the making of laws. Eventually, in 1644, the representatives demanded that they be allowed to vote as a separate body. Thus the legislature became divided into two houses.

These Puritans still considered themselves English people, loyal to the king. But they were content that England was far away and exercised little control over them. When Charles II recovered the throne in 1660, however, royal officials set about recovering their authority over the colonies. The English government revoked the Massachusetts charter in 1684. But the English Revolution of 1688 touched off successful uprisings in the colonies against the royal governors. The new rulers of England, William and Mary, felt that England should have more power over the colonies. So did Parliament, which, from this point on, was the main seat of power in England. A new charter, in 1691, made Massachusetts Bay a royal province and the king named the governor.

Connecticut and Rhode Island had been established by migrants from Massachusetts Bay. They were the only two English colonies that kept the virtual independence they had gained before 1660. Both elected their own governors throughout almost all of the colonial era.

A man living in one of the English colonies in America in the late 1600's had more chance of taking part in political life, as a voter or officeholder, than a man anywhere else in the world. This did not mean that the colonies were "democratic" in the sense that every adult could vote. Women, servants, slaves, and most men with little or no property could not vote. It did mean, however, that the wealthier men, who ran the colonial governments, had to keep in mind the interests of the voters.

The colonies' political contacts beyond their borders were nearly always with London rather than with each other. Since the colonies were independent of each other, they found it hard to cooperate.

The Ties of Commerce

Although political ties were weak, commercial ties linked the colonies strongly with each other as well as with England. Ships laden with the products of farm and forest sailed from the colonies in increasing numbers for Europe. They returned with the manufactured goods and the people so needed in America.

Tobacco soon became the most valuable colonial export. By the 1620's, the Virginians produced large quantities and sold it at good prices. During the century, tobacco dominated the colony's economy to such an extent that it was used as a kind of money. Tobacco growing soon spread north into Maryland and south into the Carolinas.

The Puritans fought against King Charles I and his supporters. The king was captured and executed in 1649. Parliament declared the monarchy abolished and established the Commonwealth under the rule of Oliver Cromwell, a Puritan. In 1660, Parliament invited Charles II to occupy the throne, thereby ending the Commonwealth.

In 1688 Parliament deposed King James II because of his arbitrary rule and his Catholic sympathies. Parliament invited his Protestant daughter and son-in-law, Mary Stuart and William of Orange, to occupy the throne according to the terms of a Bill of Rights.

Europeans eagerly purchased American furs, timber, and fish. The trading posts that dotted the North Atlantic coast from the late 1500's attracted Indians with furs and skins to trade for implements, ornaments, cloth, firearms, and alcoholic drinks. As the settlers cleared the forests, fur-bearing animals dwindled in number, and the trading posts moved inland, one jump ahead of the farmers. In England, timber was becoming scarce because of the growth of population and manufacturing. As a result, American oak, hickory, pine, and other woods were welcome. European and colonial fishermen pulled rich harvests from the Atlantic waters off New England and Newfoundland.

The settlers grew most of their own food and imported most of their manufactured goods from England. Most colonial manufactures, such as linen or wool cloth, or simple wooden or iron tools, were sold and used near the places where they were made. Shipbuilders, however, found it cheaper to build ships near a supply of good timber. American-built ships soon carried much of the transatlantic trade. They also carried goods between England and the rest of Europe.

Commerce between the colonies grew more slowly than did trade with England. But it gained an increasing importance in the late 1600's as the seaport towns of Boston, Newport, New York, Philadelphia, and Charleston demanded more supplies from the "back country" to feed and clothe their growing populations. Rich agricultural regions began to concentrate on a single crop, such as tobacco in Virginia or sugar in the West Indies. Other regions with more diversified products found a ready market for grain, lumber, fish, and cattle.

THE NAVIGATION ACTS, 1660

1. All goods and commodities imported into or exported from the colonies had to be shipped in British vessels. The captain and at least three quarters of the crew had to be British subjects.

2. Only British citizens could trade with the colonies. Anyone in authority who did not enforce this law could be dismissed immediately.

3. Major commodities produced in the colonies—such as sugar, tobacco, and cotton wool—could be exported only to British ports.

SOME ADDITIONAL PROVISIONS, 1696

1. English officers were authorized to search all colonial shipping and to confiscate goods that were prohibited to colonial import and export.

2. Any colonial laws that conflicted with Navigation Acts were null and void.

3. Any goods or merchandise leaving the colonies for Ireland or Scotland had to pass first through England and have a duty placed on them.

Until the mid-seventeenth century, the colonists shipped their produce where they wanted and sold it as they wanted. Most of it went to England or stayed within the colonies themselves. But a growing share of the valuable tobacco crop found its way to markets in the Netherlands or elsewhere in Europe. In 1651 England passed the first of several laws which required the colonies to ship their tobacco to England for sale or resale there. In turn, England prohibited the growing of tobacco in the home country, thus providing a protected market for the colonial planters. These regulations formed part of a general system of regulations called the Acts of Trade and Navigation. (See p. 50.) They were supposed to increase English and colonial commerce and shipping at the expense of other nations. Under the theory of mercantilism, a nation sought wealth, power, and self-sufficiency by having a favorable balance of trade. (If a nation exports more products than it imports, it has a favorable balance of trade. Mercantilists thought that a nation would thus gain gold and silver and would thereby grow in economic and political power.)

Under the mercantile system, colonies were needed to provide the mother country with raw materials and a market for its finished products. Colonies also supplied ships, naval bases, and crews.

Some colonists grumbled about the restrictions arising out of this system. But often the colonists managed to evade them, either by smuggling or by bribing port officials.

The Bonds of Society

Immigration and the American environment brought certain changes in the kind of life European people lived in the colonies. In Europe, wealth and hereditary titles had created vast differences between the classes. The upper classes in Europe did not have to labor with their hands. But in America even upper class men and women often had to work hard to get a successful start. The availability of land—free or at low prices—enabled relatively poor families to own farms and improve their positions. Independent farming reduced sharply the social distance between the upper and lower classes.

Social mobility was, however, largely limited to Europeans. The same condition—shortage of labor—that offered opportunity to European workers, denied opportunity to blacks once the lifetime and hereditary slavery laws, such as those passed in Virginia, were enacted. Nor did colonial society include many Indians.

By the end of the seventeenth century, other changes were also slowing down the democratizing effects of life in America. The growth of commerce in cities like Boston, Philadelphia, or Charleston made the rich richer. A new elite group consisting of the wealthy and colonial officials grew up. Many royal officials were able men. But many of them thought of England as home and considered themselves members of the English aristocracy. Such men often treated the colonies as places to make money out of their positions.

51

The Maturing Colonies,
1700-1763

STATING THE ISSUE

In the 1700's, life for most inhabitants of the colonies grew gradually more orderly, safe, and pleasant. Forests gave way to farms and plantations. The number of wild animals dwindled, and Europeans forced the Indians into the back country. Growing villages, towns, and a few cities offered townspeople and visiting farmers opportunities to trade and to see new sights and faces. The rich supply of cheap land and the demand for colonial products kept unemployment lower and pay higher than anywhere in Europe. These conditions encouraged the raising of large families and drew a steady stream of immigrants across the Atlantic.

As immigrants adapted to the new environment and as the colonial population grew, the colonists became less European and more American. During the first half of the eighteenth century, the roots of American culture took firm hold in colonial soil.

It is difficult to examine the beginnings of American culture since few statistics are available for the period and relatively few firsthand records have survived, particularly from the lower classes. It is possible, however, to learn something about eighteenth-century society from the writings of its leaders. In any society, influential leaders are part of an elite—a small group holding a large amount of power. But they often represent the values and aspirations of the men and women who follow them. For this reason, knowledge of the lives of the elite may also provide information about the rest of the society.

Chapter 3 examines the history of the American colonies during the first half of the eighteenth century. The first three readings show life as seen by a Virginia planter, a Boston minister, and a Philadelphia printer. The readings focus upon the similarities and differences of these three colonial leaders. The essay which completes the chapter describes the development of the colonies during these important years.

1400 1500 1600 1700 1800 1900 2000

1692 Twenty people are executed for witchcraft in Salem, Massachusetts
1721 Smallpox epidemic sweeps Boston
1732 Benjamin Franklin publishes **Poor Richard's Almanack**
1735 Trial of John Peter Zenger establishes freedom of the press
1741 Jonathan Edwards gives his famous sermon "Sinners in the Hands of an Angry God"
1754 French and Indian War begins

1754 Benjamin Franklin proposes Albany Plan of Union
1756 War spreads to Europe to become Seven Years' War
1758 British generals capture French fort at Louisbourg
1758 British capture Fort Duquesne and rename it Fort Pitt
1759 British capture Quebec
1763 Treaty of Paris ends French and Indian War

9 LIFE THROUGH THE EYES OF A VIRGINIA PLANTER

In the eighteenth century, large plantations run by slave labor dominated the economy of Virginia. Some of these plantations were huge, thousands of acres stretching farther than the eye could see. Some of Virginia's most prominent people owned these lands. George Washington, Thomas Jefferson, and James Madison, three of the first four Presidents, were perhaps the most notable. To be sure, the majority of whites in Virginia in the late seventeenth and early eighteenth centuries owned small farms and had few, if any, slaves. The large plantation owners, however, set the tone of Virginia society and ran its government. They were the leaders, the decision-makers and, therefore, strongly influenced the opinions and style of living of their fellow people.

For more than fifty years, William Byrd II (1674-1744) held a place of power and honor in rural Virginia. He was the son of English parents who moved to the New World and established their family securely among the elite of the colony. William Byrd II was educated in England, where his studies included the law. His fellow planters elected him at the age of twenty-two to the House of Burgesses, the lower house of the Virginia legislature. At thirty-five, he won a seat on the Council of State, the upper house. His estate at Westover on the James River remains today as an example of the setting in which wealthy planters lived.

For much of his life, Byrd kept a diary. As you read the following excerpts from it, think about these questions:

1. How did Byrd treat his slaves? his wife? visitors? his neighbors? the nearby Indians? What were his outstanding personal qualities?
2. What issues or events interested Byrd?

The Secret Diary of William Byrd of Westover

In recent years, scholars have deciphered a diary kept by William Byrd II in an antique shorthand. The frankness of some of his entries indicates clearly that the diaries were written for his eyes alone. He wrote the excerpts that follow in August and September 1709.

August 1 I rose at break of day and drank some warm milk and rode to Mr. Harrison's, where I got a permit to load tobacco on board my sloop [a sailing vessel]. . . . I ate some watermelon and stayed till about 9 o'clock, when I returned and read a chapter [probably of the Bible] in Hebrew and some Greek in Josephus. I said my prayers and went to see Old Ben [probably a black slave] and found him much better. I read some geometry. I ate fish for dinner. In the afternoon the Doctor and my wife played at piquet [a card game]. Joe Wilkinson [a nearby landowner] came and gave me an account of the tobacco that he raised this year and I agreed [to hire him as] my overseer at Burkland [one of Byrd's plantations] the next year. I read some Greek in Homer and took a walk about the plantation. I neglected to say my prayers. I had good health, good thoughts, and good humor, thanks be to God Almighty.

August 2 I rose at 5 o'clock and read two chapters in Hebrew and some Greek in Josephus. I said my prayers and drank whey for breakfast. It was terribly hot. I wrote a letter to the Governor of Barbados [in the West Indies], to whom I intend to consign my sloop and cargo. Old Ben was still better and began to complain he was hungry. I ate chicken for my dinner. In the afternoon my wife and the Doctor played at piquet and the Doctor was beat. My neighbor Harrison had the ague but was somewhat better this day. I wrote more letters to Barbados. I walked about the plantation. . . . I said a short prayer. It rained a little. I had good health, good thoughts, and good humor, thanks be to God Almighty. . . .

The Secret Diary of William Byrd of Westover, 1709-1712, Louis B. Wright and Marion Tinling, eds. (Richmond, Va: The Dietz Press, 1941), pp. 66, 68-71, 78, 79-83.

Josephus was a Jewish historian of the first century A.D. He wrote some of his works in Greek.

Homer was a Greek poet who lived before 700 B.C. He wrote the **Iliad** and the **Odyssey**.

Whey is the watery liquid left after milk has coagulated.

Ague is a condition of fever and chills; in Byrd's time it often meant a form of malaria.

54

August 13   I rose at 5 o'clock and read a chapter in Hebrew and some Greek in Josephus. I said my prayers and ate bread and butter for breakfast. Twelve Pamunkey Indians came over. We gave them some victuals [food] and some rum and put them over the river. I danced my dance. I removed more books into the library. I read some geometry and walked to see the people at work. I ate fish for dinner. I was almost the whole afternoon in putting up my books. In the evening John Blackman came from the Falls [one of Byrd's plantations] and brought me word that some of my people were sick and that my coaler was sick at the coal mine. I scolded with him about the little work he had done this summer. . . .

August 14   I sent away my sloop which came yesterday to Falling Creek. John Blackman returned to the Falls. The old man grew better in his lameness and the [slave] boy who broke his leg was much better, thanks be to God. I ate boiled mutton for dinner. In the afternoon I took a nap. My cousin Betty Harrison came over and stayed till the evening. I took a walk about the plantation with my wife who has not quarreled with me in a great while. . . .

August 15   I removed two cases of books into the library. I read some geometry. Old Ben walked a little today which made his leg swell again. Jack was better of his lameness. Mr. Isham Randolph came and dined with us. I ate fish for dinner. In the afternoon I put my books into the cases in the library, notwithstanding Mr. Randolph was here. In the evening I took a walk about the plantation.

September 2   It rained again this day, thanks be to God for his great goodness, who sent us rain almost all day and all the night following. I read some geometry. Notwithstanding the rain Mrs. Ware came to [ask] me to take tobacco for her debt to me, but I refused because tobacco was good for nothing [the price of tobacco was low]. I ate hashed pork for dinner. In the afternoon Mr. Taylor came from Surry [county] about his bill of exchange [a written order to pay a certain amount of money to a specified person]. He told me there was news by way of Barbados that the peace was expected there to be already concluded. The rain kept him here all night but Mrs. Ware went away.

September 3   I said my prayers and ate chocolate with Mr. Taylor for breakfast. Then he went away. I read some geometry. We had no court [the county court which tried local cases] this day. My wife was indisposed [Mrs. Byrd was pregnant] again but not to much purpose. I ate roast chicken for dinner. In the afternoon I beat Jenny [a house servant and probably a black slave] for throwing water on the couch. I took a walk to Mr. Harrison's who told me he heard the peace was concluded in the last month. After I had been courteously entertained with wine and cake I returned home, where I found all well, thank God.

September 5   My wife was much out of order and had frequent returns of her pains. I read some geometry. I ate roast mutton for

The Pamunkey Indians were a small tribe that remained on a reservation in Virginia.

Byrd referred frequently to his dance. It was probably a set of exercises which resembled dance steps.

The stock phrases with which Byrd ended each day's entry have been eliminated from the remainder of this reading.

During Queen Anne's War (1702-1713), battles between the English and their opponents, the French and Spanish, took place in the West Indies.

▶Did your parents ever beat you? If so, what had you done? What did you learn about yourself and your parents as a result of this beating?

The pictures on these two pages show typical scenes of life in the South. What do they reveal about how southerners viewed their roles in life?

►What sorts of things should a person do when a member of his or her family is ill? How do you expect to be treated when you are sick?

dinner. In the afternoon I wrote a letter to England and I read some Greek in Homer. Then in the evening I took a walk about the plantation and when I returned I found my wife very bad. I sent for Mrs. Hamlin and my cousin Harrison about 9 o'clock and I said my prayers heartily for my wife's happy delivery [of the baby].

September 6   About one o'clock this morning my wife was happily delivered of a son [named Parke, who died July 3, 1710], thanks be to God Almighty. I was awake in a blink and rose and my cousin Harrison met me on the stairs and told me it was a boy. We drank some French wine and went to bed again and rose at 7 o'clock. I read a chapter in Hebrew and then drank chocolate with the women for breakfast. I returned God humble thanks for so great a blessing and recommended my young son to His divine protection. My cousin Harrison and Mrs. Hamlin went away about 9 o'clock and I [rewarded] them for that kindness. I sent Peter [a servant] away who brought me a summons to the Council. I read some geometry. The Doctor brought me two letters from England.

September 11   My wife and child were extremely well, thanks to God Almighty, who I hope will please to keep them so. I recommended my family to the divine protection and passed over the creek and then rode to my brother Duke's whom I found just recovered of the ague by means of my physic. Here I ate some roast beef for dinner, and then proceeded to Colonel Duke's, whom I found to be indisposed.

Physic was medicine. Byrd, an amateur physician, cared for those on his plantation and also gave medicine and medical advice to his friends.

September 12   I rose at 5 o'clock and said my prayers and then the Colonel and I [talked] about his debt to Mr. Perry in which I promised to be the mediator. Then I met Colonel Bassett and with him rode to Williamsburg [the colonial capital]. Then I went to Mr. President's, where I found several of the Council. The President persuaded me to be sworn, which I agreed to, and accordingly went to Council where I was sworn a member of the Council. God grant I may distinguish myself with honor and good conscience. We dined together and I ate beef for dinner. In the evening we went to the President's where I drank too much French wine and played at cards and I lost 20 shillings. . . .

Mr. President refers to the presiding officer of the Council.

September 13   I rose at 5 o'clock and read some Greek in Lucian and a little Latin in Terence. I neglected to say my prayers and ate rice milk for breakfast. Several people came to see me and Mr. Commissary desired me to frame a letter to the Lord Treasurer which I did and then went to the meeting of the College [of William and Mary, then still a grammar school] where after some debate the majority were for building the new college on the old wall. I was against this and was for a new one for several reasons. . . .I received some protested bills [checks or bills of exchange upon which payment had been refused] and then we went to the President's and played at cards and I lost £4 about 10 o'clock and went home.

Lucian was a Greek satirist, and Terence was a Roman playwright.

The Commissary was the colonial representative of the Church of England.

58

FOR THOUGHT:

What do the kinds of issues and events which interested Byrd reveal about the kind of life people lived in Virginia during the early years of the eighteenth century?

10 A CRISIS IN THE LIFE OF A BOSTON MINISTER

As the seventeenth century passed, Puritan ministers in New England repeatedly warned their followers against slackening religious zeal. But many of the Puritans' children failed to join churches. As a result, the influence of the clergy declined. In many New England communities, wealthy merchants became the most influential people.

Yet Puritan ministers were still an important part of the New England elite. They were not only its spiritual leaders, but also its most learned people. Many had been educated at English universities or at Harvard College. The positions they held in Boston corresponded in some ways to those of the planters in Virginia.

Cotton Mather (1663-1728) was a leading minister of the Massachusetts Bay Colony. He was deeply concerned about the colonists' lack of piety. In 1692, a large number of persons were accused of witchcraft in nearby Salem. Mather suspected that the devil, jealous of the accomplishments of the Massachusetts Bay Colony, had set out to bring about its downfall. Mather advised against condemning the accused men and women solely on the testimony of their "victims." But he eventually approved of the execution of twenty of them. Most educated people in the seventeenth century believed in witchcraft.

Thirty years later, Mather played an important role in another episode, a role which casts a different light on his character. Like William Byrd, Mather was an avid reader. In a publication of the Royal Society, an English organization devoted to discovering and spreading scientific knowledge, he had learned that the Turks had developed an inoculation against smallpox. When an epidemic swept Boston in 1721, he urged the town's physicians to use this new technique. Only one doctor, Zabdiel Boylston, would agree to inoculate anyone. The results of the inoculation, however, were highly successful. As you read the excerpts from Mather's diary, think about the following questions:

1. What do Cotton Mather's experiences during the smallpox epidemic tell about popular attitudes in the eighteenth century?
2. What events did Mather describe? What literary, philosophical, or religious matters did he mention?

Compare the pictures on these two pages with the pictures on pages 56-57. What differences in life-style do you notice?

The Diary of Cotton Mather

Like many other people in the eighteenth century, Mather kept a diary in which he often entered his innermost thoughts. In these excerpts from the year 1721, he is deeply worried about his duty to his own children and to the community he served.

May 26   The grievous calamity of the smallpox has now entered Boston. The practice of preventing the smallpox by inoculation has never been used in America. But how many lives might be saved by it, if it were practiced? I will consult our physicians, and lay the matter before them.

May 28   The entrance of the smallpox into the town must awaken in me several thoughts about myself, besides a variety of duties to the people.

First, the glorious Lord employed me a few months ago to lecture the people of the city on approaching trouble and to predict the speedy approach of the devil. I now must humble myself exceedingly, for if I am the least vain because my prediction came true, God may do some grievous thing to me.

Secondly, I have two children that are liable to catch the disease. Should I keep them out of town? I must cry to Heaven for direction about it. I am on this occasion called to make sacrifices. If these dear children must lose their lives, the will of my Father must be submitted to.

Thirdly, my own life is likely to be in extreme danger for I must visit the sick.

June 6   My African servant is a candidate for baptism for he is afraid what may happen to him if the smallpox spreads. I must on this occasion try to make him a thorough Christian.

June 13   What shall I do? What shall I do with regard to my son Sammy? He is home from Harvard College. The smallpox is spreading in our neighborhood and he is reluctant to return to

The Diary of Cotton Mather 1709-1724, Worthington C. Ford, ed. (Boston: Massachusetts Historical Society, 1911), 7th Series, Vol. VIII, pp. 620-658 passim. Language simplified and modernized.

61

Cambridge [probably for fear of spreading the disease]. I must earnestly look up to Heaven for direction.

My daughter Lizy is in greater fear than her brother. I must improve their states of mind to make their fears less important than their piety.

June 22 I am preparing a little treatise on the smallpox. First I awaken sentiments of piety, which are called for, and then explain the best medicines and methods which the world yet has for managing the disease. Finally, I add the discovery of inoculation, as the way to prevent smallpox. It is possible that this essay may save the lives and the souls of many people. Shall I give it unto the booksellers? I am awaiting direction from God.

June 23 I am writing a letter to the physicians urging them to consider the important matter of preventing smallpox by the use of inoculations.

July 10 I must consider the various distresses of my flock as the grievous disease begins to distress the town. My prayers and sermons must be adapted to their conditions.

July 11 For Sammy, and Lizy, Oh! what shall I do?

July 16 I have instructed our physicians in the method of inoculation to prevent and to lessen the dangers of the smallpox and to save the lives of those that are properly inoculated. The devil, enraged at anything that may keep the lives of our poor people from him, has taken a strange possession of the people on this occasion. They rave, they rebuke, they curse; they talk like frantic idiots. And not only the physician who began the inoculations, but I also am an object of their fury, of their furious abuse and insults.

August 15 My dear Sammy is now receiving a smallpox inoculation. The success of the inoculation among my neighbors, as well as abroad in the world, and the urgent call of his Grandfather for it, have made me think that I could not answer to God if I neglected it. At this time, much piety must be urged upon the child.

This day Sammy's dearest companion and chamber-fellow at college died of the smallpox. He was not inoculated.

August 22 My dear Sammy, having received the smallpox from the inoculation, now has the fever necessary to produce the reaction to the inoculation. But I have reason to fear that he had already caught smallpox when he was inoculated. If he should die, besides the loss of so hopeful a son, I should also suffer a monstrous hatred from an infuriated mob, whom the devil has inspired with a most hellish rage. My continual prayers and cries, and offerings to Heaven, must be accompanied with suitable religious instructions to the child while our distresses are upon us.

August 25 It is a very critical time with me, a time of unspeakable trouble and anguish. My dear Sammy has this week had a dangerous and threatening fever, which is beyond what the inoculation had hitherto brought upon others. In this distress, I have cried unto the

▶Do you ever lose your temper when things go wrong? Why do people sometimes act this way?

Lord and he has answered with a measure of restraint upon the fever. The eruption and some degree of his fever still continue. His condition is very hazardous.

September 4 The flock must hear me take a very solemn and bitter notice, that although the arrows of death are flying around us, and our young people are afraid for their lives, yet we are not aware that any notable effects of piety have been produced among them. Instead thereof, there is a rage of wickedness among us, beyond what was ever known from the Creation to this day.

September 5 Sammy recovering strength, I must now earnestly have him consider what he shall render to the Lord!

November 3 This abominable town treats me in a most malicious and murderous manner, for my doing as Christ would have me saving the lives of the people from a horrible death. But I will go on in the imitation of my admirable Saviour and overcome evil with good. I will address a letter to the Lieutenant Governor and other gentlemen of New Hampshire to obtain from their charity a considerable quantity of wood for the poor of this loathsome town under the necessity of the hard winter coming on.

November 14 What an occasion, what an incentive for piety I have this morning. My kinsman, the minister of Roxbury, Massachusetts, being entertained at my house, said that he might undergo the smallpox inoculation and so return to his flock, which have the disease spreading among them.

Toward three o'clock in the night, some unknown hands threw a hand grenade into the chamber where my kinsman lay and which used to be my bedroom. The weight of the iron ball alone, had it fallen upon his head, would have been enough to have done part of the deadly business for which it was designed. Also the grenade was so charged, that upon its going off, it would have split, and probably killed the persons in the room, and certainly burned the chamber and speedily laid the house in ashes. But this night there stood by me the Angel of the God, whose I am and whom I serve. The merciful providence of God my Saviour, so ordered it that the grenade struck the iron in the middle of the casement window which turned it in such a way that in falling to the floor, the fuse was shaken out so the grenade did not fire. When the grenade was inspected, a paper was found tied to the fuse with a string, which had these words on it: "Cotton Mather, You Dog, Damn you. I'll inoculate you with this, with a pox to you."

November 16 Ought not the ministers of the town be called together so that we may consider what may be our duty and what could most properly be done upon the occasion of the devil possessing the town?

November 23 I join with my aged father in publishing some *Sentiments on the Small-Pox Inoculated.* Christ crowns the cause for

▶ Do you ever blame an individual for a misfortune that has happened to a large group of people? Why do people sometimes act this way?

63

which I have suffered so much, with daily victories. And many lives may be saved by our testimony. Truth also will be rescued and maintained.

December 14 The smallpox is causing terrible destruction in several parts of Europe. I will send to Holland an account of the astonishing success which we have had here with the inoculation. Who can tell, hundreds of thousands of lives may be saved by this communication.

FOR THOUGHT:

What did Mather and Byrd have in common? How did they differ?

11 THE PUBLIC CONSCIENCE OF A PHILADELPHIA PRINTER

Voluntary organizations such as the Community Chest, the Red Cross, and the Boy and Girl Scouts fill the leisure time of millions of Americans. Each year, private citizens give billions of dollars to the public activities of their choice. Voluntary organizations in the United States originated in the thirteen colonies.

Benjamin Franklin (1706-1790) is an early example of this volunteer spirit. Franklin ran away from his job as a printer's apprentice in 1723 at the age of seventeen. By 1763, he had achieved fame as a wealthy Philadelphia businessman, civic and educational leader, director of the postal system in the colonies, Pennsylvania political leader, colonial agent in London, author, publisher, inventor, and scientist. He gained further renown as a diplomat in France during the American Revolution and as a member of the Convention that drew up the United States Constitution in 1787. Franklin worked his way through the ranks of Philadelphia's mobile society to emerge as one of the outstanding members of a new national elite.

It is hard to think of a more extraordinary colonial American. Yet Franklin's life reveals the main trends of his times, and his personality shows traits that are widely shared by Americans. As you read the following excerpts from his *Autobiography*, think about these questions:

1. What were Franklin's outstanding personal qualities? Why were these particular qualities useful to him in the role he played in Philadelphia society?
2. What interested Franklin? What do these interests reveal about the society in which he lived?

Benjamin Franklin's
Autobiography

From 1771 to 1788, Franklin wrote his Autobiography, *an account of his life up to 1757. In the first part, he described many of the public activities with which he was associated.*

About this time [1737], I wrote a paper on the different accidents and carelessness by which houses were set on fire. I also included proposals for avoiding fires. This gave rise to forming a company for extinguishing fires and for mutual assistance in removing goods from burning buildings or from buildings threatened by fire. Thirty supporters of this scheme were found. According to our agreement, every member was to keep in good order and fit for use, a certain number of leather buckets with strong bags and baskets for packing and transporting goods. These were to be brought to every fire. We agreed to meet once a month and spend a social evening together discussing such ideas as occurred to us upon the subject of fires.

The usefulness of this institution soon appeared. Many more volunteers wanted to be admitted than we thought convenient for one company. They were advised to form another company, which was done. And this went on, one new company being formed after another, until they included most of the people who owned property. The small fines paid by members for absence from the monthly meetings

The Select Works of Benjamin Franklin, Including His Autobiography, Epes Sargent, ed. (Boston: Philips, Samson and Company, 1854), pp. 200-202, 206-208, 212-216. Language simplified and modernized.

►The people in this picture are taking part in volunteer activities designed to serve their community. What obligation, if any, do you have to do volunteer work of some kind?

have been applied to the purchase of pumps on wheels, ladders, firehooks, and other useful tools for each company. I question whether there is a city in the world better provided with the means of putting a stop to fires.

My business was now continually growing and my circumstances growing daily easier. My newspaper had become very profitable. For a time it was almost the only one in this and the neighboring colonies.

I had on the whole good reason to be satisfied with my life in Pennsylvania. There were, however, two things that I regretted: there was no militia nor any college.

Great Britain had declared war on Spain in 1739 and on France in 1744. Franklin was concerned because French and Spanish privateers operated in Delaware Bay.

With respect to defense, Spain had been at war against Britain for several years. Finally France joined Spain which brought us into greater danger. Because Governor Thomas had failed to get our Quaker Assembly to pass a militia law and to make other provisions for the security of the province, I determined to try what might be done by a voluntary association of the people. To promote this, I first wrote and published a pamphlet, entitled *Plain Truth*, in which I stated our defenseless situation in stirring terms. The pamphlet had a sudden and surprising effect. I was called upon to draft a plan for a militia. Having settled the draft of it with a few friends, I called a meeting of the citizens. The house was pretty full. I lectured them a little on the subject, read the paper, and explained it. Then I distributed copies I had printed which the citizens eagerly signed.

When the company separated and the papers were collected, we found about twelve hundred had signed. Other copies were distributed in the country, and at length upward of ten thousand signed. These all furnished themselves as soon as they could with arms, formed themselves into companies and regiments, chose their own officers, and met every week to be instructed in manual exercise and other parts of military discipline.

I then proposed a lottery to cover the expense of building an emplacement for artillery below the town and furnishing it with cannon. We bought some old cannon from Boston, and we wrote to England for more. Meanwhile we borrowed some cannon from Governor Clinton of New York. The volunteers kept a nightly guard while the war lasted. And among the rest I regularly took my turn of duty there as a common soldier.

When peace was concluded [1748] and the militia business therefore at an end, I turned my thoughts again to establishing an academy. The first step I took was to tell my plans to a number of my active friends. The next was to write and publish a pamphlet entitled *Proposals Relating to the Education of Youth in Pennsylvania*. This I distributed free among the principal inhabitants. As soon as I supposed they were prepared by reading it, I solicited funds for opening and supporting an academy. If I remember right, we got no less than five thousand pounds.

In the proposals for the academy, I stated their publication was not an act of mine, but of some "public-spirited gentleman." I avoided as much as I could, according to my usual rule, presenting myself to the public as the author of any scheme for their benefit.

Those who contributed funds to carry out the project chose twenty-four trustees and appointed Mr. Francis, then Attorney General, and myself to draw up constitutions for the government of the academy. When that was signed, a house was hired, masters engaged, and the school opened, I think, in the same year, 1749.

It is to be noted that the contributions to this building were made by people of different religious sects. Care was taken in nominating trustees that control should not be given to any one sect. It was for this reason that one from each sect was appointed—one Church of England man, one Presbyterian, one Baptist, one Moravian, etc. A vacancy caused by death was to be filled by an election of those who had contributed funds. The Moravian happened not to please his colleagues, and on his death they resolved to have no other of that sect. The difficulty then was, how to avoid having two of some other sect. Several persons were named and for that reason not agreed to. At length one mentioned me, with the observation that I was merely an honest man, and of no sect at all—which caused them to choose me.

The trustees of the academy after a while were incorporated by a charter from the Governor. Their funds were increased by contributions in Britain and grants of land from the proprietaries. Thus was established the University of Philadelphia [now the University of Pennsylvania].

When I disengaged myself from private business, I flattered myself that, by the sufficient though moderate fortune I had acquired, I had secured leisure for the rest of my life for philosophical studies and amusements. I purchased all of Dr. Spencer's apparatus for experiments with electricity and I proceeded in my electrical experiments with great haste. But the public now considered me a man of leisure. They laid hold of me for their purposes—every part of our civil government imposing some duty upon me. The Governor put me into the commission of the peace; the corporation of the city chose me for the common council and soon after as an alderman. The citizens at large elected me a Burgess to represent them in the Assembly.

I was reelected to the Assembly every year for ten years without my ever asking any citizen for his vote or indicating either directly or indirectly any desire of being chosen.

FOR THOUGHT:

What qualities did Franklin share with Byrd and/or Mather? How did he differ from each of them? Were the similarities among these three men greater than the differences among them?

▶ Under what conditions, if any, is a person justified to hide the fact that he or she has sponsored something?

The Moravians were a religious group from central Europe who traced their origin to the religious reformer John Huss (1369?-1415).

Proprietaries were men to whom the king had granted land.

12 THE SUCCESS OF BRITISH AMERICA

By eighteenth-century standards British America was a flourishing place. Its relatively free religious atmosphere and its abundant economic opportunities attracted thousands of immigrants. Its growing commerce created fortunes for merchants in both America and Britain and helped to raise the standard of living of hundreds of thousands of other persons. Its governments, which had a great deal of local control, generally had the support of the people. Its physical security became assured in 1763 when France lost virtually all its possessions in America. Thus, except for native Americans and black slaves, the British colonies deserved the reputation of a land of opportunity.

The Colonists Multiply

The rate of population growth is a good measure of the favorable conditions found in British America in the 1700's. At this time, the rate of growth was the fastest in the world. The colonists doubled in number every twenty-five years. A person who lived from 1700 to 1763 saw the population of the mainland colonies grow from about 250,000 to almost 1,600,000, as the graph on this page indicates. Much of this increase resulted from longer lives and more births, but much also came from the stream of immigrants.

The newcomers came from several areas. Hundreds of thousands of Scottish Presbyterians who had settled in northern Ireland now left the depressed economy of that region. Many thousands of Irish Catholics joined them. Since these settlers were usually poor, many came as indentured servants. Others moved quickly to the back country where land was cheap. Between one and two hundred thousand Germans abandoned Europe for the British colonies. They had become dissatisfied with hard economic conditions and persecutions of religious minorities. Many came as indentured servants, but some came in organized communities. They settled in large numbers in Pennsylvania, with its tolerant religious policies and vast reserves of land suited for farming.

The Africans who came to America constituted the largest non-English group in the colonies. During the 1700's, the slave trade, now open to all English or colonial merchants, reached new heights. By 1776 blacks in the mainland colonies numbered half a million, one fifth of the population. More than nine tenths of the black population

▶ Has your family ever moved? Why did they move? Were the reasons similar to those of the colonial settlers?

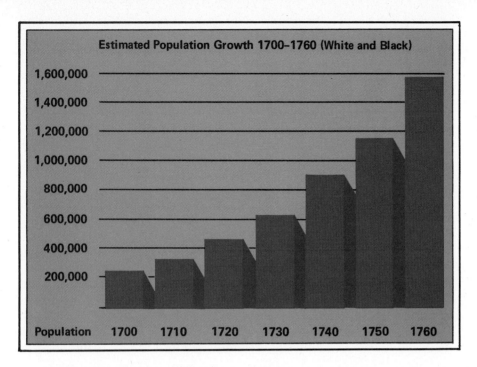

Estimated Population Growth 1700–1760 (White and Black)

| Population | 1700 | 1710 | 1720 | 1730 | 1740 | 1750 | 1760 |

lived in the plantation colonies south of Pennsylvania. Blacks outnumbered whites in South Carolina and Virginia.

The newer immigrants introduced greater diversity into the colonial population than had existed before. Many German groups remained apart, speaking their own language. Blacks, even when freed, were kept in an inferior position either by law or by custom. The immigration of the 1700's produced a population of which a large minority—perhaps a third—was non-British.

Town, Farm, Plantation, and City

In 1750 more than 90 percent of the colonists made their living directly from the land by raising crops and animals, or by taking timber and other products from the forests. Yet their patterns of life—the ways they spent their hours at work, at worship, in politics, and at leisure—differed considerably from region to region.

New England's hilly, rocky, and sandy lands discouraged the creation of large plantations. Small farms were the rule. At first the landholders of a New England town—the unit of local government—settled close together in villages, surrounded by their fields, pastures, and woodland. Community life centered on the meetinghouse where both religious services and civic affairs took place. Usually a tavern or inn also became a social center. As time went on, settlers who received grants of land in outlying towns often sold it to newcomers or divided it among their children. Farmhouses began to be scattered farther away from the villages.

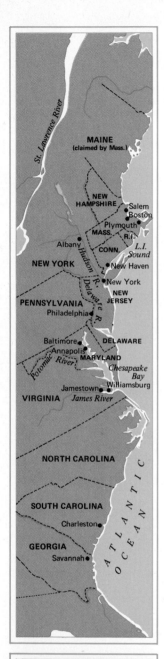

MAINE
(claimed by Mass.)

NEW
HAMPSHIRE
Salem
Boston
Plymouth
MASS.
R.I.
Albany
CONN.
L.I.
Sound
NEW YORK
New Haven

New York
NEW
JERSEY
PENNSYLVANIA
Philadelphia

Baltimore
Annapolis
MARYLAND
Chesapeake
Bay
Jamestown
Williamsburg
VIRGINIA
James River
DELAWARE

NORTH CAROLINA

SOUTH CAROLINA
Charleston

GEORGIA
Savannah

St. Lawrence River
Hudson R.
Delaware R.
Potomac River
ATLANTIC OCEAN

THE THIRTEEN COLONIES

Elsewhere in the colonies, with few exceptions, community life was more spread out. On large plantations, landowners often lived great distances from their neighbors. As a result, the county became the effective unit of local government. Where the Anglican church was strong, as in Virginia, the church parish taxed the inhabitants to provide certain civic services, such as the care of the poor.

Each kind of community—town, village, isolated farm, plantation—concerned itself with the land and its products. Hence, all of them had more in common with each other than any of them had with the colonial city. There the merchant, concerned with buying and selling, importing and exporting, dominated the life of the community.

There were few cities in 1750. Boston, Newport, New York, Philadelphia, Baltimore, and Charleston were the only ones that truly deserved to be called cities. The people who lived in these places had to cope with relatively new problems such as those Benjamin Franklin found in Philadelphia—fire and police protection, sanitation, pavements, and vice. These urban centers grew rapidly. All were larger than most English cities. Philadelphia, with a population of 40,000 by 1776, was probably the second largest city in the British empire.

Relations Among the Colonies

The eighteenth century witnessed rapid growth in kinds of communication that gave colonists more knowledge of each other. All the colonies had printing presses, and colonial newspapers circulated widely. The newspapers gradually included more news of America, rather than of Britain or other countries. This trend showed that the colonists were developing a sense of identity as British Americans rather than as just British. The postal system, which Benjamin Franklin did so much to improve, conveyed private letters as well as newspapers with speed and regularity. Much mail, however, was still carried by private persons.

Colonial religious life, on the other hand, did little to unify the colonists. The Anglican Church, which might have been able to unify its parishes in the southern colonies, did not even send a bishop to the colonies. The planters ran their parishes more or less as they pleased. Other Protestant denominations tended to be even more individualistic. Their churches were always splitting over doctrine and the personalities of ministers and lay leaders. The Great Awakening, a religious revival, swept Protestant churches during the 1740's and 1750's. It divided many Congregational, Presbyterian, and Baptist congregations and ministries. Some welcomed the emotional revivals, while others opposed them. Yet the Great Awakening increased the flow of communication from north to south and from backwoods to seacoast. It also strengthened the deep loyalties of the colonists to individualistic forms of Protestantism.

The Market Economy Grows

Of the several currents that brought colonists closer to one another in the 1700's, commerce was perhaps the most important. Many Americans no longer supplied all their own needs and sold none of their products. Wherever landholdings were large, soil was fertile, management was enterprising, or farming was specialized, farmers produced substantial surpluses for market. They also became consumers of goods produced elsewhere. They became an important part of a market economy that was often intercolonial or international.

In this way different kinds of farmers, such as the Virginia tobacco planter, the South Carolina rice grower, the Pennsylvania wheat raiser, and the Rhode Island horse breeder, helped to develop colonial commerce. So did lumbermen from New Hampshire, fishermen from Massachusetts, and the operators of small iron mines and forges scattered throughout the colonies. In the cities crafts and professional people found themselves bound tightly to the commercial world. All these persons now bought and sold in an intercolonial and international market. They became more and more sensitive to prices, the dangers of war to commerce, and governmental regulation of trade.

The trade of the southern planters went directly to British markets. But most colonists who produced goods for sale put their produce into the hands of a colonial merchant. The merchant usually commissioned the building of ships, arranged to have them manned, and sent them out of harbors laden with produce.

Countries that received colonial goods sometimes produced little that the colony wanted in return. Therefore, merchants and captains often planned triangular voyages to make the greatest profits, as the map on this page indicates. For instance, a Newport, Rhode Island, merchant might import a cargo of West Indian molasses and have it turned into rum in one of the colony's many distilleries. He could

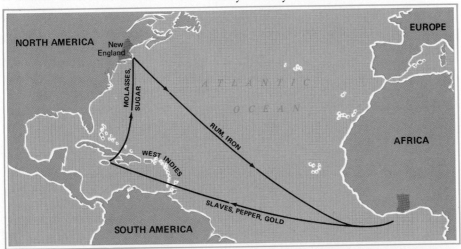

COLONIAL TRIANGULAR TRADE

make great profits with this rum—more than enough to pay the West Indian sugar planters and to cover shipping costs—by sending it to the west coast of Africa. There traders welcomed the rum which they could use to buy slaves captured in wars or raids by native chiefs. Many chiefs made a business of supplying the traders. With a cargo of slaves, the Newport captain sailed again for the West Indies. There the harsh life of the sugar plantations, which gave slaves a life expectancy of only six or seven years, demanded a steady supply of this human commodity.

Perhaps, however, the trader dropped anchor at one of the French or Spanish islands in the West Indies. Here slaves were also in demand, but molasses was cheaper. With another cargo of molasses aboard, the captain appeared a few weeks later in his home port. To avoid paying the tax of sixpence a gallon on foreign molasses, the captain or the merchant who financed him bribed a customs officer. For a penny or so a gallon, the customs officer might accept false papers from the captain. These papers would show a different port of origin, a different cargo, or a much smaller number of casks of molasses.

A profitable but illegal commerce grew up between colonial shippers and those in France, Spain, the Netherlands, and their colonies. For nearly two thirds of the eighteenth century, the British did little to enforce their customs duties. They were often at war with France and Spain and needed the cooperation of their colonies.

Conflicts Among Expanding Empires

Bitter international rivalries drew Britain, France, and Spain into war repeatedly. Each war they fought involved their colonists and the Indian tribes in America.

The British and their colonists fought three wars against the French and their Indian allies between 1689 and 1748. The French gave up Acadia (Nova Scotia), Newfoundland, and Hudson Bay. Other significant gains were made against the Spanish, who yielded the *asiento* to the British in 1713. This act contributed greatly to British and colonial participation in the slave trade. Then Spain gave way without war in a dispute over the land south of South Carolina, where the British established the colony of Georgia in 1732.

A fourth war, commonly called the French and Indian War (1754-1763), decided the fate of France in America. This time the colonists were more deeply involved than ever. In 1754, George Washington, a Virginia militia colonel, tried in vain to oust the French from Fort Duquesne, a key position at the fork of the Ohio River. He returned there a year later as a subordinate to General Edward Braddock. Braddock commanded a large force of British regulars and colonial militia. The French and their Indian allies trapped and smashed the expedition, killing Braddock.

The **asiento** was a contract in which Spain granted the South Sea Company, an English company, the right to carry 4,800 black slaves a year into Spanish colonies for thirty years.

72

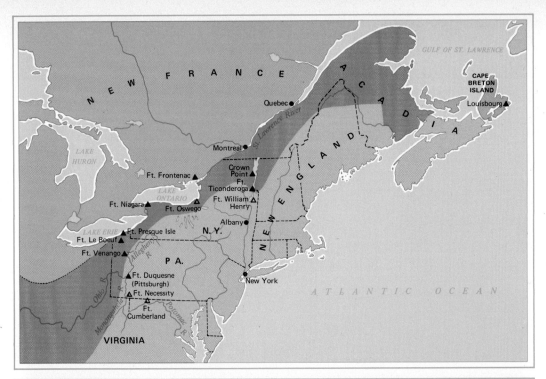

▲ French Forts	☐ French	■ Disputed Territory
△ British Forts	☐ British	

THE FRENCH AND INDIAN WAR

The struggle became European in scope in 1756 (Seven Years' War). Britain formally declared war on France, and Austria and Prussia entered the conflict. For two more years, Britain and the colonists suffered nothing but defeats and losses. The tide turned in 1758 under William Pitt, Britain's inspired Prime Minister. George Washington, aiding the British General John Forbes, returned to Fort Duquesne to capture it. It was renamed Fort Pitt. Further British victories led to a peace treaty in 1763 that ended France's rule in Canada. France also ceded Louisiana to Spain as compensation for the loss of Florida to the British.

Britain paid a high price for the successful results of this world war. It had financed Prussia to fight the European continental battles against France and Austria. The British had borne the staggering costs of maintaining supremacy at sea and of mounting dozens of campaigns in the New World and in India. The colonies contributed men to campaigns but were repaid for their expenses. Now several new questions arose. How would Britain and the colonies organize and use their rich new territories and trade? How would the ousting of France from North America affect the relationships between Britain and the colonies, now that they no longer needed each other for defense against the French? And could Britain pay off the heavy costs of the war?

73

The American Revolution

STATING THE ISSUE

The future of Great Britain and its American colonies looked bright in 1763. The Treaty of Paris signed in that year ended the French and Indian War. Britain now governed all of North America east of the Mississippi River, as well as large parts of India and some islands in the West Indies.

But the war had created some tensions between the colonists and Great Britain. English patriots were angry because many colonial merchants had continued to trade during the war with the French West Indies. Moreover, the colonists had paid only a small part of the cost of the far-flung war. Finally, British commanders had frequently criticized colonial soldiers for their lack of discipline and poor military ability. But the colonists had remained loyal to Britain. Throughout America, colonists celebrated the British victory and praised both king and mother country.

The colonists now hoped to expand their thriving trade. With the French gone from the interior of the continent and fighting with the Indians diminished, settlers began to move across the Appalachian Mountains into the Ohio River Valley and the Kentucky wilderness. In increasing numbers, immigrants arrived to swell the growing population of the colonies.

Both the costs of war and the responsibilities of victory brought new problems to Great Britain. Between 1754 and 1763, Britain's national debt had doubled. The expenses of ruling the empire had steadily increased with additional possessions in North America, the West Indies, and India. Britain needed to reorganize its increasingly complex colonial system. It wanted better control of territories but it also wanted the colonists to pay for the costs of administration.

Resentment among the American colonists rapidly began to grow. Less than twenty years after the American colonies celebrated the British victory over France, they celebrated their own victory over Great Britain in the American Revolution. The first three readings in Chapter 4 focus on the question of why the Revolution broke out. The essay at the end of the chapter examines the meaning of the American Revolution.

1400 1500 1600 1700 1800 1900 2000

1763 Parliament issues Proclamation of 1763
1765 Parliament passes Stamp Act, and colonists organize Stamp Act Congress
1766 Parliament repeals Stamp Act
1767 Parliament passes Townshend Acts
1770 Tension between colonists and British erupts into Boston Massacre
1772 Colonists raid and burn British vessel **Gaspee**
1772 John Adams organizes intercolonial Committees of Correspondence
1773 Boston Tea Party

1774 Parliament passes Intolerable Acts
1775 British fight colonial Minutemen at Lexington and Concord
1776 Thomas Paine publishes **Common Sense**
1776 Thomas Jefferson writes Declaration of Independence
1777 British surrender at Saratoga; France recognizes American government
1781 Cornwallis surrenders at Yorktown
1783 Britain recognizes American independence in Treaty of Paris

13 THE COLONISTS RESPOND TO NEW REGULATIONS

Until 1763, the American colonies had enjoyed a large measure of independence under British rule. Great Britain had controlled the colonies only loosely for a century and a half, while it had been occupied with its own problems. Customs officers had not enforced laws intended to regulate trade, and colonial merchants smuggled goods into the country without paying duties. Colonial legislatures paid the salaries of the governors. Therefore, they had considerable influence over the king's official representatives. The American colonists had become accustomed to controlling their own affairs.

But when the French and Indian War ended, Great Britain decided to tighten its control over its large and prosperous empire in North America. The British government announced a number of measures in rapid succession. The new program began with a thorough reform of the customs service. Britain appointed additional customs officers and instructed them to pay strict attention to their duties or face dismissal. In order to enforce the trade laws, the government directed customs officials to keep accurate accounts of all imports and exports, of fees collected, and of illegal trade. The governors and army and navy officers were ordered to support and protect customs officials as they carried out their duties.

To help ease its financial burdens, Parliament needed more revenue. In addition to enforcing old laws, Parliament decided to pass and enforce new ones. In 1764, the Sugar Act lowered the tariff on molasses, but provided machinery to collect duties. Merchants accused of smuggling were to be tried by judges instead of by juries of their peers. Colonial merchants complained that the duties would hurt their business. Colonial lawyers argued that the system of enforcement violated the citizen's right to a trial by jury.

These changes in taxation and administration policies touched off a vigorous debate among American colonists about the controls exercised by Great Britain. This debate was carried on in pamphlets and newspapers and in the colonial legislatures for the next twelve years. The two excerpts that follow, written in 1764, define the colonial position. As you read, keep these questions in mind:

1. Did Otis believe that the British had the authority to impose the Sugar Act duties? the right to impose them? How did he think the colonies should respond?
2. Do the ideas, attitudes, values, and goals of the New York petition resemble those of Otis? Does either one suggest grounds for resisting British authority?

The Rights of the British Colonies

James Otis was one of Boston's most brilliant lawyers. After Parliament passed the Sugar Act, he wrote The Rights of the British Colonies Asserted and Proved, *a pamphlet which became famous in the colonies. This reading summarizes the argument that Otis presented.*

James Otis, **The Rights of the British Colonies Asserted and Proved** (Boston: Edes and Gill, 1764). Language simplified and modernized.

Otis refers here to the ideas of the English scientist and mathematician, Sir Isaac Newton (1642-1727). Newton's statement of the laws of gravitation promoted the idea that the activities of people, like the motions of the planets around the sun, might be ruled by "natural laws."

Is government founded on an agreement between the people and those who govern? Or is government founded on property? It is not altogether founded on either. Then has government any solid foundation that does not change? I think it has an everlasting foundation in the will of God, the creator of nature whose laws never vary. The same Creator of the universe who made the planets revolve in beautiful order also caused the sexes to attract each other and form families. In turn, families form larger communities which need governments. Government is therefore founded on human nature.

Because government is founded on human nature, a supreme power must exist in every society, from whose final decisions there can be

76

I must confess that over the past few years I have been gravely disappointed with the white moderate. I have almost reached the regrettable conclusion that the Negro's great stumbling block in his stride toward freedom is not the White Citizens' Counciler or the Ku Klux Klanner, but the white moderate, who is more devoted to "order" than to justice; who prefers a negative peace which is the absence of tension to a positive peace which is the presence of justice; who constantly says: I agree with you in the goal you seek, but I cannot agree with your methods of direct action"; who paternalistically believes he can set the timetable for another man's freedom; who lives by a mythical concept of time and who constantly advises the Negro to wait for a "more convenient season." Shallow understanding from people of good will is more frustrating than absolute misunderstanding from people of ill will. Lukewarm acceptance is much more bewildering than outright rejection.

Martin Luther King wrote this passage when he was a prisoner in a Birmingham, Alabama, jail. To what degree did King take the same position about law and justice that James Otis did?

no appeal except directly to Heaven. I say this supreme, absolute power is originally and ultimately in the people, and that they can never give this power away since it comes from God.

Government exists to provide for the good of the whole. "Let the good of the people be the supreme law" is the law of nature. God is the only monarch who has a clear right to absolute power. Hence, it is contrary to reason that supreme, unlimited power should be in the hands of one person.

Since the purpose of government is to promote the welfare of people above all things it should provide for the happy enjoyment of life, liberty, and property. If each individual could enjoy life, liberty, and property fully, there would be no need for government. But the experience of ages has proved that by nature people are weak, imperfect beings. They cannot live independently of each other, and yet they cannot live together without conflict. To settle conflict, people need someone to help them settle their differences.

Here Otis reflects the ideas of the English philosopher, John Locke (1632-1704). Locke argued in **The Second Treatise on Government** that nature entitled people to life, liberty, and property.

By nature and by right, the individuals of each society may have any form of government they please. The same law of nature and reason applies equally to a democracy, an aristocracy, or a monarchy. Whenever the administrators of any government depart from truth, justice, and fairness, they should be opposed. If they do not improve, they should be removed by the people.

The American colonists are entitled to all the rights of nature. They are also subject to and dependent upon Great Britain. Therefore, Parliament has the authority to make laws for the general good of the colonists.

Every British subject born in America is, by the law of God and nature, and by common law and act of Parliament, entitled to all the rights of our fellow subjects in Great Britain. One of these rights is that no one's property can be taken away without his consent given either personally or through a representative. Any tax put on those not represented in Parliament deprives them of their most essential rights as free people.

I believe, however, that all acts of the king and Parliament, even those that closely affect the interests of the colonists, must be obeyed while they remain in force. Only Parliament can repeal its own acts. There would be an end of all government if subjects should take it upon themselves to judge the justice of an act of Parliament and refuse to obey it. Therefore, let Parliament lay what burden they please on us. It is our duty to obey. If Parliament can be convinced that its acts are not constitutional or not for the common good, they should repeal them.

To say that Parliament is absolute and arbitrary contradicts natural law. Parliament can in all cases declare what it thinks is good for the whole. But the declaration of Parliament alone does not make a thing good. There is in every instance a higher authority, namely God. Should an act of Parliament violate any of His natural laws, the act would be contrary to eternal truth, fairness, and justice, and consequently would have no force. Parliament would repeal such an act when it became convinced of its mistake.

> ▶ Under what circumstances, if any, is a person justified to disobey a lawful act of government?

The New York Petition
to the House of Commons

In October 1764, the New York General Assembly adopted a petition to send to Britain's House of Commons. In the petition, the Assembly gave its definition of what it believed to be Parliament's authority over the colonies. The following selection is from that petition.

Since 1683, the government of this colony has had three branches: a Governor and a Council appointed by the crown, and an Assembly.

Journal of the Votes and Proceedings of the General Assembly of the Colony of New York (New York: 1766), Vol. 2. Language simplified and modernized.

The representatives to the Assembly have been chosen by the people. Besides the power to make laws for the colony, the Assembly has enjoyed the right to tax people for the support of the government.

The founders and early settlers of the colony hoped that they had a constitution under which the rights and privileges of the people would not change. It is, therefore, with concern and surprise that they have recently seen indications that the Parliament of Great Britain plans to impose taxes upon people in New York by laws to be passed in Britain. We believe this action would absolutely ruin the colony. So it is our duty to trouble you with our claim that we should be exempt from all taxes that we have not levied ourselves.

We cannot be justly criticized for not raising adequate taxes. The king and the governors have admitted that in the past our taxes have equaled our ability to pay. Our contribution to the French and Indian War surpassed our ability to pay even in the opinion of Parliament.

Exemption from the burden of taxes we have not passed ourselves must be a principle of every free state. Without this right there can be no liberty, no happiness, no security. It is inseparable from the very idea of property, for who can call that his own, which may be taken away by another? If our contributions to the support of the government or to keep an army to subdue the Indians were necessary, why would we refuse to raise taxes?

▶ Do liberty and security depend upon the right to hold property? Why or why not?

The House of Commons should not interpret this plea as a desire for independence from the supreme power of Parliament. For from where else except Parliament can we hope for protection? We reject the thought of independence from Parliament absolutely.

The peaceful submission of the colonies to Britain during the past century denies such a motive. Has not the whole trade of North America been from the beginning controlled by Parliament? And whatever some people may pretend, his Majesty's American subjects have no desire to prevent Great Britain from regulating commerce. We think Great Britain has the power to make laws for the advancement of its own trade, as long as it does not violate the rights of the colonies. But the colonies claim the right to which they are entitled: Exemption from all duties not related to British trade.

Therefore, the General Assembly of New York asks that Parliament not levy any duties on our commerce, except those necessary to regulate trade. Instead Parliament should permit the legislature of the colony to impose all other taxes upon its own people which circumstances may require.

Furthermore, when we consider the wisdom of our ancestors in establishing trial by juries, we regret that the Laws of Trade have transferred cases from civil courts to the military courts. These military courts do not follow the civil laws, nor are they always filled by wise and honest judges. We suggest that trials held in these courts give great grief to his Majesty's American subjects.

This sentence refers to the provision of the Sugar Act of 1764 which stated that merchants arrested for violating the act should be tried in a military court rather than by a jury of their peers in a civil court.

The General Assembly of this colony has no desire to take legitimate power away from the Parliament of Great Britain. It cannot, however, avoid pleading against the loss of such rights as we have enjoyed previously.

FOR THOUGHT:

Do you think the colonists' protest against the Sugar Act in 1764 was a first step toward revolution?

14 THE CONFLICT SHARPENS

In the debate over the political relationship between Great Britain and the American colonies, the British took the position that Parliament represented all British subjects whether or not they sent representatives to it. The Americans maintained that Parliament could not tax them because they were not represented in Parliament. Yet the colonists spent little effort seeking direct representation in Parliament. They preferred to argue that their interests were largely separate from those of Britain. From their point of view, the colonies had grown and prospered without an elaborate tax program. The broader problems of the empire did not concern them.

The colonists used the arguments against "taxation without representation" in the crises caused by the passage of the Stamp Act and the Townshend Acts. In 1765, Parliament passed the Stamp Act. This act required special stamps to be bought to show that a tax had been paid on newspapers, playing cards, and legal documents such as deeds to property and college diplomas. Merchants and lawyers in colony after colony refused to do any business that required the stamps. English merchants whose trade suffered from the boycott argued against the Stamp Act. Finally Parliament repealed it in 1766. But Parliament was concerned that its authority had been challenged. It passed a Declaratory Act stating that it had the power and the right to make laws for the colonies "in all cases whatsoever."

The following year Parliament acted upon this principle by passing the Townshend Acts. With these acts, Parliament turned to a more familiar tax than stamps—import duties on glass, lead, paint, paper, and tea. But another wave of protest swept the colonies. Again colonial merchants agreed not to import goods from Britain. Again Parliament repealed the duties, except those on tea.

Conflict over trade died down until 1773 when Parliament granted the East India Company a monopoly on the sale of tea in the colonies. Colonial merchants viewed this action as discrimination against them, since tea was a profitable item to sell. Soon after a shipment of tea arrived in Boston, a band of colonists, dressed as Indians, boarded the ships and dumped the tea overboard.

▶The two pictures on this page show scenes from the Boston Massacre of 1774 and the clash between soldiers and students at Kent State College in which four students were killed. Under what conditions, if any, do citizens have a right to resist government by force?

But by the time of the Boston Tea Party, taxation and monopoly were only two of the many issues dividing the colonists and the British. In another attempt to eliminate smuggling, Britain established an American Board of Customs Commissioners with headquarters in Boston. Three new military courts were also set up in the colonies to try suspected smugglers. To help pay the cost of maintaining troops in the colonies, a Quartering Act required colonists to provide food and shelter for the soldiers. The colonists feared that all their rights as British subjects might be in danger. Finally the colonists began to question Parliament's right to pass any laws controlling them. The readings that follow show the ways some Americans interpreted British actions and answered the question of Parliament's authority over them. As you read, keep these questions in mind:

1. How did the author of the "Journal" explain the seizure of the Liberty and the presence of British troops in Boston?
2. How might Baldwin's interpretation of the Intolerable Acts have contributed to unrest in the colonies?
3. How did James Wilson define the political relationship between the colonies and Great Britain? How did this argument differ from that of James Otis?

A Journal of the Times

In 1768 the Customs Commissioners seized the Liberty, *a vessel owned by the wealthy Boston merchant, John Hancock. They charged him with smuggling wine. A riot broke out following the seizure, and General Thomas Gage, the commander of the Boston garrison, moved additional troops into the city. Following are portions of the anonymously written "Journal of the Times." It gives a contemporary explanation for the seizure of the* Liberty. *Newspapers throughout the colonies published the "Journal."*

Oliver Morton Dickerson, comp., **Boston Under Military Rule, 1768-1769** (Boston: Chapman and Grimes, 1936), pp. 18, 28-29, 79. Language simplified and modernized.

The Sugar Act (1764) had established a tax on wine.

November 3, 1768 This morning Mr. Arodi Thayer, marshal of the Court of Admiralty, came to John Hancock's house. He served Hancock with a warrant for 9000 pounds sterling and then arrested him, demanding bail of 3000 pounds. The Commissioners of the Customs are not satisfied with seizing the sloop *Liberty* for not paying the duty on a part of her cargo of wines, which before the Revenue Acts were duty free. They have gone beyond everything of the kind heard of in America. They are prosecuting the owner and each person who they imagined helped unload the wines for the value of the whole cargo plus triple damages. The public can now judge. Was the *Liberty* seized in order to create confusion, which would give an excuse for quartering troops in town instead of at the barracks?

82

November 30, 1768 A number of gentlemen passed the Town-House during the night. They were hailed several times by the three guards, but they did not answer. They were then stopped and confined to the guardhouse for a considerable time. A merchant of the town passed the guard tonight and was challenged by the soldiers. He told them that as an inhabitant he did not have to answer, nor did they have any business challenging him. The soldiers replied that this was a town under military rule. They put their bayonets to his breast and held him as a prisoner for over half an hour. He got the names of the soldiers and he is prosecuting them. Perhaps this treatment of the most respectable of our citizens is intended to impress us with the frightening idea of a military government, so that we may decide to give up such things as rights and privileges.

May 17, 1769 The indecent and outrageous behavior of the troops still grows. The citizens of the town have voted to call upon the residents to arm themselves for their defense. Violence always occurs when troops are quartered in a city, but especially when they are led to believe that they are necessary to intimidate a people in whom a spirit of rebellion is said to exist. To keep arms for their own defense is a natural right which the people have reserved to themselves, and it is a right confirmed by the English Bill of Rights.

▶ Have you or one of your friends ever been stopped by the police? How did you feel? Why?

A Plan to Enslave the Colonies

In 1774 Parliament passed four acts to punish the citizens of Massachusetts for the Boston Tea Party. The colonists called them the Intolerable Acts. The first act closed the port of Boston until the colonists paid for the tea. The second allowed those accused of committing crimes while enforcing the laws to be tried in other colonies or England. The third act changed the colonial charter so as to strengthen the power of the governor and to weaken the local government. And the fourth act required the colonists to provide food and shelter for British soldiers. These acts increased the fears and suspicions of the colonists. Ebenezer Baldwin, pastor of the First Congregational Church in Danbury, Connecticut wrote the following statement in 1774 summarizing these suspicions.

We have good reason to fear the consequences of the Intolerable Acts. I do not see how anyone can doubt that they are a fixed plan to enslave the colonies and bring them under arbitrary government.

Some may imagine it was destroying the tea that caused Parliament to change the government of Massachusetts. If it was, surely it is very extraordinary to punish a whole colony and their descendants

Ebenezer Baldwin, An Appendix Stating the Heavy Grievances the Colonies Labour from Several Late Acts of the British Parliament and Shewing What We Have Just Reason To Expect the Consequences of These Measures Will Be, published in Samuel Sherwood, A Sermon Containing Scriptural Instructions to Civil Rulers . . .(New Haven: T and S Green, 1774). Language simplified and modernized.

83

▶Is it ever just to punish a whole town or a state—or all the members of your homeroom—because of the unlawful acts of a few people? Why or why not?

for the conduct of a few individuals. I believe, however, that destroying the tea was not the reason for changing the government of Massachusetts. Rather it was a plan fixed long before, and Parliament only waited for an excuse to put it into effect. It has been reported by gentlemen of unquestionable honesty that they had incontestable evidence that more than two years ago the council ordered the crown lawyers to draw up two bills in order to change the government of Massachusetts.

Now if the British Parliament and ministry continue the course they have entered upon, it seems we must either submit to a dreadful state of slavery or must by force and arms stand up in defense of our liberties. The thoughts of either is enough to make our blood recoil with horror.

The Authority of Parliament

The events from 1764 to 1774 forced the colonists to reconsider their constitutional relationship with Great Britain. James Wilson, a Pennsylvania attorney, published a pamphlet in 1774 redefining that relationship. However, Wilson failed to note that by this time Parliament, rather than the king, was really supreme in Great Britain.

The Works of James Wilson, James DeWitt Andrews, ed. (Chicago: Callaghan and Company, 1896), Vol. II, pp. 505-543. Language simplified and modernized.

Allegiance to the king and obedience to the Parliament are founded on very different principles. The former is founded on protection, the latter on representation. Inattention to this difference has resulted in much confusion about the connection which ought to exist between Great Britain and the American colonies.

The American colonies are not bound by the acts of the British Parliament because they are not represented in it. How then can anyone claim that the colonies are dependent on Britain and must follow British laws that apply to them? With permission from the crown, the colonists made expeditions to America, took possession of the land, planted it, and cultivated it. Secure under the protection of the king, they spread British freedom. They never swore loyalty to Parliament. They never suspected that such unheard-of loyalty would be required. They never suspected that their descendants would be considered as a conquered people.

Great Britain's authority over the colonies is not justified by law nor by the right of conquest. Because British authority cannot be justified, it ought to be rejected.

There is, however, a more reasonable meaning of the colonies' dependence on Great Britain. The phrase may be used to suggest the obedience and loyalty which the colonies owe to the kings of Great Britain. Colonists took possession of America in his name. They made treaties of war with the Indians by his authority. They held the land under his grants. They established governments by virtue of his charters. No application for these purposes was made to Parliament. Nor did Parliament ratify the colonial charters.

The inhabitants of Great Britain and those of America are fellow-subjects owing allegiance to the same king. The connection and harmony between Great Britain and us will be better preserved by the crown than by an unlimited authority by Parliament.

FOR THOUGHT:

Do you think the conflicts between the colonies and Great Britain had reached the point by 1774 where a peaceful solution was unlikely?

15 REVOLT AND INDEPENDENCE

British soldiers walked the streets of Boston in 1775. Some had been sent there in 1768 to help unpopular customs officers enforce the laws. Many others had arrived as reinforcements in 1774 when Parliament set up a military government in Massachusetts to punish its resistance to British laws. On the night of April 18, 1775, General Thomas Gage sent seven hundred of these soldiers into the countryside to search for guns and other armaments he knew the people of Massachusetts were collecting. The soldiers won skirmishes with the colonial "minutemen" at Lexington and Concord. But their heavy losses—73 dead, 174 wounded, 26 missing—at the hands of farmers, shooting from behind the walls and trees that bordered the road back to Boston, signaled a challenge that Great Britain could not ignore.

War had begun. Military action spread quickly to western New England and Canada. Representatives of the rebellious colonies met in Philadelphia as a Continental Congress and took charge of military operations. They appointed George Washington general of the army and took on other duties of a central government.

But was the break of the colonies from Britain complete and final? Many colonial leaders, especially those from the Middle Colonies of New York, New Jersey, Pennsylvania, Delaware, and Maryland, hoped that colonial aggression, plus the familiar weapon of the boycott, might still cause Britain to give way. And Congress, between May 1775 and July 1776, quarreled heatedly over the question of reconciliation with Britain.

However, the course of events and the hostile attitudes of both the British government and colonial radicals prevented any chance of reconciliation. As fighting spread throughout the colonies in the following months, debate shifted to the issue of independence. The two excerpts that follow give the colonists' reasons for cutting all ties with Great Britain. As you read, consider these questions:

1. How did Thomas Paine justify independence? What was new in his arguments?
2. What authority did the Declaration of Independence give for separation from Great Britain? How did this position compare with the authority James Otis gave for obeying laws of Parliament? that James Wilson gave? Had the political ideology changed?

Common Sense

Common Sense, written and printed by Thomas Paine, was published anonymously in January 1776. It was the most famous, most widely read, and probably the most revolutionary pamphlet of those published during the debate over colonial rights.

Thomas Paine, **Common Sense** (Philadelphia: John Mycall, 1776). Language simplified and modernized.

I offer nothing more than simple facts, plain arguments, and common sense.

Volumes have been written on the subject of the struggle between England and America. People of all ranks have taken part in the controversy, but all have been ineffectual. The period of debate is over. Arms, as the last resort, must decide the contest.

The sun never shone on a more worthy cause. It is not the affair of a city, a country, a province, a kingdom, but of a continent. It is not the concern of a day, a year, or an age but of posterity.

By referring the matter from argument to arms, a new era for politics is begun, a new method of thinking has arisen. All plans and proposals made prior to the nineteenth of April [the battles of Lexington and Concord] are out of date and useless now.

As much has been said about the advantages of reconciliation with Great Britain, we should examine the other side of the argument. We should consider some of the many injuries which these colonies sustain, and always will sustain, by being connected with, and dependent on Great Britain.

I have heard some say that because America has flourished under its connection with Great Britain, that the same connection is necessary for its future happiness. Nothing can be more false than this kind of argument. America would have flourished as much, and probably more, had no European power had anything to do with it. There will always be a market for America's goods as long as people in Europe continue to eat.

We have boasted that Great Britain has protected us, without considering that it protected us because of its own interest and not because of attachment to us. It did not protect us from our enemies but from its enemies. France and Spain never were, nor perhaps ever will be, our enemies as Americans. But as subjects of Great Britain, they are our enemies.

Britain is the parent country, say some. This statement is only partly true. Europe, and not England, is the parent country of America. This new world has been the asylum for the persecuted lovers of civil and religious liberty from every part of Europe.

Whenever a war breaks out between England and any foreign power, American trade goes to ruin, because of its connection with Britain. Everything that is right or natural pleads for separation. Even the distance which the Almighty placed England from America is a strong and natural proof that the authority of the one over the other was never the design of Heaven.

It is repugnant to suppose that this continent can longer remain subject to any external power. I am clearly positively, and conscientiously persuaded that it is in our true interest to be separate and independent. Anything short of independence is mere patchwork and it can afford no lasting happiness.

▶ Is political independence necessary to "lasting happiness," as Paine says? Why or why not?

The Declaration of Independence

Thomas Jefferson wrote the Declaration of Independence. The Continental Congress adopted it on July 4, 1776, and cut formal political ties with England. It gives the best known justification for the American Revolution.

When in the course of human events, it becomes necessary for one people to dissolve the political bands which had connected them with another, and to assume among the powers of the earth the separate and equal station to which the Laws of Nature and of Nature's God entitle them, a decent respect to the opinions of mankind requires that they should declare the causes which impel them to the separation.

We hold these truths to be self-evident, that all men are created equal, that they are endowed by their Creator with certain unalienable rights, that among these are life, liberty, and the pursuit of happiness. That to secure these rights, governments are instituted among men, deriving their just powers from the consent of the governed. That whenever any form of government becomes destructive of these ends, it is the right of the people to alter or to abolish it, and to institute new government, laying its foundation on such principles and organizing its powers in such form, as to them shall seem most likely to effect [bring about] their safety and happiness. Prudence, indeed, will dictate that governments long established should not be changed for light and transient [short-lived] causes; and accordingly all experience hath shown, that mankind are more disposed to suffer, while evils

▶ What is your opinion of Jefferson's statement that "all men are created equal"?

Unalienable means "not capable of being taken away."

▶ Do you believe in the right of revolution against government? If so, under what circumstances?

TO ALL BRAVE, HEALTHY, ABLE BODIED, AND WELL DISPOSED YOUNG MEN,
IN THIS NEIGHBOURHOOD, WHO HAVE ANY INCLINATION TO JOIN THE TROOPS, NOW RAISING UNDER
GENERAL WASHINGTON,
FOR THE DEFENCE OF THE
LIBERTIES AND INDEPENDENCE
OF THE UNITED STATES,
Against the hostile designs of foreign enemies,

TAKE NOTICE,

What arguments do these recruitment posters use to encourage people to join the military? Are the arguments similar or different? Why?

are sufferable, than to right themselves by abolishing the forms to which they are accustomed. But when a long train of abuses and usurpations [seizures of power], pursuing invariably the same object evinces [reveals] a design to reduce them under absolute despotism [exercise of power], it is their right, it is their duty, to throw off such government, and to provide new guards for their future security. Such has been the patient sufferance of these colonies; and such is now the necessity which constrains [requires] them to alter their former systems of government. The history of the present king of Great Britain is a history of repeated injuries and usurpations, all having in direct object the establishment of an absolute tyranny over these States. To prove this, let facts be submitted to a candid [impartial] world.

[Here the Continental Congress listed many grievances, of which the most important follow.]

He has dissolved representative houses repeatedly, for opposing with manly firmness his invasions on the rights of the people. . . .

He has made judges dependent on his will alone, for the tenure of their offices, and the amount and payment of their salaries. . . .

He has kept among us, in times of peace, standing armies without the consent of our legislature. . . .

He has combined with others to subject us to a jurisdiction foreign to our constitution, and unacknowledged by our laws; giving his assent to their acts of pretended legislation: . . .

For cutting off our trade with all parts of the world:

For imposing taxes on us without our consent:

For depriving us in many cases of the benefits of trial by jury:

For transporting us beyond seas to be tried for pretended offences:

For taking away our charters, abolishing our most valuable laws, and altering fundamentally the forms of our governments:

For suspending our own legislature, and declaring themselves invested with power to legislate for us in all cases whatsoever.

He has abdicated government here, by declaring us out of his protection and waging war against us.

He has plundered our seas, ravaged our coasts, burnt our towns, and destroyed the lives of our people.

He is at this time transporting large armies of foreign mercenaries [hired soldiers] to complete the works of death, desolation, and tyranny, already begun with circumstances of cruelty and perfidy [treachery] scarcely paralleled in the most barbarous ages, and totally unworthy of the head of a civilized nation. . . .

Here Jefferson refers to the use of German mercenary soldiers, called Hessians, who were hired by England for use against the colonial armies.

In every stage of these oppressions we have petitioned for redress [relief] in the most humble terms: our repeated petitions have been answered only by repeated injury. A prince whose character is thus marked by every act which may define a tyrant, is unfit to be the ruler of a free people.

Nor have we been wanting in attention to our British brethren. We have warned them from time to time of attempts by their legislature to extend an unwarrantable jurisdiction over us. We have reminded them of the circumstances of our emigration and settlement here. We have appealed to their native justice and magnanimity [generous spirit], and we have conjured [appealed to] them by the ties of our common kindred to disavow these usurpations, which would inevitably interrupt our connections and correspondence. They too have been deaf to the voice of justice and of consanguinity [kinship]. We must, therefore, acquiesce [consent] in the necessity, which denounces our separation, and hold the rest of mankind, enemies in war, in peace friends.

We, therefore, the Representatives of the United States of America, in General Congress assembled, appealing to the Supreme Judge of the world. . . . do, in the name, and by the authority of the good people of these colonies, solemnly publish and declare, that these united colonies are, and of right ought to be free and independent states: that all political connection between them and the state of Great Britain is and ought to be totally dissolved. . . . And for the support of this declaration, with a firm reliance on the protection of Divine Providence, we mutually pledge to each other our lives, our fortunes, and our sacred honor.

FOR THOUGHT:

By 1776 what would it have taken for the colonies and Great Britain to resume a peaceful political relationship?

16 THE AMERICAN REVOLUTION AND ITS MEANING

HISTORICAL ESSAY

The American Revolution grew largely out of changes in Britain's colonial purposes and methods. In 1763 the American colonists seemed content with their status. If Great Britain had not attempted to tighten the loosely knit empire and to make more money out of it, the break between Britain and the colonies would probably not have come when it did or as it did.

But once the break took place changes came fast in the Americans' attitudes toward Great Britain and toward their own society. The fears, hopes, dreams, and material pressures caused by war produced some major changes in American life. Nevertheless, America after the war years looked remarkably like colonial America. The conservative nature of the American Revolution was caused largely by two circumstances. The first is that the colonists began fighting in an effort to preserve what they already had, rather than to create a new order. The second is that the war did little damage to agriculture, the basis of American economy.

Reconstructing the Empire

After the French and Indian War, the British decided that they could no longer afford to neglect their American colonies. The government issued a series of laws and decrees aimed at establishing more effective control over them.

▶ How did you feel when your parents or teachers took away a privilege you had long enjoyed?

With French power eliminated in America after 1763, colonists moved west and provoked a new Indian war, the Pontiac Conspiracy. To quiet the Indians and to gain time to organize the territory acquired from France, Parliament issued the Proclamation of 1763. This act forbade the colonists to settle west of the Appalachian Mountains. Then, in 1764, Parliament passed the Sugar Act. This act placed new duties on sugar, coffee, wine, and certain other imported products, reduced the tax on molasses, and provided ways to collect all duties more effectively.

There were only scattered protests to these first measures. But a major crisis over taxation quickly followed. In 1765, Parliament passed the Stamp Act. Colonial resistance took a number of forms. Colonial leaders refused to do any business requiring the use of stamps to show that the tax had been paid. Trade came to a halt, and courts of justice closed since virtually all legal papers needed stamps. Politicians organized bands of patriots, largely workingmen, who called themselves Sons of Liberty. They pressured reluctant business people to support the boycott and forced Stamp Act officials to resign by their use of threats and violence.

Even more significant was a meeting in New York of delegates from nine colonies. This Stamp Act Congress was the first really effective act of political cooperation among so many colonies. It adopted a series of resolutions protesting the new tax law and other new policies, such as the trials of accused smugglers by military courts. British business people hurt by the colonial boycott persuaded Parliament to repeal the Stamp Act in 1766. At the same time, Parliament restated its right to pass laws for the colonies.

Parliament continued to pass new and unpopular laws which caused the division between the colonists and Great Britain to grow larger. Occasional brawls between the colonists and the British soldiers quartered in Boston finally ended in the Boston Massacre in 1770.

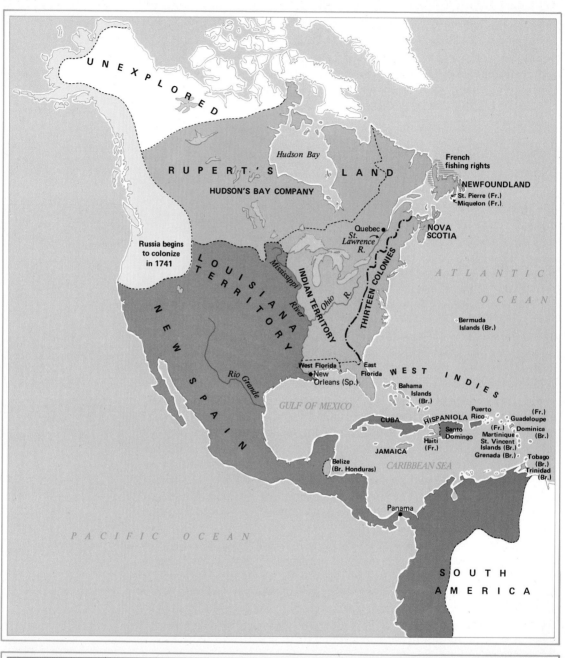

UNEXPLORED

Hudson Bay

RUPERT'S LAND

HUDSON'S BAY COMPANY

French fishing rights

NEWFOUNDLAND

St. Pierre (Fr.)
Miquelon (Fr.)

Russia begins
to colonize
in 1741

Quebec
St.
Lawrence
R.

NOVA
SCOTIA

LOUISIANA TERRITORY

Mississippi River

INDIAN TERRITORY

Ohio R.

THIRTEEN COLONIES

ATLANTIC

OCEAN

NEW SPAIN

Rio Grande

Bermuda
Islands (Br.)

West Florida

East
Florida

WEST INDIES

New
Orleans (Sp.)

GULF OF MEXICO

Bahama
Islands
(Br.)

CUBA

HISPANIOLA

Puerto
Rico

(Fr.)

Guadeloupe

Santo
Domingo

(Fr.)

Dominica

Haiti
(Fr.)

Martinique
(Fr.)
St. Vincent
Islands (Br.)

(Br.)

JAMAICA

Grenada (Br.)

Belize
(Br. Honduras)

CARIBBEAN SEA

Tobago
(Br.)
Trinidad
(Br.)

Panama

PACIFIC OCEAN

SOUTH
AMERICA

British   French
Spanish   Russian   — · — · — Proclamation Line—1763

**NORTH
AMERICA
IN 1763**

British soldiers shot five members of an unarmed mob. Similar brawls between soldiers and colonists occurred in New York and added to the growing dislike and fear between the colonists and the British.

The first colonist to fall was a black, Crispus Attucks.

The Lull and the Storm

In the spring of 1770, British-colonial relations took a marked turn for the better. The British soldiers in Boston withdrew to the fort in the harbor to prevent further incidents. A new Parliamentary ministry took office. Its leader, Lord Frederick North, had all of the Townshend duties repealed except that on tea. North allowed the Quartering Act to expire and also promised that no new taxes would be imposed on the colonies. There was rejoicing in the colonies, and for more than two years there seemed to be a real reconciliation.

Then a series of episodes produced serious conflicts that finally led to independence. The first took place in June 1772, when a group of Rhode Islanders raided and burned the *Gaspee*, a customs vessel. The British decision to try the offenders in England, assuming they could be identified, alarmed the colonists, who saw this decision as yet another blow to the right of trial by jury. The colonists organized Committees of Correspondence to keep each other informed about local conflicts between colonial and British authority and to circulate propaganda against British rule.

The British commission investigating the *Gaspee* affair failed to identify those responsible.

In 1773, the tea crisis speeded up the final break with Great Britain. The colonists saw the British East India Company's monopoly on the sale of tea as another example of colonial exploitation for British profits. The colonists prevented the sale of tea up and down the Atlantic coast. In Boston, the center of colonial protest, a band of citizens destroyed the cargo of tea ships.

Parliament responded angrily in 1774 with the Coercive Acts, labeled the Intolerable Acts by the colonists. At the same time, Parliament passed the Quebec Act, which was not intended as a colonial punishment, but which the colonists interpreted as one.

The Quebec Act granted religious freedom to Roman Catholics. It also extended Quebec's border southward to the Ohio River, thus nullifying some colonists' claims on western lands.

With the Intolerable Acts, Parliament showed that it intended to enforce British authority, regardless of the cost to trade and remaining colonial good will. All the colonies united firmly in support of Massachusetts. The Committees of Correspondence organized a Congress, which met in Philadelphia in September 1774 to deal with the mounting crisis. The fifty-five delegates from twelve colonies (Georgia was not represented) voted to support Massachusetts, to denounce Parliament's legislation for the colonies since 1763, and to form a Continental Association to enforce a complete boycott of trade with Britain.

By the spring of 1776, it became clear to most members of the Congress that reconciliation between the colonies and Great Britain was impossible without completely surrendering the colonial position.

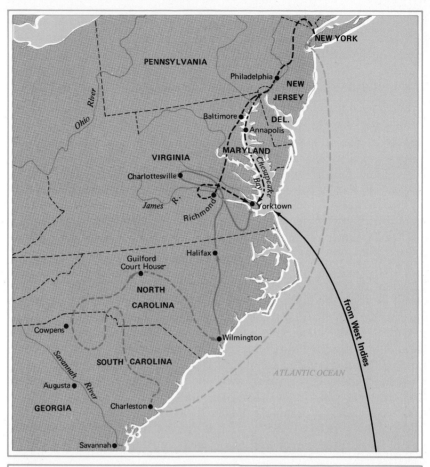

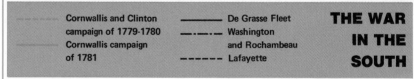

- - - - Cornwallis and Clinton campaign of 1779-1780	———— De Grasse Fleet
Cornwallis campaign of 1781	—··—··— Washington and Rochambeau
	- - - - - - Lafayette

THE WAR IN THE SOUTH

In all thirteen colonies, the Americans had removed the royal officials. The colonists were disillusioned with the king, who had stoutly supported Parliament. And their position was strengthened by Thomas Paine's bitter attack in *Common Sense* on monarchy in general and on the king in particular. The Continental Congress responded to the events of the year by adopting the Declaration of Independence.

The War and Its Strategy

The Americans' victory in the War for Independence had a number of reasons. First, they fought on home ground. Second, they received considerable help from France and Spain. And third, their commander,

94

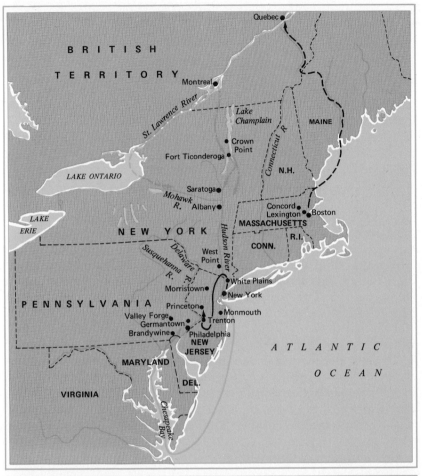

**THE WAR
IN THE
NORTHEAST**

George Washington, realized that time was on the American side if he could avoid an early defeat.

The British met with serious difficulties in using their superior strength on the distant rebellion. The war against the colonies was unpopular with many merchants, some members of Parliament, and even some generals. The British did not have the manpower needed to put down the revolt so they had to hire thirty thousand mercenary soldiers from Germany. In addition, the British navy was in bad shape.

The British campaign did not begin very well in June 1775 at the Battle of Bunker Hill. The Americans killed and wounded more than a thousand British regulars. In March 1776, the Americans suddenly fortified Dorchester Heights, which overlooked Boston and its harbor,

The Battle of Bunker Hill was actually fought on Breed's Hill.

where the British fleet was anchored. The British sailed for Halifax and did not return to Boston. Reinforced to 32,000 men, they landed six months later at New York, where Washington had moved his main army. They easily drove Washington's weaker forces into New Jersey and then Pennsylvania.

The British General William Howe and his successor, Sir William Clinton, used New York as a base of operations from then on. They sent British armies out to capture Philadelphia, Savannah, and Charleston, and to try to engage Washington in battle. Washington fought only when he had a good chance to do damage to the British forces, and he always kept a way open for retreat. Between 1776 and 1781, the main British and American armies met several times but neither could win.

British control of New York largely cut New England off from the other colonies. But British efforts to isolate New England met a spectacular failure. General John Burgoyne, leading a force of 7700 men south from Canada down the Hudson Valley, found himself blocked by American soldiers. The American commander, General Horatio Gates, forced Burgoyne to surrender his army at Saratoga, New York, on October 17, 1777. Secret aid from France and Spain contributed to the American victory at Saratoga. When news of the victory reached Paris, France recognized the American government and signed an alliance against Britain.

In the South, Britain's first attempt to capture Charleston failed in 1776. A second expedition against Charleston in early 1780 won that seaport. The British then tried for the next year and a half to mop up the opposition in the Carolinas. By late 1781, they controlled little but Charleston and Wilmington.

On the fringes of the main areas of battle, the Americans had some small but important successes. An early thrust into Canada, in the

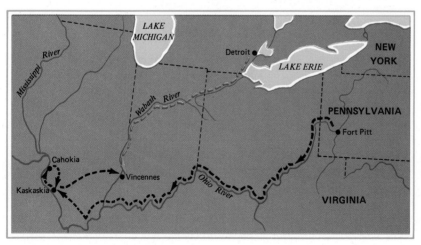

British Route
Clark's Route
Present day boundaries

NORTHWEST CAMPAIGN 1778-1779

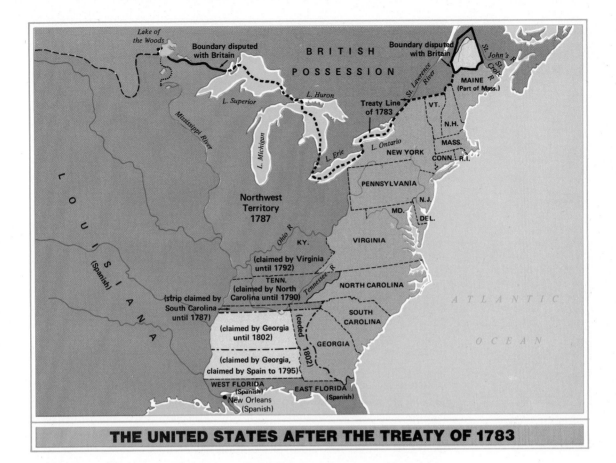

THE UNITED STATES AFTER THE TREATY OF 1783

Map labels: Lake of the Woods; Boundary disputed with Britain; BRITISH POSSESSION; Boundary disputed with Britain; St. John's R.; St. Croix R.; MAINE (Part of Mass.); L. Superior; L. Huron; St. Lawrence River; Treaty Line of 1783; VT.; N.H.; Mississippi River; L. Michigan; L. Erie; L. Ontario; NEW YORK; MASS.; CONN.; R.I.; PENNSYLVANIA; N.J; MD.; DEL.; Northwest Territory 1787; Ohio R.; KY.; VIRGINIA; L O U I S I A N A (Spanish); (claimed by Virginia until 1792); TENN. (claimed by North Carolina until 1790); Tennessee R.; NORTH CAROLINA; (strip claimed by South Carolina until 1787); (claimed by Georgia until 1802); ceded 1802; SOUTH CAROLINA; GEORGIA; (claimed by Georgia, claimed by Spain to 1795); WEST FLORIDA (Spanish); New Orleans (Spanish); EAST FLORIDA (Spanish); A T L A N T I C   O C E A N

winter of 1775-1776, failed to capture Quebec, and the Americans withdrew. Forces under Benedict Arnold, one of the leaders of that expedition, then blocked a British counterthrust at Lake Champlain the following fall. In the Ohio Valley, George Rogers Clark and a band of Virginia militiamen, aided by the French, conquered British forts at Kaskasia and Vincennes.

The French fleet sent to aid the Americans finally gave them the chance to strike a decisive blow against the British. With masterful timing, Washington and Comte de Rochambeau, commanding the American and French forces outside New York, secretly moved their troops to Virginia to trap a British army under Lord Cornwallis. Cornwallis had marched north from the Carolinas and occupied Yorktown, on a peninsula accessible to British sea power. But the French fleet prevented a British rescue fleet from reaching Cornwallis. He had to surrender.

Parliament, already dismayed at the frustrating course of the war, decided that the victory at Yorktown signaled the end of the war. Peace sentiment swelled in Britain and Lord North's ministry fell.

▶ People often vote against officials in power when a disaster hits. Why do they act that way?

Negotiations with an American peace mission in Paris followed. At that peace conference, Benjamin Franklin, John Adams, and John Jay won a remarkable diplomatic victory with the signing of the Treaty of Paris in 1783. (See map, p. 97.) Great Britain recognized both American independence and American title to the land east of the Mississippi River between the Great Lakes and Florida. Florida went to Spain. The British hoped to lure Americans away from a close attachment to the French by making such a generous settlement.

The Revolution at Home

After the revolution against Britain, relatively few changes occurred in American institutions. State governments were established under new constitutions, beginning in 1776, but they resembled the colonial governments they replaced. Under the new constitutions, the representative assemblies held most political power. Voters in most states elected their governors, whose power was reduced. In most of the colonies, the right to vote had depended on possession of some property. During the war, nearly all property qualifications for voting and officeholding were either lowered or dropped.

The new states guarded their powers jealously. They gave some authority to the new government of the United States formed under the Articles of Confederation in 1781. But they kept all authority relating to local government. The central government, which itself lacked an effective executive office, directed the army and conducted foreign relations. But it could not regulate commerce, nor did it have the authority to tax citizens directly. It had the right to request money from the states, but could not enforce its requests.

Merchants and other creditors suffered from the interruption of commerce during the war. But farmers and debtors benefited from the demand for foodstuffs and the creation of a vast supply of paper money by the revolutionary government to pay its debts. Much property owned by Loyalists was confiscated. In most cases, it went to property holders rather than to landless people. Stimulated by the war, democratic ideas affected some social relationships. Perhaps the most striking examples were the decisions of several northern states to abolish slavery. Some southern states simplified the process of freeing slaves. The numbers of freed slaves increased substantially. Most states prohibited the slave trade during the Revolution. Thus, Americans emerged from their War for Independence with a working national political system and a society and economy that were not deeply divided.

The New Government

STATING THE ISSUE

After the Revolutionary War, Americans set up a government that reflected their political ideology. The purpose of a government, they felt, was to protect the rights of individuals. Since a government with unlimited power could threaten a person's life, liberty, or property, its powers had to be carefully defined by a constitution.

The Americans also drew upon their experiences in colonial government. Individual colonies treasured their charters, in which king and Parliament had granted them important powers. In all the colonies, executive, legislative, and judicial departments had been established. Those qualifying as voters chose the members of the lower house of the legislature. The king usually appointed the governor. And either the king or the governor appointed the members of the upper house and the principal judges.

The events of the years following 1763 made a deep impression on Americans. They acquired a suspicion of a remote, central government that passed laws and issued decrees that seemed to violate established rights and to disturb usual ways of doing things. Since the colonies had been tied more closely to England than to each other, they were not used to working together. But the clashes with Britain began to forge the bonds of colonial cooperation. The Stamp Act Congress, the non-importation agreements, and the Committees of Correspondence prepared the way for the Continental Congress and the Articles of Confederation, which set up a national government.

During the 1780's, many Americans grew dissatisfied with the government established under the Articles of Confederation. As its weaknesses became apparent, movements to amend the Articles sprang up. Eventually, a new constitution was written and ratified, and a new government began. The first reading in Chapter 5 describes the way in which this new government met the challenges of independence. The remaining three readings provide materials from which you can analyze the nature of the new government.

99

1400 1500 1600 1700 1800 1900 2000

1774 First Continental Congress convenes
1775 Second Continental Congress convenes
1781 States adopt Articles of Confederation
1783 Congress ratifies Treaty of Paris
1784 Jefferson proposes ordinance for governing Northwest Territory
1785 Congress passes ordinance establishing boundaries in Northwest Territory
1786 Annapolis Convention convenes to discuss interstate commerce
1786 Daniel Shays leads rebellion of farmers in Massachusetts

1787 Constitutional Convention convenes in Philadelphia
1787 Congress passes Northwest Ordinance based on Jefferson's plan of 1784
1787-88 John Jay, James Madison, and Alexander Hamilton write **The Federalist**
1788 States ratify Constitution
1789 George Washington is elected President
1790 States agree to establish District of Columbia as site for national capitol
1791 States ratify Bill of Rights

17 THE CHALLENGE OF INDEPENDENCE

HISTORICAL ESSAY

Chapters 1-4 have each begun with three readings followed by a historical essay. Chapter 5, however, begins with a historical essay. It provides much of the information essential to an understanding of the readings which follow.

The Articles of Confederation had been drawn up in 1776 and approved by the Continental Congress in 1777. They were not ratified by all thirteen states until 1781. At this time they became the official basis for federal government.

Americans, 3 million strong, settled into peace in 1783. Most people's daily lives as citizens of states did not differ greatly from their lives as subjects of King George III. The state governments had for two years been working together under the Articles of Confederation. Yet some serious problems existed.

Many difficulties tested the strength of the national unity forged by the Revolution. States found it hard to reconcile the conflicting interests of merchants and farmers, city and country, and seacoast

100

and frontier. A few states had trouble in their direct dealings with other states. Other challenges were national in scope. The United States needed security and respect. And its citizens wanted a fair chance to engage in international trade. Governing and settling the vast western lands won by the United States in the Treaty of Paris offered another problem. Above all, the government had to convince its citizens that it was worth supporting.

The Western Country

Perhaps the most appealing opportunity for Americans lay in the West. Here millions of acres of fertile land stretched from the Appalachians to the Mississippi River. Even during the war, settlers by the tens of thousands had flooded over the mountains into the Kentucky and Tennessee country, where British influence among the Indian tribes was weak. Although Virginia and North Carolina still held title to these western lands, the settlers began to ask for new state governments west of the mountains.

With the end of the war, the lands north of the Ohio River lay open to settlement. Speculators began lobbying to get Congress to sell them large tracts of land cheaply. Meanwhile, pioneers began moving into the Ohio country, illegally "squatting" wherever they found land.

If the process of settlement was to be directed by the government and if the public lands were to provide a source of national income, some kind of land policy had to be worked out. The Continental Congress had promised in 1780 to create new states from the western lands. The new states were to enjoy the same rights as the older ones. Congress now moved to carry out this pledge by adopting the Northwest Ordinance of 1784, an act proposed by Thomas Jefferson. It divided the Northwest into ten parts, each to be governed by the settlers themselves. Each part could send a non-voting delegate to Congress as soon as its population reached twenty thousand. A part would be admitted as a state as soon as its population equaled the free population of the smallest existing state. The following year, in the Ordinance of 1785, Congress adopted a plan to survey the Northwest lands and to lay them out in townships six miles square. But before much of the Ohio country could be surveyed, Congress yielded to pressure from land speculators and to its own desire to pay off some of the war debts. It contracted to sell several million acres of Ohio lands to speculative companies at what amounted to only a few cents an acre.

The proceeds from the sale of one square mile in each township went to support public schools.

Many of these mass sales fell through within the next few years. But the land companies persuaded Congress to change the system of government in the Northwest, so that they could exert more influence upon the territorial governments than they could under

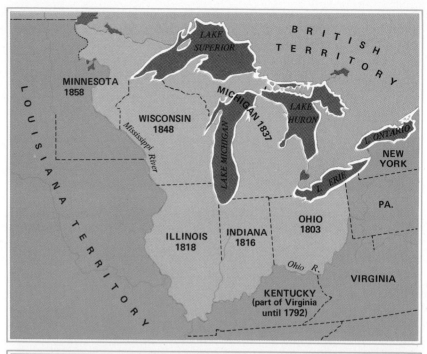

MINNESOTA
1858

WISCONSIN
1848

Mississippi River

LAKE SUPERIOR

MICHIGAN 1837

LAKE MICHIGAN

LAKE HURON

BRITISH TERRITORY

L. ONTARIO

NEW YORK

PA.

L. ERIE

LOUISIANA TERRITORY

ILLINOIS
1818

INDIANA
1816

OHIO
1803

Ohio R.

VIRGINIA

KENTUCKY
(part of Virginia
until 1792)

Northwest Territory 1787

Present state boundaries
Dates indicate year of state's
admission to Union

**STATES CARVED
OUT OF THE
NORTHWEST TERRITORY**

Jefferson's democratic scheme. Congress passed the Northwest Ordinance of 1787, which served in the future as a model for American territorial organization. It created the Northwest Territory, which could be divided into three to five new territories. Each was to be ruled by a governor and judges, appointed by Congress, until it gained five thousand adult free males. Then the settlers could elect a bicameral (two-house) legislature, whose laws, however, could still be vetoed by the governor. When the population of a territory reached sixty thousand, it could adopt a constitution and apply for statehood. (See map, above.)

Indians often lived or hunted on land the government offered for settlement. As the settlers advanced, they forced the Indians to retreat westward. Sometimes the federal government managed to acquire the land peacefully through treaty or purchase. When the Indians resisted these attempts to dislodge them, small-scale wars often followed. The Indians found that their days on the land were clearly numbered under the pressure of the land-hungry easterners.

▶How should a technologically advanced society treat people from a simpler culture who occupy lands that the more advanced people want?

102

Foreign Relations and Foreign Trade

The British gave up the territory south of the Great Lakes in the treaty that followed the Revolutionary War. Yet they violated that treaty by maintaining military posts at Detroit, in northern Michigan, and in northern New York. They kept these posts for several reasons. They wanted to continue to trade with the Indians. They hoped to put pressure on the United States to fulfill such unpleasant obligations in the treaty as paying Loyalists for confiscated property and allowing British creditors to collect debts from Americans. And they wanted to be able to exert influence in case the settlers in areas that were not states decided to break away from the United States.

The Spanish threat to the West was even more menacing. From Louisiana and the Floridas, Spain urged the Indian tribes to attack the advancing settlers. In 1784, Spain closed the lower Mississippi River to the settlers, thus blocking their only access to the sea. The Spanish also negotiated secretly with settlers in frontier areas, hoping that they would break away from the United States in return for reopening the Mississippi and restraining the Indians.

Against the British in the north and the Spanish in the south, American diplomats could do nothing. The United States lacked the military power to make European nations respect it. Moreover, the states could not cooperate to create a military force. The British were unimpressed with the possibility that the United States might become unified and powerful. They did not even bother to send a diplomatic representative to the new country. They justified their presence in the Northwest by noting that some state governments had interfered with the efforts of British creditors to collect pre-Revolutionary debts. But Congress had no power to restrain the states from such violations of the treaty of peace.

The Federal Government

The national government under the Articles of Confederation consisted of a legislature and some permanent employees who transacted government business. Congress had to rely on state courts and state militia to enforce the laws it passed. Its main sources of income were requisitions on the states, made in proportion to the value of each state's real estate, and loans from abroad. The requisitions were sometimes paid by the states on time, sometimes late or only in part, and sometimes not at all. The foreign loans came mainly from Dutch bankers, who had enough confidence in the future of the United States to keep extending credit throughout the 1780's. But the amount of the foreign debt, and the interest on it, kept increasing.

A more serious problem was the war debt the federal government still owed to Americans. Hundreds of millions of dollars in Continental paper money issued during the war had lost value. Congress had,

103

in effect, declared it worthless. This confiscation of money was a necessary act of war. Congress simply did not have the resources to pay the remaining debt, estimated at about $34 million. Some states assumed the responsibility of paying the portions of the federal debt owed to their own citizens. By 1787, they had paid off large portions of both state and federal war debts.

The States and Their Citizens

Although the states often failed to provide Congress with the money and troops it needed, they usually cooperated well with each other in interstate matters. And they usually met the needs of their citizens. The states exercised the right to control their own commerce by placing tariffs on foreign imports. But they rarely taxed each others' products in order to achieve competitive advantages and additional revenue.

In the mid-1780's the states, rather than the national government, guaranteed the individual's political and civil rights. Most states required the possession of some property in order for a person to vote, and they usually required a greater amount of property to hold office. But the franchise, or right to vote, was widely held among adult white males. The western or frontier areas, however, did not have as many representatives in the state legislatures as their populations justified.

►Should every adult in a democracy have the vote? What about criminals? the insane? people on welfare?

In 1786, some events in Massachusetts made many Americans deeply concerned about the ability of the states to survive without a strong central government. By that time most states had issued their own money. Farmers, who were always short of cash and needed it to pay their taxes, welcomed this development. But the merchants and professional men opposed it. They felt that the paper money would be issued in such large quantities that it would become worthless. In some states, merchants were so bitterly opposed that they refused to accept the paper money at all. Creditors sometimes fled a state to avoid being paid.

Massachusetts, whose government was dominated by merchants and professional people from the east coast of the state, refused to pass a paper money law. At the same time, however, it agreed to pay its Revolutionary War debt at a rate much closer to the face value of the loans than other states paid. It was trying to pay off this debt rapidly. As a result, taxes were very high. The farmers complained that they were being forced to sell or surrender their property and that hundreds of persons were being jailed for non-payment of debts. The legislature ignored these complaints. In 1786, a rebellion of western Massachusetts farmers, led by a Revolutionary War veteran, Daniel Shays, broke out. The uprising was put down after a few months with little bloodshed. But it caused intense alarm throughout the

104

United States among business and professional people. They feared that a farmers' revolt might not be easily limited to one state.

The Movement for a New Constitution

Shays' Rebellion gave a sharp impetus to a growing sentiment for a stronger central government. This sentiment had been present throughout the war and the postwar period. Alexander Hamilton of New York and others pleaded that the security and dignity of the United States demanded a stronger government. Others looked upon a strong central government as an instrument for aristocracy, corruption, and tyranny.

In 1786, delegates from five states met at Annapolis, Maryland, to discuss common commercial problems. The Annapolis Convention sent out a call for a convention to meet the following year to revise the Articles of Confederation. Those who advocated stronger government began to crystallize their ideas. Their motives were mixed. But most of them felt that the government should give more active protection against Indians, British, and Spanish in the West. They believed that it should have the power to collect taxes directly, to control commerce with other nations, and to make prompt arrangements for paying its debts. The government should also, they believed, serve as an arena for persons who wanted to serve their country, move quickly and forcefully against rebellions within states, and give the United States a new power and dignity in the world.

There had been many unsuccessful movements to strengthen the federal government. The high quality of the delegates helped greatly in making a success of the Convention of 1787 held in Philadelphia. Virginia, a leader among the states seeking a convention, sent a group of men with immense prestige. The group included George Washington; Edmund Randolph, the governor; George Mason, author of the Virginia Declaration of Rights; George Wythe, one of the most eminent legal men of the day; and James Madison. All but three delegates to the Philadelphia Convention signed the Constitution the Convention wrote.

In 1776, the Virginia Assembly adopted George Mason's Declaration of Rights. It guaranteed many of the human rights that were included later in the first Ten Amendments to the Constitution.

Congress had helped to finance the Philadelphia Convention and had supplied some of the Convention's most active members. It now moved to end its own existence by referring the new Constitution to the states. In response to the message by Congress, the states, one by one, arranged for the popular election of delegates to ratifying conventions. In several of these conventions the Federalists won easily. In several other states the Constitution was ratified only after long arguments and much pressure. The Antifederalists, who had a majority in the New York convention, for example, ratified the Constitution in July 1788, by the narrow margin of 30 to 27. They did this partly because they knew that more than the necessary nine states had already

The Federalists supported the Constitution. The Antifederalists opposed the Constitution.

ratified, but largely because Alexander Hamilton threatened that New York City might secede from the state if it failed to join the new Union. Only in North Carolina did a convention reject the Constitution. The Rhode Island legislature, which had refused to send delegates to Philadelphia, pursued its dogged independence by refusing to call a ratifying convention. These two states failed to ratify until April 1789. By then George Washington, chosen unanimously as the first President, and the recently elected First Congress had already set the new government in motion in New York City.

The government began its tasks supported by a burst of nationalist spirit and good will. This support owed much to the fact that the leaders of the new government were still those who had led the country through the Revolutionary period. But the structure of the new system also gave confidence to Americans. The Constitution, while original in some ways, had borrowed heavily both from the state constitutions and from the Articles of Confederation. While it deliberately provided solutions to the problems that had plagued the government under the Articles, it still remained very much a government of limited powers, responsible to the people and to the states.

18 THE CONSTITUTION: DISTRIBUTION OF POWERS

Most of the fifty-five men who sat in the Philadelphia Convention in 1787 agreed that the national government needed more power and that a new constitution had to be written to provide it. But they disagreed about how this should be done. The fiercest controversies centered on two major issues: the amount of power which the state governments would grant to the national government and the distribution of that power.

The Articles of Confederation had created a weak national government as a safeguard against oppression. Yet the nation's experience under the Articles had demonstrated that a national government that was too weak lacked the power to deal decisively with foreign countries or to solve such domestic problems as taxation and civil disturbances. The Convention tried to find a way to give the national government greater power than before without destroying the state governments. Its solution was to preserve the federal system used under the Articles of Confederation but to grant much more power to the national government at the expense of the states. This power was distributed into separate executive, legislative, and judicial branches, following the pattern of the state governments.

The issue of how much power the various states should have in the legislative branch nearly destroyed the Convention. Governor Edmund Randolph of Virginia had offered a plan that provided for a bicameral (two-house) national legislature, with the number of representatives from each state in each house to be based on the state's population. One house would have representatives elected "by the people." But the other house would not. The smaller states opposed the "Virginia Plan." They feared that because they would have fewer representatives in the legislature than the larger, more populous states, their interests would be subordinated to those of the larger states. William Paterson, of New Jersey, presented the "New Jersey Plan," which, like Congress under the Articles of Confederation, had a unicameral (one-house) legislature in which each state had one vote.

At the point at which the Convention seemed hopelessly deadlocked over representation, it agreed on the "Great Compromise," in part the work of Benjamin Franklin. The compromise solved the problem of representation by basing membership in the lower house (the House of Representatives) on population, and by giving each state, regardless of size, two seats in the upper house (the Senate).

The clauses in Reading 18, taken from the Constitution, reveal the practical application of the political ideas of eighteenth-century Americans. For purposes of analysis, clauses of the Constitution have been simplified and reorganized. The original version of the Constitution can be found in the Appendix. As you read, think about the following questions:

1. How did the Constitution distribute power among the three branches of the federal government (legislative, executive, judicial)? Which of these powers were taken away from the states?
2. What were the most significant new grants of power to the federal government?

Separation of Powers: Legislative Branch

Article 1

Section 1. A congress of the United States, which shall consist of a Senate and a House of Representatives, shall have the power to make all national laws.

Section 2, Clause 3. The number of representatives each state has shall be determined on the basis of the population of the state. The population of a state shall be determined by adding the number of free people, including indentured servants, and three-fifths of the

One of the compromises reached between northerners and southerners at the Convention was to count a slave as three-fifths of a person for purposes of both representation and taxation.

Under the Articles of Confederation, each state had had one vote in Congress, which had only one house.

The Seventeenth Amendment was adopted in 1913. It changed the method of electing senators. They are now elected by the qualified voters of each state.

Under the Articles of Confederation, Congress had no power to enforce its requests for money from the states. Nor could it regulate foreign trade or interstate commerce.

Bankruptcy is a legal status in which a court has declared that an individual or a corporation cannot fully pay outstanding debts. Once bankruptcy has been declared, the assets, if there are any, are often sold to pay creditors.

▶ Suppose a person developed a cure for cancer. Should he or she get an exclusive right to manufacture it and to charge high prices in order to earn a large profit? Why or why not?

Under the Articles of Confederation, Congress had been able to declare war. But it had to ask the states to furnish troops.

The state militia was similar to the present National Guard.

slaves. Each state shall have at least one representative regardless of its population.

Section 3, Clause 1. The Senate of the United States shall be made up of two senators from each state, chosen by the state legislatures. A senator's term of office is for six years. Each senator shall have one vote.

Section 8, Clause 1. Congress has the power to collect taxes of various kinds to pay the debts of the national government, to defend that nation against enemies, and to provide for the welfare of the people. Taxes must be the same for every section of the nation.

Section 8, Clause 2. Congress may borrow money.

Section 8, Clause 3. Congress may control trade with foreign nations, among the states, and with Indian tribes.

Section 8, Clause 4. Congress may make rules concerning how people may become citizens of the United States and may make laws on bankruptcy.

Section 8, Clause 5. Congress may coin money and regulate its value. It may also regulate the value of foreign money used in the United States. Congress may set standards of weights and measures.

Section 8, Clause 6. Congress may pass laws specifying how those who counterfeit securities and money should be punished.

Section 8, Clause 7. Congress may establish post offices and roads over which mail is to be carried.

Section 8, Clause 8. Congress may encourage the progress of science and useful arts by securing for authors and inventors exclusive rights to their writings and discoveries for a limited period of time.

Section 8, Clause 9. Congress may set up federal courts under the Supreme Court.

Section 8, Clause 10. Congress may decide on the punishment for crimes committed on the high seas and crimes in which foreign countries are involved.

Section 8, Clause 11. Congress may declare war.

Section 8, Clause 12. Congress may create an army and raise money to pay for its expenses. Only enough money to pay for two years' expense can be given the army at any one time.

Section 8, Clause 13. Congress may create a navy and provide money to support it.

Section 8, Clause 14. Congress may make rules governing its army and navy.

Section 8, Clause 15. Congress may call out the state militia to enforce the laws of the Union, to suppress internal rebellion, and to repel foreign invasions.

Section 8, Clause 16. Congress may organize, arm, and discipline the state militia. The state may appoint the officers of their militia, but must train them in the way Congress directs.

Section 8, Clause 17. Congress may make all rules governing the

NIXON vs. THE INVESTIGATORS

When President Nixon refused to let Watergate investigators have the tapes of White House conversations he touched off a legal conflict that is heading toward the Supreme Court. The final decision will be fateful for all Americans.

THE WATERGATE case has now produced a historic test of the constitutional powers of the Presidency.

It's a battle that pits President Nixon directly against the Watergate investigators. Out of that confrontation emerges a far larger issue than Watergate: the constitutional powers of the President vs. the constitutional powers of Congress and of the courts.

The outcome, therefore, will have a far-reaching impact. The traditional relationship between the three branches of government could be altered.

The conflict is over tape recordings of White House conversations between President Nixon and his aides. Those tapes—along with other White House records—are sought by both Senate and grand-jury investigators as evidence.

If Mr. Nixon is able to hold on to the tapes, then the American Presidency will emerge assured of its long-asserted but never-before-tested power—the power to protect the privacy of all presidential conversations and papers.

But if the President is compelled to yield those tapes, then Congress and the courts will emerge with power over the executive branch that has never before been legally established.

The winner, it now appears certain, will eventually be decided by the U. S. Supreme Court. A White House spokesman said Mr. Nixon will abide by a "definitive decision" of that court.

The final verdict, however, is not likely to come for weeks—even months.

Battle joined. This complex legal battle began July 23. On that day, Mr. Nixon sent a letter to the Senate investigating committee headed by Senator Sam J. Ervin, Jr. (Dem.), of North Carolina. A White House counsel sent another letter to Archibald Cox, the special prosecutor directing the grand-jury inquiry into Watergate.

Those letters served notice that Mr. Nixon would not give up the tapes to either the Senators or Mr. Cox.

It was a challenge quickly accepted. The Senate committee voted unanimously to issue a formal subpoena demanding the tapes and other records. Mr. Cox also issued a subpoena.

Both subpoenas were served at the White House that same day.

"Command" to the President. The subpoenas told the President, "you are hereby commanded" to produce the tapes and other requested records at 10 a.m. on Thursday, July 26.

When that deadline came, Mr. Nixon —as expected—again refused to produce the tapes.

In turning down the senatorial request, the President stood firmly on his "executive privilege" of keeping his private consultations private.

In his answer to the Cox subpoena, the President wrote U. S. District Judge John J. Sirica:

"With the utmost respect for the court of which you are chief judge, and for the [judicial] branch of government of which it is a part, I must decline to obey the command of that subpoena.

How is the principle of the separation of powers involved in the dispute between President Nixon and Congress over Watergate?

national capital and all other areas in which national military or naval installations are located.

Section 8, Clause 18. Congress may make all laws necessary and proper to carry out the powers delegated to the national government by this Constitution.

Article 4

Section 3, Clause 1. Congress may admit new states into the Union, but no new states shall be created within the boundaries of another state. No state may be formed by combining two or more states or parts of states without the consent both of the legislatures of the states concerned and of Congress.

Section 3, Clause 2. Congress shall have power to make all needful rules and regulations concerning territories or other property belonging to the United States.

Executive Branch

Article 2

The Articles of Confederation did not provide for an executive to enforce the laws.

Section 1, Clause 1. The President of the United States shall have the power to enforce all national laws. He and the Vice-President shall hold office for a four-year term.

Section 1, Clause 7. The President shall receive a salary for his services. It shall not be increased nor reduced during the period for which he has been elected. He shall not receive in that same period any additional payments from the United States nor from any state.

The heads of the executive departments have, since Washington's Administration, constituted the President's Cabinet. This body is not specifically established by the Constitution.

▶ Suppose a person appointed by the President were convicted of breaking the law. Is it just for the President to pardon such a person? Why or why not?

Section 2, Clause 1. The President shall be Commander in Chief of the Army and Navy of the United States and of the militias of the several states when they are called into the service of the United States. He may call for written reports from the heads of each of the Executive departments upon any subject relating to the work of their departments. He may grant pardons to persons convicted of crimes against the federal government or order their punishment to be delayed, except in the case of impeached government officials.

Section 2, Clause 2. The President shall have the power to make treaties with the advice and consent of the Senate. These treaties must be approved by two thirds of the senators present when the treaties are voted on. The President shall nominate and, with the advice and consent of the Senate, appoint ambassadors, other public ministers and consuls, judges of the Supreme Court, and any other officers of the United States whose appointments have not otherwise been provided for.

Some Presidents have personally delivered the State of the Union Message before Congress. Others have sent the Message to Congress to be read by a clerk. The Message is now customarily read on the first day that Congress meets.

Section 3. The President shall from time to time give Congress information concerning the state of the Union. He may suggest for congressional consideration conditions which he feels require legislation. He may call special sessions of Congress and may adjourn Congress if the two houses cannot agree on an adjournment time. He shall receive ambassadors and other public officials. He shall see that all laws are faithfully executed.

Judicial Branch

The power of receiving ambassadors carries with it the power of recognizing or not recognizing the legitimacy of new governments.

Article 3

No federal courts existed under the Articles of Confederation.

Section 1. The Supreme Court and the lower federal courts established by Congress shall have the power to hear and decide cases. Judges of the Supreme and lower courts shall hold office for life during good behavior. They shall receive salaries which cannot be reduced during their time in office.

Section 2, Clause 1. Federal courts shall have power to rule on matters affecting this Constitution, federal laws, and treaties. They have the power to rule on disagreements between the federal government and other governments or individuals. They may settle arguments between the states or between citizens of different states or between states or their citizens and foreign countries.

Section 2, Clause 2. The Supreme Court shall have original jurisdiction in cases involving a representative of a foreign government or a state. In all other cases, the Supreme Court shall have appellate jurisdiction.

Original jurisdiction means the authority to try cases for the first time. Appellate jurisdiction means the authority to try cases that have been appealed from a lower court.

States and the Federal Government

Article 1

Section 10, Clause 1. State governments must not do the following: enter into agreements with foreign nations; issue coins or paper money.

Section 10, Clause 3. No state shall, without consent of Congress, tax ships entering its ports; maintain an army or navy in times of peace; make treaties with other states or with foreign powers; engage in war unless actually invaded or in such immediate danger that delay is impossible.

Article 6

Section 2. The Constitution and the laws of the United States shall be the supreme law of the land. Judges in every state shall be bound by them, even when state laws and state constitutions conflict with the national laws.

FOR THOUGHT:

If you were rewriting the Constitution, would you keep the division between executive and legislative power?

19 THE CONSTITUTION: THE USE OF FEDERAL POWER

The framers of the Constitution knew that dividing power among the three branches of government would not necessarily keep one branch from assuming too much power. The colonial governments had been divided into executive, legislative, and judicial branches. But the governor and king had had the right to veto laws passed by the legislature. No machinery existed for overriding an executive veto. A colony could only try to change the executive's mind.

To guard against one branch of government exercising too much power, the framers of the Constitution worked out a system of checks and balances. Each branch of government was given certain ways to check the power of the others. As a further guard against arbitrary government, the delegates provided that elections to choose delegates to Congress and the President should be held regularly and fairly often. Provision was made for removing federal officeholders from their positions for misconduct. Other provisions protected state governments against specific uses of federal power, but also ensured that states would treat each other equally.

The clauses in Reading 19, taken from the Constitution, give the ways in which the framers of the Constitution tried to guard against excessive power, or improper use of power, in the federal government. Again, clauses have been reorganized, and language has been modernized. As you read, think about these questions:

1. What checks did each branch have on the powers given to other branches?
2. What were the main checks the states retained against the federal government? How did they work?

Checks and Balances

Article 1

Section 2, Clause 5. The House of Representatives shall have the right to impeach officials of the United States suspected of serious wrongdoing.

To impeach means to bring charges against officials.

Section 3, Clause 6. The Senate shall have the right to try impeached officials. If the President of the United States has been impeached, the Chief Justice of the Supreme Court shall preside at his trial. No official shall be convicted of the charges brought against him unless two thirds of the senators present at his trial find him guilty.

Article 2

Section 4. The President, Vice-President, and all civil officials of the federal government may be removed from office if Congress impeaches and convicts them of treason, bribery, or other crimes.

The Constitution defines treason, in Article 3, Section 3, as making war against the United States, or supporting its enemies by giving them "aid and comfort."

Article 1

Section 3, Clause 7. Congress can punish impeached officials found guilty only by removing them from office and disqualifying them from ever holding another federal office. After impeachment, however, officials can be tried by a regular court. If they are found guilty of crime they can be punished in accordance with the law.

Section 3, Clause 4. The Vice-President of the United States shall be the President of the Senate. But he may vote only in case of a tie.

Section 3, Clause 5. The Senate shall choose its other officers, and also a temporary president [president *pro tempore*] who shall preside over the Senate when the Vice-President is absent or acting as President.

Section 4, Clause 2. The Congress of the United States shall meet at least once every year.

Section 5, Clause 4. Neither house of Congress shall adjourn for more than three days without the permission of the other house.

Section 7, Clause 1. All bills having to do with the raising of money, or revenue, must be introduced in the House of Representatives. The Senate, however, can offer changes or amendments to revenue bills.

Section 7, Clause 2. Every bill that is passed by the House of Representatives and the Senate shall be presented to the President. If he approves the bill, he shall sign it, thus making it law. If he does not approve, he may veto the bill. If he vetoes the bill, he shall return it, with his objections, to the house where the bill originated. The house shall then reconsider the bill. If, after reconsideration, two thirds of the members of that house still vote to pass the bill, it shall be reconsidered there, and if approved by two thirds of that house also, the bill shall become law without the President's signature.

If a bill is not signed by the President within ten days (not counting Sundays) of being presented to him, it shall automatically become law unless Congress has adjourned during those ten days thus preventing the President's returning the bill to it within that time. If Congress adjourns during this ten-day period and the President does not sign the bill, the bill shall not become law.

Article 2

Section 2, Clause 2. The President shall have the power to make treaties with the advice and consent of the Senate. These treaties must be approved by two thirds of the senators present when the treaties are voted on. The President shall nominate and, with the advice and consent of the Senate, appoint ambassadors, other public ministers and consuls, judges of the Supreme Court, and any other officers of the United States whose appointments have been provided for by law.

Section 3. The President shall from time to time give Congress information concerning the state of the Union. He may suggest to Congress the matters which he feels require legislation. He may call special sessions of Congress and may adjourn Congress if the two houses cannot agree on an adjournment time. He shall see that all laws are faithfully executed.

Some colonial governments had been angered because the governor, who had the power to do so, refused to call colonial legislatures into session.

▶Isn't it undemocratic to give an elected official this much power?

This procedure of letting a last-minute bill die by simply not signing it after Congress adjourns is called a pocket veto.

How a Bill Becomes Law
(if the bill originates in the House)

HOUSE OF REPRESENTATIVES

    Congressman introduces bill; bill is placed in a "hopper."

    Clerk of House reads aloud title of bill, assigns it a number, and has it printed; Speaker of House assigns bill to appropriate committee.

▼

    Committee (or one of its subcommittees) studies bill, holds possible hearings, amends, revises, defeats, or approves bill.

    Approved bill is sent to Rules Committee which decides when and if the bill will be debated.

▼

    Bill is read and debated. Congressmen amend, revise, defeat, pass, or send bill back to committee.

    Majority vote of House approves bill.

HOUSE PASSES BILL

Conference Committee

Compromises differences and returns revised bill to both houses for approval.

BILL GOES TO SENATE

SENATE

    Clerk of Senate receives bill, assigns it a number, has it printed, and sends it to President of Senate.

    President of Senate assigns bill to appropriate committee.

▼

    Committee (or one of its subcommittees) studies bill, holds possible hearings, amends, revises, defeats or approves bill.

▼

    Bill is read and debated on floor of Senate.

    If Senate disagrees with House version, the bill is sent to a Joint Conference Committee.

    If Senate passes House version, bill is sent to President.

SENATE PASSES BILL.
BILL GOES TO PRESIDENT.

    President signs bill into law or allows bill to become law without his signature.

    If President vetoes bill, two thirds vote by both houses overrules President.

    Secretary of State affixes Seal of the United States and proclaims the bill a United States law.

Article 3

Section 1. The judges of the Supreme Court and the lower federal courts shall hold office during good behavior, shall be paid for their services, and may not have salaries reduced while in office.

Section 2, Clause 1. Federal courts shall have power to rule on matters affecting this Constitution, federal laws, and treaties. They have the power to rule on disagreements between the federal government and other governments or individuals. They may settle arguments between the states or between citizens of different states and between states or their citizens and foreign countries.

▶ What does "good behavior" mean? Suppose that a judge drinks too much? beats his wife, or her husband? is arrested several times for traffic violations?

States and the
Federal Government

Article 1

Section 9, Clause 5. Congress may not tax goods sent out of any state.

Section 9, Clause 6. Congress shall make no laws that would give the ports of one state an advantage over the ports of others.

Article 4

Section 1. Each state shall respect the laws, records, and court decisions of all other states.

Section 2, Clause 1. The citizens of one state shall be entitled to the privileges and immunities of citizens in all states.

Section 2, Clause 2. If a person charged with a crime in one state flees from that state, he shall, on request of the governor, be returned to the state from which he fled.

Section 2, Clause 3. Any indentured servant or slave who escapes from one state to another shall not become free by doing so. If his owner claims him, a runaway must be returned.

This clause has not been applied since 1865. In that year, the Thirteenth Amendment freed all slaves in the United States and its territories.

Section 4. The United States shall guarantee to every state in this Union a republican form of government. It shall protect each state against invasion and, at the request of the state, shall protect each state against domestic violence.

A republican government is one in which the law gives ultimate power to the voters, rather than to the leaders.

Article 5

The Congress, whenever two thirds of both houses shall consider it necessary, shall propose amendments to this Constitution. Or, on the application of the legislatures of two thirds of the states, a convention shall be called for proposing amendments. In either case,

A unanimous vote by states was needed to amend the Articles of Confederation.

amendments shall be valid parts of this Constitution, when ratified by the legislatures of three fourths of the states, or by conventions in three fourths of the states. Either method of ratification may be proposed by the Congress, provided that no state, without its consent, shall be deprived of its equal representation in the Senate.

FOR THOUGHT:

In addition to the formal system of checks and balances, how can public opinion help to restrain one branch of the federal government from getting or exercising too much power?

20 THE CONSTITUTION: THE RIGHTS OF CITIZENS

In the closing days of the Constitutional Convention, the delegates discussed briefly whether or not they should include a statement of individual rights. They decided not to do so, on the grounds that the state constitutions fully protected the rights of individuals. The delegates did, however, write into the Constitution several important guarantees. These were largely restrictions placed on the power of Congress and the executive.

In the battles for ratification in the states, it quickly became apparent that the Convention had misjudged the attitudes of many persons. The ideology of the Revolution was important to Americans. They took the natural rights of people seriously. The Constitution strengthened the power of the national government. This in itself reminded many people that a remote and powerful government had violated their rights in the years before the Revolution. They wanted some guarantee that the new American government could not do the same thing. Moreover, the Americans had a long tradition of expecting to find basic rights spelled out in a written document. The colonists had always looked to the charters granted by the king to the founders of the colonies to determine their political rights. They were not likely to accept readily a new government which did not define the rights of citizens as well as the rights of the government. The Antifederalists objected vigorously to the absence of a bill of rights. Five of the first eleven states that ratified the Constitution recommended strongly that a bill of rights be added promptly.

By the time the first Congress met, James Madison, who had been elected to the House of Representatives, recognized that the lack of a bill of rights could become a major focal point for opposition to the new government. Madison took the lead in framing the first ten amendments to the Constitution. They passed Congress quickly. And

116

the necessary three quarters of the states had ratified them by December 1791.

The clauses in Reading 20 are taken from the Constitution and its first ten amendments, known as the Bill of Rights. They give guarantees of individual rights. Again clauses of the Constitution have been reorganized, and the language has been modernized. As you read, think about these questions:

1. What individual rights did the Constitution and Bill of Rights guarantee?
2. In what ways did the individual rights reflect the ideology and the colonial experiences of the Founding Fathers?

Individual Rights

Article 1

Section 9, Clause 2. The privilege of the writ of habeas corpus shall not be suspended, except in cases of rebellion or invasion when the public safety requires its suspension.

Section 9, Clause 3. Congress may pass no bill of attainder. Neither may Congress pass an ex post facto law.

Section 9, Clause 8. No title of nobility shall be granted by the United States.

Section 10, Clause 1. No state shall pass any bill of attainder, ex post facto law, or law impairing the obligation of contracts, nor shall a state grant any title of nobility.

Article 3

Section 2, Clause 3. Except in impeachment cases, any trial for crime shall be decided by a jury. A trial must be held in the state where the crime took place.

Section 3, Clause 1. Treason shall consist only of making war against the United States or of helping enemies of the United States. No one shall be convicted of treason unless two persons testify that they witnessed the act, or unless the accused confesses in court.

Section 3, Clause 2. Congress shall have the power to declare the punishment of treason, but the punishment cannot extend to the families or descendants of a person found guilty of treason.

Article 4

Section 1. Each state shall respect the laws, records, and court decisions of all other states.

Section 2, Clause 1. The citizens of one state shall be entitled to the privileges and immunities of citizens in all states.

A writ of habeas corpus is a court order directing an official to show reasons for holding someone prisoner. Unless the official can show sufficient cause for holding him or her, the prisoner must be released.

A bill of attainder is a law intended to punish a particular person. An ex post facto law is a law passed to punish someone for an act that was not against the law at the time he or she did it.

117

The pictures on these two pages show a number of activities protected by the Constitution. What provision protects each activity?

A Shaker religious service

Section 2, Clause 2. If a person charged with a crime in one state flees from that state, he shall, on request of the governor, be returned to the state from which he fled.

Article 6

Section 3. No religious test shall ever be required as a qualification for any public office or public trust in the United States.

Amendment 1

Congress shall make no law that has to do with making any religion the official one or that restricts people from worshiping as they please or limits freedom of speech or of the press, or keeps them from assembling peaceably, or from petitioning the government if they think they have been treated unfairly.

Amendment 2

Since a well-regulated militia is necessary to the security and freedom of a state, the people shall be allowed to keep and to bear arms.

Amendment 3

People shall not be forced to give room and board in their homes to soldiers in times of peace. Nor shall they be forced to quarter soldiers in time of war unless a law is first passed requiring it.

Amendment 4

A warrant is an order, usually issued by a judge, which authorizes a public official to take action.

Government officials cannot make unreasonable searches or seizures of individuals or their persons, homes, or belongings. No warrant for a search shall be issued unless there is probable cause that a crime has been committed and will be exposed as a result of the search, and unless the places, persons, or things to be searched or seized are specifically described in the warrant.

Amendment 5

Grand juries never try cases. They only determine whether there is sufficient evidence for a trial.

Due process has never been specifically defined by the Supreme Court. Justice Felix Frankfurter defined it as "all those rights which the courts must enforce because they are basic to our free society."

No person shall be
(1) tried for a serious crime unless a grand jury has first examined the evidence and decided that a trial is warranted, except in cases arising in the armed forces, or in the militia in times of public danger;
(2) tried for the same crime twice [double jeopardy];
(3) forced, in a criminal case, to be a witness against himself;
(4) executed, imprisoned, or fined without due process of law;

(5) deprived of his property for public use unless he has first been given a fair price for it.

Amendment 6

Any person being tried for a criminal offense is entitled to
(1) a speedy and public trial;
(2) an impartial jury chosen from citizens of the state and district in which the crime was committed;
(3) knowledge of why he is being tried;
(4) see and hear the witnesses who testify against him;
(5) force witnesses who can give evidence in his favor to come to court to testify;
(6) assistance by a lawyer in defending himself.

This is a jury usually consisting of twelve persons. The jury weighs the facts of the case to determine whether the accused is guilty or not guilty.

Amendment 7

In law suits involving things valued at more than $20, individuals have the right to a jury trial.

Amendment 8

Individuals accused of a crime cannot be required to pay excessive bail. Individuals found guilty of crimes cannot be required to pay excessive fines, nor can cruel or unusual punishments be inflicted.

Bail usually consists of a sum of money exchanged for the release of a person who has been arrested. It serves as a guarantee that the person will appear to be tried.

Amendment 9

The fact that certain individual rights are guaranteed by the Constitution should not be interpreted to mean that rights not specifically mentioned in the Constitution are denied the individual.

Amendment 10

The Constitution delegates certain powers to the national government of the United States. All other powers are retained by the states or by the people. Except those powers specifically denied to the states by the Constitution.

FOR THOUGHT:

What responsibilities do citizens have to protect individual rights against governmental power?

Challenges to the New Nation

STATING THE ISSUE

The newly elected Congress and federal officials who gathered in New York in the spring of 1789 faced great challenges. One was internal. The Constitution of 1787 granted the federal government much greater power over states and citizens than the Articles of Confederation had. Such power offered tempting prizes for ambitious individuals and self-interested groups. Contests for power and other conflicts were inevitable in a political game whose rules were still to be written. Faced by these disruptive forces and by states jealous of their rights, could the new government continue to command loyalty and to maintain national unity?

Another challenge was external. It came from abroad. The new nation had a vast territory but relatively few people. It had no navy and few soldiers. Since the Revolutionary War, the great powers of Europe had left the United States almost undisturbed. Each of them wanted peace for its own reasons. But if war should again break out in Europe, the unprotected merchant fleet and thinly populated western lands of the United States might well invite attacks. Could the nation survive if threatened by one or more of the great powers?

Americans' hopes for dealing with these two problems depended in part on a successful response to a third challenge. This was the challenge of providing effective leadership for the federal government and for the nation. Under the Confederation, executive leadership had been weak. It had been spread among a number of leaders of Congress. The new Constitution placed strong executive power in the hands of one person, the President. But Americans were proud of their legislative traditions. And they had bitter memories of Britain's use of executive power over them. Was George Washington the kind of man who could overcome these problems? Would he be able to mediate conflicts at home and command respect abroad?

The two issues of internal unity and external threats will be dealt with in historical essays at the end of Chapter 6. Most of this chapter will concern itself with the question of leadership. It will do this by examining a variety of documents related to George Washington up to the time when he became President.

122

1787-88 John Jay, James Madison, and Alexander Hamilton write **The Federalist**

1789 George Washington becomes President

1789 Judiciary Act sets up federal judiciary system

1791 Opponents of the Federalists organize the Republican Party

1791 Congress levies tax on whiskey

1794 Federal forces end Whiskey Rebellion in Pennsylvania

1796 Pinckney's Treaty gives United States freedom of navigation on Mississippi River

1797 John Adams becomes President

1798 XYZ Affair arouses American public opinion against France

1798 Federalists in Congress pass Alien and Sedition Acts

1801 Thomas Jefferson becomes President

1803 Louisiana Purchase arranged

1804 Twelfth Amendment to the Constitution is ratified

1807 Congress passes Embargo Act

1809 Congress passes Non-Intercourse Act

1810 Macon's Bill No. 2 restores trade with England and France

1812 United States declares war on Britain

1814 Treaty of Ghent ends fighting between United States and Britain

1819 Spanish cede Florida to the United States

1823 President James Monroe issues Monroe Doctrine

21 THE CHALLENGE TO LEADERSHIP

Perhaps the greatest innovation in the new Constitution was the Presidency. Many Americans were suspicious of executive power because of their experiences with the king of England and colonial governors. Under the Confederation, committees of Congress controlled such matters as diplomacy, the army, and finance. Many states deliberately weakened the powers of their governors. Pennsylvania abolished that office for a time. The creation of the Presidency showed that a number of leading citizens thought that more individual leadership was needed. However, the first person to hold that office would have to give strong leadership without arousing fears that he would attempt to become a dictator or king.

George Washington towered above all the possible nominees for the Presidency except Benjamin Franklin, who was aged and ill. Washington's services during the Revolution had made him an international hero. He was not a military genius. But he had held his Continental Army together long enough to outlast the British. Thus, Washington won the ballot of every Presidential elector designated by voters in the separate states in 1788.

But many distinguished military leaders have failed in civil office, including the American Presidency. How wisely did the people in 1788 choose? Today, historians have far more evidence about George Washington's life and career than the electors or the people had in 1788. In the following reading, you will find a variety of things written by, to, or about George Washington. They date from his early days on the Pennsylvania frontier to the time he became President. Many of them may help you judge what kind of President he would make. Others may not.

Your task is to sift this material, to identify those pieces of evidence which would help you to predict what kind of leadership Washington would provide as President, and to evaluate them. You will work with this material for several days. On the first day your teacher will help you plan a system for taking notes on what you read. You may be asked to write an essay about the kind of President Washington would make. You must base your opinion on what you learn about him during the years before he became President. Or you may be asked to discuss this topic or other topics in class each day. In either case, you must use the information in this reading for your evidence.

The writings in this reading are divided into four chronological parts. The first part includes things written by or about Washington during the French and Indian War (1753-1758). The second includes materials from the period before the Revolutionary War (1765-1775). The third deals with Washington's services during the Revolution (1775-1783). The fourth deals with his life as a private citizen before becoming President (1783-1789).

Frontiersman and Soldier: Washington's Early Career

In 1753 twenty-one-year-old George Washington received orders from Governor Robert Dinwiddie of Virginia to journey across the Appalachian Mountains into the wilderness of the Ohio Valley. He was ordered to carry a message to the French at a military post there. The message warned them to leave the territory, which was also claimed by Virginia. The French ignored the warning. The next year Washington led some Virginia militia back to western Pennsylvania to oust the French. The resulting fighting brought the first bloodshed of the French and Indian War. Washington was forced to surrender Fort Necessity and return to Virginia defeated. He went west again a year later (1755) in command of Virginia troops serving in a small British army led by General Edward Braddock. The army was ambushed by the French and their Indian allies a few miles from present-day Pittsburgh. Washington again had to go back to Virginia in defeat. However, his conduct in commanding the retreating army won him praise. Three years later he returned once more to the forks of the Ohio. This time, as an aide to British General John Forbes, he witnessed the defeat of the French in several skirmishes and their abandonment of their main post, Fort Duquesne. Upon his return to Virginia, Washington married Martha Custis, a wealthy widow. The following documents will show you more about this part of Washington's life and career.

JOURNEY TO THE FRENCH COMMANDANT

December 23, 1753

Writings of George Washington, John C. Fitzpatrick, ed. (Washington, D.C.: United States Government Printing Office, 1931-1944), Vol. I, pp. 29-30. Material simplified and transposed.

Just after we had passed a place called the Murdering Town we met with a party of French Indians, who had been waiting for us. One of them fired at Mr. Gist or me, not 15 steps off, but fortunately missed. We took this fellow into custody. And we kept him till about 9 o'clock at night. Then we let him go. We walked all the remaining part of the night without stopping. We wanted to get as far ahead of them as possible so as to be out of their reach the next day. We were sure that they would follow our tracks as soon as it was light. The next day we continued travelling till quite dark, and got to the river. There was no way to get over but on a raft. We set about making a raft with just one poor hatchet and finished just after sunset. This was a whole day's work. Then we set off. But before we were half way over, we were jammed in the ice. Every moment we expected our raft to sink and ourselves to perish. I put out my setting pole to try to stop the raft and let the ice pass by. But the speed of the stream threw it with so much force against the pole that it jerked me out into ten feet of water. I fortunately saved myself by catching hold of one of the raft logs. Despite all our efforts we could not get the raft to either shore. We were forced, as we were near an island, to leave our raft and make for it.

The cold was so extremely severe that all of Mr. Gist's fingers and some of his toes were frozen. But the water was frozen so hard that we found no difficulty getting off the island, on the ice, in the morning.

Washington's companion was Christopher Gist, a noted backwoodsman and scout. The river in which he nearly drowned was the Allegheny.

TO RICHARD CORBIN

Alexandria, Virginia, March 1754

Writings of George Washington, Fitzpatrick, ed., Vol. I, p. 34. Material simplified and transposed.

In a conversation with you at Green Spring, you gave me some room to hope for a commission above that of major and to be ranked among the chief officers of this expedition. I neither look for, expect, nor desire the command of the whole forces. I must be fair enough to confess that it is a responsibility too great for my youth and inexperience. Knowing this, I have too sincere a love for my country

Corbin, a friend of young Washington, was a member of the Governor's Council in Virginia.

to undertake that which might cause harm to it. But if I could hope that you thought me worthy of the post of lieutenant-colonel and would favor me by mentioning it at the appointment of officers, I would appreciate the kindness.

TO JOHN AUGUSTINE WASHINGTON

Great Meadow, May 31, 1754

Writings of George Washington, Fitzpatrick, ed., Vol. I, p. 70. Material simplified and transposed.

Washington here tells his brother about a skirmish in which his soldiers ambushed their opponents.

King George II, who had been a soldier himself, heard of Washington's description of the sound of bullets as "charming." King George is said to have remarked about this description, "He would not think so if he had heard many."

Three days ago we had an engagement with the French. A party of our men met with one of theirs. Most of our men were out upon other detachments. So I had scarcely 40 men remaining under my command and about 10 or 12 Indians. Nevertheless, we won a most decisive victory. The battle lasted about 10 or 15 minutes. There was sharp firing on both sides, till the French gave up and ran. There were 12 of the French killed. Among these was Mons. de Jumonville, their commander. Twenty-one were taken prisoner.

P.S. The right wing, where I stood, was exposed to and received all the enemy's fire. I heard the bullets whistle. And, believe me, there is something charming in the sound. But I fortunately escaped without any wound.

JOURNAL OF CONRAD WEISER

September 3, 1754

"Journal of the Proceedings of Conrad Weiser," in **Minutes of the Provincial Council of Pennsylvania** (Harrisburg, 1851), Vol. VI, pp. 151-152. Material simplified.

Weiser was a well-known frontiersman. The Half-King was an Indian chief. "From one full moon to the other" means a period of about a month. "That little thing upon the meadow" refers to Fort Necessity.

Tanacharisson, otherwise called the Half King, complained very much of the behavior of Colonel Washington to him. (However, he complained in a very moderate way, saying the Colonel was a good-natured man but had no experience.) He said that the Colonel commanded the Indians as his slaves. He made them scout and attack the enemy every day by themselves. And he would take no advice from the Indians. The Half King also complained that the Colonel stayed at one place from one full moon to the other and made no fortifications but that little thing upon the meadow. He said the Colonel thought the French would come up to him in an open field. He added that, had the Colonel taken the Half King's advice and made such fortifications as the Half King advised him to make, he would certainly have beat the French off. The Half King said that the French had acted as great cowards and the English as fools in that engagement. Colonel Washington would never listen to the Indians. But he was always driving them on to fight by his directions.

TO JOHN AUGUSTINE WASHINGTON

Fort Cumberland, May 14, 1755

Writings of George Washington, Fitzpatrick, ed., Vol. I, p. 124. Language simplified.

The General has appointed me one of his aides. In this office I shall serve this campaign well enough, as I am thereby freed from all commands but his. Furthermore, I give orders to all which must be obeyed without a word.

I have now a good opportunity of forming an acquaintance, which may be useful later, if I find it worthwhile to push my fortune in the military way.

TO ROBERT DINWIDDIE

Fort Cumberland, July 18, 1755

When he came to this place, we were attacked (very unexpectedly I must admit) by about 300 French and Indians. Our numbers consisted of about 1300 well armed men, mostly regulars. They were immediately struck with such a deadly panic that nothing but confusion and disobedience prevailed among them. The officers in general behaved with incomparable bravery. And they suffered greatly for this. There were nearly 60 killed and wounded. A large proportion out of the number we had! The Virginian Companies behaved like men and died like soldiers. I believe that out of the 3 companies that were there that day, scarcely 30 were left alive. The cowardly behavior of the English soldiers exposed all those who were doing their duty to almost certain death. And at length, despite every effort to the contrary, they broke and ran like sheep before the hounds, leaving the artillery, ammunition, provisions, and everything we had with us a prey to the enemy. And when we tried to rally them in hopes of regaining our invaluable loss, it was with as much success as if we had attempted to have stopped the wild bears of the mountains. The General was wounded from behind in the shoulder and into the breast. He died of his wound three days after. I luckily escaped without a wound. However, I had four bullets through my coat and two horses shot under me.

TO JOHN AUGUSTINE WASHINGTON

Mount Vernon, August 2, 1755

I was employed to make a journey in the winter. And what did I get by it? My expenses taken care of! I was then appointed, for very little pay, to conduct a handful of men to Ohio. What did I get by this? Why, after spending a considerable amount of money in equipping and providing necessities for the campaign, I went out, was soundly beaten, and lost them all. Then I came in, and had my commission taken from me under pretense of an order from home. Then I went out as a volunteer with General Braddock and lost all my horses and many other things. This was a voluntary act and I mention it only to show that I have been on a losing course ever since I entered the service, which is now two years. So, the next time I leave my family again, I think I can't be blamed if I try to do it upon such terms as to prevent my suffering.

Washington refers here to General Edward Braddock, commander of the British expedition against the French.

▶To what degree is who you know as important as what you know?

Writings of George Washington, Fitzpatrick, ed., Vol. I, p. 149. Language simplified.

Here Washington tells Governor Dinwiddie about the defeat of Braddock's army.

Writings of George Washington, Fitzpatrick, ed., Vol. I, pp. 156-157. Language simplified.

Here Washington sums up his feelings about his experiences in the expeditions of 1754 and 1755.

127

Washington as a surveyor

Which of the characteristics that Washington is exhibiting in these pictures do you think influenced his character?

Washington among the frontiersmen at Fort Necessity

Washington reads the burial service over General Braddock during the French and Indian War.

Washington reads prayers to his camp.

Washington is crossing the Allegheny River on a raft. He was on an
official mission to warn the French to get off British-claimed land.

TO CAPTAIN JOHN ASHBY

Winchester, December 28, 1755

Writings of George Washington, Fitzpatrick, ed., Vol. I, p. 264. Language simplified.

Ashby was under Washington's command in the Virginia militia.

▶Washington accuses Ashby of using a public office to make a private profit. Should he have forced Ashby to resign? Why or why not?

I am very much surprised to hear of the great irregularities which were allowed in your camp. The rum, although sold by Joseph Coombs, I am informed is your property. There are continual complaints to me of the misbehavior of your wife. I am told she sows discontent among the men, and is head of every mutiny. If she is not immediately sent from the camp, or I hear any more complaints of such irregular behavior upon my arrival there, I shall take care to drive her out myself, and suspend you.

SPEECH TO CAPTAIN JOHNNE, CATAWBAS

Winchester, October 28, 1756

Writings of George Washington, Fitzpatrick, ed., Vol. I, pp. 486-487. Language simplified.

Britain was at war with France in Europe as well as in America. Here Washington, on behalf of Virginia, attempts to enlist the aid of a chief of the Cawtawbas, a frontier tribe usually friendly to the English.

We desire you to go to the Cherokees and tell them the road is now clear and open. We expected them to war last spring. And we love them so well that our Governor sent some few men to build a fort among them. But we are mighty sorry that they listen so much to lies the French tell as to break their promise and not come to war. They might have got a great deal of honor in war and killed a great many of the French, whose hearts are false and rotten as an old stump. If they continue to listen to what the French say much longer, they will have great cause to be sorry. For the French have no match-locks, powder, and lead but what they got from King George our father, before the war began. That will soon have run out. Then they will get no more. And all French Indians will be starving with cold. And they will have to take to bows and arrows again for want of ammunition.

Tell them we long to shake hands with them.

Let them get their knives and tomahawks sharp. We will go before them. And we will show them the way to honor, scalps, prisoners, and money enough. We are mighty sorry they stay at home idle when they should go to war and become great men and a terror and dread to their enemies. Tell them they shall have food enough and that they will be treated very kindly.

TO COLONEL HENRY BOUQUET

Fort Cumberland, July 3, 1758

Writings of George Washington, Fitzpatrick, ed., Vol. II, p. 229. Language simplified.

Bouquet was second in command to General John Forbes of the British army marching west through Pennsylvania against the French.

My men are very bare of clothes (uniforms, I mean). And I have no prospect of a supply. If I were left to pursue my own ideas, I would order the men to adopt the Indian dress. I would have the officers do it, too. And I would be the first to set the example myself. Nothing but the uncertainty of getting the General's approval causes

130

me to hesitate a moment at leaving my uniforms at this place and proceeding as light as any Indian in the woods. It is an unbecoming dress, I confess, for an officer. But I think convenience rather than show should be consulted.

TO MRS. MARTHA CUSTIS

Fort Cumberland, July 20, 1758

We have begun our march for the Ohio. A messenger is starting for Williamsburg. And I embrace the opportunity to send a few words to one whose life is now inseparable from mine. Since that happy hour when we made our pledges to each other, my thoughts have been continually going to you as another self. That an all-powerful Providence may keep us both in safety is the prayer of your ever faithful and affectionate friend.

Washington the Gentleman Farmer: Objecting to British Taxes

The French and Indian War ended successfully for the British and their American colonists. At the war's end, George and Martha Washington and their family were living contentedly on their large estate at Mount Vernon, Virginia. When George's and Martha's properties were combined, they became one of the wealthiest families in the colonies. Like many other property owners, George Washington grew increasingly resentful of British policies toward the colonies. He resented especially those involving taxation. The following documents reveal Washington's attitudes in these matters between 1765 and 1775.

TO FRANCIS DANDRIDGE

Mount Vernon, September 20, 1765

The Stamp Act imposed on the colonies by the Parliament of Great Britain is the main subject of the conversation of thoughtful colonists. They look upon this unconstitutional method of taxation as a grave attack on their liberties. And they loudly exclaim against the violation. What may be the result of this and some other ill judged measures, I will not try to determine. But I may venture to state that the advantage gained by Great Britain will fall greatly short of the expectations of Parliament. Certainly, all our wealth already flows in a manner to Great Britain. And whatever helps to cut down our imports must harm their manufacturers. The eyes of our people, already beginning to open, will see that we can do without many

▶Why do people you know sometimes wear uncomfortable or unbecoming clothing?

Writings of George Washington, Fitzpatrick, ed., Vol. II, p. 242. Language simplified.

Martha Custis was a wealthy widow with two children. Washington had proposed marriage to her just before leaving on the expedition and she had accepted.

Writings of George Washington, Fitzpatrick, ed., Vol. II, pp. 425-426. Language simplified.

Dandridge, who lived in England, was Martha Custis' uncle.

131

How is Washington portrayed
in these pictures? How are
blacks portrayed?

luxuries for which we pay Great Britain while most of the necessities of life can be found here. This consequently will introduce frugality. It will also stimulate industry. If Great Britain therefore loads its manufacturers with heavy taxes, will it not facilitate these measures? They will not force us I think to give our money for their exports. And I am certain none of their traders will part from them without a valuable consideration. Where then is the usefulness of these restrictions?

As to the Stamp Act, taken in a single view, one result of it will be to close our courts of justice. For it is nearly impossible under our present circumstances that the Act can be complied with even if we were willing to enforce it. The fact that we do not have the money to pay for the stamps would be enough alone. But there are other reasons as well to prevent compliance with the Act. And if our courts are closed, I fancy the merchants of Great Britain who trade with the colonies will be among the first to wish for a repeal of the Act.

TO GEORGE MASON

Mount Vernon, April 5, 1769

Our lordly masters in Great Britain will be satisfied with nothing less than depriving Americans of their freedom. So it seems very necessary that some thing should be done to avoid this and maintain our liberty. But the manner of doing it to achieve the end effectively is the point in question.

It is clearly my opinion that no man should hesitate a moment to use arms in defense of so valuable a blessing. Yet arms should be the last resource. We have already, it is said, proved the uselessness of addresses to the throne and petitions to Parliament. It then remains to be seen how far their attention to our rights and privileges is to be awakened or alarmed by starving their trade and manufacturers.

The northern colonies, it appears, are trying to adopt the scheme. In my opinion it is a good one. And it will have good results, if it can be carried out pretty widely. But I will not try to determine how far it is possible to do so. It cannot be denied that there will be difficulties in carrying out the scheme everywhere. These difficulties will arise from clashing interests and selfish designing men. These men are ever attentive to their own gain. They are watchful of every turn that can add to their own wealth in preference to every other consideration. In the tobacco colonies, where trade is so widely spread and is wholly carried on by middlemen, these difficulties are certainly increased. But I think that they will not be insurmountably increased if the gentlemen would take the trouble to explain matters to the people in their counties.

Writings of George Washington, Fitzpatrick, ed., Vol. II, pp. 500-501. Language simplified.

Mason was a Virginia landowner and officeholder. He joined Washington in the boycott of British goods, through which the colonists attempted to force Parliament to repeal the Townshend Acts. Mason also played an active part in the Revolutionary War in Virginia and in the writing of the Constitution of 1787. He was an authority on law.

▶Should a boycott be used to protest injustice if people such as merchants and shopkeepers, who are not responsible for causing the injustice, might be financially ruined by the boycott?

134

TO ROBERT CARY & COMPANY

Mount Vernon, July 25, 1769

If there are any articles contained in either of my orders (paper only excepted) which are taxed by Act of Parliament for the purpose of raising a revenue in America, it is my express desire and request that they may not be sent. I have very heartily entered into an Association not to import any article which is now or hereafter shall be taxed for this purpose until the said Act or Acts are repealed. I am therefore particular in mentioning this matter as I am fully determined to adhere religiously to it. And I may perhaps have written for some things unwittingly which may be under these circumstances.

TO ROBERT CARY & COMPANY

Mount Vernon, July 20, 1771

Our Association in Virginia for the non-importation of goods is not at an end except against tea, paper, glass, and painters' colors of foreign manufacture. You will please, therefore, be careful that none of the glass, paper, etc., contained in my orders are those kinds which are subject to the tax imposed by Parliament for the purpose of raising a revenue in America.

TO GEORGE WILLIAM FAIRFAX

Williamsburg, June 10, 1774

Parliament may be sure that Americans will never be taxed without their own consent. The cause of Boston now is and ever will be considered as the cause of America (not that we approve their conduct in destroying the tea). We shall not allow ourselves to be sacrificed piecemeal though God only knows what is to become of us. So many threatening evils hang over us at present. We have the Indians, a cruel and bloodthirsty enemy upon our backs. Between them and our frontier inhabitants many skirmishes have taken place. And a general war is inevitable. And those from whom we have a right to seek protection are trying by every piece of trickery and tyranny to fix the shackles of slavery upon us.

TO CAPTAIN ROBERT MACKENZIE

Philadelphia, October 9, 1774

It is not the wish or interest of that government, or any other upon this continent, separately or collectively, to set up for independence. But, at the same time, you may be sure that none of them will ever submit to the loss of those valuable rights and privileges, which are essential to the happiness of every free state and without which life, liberty, and property are rendered totally insecure.

Writings of George Washington, Fitzpatrick, ed., Vol. II, pp. 512-513. Language simplified.

Robert Cary & Company of London served as Washington's agent for selling his agricultural products and for buying and sending him manufactured goods from England and other parts of Europe.

Writings of George Washington, Fitzpatrick, ed., Vol. III, p. 60. Language simplified.

Writings of George Washington, Fitzpatrick, ed., Vol. III, p. 224. Language simplified.

Fairfax, an old friend, owned a plantation near Washington's. Washington had cared for the plantation during its owner's occasional absences. At this time, the Fairfaxes, more sympathetic to Britain than to the growing agitation for action against it, were preparing to sell their property and move to England.

Writings of George Washington, Fitzpatrick, ed., Vol. III, p. 246. Language simplified.

MacKenzie, an officer with the British army garrison in Boston, was a Virginian. He had served as a captain under Washington in the militia. Less than a year after this letter was written, he fought with the British at Bunker Hill.

Writings of George Washington, Fitzpatrick, ed., Vol. III, pp. 293-294. Language simplified.

Fighting had erupted in Massachusetts in April, 1775. Shortly after this, Washington served as a delegate from Virginia to the Second Continental Congress in Philadelphia. He was the only delegate with much military experience. This fact caused John Adams to propose Washington as commander of the Congress' army around Boston. Adams' proposal might also have been prompted by the fact that having a wealthy Virginian as a military leader would give the revolutionary cause both respectability and the appearance of Southern support.

TO MARTHA WASHINGTON

Philadelphia, June 18, 1775

It has been determined in Congress that the whole army raised for the defense of the American cause shall be put under my care. And it is necessary for me to go immediately to Boston to take command of it. You may believe me, my dear Patsy, when I assure you, in the most solemn manner, that, far from seeking this appointment, I have done everything in my power to avoid it. I am not only unwilling to part with you and the family. I am also aware that this is a trust too great for my capacity. I should enjoy more real happiness in one month with you at home than I have the most distant prospect of finding abroad if my stay were to be seven times seven years. But it has been a kind of destiny that has thrown this service upon me. And I shall hope that my undertaking is designed to serve some good purpose. It was utterly out of my power to refuse the appointment without exposing my character to such censures as would have brought dishonor upon myself and given pains to my friends. This, I am sure, would not and ought not to have been pleasing to you. And it would have lessened me considerably in my own esteem. I shall rely, therefore, confidently on that Providence which has always preserved and been bountiful to me, not doubting but that I shall return safe to you in the fall.

Washington the General: Wearing Down the Enemy

Washington's Continental Army took a heavy toll of the British at Bunker Hill in 1775. They forced them to evacuate Boston the following spring. Washington then moved his troops to New York to await an attack expected there. But a superior British army, supplied by sea, and more skillfully led, forced the Continentals across New Jersey. From then on, through years of fighting, the Continental Army's location depended on where the main British force was. It was usually in New York. In 1781, Washington, working closely with a French army under Rochambeau and a French fleet under de Grasse, suddenly moved his army south. He did this to trap a major British force under Cornwallis on the York peninsula in Virginia. The British were weary of fighting a war in which they could win battles but in which they suffered continual losses. They knew they could never fully defeat Washington and his armies. So they decided to end the war. The following documents concern this vital period in Washington's life.

BENJAMIN RUSH TO THOMAS RUSHTON

October 29, 1775

General Washington has astonished his closest friends with a display of the most wonderful talents for the government of an army. His zeal, his unselfishness, his activity, his politeness, and his manly behavior have captivated the hearts of the public and his friends. He seems to be one of those illustrious heroes whom Providence raises up once in three or four hundred years to save a nation from ruin. If you do not know him, perhaps you will be pleased to hear that he has so much military dignity in his actions that you would single him out as a general and a soldier from among ten thousand people. There is not a king in Europe that would not look like a servant by his side.

TO JOSEPH REED

Cambridge, February 1, 1776

The account given of the behavior of the men under General Montgomery agrees completely with the opinion I have formed of these people. Place them behind a parapet, a breastwork, stone wall or anything that will give them shelter, and, from their knowledge of a gun, they will bravely meet their enemy. But they will not march boldly up to a work, or stand exposed in a plain.

TO THE PRESIDENT OF CONGRESS

Cambridge, February 9, 1776

To expect the same service from raw, and undisciplined recruits as from veteran soldiers, is to expect what never did, and perhaps never will happen. Men who are used to danger meet it without shrinking. But those who have never seen service often see danger where no danger is. Three things prompt men to perform their duty regularly in time of action: natural bravery, hope of reward, and fear of punishment. The first two are common both to untutored and to disciplined soldiers. But the last most obviously distinguishes the one from the other. A coward, when taught to believe that if he breaks his ranks and abandons his colors, he will be punished with death by his own army, will take his chance against the enemy. But the man who thinks little of punishment from his own army, and is fearful of the other, may run away regardless of the consequences.

GENERAL ORDERS

New York, July 25, 1776

It is with inexpressible concern, the General sees soldiers fighting in the cause of liberty and their country and committing crimes most

Letters of Benjamin Rush, L. H. Butterfield, ed., (Philadelphia: The American Philosophical Society; Princeton: Princeton University Press, 1951), Vol. I, p. 92. Copyright © 1951 by The American Philosophical Society. Reprinted by permission. Language simplified.

Rush, a prominent physician from Philadelphia, was a member of the Continental Congress.

Writings of George Washington, Fitzpatrick, ed., Vol. IV, p. 299. Language simplified.

Reed had been president of the Second Continental Congress. He was now adjutant-general of the army.

Richard Montgomery and Colonel Benedict Arnold led invasions of Canada in 1775. A joint attack on Quebec failed. Montgomery was killed and Arnold had to fight his way back to New York. The expedition failed to take Canada. But it forced the British to divide the troops they were sending to America in order to reinforce Canada. Washington here compares the behavior of soldiers in the militia with that of trained regulars.

Writings of George Washington, Fitzpatrick, ed., Vol. IV, p. 316. Language simplified.

Writings of George Washington, Fitzpatrick, ed., Vol. V, p. 337. Language simplified.

Washington's writings include many threats of punishment, including death, for disobeying orders. However, the writings also show leniency. Severer treatment would probably have increased desertions, already frequent. It might also have led soldiers to refuse to reenlist.

Writings of George Washington, Fitzpatrick, ed., Vol. VI, p. 28. Language simplified.

destructive to the army, and which in all other armies are punished with death. What a shame and reproach will it be if British soldiers fighting to enslave us, for two pence, or three pence a day, should be more regular, watchful and sober, than men who are fighting for everything that is dear and valuable in life.

TO THE PRESIDENT OF CONGRESS

New York, September 8, 1776

History, our own experience, the advice of our ablest friends in Europe, the fears of the enemy, and even the declarations of Congress demonstrate, that on our side the war should be defensive.

TO THE PRESIDENT OF CONGRESS

Heights of Harlem, September 24, 1776

Writings of George Washington, Fitzpatrick, ed., Vol. VI, pp. 110-111. Language simplified.

This letter was written after Washington's army had been driven from Long Island, New York, by the British force.

To place any dependence upon the militia is certainly resting upon a broken staff. These men have just been dragged from the tender scenes of home life. They are unused to the din of arms, totally unacquainted with every kind of military skill, and lack confidence in themselves. When they are opposed to troops regularly trained, disciplined, and outfitted, and superior in knowledge and in arms, they become timid and ready to fly from their own shadows. Besides, the sudden change in their way of life (particularly in the lodging) makes many sick and impatient. It also creates an unconquerable desire to return to their homes. This causes shameful desertions among them and infuses the same spirit in others. Again, men used to unbounded freedom and no control cannot stand the restraint which is necessary to the good order and government of any army.

JOSEPH REED, ADJUTANT GENERAL, TO MAJOR-GENERAL CHARLES LEE

November 21, 1776

A Reprint of the Reed and Cadwalader Pamphlets with an Appendix (n.p., 1863), Appendix D. Language simplified.

Washington had thought that the American position at Fort Washington on the Hudson River could not be defended. But, because some other officers, including General Nathanael Greene, disagreed, Washington allowed the Americans to hold the fort. On November 15, 1776, the British attacked and took the fort. And the Americans suffered heavy losses.

General Washington's own judgment, seconded by us, would, I believe, have saved the men and their arms. But unluckily, General Greene's judgment was contrary. This kept General Washington's mind in a state of suspense till the stroke was struck. Oh, General! An indecisive mind is one of the greatest misfortunes that can befall an army. How often I have lamented it in this campaign!

REMARK OF JOHN ADAMS TO THE CONTINENTAL CONGRESS

February 19, 1777

Letters of Members of the Continental Congress, Edmund C. Burnett, ed. (Washington, D.C.: Carnegie Institution of Washington, 1923), Vol. II, p. 263. Language simplified.

I have been distressed to see some members of this house idolizing an image which their own hands have made. I speak here of the superstitious reverence that is sometimes paid to General Washington. I honor him for his good qualities. But in this house I feel myself his superior. In private life I shall always acknowledge that he is my superior.

TO JOHN AUGUSTINE WASHINGTON

Germantown, August 5, 1777

I have, from the first, been among those few who never counted much on a French war. I always did, and still do think, they never meant to give us more than a kind of underhand help, that is, to supply us with arms in return for our money and trade. If Great Britain has the spirit and strength to resent this, it may bring on a war. But the declaration of war, I am convinced, must come from Great Britain.

Writings of George Washington, Fitzpatrick, ed., Vol. IX, p. 22. Language simplified.

Three months after this letter was written, the French, encouraged by the American victory at Saratoga, decided to recognize the independence of the colonies and to make military and commercial treaties with Congress. These steps led France into war with Britain.

TO THE PRESIDENT OF CONGRESS

Whitemarsh, November 17, 1777

I am informed that this army has been accused of not being, in the opinion of some, as active and enterprising as it ought to have been. If the charge is just, the best way to answer it will be to tell you how many battles we won and how many the enemy won, and to show you the enclosed list of the clothing which the army now lacks. Then, I think the wonder will be how they kept the field at all, in tents, at this season of the year.

Writings of George Washington, Fitzpatrick, ed., Vol. X, p. 76. Language simplified.

Washington wrote this letter after more than two months of occasional fighting with the British around Philadelphia. The British lived in comfortable winter quarters, while the cold and hungry Continentals lived miserably at Valley Forge.

GENERAL ORDERS

Valley Forge, January 20, 1778

The General positively forbids the burning of the farmer's fences. He asks all officers to attempt to prevent it and to punish severely all those who shall commit this offense.

Writings of George Washington, Fitzpatrick, ed., Vol. X, p. 322. Language simplified.

The Continental Army desperately needed food, horses, and other supplies furnished by farmers. So, it was good policy to stay on good terms with them.

HENRY LAURENS TO ISAAC MOTTE

January 26, 1778

For about a month, we have been alarmed now and then by reports from the Commander in Chief of the near and almost inevitable scattering of the army from a lack of provisions. Nakedness is cheerfully put up with. The General has made the most affecting complaints of neglect in the main departments. He has proceeded even to say that "never was an officer so impeded as he has been." Yet I suggest with deep feeling and much regret that too little regard has been paid to his sensible, spirited, manly reports. This great and virtuous man has not acted the *half patriot*, by a hasty resignation. His complaints are well founded. No internal enemy can hurt him without his own consent. I trust he will not gratify the wishes of those who seek to remove him, if there be any.

Letters of Members of the Continental Congress, Burnett, ed., Vol. III, pp. 51-52. Language simplified.

Laurens, of South Carolina, was a member of the Continental Congress. The Congress had fled to York, Pennsylvania, when the British occupied Philadelphia.

Washington's first Inaugural

Washington arriving in New York for his first Inaugural

Washington arriving in New York for his first Inaugural

Do you think the events pictured here really happened this way? If not, why were they pictured this way?

Washington is sitting on the brown charger, overseeing the British surrender at Yorktown in 1781.

Revolution in America: Confidential Letters and Journals 1776-1784 of Adjutant General Baurmeister of the Hessian Forces. Bernard A. Uhlendorf, ed. (New Brunswick: Rutgers University Press, 1957), pp. 167-168. Language simplified.

Baurmeister's journal is one of the chief sources of information about the Hessians and other auxiliary forces of the British in America.

The Quakers, especially strong in and near Philadelphia, were a puzzling problem for Washington and the Continental Congress. As pacifists, nearly all refused to enter military service. Many often refused to aid the Americans in other ways. Such Quakers were often suspected, sometimes justly, of sympathizing with the British and were treated accordingly.

Writings of George Washington, Fitzpatrick, ed., Vol. XIII, pp. 72-73. Language simplified.

McWhorter was a chaplain with the Continental Army.

▶Was Washington justified to use a minister as a means to get information from convicted spies? Why or why not?

Writings of George Washington, Fitzpatrick, ed., Vol. XIII, pp. 254-255. Language simplified.

JOURNAL OF ADJUTANT GENERAL MAJOR BAURMEISTER OF THE HESSIAN FORCES

May 1778

On the 30th of April the rich and influential Quakers returned from their prisons. They had been confined from the time the rebels, after the battle at Brandywine, were forced to leave Philadelphia. And, in prison, they were treated roughly. The wives of four of these Quakers asked permission at the English headquarters to go and beg for the release of their husbands. General Washington, in camp at Valley Forge, received these courageous Quaker women in the most cordial manner. He had them to dinner. And for the rest of the day they were entertained by the General's wife. Through this lady's kindly intercession, all the Quakers were released.

The joy among the members of this powerful sect over the unexpected return of their brethren is extremely great. But how Congress treated them and how many unworthy and previously worthless men make up this great body is shown by the fact that it completely forgot its dignity. Congress could not pass silently over this insult. Yet, at the same time, it could not praise enough the great justice of General Washington. And this praise is not unique. Everyone is captivated by this general.

TO REVEREND ALEXANDER McWHORTER

Fredericksburg, October 12, 1778

Farnsworth and Blair are now under sentence of death. They have been convicted of being spies from the enemy and of circulating counterfeit Continental money. It is certain that these unfortunate men know much about the enemy's affairs and their plans. However, we have not been able to bring them to admit this. You can give them the benefit of your profession and you can serve another valuable purpose, too. As you prepare them for the other world, your inquiries into the condition of their spiritual concerns will naturally lead to the information we want. When you have collected in the course of your visits such information as they can give, send all of it to me.

TO HENRY LAURENS

Fredericksburg, November 14, 1778

The question of the Canadian expedition appears to me one of the most interesting that has until now disturbed our national discussions. I have one objection to it. And this objection is, in my judgment, insurmountable. It alarms all my feelings for the true and permanent interests of my country. This is the introduction of a large body of French troops into Canada and putting them in possession of the capital of that province, which is attached to them by all the ties of blood, habits, manners, religion, and former connection of government. I fear this would be too great a temptation to be resisted by any power. Let us look for a moment at the striking advantages France would get from possession of Canada. France would acquire an extensive territory abounding in supplies for the use of its islands. A vast source of the most beneficial trade with the Indian nations would be opened. France then might monopolize this trade. It would have ports of its own on this continent and would thus be independent of the uncertain goodwill of an ally. It could take over the whole trade of Newfoundland, the finest fishing ground in the world, whenever it pleased. Possession of Canada would give security to France's islands. And, finally, France would have the power to awe and control these states, the natural and most formidable rival of every sea power in Europe. Canada would be a solid acquisition for France on all these grounds. And its numerous inhabitants, subjects to it by inclination, would aid in preserving it against the attempt of every other power.

France has been acknowledged for some time the most powerful monarchy in Europe. It would now be able to dispute the control of the sea with Great Britain. And, if joined with Spain, it would be certainly superior to Great Britain. Then it would have New Orleans on our right and Canada on our left. And it would be supported by numerous tribes of Indians on our rear from one border to another. These people are generally friendly to France and France knows how to deal with them. France would then have the power, it is much to be feared, to give law to these states.

France had been giving arms and other supplies secretly to the Americans since 1776. By now, it was a full ally of the Americans and one of their chief hopes for continuing the war successfully.

EZEKIEL CORNELL TO WILLIAM GREENE

August 1, 1780

The necessity of appointing General Washington sole dictator of America is again talked of as the only means under God by which we can be saved from destruction.

Letters of Members of the Continental Congress, Burnett, ed., Vol. V, p. 305. Language simplified.

Cornell, of Rhode Island, was an army officer serving in Congress. When Congress was in flight or suffering from serious shortages of members or money, it conferred a sort of temporary dictatorship on Washington. Here Cornell seems to be talking about something more permanent.

ALEXANDER HAMILTON TO JAMES McHENRY

February 1781

The great man and I have come to an open break. Proposals of compromise have been made on his part, but rejected. I pledge my honor to you that he will find me unbending. He shall for once at least repent his ill humor. Without a shadow of reason and on the slightest grounds, he charged me in the most offensive manner with treating him with disrespect. I answered very decisively "Sir, I am not conscious of it, but since you have thought it necessary to tell me, we part!" We have often spoken our sentiments freely to each other. Except to a very few friends our difference will be a secret. Therefore, be silent.

Allan M. Hamilton, The Intimate Life of Alexander Hamilton (New York, 1910), pp. 261-262n. Language simplified.

Hamilton, a brilliant young army officer, had been serving as Washington's aide. McHenry, an army surgeon, was then one of Washington's secretaries. On this occasion, Washington had criticized Hamilton for failing to perform a task promptly.

The Works of Alexander Hamilton, Henry C. Lodge, ed. (New York, 1880), Vol. VIII, pp. 37-38. Language simplified.

Schuyler, a wealthy New York landowner, served as a general in the army. He was Hamilton's father-in-law.

► Here Hamilton argues that the public good is more important than private feelings. What do you think of Hamilton's judgment in this case?

The Revolutionary Journal of Baron Ludwig von Closen, 1780-1783. Evelyn M. Acomb, ed. (Chapel Hill: The University of North Carolina Press, 1958), p. 64. Language simplified.

Von Closen was an aide to General Rochambeau, who commanded the French forces in America. He served as a liaison officer between the two armies and saw much of Washington.

ALEXANDER HAMILTON TO PHILIP SCHUYLER

February 18, 1781

I always disliked the office of an aide-de-camp because it has in it a kind of personal dependence. I refused to serve in this capacity with two major-generals at an early period of the war. Infected, however, with the enthusiasm of the times and with an idea of the General's character (which experience taught me to be unfounded), I overcame my scruples. I accepted his invitation to enter into his family. It was not long before I discovered he was neither remarkable for delicacy nor good temper. This revived my former aversion to the station in which I was acting. And it has been increasing ever since.

I believe you know the place I held in the General's confidence and counsels. This will make it more extraordinary to you to learn that for three years past I have felt no friendship for him and have professed none. The truth is, our dispositions are the opposite of each other. And the pride of my temper would not suffer me to profess what I did not feel. Indeed, when advances of this kind have been made to me on his part, they were received in a manner that showed at least that I had no desire to court them and that I desired to stand rather upon a footing of military confidence than on a footing of private attachment.

The General is a very honest man. His competitors have slender abilities, and less integrity. His popularity has often been essential to the safety of America. It is still of great importance to it. These considerations have influenced my past conduct respecting him. And they will influence my future. I think it is necessary he should be supported.

JOURNAL OF BARON LUDWIG VON CLOSEN

March 13, 1781

Throughout my career under General Washington, I had ample opportunity to note his gentle and affable nature, his very simple manners, his very easy accessibility, his even temper, his great presence of mind. In sum, it is evident that he is a great man and a brave one. He can never be praised sufficiently. In military matters, he does not have the brilliance of the French in expression. But he is penetrating in his calculations and a true soldier in his bearing. This is the opinion of the entire army, which no one can applaud more sincerely than I.

TO LUND WASHINGTON

New Windsor, April 30, 1781

Writings of George Washington, Fitzpatrick, ed., Vol. XXII, pp. 14-15. Language simplified.

I am very sorry to hear of your loss. I am a little sorry to hear of my own. But that which gives me most concern is, that you should go on board the enemy's vessels and give them refreshments. It would have been less painful to me to have heard, that as a result of your refusal of their request, they had burnt my house and laid the plantation in ruins. You ought to have considered yourself as my representative. And you should have reflected on the bad example of communicating with the enemy and making a voluntary offer of refreshments to them in order to avert a disaster.

It was not in your power, I realize, to prevent them from sending a flag on shore. And you did right to meet it. But you should, at the instant their business was made known, have declared, explicitly, that it was improper for you to yield to the request. After which, if they had proceeded to help themselves, by force, you could but have submitted. This was to be preferred to a feeble opposition which only serves as a pretext to burn and destroy.

Lund was Washington's half-brother. He had been taking care of Mount Vernon in Washington's absence. The episode recounted here involved Lund's attitude toward a British raiding party which was seeking supplies.

I am thoroughly persuaded that you acted from your best judgment. And I believe, that your desire to preserve my property, and rescue the buildings from impending danger, were your governing motives. But to go on board their vessels, carry them refreshments, commune with a parcel of plundering scoundrels, and request a favor by asking the surrender of my Negroes, was exceedingly ill-judged. And it is to be feared, it will be unhappy in its consequences. It will be a precedent for others and may become a subject of bad feeling.

▶ Here Washington weighs public and private gains against each other. What do you think of his position?

Again the Gentleman Farmer: Thinking About the New Nation

Washington spent the years between 1783 and 1789 at Mount Vernon. There he resumed the life of farm manager. He also played the part of generous host to a large number of travelers, distinguished and undistinguished, who wanted to see the military hero at his home. However, as will be seen in the following documents, Washington kept in close touch with public affairs.

JOURNAL OF ADJUTANT GENERAL MAJOR BAURMEISTER OF THE HESSIAN FORCES

Revolution in America, Uhlendorf, ed., pp. 589-590. Language simplified.

October 1783

General Washington lives near Princeton, like a private individual. If, as is generally said, he gave prestige to the American army, it

The Hessian officer wrote this entry in his journal after the peace treaty ending the Revolutionary War had been signed but before the British army had left New York.

Washington returned to Mount Vernon late in 1783.

is certain that his frequent presence near Princeton is lending some dignity and respect to the declining Congress. As a matter of fact this great council has never been so little respected and revered as it now is, especially in New England, where the prescribed taxes cannot be collected. This is now also the case in Pennsylvania. There Congress's flight from Philadelphia is considered an unpardonable mistake. Besides, the Pennsylvanians were the first to realize that the members of Congress were misusing the money gained from the sale of confiscated property.

In view of the present misgovernment, General Washington could obtain anything he might want, even the crown of North America. The people are ready to offer it to him. But so far he has shown no desire for this gift of fortune, if, indeed, it is one.

The Magazine of American History, Vol. IV, p. 158. Language simplified.

JOURNAL OF REV. THOMAS COKE

May 26, 1785

Thomas Coke and Francis Asbury were Methodist leaders and missionaries. They were among the first to take part in the movement to end slavery.

Mr. Francis Asbury and I set off for General Washington's. The General's home is very elegant. It is built upon the great river Potomac. The General is carrying on jointly with the state some amazing plans to improve the navigation of this river. He received us very politely. He is quite the plain country-gentleman. After dinner we asked for a private interview. We described to him the grand business on which we came, presenting to him our petition for the freeing of the Negroes. We asked him to sign it if the importance of his position did not make it unwise for him to sign any petition. He informed us that he agreed with our feelings and that he had mentioned his thoughts on the subject to most of the great men of the state. He did not think it proper to sign the petition. But he said that if the Assembly took it into consideration, he would inform them of his feelings by a letter.

▶ Do you think that an elected public official should use the prestige of his or her office to support causes which he or she considers worthwhile? Why or why not?

TO JAMES McHENRY

Mount Vernon, August 22, 1785

Writings of George Washington, Fitzpatrick, ed., Vol. XXVIII, pp. 227-228. Language simplified.

McHenry, a secretary to Washington during the war, was now serving in Congress.

I have always felt that adequate powers should be given to Congress. Without them it is clear to me that we shall never establish a national character, or be respected by the powers of Europe. However, I cannot agree with you that these powers should not be enlarged to regulate commerce. Your arguments against enlarging the powers of Congress—mainly, the some states may benefit more than others by this regulation—are well taken. But we are either a united people under one head, or we are thirteen independent sovereignties, always working against each other. If we are the former, whatever a majority of the states, as the Constitution points out, decides is for the benefit of the whole should be agreed to by the minority. Let the southern states always be represented. Let them act more in union. Let them declare freely and boldly what is in the interest of and what is harmful to their people. And there will, there *must* be a spirit of compromise.

TO CHEVALIER DE LA LUZERNE

Mount Vernon, August 1, 1786

Our internal governments are daily acquiring strength. The laws have their fullest energy. Justice is well administered. Robbery, violence, or murder is not heard of from New Hampshire to Georgia. The people at large (as far as I can learn) are more industrious than they were before the war. Economy begins to prevail—partly from necessity and partly from choice and habit. The seeds of population are scattered over an immense tract of western country. In the old states, where the war was fought, it is wonderful to see how soon the ravages of war are repaired. Houses are rebuilt. Fields are enclosed. Stocks of cattle which were destroyed are replaced. And many a desolated territory assumes again the cheerful appearance of cultivation. In many places the traces of disaster and ruin are hardly to be seen. The arts of peace, such as clearing rivers, building bridges, and establishing conveniences for travelling, etc., are constantly promoted. In short, the foundation of a great Empire is laid. And I please myself with the notion that Providence will not leave its work imperfect.

Writings of George Washington, Fitzpatrick, ed., Vol. XXVIII, pp. 500-501. Language simplified.

Luzerne, now back in France, had been the French minister to the United States during the Revolutionary War.

TO DAVID HUMPHREYS

Mount Vernon, October 22, 1786

But for God's sake tell me what is the cause of Shays' rebellion? Does it proceed from licentiousness, British influence spread by the tories, or real grievances which should be redressed? If the latter, why were they delayed 'till the public mind had become so agitated? If the former, why are not the powers of government tried at once? It is as well to be without, as not to live under their exercise. Commotions of this sort, like snow-balls, gather strength as they roll, if there is no opposition in the way to divide and crumble them.

Writings of George Washington, Fitzpatrick, ed., Vol. XXIX, p. 27. Language simplified.

Humphreys had been an aide to Washington during the war. When this letter was written, he had just returned from diplomatic service in Europe to become a member of the Connecticut legislature.

Shays' Rebellion was a revolt of farmers in western Massachusetts. They protested high taxes and inadequate administration of justice. The rebellion had just broken out when Washington wrote this letter.

TO HENRY LEE

Mount Vernon, October 31, 1786

My humble opinion is that there is a call for decision. Know precisely what the rebels aim at. If they have *real* grievances, redress them if possible. Or, acknowledge the justice of them and your inability to do it in the present moment. If they do not have real grievances, use the force of government against them at once. If this is inadequate, all will be convinced that the superstructure is bad, or lacks support.

Writings of George Washington, Fitzpatrick, ed., Vol. XXIX, p. 34. Language simplified.

Lee was a Virginia landowner and had been a cavalry officer during the war. He was serving in Congress at the time this letter was written. Washington is referring to Shays' Rebellion.

These pictures show several myths about Washington which originated in the nineteenth century. What function do myths such as these have in our nation's history?

Washington crossing the Delaware River

Right top; Washington as a boy confessing to his father that he tried to cut down a cherry tree

Right bottom; Washington as a boy giving in to his mother's wishes that he not pursue a career in the navy

148

To be more exposed in the eyes of the world, and more contemptible than we are, is hardly possible.

TO JAMES MADISON

Mount Vernon, November 5, 1786

Without some alteration in our political creed, the superstructure we have been seven years raising at the expense of so much blood and treasure, must fall. We are fast sinking to anarchy and confusion!

TO HENRY KNOX

Mount Vernon, December 26, 1786

My dear General Knox, I am much more disturbed than I can express to you about the disorders which have arisen in these states. Good God! Who besides a tory or a Briton could have foreseen or predicted them! Were these people wiser than others? Or did they judge us from the corruption and depravity of their own hearts? I am persuaded that the latter was the case. And, notwithstanding the boasted virtue of America, we are far gone in everything ignoble and bad.

TO HENRY KNOX

Mount Vernon, April 2, 1787

I see, or think I see, reasons for and against my attendance at the Philadelphia Convention. The reasons on each side are so strong that I will make my decision with great care. One of the reasons against attending is a fear that all the states will not appear. I also fear that some of them, being unwillingly involved, will send their delegates so fettered as to make the whole Convention worthless. In either of these circumstances—partial representation or cramped powers—I would not like to share in the Convention. If the delegates come with powers that will enable the Convention to probe the defects of the Constitution to the bottom and point out drastic cures, I would be honored to attend. Otherwise, I will avoid it.

TO THOMAS JEFFERSON

Philadelphia, May 30, 1787

The business of this Convention is still too much in the beginning stages to form any opinion of the result. Much is expected from it by some. But little is expected by others. And nothing by a few. All will agree that something is necessary. The government—if it can be called a government—is shaken to its foundation and liable to be toppled by every blast. In a word, it is at an end. And unless a cure is soon found, lawlessness and confusion will certainly follow.

Writings of George Washington, Fitzpatrick, ed., Vol. XXIX, p. 51. Language simplified.

Madison, who had served in Congress from 1780 to 1783, was now a member of the Virginia House of Delegates. He shared Washington's views about the need for a stronger central government.

Writings of George Washington, Fitzpatrick, ed., Vol. XXIX, p. 122. Language simplified.

Knox had been major general in charge of artillery during the war. He had served as Secretary of War under Congress in 1785. At the time this letter was written, he was living in Massachusetts, where Shays' Rebellion was going on.

Writings of George Washington, Fitzpatrick, ed., Vol. XXIX, p. 193. Language simplified.

With the rebellion over, Washington was pondering the possibilities of success for the Constitutional Convention of 1787.

Writings of George Washington, Fitzpatrick, ed., Vol. XXIX, p. 224. Language simplified.

When this letter was written, Washington had been elected president of the Constitutional Convention. Jefferson, main author of the Declaration of Independence and wartime governor of Virginia, was serving as American minister to France.

NOTES OF WILLIAM PIERCE

May 1787

General Washington is well known as the commander in chief of the recent American army. He conducted these states to independence and peace. And he now appears to help in forming a government to make the people happy. Like Gustavus Vasa of Sweden, he may be called the deliverer of this country. Like Peter the Great of Russia, he appears as the politician and the statesman. And like Cincinnatus, the Roman general and statesman, he returned to his farm perfectly contented with being only a plain citizen after enjoying the highest honor of the country. And now he only seeks the approval of his countrymen by being virtuous and useful. The General was made President of the Constitutional Convention by the unanimous voice of its members. He is fifty-two years old.

"Notes of William Pierce on the Federal Convention of 1787," **The American Historical Review**, Vol. III, p. 331. Language simplified.

William Pierce was a delegate from Georgia to the Constitutional Convention.

TO MARQUIS DE LAFAYETTE

Philadelphia, June 6, 1787

Public pressure was so great that I could not resist the call to attend a convention of the states. It is to determine whether we have a government of respectability under which life, liberty, and property will be secure, or are to submit to one which may be the result of chance, springing perhaps from lawlessness and confusion and dictated perhaps by some ambitious demagogue who will not listen to the interests of his country as much as to his own ambitious views. I am not able now to tell you what may be the result of the present discussions.

Writings of George Washington, Fitzpatrick, ed., Vol. XXIX, pp. 229-230. Language simplified.

Lafayette had come to America as a boy to serve in the Continental Army during the revolution. He had served with distinction and had won Washington's friendship. He was back in France when this letter was written.

TO MARQUIS DE LAFAYETTE

Mount Vernon, February 7, 1788

It appears to me little short of a miracle that the delegates from so many different states should unite in forming a system of national government to which few objections could be raised. I am not such an enthusiastic or undiscriminating admirer of it as not to notice that it has some real, though not serious, defects. My creed is simply:

First, that the general government is not given more powers than are absolutely necessary to perform the functions of a good government. And, consequently, that no objection should be made against the amount of power given to it.

Second, that these powers are so spread among the legislative, executive, and judicial branches, into which the government is arranged, that it can never be in danger of becoming a monarchy, an oligarchy, an aristocracy, or any other tyrannical or oppressive form of government, as long as there shall remain any virtue in the body of the people.

Writings of George Washington, Fitzpatrick, ed., Vol. XXIX, pp. 409-410. Language simplified.

Here Washington gives his views on government.

151

Writings of George Washington, Fitzpatrick, ed., Vol. VI, pp. 110-111. Language simplified.

Lincoln, from Massachusetts, had served as a general during the war and as Secretary of War under Congress. He had led the Massachusetts militia in putting down Shays' Rebellion.

Washington is responding here to Lincoln's comment that he is clearly the leading candidate for the Presidency under the new Constitution.

▶What do you do when your personal wishes and comfort come in conflict with duty to family, friends, or groups to which you belong? Are you proud of your actions?

TO BENJAMIN LINCOLN

Mount Vernon, October 26, 1788

I would willingly pass over in silence the part of your letter in which you mention the persons who are candidates for the first two offices in the executive branch if I did not fear that the omission might seem to suggest a lack of confidence. Every personal consideration conspires to rivet me to retirement. At my time of life, and under my circumstances, only two things in this world can ever draw me from it: a *conviction* that the desires of my countrymen had made my services absolutely necessary joined with a *fear* that my refusal might lead people to believe that I preferred the saving of my own reputation and private ease to the good of my country. After all, if I should be forced to accept, I call Heaven to witness, that this very act would be the greatest sacrifice of my personal feelings and wishes that ever I have been called upon to make. It would be to give up rest and the enjoyments of home for trouble, perhaps for public abuse. For I should think of myself as entering upon an unexplored field, surrounded on every side with clouds and darkness.

22 THE CHALLENGE TO UNITY AND LOYALTY

HISTORICAL ESSAY

In 1789 the people of the United States began a unique experiment in government. Their new Constitution gave the federal government strong powers. However, these powers were still limited. They were also subject to popular control through regular elections and other devices. Such a government could be made to work only if citizens succeeded in keeping political conflicts peaceful and in treating political differences as legitimate. The story of the critical years from 1789 to 1801 reveals how successful Americans were in making the Constitution work.

The Federalists Absorb Their Opponents

Ratification of the Constitution was not an easy process. There were many clashes over it. And strong feelings, for and against, were aroused. However, once the Constitution was ratified, these feelings died down quickly. Some of the people who had strongly opposed the Constitution were elected to the First Congress. Many things may have attracted them to the Congress. They may have been interested in the prospect of sharing in a new kind of power. Or they may have had a desire to guard the rights of their states against the new central government. In any case they devoted their abilities to the common task of making the federal system work. By mid-1790, when all thirteen states had ratified the Constitution, open opposition to the new government had virtually disappeared. Congress' proposal for a Bill of Rights did much to quiet the fears of the suspicious. These fears were further stilled by the reputations and talents of the men who took office in George Washington's first Administration.

Washington tried hard to get men of high abilities to serve in various offices. He also set the precedent of awarding some offices to men from all sections of the nation. This policy was an important way to promote national unity. He selected trusted, former aides for two executive positions. He appointed Alexander Hamilton of New York as Secretary of the Treasury and Henry Knox of Massachusetts as Secretary of War. He drew upon the largest state, Virginia, for two more men. Edmund Randolph, its politically powerful governor, became Attorney General. And Thomas Jefferson, its most distinguished political thinker, became Secretary of State. The six Supreme Court Justices were drawn from all parts of the country. John Jay of New York became the first Chief Justice. Of the largest states, only Pennsylvania did not contribute a high-ranking federal officer.

Programs and Policies

Washington was very popular. And he made wise appointments. But these factors did not guarantee that citizens would accept the authority of the new government. The test would come when the government had to exert power where it was needed and still keep the support of a people jealous of their freedom. The political and administrative skill of Alexander Hamilton played an essential part in helping the government meet this test successfully.

As Secretary of the Treasury, Hamilton was the chief financial officer of the government. He had to obtain an income for the federal government that would free it from dependence on the states. Hamilton felt that citizens should be brought to think of the federal government, instead of the states, as the center of financial power and stability. Then, he believed, they would indentify their own interests with the success of the national government. He set out to build a sound financial structure.

In 1789, Congress quickly placed taxes on many imports. It also established port taxes that gave American-owned ships slightly lower rates. These taxes were one source of income for the government. The federal government appointed customs officers to collect the taxes. And it appointed federal marshals to help enforce the laws. A system of federal district courts, parallel in some ways to state courts, was

▶ Should the amount of political power a person wields in his or her locality be the main consideration in appointing that person to a high office in the national government? Or should other considerations take precedence?

The Constitution provided for a Supreme Court. But it did not specify the number of justices. The Judiciary Act of 1789 established the federal judiciary system. It specified that the Supreme Court "shall consist of a chief justice and five associate justices." Congress has varied the number of judges from five to ten. Since 1869, however, the figure has been set at nine.

153

created. These courts would hear cases involving the new federal laws. Between the revenue officers and the courts, the government succeeded in getting most importers to obey the laws. Smuggling, a well-established American practice, declined sharply. This reform testified to the energy and popularity of the new government.

Hamilton arranged a system of "funding" for paying off the national debt. Most of the debt had grown up during the Revolutionary War. And nearly everybody expected the new government to pay that debt. But Hamilton surprised many people with his plan. He asked that those holding federal certificates of debt be paid back at face value. Many of the people who held the certificates had bought them at very low prices at times when no one was sure that they would ever be paid off. Some of these people had been forced to sell because of hard times. James Madison and others argued that the original holders of the certificates deserved some return for the money they had lost. Hamilton also asked that the federal government be responsible for or "assume" the Revolutionary War debts of all the states. This plan was agreeable to states like Massachusetts, which had heavy debts still to be paid. But it was not agreeable to states like Virginia, which had already paid most of its debt. Virginians saw this proposal as a scheme for milking their state for the benefit of New Englanders. Madison rallied enough support in Congress to block the passage of bills for funding and assumption.

Yet nearly all national leaders, including Madison, realized that there was an important reason for paying the national debt. It would win the confidence of American citizens and of other nations in the stability of the government. Hamilton asked Jefferson to persuade Madison and his followers to back the funding program. In return, Hamilton would back the plan to establish the new national capital on the Potomac River. The Virginians reluctantly agreed. The federal government then issued new bonds to pay for funding and for taking on old debts. Both the old debts and the new bonds were held largely by business and professional people in the northern cities. They were the only group with much available capital.

Hamilton's plan for a national bank drew support from the same group. Many farmers, who often supported Madison and Jefferson, opposed it. According to Hamilton's plan, the federal government would charter the bank. The bank would act as the government's financial agent. But the capital and control of the bank would be mostly in private hands. The debate raged partly over the question of whether Congress could legally create an agency not specifically authorized by the Constitution. But, in large part, the fight over the bank represented a clash between rural southern interests and urban northern interests. Washington signed the bill authorizing the bank. It proved to be as successful in ensuring smooth and safe handling of funds and in aiding business transactions as Hamilton and the business interests had hoped it would be. But control of the bank fell to northern business interests. And its profits went largely into northern and foreign hands, just as Jefferson and the farming interests had feared.

Hamilton's financial program laid a sound basis for the stability of the new government and for the future economy. Moreover, in adopting Hamilton's program, the Federalists defined the role of the federal government broadly. Now the government had to show that it could enforce its authority.

In 1791, Congress placed an excise tax on liquor distilled within the United States. This act produced revenue. But, more importantly, it gave the federal government an opportunity to meet successfully an open challenge to its authority. Many farmers distilled whiskey from their own grain. So they avoided paying excise taxes. The farther they lived from the heavily settled coastal area, the harder it was to collect the taxes from them. In 1794, federal officials decided to collect the whiskey tax in western Pennsylvania. Farmers there resisted these efforts. They rioted and terrorized some of the tax collectors. Washington saw the importance of meeting such challenges. Henry Lee, accompanied by Alexander Hamilton, led an army of about thirteen thousand hastily recruited militiamen westward over the mountains. Resistance disappeared as word of the approaching army spread among the rebels. Washington had proved his point. He was then wise enough to temper force with leniency. The only persons arrested in the Whiskey Rebellion were eventually released.

An excise tax is a tax placed upon the manufacture, sale, or consumption of goods within a nation or a state. Federal excise taxes have been placed largely upon liquor, tobacco, and other luxury items.

The Rise of Organized Opposition

The people who designed the Constitution were realists. They expected that those who took part in government would find many reasons to disagree with each other. The delegates to the Philadelphia Convention had built a system of checks and balances into the new government. They wanted to make it difficult for one interest group to gain control of the whole government. Madison had argued in *The Federalist*, No. 10, that federalism gave protection against the evils of factions. But the authors of the Constitution had not expected that such interest groups would grow into organizations operating openly and peacefully to gain leadership and control of the government. In the 1790's, political parties were not yet a recognized part of the political process. But the beginnings of the American party system date from this period.

The Republicans (later called Democratic-Republicans) informally organized their opposition to the Federalists as early as 1791. That was the year in which Hamilton pressed his financial program on Congress. The Republicans grew in strength by battling the foreign policies of Washington and Adams. To the Republicans these policies

In 1787 and 1788, Hamilton, Madison, and Jay had written a series of newspaper articles in support of the new Constitution. Each article was signed "Publius." They were collected and published as **The Federalist.** They quickly became the most authoritative and influential statements of American political ideas.

One common practice throughout American history is to tar and feather people as a way of punishing them or to express protest. Is it ever justifiable to treat people this way?

These men are forcing tea down the throat of a tax collector whom they have tarred and feathered in protest against the tea tax of 1773.

Right; this man was tarred and feathered in 1935 because he was a suspected Communist.

Tarring and feathering a tax official in protest against a tax on whiskey passed in 1791.

seemed pro-British and anti-French. But not until 1796, with Washington's retirement from office, did they make a real effort to win the Presidency and control of Congress. They failed in both. John Adams became President, and the Federalists kept their majority in Congress.

The Republicans wanted to gain control of the government through regular elections. They promised to administer the government according to the Constitution. But they frightened many Federalists who believed that their opponents were really revolutionaries. Federalists had done a good job of representing people with business, financial, and urban interests. To many of these people, Jefferson's followers seemed to be enemies of property. Even more frightening to the Federalists was the timing of the Republican challenge. The Republicans became a recognizable group at the time that the French Revolution reached its most radical and violent stage. The revolutionary government in France had executed King Louis XVI and Queen Marie Antoinette and had gone to war with Great Britain, Austria, and Russia. Thomas Jefferson and many other Republicans sympathized with the French revolutionaries, who had cast off monarchy in favor of republican government. But conservative people shuddered as they imagined Republicans seizing property and setting up guillotines in the public squares. Republican newspapers savagely criticized Federalist leaders—even the revered Washington. And this development convinced Federalists that freedom of the press was leading to a breakdown of public order.

Events abroad influenced the tone of the political conflicts at home. The American political battle died down when the French revolutionary government fell into the hands of a more conservative group in 1795. Jefferson, in fact, greeted the election of Adams in 1796 cheerfully. His own election as Vice-President suggested that the two opposed groups could be brought together. However, Hamilton and the most conservative Federalists opposed such a reconciliation. The renewal of the war in Europe aggravated Federalist-Republican differences. Both Britain and France seized neutral American ships. Federalists and Republicans accused each other of being in league with a foreign enemy to betray American interests.

The Federalists had a majority in Congress. So they took steps to repress what to them looked clearly like subversion. In 1798, they passed, and President Adams signed, the so-called Alien and Sedition Acts. One of the acts gave the President power to deport any alien he thought was dangerous to the nation. Another provided heavy fines and jail terms for persons who criticized federal officials in "false, scandalous, and malicious" terms. This language was broad enough so that Federalist judges were able to send several Republican editors and one Republican Congressman to jail.

The Republicans responded to these challenges first with protests. In late 1798, the Kentucky and Virginia state legislatures adopted

▶ Under what circumstances, if any, do you think that people should be fined or jailed, or both, for publicly criticizing federal officials?

157

DIFFERENCES BETWEEN THE FIRST POLITICAL PARTIES	
Federalists	**Democratic-Republicans**
Party of Alexander Hamilton, John Adams, and John Marshall	Party of Thomas Jefferson and James Madison
Led by merchants, bankers, and lawyers living primarily in New England	Led by planters, farmers, and wage earners living mainly in the South and Southwest
Favored strong central government.	Favored strong state governments.
Interpreted Constitution loosely.	Interpreted Constitution strictly.
Believed in government by aristocracy.	Favored rule by the educated masses.
Passed Alien and Sedition Acts.	Supported individual liberties; passed Kentucky and Virginia Resolutions.
Pro-England	Pro-France

Favored Hamilton's financial policies:
  for protective tariff,
  for National Bank,
  for manufacturing interests,
  for assumption of state debts.
	Opposed Hamilton's financial policies:
	  against protective tariff,
	  for state banks,
	  for agrarian interests,
	  against assumption of state debts.

resolutions calling the Alien and Sedition laws illegal. They declared that the states had the power to declare federal laws unconstitutional. The resolutions were written by Jefferson and Madison, respectively. These challenges to federal authority set a precedent for later states-rights causes. But in 1798 and 1799, they drew little support from other states.

A more effective Republican response to the Federalists was made in another area. Throughout the nation, the Republicans worked to create a party organization at the local level in order to win the election of 1800. This attempt was successful. Jefferson and Aaron Burr of New York received 73 electoral votes each. The Federalists, Adams and Charles Pinckney of South Carolina, won 65 and 64 respectively. The tie between Jefferson and Burr gave states with Federalist electors the chance to decide the outcome. Hamilton considered Jefferson less dangerous than Burr. And, in the end, he persuaded the Federalists to throw the election to Jefferson. The Twelfth Amendment to the Constitution, ratified in 1804, prevented candidates of the same party from being tied in the vote for President.

Now that the Republicans were in power, what actions would they take against their political enemies? Jefferson gave a conciliatory response in his inaugural address in 1801: "We are all republicans, we are all federalists." He did not oust Federalists from appointive offices in large numbers. But he did require their loyalty to the new administration. After the turbulence of the 1790's, a calmer spirit prevailed in the nation. A challenge had been met. The leadership of a nation had been changed peacefully. Political opposition within a Constitutional framework would be tolerated and eventually praised rather than driven underground and punished.

23 THE CHALLENGE TO AMERICAN SECURITY

HISTORICAL ESSAY

In its first half-century the United States firmly established its security as a nation. It maintained its independence while growing rapidly in population, area, and economic strength. These things were achieved despite the recurrent antagonism of the great powers of Europe. Stable government and effective leadership helped meet these challenges by providing an energetic foreign policy. This policy made good use of the United States' distant location and some shrewd diplomacy to take advantage of the disputes of the great European powers themselves.

The World at Peace

After the Revolutionary War, the United States badly needed a period of peace. Fortunately, none of the major western European powers wanted war in the New World. Britain made no effort to recover the thirteen colonies. Its major goal was to increase its supremacy in world trade. And, for this, peace was much more useful than war.

France too hoped to gain power through commerce. It had encouraged American trade by an agreement which formed part of the Alliance of 1778. But France did not succeed in winning American trade from Britain. Likewise, it made no effort to recover lost colonies in the New World.

Spain had more to lose through war than either Britain or France. Its military and naval strength had declined rapidly during the eighteenth century. It had gained Louisiana from France in 1762 and Florida from Britain in 1783. But its widespread colonies were thinly populated and highly vulnerable to attack.

Besides peace, the United States wanted several things from other nations. However, it had little to bargain with. The government was uncertain. And the nation lacked military strength. Americans wanted the British to leave their military posts in the Northwest Territory. They also wanted them to sign more favorable trade agreements. The French had guaranteed the Treaty of Paris of 1783. But they had little interest in helping to oust the British from their American frontier posts. The French were allied to the Americans. However, they limited their American trade to the West Indies. Americans tried to increase their trade with Mediterranean ports. But they found that pirates crippled their commerce. Congress lacked funds either to bribe the pirates, as the European powers did, or to build a navy to protect American ships. The United States could not force Spain to grant free navigation of the Mississippi. And it could not stop the Spanish from plotting with the Indians and the settlers of the Southwest.

The creation of the new Constitution in 1787 and a stronger central government in 1789 brought the United States some small diplomatic successes. Spain agreed to reopen the Mississippi. France eased some of its restrictions on West Indian trade. And Britain sent a minister to represent it in the United States. But major changes in the position of the United States had to wait for more dramatic events abroad.

The World at War

The French Revolution of 1789 produced one of the greatest upheavals of modern times. France tried to spread the revolution to other countries and to extend French control to other parts of Europe. Most European powers desperately resisted both the revolutionary ideas and the expansion of France.

When Britain went to war against France in 1793, both the dangers and the opportunities were quickly brought into focus. Both nations wanted American supplies. But neither wanted the United States to trade with the other. France opened its West Indian ports to United States trade. Britain retaliated by seizing hundreds of American ships. These ships were bound for France or French colonies, or were carrying produce from either France or its colonies. The British also increased their agitation among the Indians in the Northwest.

Most Americans sympathized with the French Revolution, at least in its early stages. And they were enraged. The United States moved closer to war with Britain. But France, in its turn, seized many American ships bound for Britain. Britain had also opened its West Indian ports to American trade.

The pressures on the warring European powers produced some diplomatic benefits for the United States. John Jay was sent as a special envoy to negotiate a treaty with Britain. He brought home several agreements. The British finally gave up their frontier posts on United States soil. They gave American ships the same privileges in British ports as those enjoyed by any other foreign nation. And they allowed a small amount of trade with the West Indies.

160

In the United States, hostility against Great Britain was very strong. Many Americans denounced Jay as a traitor because he had failed to convince the British to stop seizing American ships. But President Washington wanted to keep relations with Britain from growing worse. He realized that Jay's Treaty was the best the new, weak nation could get at the time. He threw his influence behind the treaty. And the Senate ratified it.

Meanwhile, Spain had withdrawn from the coalition of European nations fighting France. Spain quickly offered the United States a highly favorable treaty. It included freedom of navigation on the Mississippi River and the "right of deposit" at the port of New Orleans. The United States thus frustrated Spanish hopes of establishing a strong colony in the Mississippi Valley and of persuading the settlers of Kentucky and Tennessee to secede from the Union. In 1796, the Senate ratified Pinckney's Treaty unanimously.

Further dangers and benefits to the United States followed shortly. The temporary improvement in relations between Great Britain and the United States provoked the French to a new wave of attacks on American ships and cargoes. The French government gave insulting treatment to three American envoys to France in 1797. This insult increased American sentiment for war. Congress, in 1798, authorized the capture of French armed ships. An unofficial naval war continued for more than two years. It was fought largely in the West Indies against French privateers. But John Adams, who succeeded Washington as President, did not wish to fight a war with France. He made the unpopular decision to send new envoys to France. In 1800, they reached agreements with France which ended both the naval hostilities and the Franco-American treaty of alliance of 1778.

Reducing tension with France contributed to a far more important development. Louisiana included a tract of land ranging from the Gulf of Mexico northward to Canada and westward to the Rocky Mountains. It had passed from Spain back to France in a deal arranged in 1800. Control of that vital area by a nation as powerful as France alarmed both President Jefferson and the western farmers. In 1803 Jefferson sent James Monroe to France. He was to aid Robert R. Livingston, the American ambassador to France, in an attempt to buy New Orleans and West Florida from Napoleon for $10 million. Such a purchase would guarantee Americans control of the Mississippi.

Napoleon had intended to use Louisiana to further a plan to restore French power in the New World. But a revolt in Haiti, a French island in the West Indies, and an epidemic there of yellow fever frustrated his plan. Napoleon decided instead to sell all of Louisiana. For the bargain price of $15 million, the United States doubled its land area and acquired the potential agricultural wealth of the vast western half of the Mississippi Valley. Moreover, the Louisiana Purchase removed the threat that a strong foreign power would occupy territory bordering the United States.

Thomas Pinckney was minister to Great Britain from the United States. He negotiated an agreement whereby Spain recognized the boundaries established by the Treaty of Paris of 1783: the Mississippi River in the west and the 31st parallel in the south. The United States also gained free navigation of the Mississippi and the right to deposit goods at New Orleans to await ocean shipment without paying a duty to Spain.

President Adams sent three Americans to Paris to negotiate with the French. The go-betweens for the French government, known as X, Y, and Z, demanded a bribe from the American Commissioners as the price for any agreement. When Adams told Congress about the "XYZ Affair," a cry went up for war against France.

▶The Constitution does not explicitly give the national government the right to acquire new territory. But it does not forbid it to acquire territory either. Do you think that Jefferson was violating the Constitution when he purchased the Louisiana Territory?

Shortly after the purchase, Jefferson launched the first great exploring expedition in American history. Under the leadership of Meriwether Lewis and William Clark the expedition explored the new territory. They pushed up the Missouri River, across the Great Plains and Rocky Mountains, to the Pacific Ocean. The mission proved that an overland route to the Pacific was possible. And it ultimately stimulated new settlement and trade.

The Trial and Failure of Neutrality

The war between Britain and Napoleonic France resumed in 1803. And both powers again threatened American neutrality. Great Britain smashed the combined French and Spanish fleets in 1805 off Trafalgar, on the coast of Spain. Then its navy patrolled the seas unchallenged. Napoleon's armies, however, dominated most of western and central Europe. The British announced a blockade of the thousands of miles of coastline held by Napoleon. To guard all of these shores was impossible. But the British found a way to halt supplies bound for Napoleonic Europe. They stopped, searched, and seized American ships and cargoes right outside American ports and often within American territorial waters. The British suffered from a shortage of seamen for their huge fleet. So they also took many sailors from American ships and forced them into British naval service. Sometimes the sailors they seized were British subjects who had deserted from the British navy to serve on American ships. But usually the sailors who were "impressed," as the practice was called, were American citizens. The United States protested strongly against impressment. But to no avail.

Napoleon retaliated against the British attempt to strangle the French-controlled economy. He declared a counter-blockade of Britain. French ships seized any neutral ships which obeyed the British blockade. Americans lost more ships to France than to Britain. Crews of ships seized by the French also suffered harsh treatment. American relations with France deteriorated rapidly.

To preserve both American trade and American neutrality, Presidents Jefferson and Madison (who was elected in 1808) put economic pressure on Britain and France. In December 1807, Jefferson got Congress to place an embargo on foreign trade. It prohibited American merchant ships from sailing to foreign ports. New Englanders depended heavily on shipping. They opposed the act bitterly and violated it freely. But American trade was reduced enough to hurt Britain badly. British citizens pleaded with their government to relax its pressure on American trade so that the American embargo would be dropped. But pressure from maritime interests in the United States on the American government was even greater. Congress repealed the Embargo Act a few days before Jefferson left office in March

In 1806, Napoleon issued the Berlin Decree, in which he declared that all trade with Great Britain was illegal. Since he lacked naval power, this was only a paper blockade. Great Britain retaliated with the Orders in Council which blockaded most European ports.

In 1807, Napoleon issued the Milan Decree which declared that any ship observing the British blockade was subject to seizure by the French.

1809. It substituted a Non-Intercourse Act. This act allowed trade with all ports not under French or British control. It did not achieve the desired purpose of getting the belligerents to cease their attacks on American ships. Congress substituted another Act in 1810, Macon's Bill No. 2. It restored trade with the two belligerents. But it offered to prohibit imports into America from either belligerent, if the other met American terms.

Napoleon took clever advantage of this confusing offer. He promised to repeal his restrictions against American commerce. He never fulfilled this promise. But it convinced an over-optimistic President Madison and Congress that France was ready to cooperate. So the United States adopted the threatened prohibition against British

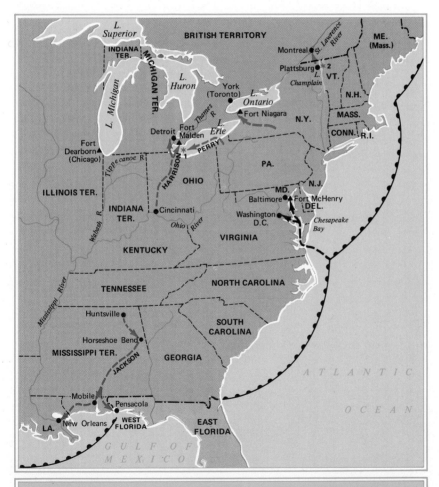

British Moves
U.S. Moves
British Blockade

1 ✳ Oliver Perry's Victory on Lake Erie
2 ✳ Macdonough's Victory at Plattsburg

CAMPAIGNS OF THE WAR OF 1812

imports in March 1811. The American economic weapon worked well. Britain ended its restrictions on June 16, 1812. Unfortunately, the United States Congress, in response to President Madison's request, declared war on June 18. It did not learn of the British concession until weeks later.

To those who wanted military glory and additional territory, the War of 1812 was a disappointment. Some ships of the small American navy fought brilliant battles with British warships. And American privateers captured hundreds of British merchant ships. But the British navy still ruled the seas. It blockaded American ports and gradually cut down the losses of its ships. Meanwhile, British troops beat back such American attempts to invade Canada as a raid on York, Ontario, where government buildings were burned. The British retaliated with a raid on Washington. There they burned the Capitol, the White House, and other buildings.

The United States had been unprepared for war. Thus, it had great difficulty financing any military effort. Moreover, strong anti-war sentiment had actually created a secessionist movement by 1814. Federalist delegates from Connecticut, Rhode Island, Massachusetts, New Hampshire, and Vermont held a secret convention in Hartford, Connecticut. They drew up a resolution calling for several constitutional amendments. These amendments were aimed at making states less liable to federal draft, taxation, and embargoes. The resolution included a statement of the philosophy of the Virginia and Kentucky Resolutions. Now it was New England's turn to claim that a state could use its authority to act against federal laws it considered unconstitutional. The convention met too late, however, to have any effect on the outcome of the war.

The British threatened to invade the country from the north. But small, makeshift American fleets defeated similar British fleets on Lake Erie and Lake Champlain. Thus, they established command of these waterways. An equally serious threat came at New Orleans. There a large force of British veterans landed in late 1814 after Napoleon had been defeated. Western militiamen led by General Andrew Jackson crushed the attacking force in early 1815.

Negotiations to end the conflict had actually begun almost as soon as war had been declared. Not until August 1814, however, did British and American representatives meet in Ghent, Belgium. The peace they signed in December recognized that neither party had won. Their main agreement in the Treaty of Ghent was simply to stop fighting. Jackson's victory at New Orleans came two weeks later, before news of the treaty reached the United States.

The Collapse of the Spanish Empire

With the war ended, the United States continued to reap benefits from the squabbling among European nations. When Napoleon had

▶ Do you think that citizens ever have the right to violate laws which they consider unconstitutional? Why or why not?

In September 1813, Captain Oliver Hazard Perry destroyed the British vessels at Put-in-Bay, near the western end of Lake Erie. The following year Captain Thomas Macdonough destroyed the British ships on Lake Champlain.

The five American commissioners were John Quincy Adams, Henry Clay, Albert Gallatin, Jonathan Russell, and James A. Bayard.

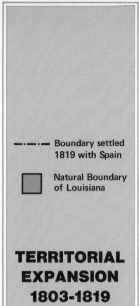

Boundary settled
1819 with Spain

Natural Boundary
of Louisiana

**TERRITORIAL
EXPANSION
1803-1819**

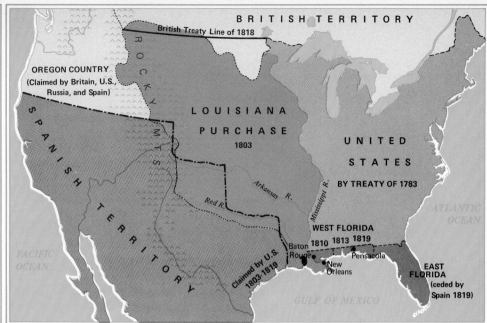

BRITISH TERRITORY

British Treaty Line of 1818

OREGON COUNTRY
(Claimed by Britain, U.S.,
Russia, and Spain)

ROCKY MTS

SPANISH MTS

SPANISH TERRITORY

LOUISIANA
PURCHASE
1803

UNITED
STATES
BY TREATY OF 1783

Arkansas R.

Red R.

Mississippi R.

Claimed by U.S.
1803-1819

WEST FLORIDA
1810 1813 1819

Baton
Rouge
New
Orleans

Pensacola

EAST
FLORIDA
(ceded by
Spain 1819)

PACIFIC
OCEAN

GULF OF MEXICO

ATLANTIC
OCEAN

taken over Spain, revolts against Spain broke out in the Spanish colonies in America. The United States took advantage of this unrest to encourage a revolution in West Florida in 1810. It welcomed the new territory when the rebels asked to have it annexed. Spain ceded East Florida to the United States in 1819. The cession was part of an extensive settlement by which the boundary between the United States and the western Spanish possessions was carefully defined for the first time.

To Americans, a great prospect was opening. It was the vision of a Western Hemisphere in which the United States would hold a dominant position. Two possible sources of danger, however, appeared on the horizon. The major European powers might try to deprive the new Latin American nations of their independence. And Russia, who owned Alaska, might extend control down the Pacific coast of North America.

The British navy was the strongest force for resisting any ambitions of European nations. Moreover, Britain opposed the restoration of European control of Latin America and further Russian expansion. Both Britain and the United States issued strong protests against Russian claims. Then, in 1823, the British Foreign Secretary, George Canning, proposed to the United States that the two nations jointly declare their opposition to European intervention in Latin America. But the shrewd American Secretary of State, John Quincy Adams, recognized that the United States could be sure of British support in keeping Europeans out of the New World. He believed the long-range interests of the United States would be better served by an independent policy statement. This statement came in December 1823, in President James Monroe's annual message to Congress. A few scattered excerpts in the message were later called the Monroe

Doctrine. The Doctrine declared that the Americas were no longer open to European colonization. It also said that the United States had no intention of interfering in the internal affairs or the political disputes of European countries. British power was the real deterrent to European action. So, little attention was paid at the time to Monroe's pronouncement. Only later did it become an important and effective part of American foreign policy. But again the United States had profited from disputes among European nations.

The Growth of a National Spirit

STATING THE ISSUE

Many new nations have emerged in Africa and Asia since the end of World War II. Only a few of these new countries have developed without violence and internal dissension. Some of them have been torn by bitter revolutions and internal fighting. In the modern world, nation-building and violence often go hand in hand.

Between 1815 and 1830, the United States was an emerging new nation. The American Revolution had established the independence of the former British colonies, and the War of 1812 had reaffirmed it. The Louisiana Purchase and the acquisition of Florida had doubled the size of the original thirteen colonies. New settlements had sprung up throughout the Ohio and Mississippi valleys. But no one could be sure whether the United States would survive as one united nation, divide into several countries, or break out in civil war.

The national government set up by the Constitution had established a state—a politically organized body of people. But to become a nation, these people had to develop self-consciousness and national pride. They also had to establish firm lines of communication among themselves. Finally they had to learn to participate in the government if they wanted their new nation to become a democracy.

Readings 24-26 focus on the factors that helped the newly created state to become a nation between 1815 and 1830. The essay at the end of this chapter summarizes the major events in the history of these vital years. Chapter 8 will discuss how American life became more democratic through the process of participation.

1400 1500 1600 1700 1800 1900 2000

1790 Samuel Slater builds first American cotton-spinning machine
1793 Eli Whitney invents cotton gin
1801 John Marshall becomes Chief Justice of Supreme Court
1803 Supreme Court declares law unconstitutional for first time in **Marbury** vs. **Madison**
1807 Robert Fulton invents steamboat
1809 James Madison becomes President
1816 Congress passes a protective tariff
1816 Dartmouth College Case strengthens federal government
1817 James Monroe becomes President

1819 Supreme Court strengthens the role of federal government in **McCulloch** vs. **Maryland**
1819 First major depression
1820 Congress passes Missouri Compromise
1823 Erie Canal completed
1824 **Gibbons** vs. **Ogden** gave Congress the right to regulate interstate commerce
1825 John Quincy Adams elected President by House of Representatives
1828 Noah Webster publishes an American dictionary

24 THE NEED FOR NATIONAL COMMUNICATIONS

By 1820, the American population had grown to 9½ million, more than twice what it had been when the Constitution was ratified. During the same period, the land area of the United States had more than doubled. Americans quickly began to move into the new land. In 1790, only 100,000 Americans lived west of the Appalachian Mountains. By 1820, more than 2 million people had moved into the Mississippi River Valley.

To many observers, the addition of new territory and the spread of American settlements over a vast area seemed to threaten the future of the new nation. The American people lived in bustling cities, river towns, seaports, tiny rural villages, isolated plantations, or far-flung frontier settlements cut off from the coast by vast mountain barriers. These communities often had little to do with each other. This isolation led many American leaders to argue that the government should build and maintain a vast transportation network to promote national unity.

The first selection that follows gives the proposal of a famous senator, John C. Calhoun. He suggested a way to overcome the problems caused by the physical barriers to American unity. The second selection explains how Americans felt about the completion of one of the first great engineering feats—the Erie Canal. As you read, try to answer the following questions:

1. According to Calhoun, what were America's important natural advantages and disadvantages?
2. How did the Erie Canal help satisfy the requirements for nationhood discussed at the beginning of this chapter?

Calhoun's Program for National Unity

John C. Calhoun (1782-1850), along with Daniel Webster and Henry Clay, dominated national politics from the War of 1812 to 1850. Calhoun eventually became a leading spokesman for southern sectionalism and states' rights. But early in his career, he was a strong supporter of nationalistic legislation. Following are portions of a speech that he delivered in the House of Representatives on February 4, 1817.

Congress ought to take charge of building roads and canals. If we were only to consider the financial advantages of a good transportation system, it might then be left to private enterprise. But when we come to consider how intimately the strength and political prosperity of the republic are connected with transportation, we find the most urgent reasons why we should apply our national resources to it.

In many respects, no country of equal population and wealth possesses potential power equal to ours. In muscular power, in hardy and enterprising habits, and in lofty and gallant courage, our people are surpassed by none. In one respect, and, in my opinion, in one only, are we materially weak. We occupy an enormously large land area in proportion to our population. Only with great difficulty can the common strength of our nation be brought to bear on any point that may be menaced by an enemy.

It is our duty, then, in so far as possible, to correct this weakness. Good roads and canals, carefully laid out, are the proper remedy. In the recent War of 1812, how much we suffered for the lack of them. Our military movements were slow, while our transportation costs were high. In the event of another war, the savings in the cost of transporting materials and men would go far toward repaying us for the expense of constructing roads and canals.

What can be more important than unity of feelings and sentiments among the people in every part of the country? And what can help

Works of John C. Calhoun, Richard K. Crallé, ed. (New York: D. Appleton and Company, 1856), Vol. II, pp. 188-191. Language simplified and modernized.

169

In what ways could the subjects of these three pictures have contributed to the development of national consciousness?

CHICAGO'S FIRST POST-OFFICE

In the 1800's, this road was an important route west to the Alleghenies.

to produce unity more than a transportation system? No free state ever occupied a country as large as this one. Let it not, however, be forgotten that the size of our nation exposes us to the threat of disunity. We are great and growing rapidly. This is our pride and our danger, our weakness and our strength.

We must correct every tendency to disunion. Whatever hinders communication between the distant parts of the country and Washington, D.C., the center of the republic, weakens the union. The larger the area within which trade goes on, the greater are the social contacts among people. In turn, the more strongly are we bound together.

Nothing—not even differences in language—tends more than distance to divide people from each other. Let us, then, bind the republic together with a perfect system of roads and canals. Let us conquer space. The most distant parts of the republic will be brought within a few days' travel of the center. A citizen of the West will read the news of Boston still moist from the press. The mail and the press are the nerves of the nation.

To aid us in this great work of maintaining the integrity of this republic, our country has most admirable advantages. It is belted around with lakes and oceans and cut in every direction by bays and rivers. It is blessed with a form of government which combines liberty and strength. We may reasonably raise our eyes to a most splendid future if we only act in a manner worthy of our advantages.

▶ Do you think that a good transportation system is still of primary importance in the United States or have other considerations become more important?

171

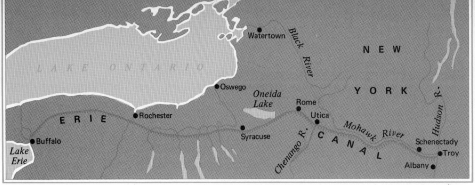

THE ERIE CANAL

Building a Great Canal

On October 10, 1823, a great public celebration was held in Albany in honor of the approaching completion of the Erie Canal. William Bayard, one of the speakers for the occasion, made the following remarks.

Albany Gazette, October 14, 1823. Language simplified.

The completion of more than three hundred miles of canal in less than seven years will have a most important influence on the prosperity of our state, on the social and moral character of our people, and on the political power and importance of this nation.

It would be useless to speak at this moment of the advantages of this canal. You have the best proofs of them in the joy of the people who surround you. The great enterprise we celebrate, destined as it is to connect the valleys of the Ohio and the Mohawk, will hereafter create a homemarket for our products. Our canal is the beginning of a system of internal improvements which, while they lessen the cost, will increase the amount of our domestic productions. Hereafter our wheat will compete in the European markets.

This canal will unite a large portion of our people in the strong ties of a community of commercial interest, and under God, as we trust, secure forever, the union of these states. Thus our republican institutions will be preserved, the example of a representative government, founded on the people's will, be maintained in its purity—and the once fond wish of the patriot be realized, in the permanence of our Constitution.

FOR THOUGHT:

What kinds of people might develop a feeling of national consciousness through the creation of a national transportation system?

25 A COMMON LANGUAGE AND HISTORY

After the War of 1812, the government made a strong effort to build an improved transportation and communication system. This effort may be interpreted as a step in nation-building. But national self-consciousness and pride do not automatically follow new highways. They rest in part on a common cultural heritage and language.

National self-consciousness grows from the pride which a people take in their history and in the leaders who have helped to build the nation. The essential elements of a people's national tradition stay alive in many different ways: through stories, songs, and poems that are handed down orally; through written histories and textbooks; and through the work of painters, architects, and sculptors. Recently established nations in Asia or Africa place murals and statues in almost every public square to celebrate the national heroes and heroines who led their countries' struggles for independence. Similarly, American artists of the early nineteenth century celebrated the memories of the people who joined in the American struggle for independence.

The following selections reflect the concern shared by many Americans during this period about their language and the events in their history. As you read, keep these questions in mind:

1. What were Webster's objections to the use of conventional English dictionaries by Americans?
2. How does the strong public interest in Trumbull's painting help explain the requirements for nationhood discussed in the beginning of this chapter?

Noah Webster on the Reasons for an American Dictionary

Noah Webster (1758-1843) began to work on An American Dictionary of the English Language *in 1800. He completed it in 1828. The following selection is taken from his preface to that dictionary.*

It is not only important, but in a degree necessary, that the people of this country should have an *American Dictionary of the English Language.* Although the body of the language is the same as in England, and it is desirable to continue that sameness, yet some differences must exist.

The principal differences between the people of this country and of all others arise from different forms of government, different laws, institutions, and customs. Thus the practice of *hawking* and *hunting* and the *feudal system* of England originated terms which formed a necessary part of the language of that country.

But in the United States, many of these terms are not part of our present language. And they cannot be, for the things which they express do not exist in this country. They can be known to us only as out-of-date or foreign words. On the other hand, the institutions in this country which are new and peculiar give rise to new terms or to new applications of old terms unknown to the people of England. They cannot be explained by them, and will not be inserted in their dictionaries unless copied from ours. Thus the terms *land-office, regent*

Noah Webster, **An American Dictionary of the English Language** (New York: S. Converse, 1828), Vol. I, Preface. Language simplified and modernized.

Hawking is hunting game with a trained falcon, a variety of hawk. **Hunting,** for the English upper classes, is pursuing game for sport. The **feudal system** was the political, economic, and social organization of medieval Europe.

Land-office was a
government office which sold
public lands to settlers and
land speculators. A **regent** is
a member of the governing
board of a university. In the
United States, a **plantation**
was a large farm on which
cotton or tobacco was
grown. In Britain, **plantation**
meant a group of planted
trees or plants. A **selectman**
is a member of a board of
town officers in New
England chosen to manage
certain public affairs.

of a university, *plantation, selectmen, senate, congress, courts,* and *assembly* are either words not belonging to the language of England, or they are applied to things in this country which do not exist in that. No person in this country will be satisfied with the English definitions of the words *congress, senate, assembly, court,* etc.

But this is not all. In many cases, the nature of our governments and of our civil institutions requires an appropriate language in the definition of words, even when the words express the same thing as in England. Thus the English dictionaries inform us that a *justice* is one appointed by the *king* to make right judgments. He is a *lord* by his office. Justices of the peace are appointed by the king's *commission* [authority]—language which is inaccurate in respect to this officer in the United States.

A great number of words in our language require that they be defined in phrases suitable to the condition and institutions of the people in these States. The people of England must look to an *American Dictionary* for a correct understanding of such terms.

The necessity, therefore, of a dictionary suited to the people of the United States is obvious.

An Artistic Expression
of Nationalism

In 1818 the well-known American painter, John Trumbull, painted the signing of the Declaration of Independence for the Capitol rotunda. The Capitol painting was widely reviewed in American newspapers and magazines. Benjamin Silliman, a prominent chemist at Yale University, wrote the review from which this selection is taken.

The American Journal of
Science and Arts, 1818,
Vol. I, pp. 200-203.
Language simplified and
modernized.

This is the greatest work which the art of painting has ever produced in the United States. The picture is magnificent both in size and in execution. The dimensions of the canvas are eighteen feet by twelve.

This picture forms one of a series by Mr. Trumbull, in which he intended to represent the most important civil and military events of the American Revolution, with portraits of the most distinguished actors in the various scenes. The government of the United States has ordered four of the subjects originally proposed by Mr. Trumbull, to be painted by him, and to be deposited in the national Capitol.

No event in human history ever shed a more wholesome influence over the destinies of so great a group of people as the American Revolution did. The wisdom of no political act was ever so soon and so powerfully demonstrated, by such magnificent consequences. And justly may the nation be proud of the Revolution and of those distinguished men, its authors, whose patriotism was calm, dignified, persevering, and always under the guidance of reason and virtue.

▶Do you think that men
alone were the force behind
the Revolution?

In what ways could these two paintings, both by John Trumbull, contribute to the growth of national consciousness?

The painting represents the Congress at the moment when the committee advanced to the table of the President to make their report. It contains faithful portraits of all those members who were living when the picture was begun, and of all others of whom any authentic representation could be obtained.

The figures are as large as life. And it may safely be said that the world has never beheld a more noble group of men. It was the native and untried nobility of great talent, cultivated intelligence, superior manners, high moral aim, and devoted patriotism. The crisis demanded the utmost firmness of which the human mind is capable—a firmness not produced, for the moment, by passion and enthusiasm, but resting on the most able comprehension of both duties and dangers.

▶Do you think art should be used to encourage feelings of nationalism? Why or why not?

This moral effect has been produced in the fullest and finest manner by this great painter. No true American can view this picture without gratitude to the men who, under God, defended their liberties, and to the artist who had commemorated the event, and passed on the very features and persons of the actors to future generations. Such artistic efforts tend powerfully also to promote patriotism, and to prompt the rising generation to imitate such glorious examples.

FOR THOUGHT:

To what degree do the excerpts in this reading reflect rising national spirit? To what degree might they have promoted this feeling?

26 EMERGENCE OF A NATIONAL ECONOMY

In 1800, more than 90 percent of the American people lived on farms or in small villages. These farms and villages formed thousands of separate economies.

Large southern planters and merchants on the Atlantic coast carried on heavy trade with Europe, primarily with Great Britain. But the subsistence farm was the typical unit of the American economy. In this "family economy," the whole family including the children spent most of their time producing the basic necessities of life: food, fuel, clothing, and shelter.

By 1820, about 500,000 family economies participated in large "local economies." For example, neighboring farmers traded crops and shared labor with each other. At village stores or markets, farmers exchanged their excess crops and homemade products. The village usually served as the center for the local market, and small, local industries produced lumber, flour, bricks, wagons, and nails. These products rarely went beyond the local market, which ordinarily was not larger than thirty miles in diameter.

During the next few decades of the nineteenth century, the economy gradually became less local and more national. America had always been involved in the world economy. European countries wanted American farm products, such as cotton, tobacco, rice, and sugar. In turn, America needed European manufactured goods. However, transportation problems had held back trade between distant points within the nation. As more roads, canals, and bridges were built, trade between the various sections increased. More and more local economies began to take part in the same general economy. In turn, economic interdependence between sections of the country increased. Each section specialized in those products it could produce most efficiently and could sell in other areas of the country. Thus economic development in America encouraged the growth of nationalism in the first half of the nineteenth century. As you read the following selections describing this change in the American economy, try to answer these questions:

1. How did the development of the cotton culture in the South and the Southwest early in the nineteenth century affect the American economy?
2. Why did textile manufacturing develop rapidly in New England after 1815?

The Growth of an Interdependent Economy

This account of economic developments in the United States in the early nineteenth century is taken from the works of the American economic historian, Guy S. Callender.

The influence which rapidly changed local economies into a national economy was the introduction of cotton culture into the South and its extension after 1815 over the Southwest. About the same time, there was a considerable extension of sugar culture in Louisiana, and tobacco culture in Kentucky and Tennessee. Here was a group of products that were much in demand everywhere. They had large value in small bulk so that the cost of transporting them for long distances over the poor roads of new settlements was not too great. The soil and climate of a vast region were well suited to the production of cotton, the demand for which was increasing at an extraordinary rate. This region was covered by a network of navigable streams that could easily and cheaply float this valuable product to the coast. The steamboat perfected a natural transportation system entirely adequate for a community devoted to producing a few such products and exchanging them with the outside world.

Guy S. Callender, **Selections from the Economic History of the United States, 1765-1860** (Boston: Ginn and Company, 1909), pp. 272-274.

The Southwest, in the early nineteenth century, included the present states of Alabama and Mississippi.

Robert Fulton invented the steamboat in 1807. By 1815, steamboats operated regularly on the Mississippi River.

The Gulf States included Louisiana, Mississippi, and Alabama.

The effect of these economic advantages was not limited to the South. Very soon they were felt by every other section of the country. The great profit to be made by growing cotton and sugar caused the people of South Carolina and the Gulf States to devote themselves chiefly to these crops. Planters with slave labor took over the production of cotton and sugar. Mixed farming could not be profitably carried on by slaves in the South. Hence the planters were glad to buy their farm supplies, so far as possible, from other producers.

The livestock could be driven overland to the plantations, and the great network of rivers with their flatboats and steamboats provided an easy means of transportation for other supplies. All kinds of produce from such important products as pork, bacon, lard, beef, butter, cheese, corn, flour, and whiskey, to such minor ones as apples, cider, vinegar, soap, and candles went down the Ohio and Mississippi in great quantities. This was the first important market which the farmers of Tennessee, Kentucky, and the Northwest had. It made an improvement in their economic situation almost as remarkable as the introduction of cotton culture produced in the Southwest.

The Northwest, in the early nineteenth century, included the region beyond the Appalachians from Tennessee and Kentucky northward.

The prosperity of the South and West now in turn influenced the East. The people of these sections were able for the first time to buy freely from other communities. The products they bought were partly imported from abroad and partly produced in New England and the Middle States. Accordingly, both the commercial and manufacturing interests of this section were greatly stimulated. New York reached out with its Erie Canal to win a larger share of the growing internal trade, and a keen rivalry sprang up among the commercial cities of the seaboard which has lasted to the present day. Manufacturers also began to feel the influence of their expanding home market.

This account should make clear the general character of internal commerce. Its basis was a territorial division of labor among the three great sections of the country resting upon foreign commerce. The South was able to devote itself chiefly to the production of a few basic crops, turning out a great surplus of them for export and depending upon the other two sections for much of its farm produce, nearly all of its manufactures, and to a large extent for the shipment of its products. Both its exports and imports were carried largely by northern shipping, went through northern ports, and were either actually in the hands of northern merchants or financed by northern money. The Northwest devoted itself chiefly to farming, depending at first entirely upon the South for its markets, but gradually winning after 1840 a home market in the Northeast and a foreign one in Europe. New England and the Middle States were devoted principally to commerce and manufactures. They were able to supply the needs of the other two sections, depending at first upon their own farmers for their farm supplies and later drawing them partly from the southern seaboard slave states and partly from the Northwest.

178

RIVER TRADE OF NEW ORLEANS 1813–1830

	Number of Steamboats entering New Orleans	Tonnage Received in New Orleans	Value of Cargo Deposited
1813–14	21	67,560	—
1814–15	40	77,220	—
1815–16	—	94,560	$ 9,749,253
1816–17	—	80,820	8,773,779
1817–18	—	100,880	13,501,036
1818–19	191	136,300	16,771,711
1819–20	198	106,706	12,637,079
1820–21	202	99,320	11,967,067
1821–22	287	136,400	15,126,420
1822–23	392	129,500	14,473,725
1823–24	436	136,240	15,063,820
1824–25	502	176,420	19,044,640
1825–26	608	193,300	20,416,320
1826–27	715	235,200	21,730,887
1827–28	698	257,300	22,886,420
1828–29	756	245,700	20,757,265
1829–30	989	260,900	22,065,518

FEDERAL EXPENDITURES FOR RIVERS AND HARBORS 1822–1830
(in thousands of dollars)

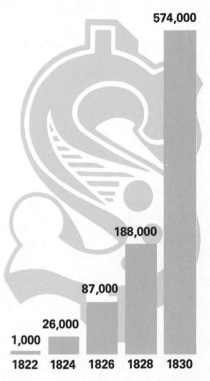

Year	Amount
1822	1,000
1824	26,000
1826	87,000
1828	188,000
1830	574,000

How might the activities indicated on these charts and map have promoted the development of national consciousness?

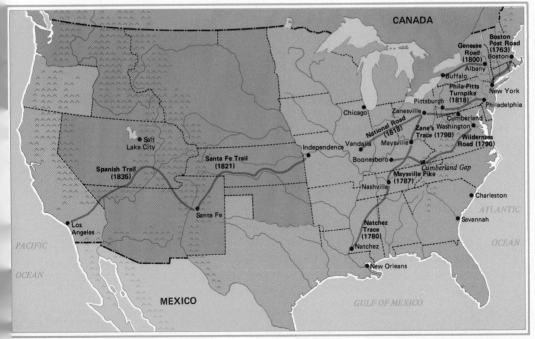

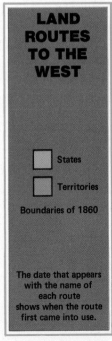

LAND ROUTES TO THE WEST

- ☐ States
- ☐ Territories

Boundaries of 1860

The date that appears with the name of each route shows when the route first came into use.

The Growth of
Textile Manufacturing

Two important developments spurred the growth of textile manufacturing in the United States. In 1790, a young Englishman named Samuel Slater introduced the English factory system by developing a water-powered machine to spin cotton thread. In 1793, Eli Whitney invented a cotton gin which rapidly separated the cotton seeds from the fibers. This selection, written by an American economic historian, Victor S. Clark, describes the growth of textile manufacturing in the early nineteenth century.

Victor S. Clark, **History of Manufacturers in the United States, 1607-1860** (Washington, D.C.: Carnegie Institution of Washington, 1916), Publication No. 215A, pp. 543-551. Language simplified.

A depression followed the War of 1812. To add to American economic problems, the British dumped their manufactured goods on the American market in an effort to cripple the infant industries.

Spindles are the rods that hold the bobbins on which thread is wound as it is spun.

A loom is a machine for weaving thread or yarn into cloth. Waterpower replaced hand operation of looms.

The Merrimac River flows from New Hampshire through Massachusetts to the Atlantic Ocean.

While early efforts in textile manufacturing were beginning in remoter parts of the country, the cotton manufactures of New England and the Middle States were passing through hard times. Mills that survived the dark years between 1815 and 1820 were generally fitted by location, management, equipment, and resources to continue the industry successfully. Cotton-spinning by 1820 had nearly recovered the position it occupied in 1815. About one-third of the spindles of New England and New York were making yarn for power-looms. The ratio of looms to spindles was higher in Massachusetts than in neighboring states. New Jersey and Delaware mills were engaged chiefly in spinning for Philadelphia manufacturers. Except for this small but important instance, however, the centralized system of manufacture was rapidly extending.

This concentration affected all aspects of the industry. More processes were performed in one establishment; the capacity of individual mills was enlarged; the plants began to group in narrow areas. Technical and commercial limitations no longer restricted the size of factories so much as formerly. But most mills and most spindles, even in old manufacturing districts, were still moved by small water-powers. The series of large water-power developments which gave rise to the new manufacturing cities of the Merrimac River was anticipated or repeated in a smaller way at several mill villages on rivers that led to the New England sounds.

Between 1820 and 1832, the number of spindles in Rhode Island increased in round numbers from 70,000 to 240,000. There may have been one mill loom in use for every 160 spindles in 1820; there was one for every forty spindles in 1832. Connecticut increased its spindles from 30,000 to 140,000 and its loom capacity in the same ratio as Rhode Island. Massachusetts, with more capital and room for growth, raised its spindles from 52,000 to 340,000, and used relatively more factory looms than its neighbors. It had now passed Rhode Island as our leading cotton-manufacturing state.

The Boston Manufacturing Company produced its first cloth in 1815, built a second larger mill two years later, and added a third factory and a bleachery in 1820. This convinced Boston capitalists that cotton goods could be made profitably in New England and that the Waltham method best suited our conditions of production. Therefore, measures were taken to start this system of manufacture in other places. Soon after 1820, two groups of large factories were promoted. The first was at Lowell, Massachusetts, and made that city until the Civil War the leading textile center of America. The other was at Dover and Somersworth, in New Hampshire. The latter mills were built with Boston money, but by different investors from those who supported Waltham and were engaged in founding Lowell. As a result of this movement, Boston became the financial and commercial supporter of New England's textile development during the years that followed 1820.

The Merrimac Company, which was the original Lowell corporation, was organized in 1822 with $600,000 capital. And ten years from the time it shipped its first goods to Boston, its factories contained over 30,000 spindles and 1,000 looms.

Meantime, in 1825, the Hamilton Company was organized, with $600,000 capital, to make drillings—a fabric which it originated—and fancy clothes. In 1828 the Appleton and Lowell companies were chartered, both of which manufactured coarse-goods to supply a demand that had outgrown the capacity of Waltham. And in 1830, the Suffolk, Tremont, and Lawrence companies were started. By the end of 1834, these six companies operated 19 cotton mills at Lowell, with 110,000 spindles and 4,000 looms. This represented the most remarkable decade of progress, in a single place and industry, as yet achieved in our manufacturing history.

FOR THOUGHT:

Would the economic dependence of the various parts of the country cause national feeling to grow? How could you test your answer?

A bleachery is a place where cloth is bleached or whitened.

Under the Waltham method of manufacturing, introduced in Waltham, Massachusetts, all the processes involved in turning raw cotton into furnished cloth were completed in one factory.

▶ Do you think factories should produce goods that people want or that people need?

27 THE DIMENSIONS OF NATIONHOOD

HISTORICAL ESSAY

Two opposite developments took place in the United States during the first quarter of the nineteenth century. On the one hand, national consciousness and pride increased tremendously because of spectacular social and economic growth after the War of 1812 with

England. At the same time, sectional and class feelings grew rapidly. Northerners, southerners, and westerners developed somewhat different societies. Farmers, mechanics, slaveholders, and manufacturers began to see different visions of America's future. These developments created a difficult political problem: how to encourage national growth and at the same time satisfy the various sections and interests within the country.

The "Era of Good Feelings"

Jefferson's friend and Secretary of State, James Madison, succeeded to the Presidency in 1809. He won a second term four years later. In 1817, another political associate of Jefferson, James Monroe, won an easy victory in the electoral college. By this time, the Federalists had become so weak that their Presidential candidate, Rufus King, was able to carry only three states. Because of this overwhelming electoral victory and because Monroe's administration was generally received with favor, historians have commonly referred to his two terms of office (1817-1825) as an "Era of Good Feelings." In this period, little formal political opposition existed, contrasting sharply with the fierce party fighting at the end of the eighteenth century. But the sectional tensions and opposing economic forces did not disappear. The "Era of Good Feelings" ended with a disputed national election in 1824 and the appearance of new political factions.

The most important domestic laws of the period reflected the growth of American nationalism. In 1816, Congress passed the first American tariff designed mainly to protect new industries rather than to provide income for the federal government. The tariff was a direct response to the rapid growth of cotton mills during the war years. When trade with England began again, Congress believed it was in the national interest to protect new industries. But within ten years, the tariff would be sharply disputed between northerners and southerners.

Internal Improvements

During the early part of the century, people all over the country felt the need for roads and canals to tie the different parts of the country together. But the administrations of Jefferson, Madison, and Monroe were less willing to support this measure than they were the tariff. They had two reasons for this attitude. First, many people doubted the government's constitutional right to build roads and canals. Second, many people in New England and the South could not see the advantages of improved roads and canals. Many New Englanders feared that better transportation facilities would drain off the labor supply in eastern cities. Therefore, federal responsibility for internal improvements became a lively political issue. It soon became associated with Henry Clay, the dynamic young Speaker of

182

the House of Representatives. Later, it became one of the most important issues of the Whig party which Clay helped to organize in the 1830's.

Slowly, a national transportation and communication network was built. Western farmers were able to use it to sell their crops in eastern markets. Eastern manufacturers could market their goods throughout the country. As a result, Americans became less dependent on the European economy. Throughout the seventeenth and eighteenth centuries, most Americans had lived on self-sufficient farms. A few had produced farm products for sale in Europe and had bought manufactured goods there. The changes in the economy in the early nineteenth century have been described as a "market revolution." Americans were developing a national economy. More and more Americans sold their labor or their farm products in the market to the highest bidder. Their prosperity as individuals became tied to the general level of prosperity in the country as a whole.

The Strengthening of the Supreme Court

During this period the Federalists declined as a political party. But the Republicans began to support many of the nationalistic measures that Federalists originally favored, such as the tariff and the bank. Federalist ideas also continued to have an impact on the government through decisions of the Supreme Court. In 1801, John Marshall was appointed Chief Justice of the Supreme Court. For the next thirty-four years, Marshall was the guiding influence on the Court. Because of his influence, the most important decisions of the Court represented a national rather than a states-rights point of view.

In *Marbury vs. Madison* (1803), Marshall said that the Supreme Court could declare a law of Congress unconstitutional. In 1816, the Marshall court decided two more vital cases. The first concerned the right of the New Hampshire legislature to change the royal charter under which Dartmouth College had been established in 1769. Marshall ruled that the charter was a contract and was, therefore, protected from state interference by the Constitution. The Dartmouth College Case was important for two reasons. First, it declared that a state could not pass laws contrary to Constitutional provisions. Second, it placed existing corporations beyond the control of individual states and thus encouraged business growth. Corporations felt freer to make plans when they knew that business rules would not be changed by state actions.

In 1819, the Court ruled in the case of *McCulloch vs. Maryland.* The issue concerned the legal right of Maryland to tax a branch of the Bank of the United States. The decision involved two questions: the constitutionality of the Bank, and the constitutionality of the tax. Marshall started with the assumption that the federal government represented one united nation and not a group of independent states. He said that the Constitution gave the federal government the power to do what was "necessary and proper" for the general welfare. Although the Constitution did not give the federal government the specific power to establish a bank, it could be reasonably assumed that the government needed a bank to carry out its other powers.

Marshall's insistence that the language of the Constitution should be interpreted broadly made it possible for the federal government to expand its powers and functions during the nineteenth century. After deciding that the Bank was constitutional, Marshall and the Court said that the state could not tax it, since the power to tax any institution can be used in such a way as to destroy it.

Another important case, *Gibbons vs. Ogden* (1824), involved the question of New York State's right to grant a monopoly to a steamboat company that operated in the waters between New York and New Jersey. Marshall and the Court held that the Constitution reserved to Congress the right to regulate commerce between the states. The immediate effect of this decision was to send steamboats chugging across bays and harbors and up and down rivers without worrying about state restrictions. It thus encouraged national commerce. Years later government regulation of business and labor would be justified on this same principle.

The Growth of Sectionalism

Despite the forces in this period which encouraged national feeling and political unity, Americans in the three great geographic sections—the Northeast, the South, and the West—were also developing a greater sectional consciousness. In the Northeast, economic interests were divided. Farming remained important in northern New England, upstate New York, and much of Pennsylvania. Traditionally, because of its large cities and seaports, the Northeast had been the commercial center of the nation. But by 1820 manufacturing had become more important than foreign trade.

▶Do you feel a stronger loyalty to your hometown, your state, or your country?

The Northeast was also divided politically. Federalists in New England resented having had no power in the federal government for so long. Manufacturers wanted higher tariffs, but they were opposed by shipowners and merchants who feared that the tariff would interfere with foreign trade. Northerners distrusted the rising power of the West. They were anxious to keep their supply of inexpensive labor. They also looked with distaste on the institution of black slavery in the South.

Meanwhile, the South still produced farm products almost exclusively, but the particular crops had changed. During the colonial period the principal crop for export had been tobacco. Hemp, grain, rice, and sugar were also grown. Originally cotton had been a minor crop because of the difficulty in separating the fiber from the seeds. But in 1793 Eli Whitney's cotton gin solved this problem. In 1800 only about 70,000 bales of cotton were produced in the South. By 1825 cotton production had increased 700 percent. As cotton production increased, so did the number of black slaves, although importing additional slaves became illegal in 1808. From 1800 to 1820, by which time every northern state had begun to abolish slavery, the number of slaves in the South had almost doubled, growing from about 800,000 to more than 1½ million.

During the first quarter of the nineteenth century, the Old Northwest was the most rapidly growing section of the country. By 1820, Ohio, which had not been admitted to the Union until 1803, had a larger population than Massachusetts. The people who settled this section came from both the South and the Northeast. Northern Ohio, Indiana, and Illinois, for example, were largely settled by New Englanders. But the southern parts of these states were settled by southerners, who generally supported the idea of slavery even if they had no slaves themselves. Large slaveholders who moved westward usually settled on the rich cotton lands along the lower Mississippi River.

In politics, the Northeast had traditionally supported Federalists while the South had supported Republicans. Because the West was settled by people from both the Northeast and South, it was politically mixed. Westerners supported the War of 1812 with great enthusiasm because they wanted the British-supported Indians removed from their frontier. After the war, they usually supported a strong national government because they wanted federal help to solve their most difficult problem, transportation.

Sectional balance became a major political problem after 1819 when the United States suffered its first major depression. In the years immediately following the War of 1812, the economy began to expand. Agricultural production soared as American farmers took advantage of the newly reopened European markets. Settlers and speculators bought up vast amounts of western land on credit, and new untested manufacturing enterprises rapidly attracted investors. But the economy began to contract as quickly as it had expanded. Farmers found they had produced more than they could sell. Banks began to call in loans that borrowers could not repay. Land values fell, and the banks ended up owning much of the land. The South and West were most severely hurt. People in these sections tended to blame banks, in general, and the Bank of the United States, in particular, for the hard times. Since they associated the Bank with wealthy financial interests in the northeastern states, the panic not only brought economic distress but sharpened sectional antagonisms as well.

In what ways could the symbols on this page, all of which began to be widely used during the period from 1815-1830, contribute to national consciousness?

UNCLE SAM WILSON OF TROY SUPPLIED BEEF TO THE UNITED STATES ARMY DURING THE WAR OF 1812 - STAMPING HIS BARRELS WITH THE LETTERS 'U.S.' THIS BEEF BECAME KNOWN TO THE ARMY AS *UNCLE SAMS* AND THIS FAMILIAR APPELLATION WAS THEREAFTER BESTOWED ON OUR OWN GOVERNMENT

Slavery and Sectionalism

At the same time that the American people were coping with the problems of depression, they were forced to deal with another problem—the role of slavery in the American future. By 1819, the Union had grown to twenty-two states, evenly divided between free and slave states. In 1818, Missouri applied for admission as a state. In 1819, James Tallmadge, a congressman from New York who hated slavery, proposed an amendment to the Missouri statehood law forbidding slavery there. This proposal touched off a serious sectional debate. Northern political leaders were already unhappy because of the clause in the Constitution which allowed southern states to count three-fifths of their slaves in calculating the number of representatives they could send to Congress. These northern leaders denounced the slave system and insisted that Congress had a right to prohibit it in a new state. Southerners warned that they would never support a system of government that refused to let them take their property into new territory.

In the end, the Missouri Compromise was reached. It admitted Maine to the Union as a free state and Missouri as a slave state. It also prohibited slavery from the remainder of the Louisiana Purchase north of the parallel 36°30′.

The End of Political Unity

By 1824, Monroe's last year in office, the great political leaders who had developed with the American Revolution were fast passing from the scene. The political leadership of the new nation was falling into the hands of a younger generation. The election of 1824 symbolized this change. The leading candidates were all Republicans and strong nationalists, and could be distinguished from each other more by their sectional support than by differences in their political platforms. John Quincy Adams, son of the second President, was New England's favorite son. Kentucky nominated Henry Clay, spokesman for the West. Tennessee and other states supported Andrew Jackson. Although Jackson had the broadest national support because of his military reputation, he was particularly strong along the frontier. Calhoun, who was the South's favorite son, originally sought the Presidency, but later decided to run for Vice-President. When the votes were counted for President, Jackson received the largest electoral vote, but not the majority required by the Constitution. As a result, the choice of President fell to the House of Representatives. When Clay advised his supporters to vote for Adams, the latter was elected.

After the election of 1824, the political unity, which on the surface had characterized the Republican era, disintegrated altogether. When Clay was named Secretary of State, Jackson's followers claimed that he had been robbed of the election because of a "corrupt bargain" between Adams and Clay. The new President was hardly in office before the Jackson men began to plan for 1828.

Democratizing American Society

CHAPTER
8

People usually think of democracy in political terms. In a political democracy, citizens have an opportunity to influence their government by voting for one party or candidate instead of another. They can also persuade public officers to support particular measures. But democracy has other meanings. Applied to a social system, it means a society in which every person has a chance to change his or her social status. People can move either up or down the social ladder. In economic terms, democracy means that all people have equal opportunities to seek any job and to improve their standard of living. In its broadest meaning, a democratic society offers all people the maximum opportunity to develop to the fullest extent of their ability and willingness to work.

Eighteenth-century America was not a democracy by today's standards. Women, large numbers of men without property, and most blacks could neither vote nor hold public office. Moreover, the lines between classes were clearly drawn despite some limited social mobility. Differences in education, dress, and occupation divided the upper classes from ordinary farmers and indentured servants. Laws and customs also limited economic opportunities. The national government owned western lands which it sold only in large parcels. This practice kept many people from owning their own farms. Moreover, state and national governments had set up monopolies which gave one person or one company the sole right to build a bridge or establish a bank. Such monopolies closed wide areas of economic life to newcomers.

The restrictions on political, social, and economic democracy began to collapse one by one in the early history of the Republic. The movement to democratize American life reached its peak during the Jacksonian Period. Andrew Jackson was President only from 1829 to 1837. But he so dominated the period from 1824 to 1840 that historians frequently refer to it as the "Age of Jackson." Chapter 8 examines the ways in which the United States became more democratic during this exciting period.

1828 John C. Calhoun writes **The South Carolina Exposition and Protest**
1828 Congress passes Tariff of Abominations
1829 Andrew Jackson becomes President
1830 Senators Daniel Webster and Robert Hayne debate states' rights
1831 Alexis de Tocqueville visits United States and writes **Democracy in America**
1832 President Jackson vetoes renewal of charter of National Bank
1833 Henry Clay works out a compromise tariff

1833-34 The "Bank panic" takes place
1834 The National Trades' Union is organized
1834 Opponents of President Jackson organize Whig Party
1836 Democratic Party holds first national nominating convention
1837 Martin Van Buren becomes President
1841 William Henry Harrison becomes President

28 THE DEMOCRATIZATION OF AMERICAN LIFE: AN EXERCISE IN HYPOTHESIS FORMATION

Any investigation of the past begins with the identification of a problem. Once historians identify a problem, they begin to gather data about it. They read widely in textbooks, documents written at the time, diaries, letters, and similar source materials and gather statistics, if any are available. As they accumulate information, they also begin to develop hypotheses—tentative answers to the questions that were the beginning point of the investigation. These hypotheses help to focus attention on important evidence. The sooner historians develop hypotheses, the sooner they can begin to gather meaningful evidence.

Hypotheses often need to be revised. Suppose historians read a passage written in 1820 by a person who disagreed with the majority of the people at the time. The ideas in the passage might seem well worth investigating. Yet, when historians gather evidence from more typical people, they may decide that the original hypothesis was not accurate. In this case, they might revise the hypothesis in the light of new evidence or abandon it completely. They would then develop new hypotheses more in keeping with the majority of the evidence.

Reading 28 presents six short excerpts written by Americans or travelers to America during the first half of the nineteenth century. No attempt has been made to select passages which represent—or do not represent—majority views. Hence, any hypotheses developed from these passages must be viewed as highly tentative.

In preparation for class, read each passage carefully. After you have read a passage, write down in one simple sentence in your notebook any hypothesis which you think the passage implies. Then when you have finished all the passages, write in one sentence one or more hypotheses which pull together the ideas from the entire set of passages. Because of the nature of this lesson, there are no study questions.

A Discovery Exercise

1

"Annual Report of the Treasury Department at the Opening of the First Session of 22nd Congress," in **The American Quarterly Review**, Vol. XI (June 1832), p. 280. Language simplified and modernized.

Land is now sold in tracts of eighty acres, at $1.25 an acre. For $100, an unimproved tract of eighty acres may be purchased. In any of the states west of the Ohio River, a laborer can earn 75¢ per day. If his living costs 25¢ a day, he can, by the labor of two hundred days, or about eight months, purchase a farm. Again, a laborer can get his board and $10 per month the year round. This would amount to $120. If he uses $20 to buy clothing, he will still have earned the purchase money of a farm in one year.

2

Charles River Bridge vs. **Warren Bridge**, 11 Peters, 420 (1837). Language simplified and modernized.

In 1785, the Massachusetts legislature had incorporated a company called "The Proprietors of the Charles River Bridge."

The act of incorporation gives "The Proprietors of the Charles River Bridge" the rights of a corporation to build the bridge. It also sets up a toll rate to which the company is entitled. This is the whole grant. There is no exclusive privilege given the company over the waters of the Charles River, above or below the bridge. Nor does it have the right to build another bridge. Neither can it prevent other persons from building another bridge. Nor can it get a commitment from the state that another bridge shall not be built. The act does not promise to limit competition.

3

In 1834, the city-wide unions of skilled craftsmen from New York, Philadelphia, and four other cities joined together in a National Trades' Union in an effort to gain improved working conditions. Membership had risen to 300,000 by 1837 when a business collapse destroyed the craft-union movement.

Resolved, That this Convention of the National Trades' Unions recommend that working people of these United States who have not already formed themselves into societies for the protection of their industry, do so forthwith.

Resolved, That this committee view with serious alarm the terrible condition of the male and female children in the cotton and woolen

►These pictures show a prisoner in a jail and a patient in a mental hospital. Should these American citizens be allowed to vote? Why or why not?

factories of this country. They are put to work at an early age and spend long hours at work each day.

Resolved, That the laws existing in parts of our country, under which Traders' Unions are declared illegal, are a clear violation of the Constitution of these United States. They interfere with the lawful rights of every citizen. This Convention asks every laboring person to consider seriously the need to repeal them.

Trades' Union National Convention, **The Man**, Vol. II (August 30, 1834), p. 357.

A number of state courts had ruled that unions were conspiracies which interfered with trade. Hence, strikers were subject to criminal prosecution.

4

Let us suppose you arrived at a New England inn as I did and that you talked with the landlord while he got refreshments for you. He will then sit by your side and carry on the most familiar conversation. He will start asking you about your business and so forth. Then he will raise a political question, for here every individual is a politician. He will force you to answer. Then he will contradict and deny what you said. Finally, he will start a quarrel should you not agree with all of his opinions.

Report of an English Traveler in the United States. C.W. Janson, **The Stranger in America** (London: James Cundee, 1807), p. 85. Language simplified and modernized.

5

Should the right to vote, the characteristic and the highest privilege of a freeman, be taken away because of an accident? I am rich today, but my wealth consists of merchandise. It may be in storehouses. It may be upon the ocean. Suppose I have been unable to get insurance, or there is a legal defect in my policy. Fire or storms devour wealth in an hour. Am I any the less competent to vote? Have I less of the capacity of a moral and intelligent being? Am I less of a good

George S. Camp, **Democracy** (New York: Harper and Brothers, 1841), pp. 145-146. Language simplified and modernized.

► What do you think are the qualities of a good citizen?

Workingman's Advocate (March 6, 1830). Language simplified and modernized.

Except for large cities, few communities provided public education on any regular basis. Some communities set up charity schools for poor children. Otherwise, schools in America were private and were usually run by churches.

citizen? Is it not enough that I have lost my fortune—must I also be barred from voting by the community?

6

It appears, therefore, to the committee that there can be no real liberty without education. The members of a republic should all be taught the nature and character of their equal rights and duties as human beings and citizens. Education should develop a just disposition, virtuous habits, and a rational, self-governing character.

29 WORKING WITH HYPOTHESES, II

A hypothesis is a tentative answer to a question. To find out whether it is right or wrong, historians must go through several steps. Even after taking all these steps, historians still cannot be entirely sure that the answer to the original question is completely right. Additional evidence may turn up in new documents. Or the historian may have made errors in logic as he or she thought about the problem. Nevertheless, a disciplined way to think about hypotheses helps to reduce the chance of errors.

Once historians have developed hypotheses, they ought to think through what the hypotheses imply. Suppose a person begins with the hypothesis that the colonists won the American Revolution because they had foreign aid. "If this hypothesis is right," he or she might say, "then foreign aid should have played a key role in each of the decisive battles. If it did not, then something in addition to foreign aid must have been involved."

Given this idea, the historian should then set out to determine the role of foreign aid in key battles: Lexington, Saratoga, Yorktown, and others. To do so, the historian would have to decide what sources would contain useful facts. Then he or she would have to read those sources, decide whether or not the evidence in them was accurate, take down notes about the evidence, and decide whether or not the hypothesis was valid or needed to be changed. Once that decision has been made, the historian will have developed a generalization, the end product of the investigation.

While analyzing Reading 28, each student developed a hypothesis about Jacksonian society. Readings 29 and 30 provide evidence with which these hypotheses can be tested. No study questions are provided because of the nature of the readings. Before you begin to read, you should write out one or two of the logical implications of the hypothesis you developed. Then you should study the material in Reading 29 to gather evidence. As you study, you may form new hypotheses or new ideas about the implications of the hypothesis you started with. Write out the implications of your hypothesis and include evidence collected from the reading.

Public Land Laws

Most of the public lands in the United States belonged to the national government. It acquired these public lands when the original thirteen states gave up their western land claims to it. Through treaties and agreements, the government also acquired territory formerly claimed by Britain, France, and Spain. The government sold these lands to settlers and speculators. This chart gives the land laws passed by the governments under the Articles of Confederation and under the Constitution.

Year	Minimum Purchase	Minimum Price Per Acre	Terms of Sale
1787	640 acres	$1.00	One third of purchase price in cash; the remainder in three months
1796	640 acres	$2.00	Half of purchase price to be paid within 30 days; half to be paid at end of 12 months
1800	320 acres	$2.00	One quarter of purchase price payable in cash; one quarter payable in 2 years; one quarter payable in 3 years; one quarter payable in 4 years
1804	160 acres (north of the Ohio River)	$2.00 ($1.64, if the entire payment in cash)	Same as in 1800
1820	80 acres	$1.25	Full purchase price in cash
1832	40 acres	$1.25	Full purchase price in cash

▶ Should government have set high land prices in order to make money and hence lower taxes? Or should it have set low prices in order to help poor people buy their own farms? Why?

A Frenchman Views
American Society

The French government sent Michel Chevalier, a young engineer, to the United States in 1834 to study American transportation and public works. Chevalier was a keen observer of American society. He described his observations and impressions in Society, Manners and Politics in the United States, *from which this excerpt is taken.*

Michel Chevalier, **Society, Manners and Politics in the United States: Being a Series of Letters on North America** (Boston: Weeks, Jordan and Company, 1839), pp. 398-401. Language simplified and modernized.

The proletariat is the laboring class that works for others, usually in manufacturing.

Capital is wealth either in the form of property or money.

In the northern states, with the exception of the Negro caste, there are only two classes: the middle class and the common people. The middle class consists of manufacturers, merchants, lawyers, physicians, a small number of large landowners, and persons devoted to literature and the fine arts.

The common people are the farmers and mechanics. In general, the farmers own their own farms. In the West, this is true without exception. Great landholders do not exist, at least as a class, in the North and the Northwest. There is strictly speaking no proletariat. There are day laborers, both in the cities and the country, and many workmen without capital. Yet these men, most of whom are recent immigrants, are apprentices. They, in turn, become proprietors and master-workmen and not infrequently rich manufacturers or wealthy speculators.

There is no dividing line between these two classes, however. The two classes live in the same ways, lead the same life, and differ only in terms of the religious sect to which they belong and the pews they occupy in church.

In the southern states, slavery produces a society quite different from that of the North. Half of the population there, that is the slaves, consists of the proletariat in the strictest sense. Slavery requires great landed property, whose owners form an aristocracy.

Between these two extremes in the South, an intermediate class of working men and men of leisure has sprung up. Those in commerce, manufactures, and the professions are on the one side. On the other are the landholders, who live on their estates by the sweat of their slaves. They have no taste for work, are not prepared for it by education, and take little responsibility for the daily business of the plantation.

In the United States, landowners usually divided property equally among sons instead of following the English practice of primogeniture, which left entire estates to the eldest son.

Dividing estates equally among all the sons must have increased the numbers of this leisure class. It is numerous in the old southern states of Virginia, the Carolinas, Georgia, and Louisiana. But we do not find this class in the new states of the South. The new generation there, anxious to make money, has become as industrious as the Yankees. Growing cotton offers a wide field of activity. In Alabama and Mississippi, cotton lands are sold at a very low price. The internal

194

WAYNE OATES

CONFESSIONS OF A WORK AHOLIC

The Facts about Work Addiction

►This book argues that the United States is full of "workaholics," people who are addicted to work in the same way that some people are addicted to alcohol. Do you know any workaholics? Why do you think some people devote themselves single-mindedly to work? How important is work in your life?

The internal slave trade refers to the practice of raising slaves in the states of the upper South, such as Virginia, and selling them in Alabama and Mississippi.

slave trade furnishes abundant hands which are easily bought on credit. The sons from the old southern states sell off their property at home, get a loan, which they are sure of being able to repay promptly, and go to the Southwest to establish a cotton plantation.

Thus the part of the middle class which works little or not at all is disappearing in the United States. In the western states, which are the true New World, it no longer exists at all, either in the North or the South. In the West, you meet with no one who is not engaged in agriculture, commerce, manufactures, the professions, or the Church. The United States, then, has no aristocracy, no idle middle class, and no class of mere laborers, at least in the North.

An Immigrant Examines the American Character

Francis Grund was born in Austria and came to this country in 1827. He became a successful journalist. The following excerpt is from his work The Americans in Their Moral, Social and Political Relations.

Francis Grund, The Americans in Their Moral, Social and Political Relations (London: Longman, Rees, Orme, Brown, Green and Longman, 1837), Vol. 2, pp. 1-5, 226-229.

There is probably no people on earth for whom business is as much pleasure and industry as much amusement as with the people of the United States of America. Active work is not only the principal source of their happiness and the foundation of their natural greatness, but they are absolutely wretched without it. Business is the very soul of an American. He pursues it, not as a means of winning for himself and his family the necessary comforts of life, but as the fountain of all human happiness.

From the earliest hour in the morning till late at night, the streets, offices, and warehouses of the large cities are filled with people of all trades and professions. Each person follows his vocation as if he never dreamt of the possibility of becoming tired. If a lounger should happen to be parading the street, he would be sure to be jostled off the sidewalk, or to be pushed in every direction until he keeps time with the rest.

▶How important do you think work is? Do you think it should be "the principal source of happiness"?

Life consists in motion. The United States present certainly the most animated picture of universal bustle and activity of any country in the world. Such a thing as rest does not even enter the mind of an American. The rates of fares and passages are low and well suited to the means of most of the population. There is scarcely an individual so poor as to be unable to afford a "dollar or so," to travel a couple of hundred miles from home "in order to see the country and the improvements which are going on." On the steamboats, meals are generally included in the price of passage. It is also as cheap, or cheaper, to travel than to stay at home.

The influence of these proceedings on the laboring classes is incredible. They have the same opportunity of widening their knowledge by traveling and personal observation of the manners of different people, which in other countries is enjoyed by gentlemen of moderate fortune.

The absence of vehicles exclusively for wealthy travelers forces them to make their journeys with people they may chance to meet on the road. If these happen to be mechanics or traders, an exchange of thought takes place which is often profitable to both parties. The laboring classes can hardly fail to improve in manners. The higher and wealthier classes, who in most countries are totally ignorant of the sentiments and wants of the lower classes, receive much valuable instruction. This new knowledge is sure of finally reaching the halls of Congress.

The Price of American Prosperity

Not everyone agreed that the opportunities which American democracy offered for economic and social advancement were an unmixed blessing. The following excerpt is by an American journalist who left the United States in 1861 to spend the last half of his life in England.

We talk in America of our great, our enlightened, our free, and above all, our happy country! I never thought America *was* a happy country—only that it ought to be. In all the years of peace and plenty, we were not happy. In no country are the faces of the people marked with harder lines of care. In no country that I know of is there so much hard, unending labor; in none so little of enjoyment of life. Work and worry eat out the hearts of the people, and they die before their time. It is a hard story, but it is a true one.

The scarcity and high price of labor force the small farmers to do their own work. They raise large crops with heavy and continuous labor. The owner of a hundred acres is a slave to his land, a slave to his cattle, a slave to the necessities of his position. His family must live as well and dress as well as their neighbors.

It is seldom that an American retires from business to enjoy his fortune in comfort. Money-making becomes a habit. He works because he always has worked, and knows no other way. Of the few who retire, many become hypochondriacs, and some commit suicide.

Then why the universal and everlasting struggle for wealth? Because it is the only thing needful, the only secure power, the only real distinction. Americans speak of a person being *worth* so many thousands or millions. Nowhere is money sought so eagerly. Nowhere is it so much valued. In no civilized country does it bring so little to its possessor.

Thomas Low Nichols, **Forty Years of American Life** (London: Longmans, Green & Co., 1874), pp. 401-406.

A hypochondriac is a person who has imaginary physical ailments.

197

The real work of America is to make money for the sake of making it. It is an end, and not a means. The value of a dollar consists in its power to make dollars. "Get money, honestly if you can, but get it." In politics and business, and in many other matters, money is the great object, and principles are thrown to the wind.

The first element of happiness is contentment. There is no such thing in America as being contented with one's position or condition. The poor struggle to be rich, the rich to be richer. Every one is tugging, trying, scheming to get ahead. It is a great scramble, in which all are troubled and none are satisfied. In Europe, the poor, as a rule, know that they must remain poor, and they submit to their lot, and try to make the best of it. In England the peasant does not expect to become a noble. Most people live and die in the position to which they are born. The exceptions are too rare to excite much effort or discontent. Not so in America. Every other little ragged child dreams of being President or a John Jacob Astor. The dream may be a pleasant one while it lasts, but what of the disappointing reality?

The chief source of human happiness is the enjoyment of the domestic affections. In the countries of the Old World, the loves of parents and children for each other—the family affections—make up a large portion of the enjoyment of life. America strangely lacks these affections. It would be too much to say that Americans were without natural affection. But it is strange how little they appear to have.

John Jacob Astor (1763-1848) was a famous fur trader and capitalist.

30 WORKING WITH HYPOTHESES, III

Like Reading 29, the present reading contains evidence about the nature of American society during the Jacksonian Period. You are to continue the exercise begun yesterday, adding to the material which you put together in your notes. In preparation for class, write one paragraph, no longer than a hundred words, in which you state the conclusions you have drawn from your work with Readings 28 through 30.

President Jackson's First Annual Message to Congress

Although Andrew Jackson received more popular and electoral votes than any other candidate in the Presidential election of 1824 (see p. 187), the House of Representatives elected John Quincy Adams to the Presidency. Jackson and his supporters believed that he had been "robbed." Jackson won the election of 1828. In his first message to Congress, from which this excerpt is taken, he expressed his ideas on the proper relationship between citizens and public officers.

The right to elect the President belongs to the people. Their choice should never be defeated, either by the electoral college or by the House of Representatives. Experience proves that as the number of officials to carry out the will of the people increases, so does the danger that their wishes will be frustrated. Some officials may be unfaithful. All may make errors. So far as the people can speak conveniently, it is safer for them to express their own wills.

In the election of the President, as in all other matters of public concern, as few obstacles as possible should exist to the free expression of the public will. Let us, then, try to change our system so that no citizen may become President except as a result of a fair expression of the will of the majority.

The duties of all public officers are, or at least could be made, so plain and simple that men of intelligence may readily qualify to perform them. I believe that more is lost by men remaining in office for a long period of time than is gained through their experience. I submit, therefore, to your consideration whether government efficiency would not be promoted and officeholders' industry and integrity improved by a law which limits officials to a four-year term.

A Compilation of the Messages and Papers of the Presidents, James D. Richardson, ed. (Washington, D.C.: Government Printing Office, 1896), Vol. II, pp. 447-449. Language simplified and modernized.

Method of Electing Presidential Electors, 1800-1840

The Constitution provides that state legislatures shall determine the way in which the electors, who elect the President, will be chosen. This chart gives the percentage of states in which the state legislatures, rather than the ordinary voters, chose the Presidential electors between 1800-1840.

U.S. Bureau of the Census, Historical Statistics of the United States, Colonial Times to 1957 (Washington, D.C.: Government Printing Office, 1960), p. 681.

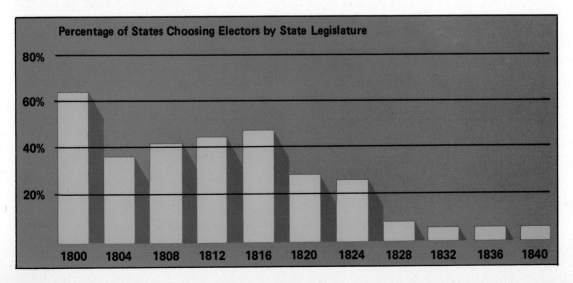

Percentage of States Choosing Electors by State Legislature

The Nominating Convention

In a political democracy, citizens have a voice in choosing political candidates. Before the Jacksonian Period, a group of influential leaders in Congress had selected Presidential candidates. Candidates for local and state offices were either selected by caucuses, meetings of party members, or they simply announced their candidacy. In the 1820's and 1830's, with the development of well-organized political parties, the caucus gave way at all levels of government to the nominating convention. Delegates to the convention were elected, at least in theory, by party members. These delegates selected the candidates, adopted a party platform, and planned for the election campaign.

Thomas Ford, a Jacksonian Democrat and governor of Illinois from 1842 to 1846, observed these party developments closely in his state. In A History of Illinois *he evaluated the nominating conventions as they functioned in his state.*

Thomas Ford, **A History of Illinois** (Chicago: S.C. Griggs, 1854), pp. 201-206. Language simplified and modernized.

▶Do you and your friends "consult a little caucus" before you run for office in your class or club? Why or why not?

A precinct is a small electoral district that contains a polling place.

Our old way of conducting elections required each person seeking an office to announce himself as a candidate. The more careful, however, always first consulted a little caucus of influential friends. The candidates then traveled around the country or state, making speeches, talking with people, trying to win votes, whispering lies against their opponents, and defending themselves against the attacks of those opponents.

As party spirit increased more and more, it became necessary to find a way of concentrating party strength. Some settlers from New England and New York introduced into Illinois the convention system of nominating candidates.

The system has some advantages and disadvantages in Illinois. Those in favor of it say it is the only way of giving voice to the will of the majority. On the other side, it is argued that the whole convention system is a fraud on the people; that conventions themselves are got up and packed by cunning, active, intriguing politicians, to suit the wishes of a few. Some active men organize conventions by getting a few friends in each precinct of a county to hold primary meetings, where delegates are elected to county conventions. These delegates meet at the county seats, and nominate candidates for the legislature and for county offices and appoint other delegates to district and state conventions to nominate candidates to run for Congress and for governor.

The great difficulty lies in the primary meetings. In the eastern states, where conventions began, they had township governments—little democracies—where all the people met at least once a year, to lay taxes for roads and for the support of schools and the poor. This accustomed all the people to take a lively interest in their government. While they were assembled, they elected delegates to conventions. In this way, a convention reflected the will of a party.

But how is it in Illinois? We have no township government, no occasions for a general meeting of the people, except at the elections themselves. The people do not attend the primary meetings. Only a few who live closest to the meeting places attend. These are too often the professional politicians and the loafers about town. Having little business of their own, they are ever ready to attend to the affairs of the public. This throws the political power out of the hands of the people, merely because they will not exercise it. Thus, political power falls into the hands of idlers and a few active men, who control them.

A Plea for Expanded
Business Opportunities

The state legislatures chartered banks, insurance companies, manufacturing companies, and other corporations. Wealthy people used their influence to win special privileges from the legislators. Jacksonian Democrats, such as William Leggett, an editorial writer for the New York Evening Post, *argued for reforms that would increase opportunities for ordinary citizens to set up new businesses. This editorial, written by Leggett, appeared in the* Evening Post *on December 30, 1834.*

A week from today the Legislature will meet in Albany. Seldom has a meeting of the Legislature been looked forward to with such interest. The message of Governor Marcy will probably be delivered to both Houses of the Legislature on the first day of the session. That message will either raise him to a most enviable height, or sink him to the level of the herd of petty, selfish, short-sighted, and low-minded politicians.

A Collection of the Political Writings of William Leggett, Theodore Sedgwick, Jr., ed. (New York: Taylor and Dodd, 1840), pp. 140-141. Language simplified and modernized.

He has the rare opportunity, by one single act, to put his name among those of the greatest benefactors of mankind. We hope he will stand forth as the honest, bold supporter of the great principle of equal rights. We urge the Governor to oppose all exclusive privileges. We earnestly recommend instead the adoption of a general law of joint-stock partnerships which would allow voluntary associations of people, who possess no special privileges. Businessmen would be open to the same free competition as the merchant, the mechanic, the laborer, and the farmer.

If the Governor should take such a stand, his name will go down in history forever associated with that of the patriotic and democratic Jackson, who, at the head of the national government, has done so much to restore to the people their rights, and stop unequal, aristocratic legislation.

A joint-stock partnership or company is a form of business organization that allows people to combine their capital by purchasing shares of stock. Each share of stock represents ownership and usually entitles its owner to a vote at a shareholders' meeting.

Percentage of Adult White Males Voting in Presidential Elections, 1824-1844

Chart prepared at the Curriculum Development Center, Carnegie-Mellon University. Based on data from Richard P. McCormick, "New Perspectives on Jacksonian Politics," The American Historical Review, Vol. LXV (January 1960), p. 294.

One way to measure the vitality of political democracy is to look at the number of citizens who vote for public officials. This chart shows the percentage of qualified voters who actually voted in Presidential elections between 1824 and 1844. The chart is based on selected states for which election data was available.

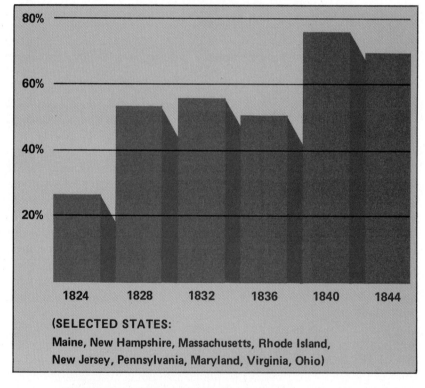

80%

60%

40%

20%

1824   1828   1832   1836   1840   1844

(SELECTED STATES:

Maine, New Hampshire, Massachusetts, Rhode Island, New Jersey, Pennsylvania, Maryland, Virginia, Ohio)

Voting Qualifications, 1800-1840

Each state sets up certain requirements that its citizens must meet in order to vote. This chart gives the voting qualifications in all states between 1800 and 1840.

Original 13 States

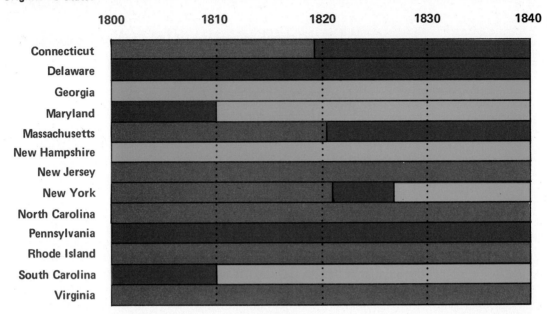

	1800	1810	1820	1830	1840
Connecticut					
Delaware					
Georgia					
Maryland					
Massachusetts					
New Hampshire					
New Jersey					
New York					
North Carolina					
Pennsylvania					
Rhode Island					
South Carolina					
Virginia					

(States listed in order of date of admission to the Union)

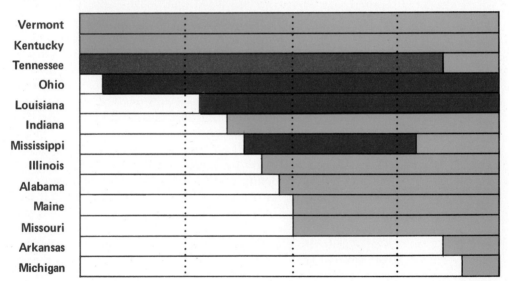

Vermont					
Kentucky					
Tennessee					
Ohio					
Louisiana					
Indiana					
Mississippi					
Illinois					
Alabama					
Maine					
Missouri					
Arkansas					
Michigan					

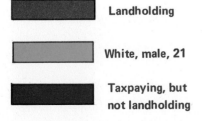

Landholding

White, male, 21

Taxpaying, but not landholding

Chart prepared at the Curriculum Development Center, Carnegie-Mellon University. Based on data from Richard P. McCormick, "Suffrage, Classes and Party Alignments: A Study in Voter Behavior," in **Mississippi** Valley Historical Review, Vol. XLVI, No. 3 (December 1959), pp. 397-410, and Chilton Williamson, **American Suffrage from Property to Democracy: 1760-1860.** (Princeton, N.J.: Princeton University Press, 1960).

Alexis de Tocqueville's Observations on American Political Life

Alexis de Tocqueville, a young Frenchman, came to the United States in 1831 to study prison reforms. He was also deeply interested in America's experiment with democracy. For nine months he traveled throughout the United States. Upon his return to France he published Democracy in America, *a two-volume work from which this selection is taken, in which he gave his observations and analysis of American ideas, attitudes and institutions.*

Alexis de Tocqueville, **Democracy in America,** ed. and trans. by Henry Reeve (Cambridge, Mass.: Sever and Francis, 1862), Vol. 1, pp. 318-319. Language simplified and modernized.

It is possible to imagine the surprising liberty that the Americans enjoy. Some idea may also be formed of their extreme equality. But the political activity that is everywhere in the United States must be seen in order to be understood. No sooner do you set foot upon American ground than you are stunned by a kind of tumult. A confused noise is heard on every side, and a thousand simultaneous voices demand the satisfaction of their social wants. Everything is in motion around you. Here the people of one quarter of a town are meeting to decide upon the building of a church. There the election of a representative is going on. A little farther, the delegates of a district are hurrying to the town in order to discuss some local improvements. In another place, the laborers of a village quit their plows to discuss a project for a road or a public school. People call meetings for the sole purpose of declaring their disapproval of the conduct of the government. In other assemblies, citizens salute the authorities of the day as the fathers of their country.

It is difficult to say what place is taken up in the life of an inhabitant of the United States by his concern for politics. To take a hand in the regulation of society and to discuss it is his biggest concern and the only pleasure an American knows. Even the women frequently attend public meetings and listen to political speeches as a recreation from their household labors. Debating clubs are, to a certain extent, a substitute for the theatre. An American cannot converse, but he can discuss. He speaks to you as if he were addressing a meeting.

31 THE IMPACT OF JACKSONIAN DEMOCRACY

HISTORICAL ESSAY

Andrew Jackson brought new qualities to the Presidency. He was very different from the man he succeeded, John Quincy Adams.

Adams was a man of exceptional intellect and education. He had already served his country ably as a diplomat abroad and as Secretary of State. He believed that the federal government should play a positive role in American social and economic life. He tried during his administration to establish a national university, as well as to encourage such internal improvements as roads and canals.

If Adams had been President ten years earlier, he might have been very successful. In the middle of the 1820's, however, he was out of place. Adams came from a prominent family. His political opponents tagged him as an aristocrat. His background, together with his cold temperament, proved his undoing as President. In the election of 1828, Jackson received 178 electoral votes to Adams' 83. Jackson drew strong support from every section except Adams' New England.

Jackson was the first American President to come from the ranks of the common people. His parents had been poor Scotch-Irish immigrants. Jackson rose from total obscurity to a prominent position as lawyer, planter, soldier, and land speculator in Tennessee. In many ways, his career was typical of what was happening everywhere in the highly fluid social conditions of early nineteenth-century America. Western farmers, working people in the cities, and business people all believed that Jackson sympathized with them, so they gave him support.

Growth and Limits of Equality

The idea of equality in America had been expressed in the Declaration of Independence. But it had not been put completely into political practice. As the chart on page 203 shows, before the War of 1812, several states limited the right to vote to property owners. In the years following the war, however, the new western states that entered the Union gave every white male twenty-one years old the right to vote. Several eastern states also took steps to liberalize their voting qualifications. At the same time, the people gained the right to elect more and more of their officials. State legislatures transferred their power to choose Presidential electors to the voters.

Indiana entered the union in 1816, Illinois in 1818, and Alabama in 1819.

Because Jackson believed in the principle of equality, he had great faith in the common people. His respect for the abilities of ordinary citizens led him to rely on what became known as the "spoils system." He replaced government jobholders with his own supporters. He believed that they represented the public will and that ordinary people were capable of carrying on the business of government.

The term "spoils system" comes from the phrase "to the victor belong the spoils." "Spoils" are the fruits of victory and, in politics, the "spoils system" means awarding government jobs to one's political supporters.

Jackson's attitude toward the public lands in the West also shows his belief in equality. Political leaders disagreed over whether these lands should be sold by the government in order to raise revenue or distributed to settlers at cheap prices. Jackson favored the latter course as a way of making it possible for the largest number of people to own their own land and get a start in the world.

Jackson also sought advice from his "kitchen cabinet," that is, close personal friends who held no official positions in government.

GENERAL JACKSON SLAYING THE MANY HEADED MONSTER.

The pictures on these pages are all of Andrew Jackson. How did each artist picture him? What aspects of his career did each artist emphasize? Which picture, if any, most accurately portrays Jackson?

Equality as a condition of life and as an ideal was important during this period. But neither the condition nor the ideal included everybody. Blacks, Indians, and women did not enjoy equality. An abolition movement began to develop during the Jacksonian Period. Yet those reformers who believed that the principle of equality should apply to everybody were still a tiny minority. Jackson himself supported slavery and owned slaves. Along with almost all of his followers, he believed that the principle of equality should apply only to white males. Many state constitutions had originally allowed free blacks to vote. They were later changed to deny the vote to blacks at the same time that more whites voted.

▶Does knowledge that Jackson owned slaves change your feelings about him? Why or why not?

Meanwhile, something similar happened to the Indians. Jackson favored a land policy that would distribute western lands widely among settlers and thus promote economic opportunities in the West. But he also forced Indian tribes to move to lands west of the Mississippi River. Usually, they had to give up better land than they received. In the 1830's, the Indian, like the black, was still a long way from equal membership in American democracy.

The New Tariff and the Issue of Nullification

Jackson believed that the President should be a strong executive. He believed that the President should use all of his Constitutional powers, and that he should not be subordinated to either the legislature or to the judiciary. President Jackson applied his two basic principles—the belief in equality and the belief in a strong executive—in dealing with the two major issues of his Administration: the bank and the tariff.

The most nagging sectional issue during this period centered on the federal government's use of the tariff. Southerners believed that the tariff was contrary to their interests. Opposition to the tariff was particularly strong in South Carolina. John C. Calhoun, the state's leading political figure, became the spokesman for the anti-tariff position. Calhoun, who served as Vice-President under both Adams and Jackson, had favored the Tariff of 1816. During the 1820's, as opposition to the tariff hardened in his own state, he changed his position. In 1828, Congress passed a tariff bill with particularly high duties. In protest against this "Tariff of Abominations," Calhoun wrote an essay entitled *The South Carolina Exposition and Protest.*

Calhoun reasoned that the various states had organized the federal government. They had given it certain powers for the purpose of protecting the states' interests and rights. If the federal government passed a law that threatened the rights or interests of a state, that state had the right to declare the law unconstitutional and, therefore, null and void within its boundaries. The Congress could then either accept state nullification of a federal law or it could work to get a Constitutional amendment passed which would make the law part

PRE-CIVIL WAR TARIFFS

Name of Tariff	Provisions	Public Reaction
Tariff of 1789	Placed specific duties on 30 items, including molasses, hemp, steel, and nails; average of 8½% *ad valorem*° on listed items; 5% duty on all other goods.	Designed primarily to raise revenue; it met with wide acceptance.
Tariff of 1792	Increased 5% duty to 7½%.	Farmers and New England shippers protested.
Tariff of 1816	A protective tariff, it placed duties of 25% on most woolen, cotton, and iron manufactures.	General support from all sections, small protest from New England commercial interests and the South and Southwest.
Tariff of 1824	Increased duty on cotton and woolen goods to 33⅓%; increased duty on raw wool to 15%.	Favored by western farmers and manufacturers in New England; opposed by South and Southwest.
Tariff of 1828 (Tariff of Abominations)	Duty of 50% *ad valorem*° plus 4¢ a pound on raw wool, 45% *ad valorem* on woolens, increased duties on iron and hemp.	Supported by western farmers and middle states; Southwest and New England divided; South opposed.
Tariff of 1832	Increased duty on woolens; placed cheap raw wool and flax on duty-free list; reduced average duties to 35%.	South Carolina adopted Ordinance of Nullification and threatened secession.
Tariff of 1833	Expanded the number of items on duty-free list; provided for gradual reduction of all duties above 20%.	South supported this compromise tariff; New England and middle states opposed it.
Tariff of 1842	Returned tariff to 1832 level; duties averaged 23%–35%.	Democrats opposed it; Whig party passed it.
Walker Tariff of 1846	Reduced average rates to 25%; placed several items on duty-free list.	South supported it; New England and middle states opposed it.
Tariff of 1857	Increased the duty-free list; reduced tariff to average of 20%.	South and Southwest supported it; northern industrialists opposed it.

°*Ad valorem* duties are levied according to value of the goods. Other duties are levied according to weight or quantity.

of the Constitution. If the law were made part of the Constitution, the state could decide either to remain in the Union and accept the law or become independent.

Calhoun then showed that the southern states were a great exporting and importing area which the tariff injured. Southern planters sold their cotton at low prices in competitive markets abroad. But they bought their manufactured goods at high prices in a protected market at home.

Calhoun kept his authorship of the *South Carolina Exposition and Protest* secret in 1828, but a famous debate in the Senate gave the ideas it contained wide public exposure. Daniel Webster from Massachusetts argued for the supremacy of the Union, and Robert Hayne from South Carolina presented Calhoun's point of view.

Jackson's position on the tariff was not very clear. He was sensitive to the charge that the tariff helped manufacturers more than southern farmers. At the same time, however, he wanted tariff revenues to help the government pay its debts. Jackson also felt that the rights of the states had to be protected from federal power. However, his belief that as President he represented all the people in the nation made it impossible for him to accept the idea that a state could defy federal authority.

The opposing ideas of Webster and Hayne, as well as those of Jackson and Calhoun, were put to the test in 1832. A state convention in South Carolina declared the tariffs of 1828 and 1832 unconstitutional and hence not binding on the people of the state. Calhoun's own views had become public knowledge by now. He resigned his position as Vice-President to represent his state in the Senate and lead the fight for nullification.

In what was probably America's greatest political crisis since the adoption of the Constitution, Jackson stood resolutely by the power of the federal government. He sent a warship to Charleston harbor. But South Carolina remained defiant, and violence was avoided only when Henry Clay worked out a compromise tariff in 1833. Once again, the American people found a practical way to prevent sectional hostility from destroying the Union.

The "Bank War"

The second major issue of Jackson's administration involved his battle with the Bank of the United States. The Second Bank of the United States had been chartered by Congress in 1816 to act as a depository for government funds, to issue paper money, to sell government bonds, and to do a commercial banking business. Since 1822, the Bank had been run by Nicholas Biddle, a highly able financier who came from an aristocratic Philadelphia family.

Jackson based his opposition to the Bank on two assumptions. In the first place, he was highly suspicious of the reckless speculation in land and business activity so characteristic of the time. Numerous state banks, willing to offer generous terms to prospective borrowers and investors, made the most of the speculation. Many of these banks rested on shaky foundations. They went through periods of spectacular prosperity, but frequently periods of spectacular failure followed. The result was that the American economy in the decade following the War of 1812 had become highly unstable. Individual speculators made and lost fortunes in rapid succession. Jackson, himself, had tried his hand at land speculation and had suffered disastrous financial losses. He had recovered by turning to farming. He came to the White House

Congress had allowed the First United States Bank to die in 1811 at the end of its twenty-year charter.

210

convinced that the early republic's emphasis on the value of land was a source of national strength and that banks and speculators threatened American values.

Jackson also opposed the Bank because it depended on special privilege, which had no place in a democratic society based on equal opportunity for all. Its great power was based largely on funds that the federal government deposited in it.

The Supreme Court had upheld the constitutionality of the Bank in *McCulloch* vs. *Maryland*. However, this development did not dissuade Jackson. He let it be known that he disagreed with Marshall and would veto any attempt by Congress to recharter the Bank. When Congress passed such a bill in July 1832, Jackson quickly vetoed it.

Congress failed to pass the Bank bill over Jackson's veto. The Bank controversy immediately became the central issue in the Presidential election of 1832. In this campaign, the anti-Jackson forces rallied around Jackson's chief opponent, Henry Clay. They claimed that the President was trying to put himself above the Constitution and play the role of a king. Jackson won the election easily, largely because of his attack on the Bank. On the one hand, farmers who shared his prejudices against banks supported him. The farmers were joined by small businessmen and speculators who felt that the Bank of the United States favored established business interests over newcomers like themselves. Thus, Jackson attracted support for his policies from different kinds of people for different kinds of reasons. The belief that held these people together, however loosely, was equality of opportunity.

▶ "Politics make strange bedfellows." This saying could be applied to Jackson's opponents. Can it be applied to people you know or organizations to which you belong? Why do people sometimes behave in this way?

What historians refer to as the "Bank War" did not end with Jackson's veto and reelection in 1832. Jackson transferred government funds from the National Bank to state banks, which his opponents called "pet banks." Nicholas Biddle retaliated by calling in bank loans to such an extent that a depression (the "Bank panic") took place in the winter of 1833-1834. Jackson's support in the Congress remained firm, however, and the bank finally closed its doors in 1836 when its charter expired.

A New Two-Party System

One of the most important developments during the Jacksonian Period was the re-emergence of the two-party system. The election of 1828 marked the end of the power of the National-Republicans. The Jacksonians began to call themselves Democrats and to build a strong organization on both the state and national level. In 1836, the Democratic party held its first national nominating convention.

At first, the anti-Jacksonians were a poorly organized coalition centered around National-Republicans like Adams, Clay, Webster, and Calhoun. Opposition to Jackson was about all that held these political leaders together. Under the impact of the Bank crisis, however, these men began to draw up a program, which supported internal improvements and sound business enterprise. They made a special appeal to business people in the North and to large southern planters with strong commercial ties in the North. These political leaders called themselves Whigs, after the party in England that had stood for liberty before the time of the American Revolution. Calhoun and the supporters of states' rights worked with the Whig party for a short period but returned to the Democratic party after 1837.

In 1836, Jackson retired from the Presidency. His successor and close political adviser from New York, Martin Van Buren, won a narrow victory over the Whigs. But Van Buren had to cope with a long period of economic depression during which the Bank issue continued to be debated hotly. Van Buren continued Jackson's economic policies. He refused to expand the supply of paper money. He also supported legislation which finally took federal deposits out of private banks altogether and deposited them in separate government depositories called subtreasuries.

In the election of 1840, the Whigs found Van Buren vulnerable on two counts. In the first place, his opponents accused him of continuing the depression through disastrous financial policies. In the second place, they accused him of not being a typical representative of American democracy. The Whigs held their first national convention in 1840. They nominated William Henry Harrison, an old Indian fighter, as their candidate for President. Harrison had won popularity as a war hero in the Battle of Tippecanoe. The Whigs appealed to the voters by emphasizing Harrison's rustic background which they contrasted with Van Buren's "aristocratic" manners. They campaigned vigorously with massive rallies and torchlight parades and used log cabin replicas to symbolize the simple beginnings of their candidate.

The result was a large victory for the Whigs. The American voters went to the polls in greater numbers than ever before to vote for Harrison. The election of 1840 revealed the lasting impact of Jacksonian democracy on American politics. From now on, every American Presidential candidate, Democratic, Whig, or Republican, would be known as "the people's candidate."

The Battle of Tippecanoe took place in 1811. A number of Indian tribes had formed a confederacy to defend their land against advancing white settlers. Harrison led the troops that finally defeated the Indians at Tippecanoe Creek.

The Spirit of Reform

STATING THE ISSUE

Today's college and high school students have grown up in an era of protest. Many students have taken part in movements to stop war, abolish poverty, or gain equal rights for all citizens. Protest and reform movements have long played an important role in American history. Americans have probably enjoyed more freedom and prosperity than any other people in the world. Still, a substantial number of Americans have always been dissatisfied with their lot and with the lot of others and have struggled to improve it.

American reformers have used two major ways to achieve their goals. Most reformers have struggled within society in an attempt to correct injustices for a large number of people, often by demanding changes through the government. Other reformers have refused to work through society's institutions. They have attempted to start revolutions or they have retreated from the world to build perfect communities for themselves.

In the period before the Civil War, American reformers took part in both types of movements. They organized a large number of movements designed to bring about widespread reforms in such areas as education, women's rights, the abolition of slavery, and the treatment of the insane. A few reformers, such as John Brown, tried to bring about change by armed revolt. Larger numbers left society to found ideal or "utopian" communities designed to set up "perfect" societies.

These reformers often quarreled among themselves about tactics and specific goals. However, they usually agreed upon one issue—the importance of trying to perfect the society in which they lived. The first three readings in Chapter 9 examine the quest for perfection in the United States during the decades before the Civil War. The historical essay at the end of the chapter places the reform movement of that period in the wider tradition of American reform.

213

1828 American Peace Society is founded

1828 Andrew Jackson is elected President

1830 Joseph Smith establishes the Church of Jesus Christ of Latter-Day Saints (Mormon Church)

1831 William Lloyd Garrison publishes first issue of **The Liberator**

1832 Samuel Gridley establishes Perkins Institute for the Blind

1833 William Lloyd Garrison establishes American Anti-Slavery Society

1839 Theodore Weld publishes **American Slavery As It Is: Test of a Thousand Witnesses**

1840 Liberty Party is formed

1843 Dorothea Dix writes **Memorial to the Legislature of Massachusetts** about treatment of insane

1847 Frederick Douglass publishes **North Star**

1847 Under leadership of Brigham Young, Mormons settle in Salt Lake City

1848 John Humphrey Noyes establishes Oneida community

1848 Dorothea Dix and Elizabeth Cady Stanton lead first women's rights convention in Seneca Falls, New York

1849 Henry David Thoreau publishes "Civil Disobedience"

1857 Thomas Hopkins Gallaudet establishes college for deaf

32 UTOPIAN EXPERIMENTS IN THE UNITED STATES

In 1516 an Englishman named Sir Thomas More published *Utopia*. The book described an imaginary island with an ideal moral, social, and political system. During the nineteenth century, a number of European thinkers took up More's ideas. They began to plan and then found experimental communities. The ideas of the Utopians spread quickly to the United States. Between 1840 and 1850, Americans founded more than forty Utopian communities. Although these communities differed from each other, they had one belief in common—that humans could become perfect if they lived in a completely different society where people cooperated instead of competing.

Some of these Utopian experiments involved only a handful of people. Others were quite large, enrolling several hundred men, women, and children. Some of them were designed to preserve a particular religious way of life brought from Europe. Others tried to provide alternative life-styles for people tired of conventional religious or social restrictions. Some societies required their members to give all their property to the group. Others permitted private property. Some societies had one leader. Others made decisions in group meetings. But all Utopian communities had a common goal—to provide a better way of life through group living.

214

In recent years some Americans have founded communal communities, some on the land and others in cities. To what degree do these communes appear to be based on the same principles as those of nineteenth-century Utopians?

The community in Oneida, New York, described in this reading, was founded in 1848 by John Humphrey Noyes. Noyes came from an old and respected New England family and had attended Dartmouth College. In the 1830's he abandoned the law after becoming a convert to religion during a revival meeting. Later, while attending Yale Theological Seminary, he decided that current religious teachings were all wrong and that Christ demanded perfection here on earth. After preaching for about fifteen years, Noyes left Putney, Vermont, to found the Oneida community. As you read this account of life at Oneida, think about the following questions:

1. How did the people at Oneida differ from typical Americans in respect to work and family life?
2. What was the goal of the "system of criticism" at Oneida?

An American Utopia as It Saw Itself

The Oneida Association, one of the most successful American communes, lasted from 1848 to 1881. The following document was drawn up by the membership in 1851.

Constance Noyes Robertson, Oneida Community: An Autobiography, 1851-1876 (Syracuse: Syracuse University Press, 1970), pp. 53-56. Language simplified.

The residents of Oneida sometimes travel about the country. They had frequently asked that we would furnish them with a brief pamphlet containing all necessary information about the history, principles, and condition of the Oneida Association. They could then give this pamphlet to inquirers, and so save a world of talk.

Question 1—Where is the Association located?

Answer—On the Oneida Creek, in the town of Lenox, Madison County, N.Y., three miles south of Oneida Depot.

Q 2—What is the number of members?

A—About 150; of whom ⅓ are men, ⅓ women, and ⅓ children.

Q 3—Do all these live in one house and eat at one table?

A—The main building is 60 feet long, 35 feet wide, three stories high, with a habitable attic. The basement is divided into three equal rooms. The first is the dining room, where we all eat together. The second is the kitchen. The third is the cellar. Over the dining room is a parlor of the same size for general gatherings. The rest of the house is divided into sleeping rooms, which, with those in the children's house and out-buildings, accommodate the whole family.

Q 4—How long has the Association been organized?

A—Nearly four years. Many of the first members, however, were immigrants from Putney, Vermont. There they had been organized as an Association nine years previously.

Q 5—What are your principles?

A—Our fundamental principle is religion.

216

Q 6—What denomination do you belong to?

A—To none of the popular denominations. We are generally called Perfectionists.

Q 8—Do you believe in the Bible?

A—Most heartily, and study it more than all books. It is, in fact, our only written creed and constitution.

Q 13—What are your rules and regulations?

A—The Bible, as I said before, is our only written constitution. We have no systematic code of by-laws. Or rather, we have no book of rules. Unwritten by-laws are constantly growing in us and among us by the suggestion of experience. Wisdom is the common law of all countries. And this is our code.

Q 14—You must have officers. How do you elect them?

A—We do not elect them—we find them out. God and education make officers. In a well ordered society, they are sure to reach their places by a natural process.

Q 15—What do you rely upon for the regulation of members?

A—On religious influence, free criticism, and education.

Q 16—What are your means of religious influence?

A—We have meetings every evening. They are generally devoted to religious conversation and reading though business and other topics are not excluded. Then we have a religious meeting on Sunday open to the public. The Bible is the daily study of men, women, and children.

Q 17—What is your system of criticism?

A—We tell each other plainly and kindly our thoughts about each other in various ways. Sometimes the whole Association criticizes a member in meeting. Sometimes it is done more privately, by committees, and sometimes by individuals. In some cases, criticism is directed to general character, and in others to special faults and offenses. Generally, criticism is invited by the person criticized and is regarded as a privilege. It is well understood that the moral health of the Association depends on the freest circulation of this plainness of speech. And all are eager to balance the accounts in this way often.

▶ How would you like to live in a community where everyone offered "constructive criticism" about the way you lived?

Q 18—What are your provisions for education?

A—We have a daily school for children in which common learning is taught in connection with the fear of God and the law of love. But it is understood among us that the whole Association is a school. And all members, old and young, are supplied with books and familiarize themselves with various branches of learning as they can.

Q 19—Do you hold to community property?

A—No, but we teach the law of love rather than the "grab game," i.e., the game in which the prizes are not distributed by any rules of wisdom and justice, but are seized by the strongest and craftiest.

Q 22—Do parents take care of their own children?

A—Yes, if they please. But members come to regard the whole Association as one family and all children as children of the family. The care of the children, after the period of nursing, is given to those

▶ Should children be entrusted to the regular care of adults other than their parents? Why or why not?

217

who have the best talent and the most taste for the business, so the parents are made free for other pursuits.

Q 23—What are your regulations about labor?

A—Labor in the Association is free. We find that free labor is more profitable than slave labor. Our men and women organize themselves or are organized by the General Managers, into groups under Chiefs for the various departments of work. These groups are frequently changed and constant rotation goes on so that all have variety of occupation, and opportunity to find out what each one is best adapted to.

Q 24—What do you do with the lazy ones?

A—This sort of person cannot live under our system of religious influence, criticism, and education. We have to criticize members more often for working too much than for being lazy.

Q 27—How much land have you?

A—About 275 acres, mostly very good meadowland.

Q 28—What do you raise?

A—Most of the things usually raised by farmers. We have this year a considerable stock of broom-corn which we shall manufacture for market. We have large orchards of various and choice fruit trees. And our vegetable garden has been productive and profitable.

Q 29—Are you engaged in any manufactures?

A—We have a mill, three stories high, on good water power. In this building there is a sawmill, a gristmill, and a machine shop. The gristmill makes the best flour and is getting many customers. The machine shop is doing some business and getting ready for more. Then we have a shoe shop and a blacksmith shop in active operation. And we are preparing for wagon-making.

Q 30—What are your expenses?

A—The only estimate we have is recorded in our Second Annual Report. According to this report, the expense for board is 45¢ per week for each individual, or about $24.00 per year, and for clothing $10.50 per year.

Q 31—Does the Association support itself?

A—During the first three years, we were engaged in preparatory labors, building mills, etc., and could not be said to have supported ourselves. Except that we increased the value of the homestead. This year we have begun to use the things we have built. We expect to be able to show in our Annual Report in February, that the Oneida Association is a self-supporting institution.

FOR THOUGHT:

Through what means did the Utopians hope to perfect society? What would have to happen before their reforms would affect all or a large number of Americans?

33 AMERICAN WOMEN
TAKE UP REFORM

At various times in American history large numbers of people have been reformers. Extension of the suffrage, reform of the federal civil service, control of monopolies, prohibition of the sale of alcoholic beverages—each of these has held the spotlight at a given time in American history.

The reform movement before the Civil War, however, was all-inclusive. So many different kinds of reformers lived in Boston, for example, that some boardinghouses advertised rooms "for reformers only." There one could find people who believed that specific religious groups, such as Baptists, Methodists, or Mormons, were commissioned to save the world. They mingled with people who called themselves "come-outers" because they felt compelled to leave their churches in order to reform society. Other reformers believed that the formula for a better world lay in eating dark bread and taking cold showers. Still others claimed that men and women would find happiness only by giving away their money and property and living together without marriage or government.

A few of these reformers were simple-minded eccentrics. Most of them, however, were strong-minded idealists. Despite their disagreement over precise cures for the ills of society, these reformers tended to agree on certain basic principles. They believed, for example, that many social injustices would disappear if all people had an equal chance to improve themselves through education. They believed that women had as much to contribute to reform as men. Women played leading roles in many reform movements. The crusade to give women greater political rights was itself a leading reform movement of the period.

The following selections describe the roles of women in several reform movements during this period. As you read, think about the following questions:

1. What specific reforms did these women demand?
2. What arguments did they use to support their demands?

Dorothea Dix on the Insane

Dorothea Dix (1802-1887) was a teacher in a Boston girls' school in 1841, when she accidentally discovered the mistreatment of a group of insane people in a local jail. During the next two years, she investigated conditions in jails and asylums throughout Massachusetts. Then she wrote a report to the Massachusetts legislature.

219

Francis Tiffany, **Life of Dorothea Lynde Dix** (Boston: Houghton Mifflin Company, 1891), pp. 76-82. Language simplified and modernized.

Massachusetts soon took steps to provide better care for its mental patients. And Dorothea Dix broadened her efforts throughout the United States and Europe.

I come to present the strong claims of suffering humanity. I come to place before the legislature of Massachusetts the condition of the miserable, the desolate, the outcast. I come as the advocate of helpless, forgotton, insane, and idiotic men and women; of beings sunk to a condition from which the most unconcerned would start with real horror; of beings wretched in our prisons, and more wretched in our poorhouses. And I cannot suppose it is necessary to use earnest persuasion, or stubborn argument, in order to fix attention upon a subject, only the more strongly pressing in its claims, because it is revolting and disgusting in its details.

I must confine myself to few examples. But I am ready to furnish other and more complete details, if required. If my pictures are displeasing, coarse, and severe, my subjects, it must be recalled, have no pleasant features. The condition of human beings, reduced to the extremest states of degradation and misery, cannot be described in pleasant language.

I proceed, gentlemen, briefly to call your attention to the present state of insane persons confined within this Commonwealth in cages, closets, cellars, stalls, pens! Chained, naked, beaten with rods, and lashed into obedience.

To illustrate my subject, I offer the following extracts from my Notebook and Journal:

Lincoln, [Massachusetts. All the other locations are also in Massachusetts.] A woman in a cage. *Medford.* One idiotic subject chained, and one in a close stall for seventeen years. *Pepperell.* One often doubly chained, hand and foot, another violent, several peaceable now. *Brookfield.* One man caged, comfortable. *Granville.* One often closely confined, now losing the use of his limbs from lack of exercise. *Charlemont.* One man caged. *Savoy.* One man caged. *Lenox.* Two in the jail, against whose unfit condition there the jailer protests.

Gentlemen, I commit to you this sacred cause. Your action upon this subject will affect the present and future condition of hundreds and of thousands.

In this legislation, as in all things, may you exercise that "wisdom which is the breath of the power of God."

The Legal Status of Women

In 1860, David Dudley Field, a noted judge, described the legal status of married women in the United States.

A married woman cannot sue for her services. All she earns legally belongs to the husband. However, his earnings belong to him, and the wife legally has no claim on them. Where children have property and both parents are living, the father is the guardian. If a wife dies without a will, the husband is entitled to all her personal property. He is also entitled to a life interest in all of her real estate even though this property may have come to her through a former husband and the children of that marriage are still living. If a husband dies without a will, the widow is entitled to one third of the personal property and to a life interest in one third only of the real estate. If a wife is personally injured, either in reputation by slander or in body by accident, compensation must be sought in the name of herself and her husband. When the compensation is paid, it belongs to the husband. The father may by deed or will appoint a guardian for the minor children. They may thus be taken entirely away from the supervision of the mother at his death.

Ida Harper, **Life and Work of Susan B. Anthony** (A National Woman Suffrage Publication, 1898) Vol. I, pp. 185-186. Language simplified.

Seneca Falls Declaration of Sentiments and Resolutions

The Seneca Falls Convention on women's rights was called in 1848 by Lucretia Mott and Elizabeth Cady Stanton. The delegates to the convention drew up a Declaration of Independence which marked the beginning of the women's rights movement in America.

When, in the course of human events, it becomes necessary for one portion of the family of man to assume among the people of the earth a position different from that which they have occupied up to now, but one to which the laws of nature and of nature's God entitle them, a decent respect to the opinions of mankind requires that they should declare the causes that impel them to such a course.

History of Woman Suffrage, E.C. Stanton, S.B. Anthony, and M.J. Gage, eds. (New York: Charles Mann, 1889), Vol. I, pp. 70-73. Language simplified and modernized.

We hold these truths to be self-evident: that all men and women are created equal; that they are endowed by their Creator with certain inalienable rights; that among these are life, liberty and the pursuit of happiness; that to secure these rights governments are instituted, deriving their just powers from the consent of the governed. Whenever any form of government becomes destructive of these ends, it is the right of those who suffer from it to refuse allegiance to it, and to insist upon the institution of a new government, laying its foundation on such principles, and organizing its powers in such form, as to them shall seem most likely to effect their safety and happiness. Prudence, indeed, will dictate that governments long established should not be changed for light and transient causes. And all experience hath shown that mankind are more disposed to suffer while evils are

These pictures show women performing jobs that until recently were generally open only to men. In what ways are these women heirs to the women's reform movement of the years before the Civil War? How might your life be affected by the new jobs that the women in these pictures are performing?

5

6

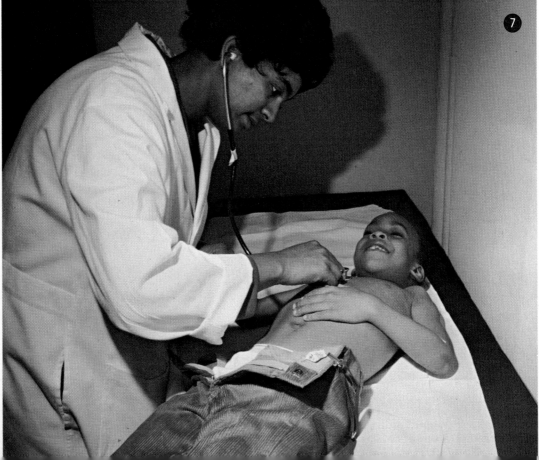

7

sufferable, than to right themselves by abolishing the forms to which they are accustomed. But when a long train of abuses and injustices pursuing the same object, reveals a design to reduce them under absolute despotism, it is their duty to throw off such government, and to provide new guards for their future security. Such has been the patient sufferance of the women under this government, and such is now the necessity which forces them to demand the equal position to which they are entitled.

The history of mankind is a history of repeated injuries and injustices on the part of man toward woman, having as its direct object the establishment of an absolute tyranny over her. To prove this, let facts be submitted to a candid world.

He has never permitted her to exercise her inalienable right to vote.

He has forced her to submit to laws, which she had no voice in making.

He has taken from her all right in property, even to her wages.

He has monopolized nearly all the profitable employments. And from those she is permitted to follow, she receives but scanty payment.

He closes against her all the avenues to wealth and distinction which he considers most honorable to himself. As a teacher of theology, medicine, or law, she is not known.

He has denied her the opportunity to obtain a thorough education for all colleges are closed to her.

Resolved, That woman is man's equal—was intended to be so by the Creator, and the highest good of the race demands that she should be recognized as such.

Resolved, therefore, That, being given by the Creator the same capabilities, and the same sense of responsibility for their exercise as men, it is the right and duty of woman, equally with man, to promote every righteous cause by every righteous means. Especially, it is her right to participate with her brother in teaching the great subjects of morals and religion, both in private and in public, by writing and by speaking, by any proper means and in any proper assemblies. This is a self-evident truth growing out of the divinely implanted principles of human nature. Any custom or authority against it, whether modern or old, is to be regarded as a self-evident falsehood, and at war with mankind.

▶ What jobs, if any, should be reserved exclusively for men or for women?

▶ Should girls be brought up to think that almost any role in life is appropriate for them? Why or why not?

Women and Blacks

At a meeting of women reformers in 1863, Angelina Grimke Weld, a prominent abolitionist, made the following statement.

Resolved, There never can be a true peace in this Republic until the civil and political rights of all citizens of African descent and all woman are ensured.

History of Woman Suffrage, Stanton, et. al., eds., p. 86. Language simplified and modernized.

I rejoice exceedingly that the resolution should combine us with black people. I feel that we have been with them. I feel that the iron has entered into our souls. True, we have not felt the slave-holder's lash. True, we have not had our hands chained. But our hands have been crushed. Was there a single institution in this country that would throw open its doors and acknowledge woman's equality with man until twenty years ago? Have I not heard women say—I said this to my brother, "Oh brother, that I could go to college with you! that I could have the instruction you do! But I am crushed! I hear nothing, I know nothing, except in the fashionable circle." A teacher said to a young lady, who had been studying for several years, on the day she finished her course of instruction, "I thought you would be very glad that you were soon to go home, so soon to leave your studies." She looked up and said, "What was I made for? When I go home I shall live in a circle of fashion and folly. I was not made for embroidery and dancing. I was made a woman. But I cannot be a true woman, a full-grown woman in America."

But woman is full-grown today, whether man knows it or not. She is equal to her rights and equal to the responsibilities of the hour. I wanted to be identified with the black man. Until he gets his rights, we never shall have ours.

FOR THOUGHT:

Through what means did these women hope to perfect society? How did their means differ from those used by the Utopians?

34 THE ABOLITIONIST MOVEMENT

Slavery became increasingly important in the South after Eli Whitney invented the cotton gin in 1793. Whitney's invention made cotton cultivation more profitable than it had been before. Southern planters quickly opened plantations on rich lands in Mississippi, Alabama, and Louisiana. As cotton growing moved to the Southwest, the demand for slaves increased accordingly. Between 1820 and 1840, cotton production quadrupled. The number of slaves grew from 1,538,000 to 2,487,355.

Since the eighteenth century, slavery had been a controversial part of American life. In the years following the Revolution, it had been abolished gradually throughout the North. Even in the South widespread opposition to slavery grew up during the first three decades of the nineteenth century. By 1840, however, almost all southerners defended slavery. This response came in part as a direct reaction to the activities of the American Anti-Slavery Society. Meeting in Philadelphia in 1833, the organizers of the society admitted that several state constitutions protected slavery. They insisted, however, that immediate emancipation of the slaves was the only morally correct course for the nation to take. They also pledged themselves to establish local antislavery organizations and to launch a massive campaign to convince their fellow citizens that slavery was a monstrous evil.

The abolitionists had strong religious convictions and were also skillful organizers and effective writers. By 1840, they had recruited about 200,000 members and established over 2000 local antislavery societies. These societies supported the work of antislavery agents such as Theodore Dwight Weld, who lectured and wrote in behalf of their cause. The selections in Reading 34 show some of the ways in which the abolitionists went about trying to destroy slavery. As you read these selections, try to answer the following questions:

1. What were the objectives of the American Anti-Slavery Society, and how did the society try to achieve its objectives?
2. What special contributions did Frederick Douglass make to the abolition movement?

Instructions to an Abolitionist Agent

Theodore Weld was one of the most successful abolitionist agents. In 1834, the American Anti-Slavery Society, which he had helped to found, appointed him to carry the abolitionists' message into Ohio. At the time of his appointment, the society sent him a letter containing instructions. Portions of those instructions are given here.

Letters of Theodore Dwight Weld, Angelina Grimke Weld, and Sarah Grimke, Dwight L. Dumond and Gilbert H. Barnes, eds., (New York: Appleton-Century-Crofts, 1934), Vol. I, pp. 124-128. Language simplified and modernized.

To Mr. T. D. Weld
Dear Sir:

You have been appointed an agent of the American Anti-Slavery Society. You will receive the following instructions from the executive committee. They are a brief expression of the principles they wish you to teach and the course of conduct they wish you to pursue.

Our object is the overthrow of American Slavery. We expect to accomplish this, mainly by showing to the public its true character, its denial of the first principles of religion, morality and humanity, and its inconsistency with our beliefs as a free, humane, and enlightened people.

226

You will teach everywhere, the great fundamental principle of IMMEDIATE ABOLITION, as the duty of all masters, on the ground that slavery is both unjust and unprofitable. Insist mainly on the SIN OF SLAVERY, because our main hope is in the consciences of men.

We oppose the idea of payment to slaveholders, because it implies that slavery is right. It is also unnecessary. The abolition of slavery will be an advantage, as free labor is more profitable than the labor of slaves.

The people of color should at once be emancipated and recognized as citizens. Their rights should be secured, equal in every way to others, according to the fundamental principle laid down in the American Declaration of Independence.

In covering your territory you will generally find it wise to visit first several prominent places, particularly those where our cause has friends. In going to a place, you will naturally call upon those who are friendly to our objectives and take advice from them. Also, call on ministers of the gospel and other leading characters. Work especially to enlighten them and secure their favor and influence. Ministers are the hinges of community, and ought to be moved, if possible.

Form branch societies, both male and female, in every place where it is practical. Encourage them to raise funds and apply them in purchasing and circulating free antislavery publications.

You are not to take up collections in your public meetings. The practice often prevents persons from attending, whom it might be desirable to reach.

▶Would it be immoral to compensate slaveholders? Or would this act be moral if it resulted in the abolition of slavery?

Selections from an Abolitionist Best Seller

Theodore Weld, his wife Angelina Grimke Weld, and her sister, Sarah Grimke, compiled evidence from thousands of southern newspapers for a book American Slavery as It Is: Testimony of a Thousand Witnesses. *The book, published in 1839, immediately became a best seller. It later served as a source for Harriet Beecher Stowe's* Uncle Tom's Cabin.

We will first prove by a number of witnesses, that slaves are whipped with such inhuman severity, as to cut and mangle their flesh in the most shocking manner, leaving permanent scars and ridges. After establishing this, we will present a mass of testimony about a great variety of other tortures. The testimony, for the most part, will be that of the slaveholders themselves, and in their own chosen words. A large portion of it will be taken from the advertisements, which they have published in their own newspapers, describing the scars

American Slavery as It Is: Testimony of a Thousand Witnesses (New York: American Anti-Slavery Society, 1839), pp. 62-63, 77, 125, 127. Language simplified and modernized.

made by the whip on the bodies of their own runaway slaves. We shall insert only so much of each advertisement as will clearly set forth the precise point under consideration. In the column under the word "witnesses" will be found the name of the individual who signs the advertisement, or for whom it is signed, with his or her place of residence, the name and date of the paper in which it appeared, and generally the name of the place where it is published. Opposite the name of each witness will be an extract from the advertisement containing his or her testimony.

Witnesses	Testimony
Mr. Robert Nicoll, Dauphin St. between Emanuel and Conception Sts., Mobile, Alabama, in the "Mobile (Alabama) Commercial Advertiser."	"Ten dollars reward for my woman Siby, very much scarred about the neck and ears by whipping."
Maurice Y. Garcia, Sheriff of the County of Jefferson, La., in the "New Orleans Bee," August 14, 1838.	"Lodged in jail, a mulatto boy, having large marks of the whip, on his shoulders and other parts of his body."
James A. Rowland, jailor, Lumberton, North Carolina, in the "Fayetteville (N.C.) Observer," June 20, 1838.	"Committed, a mulatto fellow—his back shows lasting impressions of the whip, and leaves no doubt of his being a slave."
Mr. Micajah Ricks, Nash County, North Carolina, in the Raleigh "Standard," July 18, 1838.	"Ranaway, a Negro woman and two children; a few days before she went off, I burnt her with a hot iron, on the left side of her face, I tried to make the letter M."
Mr. Asa B. Metcalf, Kingston, Adams Co., Miss., in the "Natchez Courier," June 15, 1832.	"Ranaway Mary, a black woman, has a scar on her back and right arm near the shoulder, caused by a rifle ball."
Mr. William Overstreet, Benton, Yazoo Co., Miss., in the "Lexington (Kentucky) Observer," July 22, 1838.	"Ranaway a Negro man named Henry, his left eye out, some scars from a dagger on and under his left arm, and much scarred with the whip."
J. A. Brown, jailor, Charleston, South Carolina, in the "Mercury," Jan. 12, 1837.	"Committed to jail a Negro man, has no toes on his left foot."

Frederick Douglass
Joins the Cause

Frederick Douglass, an escaped slave, became a renowned orator in both the United States and Great Britain. In later life, he recalled his unusual contribution to the abolitionist cause.

Among the first duties assigned to me on entering the ranks was to travel in company with Mr. George Foster, to secure subscribers to the *Anti-Slavery Standard* and the *Liberator*. With him I traveled and lectured through the eastern counties of Massachusetts. Much interest was awakened. Large meetings assembled. Many came, no doubt, from curiosity to hear what a Negro could say in his own cause. I was generally introduced as a "chattel"—a "thing"—a piece of southern property—the chairman assuring the audience that *it* could speak. *Fugitive slaves*, at that time, were not so plentiful as now [1855]. And as a fugitive slave lecturer, I had the advantage of being a "bran-new fact"—the first one out. Up to that time a colored man who confessed himself a runaway slave was considered a fool. This was not only because of the danger of being captured to which he exposed himself, but because it was a confession of a very low origin.

Frederick Douglass, **Life and Times of Frederick Douglass** (Boston: De Wolfe Fiske and Company, 1895), pp. 268-69. Language simplified and modernized.

The Reform Philosophy
of Frederick Douglass

Frederick Douglass made this statement in a speech in 1857.

Let me give you a word of the philosophy of reform. The whole history of the progress of human liberty shows that all concessions yet made to her have been born of earnest struggle. The conflict has been exciting, agitating, all-absorbing. If there is no struggle there is no progress. Those who claim to favor freedom and yet denounce agitation are men who want crops without plowing up the ground. They want rain without thunder and lightning. They want the ocean without the awful roar of its many waters.

This struggle may be a moral one, or it may be a physical one. And it may be both moral and physical. But it must be a struggle. Power gives nothing without a demand. It never did and it never will. Find out what any people will quickly submit to and you have found out the exact measure of injustice and wrong which will be imposed upon them. And these will continue till they are resisted with either words or blows, or with both. The limits of tyrants are set by the endurance of those whom they oppress. In the light of

Two Speeches by Frederick Douglass (Rochester: C.P. Dewey, 1857), pp. 21, 22. Language simplified and modernized.

▶ Under what conditions, if any, should reformers persist in their activities if violence may result?

these ideas Negroes will be hunted in the North. They will be held and flogged in the South so long as they submit to those devilish outrages, and make no resistance, either moral or physical. Men may not get all they pay for in this world, but they must certainly pay for all they get. If we ever get free from the oppressions and wrongs heaped upon us, we must pay for their removal. We must do this by labor, by suffering, by sacrifice, and, if needs be, by our lives and the lives of others.

An Editorial from
Frederick Douglass' Newspaper

The first issue of Douglass' newspaper, The North Star, carried an editorial. An excerpt from it appears below.

We neither question the good faith nor the abilities of our white friends and fellow workers when we assert that the man who has suffered wrong should be the man to demand justice—that the man struck is the man to cry out—and that he who has endured the cruel pangs of slavery must advocate liberty. We must be our own advocates and representatives, not alone but independent, not separate from but in connection with our white friends. In the grand struggle for liberty and equality now waging, it is appropriate, necessary, and right that authors, editors, and orators should arise in our ranks. In these capacities we can contribute the most permanent good to our cause.

FOR THOUGHT:

In what ways were the methods of reform used by the abolitionists similar to or different from those used by the Utopians? by women reformers?

35 THE TRADITION OF AMERICAN REFORM

HISTORICAL ESSAY

A high percentage of nineteenth-century American reformers came from the vicinity of Boston, Massachusetts. Boston was filled with reminders of the American Revolution. Most of the people who became active in reform causes before the Civil War were born early in the nineteenth century. Their fathers and grandfathers had fought in the Revolution. The ideals of the Declaration of Independence, like the sight of Boston Common, Bunker Hill, and Faneuil Hall, were a part of the living past for these men and women.

Another factor helps to explain the importance of Boston as a center of reform. Three hundred years earlier, the Puritans had come to New England to pursue their own religious beliefs and to build a Christian society which would serve as a model for the old world. Many active reformers were descended from the Puritans. Most of them, whatever their own personal background, felt a tie between their mission to reform American society in the nineteenth century and the earlier mission of the Puritans.

The Role of the Church

In the case of some reform causes, most notably abolition, churches played an important role on both sides. Some church people argued that the Bible treated slavery as a legitimate institution and that people should not tamper with it. Others argued that slavery denied the spirit of Christianity and should be abolished. The churches also faced a practical problem because they drew their membership from Americans all over the country. By agreeing with the reformers and condemning slavery, the churches might drive out southern members and disrupt their organizations.

Because churches took official positions on slavery slowly, many reformers turned upon the churches themselves as obstacles to reform. These reformers were anti-church but not anti-religious. They believed that if a person expected to find favor from God in the next world, he or she must struggle against everything unjust and evil in this world.

Perfectionism, Transcendentalism, and Reform

A new school of philosophy in America called transcendentalism also contributed to the ideology of the reformers. The founder of the movement was Ralph Waldo Emerson. In the philosophy of transcendentalism, which Emerson proclaimed, a person became "a God in ruins." By this phrase Emerson meant that all nature, including humans, was a part of God. A person could become divine, he thought, by expressing the spiritual quality within herself or himself and living according to his or her most profound moral intuitions.

Emerson lived in Concord, Massachusetts, from 1834 until 1882. He had a wide following as a writer and lecturer throughout the northern and western states. The heart of his philosophy appealed strongly to Americans. Human beings were godlike, he argued, and should stand on their own two feet and pursue their own convictions. One of his most famous essays was called "Self Reliance." This emphasis on individualism gave a kind of philosophical support to the ideals of Jacksonian democracy. It also stimulated the reform

Boston Common is a public area which the Revolutionary War patriots used as a meeting place. In the Battle of Bunker Hill, fought in 1775, the Americans inflicted heavy losses on the British. The patriots also used Faneuil Hall, an old market building and public hall, as a meeting place.

▶Should a church take a stand on a social issue if some members of the congregation will probably leave in protest? Why or why not?

movement. If all human beings were a part of God, then it was wrong to treat anyone unjustly. Moreover, if a person knew in his or her heart that an institution such as slavery was wrong, then he or she was obliged to try to change it.

The case of one of Emerson's most famous followers, Henry David Thoreau, illustrates the meaning of transcendentalism. Like Emerson, Thoreau lived in Concord. He believed that slavery was wrong. In 1846, he refused to pay taxes because he felt that tax money was being used to support a government that protected slavery. The authorities put Thoreau in the Concord jail overnight. On his release he wrote an essay entitled "Civil Disobedience." In it he justified his refusal to obey what he thought were unjust laws. Thoreau believed it was wrong to support slavery in any way. He preferred to go to jail rather than violate his deepest moral convictions. "Civil Disobedience" is still widely read throughout the world. It influenced Mohandas Gandhi, who attempted to get England to grant independence to India in the 1930's and 1940's. It also influenced American civil rights leaders such as Martin Luther King, Jr.

The reform spirit before the Civil War was also nourished by an emphasis on equality in American life. This emphasis characterized the thinking of many Americans during the time of Andrew Jackson. If the common people were good enough to win political power and to fill responsible positions in government, then, the reformers argued, any institutions which kept them from enjoying equal opportunities should be changed.

Historians often use the word "perfectionism" to stand for all of the influences just mentioned: the idealism of the Declaration of Independence, the moral emphases of Christianity and transcendentalism, and the Jacksonian emphasis on equality. Large numbers of Americans before the Civil War believed that society could and should be made more perfect. This perfectionist faith supported northern reformers and helped to distinguish the North from the South.

Mormonism

Perfectionism and religious zeal went hand in hand. They led to the development of new kinds of churches. The most important of these new religious groups was the Church of Jesus Christ of the Latter Day Saints. It was organized in Fayette, New York, in 1830. Joseph Smith founded this church after he claimed that he had received a special revelation from God in the form of the Book of the Mormon. Smith accepted the authority of the Bible. But he taught that God intended to establish the pure form of Christianity in Mormonism. The Mormon church was characterized by a centralized form of economic and social life. This way of life clashed sharply with the individualism of the times. Mormon group solidarity, together with

232

reports of such unorthodox ideas as their belief in polygyny, aroused the antagonism of their neighbors. Searching for more congenial surroundings, the Mormons moved from New York to Ohio, Missouri, and Illinois. In 1844, a mob in Nauvoo, Illinois, killed Joseph Smith and drove the Mormons out.

Brigham Young succeeded Smith as leader of the Mormons. By this time Young and most of his followers had come to feel that they would only find security outside the populated areas of the United States. In 1847, Young led a small group of Mormons west to the Great Salt Lake Valley in what is now the state of Utah. By 1850 more than 11,000 fellow believers had joined him. Mormonism has since become a powerful world-wide religious order. It is one of the most original religious organizations ever developed in the United States.

The Variety of Reform Movements

An enormous variety of reform causes concerned Americans before the Civil War. All groups, however, made one basic assumption. They believed that any pattern of behavior or any social arrangement which degraded the dignity of the individual should be reformed.

Children, forced to work in factories twelve hours a day, could not go to school to prepare themselves for a better life. Rather than press for factory legislation, reformers tried to pass laws requiring all children to go to school. Horace Mann led the fight for free public education. By 1860 many states had passed compulsory school laws. Before the Civil War few children studied beyond the elementary school. Today's concern that every qualified student finish high school and, if possible, continue on to college grew directly from the pre-Civil War reform spirit expressed in the work of Horace Mann.

Americans' contemporary concern for world peace also has roots in the early nineteenth century. In 1828, reformers founded the American Peace Society in New York City. This organization denounced the use of force in international disputes and urged the establishment of an organization like the United Nations. Local peace societies sprang up throughout the country. And students in schools and colleges received special prizes from the society for their essays and orations.

Important movements also developed to improve prisons and provide care and educational opportunities for the deaf and the blind. In 1832, Samuel Gridley Howe, a graduate of Harvard Medical School, established Perkins Institute in Boston for the purpose of instructing blind children. In 1857, a Yale graduate and minister, Thomas Hopkins Gallaudet, established a college in Washington, D.C., for the education of the deaf.

Polygyny is the practice of a husband having two or more wives at the same time.

►This picture shows several young men who deliberately broke a law that they thought was unjust. Under what circumstances, if any, is a person justified to break laws? Do you think it is important for people to make a public affirmation of their stand.

The Movement to Abolish Slavery

The antislavery movement, however, occupied the center of the stage. Although the American Anti-Slavery Society was not founded until 1833, slavery had troubled America's conscience long before that. Quakers had organized the first antislavery society in America in 1775. All the northern states took steps to abolish slavery in the years following the Revolution. Even in the South feeling against slavery ran high. A movement providing for gradual emancipation of slaves and for their colonization in Africa remained a powerful influence in the upper South as late as the 1820's. By the 1830's, however, slavery had become accepted in the South as an essential part of the economy. And southerners resented any criticism of it.

William Lloyd Garrison became the most famous abolitionist. The son of a poor family from Newburyport, Massachusetts, Garrison received little formal education. While he was working for a Quaker journalist in Baltimore, Garrison became interested in slavery. In 1831, he founded his own paper, the *Liberator*, in Boston, to crusade against slavery. In the first issue, Garrison indicated how he intended to carry out his crusade:

I *will be* as harsh as truth, and as uncompromising as justice. On this subject I do not wish to think, or speak or write with moderation . . . . I am in earnest—I will not equivocate—I will not excuse—I will not retreat a single inch—AND I WILL BE HEARD.

Garrison was true to his word. In the following years, the *Liberator* became the most famous antislavery newspaper in the country. Its subscription list was always relatively small. But other papers North and South quoted the *Liberator* freely, spreading the influence of its crusading editor.

During the 1830's, great troubles vexed the abolitionists despite their growth in numbers. Trouble arose both in the South and in the North. The South took action almost immediately to keep abolitionism from spreading below the Mason-Dixon line. Southern states passed laws making it a crime to circulate antislavery literature or to criticize slavery in public. Some states actually posted a reward for the capture of Garrison, dead or alive. Therefore, abolitionists had to find their audiences in the North. Even there the reception at first was very hostile. Opposition grew partly from the fact that considerable anti-black feeling existed in the North before the war. Blacks went to segregated schools. They rode in segregated trains. They even sat in segregated pews in white churches. Abolitionists opposed these practices and thus angered many northern whites. Northern business people also opposed abolitionists for fear that agitation would disrupt trade between North and South. As a result, abolitionists often found it hard to get a hearing in the North. Mobs broke up their meetings. And they were sometimes beaten. A mob even killed one of their number, Elijah Lovejoy, in Alton, Illinois, in 1837.

This harassment also had a positive effect, however. By the end of the 1830's, many people in the North had begun to feel that abolitionists were being denied their fundamental right of free speech. On this ground, they began to take new interest in the antislavery movement.

Most abolitionists limited their activities to paying dues to an antislavery organization, listening to abolitionist orators, reading antislavery newspapers and pamphlets, and occasionally writing legislators to support antislavery measures. A small number, however, struck directly at slavery by developing a secret organization called the underground railroad. It began in the early 1830's. It helped hundreds

The southern boundary of Pennsylvania was run in the 1760's by Charles Mason and Jeremiah Dixon at about 39° latitude. This line was extended in 1820 as the boundary between slave and free states under the Missouri Compromise. The term "Mason-Dixon line" thus came to mean the boundary between slave and free states.

of slaves to escape from the South every year. The underground railroad was particularly strong in border states. Most of the money to support it came from white people in the North sympathetic to the antislavery cause. Some of its most important agents, however, were escaped slaves, like the courageous Harriet Tubman. After escaping from a Maryland plantation into Pennsylvania, she returned many times to the South and developed a line of underground stations extending from Maryland to Canada.

Disagreements divided American abolitionists. People who devote their lives to reform causes are usually strong minded and uncompromising. Frequently, they find it difficult to get along with each other. In 1840, the American Anti-Slavery Society split into two factions. One faction began to concentrate on political means to destroy slavery. Some of them helped to organize the Liberty party. Others began to work through the Whig or Democratic parties. These political abolitionists worked to abolish slavery in the District of Columbia and to exclude slavery from federal territories. In the 1850's, the Republican party took over this position.

The other faction, which grouped around Garrison, believed that abolitionists could not become involved in politics without compromising their principles. They should, therefore, stay aloof from political activity. They advocated extreme measures, such as the secession of the North, so that slavery would no longer stain the entire Union. One of Garrison's slogans carried in the *Liberator* proclaimed, "No union with slaveholders." Because the Constitution of the United States seemed to protect slavery, radical abolitionists refused to honor it. At a public meeting Garrison burned a copy of the Constitution, saying "thus perish all compromises with tyranny."

For thirty years, the radical abolitionists continued to demand immediate emancipation and to denounce people whose position was more conservative than their own. In one sense they failed. They did not convert the slaveholders. And the majority of people in the North continued to look on them as dangerous fanatics. In another sense, even with all their shortcomings, they succeeded. The abolitionists represented the American conscience. They helped to force the great issue which Abraham Lincoln defined by saying that the American nation could not remain indefinitely half slave and half free. People who denounce contemporary reformers for their uncompromising stands might well reflect upon the influence of this remarkable band of impassioned people who believed that it was preferable to divide a nation rather than condone injustice. They represent a great American tradition—the belief that free people must give their time, money, and energy, indeed their very lives, so that justice and freedom may reign supreme in the land.

Slavery in
the South

STATING THE ISSUE

What was the impact of slavery on southern life? This big question dominates the history of the South in the decades before the Civil War. To help you formulate your own tentative answers to this question, we are departing from the format followed thus far in this volume.

Reading 36 consists of pictures, tables, and other original materials which illustrate the impact of slavery on southern life. Examine each piece of visual evidence carefully. Then develop tentative answers to the major question of this chapter: What was the impact of slavery on southern life?

1400 1500 1600 1700 1800 1900 2000

1829 David Walker's essay **Appeal** urges slaves to use force to gain their freedom
1831 Nat Turner leads slave rebellion in Virginia
1836 Virginia legislature orders censoring of abolitionist literature
1844 James K. Polk is elected President
1846–48 United States fights a war with Mexico
1848 Free Soil party is formed and adopts anti-slavery platform
1848 Zachary Taylor is elected President
1850 Congress adopts Compromise of 1850
1851 Slave trade is abolished in District of Columbia

1852 Harriet Beecher Stowe writes **Uncle Tom's Cabin**
1853 Slaves revolt in New Orleans
1854 George Fitzhugh publishes pro-slavery book **Sociology for the South**
1856 Slaves revolt in North Carolina
1857 In Dred Scott decision Supreme Court rules slavery legal in territories
1859 John Brown raids federal arsenal at Harper's Ferry, Virginia
1860 Frederick Law Olmsted's **Journey in the Back Country** is published

36 THE IMPACT OF SLAVERY ON SOUTHERN LIFE

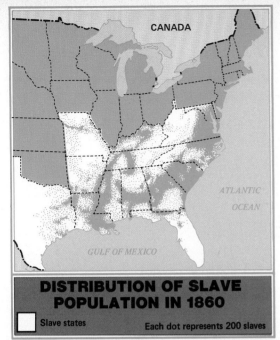

DISTRIBUTION OF SLAVE POPULATION IN 1860

☐ Slave states   Each dot represents 200 slaves

ESTIMATED AVERAGE SLAVE PRICES 1828–1860

Year	Price
1828	$ 700
1835	900
1837	1,300
1839	1,000
1840	700
1844	600
1848	900
1851	1,050
1853	1,200
1859	1,650
1860	1,800

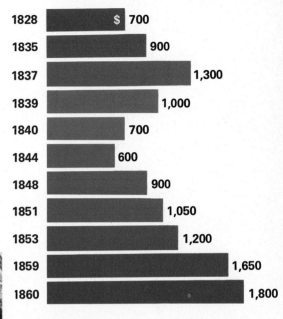

A SLAVE-HUNT.

240

SALE OF VALUABLE SLAVES,
IN THE CITY OF WILLIAMSBURG, AND OF OTHER PRO-
PERTY, AND RENTING OF REAL ESTATE.

I SHALL sell for cash, to the highest bidder, in the said city, before
the Court House door, on MONDAY, the 10th day of February,
1851, (that being James City County Court day,) some thirty valuable
Slaves, belonging to the estate of the late James M Maupin, consisting
of Men, Women and Children. It is seldom purchasers can have so
favorable an opportunity to be supplied with Slaves of such value as
will then be sold. The sale will commence at 1 o'clock, and those at
a distance, and others wishing to purchase, will do well to attend
punctually.

I shall also sell, upon a suitable credit to the highest bidder, com-
mencing the sale, as heretofore advertised, on the 29th day of January, 1851, the perishable estate of the deceased, consisting of a large
and desirable variety of articles of husbandry; such as Horses, (among
them an excellent pair of match Carriage Horses,) Mules, Oxen and
other Cattle, Hogs, Wagons, Ox and Tumbrel Carts, and a great variety of Farming Implements, some of the most modern and improved
construction and use ; such as a Wheat Threshing Machine,
Wheat Fan, Wheat Drill, Corn Sheller and Grinder, &c., &c. Also,
Corn, Oats, Fodder, Straw, Shucks, &c., &c. Also, will
be then sold an excellent Carriage and Harness; also, the
Household and Kitchen Furniture, of great variety and value. Many
items of the Household Furniture are of the most costly and modern
style. The Farms in the neighborhood, belonging to said estate, will
be rented out, upon one of which is now growing a large and promising crop of wheat. Also, the lots of land and tenements in and adjoining the said city. The sale will take place upon the premises respectively, but the renting will be in Williamsburg, and the sales and
renting will be continued, from day to day, until completed.
Jan. 17—cwtds   RO. H. ARMISTEAD, Executor, &c.

☞ Whig requested to copy.

SLAVEHOLDERS AND SLAVES, 1850 AND 1860

1850 Number of slaves	100–200	200–300	300–500	500–1,000	Over 1,000	Total Number of Slaveholders (including those with less than 100 slaves)
Alabama	216	16	2	–	–	29,295
Georgia	147	22	4	2	–	38,456
Louisiana	244	36	6	4	–	20,670
Mississippi	189	18	8	1	–	23,116
North Carolina	76	12	3	–	–	28,303
South Carolina	382	69	9	2	2	25,596
Virginia	107	8	29	–	–	55,063

1860 Number of slaves	100–200	200–300	300–500	500–1,000	Over 1,000	Total Number of Slaveholders (including those with less than 100 slaves)
Alabama	312	24	10	–	–	33,730
Georgia	181	23	7	1	–	41,084
Louisiana	460	63	20	4	–	22,033
Mississippi	279	28	8	1	–	30,943
North Carolina	118	11	4	–	–	34,658
South Carolina	363	56	22	7	–	26,701
Virginia	105	8	1	–	1	52,128

New Slavery Book Kindles a Dispute

By SOMA GOLDEN

More than a century after the Civil War ended slavery, a new book written by two economists has stirred up an unusually heated scholarly debate over the institution of slavery and its effect on black Americans.

With high-speed computers, mountains of data, textbook theories, and fancy mathematics, the economists have invaded the territory of historians, the traditional arbiters of what slavery was and was not. And the historians, a group with little internal cohesion, are stumbling about, uncertain just how to respond.

Although the dispute has been building for years, it burst into full force this week with publication of "Time on the Cross," a two-volume analysis of slave history by economists Robert W. Fogel and Stanley L. Engerman, both professors at Rochester, both quasi historians and both skilled mathematicians.

Like Union General William T. Sherman on his march from Atlanta to the sea, Professors Fogel and Engerman slashed their way through the history books of slavery, leaving almost nothing behind them intact. With a mixture of intellectual delight and academic challenge, they attacked one after another the traditional views of the Old South and came up with tenets of their own, among them the following:

¶Slavery was not a dying, profitless business, but the "growth industry of its day," as Professor Fogel puts it.

¶Slave agriculture was not backward and inefficient, but about 35 per cent more efficient than "free" farming.

¶Slaves were not lazy, incompetent workers; they were tough team laborers, more efficient than their white counterparts.

¶Slave families were not generally torn apart by wicked white traders selling them "down the river"; instead, slaveholders had an economic incentive to keep the family unit together and to keep worker morale high.

¶Slave women were not used on stud farms to breed new slaves nor were they typically forced to bed with slaveholders; indeed, slave women generally abstained from sexual activity in their teens.

¶Slaves were not worked to exhaustion; instead, they were relatively well fed, housed and clothed because of their key part in the production process.

And on and on it goes for 453 pages, ringing with the sound of breaking icons. The book, which is divided into a volume for lay readers and one for technicians, gathers together for the first time the fruits of 18 years of labor by the authors and other Cliometricians. The self-styled New Economic Historians, who have tried to wed Clio, the muse of history, to mathematics. It is a merger that has raised both cheer and havoc among historians.

37 SLAVERY
ON AND OFF
THE PLANTATION

Since the Civil War, historians have been trying to determine what it was like to be a black slave in the South. Their task has been difficult. In the first place, slaves led different kinds of lives depending upon where they lived, who their masters were, and what kind of work they did. Some slaves worked as field hands on plantations. Others worked on small farms. Some were house servants on plantations or in cities. Others were skilled in various crafts and were often hired out for wages by their masters. Slaves who lived and worked under such different circumstances clearly had different experiences.

The great plantation has been glamorized in historical fiction and in the movies. However, it was not the typical unit of southern economic and social life. A few plantations had a slave population numbering in the hundreds. But only 1 percent of the slaveowners held more than a hundred slaves each. Two thirds of all slaveholders owned fewer than twenty slaves each. Twenty percent owned only one slave. Nevertheless, more than half of the 4 million slaves in the South in 1860 lived in groups of ten or more and worked in the fields planting and harvesting crops. Plantation slavery, then, was the experience of the majority of slaves.

What was plantation slavery like before the Civil War? Different sources suggest different answers. Former slaveholders, writing after the Civil War, stressed the harmony of plantation life and the kindness and generosity of the masters. Northern historians, writing at the same time, emphasized the cruelty of the slaveholder and the suffering of the slave. Former slaves, testifying about their experiences, often gave inconsistent reports.

The following reading contains two selections. In the first, a southern plantation is described by a northern traveler who visited the South in the 1850's. In the second, the life of urban slaves is discussed by a modern American historian. As you read keep these questions in mind:

1. Does Olmsted find that slaves were treated well or that they were dissatisfied?
2. What were the advantages of being a slave in the city?

A Mississippi Plantation

In the late 1850's, Frederick Law Olmsted visited a plantation in lower Mississippi. His observations on the daily life of the slaves are given here.

Frederick Law Olmsted, **A Journey in the Back Country** (New York: Mason Brothers, 1860), pp. 46-51. Language simplified and modernized.

An overseer directed the work of the slaves. He usually had experience in managing a plantation.

A wheelwright made and repaired wheels for wagons and carriages.

A midwife assists women in childbirth.

The hoe-gang hoed the fields to loosen the soil around the plants and to destroy weeds.

Irons were rings and chains made of iron and placed on slaves' wrists or ankles to prevent them from escaping.

A driver's job was to keep the slaves working steadily.

It was a first-rate plantation. On the highest ground stood a large and handsome mansion. But it had not been occupied for several years. The owner lived several hundred miles away. And the overseer had not seen him for more than two years.

There were 135 slaves, big and little. Sixty-seven of them went to the fields regularly. They were equal, the overseer thought, to sixty able-bodied hands. Besides the field-hands, there were three mechanics (blacksmith, carpenter, and wheelwright), two seamstresses, a cook, one stable servant, one cattle-tender, one hog tender, one teamster, one house servant (the overseer's cook), and one midwife and nurse. These were all first-class hands. The overseer said that most of them would be worth more, if they were for sale, than the best field-hands. There was also a driver of the hoe-gang, who did not work himself, and the foreman of the plow-gang. These two acted alternately as police officers in the field and in the slave quarters.

There was a nursery for babies at the quarters. Twenty women, at this time, left their work four times each day for half an hour to nurse the young ones. The overseer counted these women as half hands. In other words, they were expected to do half an ordinary day's work.

The overseer had no runaways out at this time. But he had just sold a bad one to go to Texas. He had been whipping the fellow when he turned and tried to stab him. The slave then broke from him and ran away. The dogs had caught him almost immediately. After catching him, the overseer kept him in irons until he had a chance to sell him.

In the field, we found thirty plows. They moved together, turning the earth from the cotton plants. We also found thirty to forty hoers, most of whom were women. A black driver walked about among them with a whip, which he often cracked at them. Sometimes, he allowed the lash to fall lightly upon their shoulders. He also constantly urged them with his voice. All worked very steadily. The presence of a stranger on the plantation must have been rare. I saw none raise or turn his head to look at me. A watertoter attended each gang.

I asked at what time the slaves began to work in the morning. "Well," said the overseer, "I do better by my slaves than most. I keep 'em right smart at their work while they are working. But I generally knock 'em off at 8 o'clock on Saturday mornings and give 'em all the rest of the day to themselves. I always give 'em Sunday off. At pickin' time, and hoein' time, I sometimes keep 'em to it till about sunset on Saturdays. But I never work 'em on Sundays."

"How early do you start them out in the morning, usually?"

"Well, I don't never start my slaves 'fore daylight except in pickin' time. Then maybe I get 'em out a quarter of an hour before daylight. But I keep 'em right smart to work through the day." He showed an evident pride in the vigilance of his driver. And he called my attention to the large area of ground already hoed over that morning—well hoed, too, as he said.

At half past nine o'clock, the drivers, each on an alternate night, blew a horn. At ten, the driver visited every cabin to see that its occupants were at rest, rather then spending their strength in fooleries. He also made sure the fires were safe—a very unusual precaution.

The Negroes are generally free, after their day's work is done, till they are called in the morning. I did not learn when washing and patching were done, wood hauled and cut for the fires, corn ground, etc. Probably all chores that did not have to be done daily were reserved for Saturday. Custom varies in this respect. In general, the Negroes have to look out for fuel for their cabins themselves. They often have to go to "the swamp" for it. If it has been hauled, they have to cut it to a convenient size, after their day's work is done.

The allowance of food was a peck of corn and four pounds of pork for each slave per week. When they could not get "greens," each generally received five pounds of pork. They had gardens, and raised a good deal of food for themselves. They also had chickens and usually plenty of eggs. The overseer added, "The man who owns this plantation does more for his slaves than any other man I know. Every Christmas he sends me up a thousand or fifteen hundred dollars' [about eight to eleven dollars per slave] worth of molasses, coffee, tobacco, calico, and Sunday treats for 'em. Every family on this plantation gets a barrel of molasses at Christmas." (This was not an uncommon practice in Mississippi, though the quantity is rarely so generous. The amount is usually made somewhat proportionate to the value of the last crop sold.)

The overseer also added that the slaves are able if they choose, to buy certain comforts for themselves—tobacco, for instance—with money earned by Saturday and Sunday work. Some of them went into the swamps on Sunday and made boards. One man sold fifty dollars' worth last year.

A peck is a unit of measurement equivalent to a fourth of a bushel or eight quarts.

▶ Do you think that reformers should try to take care of a people's material needs such as food, shelter, and clothing before trying to take care of non-material needs such as political and social freedom? Why or why not?

Calico is printed cotton cloth.

Slavery in the City

The following excerpt, by a modern American historian, discusses the life of urban slaves in the 1850's.

245

Olmsted described southern plantations from the perspective of a northern newspaperman. Suppose you were a traveller and wanted to describe the African village shown on this page. How would your background influence what you chose to describe? Would someone from a different background, such as a person who lived in this village, emphasize the same things you did? How accurate would either of these descriptions be?

Urban blacks not only dressed much better than those in the countryside, they also ate better. Both the quantity and the quality of their food were higher. And, just as importantly, the diet had a greater variety. A Charleston slaveholder, comparing the cost of keeping bondsmen in a city and on a plantation, put the differences neatly when he said that the town slaves were "in general clothed more expensively, and more daintily fed." This could be expected since so many were house servants and ate out of their master's kitchen. But even those who "lived out" and "boarded out" probably fared better than country house servants and certainly far better than field hands . . . .

The food of urban slaves differed both in amount and character. Since little was grown on town lots, it was not confined by what might be raised by the master. This meant that the range of foods consumed would be much greater. Bondsmen usually ate whatever whites did, though not as much and not always openly. "They live with us—" explained a Charleston minister, "eating from the same storehouses, drinking from the same fountains." The result was a varied fare, including not only meat, vegetables, fruit, bread, and milk, but also delicacies—cakes, pies, and candies. Moreover, the location of most cities on oceans and rivers provided seafood through most of the year.

The town slave, however, was never wholly dependent on his master or employer for food. The city abounded with grocery stores, bake shops, and confectioners. The market opened early and closed late. And hucksters plied their trade in all seasons. Legally, merchants could not sell to slaves who did not have a written order from their owners. But this was seldom enforced. Officials considered themselves successful if they kept some control over liquor sales. In fact, they generally acted as if purchases of food were legal, if not made in large amounts. . . . Few shopkeepers turned down slaves who could pay for the food, whether they carried a "ticket" or not.

Shops also grew up that catered to blacks. Sometimes these were run by free blacks, sometimes by whites, and even occasionally by slaves . . . . Every city had many such places, offering a congenial opportunity for eating and drinking and filling in any gaps in the diet offered by the master.

Richard C. Wade, **Slavery in the Cities** (New York: Oxford University Press, 1964), pp. 132-134.

► Should all of the laws created by a community be enforced equally? Or should some laws be enforced more strictly than others?

FOR THOUGHT:

Does the evidence in these two excerpts support any of the hypotheses you developed after studying the materials in Reading 36? Does this evidence suggest new hypotheses?

38 THE DEFENSE OF SLAVERY

Until the early 1830's, few Americans, either in the North or the South, tried to defend slavery. They merely pointed out that it was so deeply ingrained in the southern way of life that it could not be done away with overnight. Several events, which happened in the South at this time, however, encouraged the defense of slavery. In 1831, Nat Turner, a black preacher, led a slave revolt in Virginia. Fifty-seven white people were killed. State and federal troops crushed the revolt, and Turner and his supporters were executed. But the slaves' bid for freedom terrified slaveholders. At about the same time, William Lloyd Garrison began to publish his radical antislavery newspaper, the *Liberator*. The paper put slaveowners on the defensive. Finally, the booming cotton economy in the deep South increased the demand for slave labor.

Nat Turner had made, and Garrison was beginning to make, an impact on southern thinking. But in 1832, southern leaders still argued in public over the merits and evils of slavery. In that year, the members of the Virginia Constitutional Convention debated emancipation proposals. These proposals received considerable support. From that time on, however, it became increasingly difficult and dangerous for southerners to criticize slavery in public.

During the twenty-five years before the Civil War, southern leaders almost unanimously defended slavery. They did this whether they held slaves or not. The "proslavery argument" which they developed took various forms. One argument held that slavery could be justified because the Bible recognized it. Another held that it could be justified because blacks were naturally inferior to white people. The selections in Reading 38 explore the social, political, and economic arguments for slavery. As you read, consider these questions:

1. How did Fitzhugh and Senator Brown attempt to answer the criticism of the abolitionists?
2. To what extent would Mrs. Chesnut have agreed or disagreed with Fitzhugh's evaluation of slavery?

These pictures show a southern view of slaves and factory workers. What kinds of pictures would an abolitionist draw to portray the same thing?

BLACK AND WHITE SLAVES.

Slavery and the "Most Contented and Prosperous People on Earth"

George Fitzhugh was a Virginia slaveholder and a widely read proslavery writer. The following selection is taken from his book, Sociology for the South, *published in Richmond in 1854.*

George Fitzhugh, **Sociology for the South** (Richmond, Virginia: 1854), pp. 47-48.

In the slaveholding South all is peace, quiet, plenty, and contentment. We have no mobs, no trade unions, no strikes for higher wages, no armed resistance to the law, little jealousy of the rich by the poor. We have few in our jails, and fewer in our poor houses. We produce enough of the comforts and necessities of life for a population three or four times as numerous as ours. Population increases slowly, wealth rapidly. Wealth is more equally distributed than in the North. There a few millionaires own most of the property of the country. (These millionaires are men of cold hearts and weak minds. They know how to make money. But they do not know how to use it, either for the good of themselves or of others.) High intellectual and moral achievements, refinement of heads and heart, give status to a man in the South, however poor he may be. Money is, with few exceptions, the only thing that ennobles in the North. We have poor among us. But no one is over-worked and under-fed. We do not crowd cities because lands are abundant and their owners, kind, merciful, and hospitable. The poor are as hospitable as the rich, the Negro as the white man. Nobody dreams of turning a friend, a relative, or a stranger from his door. Our society shows no signs of decay. We see a long course of continuing improvement before us with no limits in sight. We have come closer than the free states to real liberty and equality among our white population. Few of our whites ever work as day laborers. None work in other menial jobs. One free citizen does not lord it over another. From this comes that feeling of independence and equality that distinguishes us, that pride of character, and self-respect, that gives us superiority when we come in contact with northerners. It is a distinction to be a southerner, as it was once to be a Roman citizen.

Until the last fifteen years, our great error was to imitate northern habits, customs, and institutions. Our circumstances are so different from theirs that whatever suits them is almost sure not to suit us. Until that time, in truth, we distrusted our social system. We thought slavery morally wrong. We thought it would not last. We thought it unprofitable. The Abolitionists assailed us. We looked more closely into our circumstances. We became satisfied that slavery was morally right, that it would continue to exist, that it was as profitable as it was humane. This gave us self-confidence, self-reliance. Since then our improvement has been rapid. Now we may safely say that we are the happiest, most contented and prosperous people on earth.

The Attitude of Non-Slaveholding Southerners Toward Slavery

Senator William H. Seward of New York argued in a Senate speech that the non-slaveholders in the South, who made up a majority of the white population, might be expected to oppose slavery. Senator Albert G. Brown of Mississippi answered Seward on December 22, 1856. Portions of his answer are given here.

There are, according to Senator Seward, 350,000 slaveholding aristocrats in the South. He says that they are men at war with liberty and dangerous to the republic. Only one out of every one hundred of the entire population owns slaves. If you include the children, relatives, and dependents of the slaveholders, he says that the ratio is one in fifteen. Consequently, fourteen out of every fifteen white southerners have no direct interest in slavery. The non-slaveholders, according to the Senator, are mere "hewers of wood and drawers of water" to the slaveholding aristocrats.

This opens a wide field for speculation. If the Senator expects by such appeals to turn the non-slaveholders against slavery, he will not be successful. They may have no financial interest in slavery, but they have a social interest at stake. And it is worth more to them than the wealth of all the Indies.

Suppose for the sake of argument that the Senator from New York should succeed in abolishing slavery. What would the social relationship between the two races then be in the South? Could they live together in peace? No one pretends to think that they could. Would the white man be allowed to maintain his superiority if the Negroes were free? Let us examine this question. In my state, there are about 350,000 whites and about an equal number of blacks. Suppose the Negroes were all set free. What would be the immediate and necessary consequence of that? A struggle for supremacy would follow immediately. No more white people would move into the state. The whites already there would have little reason to struggle in the unequal contest between them and the blacks with their millions of sympathizing friends in the free states. The result would be that the wealthy men would gather up their movable property and seek a home in some other country. The poor men, those of little means—the very men

Speeches, Messages, and Other Writings of Hon. Albert G. Brown, Michael W. Cluskey, ed. (Philadelphia: Jas. B. Smith and Company, 1859), pp. 484-485. Language simplified and modernized.

This biblical quotation is from **Joshua 9:21** and means menial workers or servants.

the Senator from New York relies on to aid him in carrying out his great scheme of emancipation—would alone be forced to remain behind. Their poverty, not their will, would compel them to stay in Mississippi.

In a few years, with no one going to the state, and thousands upon thousands leaving it in one steady stream, the present balance between the races would be, in a few years, some three, four, or five to one in favor of the blacks. In this state of things, it is not difficult to see what the white man's condition would be. If he were allowed to maintain his equality, he might think himself fortunate. Superiority would not be dreamed of. The Negroes, who would be vastly in the majority, would probably claim social superiority over the whites. If the white man, reduced to such a condition, were allowed to marry his sons to Negro wives, or his daughters to Negro husbands, he might bless his stars. If the Senator from New York expects the aid of non-slaveholders in the South in bringing about this state of social relationships, let me tell him that he is greatly mistaken.

A Southern Woman
Looks at Slavery

The following selections are taken from the diary of Mary Boykin Chesnut, mistress of a southern plantation. Her husband was a Civil War general. Mrs. Chesnut describes life in the South as it appeared to the mistress of a plantation.

A Diary from Dixie, Ben Ames Williams, ed. (Boston: Houghton Mifflin and Company, 1949), pp. 10, 11, 142.

She spends hours every day cutting out baby clothes for the Negro babies. This department is under her supervision. She puts little bundles of things to be made in everybody's work basket and calls it her sewing society. She is always ready with a full wardrobe for every newcomer. Then the mothers bring their children for her to prescribe and look after whenever they are sick. She is not at all nervous. She takes a baby and lances its gums quite coolly and scientifically. She dresses all hurts, bandages all wounds. These people are simply devoted to her, proving they can be grateful enough when you give them anything to be grateful for. Two women always sleep in her room in case she should be ill, or need any attention during the night. And two others sleep in the next room—to relieve guard, so to speak. When it is cold, she changes her night clothes. Before these women give her the second dress, they iron every garment to make sure that it is warm and dry enough. For this purpose, smoothing irons are always before the fire. And the fire is never allowed to go down while it is cool enough for the family to remain at Mulberry. During the summer at Sandy Hill it is exactly the same, except that

▶ Do you think every society will always have at least one group that claims it is superior to all the other groups? Why or why not?

▶ Do you think that the personal characteristics of the plantation mistress described by Mrs. Chesnut should be developed by all members of a society? Why or why not?

then she gets up and changes everything because it is so warm! It amounts to this. These people find it hard to invent ways of passing the time. And they have such a quantity of idle Negroes about them that some occupation for them must be found.

I have seen a Negro woman sold upon the block at auction. I was walking. The woman on the block overtopped the crowd. I felt faint, seasick. The creature looked so like my good little Nancy. She was a bright mulatto, with a pleasant face. She was magnificently gotten up in silks and satins. She seemed delighted with it all, sometimes ogling the bidders, sometimes looking quite coy and modest. But her mouth never relaxed from its expanded grin of excitement. I dare say the poor thing knew who would buy her. My very soul sickened. It was too dreadful. I tried to reason. "You know how women sell themselves and are sold in marriage, from queens downwards, eh? You know what the Bible says about slavery, and marriage. Poor women, poor slaves."

FOR THOUGHT:

What evidence did you find to support the hypotheses you have developed? Do you have additional hypotheses to advance? What do you now conclude about the impact of slavery on southern life?

39 A COTTON KINGDOM BUILT ON SLAVERY

HISTORICAL ESSAY

Slavery dominated the social, economic, and political life of the South before the Civil War. To understand what slavery was really like, it is necessary to distinguish between theory and practice.

Slavery in Theory and Practice

In theory, American slavery was extremely harsh. Some South American countries guaranteed slaves certain basic rights by law. But slaves in the United States had no rights. The law defined them as property rather than as persons. Americans considered the freedom of a person to control his or her property in his or her own way a basic right. So slaveholders could buy and sell slaves just as they could any other property. Slaves had no right to marry, to govern their own children, to learn to read or write, to worship as they pleased, or to sell their own labor.

In practice, slavery was probably not as severe. Slaves were valuable property. And common sense led most people to protect and care for their property. Moreover, both slaves and slaveowners frequently lived and worked together on close terms and developed strong ties of affection for each other.

On the other hand, the use of violence and brutality helped the slaveowners and overseers to wield absolute power over their slaves. Many masters controlled unruly slaves with the whip. But, no matter how barbarously an owner treated a slave, the slave had no legal recourse. His or her testimony against a white person could not be heard in court.

The Social Structure of the Pre-War South

It is impossible to understand life in the South before the Civil War without distinguishing between the South as it actually was and the romantic descriptions of the South given in the movies and the historical novels of the first half of the twentieth century. The stately mansion house attended by hundreds of faithful blacks, shielded by graceful magnolias, and surrounded by vast well-tended cotton fields was not entirely a myth. Such places did exist in the South. But they were even less common than millionaires' mansions are in today's society.

At the risk of some oversimplification, the free population of the South can be divided into five large social classes. The first group consisted of planters. They represented the top of the southern economic and social order. A person needed 20 slaves devoted to agriculture and a minimum of 500 to 1000 acres of land to belong in this elite class. The census of 1860 counted only about 46,000 planters. Of this number only about 2000 were large planters who owned 100 or more slaves. In the entire South in 1860, only 13 planters owned more than 500 slaves.

It is clear, therefore, that vast plantations are far more common in romantic legends than they ever were in historical fact. The great majority of planters lived simply on small plantations. But statistics cannot tell the whole story. The planters had an influence far greater than their numbers indicate. The large planters represented the social ideal for almost all white southerners. They came as close to being aristocrats as any people have in American history. They patterned their lives after the style of the English country gentry. And their distaste for commerce and industry helped to keep the South agricultural. In politics, they were the most important group in the South. Their political power rested on a sound economic base because the planters, large and small, produced most of the crops which the South sold to the North and in Europe.

Farmers were the largest group in the South. They were comparable to the middle class in the North. In states such as North Carolina and Louisiana, two thirds of all farms contained less than one hundred

▶ Do you think it is important for a society to have one group, such as the planters of the pre-Civil War South, to hold up as an ideal for the other groups in the society? Why or why not?

254

acres. Some farmers owned a few slaves and worked alongside them in the fields. But most farmers did not have enough capital to buy slaves. Usually, farmers owned their own land and lived in a two-room log house. They grew enough cotton or tobacco to get money for taxes and store-bought goods which they could not produce themselves. And they spent most of their energy raising food crops and livestock. These farmers were the backbone of the South. They were not as well educated as farmers in the North. But they were hardworking and ambitious. Some farmers were successful enough to buy slaves and become planters. Others left their farms to work as overseers on large plantations so that they might save money and start their own plantations. They were staunch defenders of slavery. And they made up the bulk of the Confederate Army after 1860.

Business and professional people made up a third class. Merchants were its most important members. They worked out of major southern cities and sold planters' crops for a commission. They also frequently helped planters to purchase supplies for the coming year. Many planters were constantly in debt to such merchants.

A small number of southern manufacturers made up a fourth group. Most of them were in the lumber, tobacco, textile, flour-milling, or iron industries. Their role was not nearly as important as that of manufacturers in the North. Industry was less developed in the South. At the time of the Civil War, for example, the town of Lowell, Massachusetts, had as much textile manufacturing machinery as the whole South. In addition, the southern industrialist, like the lawyer, doctor, and teacher, enjoyed less prestige than the planter.

Three kinds of people composed a final group. They were outside the mainstream of southern life. The first of these consisted of mountain people, who lived in isolated areas of the Appalachian and Ozark Mountains. They practiced a hardy, subsistence agriculture, spurned slavery almost entirely, and clung to traditional folkways. These mountain people were the one group that refused to support the Confederacy in the Civil War.

▶What, if any, benefits might a group or an individual derive from being outside the mainstream of the life of a society?

At the bottom of the white social ladder were the "poor whites." They numbered perhaps half a million people in 1850. They carried on a meager existence in squalid cabins on some of the most wornout land in the South. Energy-sapping diseases, such as hookworm and malaria, beat them down. And their most important characteristic was an unrelenting determination to keep black slaves in their place—at the absolute bottom of the southern social system.

Free blacks were most decisively outside the mainstream of southern life. They numbered about a quarter of a million before the Civil War. Some of them had been freed by their masters. Others were descendants of freed slaves. A few had been allowed to work, save money, and purchase their own freedom. Almost all free blacks lived hazardous lives. Laws limited their freedom to work, move around the country, or meet together. A few free blacks in the South prospered. Some even owned slaves. But the majority lived in poverty and an atmosphere of fear and suspicion. Free blacks had little place in a society based on black slavery.

The Cotton Kingdom

Agriculture provided the economic base for the southern way of life. In the upper South, farmers raised many different kinds of crops. Virginia still grew more tobacco than any other state. But it also produced large quantities of wheat. In 1850, the South grew more than half the nation's corn and four fifths of its peas and beans. But southern agriculture concentrated on the cultivation of staple crops for sale in the world market. Rice plantations dotted the coasts of Georgia and South Carolina. Sugar plantations flourished in lower Louisiana. Cotton, of course, was the greatest crop. Cotton fields spread from North Carolina to Texas.

The South earned its description as "The Cotton Kingdom." In 1820, the cotton crop was 160 million pounds. In the decades that followed, more and more people in Europe and America chose cotton over woolen and linen clothing. And the American cotton crop grew spectacularly. By 1860, the South grew over a billion pounds of cotton. This crop accounted for two thirds of all American exports.

Many of the great southern plantations were highly efficient agricultural units. However, increased cotton production resulted not from more efficient means of production, but from expanded acreage. From about 1820 until the outbreak of the Civil War, the center of the Cotton Kingdom moved steadily south and west to the new, rich soils of Alabama, Mississippi, Arkansas, and Texas. During the "Age of Jackson" speculators bought and sold land frenziedly. Nowhere was speculation more rampant than in the southern states. There people vied with each other to control valuable cotton land.

The expansion of cotton agriculture into the Southwest helped to fasten slavery even more tightly upon the South. As new lands opened to cultivation, the demand for slave labor increased. States in the upper South, such as Maryland, Virginia, Kentucky and Tennessee, found themselves caught up in a profitable domestic slave trade with the new cotton states. Estimates suggest that almost a half million slaves were moved from the upper to the lower South in the twenty years before the war. During this period, the price of a good field slave rose as high as $1700. And about 60 percent of all slaves worked on cotton plantations.

The Economic Impact of Slavery

Was slavery economically profitable for the South? Historians have argued this question for a long time. Without any doubt some southerners found slavery profitable. John H. Randolph bought a modest Louisiana plantation in 1841, with a down payment of $863. Before the outbreak of the Civil War, he had expanded his holdings to several thousand acres. He had increased his slaves from twenty-three to almost two hundred, and built an elegant fifty-one room mansion which still stands. Other southerners enjoyed similar successes, although usually on a smaller scale. People made fortunes buying and selling slaves. Some successful planters began as slave traders.

John H. Randolph (1773-1833) served in the House of Representatives and in the Senate. He was a bitter opponent of the Missouri Compromise.

Against this evidence historians have argued that because slaves had no personal economic incentives, they were bound to be inefficient workers. Because their masters controlled their working conditions and compensation absolutely, slaves were not encouraged to experiment with new, more efficient ways of work.

The evidence suggests, however, that the average well-run plantation could make a reasonable profit. Certainly slaveholders themselves thought slavery was profitable—an important reason they defended it so strongly.

At the same time, slavery had an unfavorable economic impact on the South in the long run. While cotton fields expanded in the South, factories expanded in the North. The South contributed vastly to the national wealth by producing the American commodity most in demand on the world market. But it still found itself dependent on the North. The South depended on the North for more than manufactured goods. Many planters shipped their cotton in northern ships through northern harbors. And they borrowed money from northern banks.

The Psychological Effects of Slavery

The psychological effects of slavery on the slave have been as important as the long-run economic consequences of slavery on the South. Slaves learned that complete subservience was their best path to self-preservation. Unlike many other Americans, slaves were not encouraged to be ambitious and self-reliant.

Slavery also influenced deeply the lives of white people in the South. After about 1830, most southern whites ceased to apologize for slavery. They began to defend it fiercely. The best minds in the South attempted to show that southern civilization based on slave labor was superior to northern civilization based on free labor. New England writers such as Emerson and Thoreau wrote essays and poems celebrating the values of equality and individualism. Southern novelists, such as William Gilmore Simms and William Caruthers, wrote novels celebrating the aristocratic quality of southern life. Southern planters referred to themselves as "cavaliers" after English aristocrats of the seventeenth century. They also copied many of the traditions of the old English aristocracy.

257

Southerners from lower levels of society also defended slavery. They feared that antislavery agitation would incite slaves to revolt, resulting in bloodshed and massacres. Although there were few slave revolts before the Civil War, this fact did not allay the white southerner's fears.

Lower class white people deeply feared that their own social and economic position would be threatened if blacks were freed. These poor whites lived in miserable conditions. But, as long as slavery existed, they could take comfort in not being at the bottom of society.

Southern Attitudes Affect Civil Liberties

These fears led the South to take severe measures in the years before the Civil War to protect itself from all criticism of slavery. Southern states passed laws making it a crime to write or speak against slavery or to have antislavery literature. Mails were censored.

And mobs frequently attacked individuals suspected of holding antislavery views and drove them from the South. Such measures were "democratic" in the sense that the great majority of southerners supported them. At the same time, the South, because of its position on slavery, denied its citizens basic civil liberties.

The denial of these liberties also occurred, to a lesser degree, in the North. Opponents of the abolitionists mobbed antislavery meetings in attempts to break them up.

As the abolitionists grew more numerous and more vocal, southerners retreated into angry and frightened isolation. They felt that their property was under attack. Moreover, they did not believe that they could ever live together in peace and harmony with a free black population. The issue of slavery became a problem not only in the South. It became an American problem.

National Growth and Its Effect
on the Environment

STATING THE ISSUE

During the first half of the nineteenth century, American population increased more than 30 percent every ten years. European immigrants supplemented the rapidly growing native population. Established cities in the East grew at an astonishing rate, while new cities sprang up in the West. The market economy, which had begun to develop after the War of 1812, expanded rapidly in the 1840's and 1850's. Railroads began to link the nation together. The development of new factories and new machinery expanded economic opportunities. Products from American farms and factories played an increasingly important role in world trade.

Americans also continued to push westward. In the 1840's, they built large settlements on the shores of the Pacific Ocean. They began to press upon the Mexican border in the Southwest and the British border in Oregon. Many Americans believed that their flag was destined to fly over the entire continent.

Americans responded to the pace and pattern of national growth in different ways. Most believed that the nation's growth demonstrated the effectiveness of democratic institutions. They felt this growth heralded the future greatness of the nation. Others feared that Americans were ignoring the need to preserve the natural beauty and resources of the continent in their reckless rush for land and wealth. Still others worried that continued expansion would strengthen sectional differences and eventually cause the break-up of the Union.

The first three readings in Chapter 11 analyze the ways in which the nation expanded between 1840 and 1860. They also relate this expansion to new ecological problems. The historical essay at the end of the chapter describes the growth of the United States at mid-century.

1836 Mexican army defeats Texans at Alamo

1836 Sam Houston becomes president of Republic of Texas

1836 Ralph Waldo Emerson gives famous lecture "The American Scholar"

1844 James K. Polk is elected President

1845 Texas enters the Union

1846 United States declares war on Mexico

1846 Oregon Treaty sets boundary of United States and Canada at 49th parallel

1847–54 Crop failures in Europe cause thousands of Irish and Germans to emigrate to America

1848 Treaty of Guadalupe Hidalgo ends war with Mexico

1848 Zachary Taylor is elected President

1850 Nathaniel Hawthorne publishes **The Scarlet Letter**

1850 President Taylor dies; Millard Fillmore becomes President

1850 California joins the Union

1851 Herman Melville publishes **Moby Dick**

1853 Congress approves Gadsden Purchase from Mexico

1854 Henry David Thoreau publishes **Walden**

1864 George Perkins Marsh publishes **Man and Nature**

40 PROBLEMS OF GROWTH

In the two hundred years since the Revolution, the United States has grown at a spectacular rate. This growth involved territorial expansion, an increasing population, and the development of the most productive agricultural and industrial system in the world.

Most Americans assumed that growth was good because it meant more prosperity for more people. In recent years, however, many have begun to question the benefits of unlimited growth. They argue that communities which grow rapidly without proper planning frequently end up in conflict. Moreover, these communities often cannot provide people with basic necessities such as clean air, pure water, adequate housing, and sound sanitary systems. In other words, rapid growth makes it more difficult for people to relate to each other and to their natural environment.

Around 1840, the United States entered a period of new expansiveness. Reading 40 will give you an idea of the scope and implications of American growth during this period. Study questions accompany each excerpt in the reading.

Assessing Growth: Some Data

U.S. Bureau of the Census, A Compendium of the Ninth Census, June 1, 1870 (Washington, D.C.: Government Printing Office, 1872), pp. 8-9.

		FIGURE 40A	**U.S. POPULATION DISTRIBUTION BY REGIONS, 1840-1860**					
	Total U.S. Population	*South*		*West*		*Northeast*		
Year	(does not include territories)	Population	% of Total Pop.	Population	% of Total Pop.	Population	% of Total Pop.
1840	17,019,641	4,749,875	27.9	4,960,580	29.1	7,309,186	42.9
1850	23,067,262	6,271,237	27.2	7,494,608	32.5	9,301,417	40.3
1860	31,183,744	7,993,531	25.6	11,796,680	37.8	11,393,533	36.5

1. What happened to total population?
2. Which region gained population most rapidly?
3. Might people in any of these regions have felt threatened by the population trends? Why?

U.S. Bureau of the Census, Statistical View of the United States; A Compendium of the Seventh Census (Washington, D.C.: Government Printing Office, 1854), p. 61.

FIGURE 40B   MIGRATION WITHIN THE STATES, 1850

	Population Born in State	Population Born in Other States	Population Born Outside U.S.	Total
Northern Seaboard				
Connecticut	284,978	39,117	38,374	383,099
Massachusetts	679,624	139,419	163,598	985,450
New York	2,092,076	296,754	655,224	3,048,325
Pennsylvania	1,787,310	165,966	303,105	2,258,160
Midwest				
Illinois	331,089	399,733	111,860	846,034
Indiana	520,583	398,695	55,537	977,154
Michigan	137,637	201,586	54,593	395,071
Ohio	1,203,490	529,208	218,099	1,955,050
South				
Georgia	394,979	119,587	6,452	521,572
North Carolina	529,483	20,784	2,565	553,028
South Carolina	253,399	12,601	8,508	274,563
Virginia	813,891	57,502	22,953	894,800

1. To which states did Americans move in large numbers?
2. Which states received large numbers of immigrants?
3. How might these migration trends affect sectional attitudes and loyalties?

U.S. Bureau of the Census,
A Compendium of the U.S.
Census for 1850 and A
Compendium of the Ninth
Census, June 1, 1870
(Washington, D.C.:
Government Printing Office,
1872), pp. 40, 798-799.

FIGURE 40C   PERSONAL INCOME PER CAPITA BY REGIONS, 1840-1860°

Regions	1840	1860
Northeast	135%	139%
North Central	68%	68%
South	76%	72%

°Per capita personal income is shown in percentages with the average income for the country considered to be 100%.

1. In which areas were people becoming more prosperous? less prosperous?
2. How might these trends in personal income affect some sectional attitudes?

American Economic History,
Seymour E. Harris, ed. (New
York: McGraw-Hill Book
Company, 1961), p. 528.

FIGURE 40D   AMERICANS EMPLOYED IN MANUFACTURING, 1840-1860

Persons Employed in Manufacturing

	1840	1850	1860
Northern Seaboard			
Connecticut	27,932	50,731	64,469
Massachusetts	85,176	177,461	217,421
New York	173, 193	199,349	230,112
Pennsylvania	105,883	146,766	222,132
Midwest			
Illinois	13,185	11,559	22,968
Indiana	20,590	14,440	21,295
Michigan	6,890	9,344	23,190
Ohio	66,265	51,491	75,602
South			
Georgia	7,984	8,368	11,575
North Carolina	14,322	14,601	14,217
South Carolina	10,325	7,066	6,994
Virginia	54,147	29,110	36,174

1. Which states had the largest numbers of workers employed in manufacturing? the smallest?
2. Which states gained the most workers in manufacturing between 1840 and 1860? Which states lost workers?
3. How might this pattern of employment affect sectional interests and attitudes?

262

A passenger pigeon hunt

Carrier pigeon population in 1800 (est.) _ _ _ _ _ 5,000,000,000

Carrier pigeon population in 1914 _ _ _ _ _ _ _ _ _ _ _ _ _ _ 0
(The last carrier pigeon, Martha,
died in the Cincinnati Zoo in 1914)

Buffalo population in the seventeenth century (est.) _ _ _ _ _ 60,000,000

Buffalo population in 1884 (est.) _ _ _ _ _ _ _ _ _ _ _ _ _ _ _ Several hundred

▶What reason, if any, can you give that people should not kill all the animals they want to if the animals are in plentiful supply?

A buffalo hunt

U. S. Bureau of the Census, **Sixteenth Census of the United States Population** (Washington, D.C.: Government Printing Office, 1942), Vol. I, p. 20.

FIGURE 40E	PERCENTAGE OF POPULATION LIVING IN CITIES BY REGIONS, 1840-1860		
Area	**1840**	**1850**	**1860**
Northeast	18.8%	27.2%	36.0%
North Central	3.9%	9.7%	13.8%
South	4.9%	7.0%	8.7%

1. What areas of the country had the largest percentage of people living in cities? the smallest?
2. Which area gained the largest percentage of urban dwellers? the smallest?
3. What do these data suggest about sectional differences?

The Use of Resources

Clement Eaton, **History of the Old South** (New York: The Macmillan Company, 1966), pp. 21-22.

Tobacco was planted for four or five years in succession in the same field. This practice exhausted the fertility of the soil, but brought quick returns. Such rapid exploitation of the land, as well as the ravages of erosion, led to the abandonment of old fields and the clearing of new fields. This wasteful, frontier method of agriculture was followed primarily because of the high cost of labor and the large reserves of land in America. It was not because of ignorance or carelessness. Nevertheless, it had bad results. Every planter realized the need to acquire extensive reserves of land. This need led to the growth of lonely plantations and the scattering of population. Consequently, the tobacco planters marched slowly to the West. They left behind them abandoned tobacco fields that in time became covered with pine trees and broom grass. By the time of the Revolution much of Tidewater Virginia and Maryland had been left in a state of desolation.

Tidewater Virginia is the area along the coast.

FIGURE 40F	LUMBER PRODUCTION IN THOUSANDS OF BOARD FEET
Year	**Production**
1829	850,000
1839	1,604,000
1849	5,392,000
1859	8,029,000

1. How rapidly did the production of lumber grow?
2. In which decade did lumber production increase most rapidly?

FOR THOUGHT:

How long could growth such as this go on without creating problems?

41 WESTWARD EXPANSION AND ECOLOGY

In the 1820's, the western line of American settlement extended to the Missouri River. By 1853, today's boundaries of the continental United States had been reached, and most of the area between the Atlantic coast and the Mississippi River had numerous settlers. Reading 41 focuses on the relationship between this period of spectacular expansion and the later awareness of some ecological problems.

In recent years Americans have become increasingly concerned with environmental problems. City dwellers worry about air and water pollution. Those who live in the country are concerned about the possible harmful side effects of pesticides and chemical fertilizers. And almost everyone has read about or been affected by the shortages in essential resources, such as natural gas and petroleum.

Although environmental, or ecological, problems seem new, their roots go deep into American history. Since the first settlements in Virginia and Massachusetts, Americans have been changing their natural environment in radical ways. The two excerpts in Reading 41 will help you to understand some of these early changes and their effect on today's environment. The first excerpt explains what it was like to have been a hunter when the American forest was still unspoiled. The second excerpt connects American behavior on the frontier with environmental problems today. As you read, think about the following questions:

1. What was the factual basis for the hunter's "tall story"?
2. In what ways was life on the frontier wasteful? How do you account for that wastefulness?

The Unmatched Bounty of the Land

Nothing in their European experience had prepared the early settlers for the rich and apparently endless stretches of American forest. In this selection, a modern historian recreates what it must have been like to live and hunt in that forest.

266

What attitudes toward the environment do each of these pictures show?

Richard G. Lillard, **The Great Forest** (New York: Alfred A. Knopf, Inc., 1948), pp. 39-40.

▶ Does your family have special times to swap stories or experiences, perhaps at dinner or in the evening on a summer vacation? If so, what do these times add to your life?

The Cumberland Gap is an opening in the Cumberland Mountains where Virginia, Tennessee, and Kentucky meet.

Now was the time of day for leisurely hours of hunting anecdotes, factual or exaggerated, tales of adventure that amazed or frightened settlers straight from sober European countrysides and thrilled young boys. In the seventeenth century five Virginians in three or four days killed and salted sixty deer, while shooting freely at turkeys in flocks of four to five hundred. In the next century, six men exploring in the Cumberland Gap country over a three-month period killed thirteen buffalo, eight elk, fifty-three bear, twenty deer, four geese, one hundred and fifty turkeys, and uncounted rabbits, squirrels, and small game birds. "We might have killed three times as much meat, if we had wanted it." One Pennsylvania hunter, when he was a boy of thirteen, shot a panther fourteen feet long from the end of the nose to the end of the tail. By middle age, this hunter had killed three thousand deer, five or six hundred bear, hundreds of panthers, wolves, and wildcats, and many thousands of turkey and rabbit. As late as 1864, when a New Yorker asked a man near Raquette Lake in the Adirondacks how many deer he had killed in the past year, the answer came: "Well, about two hundred. The wolves were so thick, that they drove them away." A man in Alabama remembered: "Many a time I've kilt seventy-five or eighty squirrels out of one big beech tree." A squatter in Arkansas said he wouldn't kill a turkey under forty pounds. Once he shot one so fat that it couldn't fly far, "and when he fell out of the tree, after I had shot him, on striking the ground he bust open . . ."

Good storytellers converted fact into yarns. And tales by hunters like John Darling of New York, Davy Crockett of West Tennessee, and John Lybrook of the Valley of Virginia, or tales about hunters, entered into the lore of the area. . . . One old Vermont hunter told a story common, with local variations, from the Green Mountains [which are in Vermont] to the Ozarks [which are in Missouri, Arkansas, and eastern Oklahoma].

I was once passing down the banks of the Hudson, in search of game, and suddenly heard a crackling on the opposite bank. Looking across the river, I saw a stately buck, and instantly drew up and let fly at him. The very moment a huge sturgeon leaped from the river in the direction of my shot. The ball went through him and passed on. I flung down my gun—threw off my coat and hat, and swam for the floating fish, which I towed to shore, and went to see what more my shot had done for me. I found it had passed through the heart of the deer, and struck into a hollow tree beyond; where the honey was running out like a river! I sprung round to find something to stop the hollow with, and caught hold of a white rabbit. It squeaked like a stuck pig. So I thrust it away from me in a passion at the disappointment, and it went with such force that it killed three cock partridges and a wood cock!!!

268

The Wasteful Settler

Ever since the late nineteenth century, American historians have evaluated the influence of the frontier on American history. Until recently, most historical writing emphasized the positive effect of the frontier in shaping democratic institutions. The tendency today is to point out the harmful as well as the beneficial effects of the frontier experience. In the following selection, a modern historian gives his views on the influence of the frontier.

The quest for wealth on America's frontiers contributed to the emergence of another national trait that has [lasted] into the twentieth century: flagrant wastefulness. No other western nation of the twentieth century so recklessly squanders its resources, or so heedlessly destroys its own creations. The United States, to visiting foreigners, is the land of the throwaway; paper handkerchiefs and paper plates, metal cans and plastic containers, no-deposit-no-return bottles are all made to be used once, then discarded. To a thrifty European the American factory is an assembly line to produce gadgets that will disintegrate after short use. The American home [is] a reverse assembly line to reduce those gadgets to basic rubble as rapidly as possible. In Britain a man prides himself on the vintage of his car, in America on its recency. Europeans will never cease to be shocked by the extravagant waste of paper bags in an American supermarket, or by the reckless manner in which nearly new machinery is thrown into the dump heap to make room for something better. They are equally astounded by the reluctance of the United States to preserve its dwindling resources, for not until the twentieth century did a conservation movement attract popular support. Even today, nature's bounties are squandered with an abandon unknown in other lands.

Wastefulness came naturally to the frontiersman. Who would think of preservation amidst overwhelming abundance? . . . Why protect trees in a land where they grew by the billions? Why preserve soil when a move to virgin fields was cheaper than fertilizer? To these questions the pioneer had obvious answers. "Nothing on the face of the broad Earth is sacred to him," wrote an Englishman from the Far West. . . . So the frontiersman felled forests, mined the soil with his wasteful farming methods, slaughtered game, honeycombed mountains with his mining shafts, overcropped pasturage with his herds, drained lakes, and altered the landscape as he moved in quest of wealth.

On the forested frontiers, trees were particular enemies, symbolizing the wilderness that must be destroyed. "He seems to have declared war on the whole species," observed a French traveler in 1817. "He

Roy A. Billington, **America's Frontier Heritage** (Albuquerque: University of New Mexico Press, 1966), pp. 168-170.

▶ Suppose a company owned a mountain covered with trees. Should it be allowed to cut down all those trees? Why or why not?

269

does not spare a single one." All fell before his ax: trees needed for windbreaks, trees that added beauty to the countryside, trees that would have provided cooling shade in summer, even maple groves that would have yielded sweets for the community. Travelers along the Old National Road that after 1818 linked the seaboard and the Ohio River complained of the bleakness of the countryside after the pioneers had passed on, leaving a desolate plain behind them. . . .

The soils of America suffered the same fate. With land cheap and both labor and fertilizers expensive, pioneers discovered that they could economize by plundering the soil through successive plantings, then move on. . . . Soils were depleted so rapidly that their exhaustion was a primary factor in the westward movement. . . ."Now lands which at one time would yield 30 to 40 bushels of wheat to the acre," wrote a Wisconsinite in the 1870's, "cannot be depended upon to yield 10 or 12." Oldtimers in Nebraska, so the story goes, used to brag to younger men: "Why, son, by the time I was your age I had wore out three farms."

. . . Today reforestation has restored damaged hillsides, and chemical fertilizers have revitalized butchered soils, but exploitive tendencies were too firmly embedded to be abandoned with the passing of the frontier. . . . Today's Texan who throws away his Cadillac because the ash trays need cleaning (to quote a modern tall tale) differs only in degree from the Kentucky farmer who told a traveler in 1818 that he was moving to new land rather than carry away the pile of manure that had accumulated near his barn. Today's American who wastes half his plateful of food (or asks for a "Doggie Pack" for the remainder) is comparable to the Ohio landlord who invited a stranger to eat all he wanted without charge as the whole bountiful table was to be thrown away. Abundance encourages a modern generation to perpetuate the wasteful habits that abundance bred into the pioneers.

FOR THOUGHT:

How has the unique history of America encouraged a wasteful approach to the use of resources?

42 THE EMERGENCE OF A CONSERVATIONIST TRADITION

Although conservation did not become an important political movement until about 1900, the ideological roots of the movement

270

go back into the nineteenth century. Most Americans welcomed the remarkable material progress which the nation began to achieve after 1815. But there were some doubters—critics who felt the price was too great. Some argued that Americans were so anxious to find wealth and power that they ignored nature as a moral and spiritual resource. They felt Americans manipulated nature primarily for personal gain. Others were concerned with the physical results of rapid growth. The slaughter of wildlife and the apparently careless reduction of American forests worried them.

The first selection in Reading 42 is taken from the work of Henry David Thoreau, the Transcendentalist whom you read about in Chapter 9. The second selection is from the work of George Perkins Marsh, a talented New England scholar. In the middle of the nineteenth century, Marsh formulated many of the principles which later

▶This picture was taken in Grand Teton National Park, a national park where the wilderness has been preserved. How much does access to the wilderness mean to you? Should the government try to preserve wilderness areas or should it permit lumbering in all of the national parks?

provided a foundation for the science of ecology. As you read, consider the following questions:

1. Why did Thoreau place so much value on his life in the woods?
2. According to Marsh, how did people disturb nature? How should people cooperate with nature to correct the harm that had been done?

A Transcendental View of Nature

In 1845 Henry David Thoreau, a surveyor, pencil-maker, poet, and graduate of Harvard College, built a small cabin on the edge of Walden Pond near Concord, Massachusetts. He lived alone in the cabin for two years. In 1854 he published a book about his experiences. The following selection is taken from his book.

Henry David Thoreau, **Walden or Life in the Woods** (Boston: Houghton Mifflin Company, 1896), pp. 202-204, 206-207, 216. Language simplified and modernized.

▶How much does contact with nature mean to you? Could it mean more?

This is a delicious evening. As I walk along the stony shore of the pond in my shirt-sleeves, all the elements are unusually friendly to me. The bullfrogs trump to usher in the night, and the note of the whip-poor-will is borne on the rippling wind from over the water. Sympathy with the fluttering alder and poplar leaves almost takes away my breath. Yet, like the lake, my serenity is rippled but not ruffled. These small waves raised by the evening wind are as remote from storm as the smooth reflecting surface. Though it is now dark, the wind still blows and roars in the wood, the waves still dash, and some creatures lull the rest with their notes. The repose is never complete. The wildest animals do not repose, but seek their prey now. The fox, and skunk, and rabbit, now roam the fields and woods without fear. They are Nature's watchmen—links which connect the days of animated life.

For what reason have I this vast range of forest abandoned to me by men? My nearest neighborhood is a mile away, and no house is visible from any place but the hill-tops.

For the most part it is as deserted where I live as on the prairies. It is as much Asia or Africa as New England. I have, as it were, my own sun and moon and stars, and a little world all to myself.

In the midst of a gentle rain, I was suddenly aware of the sweet and kind society in Nature. The fancied advantages of human neighborhood became insignificant, and I have never thought of them since. Every little pine needle expanded and swelled with sympathy and befriended me. I was so aware of something kindred to me, even

272

in scenes which we are accustomed to call wild and dreary. I thought no place could ever be strange to me again.

The innocence and generosity of Nature—of sun and wind and rain, of summer and winter—such health, such cheer, they afford forever! And such sympathy they have with our race. Shall I not have intelligence with the earth? Am I not partly leaves and vegetable mould myself?

George Perkins Marsh and the Beginnings of Ecology

In 1864 Marsh published his views on the environment in a book entitled Man and Nature. *At a time of abundant natural resources, most Americans found his warnings exaggerated. Marsh did more than focus on the errors of the past, however. Most of* Man and Nature *was concerned with ecology. He discussed the balance of nature and pointed out how all things in nature are interrelated. If people disturbed any part of nature, they could upset the balance. Marsh's arguments are summarized in the following excerpt.*

Careless use of land destroys the balance of nature and leads to new problems. When forests are cleared at random, the moisture stored in them evaporates. This moisture returns to earth in the form of heavy rains that wash away the remains of the land surface. Thus, well-wooded hills become ridges of dry rock. Debris from these ridges are washed into the rivers and streams of lowland areas. Unless land is saved from such destruction, it soon becomes a wasteland of barren hills and swamps. Land surface in Asia Minor, North Africa, Greece, and even parts of Alpine Europe has been completely worn away in this manner by centuries of overuse.

Because of the rapid destruction of its resources, the earth will soon be unlivable. Continued abuse will result in a decline of the productivity of the land, and may eventually threaten the existence of the human race.

Limits should be placed on the reckless hunting of smaller wild birds. Many of these birds have no value as food. Instead, they render an important service by checking the spread of millions of insect pests. Insects themselves, if their numbers are kept in balance, play an indispensable role. For example, the trout feeds on mosquitoes. These fish also prey upon the May fly which is most destructive to young salmon. Trout cannot survive without mosquitoes. Thus, the destruction of the trout's main food supply also threatens the survival of the salmon.

George P. Marsh, **The Earth as Modified by Human Action: A New Edition of Man and Nature** (New York: Scribner, Armstrong and Company, 1874), pp. 43-44, 50, 124-125, 139. Language simplified and modernized.

▶What difference does it make if people learn to think of themselves as part of nature rather than as outside of nature and superior to it?

People must become co-workers with nature to repair the damage that has been done. To reclaim wasteland, people must work with nature to overcome the damage caused by misuse of the land. Forests should be replanted. By absorbing the excess water, these trees will protect the land from floods. Rivers and streams will then return to their natural levels.

FOR THOUGHT:

How are the ideas of Thoreau and Marsh related to the developments you read about in Readings 40 and 41?

43 THE GROWTH OF AMERICA AT MID-CENTURY

HISTORICAL ESSAY

As the American people approached the disaster of secession and Civil War, they lived in the world's most prosperous and rapidly growing nation. This essay discusses economic, cultural, and territorial growth in that nation from about 1840 to 1860.

The annual value of manufactures in America practically doubled between 1850 and 1860. Industry, however, had been growing steadily throughout the century. After the War of 1812, the total annual value of manufactured goods produced in America had been less than $200 million. By 1859, the northeastern states alone produced goods worth more than $1 billion.

Population Growth and Mobility

The rapid increase of factory production was related to the growth and mobility of the American population. From 1800 to 1850, American population increased more than 30 percent every ten years. Large numbers of this increasing population moved from east to west and from country to city.

The arrival of great numbers of European immigrants swelled the population figures and added to the movement of people within the country. During the 1830's, only about 500,000 immigrants came to this country. During the 1840's, this number tripled to over 1,500,000. And during the 1850's, it climbed to about 2,500,000. Most of the immigrants came from Ireland and from Germany. The majority of the Irish settled in cities on the eastern seaboard where most of them worked as factory hands or as day laborers. Many of the Germans moved to the Midwest where they became farmers or merchants.

American Ingenuity and Enterprise

Population growth can weaken the economy of a country that has limited natural and capital resources. In the United States with its vast resources, population growth spurred economic growth. More people worked to produce more goods for a constantly expanding domestic market.

During the 1850's, thousands of Americans decorated their parlors with a steel engraving entitled "Men of Progress." This engraving included the portraits of American scientists and inventors, such as those listed in Figure 43A. In the 1700's, America had to rely on imported talents, such as those of Samuel Slater. Slater left England secretly to help build textile machinery in Rhode Island. By the 1850's, the United States had become a world leader in many fields of technology. At the London Exhibition of 1851, American machines made a tremendous impression. Many Europeans sent special commissioners across the Atlantic to study some of the American methods of manufacturing.

FIGURE 43A   INVENTIONS AND DISCOVERIES BEFORE 1860

Inventor or Discoverer	Date	Contribution
Eli Whitney	1793	cotton gin
	1798	interchangeable parts
Robert Fulton	1807	steamboat
Peter Cooper	1830	locomotive
Cyrus H. McCormick	1831	reaper
Charles Goodyear	1839	vulcanization of rubber
Samuel F. B. Morse	1844	telegraph
Elias Howe	1846	sewing machine
Richard Hoe	1846	rotary printing press
William Morton	1846	ether
William Kelly	1851	Kelly process of converting pig iron into steel
Elisha Otis	1852	passenger elevator (made skyscrapers possible)
Edwin Drake	1859	oil drilling

American technology helps to explain the expansion of American industry before the Civil War. In popular terms, Americans believed this technological success was due to "Yankee ingenuity" or "American know-how." Historians do not agree on a precise explanation. Most historians believe that the explosion in technology reflected the fact that the United States usually had fewer workers than its industries needed. Therefore, Americans welcomed labor-saving devices. Another explanation is that Americans valued new ways of doing things because they lived in a new country. They preferred to give up

▶Do you admire people who can make or fix things? Why or why not?

traditional ways of doing things. Some believed that American education explained the efficiency and cleverness of the American worker. Whatever the explanation, Europeans considered American tools far superior to their own. Many artisans emigrating to America left their tools at home.

The growth of a national railroad system was the most spectacular aspect of the American industrial revolution before the Civil War. Railroads expanded the market for agricultural and manufactured products. They also increased the value of property. The railroads represented the largest industrial investment in the country before the Civil War. By 1860, private investors in America and Europe, and federal, state, and local governments invested over a billion dollars in railroads. The federal government also aided railroad construction by granting federal land along the right-of-way to the railroad companies. The construction and maintenance of the railroads helped to spur the growth of the iron and steel industry and, in turn, to support the entire industrial enterprise.

Industrialization Creates a Working Class

The growth, mobility, attitudes, and education of the American people influenced the development of industry. The city and factory also made great changes in people's lives. Most of the unskilled laborers and factory workers came from unsuccessful farms or were European immigrants. The immigrants, especially the Irish, did most of the heavy construction work in building canals, railroads, and factories. They lived in crude shanties on the fringes of construction projects or in the worst parts of the cities.

For skilled workers, two systems of labor were used in most factories. One, practiced in the textile mills of Lowell and Waltham, Massachusetts, employed young farm girls. The girls lived in supervised boardinghouses. They usually worked for a few years, saved their money, and then returned to their homes to get married. The second labor system employed whole families—father, mother, and young children—to tend the looms.

▶ Would you rather work at a leisurely pace for twelve hours or at a very rapid pace for eight? Why?

Today, working conditions before the Civil War seem hard and wages low. Men, women, and children worked twelve to fifteen hours a day. Skilled workers earned four to ten dollars a week. Unskilled workers, including many women and children, earned one to six dollars a week. Yet working conditions and wages in America were better than in Europe.

Industrialization, nevertheless, changed American society. A distinct working class developed during the period. Class lines remained flexible. But the unpropertied industrial worker and city dweller became a normal part of American society.

276

An American Literature

Along with the growth of the economy, an American literature began to develop. In the early 1800's, educated Americans complained that most American writers imitated English novels. James Fenimore Cooper was the first American novelist to concentrate on American themes. Two of his books, *The Last of the Mohicans* and *The Deerslayer*, dramatized the role of the pioneer and Indian in the American wilderness. Cooper's popularity began in the 1820's. But few writers of his time displayed equal talent.

By the 1850's, this criticism of American literature was no longer true. Between 1850 and 1855 some of the most famous works in the history of American literature appeared. Nathaniel Hawthorne wrote *The Scarlet Letter* and *The House of the Seven Gables*. Herman Melville wrote *Moby Dick* and Henry David Thoreau published *Walden*. At this time, Walt Whitman also wrote *Leaves of Grass*, one of the most important volumes of poetry written by an American.

These writers were major literary artists. They often criticized American society. Hawthorne and Melville, for example, believed that Americans placed too much value on individual progress. They felt Americans should develop a greater sense of community. Thoreau and Whitman criticized the American desire for money and material possessions. None of these writers approved of slavery. They aimed to make great literature out of the American experience and to uphold the values of human dignity and freedom. With the publication of their works in the 1850's, the American nation expressed its cultural Declaration of Independence.

Territorial Expansion

Finally, the United States expanded its national boundaries between 1830 and 1850. In theory, the 30,000 American settlers living in Texas in 1830 were Mexicans, subject to Mexican law. Actually, they thought of themselves as Americans. They objected to Mexican restrictions upon their rights. In April 1830, the Mexican government prohibited slavery in Texas and any further settlement of Americans. During the next few years, relationships between the colonists and the Mexican government worsened. By 1835, the Texans had decided to secede from Mexico. Both sides raised armies. In February 1836, at the siege of the Alamo, the Mexican army overwhelmed and massacred the Texans' small force. The heroic stand of the Texans gained them the support of millions of Americans. Later that year, the Texan army under Sam Houston defeated the Mexicans at San Jacinto near Galveston Bay. In October 1836, Houston became president of the Republic of Texas. Both Texans and Americans then called for Congress to annex Texas to the United States.

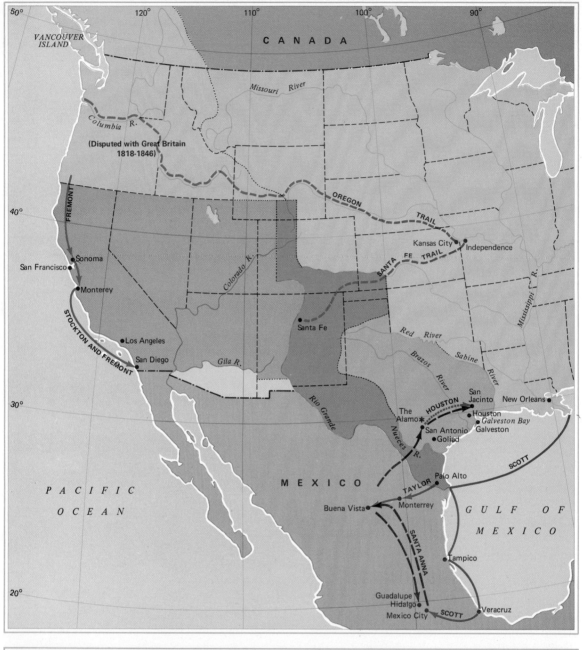

50°

VANCOUVER
ISLAND

120°   110°   100°   90°

C A N A D A

Missouri   River

Columbia   R.

(Disputed with Great Britain
1818-1846)

40°

FREMONT

OREGON

TRAIL

SANTA   FE   TRAIL

Kansas City

Independence

San Francisco
Sonoma

Monterey

STOCKTON AND FREMONT

Los Angeles

San Diego

Colorado R.

Gila R.

30°

Rio Grande

Santa Fe

Red   River

Brazos
River

Sabine
River

Nueces R.

HOUSTON
San
Jacinto

New Orleans

The
Alamo *

Houston
Galveston Bay
Galveston

San Antonio
Goliad

Mississippi   R.

PACIFIC

OCEAN

M E X I C O

TAYLOR

Palo Alto

SCOTT

GULF   OF

MEXICO

Buena Vista

Monterrey

SANTA ANNA

Tampico

20°

Guadalupe
Hidalgo
Mexico City

SCOTT

Veracruz

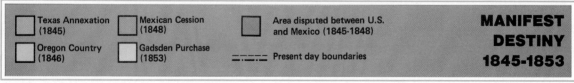

Texas Annexation
(1845)

Mexican Cession
(1848)

Oregon Country
(1846)

Gadsden Purchase
(1853)

Area disputed between U.S.
and Mexico (1845-1848)

Present day boundaries

**MANIFEST
DESTINY
1845-1853**

Many Americans opposed the annexation of Texas, however. Jackson was President in 1836 when the issue was first raised. He personally favored annexation. But he did not want to take any action that might result in war with Mexico or divide the Democratic party. A split in the Democratic party was a real possibility. Many people in the North believed that annexation was a southern plot to expand slave territory.

For the next eight years, the Texans' problem simmered. President Van Buren avoided the issue. John Tyler, who became President in 1841 when William Henry Harrison died after one month in office, arranged for a secret annexation treaty with Texas. However, the antislavery forces in the Senate defeated the treaty.

Meanwhile, Americans colonized the Far West. Since 1818, the Oregon country had been occupied jointly by the United States and Great Britain. Oregon had not attracted settlers as quickly as Texas, however. It was too far away to attract people at first. By 1840, only a few hundred Americans lived in Oregon. Most of them were missionaries and trappers. In the early 1840's, however, large numbers of pioneers began the long trek to the rich farm lands in the Pacific Northwest. As American settlement increased, so did American interest in solving the dispute over ownership of Oregon. Both England and America had good claims to the territory. America's claim went back to the Lewis and Clark expedition of 1803-1806. Many expansionists believed that America had a manifest destiny to spread its institutions the length and breadth of the continent. They insisted that Americans push as far north as the 54th parallel, several hundred miles above the present border with Canada. These expansion-minded patriots adopted the slogan "54°40′ or fight!"

Texas and Oregon

At the time of the 1844 election, much of the political debate centered on the Texas and Oregon questions. The Whigs had become disgusted with President Tyler because of his unwillingness to support their programs. They nominated Henry Clay. Meanwhile, the Democrats had their own problems. Neither of their two leading candidates, former President Martin Van Buren and Lewis Cass of Michigan, could win enough votes for the nomination. Finally, the Democrats settled on James K. Polk of Tennessee as a compromise candidate. Polk campaigned on a platform which called for the annexation of Texas and insisted on American claims to the Oregon territory. He won in a very close election.

Polk came into office determined to resolve the Texas and Oregon questions to the advantage of the United States. Just before his inauguration in 1845, Congress approved the admission of Texas into the United States. With the Texas issue apparently out of the way,

Polk turned to Oregon. He made an offer of a compromise boundary along the 47th parallel to the British. When they rejected his offer, he claimed the whole Oregon territory. For a while, war between the United States and Britain seemed likely. Finally, in June 1846, both countries agreed to divide the territory along the 49th parallel. Britain, however, kept Vancouver Island.

War with Mexico

The settlement with Britain came at a fortunate time. The United States had declared war with Mexico on May 13, 1846. When Texas had declared its independence from Mexico, it claimed the Rio Grande as its western boundary. The accepted Texas boundary had been the Nueces River. This boundary was farther east than the Rio Grande. (See map, p. 278.) In 1845, Polk had sent an army to the Rio Grande to support the Texans' claim. He had also sent a minister to Mexico to offer to pay certain debts the Mexican government owed Americans. He hoped that Mexico would accept this offer in exchange for the Rio Grande boundary. At the same time, Polk had authorized the minister to purchase New Mexico and California from Mexico. But Mexico had refused to negotiate. After a skirmish between American and Mexican troops, the United States declared war.

Few modern American historians justify the war with Mexico. The honor and security of the United States do not seem to have been at stake. Rather the American government was determined to expand the continental boundaries of the nation.

The war ended in 1848 with the signing of the Treaty of Guadalupe Hidalgo. Mexico recognized the Rio Grande boundary and ceded New Mexico and California to the United States. The United States agreed to pay Mexico $15 million and to assume the claims of American citizens against Mexico.

From one point of view, the acquisition of the territories of Oregon, California, New Mexico, and Texas represented a great accomplishment. It indicated the growth of a great nation. From another point of view, it was terribly costly. The war with Mexico was not popular in the United States. Thousands of Americans, mostly in the northern states, feared that any new territory won from Mexico would encourage the expansion of slavery. Economically, culturally, and geographically the nation expanded as never before. But sectional tensions continued to build up under the surface of national unity. The future peace, unity, and prosperity of Americans would depend upon their ability to organize these new territories without letting the debate over slavery tear the nation apart.

With the Gadsden Purchase in 1853, the United States paid Mexico $10 million for 54,000 square miles of territory along the southern New Mexico border. Since the Gadsden Purchase, the boundaries of the continental United States have remained fixed.

Civil War and Reconstruction
1850-1877

STATING THE ISSUE

This chapter begins with a historical essay which focuses on the difficulties that northerners and southerners had in solving their problems during the 1850's. The second part of the chapter contains a selection of documents relating to one of the most dramatic examples of the failure of compromise during the period—the career of abolitionist John Brown. A second historical essay covering the period of war and reconstruction forms the third part of the chapter.

CHAPTER
12

1846 David Wilmot introduces proviso barring slavery in newly acquired territories

1848 Zachary Taylor becomes President

1849 Gold is discovered in California

1850 Congress adopts Henry Clay's Compromise of 1850

1852 Harriet Beecher Stowe publishes *Uncle Tom's Cabin*

1854 Congress passes Kansas–Nebraska Act

1854-56 Violence over slavery issue breaks out in Kansas

1856 Republican Party is organized

1856 James Buchanan is elected President

1857 Dred Scott decision permits slavery in territories

1859 John Brown seizes federal arsenal at Harper's Ferry

1860 Abraham Lincoln is elected President

1860 South Carolina secedes from the Union

1861 Jefferson Davis is elected President of the Confederate States of America

1861 Southern forces fire on Fort Sumter, beginning Civil War

1863 Congress passes first draft law

1863 Emancipation Proclamation is passed

1865 General Robert E. Lee surrenders to northern forces at Appomattox Courthouse, ending Civil War

1870 President Andrew Johnson is impeached

44 THE FAILURE
OF COMPROMISE
1850-1859

One way of writing American political history is to stress the importance of compromise. The Constitution was a compromise between states with different interests and between citizens with conflicting ideas about democracy. In 1820, the balance between free and slave states was kept through compromise. In 1832, a confrontation over states rights that might have led to war was avoided by a compromise. South Carolina suspended its nullification act in return for a more acceptable tariff bill. The period with which this essay is concerned opened with compromise and closed in civil war. The question to consider is why the attempts at compromise failed.

The Mexican War and the Need for Compromise

Many people in the North had opposed the Mexican War. They suspected that it was a southern plot to extend slavery. In 1846, David Wilmot, a congressman from Pennsylvania, introduced an amendment to a bill designed to appropriate $2 million for negotiating a settlement with Mexico. Part of his amendment proposed that slavery should be barred from any territory acquired from Mexico. A bitter and prolonged debate between those who supported slavery and those who opposed it broke out. Finally, the Wilmot Proviso, as the amendment was called, passed the House of Representatives. But it failed to pass the Senate.

The issue raised by the Proviso in 1846 became a pressing, practical problem two years later. After the Mexican War, California and New Mexico belonged to the United States. In 1848, President Polk urged northerners and southerners to compromise their differences. He proposed to extend to the Pacific the line drawn by the Missouri Compromise. This line separated free from slave territory within the Louisiana Purchase at 36° 30'. But his proposal failed to win support.

In 1848, the American voters elected the Whig candidate, Zachary Taylor, a hero of the Mexican War, to the Presidency. Meanwhile, prospectors discovered gold near Sacramento, California, setting off a rush for the gold fields. By the end of 1849, more than 100,000 prospectors and settlers had poured into California. The question of statehood could not be delayed. With the encouragement of President Taylor, Californians held a convention. At the convention they drew

STETSON'S BIG DOUBLE SPECTACULAR
UNCLE TOM'S CABIN -CO-

"YOU BLACK DOG, I WILL TEACH YOU TO DO AS I SAY."

The pictures on this page were used to illustrate several versions of Uncle Tom's Cabin. How did they portray slavery? How might you have reacted to these pictures if you had been a northerner? a southerner?

up a constitution. Then they applied for immediate admission as a state.

The debate in Congress over slavery grew particularly intense because the nation consisted of fifteen free and fifteen slave states. Congressmen hesitated to upset that balance. Moreover, northerners wanted slavery outlawed in Washington, D.C. And southerners agitated for an effective fugitive slave law that would guarantee the return of runaway slaves. Slaves had been escaping in increasing numbers since the underground railroad had been organized in the 1830's. Runaways were a constant source of irritation to the South. Some of them, such as Frederick Douglass, had joined the abolitionist forces as eloquent orators and journalists. All these issues surrounded the admission of California as one of the greatest Senate debates in American history took shape. It marked the last appearance of Daniel Webster, Henry Clay, and John C. Calhoun.

Calhoun died in March 1850, Clay in June 1852, and Webster in October 1852.

The Compromise of 1850

There were four main points of view represented in Congress. First, in order to avoid a confrontation, President Taylor urged the early admission of California and New Mexico. Each state was to decide for itself whether or not it would allow slavery. Clay and Webster expressed a second point of view. They called for concessions for both sections. For the North, they supported admission of California as a free state and passage of a law prohibiting the slave trade in Washington, D.C. For the South, they supported passage of an effective fugitive slave law, organization of New Mexico as a territory with no restrictions on slavery, and declarations that the federal government could not interfere with slavery in the District of Columbia or with the interstate slave trade. A third point of view was represented by John C. Calhoun. He advocated silencing the abolitionists and guaranteeing the right of southerners to take slaves to all new territories. William Seward of New York presented a fourth point of view. He maintained that abolitionists obeyed a moral law that was higher than the Constitution.

▶By a "higher law" Seward meant a law based on natural rights or on principles of justice. These rights and principles preceded the law of the Constitution made by human beings. Should citizens of a democracy appeal to abstract principles such as these? Why or why not?

The debate over these proposals was violent. Some members actually threatened each other with weapons. In July, the deadlock was broken by President Taylor's sudden death. Vice-President Fillmore, who succeeded to the Presidency, supported the Clay-Webster proposals. They became law in September 1850.

Northern and Southern Views of the Compromise

While thousands of Americans applauded the Compromise of 1850, thousands of others denounced it. Many northerners bitterly resented the Fugitive Slave Law. It provided for special United States commissioners. They were authorized to hold hearings, issue warrants for the arrest of suspected fugitives, and return them to their masters. The commissioners did not allow suspected runaways, who claimed to be free citizens, to testify. The commissioners also received a larger fee when they returned a suspect to the South, than when they set her or him free.

Antislavery people in the North, such as Senator Seward, found the law morally objectionable. They believed that the federal government was using its power to support slavery. Prominent northern abolitionists and intellectuals announced publicly that they would not obey the law. Some northern states passed "personal liberty" laws. These laws made it illegal for slaveholders to capture runaways.

The Fugitive Slave Law drove many northerners to join the abolitionists. They felt the government was trying to force them to support an immoral institution. The publication in 1852 of Harriet Beecher Stowe's novel, *Uncle Tom's Cabin*, intensified northern opposition to slavery. The book focused on the cruelty of slavery and stressed the persecution of runaway slaves. Within a year, several hundred thousand copies of *Uncle Tom's Cabin* circulated throughout the North. The popularity of the book contributed to the growing antislavery sentiment in the North.

Many southerners also denounced the Compromise of 1850. Calhoun died while the Senate was still debating the issue. But other southern leaders continued to voice his views. After California's admission, there were sixteen free and fifteen slave states. And the free states were growing more rapidly in population. Extremist southern politicians believed that the South could gain little from compromise. They insisted that the abolitionists be silenced and that slavery be protected everywhere in the territories. If the national government failed to do this, southern extremists believed that secession was the only solution.

Slavery in the Territories: The Kansas-Nebraska Act

Perhaps the most important reason for the failure of the Compromise was its inability to dampen the fires of controversy over slavery in the territories. The laws of 1850 applied only to territory gained by the United States through war with Mexico. The Compromise did not include the vast plains west of Missouri and Iowa which had been part of the Louisiana Purchase. In theory, slavery in that area had been prohibited by the Missouri Compromise. But the question had not arisen because the region remained unorganized.

Then in 1854, Stephen A. Douglas confused the issue. He introduced legislation to organize the territories of Kansas and Nebraska and to

►Henry David Thoreau went to jail rather than pay taxes to a government which supported slavery. Was he justified in taking this stand? Why or why not?

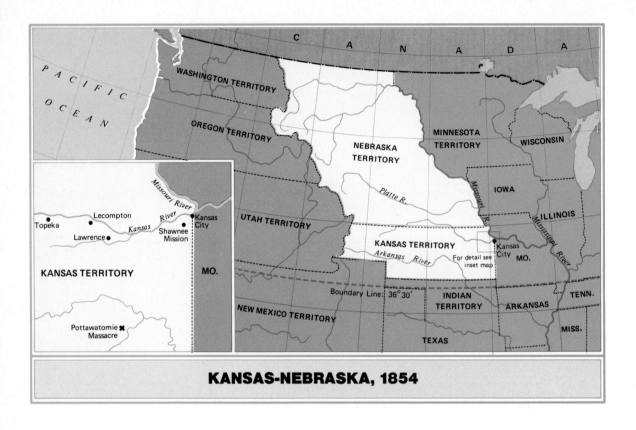

KANSAS-NEBRASKA, 1854

allow their admission to the Union as states with or without slavery. The issue of slavery would be decided by the inhabitants. If Congress passed the bill, slavery could exist in Louisiana Purchase territory north of the 36th parallel if the settlers wanted it. Douglas urged the passage of the Kansas-Nebraska bill on the grounds of "popular sovereignty." Americans had fought a revolution in order to be able to decide important matters for themselves, he said.

After a furious debate, the bill became law in May 1854. The South accepted the Kansas-Nebraska Act without excitement or particular interest. In the North, however, opposition was intense and immediate. The Massachusetts Senate voted unanimously to send a formal resolution of protest to Congress. That body was already flooded with evidence of northern displeasure, including a petition from three thousand New England clergymen.

"Bleeding Kansas": A Rehearsal for War

The Kansas-Nebraska Act hastened the decline of the Whig Party and helped create the new Republican Party. Moreover, it encouraged violence in Kansas. Settlers from the North and the South poured into "Bleeding Kansas." Their goal was to establish a territorial government sympathetic to their particular views. Antislavery groups in New England raised money to support colonies of antislavery settlers. Similar organizations sprang up in the South. Fraud and bloodshed accompanied the territorial elections which took place in 1854. About two hundred people died in the violent struggle, and federal troops did not restore temporary order until September 1856. Kansas did not become a state until 1861. The struggle in Kansas foreshadowed the violence and bloodshed of the Civil War. And it dramatized urgently the great issue of the extension of slavery.

Three Additional Incidents Undermine Compromise

Three other events that occurred in the late 1850's helped to dramatize the slavery problem and weaken the possibilities of maintaining any kind of compromise. The first happened on the floor of the United States Senate in May 1856. Senator Charles Sumner, from Massachusetts, was one of the most outspoken opponents of slavery in Congress. On May 19, he made a speech bitterly denouncing the "slave power" in the South for its "crime against Kansas." He also questioned the integrity of several southern senators, including Andrew Butler from South Carolina. The next day Representative Preston Brooks, Butler's nephew, attacked Sumner in the Senate chamber with a heavy cane. Sumner was severely injured and spent two years recovering. His empty seat in the Senate reminded northerners of the unwillingness of slaveholders to tolerate criticism.

The second dramatic event was a decision passed down by the Supreme Court in March 1857. The case involved Dred Scott, a slave. Scott had sued for his freedom after his master had taken him for a long period from the slave state of Missouri to the free state of Illinois and the free territory of Wisconsin. The Missouri Compromise had made slavery illegal in these areas. Chief Justice Roger Taney spoke for the majority of the Court, which sympathized with the South's position. He ruled that no slave or descendant of a slave could be a citizen. Therefore, Dred Scott had no right to sue in a federal court. In addition, he said that Scott could not have been freed by the provisions of the Missouri compromise because that law was unconstitutional. The Court reasoned that it violated the Fifth Amendment of the Constitution. This amendment prohibits Congress from depriving persons of property without due process of law. Northerners saw in the Dred Scott decision another example of conspiracy to spread slavery throughout the nation.

The Dred Scott decision marked the second time in American history that a law was declared unconstitutional. The first instance was in *Marbury vs. Madison* (1803).

The third dramatic event was a raid by a northern abolitionist named John Brown on the government arsenal at Harper's Ferry, Virginia. Brown hoped to free the slaves. This incident drove another wedge between North and South. It is the subject of Reading 45.

THE EVOLUTION OF THE TWO-PARTY SYSTEM

Date	Hamiltonians	Jeffersonians
c.1791	Federalists	Democratic-Republicans
c.1820		Republicans "Era of Good Feelings"
1824–1825	National Republicans	Democratic-Republicans
1834	Whigs	Democrats (Jacksonian)
	{ Northern Whigs { Antislavery Democrats	Southern Democrats
1854	Republicans	Democrats
Present	Republicans	Democrats

New Party Alignments

Another development which hurt the possibility of compromise was the emergence of a major political party with strong antislavery support. Since 1836, the Whig and Democratic Parties had been the chief political organizations in the United States. Both were national, not sectional, parties. Both bid for and attracted support in all parts of the nation. As the abolitionists grew more numerous and vocal in the 1830's and 1840's, the Whigs and Democrats faced a dilemma. Taking a position on either side of the slavery argument would mean losing important votes in either the North or the South. Consequently, the two major parties were very cautious about dealing with an issue that threatened to divide their supporters.

A group of northern abolitionists became disgusted with the parties' failure to take a stand on slavery. In 1840, they organized their own Liberty Party. The Liberty Party got only 7,069 votes in 1840 and 62,000 votes in 1844. In 1848, antislavery forces created a new Free Soil Party. It attracted numerous supporters from both Whigs and Democrats. In the election of 1848, Martin Van Buren, the Free Soil candidate, received 291,000 votes, over 10 percent of the votes cast. The Free Soil Party took votes away from Lewis Cass, the Democratic candidate. By doing this, it helped swing the election to the Whig candidate, Zachary Taylor.

288

In the election of 1852, the Free Soil vote declined. This was largely because the Compromise of 1850 had eased tensions over slavery temporarily. By 1856, however, the issue of slavery in the territories dominated the election. Two new parties emerged. One was the short-lived American party. It was the official arm of an anti-Catholic, anti-immigrant organization popularly known as the "Know-Nothing party." The other, a direct heir of the Free Soil movement, was the Republican Party. The Republicans attracted antislavery people from both the Whigs and Democrats. Their platform favored internal improvements, tariffs, and a homestead law designed to appeal to both the East and the West.

A homestead law would allow a person to acquire certain amounts of public land by paying a small fee and by living on that land for a specified number of years.

The Republicans said that since the Constitution recognized slavery, it should be protected in states where it already existed. But they held that slavery was morally wrong and should not be allowed in the territories. In the election of 1856, the combined total of Republican and American party votes exceeded the Democratic vote. But the Democrat James Buchanan won by a large majority. By 1858, however, the Republicans were able to win most state elections in the North. They also made important gains in Congress. Meanwhile, the Democrats fell more under the influence of extreme proslavery politicians. This was the political atmosphere in the United States when John Brown attacked a government arsenal at Harper's Ferry, West Virginia, on October 16, 1859.

45 JOHN BROWN: AN EXERCISE IN HISTORICAL INQUIRY

Few Americans are more famous or more controversial than John Brown. He has been called a revolutionary hero, a Christian martyr, a murderous fanatic, a lunatic, and a traitor. Both his contemporaries and modern historians have been divided about his role in American life. This exercise has been designed to help you understand how these widely differing judgments of his career were made.

The materials in Reading 45 include eight brief biographies of people who might have been contemporaries of John Brown. The reading also consists of documents by and about John Brown. First, study the biographical material carefully. When you have done this, your teacher will help you and your classmates decide which of these nine people you will represent as you examine the documents by and about John Brown. Then, read all of the written materials and examine the visual evidence in the rest of the reading as if you were the person you have chosen to represent. Take notes from the point of view of that person. While you read these materials or when you have finished your study of them, your teacher will probably ask you to take part in one or more of the following activities: write a paper, participate in a debate, or take part in class discussions. In these activities you will take the point of view of the person you are representing.

While you are examining materials from the perspective of someone else, you will also be making up your own mind about John Brown. You will be forming your own responses to the following questions. What manner of man was he? Was he justified in what he did? Would the history of the United States have been different if he had never lived? If you had been able to interview him in his prison cell during the week before he was executed, what would you have asked him?

Eight Biographies

Rhett------: Reporter for the *Southern Star*, Montgomery, Alabama. Born 1810 of poor white parents in South Carolina. Little formal education. Began as printer's apprentice. Ardent admirer of Andrew Jackson and author of articles supporting African colonization.

Sarah------: Prominent abolitionist and teacher. Founding member of the Philadelphia Female Antislavery Society. Active in community affairs. Born in Philadelphia in 1806 into a prominent family of free blacks. Raised in comfortable circumstances and educated privately by tutors. Founded one of the first private schools for black children in Philadelphia.

Col. Jason------: Officer in the United States Army. Born on a Virginia plantation in 1820. West Point graduate. Served with distinction in the Mexican War. Extremely religious and patriotic. Author of a book on Virginia patriots. Married to the sister of a very well-known female abolitionist.

The Honorable Henry------: Republican congressman from Ohio. Born in upstate New York in 1800. Lawyer. Entered politics as a Whig in the 1830's. Admirer of Henry Clay and Daniel Webster. Supported the Compromise of 1850, including the Fugitive Slave Law. Opposed the Kansas-Nebraska Act. Very ambitious.

Hans------: Editor of German language newspaper in Chicago. Born in Germany in 1815. Left Germany as a political refugee after the Revolution of 1848. Active in getting immigrants to settle farmlands in western territories. Great admirer of Jefferson and the Declaration of Independence.

Margaret------: Owner of boardinghouse located near a black section of Boston. Born in Dublin in 1830. Emigrated in 1850. Widow with five children. Has mixed feelings about the activities of the Boston abolitionist societies.

Jane------: Elderly free black servant in Richmond. Date and place of birth in Africa unknown. Was given her freedom in 1855. Two of her children still in slavery. Has learned to read and write.

Andrew and Eliza------: Settlers near Pottawatomie, Kansas. Left five slaves behind in Kentucky. Supporters of the Democratic party. Admirers of Stephen A. Douglas. Recently purchased 500 acre farm. Six children.

John Brown Before 1850

The documents in this section were written by John Brown. They include an autobiographical account, a letter to his brother, and two letters to his wife. Brown put the autobiographical account into a letter written to the son of a friend on July 15, 1857. Most of what is known about Brown's early life comes from this account. Brown wrote the second letter, to his brother, while he was a successful businessman in Pennsylvania. He wrote the two letters to his wife after he had moved to Ohio and was involved in the first of a long series of business failures.

AUTOBIOGRAPHICAL ACCOUNT

John was born May 9, 1800, at Torrington, Litchfield County, Connecticut. He was the child of poor but respectable parents. On his father's side he was a descendant of one of the company of the Mayflower who landed at Plymouth in 1620. His mother was descended from people who came at an early period to New England from Amsterdam in Holland. Both grandfathers served in the war of the revolution. His father's father died in a barn in New York while in the service in 1776.

When he was five years old his father moved to Ohio. It was then a wilderness filled with wild beasts and Indians. During the long journey, which was performed mostly with an ox-team, he was called upon to help a boy five years older. (This boy had been adopted by his father and mother.) As a result, he learned to think he could accomplish smart things in driving the cows and riding the horses.

After getting to Ohio in 1805, he was for some time afraid of the Indians and their rifles. But this soon wore off. He used to hang around them as much as he could. And he learned a little of their language. His father learned to dress deer skins. And when he was six, John was dressed in buckskin. He remembered the process of dressing deer skin so well that he could dress his own animal skins after that. He also learned to make whip lashes, which he sold now and then, and many other useful things.

At six he began to ramble in the wild new country. He found birds and squirrels and sometimes a wild turkey's nest. But about that time

The Life and Letters of John Brown, Franklin B. Sanborn, ed. (Boston: Roberts Brothers, 1891), pp. 12-17. Language simplified.

he was also placed in the school of hardship, a most necessary part of his early training. These trials were the beginning of a severe but much needed course in discipline. It is to be hoped that he has learned this course before the Heavenly Father sees it best to take all the little things out of his hands which he had ever placed in them. You may laugh when you read about them. But these were sore trials to John, whose earthly treasures were very few and small. When John was six, a poor Indian boy gave him a yellow marble. It was the first he had ever seen. He thought a great deal of this and kept it a good while. But at last he lost it. It took years to heal the wound. And I think he cried at times about it. Five months after this he caught a young squirrel. He tore off the squirrel's tail in catching it and got severly bitten himself. However, he held on to the little squirrel and finally got him perfectly tamed. He almost idolized his pet. This, too, he lost. And for a year or two John was in mourning. He looked at all the squirrels and tried to discover his pet, Bobtail. John also had another misfortune which set rather hard on him while he was a boy. By some means—perhaps by gift of his father—he had become the owner of a little lamb. It did fine until it was about two-thirds grown. Then it sickened and died. This caused another long mourning season, so strong and earnest were his attachments.

I must not neglect to tell you about the very bad and foolish habit John had of telling lies. He did this generally to protect himself from blame or from punishment. He could not stand being reproached. I now think that if he had been encouraged more often to be entirely frank, he would not have been guilty of this fault so often. And he would not have been forced to struggle so long with so mean a habit.

John was never quarrelsome. But he was very fond of the hardest and roughest kind of games and could never get enough of them. Indeed, when he was sometimes sent to school, the chance to play these games was almost the only compensation for the confinement and restraints of school. I need not tell you that, with such a feeling and with little chance of going to school at all, he did not become much of a scholar. He would always choose to stay home and work hard rather than be sent to school. And, during the warm season, he usually went barefooted and bareheaded. He particularly enjoyed being sent off through the wilderness alone to very great distances. He did this so often that by the time he was twelve he was sent off more than a hundred miles with herds of cattle. Moreover, he would not allow anyone to help him in such a job. This feeling was very characteristic of John.

When he was eight, John's mother died. Although his father's second wife was a sensible, intelligent, fine woman, John never thought of her as his mother. He continued to pine after his own mother for years.

When the war broke out with England, his father supplied the troops with beef cattle. During the war, John had a chance to form his own boyish judgment of men and deeds. He also had the opportunity to meet some who have become important figures in the country since then. What he saw during the war made him so disgusted with military affairs that he would neither train nor drill. He paid fines and got along like a Quaker until he was too old for military duty.

Brown is referring to the War of 1812.

During the war something happened that made him a most determined abolitionist. It led him to declare eternal war with slavery. He was staying for a short time with a very gentlemanly landlord who has since become a United States Marshal. The man held a slave boy near John's own age. The boy was very active, intelligent, and of good feeling. John was indebted to him for many little acts of kindness. The master made a great pet of John. He had him sit at the table with his company and friends. And he called their attention to every little smart thing John said or did. But the Negro boy, who was fully if not more than equal, was badly clothed, poorly fed and lodged, and beaten before John's eyes with iron shovels or anything else that came to hand. This caused John to think about the wretched, hopeless condition of fatherless and motherless slave children who had no one to protect or provide for them. He would sometimes raise the question: Is God their father?

When he was ten, an old friend persuaded him to read a little history. He also offered him the free use of a good library. In this way, John acquired some taste for reading. This formed the main part of his early education and kept him away from bad company. By this means, he grew very fond of the company and conversation of old and intelligent people.

He never tried to dance in his life. Nor did he ever learn to know one card in a pack from another. He learned nothing of grammar. Nor did he get at school much knowledge of common arithmetic. This will give you some general idea of the first fifteen years of his life. During this time he became very strong and large for his age. And he was eager to work like a grown man at almost any kind of hard work.

He read the lives of great, wise, and good men and their sayings and writings. By doing this he grew to dislike vain and foolish conversation and people. Since he was extremely bashful, he was often grateful for the kind way in which older and more intelligent people treated him at their houses and in conversation.

Very early in life he became ambitious to excel in doing anything he took on. I would recommend this feeling to all young people both male and female. It will certainly tend to admit them to the company of the more intelligent and better part of every community. By all means try to excel in some praiseworthy pursuit.

293

John had been taught from earliest childhood to "fear God and keep his commandments." Although he was very skeptical, he had always felt much serious doubt about his future well being. And about this time he became something of a convert to Christianity. And ever after he was a firm believer in the divine truth of the Bible. He became very familiar with this book. And he has a most unusual memory of its entire contents.

Many people seem to have no definite plan of life. Others never stick to any plan they do form. This was not the case with John. He followed tenaciously whatever he set about to do as long as it served his general purpose. Hence, he rarely failed to bring about the things he worked at.

From fifteen to twenty years of age, he spent most of his time working at the tanner and currier's trade at Bachelor's Hall. He also did all the cooking. And for most of the time he was forcman of the establishment under his father. During this time he found much trouble with some of the bad habits I mentioned and with some I have not told you of. But his close attention to business, his success in managing it, and the way he got along with a group of men and boys, made him a favorite with the more serious and intelligent older people. This got him so much attention from those he esteemed that he became very vain. And he reached manhood quite full of conceit and self-confidence, in spite of his bashfulness. A younger brother sometimes used to remind him of this and repeat to him the following expression: "A King against whom there is no rising up." He formed the habit of being obeyed early in life.

From fifteen years and upward he felt very anxious to learn. But he could only read and study a little. He not only lacked the time, but also had an inflammation of the eyes. However, he managed with the help of books to learn some common arithmetic and surveying. He practiced surveying more or less after he was twenty years old.

At a little past twenty, led by his own inclination and prompted by his father, he married a remarkably plain, but neat, hardworking, and economical girl. She had an excellent character, earnest piety, and good common sense. And she was about one year younger than himself. By her mild, frank, and very consistent conduct this woman maintained a most powerful and good influence over him. Her plain but kind admonitions generally had the right effect. And they did not arouse his proud, stubborn temper.

John began early in life to like fine cattle, horses, sheep and swine. As soon as circumstances allowed, he began to be a practical shepherd. It was a calling for which he had a kind of enthusiastic longing in early life. And, as a business, it promised to give him the means of carrying out his greatest object.

Your Friend,
J. Brown

Tanners and curriers are skilled workers who convert hides into leather.

LETTER TO HIS BROTHER

The Life and Letters of John Brown, Sanborn, ed., pp. 20-21. Language simplified.

Randolph, Pennsylvania, Nov. 21, 1834

Dear Brother,

Since you left me, I have been trying to find some way of doing something practical for my poor fellow-men who are in bondage. My wife and my three boys and I have decided to get at least one negro boy or youth and bring him up as we do our own. We will give him a good English education, teaching him what we can about history of the world, about business, and about general subjects. And, above all, we will try to teach him the fear of God. We think of three ways to obtain one. First, we will try to get some Christian slaveholder to release one to us. Second, we will get a free one if no one will let us have one that is a slave. Third, if that does not succeed, we have all agreed to do without many things in order to buy one. We are now doing all we can to bring this about. And we confidently expect that God will soon bring them all out of the house of bondage.

For years I have been trying to find a way to get a school going here for blacks. And I think that on many accounts it would be a most favorable location. Children here would have nothing to do with vicious people of their own kind, nor with openly vicious persons of any kind. There would be no powerful influence against such a thing. And, if there were any, I believe that the thing might be done in such a way as to have almost the whole influence of the place in favor of such a school in the future. Write me how you would like to join me. And try to get on from Hudson and thereabouts some first-rate abolitionist families with you. I do honestly believe that our combined efforts alone might soon, with the good hand of our God upon us, bring it all about.

Your brother,
John Brown

LETTERS TO HIS WIFE AND CHILDREN

The Life and Letters of John Brown, Sanborn, ed., pp. 24-25. Language simplified.

New York, December 5, 1838

Dear wife and children,

A kind merciful God has kept me till now. I arrived here four days ago. But I shall probably leave soon. I have not had the pleasure of hearing from you since I left. I hope I may before I leave. I have not yet succeeded in my business. But the outlook is such that I do not despair of final success. As to that, may God's holy will be done. My unceasing and anxious care for the present and everlasting welfare of every member of my family increases as I get separated farther and farther from them. Forgive the many faults and foibles you have seen in me. And try to profit by anything good either

▶Do you expect your parents to look over your homework, as John Brown examined the lessons he set for his children? Why or why not?

The Life and Letters of John Brown, Sanborn, ed., p. 26. Language simplified.

▶Rather than pay debts at a sacrifice, some people declare bankruptcy. What do you think of that practice?

The Life and Letters of John Brown, Sanborn, ed., pp. 265-266. Language simplified.

in my example or my advice. Try not to get weary of doing good. If the older boys read and copy my old letters as I suggested, I want to have them preserved with care. The time of my return is very uncertain, but will be as soon as I can manage. I will write you again when I have the chance. God Almighty bless and keep you all.

Your affectionate husband and father,
John Brown

New Hartford, June 32, 1839

My dear wife and children,

I write to let you know that I am in comfortable health. I expect to be on my way home in the course of a week if nothing befalls me. If I am detained longer, I will write you again. The cattle business has succeeded about as I expected. But I now fear that I shall fail to get the money I expected on the loan. Should that be the will of Providence, we must consider ourselves very poor. For our debts must be paid, if paid at a sacrifice. Should that happen (though it may not) I hope God, who is rich in mercy, will grant us the grace to accept our circumstances with cheerfulness and true resignation. I want to see each of my dear family very much. But I must wait God's time. Try to do the best you can. And do not be discouraged. Tomorrow may be a much brighter day. Cease not to ask God's blessing on yourselves and me.

Your affectionate husband and father,
John Brown

John Brown in Kansas

Brown went to Kansas in October 1855. By that time armed violence between proslavery and antislavery settlers was already common. The next spring a band of proslavery settlers burned and looted the town of Lawrence. And civil war broke out. On the night of May 24, 1856, John Brown and six companions, including four of his sons, visited the cabins of five proslavery families near Pottawatomie Creek. The two documents in this section focus on this event. The first is the testimony given by one of these settlers to a congressional investigating committee. The second and third are letters in which Brown gives his version of the war in Kansas and his role in it.

TESTIMONY OF JAMES HARRIS

On Sunday morning, May 25, 1856, about two A.M., my wife and child and myself were in bed in the house where we lived, near Henry Sherman's. We were aroused by a group of men who said they belonged to the northern army. Each was armed with a sabre and two revolvers. I recognized two of them. One was Mr. Brown, whose given name

I do not remember. He is commonly known as "old man Brown." The other was his son Owen Brown. They came into the house and approached the bed where we were lying. They ordered us and three other men who were in the house to surrender. They said that the northern army was upon us and it would be useless for us to resist. The names of the other men who were in the house with me were William Sherman and John S. Whiteman. I did not know the other man. They were staying with me that night. They had bought a cow from Henry Sherman. And they intended to go home the next morning.

When the men came up to the bed, some had drawn sabres in their hands and some had revolvers. Then they seized two rifles and a bowie-knife which I had there in the room. (There is only one room in my house.) Afterwards, they ransacked the whole place in search of ammunition. Then they took out one of the three men who were staying in my house. (This was the man whose name I do not know.) He came back. Then they took me out. They asked me if there were any more men around the place. I told them there were not. They searched the place, but found no others but us four. They asked me where Henry Sherman was. (Henry was a brother to William Sherman.) I told them he was out on the plains in search of some cattle he had lost. They asked me if I had ever aided proslavery men in coming to the territory of Kansas, or if I had ever taken part in the troubles at Lawrence. They asked me whether I had ever done the Free-State party any harm, or ever intended to do that party any harm. They asked me what made me live at such a place. I answered that I could get higher wages there than anywhere else. They asked me if there were any bridles or saddles around my place. I told them there was one saddle, which they took. They also took Henry Sherman's horse, which I had at my place, and made me saddle him. Then they said if I would answer no to all the questions they asked me, they would let me loose. Old Mr. Brown and his son then went into the house with me. The other three men—Mr. William Sherman, Mr. Whiteman, and the stranger—were in the house all this time. After old man Brown and his son went into the house with me, old man Brown asked Mr. Sherman to go out with him. And Mr. Sherman then went out with old Mr. Brown. Another man came into the house in Brown's place. I heard nothing more for about fifteen minutes. Two of the northern army, as they called themselves, stayed with us until we heard a cap burst. And then these two men left. That morning, about ten o'clock, I found William Sherman dead in the creek near my house. I was looking for him, as he had not come back. I thought he had been murdered. I took Mr. William Sherman out of the creek and examined him. Mr. Whiteman was with me. Sherman's skull was split open in two places. And some of his brains were washed out by the water. A large hole was cut in his breast. And his left hand was cut off except a little piece of skin on one side. We buried him.

"The Last Moments of John Brown" painted in
1884 by Thomas Hovendon

Use the materials on these
three pages as resources in
your study of John Brown.

298

Painted by John Steuart Curry

JOHN BROWN AT HARPER'S FERRY.

JOHN BROWN TO HIS FAMILY, JUNE 1856

It is now about five weeks since I had any chance of writing you. During that period we here have passed through an almost constant series of very trying events. We were called to the relief of Lawrence on May 22nd. On our way to Lawrence we learned that it had been destroyed already. So we set up camp for the night. Next day our little company left. During the day we stopped and searched three men.

Lawrence was destroyed in this way. Their leading men had (as I think) decided, in a very cowardly way, not to resist any action of a Government official, even if the action might be a wholly bogus affair. As a result, a man called a United States marshal came with a horde of ruffians which he called his posse. And, after arresting a few persons, he turned the ruffians loose on the defenseless people. They robbed the inhabitants of their money and other property and seized the women's jewelry. They also burned a considerable part of the town.

A few days later, we met with quite a number of proslavery men. We took quite a number of prisoners. We let our prisoners go. But we kept some four or five horses. After this, we were immediately accused of murdering five men at Pottawatomie. Since then, great efforts have been made by the Missourians and their ruffian allies to capture us.

Since then we have, like David of old, had our dwelling with the serpents of the rocks and wild beasts of the wilderness. We are obliged to hide away from our enemies. We are not disheartened. But we have almost no food, clothing, and money. God has not given us over to the will of our enemies, but has delivered them into our hand. He will, we humbly trust, still keep and deliver us. We feel assured that He who sees not as men see, does not lay the guilt of innocent blood to our charge.

JOHN BROWN TO HIS FAMILY, SEPTEMBER 7, 1856

I have one moment to write you to say that I am yet alive. On the morning of August 30th an attack was made by about four hundred ruffians on Osawatomie. Their scouts shot our dear son Fred dead without warning. He thought they were Free State men as near as we can learn. One other man was murdered by them about the same time that Fred was killed. And one was badly wounded. At this time I was about three miles off. I had some fourteen or fifteen men overnight who had just enlisted to serve under me as regulars. I collected there as well as I could in about three quarters of an hour. And, with some twelve or fifteen more, I attacked them from a wood with thick undergrowth. With this force we threw them into confusion for about fifteen or twenty minutes. During this time we killed and

The Life and Letters of John Brown, Sanborn, ed., pp. 266-267. Language simplified.

David was a biblical leader of Israel.

The Life and Letters of John Brown, Sanborn, ed., pp. 268-269. Language simplified.

wounded from seventy to eighty of them. Then we escaped as well as we could. One of us was killed while escaping. Two or three were wounded and as many more missing. In all, four or five Free State men were butchered during the day. I was struck by a partly spent rifle shot. It bruised me some but did not injure me seriously. "Hitherto the Lord hath helped me" nothwithstanding my afflictions. Things seem rather quiet just now. But what another hour will bring I cannot say.

John Brown and Other Abolitionists

Brown's activities in Kansas made him a celebrated figure among some radical abolitionists. The following selections document Brown's relations with two noted abolitionists, Frederick Douglass and Thomas Wentworth Higginson. The first selection is taken from the autobiography of Frederick Douglass. The second and third are letters between Brown and Higginson. And the fourth is a letter about Brown, written by F. B. Sanborn, an abolitionist, to Higginson.

Frederick Douglass, **Life and Times of Frederick Douglass** (Hartford, Conn: Park Publishing Co., 1881), pp. 318-321. Language simplified.

FREDERICK DOUGLASS ON JOHN BROWN

Brown's plan was to take twenty or twenty-five discreet and trustworthy men into the mountains of Virginia and Maryland. There they would be stationed in squads of five, about five miles apart, on a line of twenty-five miles. Each squad was to cooperate with all, and all with each. Secure and comfortable retreats in the mountains would be chosen for them. There they could easily defend themselves in case of attack. They were to live upon the country about them. They were to be well armed. But they were to avoid battle or violence, unless forced by pursuit or in self-defense. In that case, they were to make it as costly as possible to the attacking party, whether that party should be soldiers or citizens. He further proposed to have a number of stations from the line of Pennsylvania to the Canada border. Here those slaves that his men might persuade to run away would be supplied with food and shelter. They would also be sent from one station to another till they reached a place of safety either in Canada or the northern states. He proposed to add to his force in the mountains any courageous and intelligent fugitive who might be willing to remain and endure the hardships and brave the dangers of this mountain life. He thought that these people, if properly chosen, would be valuable assistants. They would know the surrounding country well. The work of going into the valley of Virginia and persuading the slaves to flee to the mountains was to be given to the most courageous and wise man in each squad.

I hated slavery and made its abolition the object of my life. Thus, I was ready to welcome any new method of attack upon the slave

302

system which gave any promise of success. I readily saw that this plan could work very well in one respect. It would make slave property in Maryland and Virginia valueless by making it insecure. Men do not like to buy runaway horses. They do not like to invest their money in a property that is likely to take legs and walk off with itself. If the plan should fail and John Brown should be driven from the mountains, something would have happened to keep the nation awake to the existence of slavery. Hence, I agreed to John Brown's plan for running off slaves.

To put this plan to work, money and men, arms and ammunition, food and clothing were needed. And these were not easily obtained. And nothing was immediately done. Captain Brown was poor. And he was unable to arm and equip men for the dangerous life he had mapped out. So the work lingered till after the Kansas trouble was over and freedom was a fact in that territory. This left him with arms and men. For the men who had been with him in Kansas believed in him. And they would follow him in any humane but dangerous work he might undertake.

BROWN TO THOMAS WENTWORTH HIGGINSON, FEBRUARY 2, 1858

I have been told that you are both a true man and a true abolitionist. And I partly believe the whole story. Last fall I tried to raise from $500 to $1,000 for the secret service. I succeeded in getting $500. I now want to get from $500 to $800 within the next sixty days. It will be used to perfect by far the most important undertaking of my whole life. I have written Rev. Theodore Parker, George L. Stearns, and F. B. Sanborn, Esq. on the subject. But I do not know whether Mr. Stearns or Mr. Sanborn are abolitionists. I suppose they are. Can you be persuaded to work at Worcester [Massachusetts] and elsewhere to raise some part of that amount from antislavery men and women, or any other people? I wish to keep entirely secret about where I am. And I will be greatly obliged if you will consider this communication strictly confidential. Please be so kind as to write N. Hawkins on the subject in care of Wm. L. Watkins, Esq., Rochester, New York. I should be most happy to meet you again and talk matters over more freely. I hope this is my last effort at begging.

T. W. HIGGINSON TO N. HAWKINS (BROWN), FEBRUARY 8, 1858

I am always ready to invest money in treason. But at present I have none to invest. As for my friends, those who are able are not quite willing. And those who are willing are at present bankrupt. Besides this, I have most of our fugitives to look after. And I have just consented to raise something for the Underground Railroad in Kansas, which is in full operation now. But I'll raise something, if

▶Are people justified in taking any action possible to wipe out a practice such as slavery which they consider morally wrong? Why or why not?

From **The Thomas Wentworth Higginson Papers** in the Boston Public Library, Boston, Massachusetts. Reprinted by permission. Language simplified.

The "secret service" refers to Brown's secret activities.

Theodore Parker and George L. Stearns were leading abolitionists.

From **The Thomas Wentworth Higginson Papers**. Reprinted by permission. Language simplified.

only $5, and send it on. I may be able to persuade our Committee who have a little money left.

F. B. SANBORN TO T. W. HIGGINSON, FEBRUARY 11, 1858

From **The Thomas Wentworth Higginson Papers**. Reprinted by permission. Language simplified.

▶Do you trust anyone enough to give them money for a secret project? If yes, why do you trust that person so much?

I have received two letters from J. B. in which he speaks of a plan but does not say what it is. Still I have enough confidence in him to trust him with the small sum he asks for—if I had it—without knowing his plan. Morton writes me from Gerrit Smith's that with from $500 to $800 J. B. hopes to do more than has yet been done. He wishes to raise the money in two months. Meanwhile he is staying up with Douglass (Fred) at Rochester. He avoids publicity as much as possible. In his last letter he says he shall probably continue to see me. And I think he will be in Boston before long. He expects to "overthrow slavery in a large part of the country." E. B. Whitman writes me from Lawrence that Brown has disappeared and has been of little service to them. He adds that some say Brown is insane. This, of course, is not so.

If you can aid Brown in any substantial way, please do so. For I do not well see how I can, though I shall try. Mr. Smith has sent him $100. Has B. written to you? I judge so. I should not wonder if his plan includes an uprising of slaves, though he has not said as much to me.

The Union is evidently on its last legs. And Buchanan is laboring to tear it to pieces. Treason will not be treason much longer. It will be patriotism.

Write me if you can do anything for B.

John Brown at Harper's Ferry

Early in the morning of October 17, 1859, John Brown led eighteen men—including five blacks—in an attack on Harper's Ferry, Virginia. There he seized the government arsenal and armory. John Daingerfield, a clerk in the armory, was taken prisoner by Brown. He supplied the following account of the raid. It was first published in 1885.

The Life and Letters of John Brown, Sanborn, ed., pp. 556-560. Language simplified.

I walked towards my office. It was just within the armory inclosure and not more than a hundred yards from my house. As I proceeded, I saw a man come out of an alley, then another and another, all coming towards me. I asked what all this meant. They said, "Nothing, only they had taken possession of the Government works." I told them they talked like crazy men. They answered, "Not so crazy as you think, as you will soon see." Up to this time I had not seen any arms. Presently, however, the men threw back the cloaks they wore, and disclosed Sharp's rifles, pistols, and knives. Seeing these, and fearing something serious was going on, I told the men I believed I would return home. They at once cocked their guns, and told me I was a prisoner. This surprised me. But I could do nothing, being unarmed. I talked with them some little time longer. And again I tried to go home. But one of the men stepped before me, presented his gun, and told me if I moved I would be shot down. I then asked what they intended to do with me. They said I was in no personal danger. They only wanted to carry me to their captain, John Smith. I asked them where Captain Smith was. They answered, at the guard house, inside of the armory inclosure. I told them I would go there. That was the point for which I first started. (My office was there. And I felt uneasy lest the vault had been broken open.)

The captain's real name, of course, was John Brown.

Upon reaching the gate, I saw what indeed looked like war. There were negroes armed with pikes, and sentinels with muskets all around. I was turned over to "Captain Smith," who called me by name. He asked if I knew Colonel Washington and others, mentioning familiar names. I said I did. And he then said, "Sir, you will find them there," motioning me towards the engine-room. We were not kept closely confined. And we were allowed to talk with him. I asked him what his object was. He replied, "To free the negroes of Virginia." He added that he was prepared to do it. And he said that by twelve o'clock he would have fifteen hundred men with him, ready armed.

Up to this time the citizens had hardly begun to move about. They knew nothing of the raid. When they learned what was going on, some came out with old shotguns. They were shot by concealed men. All the stores, as well as the arsenal, were in the hands of Brown's men. Since there were hardly any private weapons, it was impossible to get either arms or ammunition. At last, however, a few arms were obtained. And a body of citizens crossed the river and advanced from the Maryland side. They made a vigorous attack. In a few minutes they caused all the invaders who were not killed to retreat to Brown inside the armory gate. Then he entered the engine-house, carrying some of his prisoners along, for he made selections. After getting into the engine-house, he made this speech: "Gentlemen, perhaps you wonder why I have selected you from the others. It is because I believe you to be more influential. And I have only to say now, that you will have to share precisely the same fate that your friends extend to my men." He began at once to bar the doors and windows and to cut portholes through the brick wall.

Then a terrible firing began outside. And in a few minutes every window was shattered. Hundreds of balls came through the doors. These shots were answered from within whenever the attacking party could be seen. This was kept up most of the day. Thousands of balls were imbedded in the walls. Holes were shot in the doors almost large enough for a man to creep through. But, strangely, not a prisoner was hurt. At night the firing ceased, for we were in total darkness, and nothing could be seen in the engine-house.

During the day and night I talked much with Brown. I found him as brave as a man could be. He was sensible upon all subjects except slavery. He believed it was his duty to free the slaves, even if in doing so he lost his own life. During a sharp fight one of Brown's sons was killed. He fell. Then, trying to raise himself, he said, "It is all over with me," and died instantly. Brown did not leave his post at the porthole. But when the fighting was over he walked to his son's body. He straightened out his limbs, took off his trappings, and then, turning to me, said, "This is the third son I have lost in this cause." Another son had been shot in the morning, and was then dying, having been brought in from the street. Often when his men would want to fire upon some one who was seen passing, Brown would stop them, saying, "Don't shoot; that man is unarmed." The firing was kept up by our men all day and until late at night. During that time several of his men were killed. But none of the prisoners were hurt, though in great danger. During the day and night many propositions, pro and con, were made, regarding Brown's surrender and the release of the prisoners, but without result.

Colonel Lee came with the Government troops in the night. He at once sent a flag of truce by his aid, J. E. B. Stuart, to notify Brown of his arrival. In the name of the United States he demanded his surrender, advising him to throw himself on the clemency of the Government. Brown did not accept Colonel Lee's terms. He decided to await the attack.

When Stuart was admitted and a light brought, he exclaimed, "Why, aren't you old Osawatomie Brown of Kansas, whom I once had there as my prisoner?" "Yes," was the answer, "but you did not keep me." This was the first hint we had of Brown's real name. When Colonel Lee advised Brown to trust to the clemency of the Government, Brown responded that he knew what that meant—a rope for his men and himself. He added, "I prefer to die just here." Stuart told him he would return at early morning for his final reply and left him. When he had gone, Brown at once barricaded the doors, windows, etc. He tried to make the place as strong as possible. All this time no one of Brown's men showed the slightest fear. They calmly awaited the attack, selecting the best situations to fire from. They arranged their guns and pistols so that a fresh one could be taken up as soon as one was discharged.

During the night I had a long talk with Brown. I told him that he and his men were committing treason against the State and the United States. Two of his men, hearing the conversation, said to their leader, "Are we committing treason against our country by being here?" Brown answered, "Certainly." Both said, "If that is so, we

▶ Should Brown have gone to the side of his dying son? Why or why not?

Robert E. Lee was a colonel in the Second U.S. Cavalry. J.E.B. Stuart was a lieutenant in the First U.S. Cavalry. Both officers would play a major role in the Confederate Army during the Civil War.

306

don't want to fight any more. We thought we came to liberate the slaves. We did not know that was committing treason." Both of these men were afterwards killed in the attack on the engine-house.

▶In this case, loyalty to country seemed to be more important than another principle—freeing slaves. Which seems more important to you? Why?

Lieutenant Stuart came in the morning for the final reply to the demand to surrender. I got up and went to Brown's side to hear his answer. Stuart asked, "Are you ready to surrender, and trust to the mercy of the Government?" Brown answered, "No, I prefer to die here." His manner did not show the least fear. Stuart stepped aside and made a signal for the attack. It was instantly begun with sledge-hammers to break down the door. It would not yield. So, the soldiers seized a long ladder for a battering-ram, and commenced beating the door with that. The people within fired incessantly. I had assisted in the barricading, fixing the fastenings so that I could remove them on the first effort to get in. But I was not at the door when the battering began. And I could not get to the fastenings till the ladder was used. I then quickly removed the fastenings. And, after two or three strokes of the ladder, the engine rolled partially back, making a small opening. Through it Lieutenant Green of the Marines forced his way. He jumped on top of the engine, and stood a second, amidst a shower of balls, looking for John Brown. When he saw Brown he sprang about twelve feet at him. He gave an under thrust of his sword, striking Brown in the middle of the body and raising him completely from the ground. Brown fell forward with his head between his knees. Green struck him several times over the head, and, as I then supposed, split his skull at every stroke. I was not two feet from Brown at that time. Of course I got out of the building as soon as possible. And I did not know till some time later that Brown was not killed. It seems that Green's sword, in making the thrust, struck Brown's belt and did not penetrate the body. The sword was bent double. Brown was not killed when struck on the head because Green was holding his sword in the middle, striking with the hilt, and making only scalp wounds.

When Governor Wise came and was examining Brown, I heard the questions and answers. No lawyer could have used more careful reserve. At the same time, Brown showed no disrespect. Governor Wise was astonished at the answers he received from Brown. After some argument between the United States and the State of Virginia as to which had jurisdiction over the prisoners, Brown was carried to the Charlestown jail. After a fair trial he was hanged.

Henry A. Wise was governor of Virginia.

Of course I was a witness at the trial. And I must say that I have never seen any man display more courage than John Brown showed under the trying circumstances in which he was placed. I could not go to see him hanged. He had made me a prisoner. But he had spared my life and that of other gentlemen in his power. And when his sons were shot down beside him, almost any other man similarly placed would at least have taken life for life.

▶Do you admire Brown for not killing his hostages? Why?

Evidence About John Brown

Brown freed no slaves at Harper's Ferry, but ten of his men were killed. Brown was tried under Virginia law, and he and six others were hung. The evidence introduced regarding him attracted great public attention. Portions of that evidence follow.

From **The Henry A. Wise Papers** in the Library of Congress, Washington, D.C. Language simplified.

EVIDENCE OF EDWIN WETMORE, NOVEMBER 11, 1859

Edwin Wetmore says that he has been acquainted with John Brown (now under sentence of death in Virginia) since early childhood. He always regarded him as strictly honest and upright in all his dealings and of a gentle and mild disposition. This was his opinion of him until about a year ago. At that time, he had a conversation with him. Brown gave him an account of the death of his sons in Kansas. He also gave him what was supposed to be a history of his adventure there. From his statements then and the whole manner and appearance of the man he regarded him as demented and actually insane. His whole character seemed changed. He appeared fanatic and furious and incapable of reasoning or of listening to reason. Wetmore then stated and still believes that he was insane upon the subject of slavery and that he was a monomaniac.

Monomania is a form of mental illness which shows itself in excessive concentration on a single object or idea.

EVIDENCE OF E. N. SILL, NOVEMBER 14, 1859

From **The Henry A. Wise Papers**. Language simplified.

I have had some acquaintance with John Brown who is now under sentence of death in the State of Virginia. For many years, I was well acquainted with his father, a most excellent but very peculiar man. I have also known several of his brothers well. All of these men have had more than ordinary character. And several of them have had very striking idiosyncrasies. John Brown had moved to Kansas with his family. But he returned to this area soon after the beginning of difficulties between the free state men and other parties. He told me the story of the wrongs against himself and family and free state friends. And he asked my aid to purchase arms for their defense. He said not one word of any acts of retaliation in Kansas, Missouri, or elsewhere. He said nothing of any plan to liberate slaves. He spoke only of defense. And in this matter I fully sympathized with him. And I was more than willing to give the desired aid. But, because of his peculiarities, I thought that Mr. Brown was an unsafe man to be commissioned with such a matter. And I neither then, nor at any other time, contributed anything to him or through him, for this or any other purpose. I admire Mr. Brown's courage and devotion to his beliefs. But I have no confidence in the sanity of his judgment in matters concerning slavery. I have no doubt that, upon this subject, especially upon his relation to the abolition of slavery, he is as surely a monomaniac as any inmate of any lunatic asylum in the country.

Idiosyncrasies are eccentric or peculiar habits.

▶Do you know people who are fanatical about only one subject? What do you think of them?

EVIDENCE OF DAVID L. KING, NOVEMBER 15, 1859

From **The Henry A. Wise Papers**. Language simplified.

I have been slightly acquainted with John Brown for from five to eight years. I have considered him as lacking a "balance wheel." About the first of April last I had some business with one of Brown's sons on a farm about four miles from this village. On my return I was asked to take John Brown and two of his Kansas followers in my wagon to town. On the way I passed the time in conversation with Mr. Brown. And I became convinced that on the subject of slavery he was crazy. He was armed to the teeth. And he remarked among other things, that he was an "instrument in the hands of God to free the slaves." I asked his followers if they were relatives of Mr. Brown. They said no. They were all "Sons of Liberty" and were on their way to Kansas to take part in the good work. They said that they always went armed and would never be taken alive.

PORTION OF AN INTERVIEW WITH MRS. JOHN BROWN

The New York Times, November 18, 1859. Language simplified.

I then put the question which I had been most anxious to ask, "It is the common talk of the newspapers that Captain Brown is insane. What do you say about that?"

"I never knew of his insanity," she replied, "until I read it in the newspapers. He is a clear-headed man. He has always been, and now is, entirely in his right mind. He is always cool, deliberate, and never over-hasty. But he has always considered that his first views of duty and his first impulses to action were the best and the safest to follow. He has almost always acted upon his first suggestions. No, he is not insane. His reason is clear. His last act was the result, as all others have been, of his truest and strongest conscientious convictions."

John Brown's Last Speech and Execution

Following are John Brown's last speech to the court, made on November 2, 1859, and an account of his execution, which took place on December 2, 1859.

BROWN'S LAST SPEECH

From **The John Brown Papers**, Chicago Historical Society, Chicago, Illinois. Reprinted by permission. Language simplified.

I have, may it please the Court, a few words to say.

In the first place, I deny everything but what I have all along admitted—my plan to free the slaves. I certainly intended to have made a clean thing of that matter, as I did last winter, when I went into Missouri. There I took slaves without the snapping of a gun on either side. I moved them through the country, and I finally left them in Canada. I planned to have done the same thing again, on a larger scale. That was all I intended. I never did intend murder, or treason, or the destruction of property. I never intended to incite slaves to rebellion.

I have another objection. And that is, it is unjust that I should suffer such a penalty. Had I interfered in the manner which I admit in behalf of the rich, the powerful, the intelligent, the so-called great, or in behalf of any of their friends—either father, mother, brother, sister, wife, or children, or any of that class—and suffered and sacrificed that I have in this interference, it would have been all right. And every man in this court would have deemed it an act worthy of reward rather than punishment.

This court acknowledges, as I suppose, the validity of the law of God. I see a book kissed here which I suppose to be the Bible, or at least the New Testament. That teaches me that all things that I would have men do to me, I should do to them. It teaches me, further, to "remember them that are in bonds, as bound with them." I tried to act according to that instruction. I say, I am yet too young to understand that God is any respecter of persons. I believe that to have interfered as I have done—as I have always freely admitted I have done—in behalf of His despised poor, was not wrong, but right. Now, if it is deemed necessary that I should give my life to further the end of justice, and mingle my blood further with the blood of my children and with the blood of millions in this slave country whose rights are disregarded by wicked, cruel, and unjust enactments—I submit. So let it be done!

Let me say one word further.

I feel entirely satisfied with the treatment I have received on my trial. Considering all the circumstances, it has been more generous than I expected. But I feel no guilt. I have stated from the first what was my intention and what was not. I never have had any design against the life of any person. I have never had any disposition to commit treason, or excite slaves to rebel, or make any general insurrection. I never encouraged any man to do so. I have always discouraged any idea of that kind.

Let me say, also, a word about the statements made by some of those connected with me. I hear it has been stated by some of them that I have persuaded them to join me. But the contrary is true. I do not say this to injure them, but because I regret their weakness. Each of them joined me of his own accord. And most of them joined at their own expense. I never saw or spoke with a number of them till the day they came to me.

Now I have done.

▶ Should Brown have left this paragraph unsaid in order to help save the lives of his friends? Why do you feel as you do?

The Life, Trial, and Execution of John Brown (New York: Robert W. Dewitt, 1859), pp. 100-101. Language simplified.

THE EXECUTION OF JOHN BROWN

At eleven o'clock on Friday, December 2nd, John Brown was brought out of the jail accompanied by Sheriff Campbell and assistants, and Capt. Avis, the jailer.

Brown was accompanied by no ministers. He desired no religious services either in the jail or on the scaffold.

On reaching the field where the gallows was erected, the prisoner said, "Why are none but military allowed in the inclosure? I am sorry citizens have been kept out." On reaching the gallows he observed Mr. Hunter and Mayor Green standing near. To them he said, "Gentlemen, goodbye." His voice did not falter.

The prisoner walked up the steps firmly, and was the first man on the gallows. Avis and Sheriff Campbell stood by his side. After shaking hands and bidding an affectionate farewell, he thanked them for their kindness. When the cap was put over his face, and the rope around his neck, Avis asked him to step forward on the trap. He replied, "You must lead me, I cannot see." The rope was adjusted, and the military order given, "Not ready yet." The soldiers marched, countermarched, and took position as if an enemy were in sight. They were thus occupied for nearly ten minutes. The prisoner was standing all the time. Avis asked if he was tired. Brown said "No, not tired. But don't keep me waiting longer than is necessary."

▶ Does making a person wait with a rope on his neck for ten minutes seem like "cruel or unusual punishment" to you?

While on the scaffold, Sheriff Campbell asked him if he would take a handkerchief in his hand to drop as a signal when he was ready. He replied, "No, I do not want it—but do not detain me any longer than is absolutely necessary."

He was swung off at fifteen minutes past eleven. A slight grasping of the hands and twitching of the muscles were seen. And then all was quiet.

The body was several times examined. And the pulse did not stop until thirty-five minutes had passed. The body was then cut down, placed in a coffin and conveyed under military escort to the depot. There it was put in a car to be carried to the ferry by a special train at four o'clock.

John Brown
as Others Have Seen Him

The following selections present several views of John Brown. The first four are the views of Brown's contemporaries. The fifth is the view of an American poet writing nearly seventy years after Brown's execution. The last is the view of a modern American historian.

WILLIAM LLOYD GARRISON, 1859

Was John Brown justified in his attempt? Yes, if Washington was in his. If Warren and Hancock were in theirs. If men are justified in striking a blow for freedom, when the question is one of a three-penny tax on tea, then, I say, they are a thousand times more

The Liberator, Boston, Massachusetts, December 16, 1859. Language simplified.

Joseph Warren and John Hancock were two patriot leaders during the American Revolution.

311

justified when it is to save fathers, mothers, wives and children from the slave-gang and the auction block, and to restore to them their God-given rights. Was John Brown justified in interfering in behalf of the slave population of Virginia to secure their freedom and independence? Yes, if LaFayette was justified in interfering to help our revolutionary fathers. If Kosciusko, if Pulaski, if Steuben, if DeKalb, if all who joined them from abroad were justified in that act, then John Brown was incomparably more so. If you believe in the right of assisting men who are of your own color to fight for freedom—God knows nothing of color or complexion, human rights know nothing of these distinctions—then you must cover, not only with a mantle of charity, but with the admiration of your hearts, the effort of John Brown at Harper's Ferry.

EDITORIAL
FROM A SOUTHERN NEWSPAPER, 1859

Some of the northern papers are lecturing the South on the subject of the outbreak. They remind our people that they are quietly sitting on the crust of a volcano, ready at any moment to burst forth and destroy them. This, they say, is the lesson the recent outbreak teaches. No foolhardy enthusiasts ever missed the mark further. It teaches a lesson to the fanatics of the North. It shows them that the slaves their misdirected efforts would save are so well satisfied with their condition that they will not join them in their rebellion. And by the time the outraged sovereignty of Virginia has been satisfied, they will learn one other great lesson. They will learn that the South can produce enough hemp to hang all the traitors the great "northern hive" can send among her people to stir up rebellion!

JEFFERSON DAVIS, DEMOCRATIC SENATOR FROM MISSISSIPPI, 1859

What is that stage to which the Union has advanced? The slave states had a majority in both branches of Congress once. Now the free states are seventeen. And the slave states are only fifteen in this Union. There has been a transfer of the majorities in Congress from the slave to the free states. The Government, Senator Seward tells us, has advanced another state. It will no longer intervene in favor of protection for our slaves. We may be robbed of our property. But the general Government will not intervene for our protection. When the government gets into the hands of the Republican party, the arm of the general Government, we are told, will not be raised for the protection of our slave property. Then intervention in favor of slavery and slave states will no longer be tolerated. We may be invaded.

312

LaFayette, Kosciusko, Pulaski, Steuben, and DeKalb were Europeans who served in various capacities with the Continental Army during the American Revolution.

▶ Is an individual, group, or government ever justified in intervening in a conflict between opposing factions in another country? If so, under what circumstances?

The Southern Watchman, Athens, Georgia, November 3, 1859. Language simplified.

Rope was commonly made from hemp, an Asiatic plant.

The Congressional Globe, Washington, D.C., 1860, p. 69. Language simplified.

And the black Republican Government will permit our soil to be violated and our people attacked and will raise no arm in our defense. When the Government gets into black Republican hands, state sovereignty will no longer be a bar to encroachments on our rights. Then John Brown, and a thousand John Browns, can invade us. And the Government will not protect us. There will be no army, no navy sent out to resist such an invasion. But we will be left to the tender mercies of our enemies. Has the South then no right to complain? Has the South then no right to fear when we are told that our property will not be protected when the Republicans get hold of the Government? Have we then no right to announce on this floor that if our property and our sovereignty are not to be protected, we are freed from our allegiance and will protect ourselves out of the union, if we cannot protect them in the Union? Have we no right to say that to secure our rights and protect our honor we will cut the ties that bind us together, even if it rushes us into a sea of blood.

ABRAHAM LINCOLN, 1860

You charge that we stir up rebellion among your slaves. We deny it. And what is your proof? Harper's Ferry! John Brown? John Brown was no Republican. And you have failed to involve a single Republican in his Harper's Ferry enterprise.

From a speech by Abraham Lincoln in New York City, February 27, 1860. Language simplified.

John Brown's effort was peculiar. It was not a slave rising. It was an attempt by white men to start a revolt among slaves. And the slaves refused to participate. In fact, it was so absurd that the slaves, with all their ignorance, saw plainly enough it could not succeed. That affair, in its philosophy, corresponds with many historical attempts to assassinate kings and emperors. A person like Brown broods over the oppression of a people till he believes that he has been commissioned by Heaven to free them. He makes the attempt. But it ends in little else than his own execution.

And what would you gain if you could, by the use of John Brown and the like, break up the Republican organization? Human action can be modified to some extent. But human nature cannot be changed. There is a judgment and a feeling against slavery in this nation. It cast at least a million and a half votes. You cannot destroy that judgment and feeling by breaking up the political organization which rallies around it. You can scarcely scatter an army which has been formed into order in the face of your heaviest fire. But if you could, how much would you gain by forcing the feeling which created it out of the peaceful channel of the ballot-box into some other channel? What would that other channel probably be? Would the number of John Browns be lessened or enlarged by the operation?

Here Lincoln refers to the people who voted for the Republican Party in 1860.

313

Stephen Vincent Benét, **John Brown's Body** (New York: Holt, Rinehart and Winston, Inc., 1927), p. 56. Copyright renewed © 1955, 1956, by Rosemary Carr Benét. Used by permission.

Brown used the name "Shubel Morgan" as an alias in Kansas.

Mores are moral attitudes.

STEPHEN VINCENT BENET
1928

He had the shepherd's gift, but that was all.
He had no other single gift for life.
Some men are pasture Death turns back to pasture,
Some are fire-opals on that iron wrist,
Some the deep roots of wisdoms not yet born.
John Brown was none of these,
He was a stone,
A stone eroded to a cutting edge
By obstinacy, failure and cold prayers.
Discredited farmer, dubiously involved
In lawsuit after lawsuit, Shubel Morgan
Fantastic bandit of the Kansas border,
Red-handed murderer at Pottawattomie,
Cloudy apostle, whooped along to death
By those who do no violence themselves
But only buy the guns to have it done,
Sincere of course, as all fanatics are,
And with a certain minor-prophet air,
That fooled the world to thinking him half-great
When all he did consistently was fail.

So far one advocate.
                    But there is this.

Sometimes there comes a crack in Time itself.
Sometimes the earth is torn by something blind.
Sometimes an image that has stood so long
It seems implanted as the polar star
Is moved against an unfathomed force
That suddenly will not have it any more.
Call it the *mores*, call it God or Fate,
Call it Mansoul or economic law,
That force exists and moves.
                            And when it moves
It will employ a hard and actual stone
To batter into bits an actual wall
And change the actual scheme of things.
                                    John Brown
Was such a stone—unreasoning as the stone,
Destructive as the stone, and, if you like,
Heroic and devoted as such a stone.

C. VANN WOODWARD, 1952

Southern zealots of secession had no better ally than John Brown. Non-slaveholders saw dramatized before them the menace of a slave uprising. They readily concluded that their wives and children, as much as the home of the planter, were threatened with the horror of insurrection. They frequently became more fanatical secessionists than the planters. In face of the northern [glorification] of Brown there was little that southern moderates could say in answer to such pronouncements as that of the New Orleans *Picayune* of December 2: "Crime becomes godliness, and criminals, red from the slaughter of innocent, are exalted to eminence beside the divine gospel of Peace." The Charleston *Mercury* of November 29 rejoiced that Harper's Ferry, "like a slap in the face," had roused Virginia from her hesitant neutrality and started her on the road to secession. "I have never before seen the public mind of Va. so deeply moved," wrote a Virginian sadly. "The people are far in advance of the politicians, and would most cheerfully follow the extremist counsels. Volunteer companies, horse & foot, are springing up everywhere."

This crisis psychology of 1859 persisted and deepened in the fateful year of 1860 into a pathological condition of mind. Delusions of persecution and impending disaster flourished. Out of Texas came wild rumors of incendiary fires, abolitionists plotting with slaves, and impending insurrection on a vast scale. Rumors of large stocks of strychnine in the possession of slaves and of plans for well-poisoning were widely believed, though unproved. . . .

In the course of the crisis each of the antagonists, according to the immemorial pattern, had become convinced of the depravity and [evilness] of the other. Each believed itself persecuted, menaced. "Let the 'higher law' of abolitionism be met by the 'higher law' of self-preservation," demanded the Richmond *Enquirer*. Lynch law was the only answer to pikes. "What additional insults and outrages will arouse it [the North] to assert its rights?" demanded Garrison. And Garrison's opposite number in Mississippi, Albert Gallatin Brown, cried: "Oh, God! to what depths of infamy are we sinking in the South if we allow these things to pass." Paranoia continued to induce counterparanoia, each antagonist infecting the other reciprocally, until the vicious spiral ended in war.

C. Vann Woodward, "John Brown's Private War," in *America in Crisis*, Daniel Aaron, ed. (New York: Alfred A. Knopf, Inc., 1952), pp. 128-129. Reprinted by permission.

Strychnine is a poison.

Paranoia is a tendency toward excessive suspiciousness of others.

FOR THOUGHT:

Do you think that war between the North and the South was the *inevitable* consequence of John Brown's raid on Harper's Ferry? Why or why not?

46 THE CIVIL WAR, 1860 - 1865

Lincoln Elected: The South Secedes

In 1860, the Republicans turned to Abraham Lincoln as their candidate. The Democratic party had always claimed strong support from all sections of the country. But by this time it had divided into northern and southern factions. As a result, Lincoln's election was almost a foregone conclusion. It was not, however, a national victory. Lincoln failed to receive a single electoral vote from a slave state.

The genius of the American political system had been its ability to absorb disagreements and to devise compromises that had prevented open rebellion. More often than not, the differences between the major parties had not been great. But in 1860 the flexibility of the political party system broke down. The South interpreted the Republican victory as a triumph for the North and for abolition.

▶If Lincoln thought slavery wrong, was it immoral of him to protect slavery in the South? Why or why not?

Lincoln was not an abolitionist. He believed that slavery was wrong and he opposed its extension. At the same time he felt obligated to uphold the Fugitive Slave Law and to protect slavery in the South. Some abolitionists refused to vote for him. They believed that his position on slavery was much too moderate. The political leaders in the South, however, believed that Lincoln's election proved that the balance of political power had definitely shifted to the North.

When Lincoln's electoral victory became known, South Carolina called a state convention. On December 20, 1860, the convention announced South Carolina's secession from the Union. Mississippi, Florida, Georgia, Alabama, Louisiana, and Texas quickly followed South Carolina. Early in February 1861 delegates from these states met in Montgomery, Alabama. There they formed a new government, the Confederate States of America. They adopted a constitution modeled after the United States Constitution. And they elected Jefferson Davis President.

Secession took place during President Buchanan's last months in office. Buchanan was a Democrat, sympathetic with the grievances of the South. But he was unwilling to admit the right of secession. At the same time, he did not feel authorized to use force to prevent secession.

Meanwhile, eight slave states had not seceded. People of good will from all parts of the country tried to find some compromise that would keep the Union intact. The Senate organized a special committee for this purpose. At the request of the Virginia Legislature a convention of delegates from twenty-one states met in Washington to search for a solution. All attempts at compromise failed.

Lincoln was inaugurated March 4, 1861. During the period between his election and inauguration he had remained largely silent. But he had made it clear that he would not support any compromise that might encourage the further spread of slavery. In his inaugural address he said that he had no intention of interfering with slavery in the states. And he urged the seceded states to return to the Union. He warned that he was sworn to uphold the Constitution and protect federal property. But he said there would be no violence "unless it be forced upon the national authority."

Attack on Fort Sumter: Civil War Begins

Lincoln's policy of firmness in the face of secession was put to the test almost immediately. During the previous few months the seceding states had claimed the federal property in their states. Southern troops had seized federal forts and arsenals in Georgia, Alabama, Florida, Louisiana, Arkansas, and Texas. In Charleston, South Carolina, Major Robert Anderson, who commanded the United States troops there, had retreated to Fort Sumter in Charleston Harbor. President Buchanan had dispatched an unarmed ship to bring supplies to Fort Sumter. But South Carolina shore guns had driven the ship away. Lincoln had to decide what the federal government should do to support Major Anderson's garrison at Fort Sumter. He decided to try to supply the fort peacefully without sending armed force. This was consistent with his inaugural promise. And he notified South Carolina of his decision.

Now the South had to decide what action to take. Jefferson Davis made the decision for the Confederacy. Fort Sumter was to be evacuated or captured. On April 12, 1861, South Carolina guns opened fire on Sumter. On April 13, Major Anderson surrendered. The next day President Lincoln declared that "insurrection" existed. He called for the raising of a volunteer army in the North. In the next weeks Virginia, Arkansas, Tennessee, and North Carolina seceded. The Civil War had begun.

War Aims

The war aims of the North and South were directly opposed. The South wanted the North to recognize the independence of the Confederate states and to recognize their right to legislate for themselves in all matters, including slavery. The North wanted to restore the Union. In addition, many northerners wanted to free the slaves. During the early years of the War, Lincoln insisted that his first purpose was to save the Union and "not either to save or destroy slavery."

The Crittenden Compromise, suggested in 1860, was considered most seriously. Senator John J. Crittenden of Kentucky proposed that the 36° 30′ line be extended to the Pacific, with slavery allowed and protected south of it and banned north of it. Lincoln was opposed to this compromise because it would have permitted the extension of slavery.

The western part of Virginia refused to secede. In 1863, that area was admitted to the Union as the state of West Virginia.

317

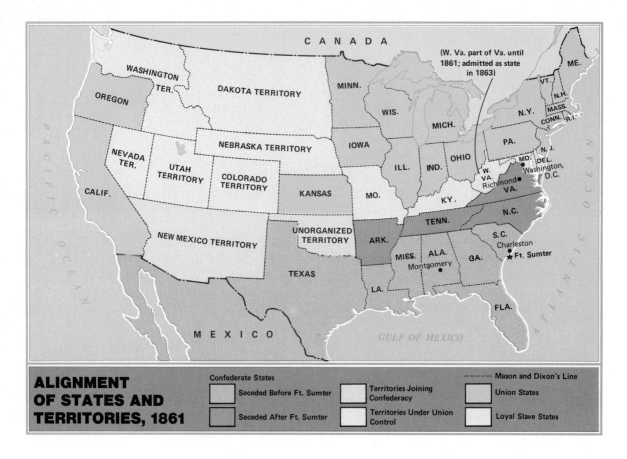

ALIGNMENT OF STATES AND TERRITORIES, 1861

Confederate States
- Seceded Before Ft. Sumter
- Seceded After Ft. Sumter

- Territories Joining Confederacy
- Territories Under Union Control

- Mason and Dixon's Line
- Union States
- Loyal Slave States

Comparative Strength

At first, each side had some advantages. The South needed only to fight defensively and maintain a stalemate to win its point. Most of the best officers in the United States army were southerners. They returned to the South after secession. The ruling classes in England and France sympathized with the South. Southern leaders hoped to exchange cotton for European economic and military support.

The North had superior military capacity from the beginning. Twenty million people lived in the North as opposed to nine million (including slaves) in the South. The North had a manufacturing capacity seven times greater than that of the South. It had a much more extensive railroad system, most of the country's merchant marine and navy, and a near monopoly in the firearms industry.

The first important battle of the War was fought at Bull Run, Virginia (July 21, 1861), only a few miles outside of Washington. There smaller Confederate forces routed a large Union army. The Confederate victory was in part due to the firm stand of General T. J. Jackson, then nicknamed "Stonewall."

318

Lincoln's Problems at Home and Abroad

Meanwhile, Lincoln encountered political and diplomatic difficulties. When the southern states seceded and their congressmen left Washington, the control of Congress naturally fell into the hands of northern Republicans. Within the Republican Party a group of "Radicals" took over the leadership of the Congress during the early years of the War. The Radicals had strong abolitionist support. And they urged Lincoln to move more aggressively against the South to free the slaves. Under the leadership of Representative Thaddeus Stevens, they dominated the Joint House and Senate Committee on the Conduct of the War. They remained a thorn in Lincoln's side throughout the conflict.

Lincoln was as anxious as anyone to bring the War to a speedy end. He believed, however, that it was his constitutional duty to direct the war effort. He was unwilling to issue a proclamation emancipating all slaves. He feared that it would encourage the South to fight to the bitter end. He also felt it would alienate the slaveholding border states that had reluctantly sided with the Union. Lincoln's insistence on moving cautiously against slavery caused much friction between him and the Radicals in Congress.

The diplomatic picture was not much brighter during the early years of the War. England maintained neutrality. It apparently intended to consider the struggle between North and South a war, rather than a domestic rebellion. Lincoln threatened to break off diplomatic relations if England entered into official negotiations with commissioners representing the Confederacy. In November 1861, an American warship stopped the British steamer *Trent*. Two Confederate commissioners en route to England were removed from the ship. This interference with a British ship on the high seas inflamed British public opinion. The threat of war with Britain subsided only when Secretary of State William Seward released the Confederates.

For several months, it seemed that 1862 would repeat the disappointments of the previous year for the North. McClellan remained reluctant to engage the enemy in Virginia. And the brilliant leader of the Confederate army, General Robert E. Lee, defeated the North in a second battle at Bull Run (August 1862).

The North Gathers Strength

Two events, however, made the North more optimistic. The Union mounted an effective naval blockade along the southern coastline. And Lincoln discovered that General Ulysses S. Grant could win battles. Grant was a West Point graduate. He had served in the Mexican War and later retired from the army. When the War started, he returned to military service at the head of a regiment of Illinois volunteers. In April 1862, Grant moved south. With heavy losses on

Lincoln had offered Lee the command of the Union armies. Lee, who had opposed both secession and slavery, felt his first loyalty belonged to Virginia. When Virginia seceded, he joined his state. Generals on both sides had high regard for Lee's character and ability. Lincoln had appointed McClellan commander of the Army of the Potomac after the first defeat at Bull Run.

both sides, he defeated the main Confederate army in the west at Shiloh, Tennessee, near the Mississippi border. At about the same time, Union gunboats bombarded New Orleans. And Union troops moved into the city. The strategy of dividing the Confederacy along the Mississippi and Tennessee rivers began to bear fruit.

The First Strike at Slavery

Despite limited success on the battlefield, the balance of power definitely shifted to the North by 1863. On January 1, Abraham Lincoln issued the Emancipation Proclamation. It declared that all slaves in areas still in rebellion were free. The proclamation applied only to the Confederate states, over which the federal government had no control. So it did not effectively free any slaves. It did, however, strengthen Lincoln's hand with the Radical Republicans in Congress. And it helped to influence public opinion abroad, especially in England. The English, proud of their own freedom, were unwilling to give moral or material support to the South.

In 1863, the war to save the Union also became a war to free the slaves. Northern blacks naturally wanted to participate in such a war. Thousands of black men had responded to Lincoln's call for volunteers in 1861. But they had been turned away. By the time the Union army had begun to draft soldiers, however, black men were being accepted into the northern army. And Union black regiments had seen action in several southern states. More than 180,000 black men enrolled in the Union army by the end of the War. Over 38,000 black soldiers lost their lives in the War. Many black soldiers were decorated for bravery.

An End in Sight

Two decisive encounters, in the spring and summer of 1863, foreshadowed the South's defeat. In May, Grant lay siege to 30,000 Confederate troops in Vicksburg, Mississippi. When Vicksburg fell on July 4, the Union gained control of the entire Mississippi River. At the same time in the east, General Robert E. Lee launched a final daring attempt to split the Union. He invaded the North and hoped to cut the main east-west railroads in Pennsylvania and Maryland. On July 1, Lee's army of 70,000 men attacked a Union force of 90,000 commanded by George Meade at Gettysburg, Pennsylvania. After three days of furious, bloody fighting, the Confederate forces withdrew in retreat to Virginia.

The Union victories at Vicksburg and Gettysburg introduced the final phase of the war. In March 1864, Grant assumed general command of the Union armies. He took personal command of the Army of the Potomac and began to move slowly, but relentlessly,

The Thirteenth Amendment was adopted in 1865. It freed all slaves in the United States and its territories.

Appeals for volunteers did not provide the necessary human resources in 1863. Congress passed the first draft law. One of its most resented features allowed a man to escape the draft by hiring a substitute to serve in his place or by paying a $300 fee to the authorities. They, in turn, paid a bounty to a substitute.

against Lee's smaller army. At the same time, General William T. Sherman moved south and east from Chattanooga, Tennessee, into Georgia. Sherman's march through Georgia to the sea further fragmented the South. It had already been split vertically by Union victories in the river valleys of the west.

The Election of 1864

The war seemed to be going better. But, in 1864, gloom and frustration marked the public mood in the North. The fighting had dragged on for three frightful years. It was an election year, and Lincoln was in trouble. On one side, Peace Democrats in the North who wanted a negotiated settlement with the South harassed the President. They drew their political strength largely from working classes in the cities. There intense resentment existed against the government's draft laws. In the summer of 1863 in New York City, this resentment had erupted into four days of rioting, looting, and lynching of blacks. Union troops fresh from the battlefields at Gettysburg had been called in to restore order. On the other side, Lincoln still had trouble with the Radicals in his own party. Many of them preferred another candidate in 1864. Nevertheless, the Republicans nominated Lincoln for re-election. General McClellan opposed him as the Democratic candidate and ran on a peace platform. Lincoln easily won in the electoral vote (212-21). But the popular vote shows how divided northern opinion was about his leadership. Lincoln received only 2.2 million votes to McClellan's 1.8 million.

By the time of Lincoln's inauguration in March 1865, the South's fate was sealed. In Georgia, Sherman pursued a policy of destroying factories, warehouses, bridges, railroads, and anything else that might contribute to the Confederate cause while his troops "lived off the land." In April 1865, Grant's relentless pounding forced Lee out of Richmond. On April 9, Lee surrendered the tattered remains of his army at Appomattox Courthouse in Virginia. The remaining Confederate generals soon followed Lee's example.

The Death of Lincoln

In his Second Inaugural Address, Abraham Lincoln called upon his countrymen to proceed "with malice toward none; with charity for all . . . to bind up the nation's wounds" and "to do all which may achieve and cherish a just and lasting peace among ourselves, and with all nations." Six weeks later, only a few days after Appomattox, Lincoln was killed by an assassin while attending the theater. We will never know how much difference his presence and leadership might have made during Reconstruction.

Andrew Johnson, Democrat from Tennessee and the only southerner to remain in Congress after secession, was selected as the Republican or Union party's Vice-Presidential candidate, as a replacement for Hannibal Hamlin.

▶To win a war, should it be permissible to destroy anything that might contribute to the enemy's cause or to take any action that might reduce the enemy's chances of winning? Why or why not?

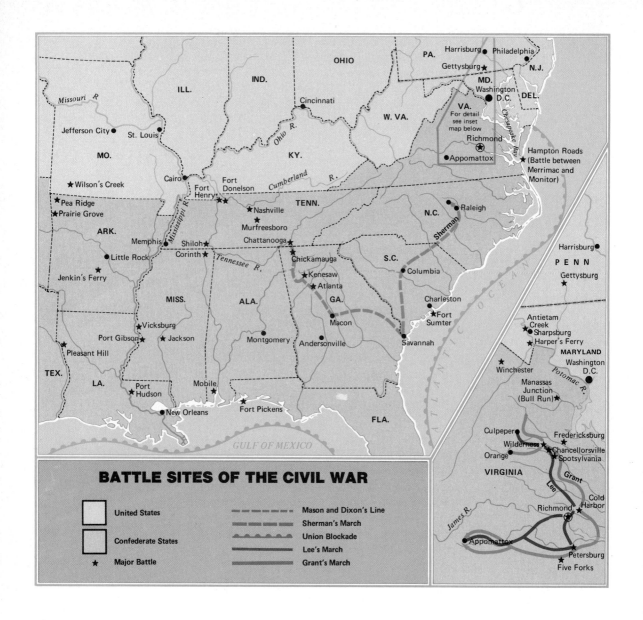

BATTLE SITES OF THE CIVIL WAR

☐ United States	
☐ Confederate States	
★ Major Battle	

- – – Mason and Dixon's Line
- —— Sherman's March
- ～～～ Union Blockade
- —— Lee's March
- —— Grant's March

47 RECONSTRUCTION,
1865-1877

HISTORICAL ESSAY

What were the most important problems confronting the American people as they tried to reconstruct the Union? What strategies did the political leaders pursue? Did Reconstruction work or was it a failure? The remainder of this essay is built around these questions.

A New Role for the Freed Slaves

Many of the problems involved in Reconstruction were visible in the form of shelled cities, wrecked railroads, and abandoned fields. The southern economy would need to be rebuilt. But who would do the building? In the past, slaves had been the work force in the South. What kind of work force would take their place? Would the freed slaves be given land? Could they be forced or persuaded to work?

Involved in all questions about the freed slaves was something not so visible—the attitude of white Americans toward black Americans. And most southerners accepted the abolition of slavery as part of the price of defeat. However, almost all of them continued to believe that blacks were more suited for slavery than for freedom. They also believed that large numbers of whites and blacks could never live together in harmony except under white dominance.

The refusal to admit the injustice of slavery was unique to the South. But the belief that a basic inequality existed between the races was almost universal in the country. Laws that prevented blacks from voting in northern states were only one example of the general prejudice against them outside the South. Widespread prejudice meant that attempts to legislate equality for the freed slaves would be resisted violently in the South. And in the long run, except for a few unyielding reformers, such legislation would win only half-hearted support from people in the North.

Americans in the North also found it increasingly difficult to concentrate on Reconstruction during the postwar years. Reconstruction of a lasting union without slavery had to compete with new economic opportunities for the attention and energy of the American people.

The President Against the Radicals

Finally, there was the problem of assigning political responsibility for Reconstruction. Lincoln had taken the position that the Confederate states rebelled against the Union. He argued that a state could not legally secede. The President, as Commander-in-Chief of the Army, had the right to grant pardons. Lincoln felt that the President should help southern states to resume their proper place in the Union. If 10 percent of the people in a southern state professed loyalty to the federal government and recognized the end of slavery, Lincoln was prepared to have them send representatives to Congress.

▶ Under what circumstances, if any, should governments have the right to demand public declarations of loyalty from citizens?

323

Lincoln ran into trouble with Congress. The Radical Republicans in Congress felt that the President was exceeding his authority. They argued that the Confederate states were conquered provinces, subject to congressional control. They should not be readmitted to the Union until Congress was convinced that they were, in the words of Representative Thaddeus Stevens of Pennsylvania, "republican in spirit and placed under the guardianship of loyal men."

Andrew Johnson succeeded Lincoln. He was a former Jacksonian Democrat from eastern Tennessee. He hated slavery and slaveholders. Johnson had been a staunch Union supporter during the secession crisis. Honest and courageous, he lacked Lincoln's patience and sense of the public mood. When Johnson came to the White House, he faced the immediate problem of reaching an agreement with Congress on Reconstruction policy. Congress had already demonstrated its unwillingness to go along with Lincoln's plan of Reconstruction. But Johnson pursued a similar policy. By the end of 1865, all the southern states had satisfied his requirements for Reconstruction. However, Congress still refused to admit southern representatives. The executive and legislative branches of government had reached a deadlock over the question of responsibility for reconstructing the Union.

Black Codes and Civil Rights

Developments in the southern states also disturbed many congressmen. Beginning in the fall of 1865, southern legislatures passed a series of laws known as "Black Codes." These laws attempted to regulate the terms on which blacks would continue to work on plantations. Some provisions in the laws were designed to protect former slaves. But the laws inhibited blacks from leaving their plantations and moving around the country like other free people. Abolitionist Republicans in the Congress believed that southerners designed the "Black Codes" to preserve the basic features of slavery. Therefore, they attempted to secure freedom for the blacks by passing a Civil Rights Act. They also authorized federal agents working with the Freedmen's Bureau to try persons accused of denying blacks their rights. Both laws were passed by Congress over the vetoes of President Johnson.

In the congressional elections of 1866, Johnson decided to go to the voters to campaign for his Reconstruction policy. By this time he had gained the backing of northern Democrats. But the Republicans opposed him solidly. Johnson ignored the hostility of northern audiences. And he vehemently attacked his Republican opponents in the Congress by name. The Radicals, however, represented the public mood more accurately than Johnson did. They piled up heavy majorities in both houses. When the new Congress met, the period of Presidential Reconstruction ended.

Most of the "Black Codes" recognized the right of blacks to marry, to own property, and to sue and testify in court, at least in cases involving other blacks. Most of the "Codes" also specified that blacks could work only as farmers or domestic servants who could not change jobs without the loss of pay.

The Civil Rights Act of 1866 declared that states could not deny blacks the right to testify in court or to own property. It made blacks citizens and gave the federal courts jurisdiction over cases involving deprivation of rights. It was later declared unconstitutional because it violated states' rights.

POST CIVIL WAR AMENDMENTS

The Thirteenth Amendment ended slavery and gave Congress the power of enforcement.

The Fourteenth Amendment 1. declared that everybody born or naturalized in the United States is a citizen of both the nation and the state he or she lives in. A state cannot make laws limiting the rights of citizens, nor refuse due process of the law.

2. apportioned representatives on the basis of the entire population of the state (thus nullifying Article 1, Section 2, Clause 3)—except non-taxpaying Indians—and threatened to reduce the number of representatives in any state that denied the vote to male citizens over 21.

3. denied public office to most former U. S. officials who had joined the Confederacy, and repudiated the Confederate war debt.

4. gave Congress the power of enforcement.

The Fifteenth Amendment said that neither the federal nor the state government could deny the right to vote because of race, color, or previous condition of slavery. It gave Congress the power of enforcement.

Congress Gains Control

Radical Republicans controlled Reconstruction policy from 1867 to about 1872. When Congress convened in March 1867, the Radicals commanded a two-thirds vote in each house. This was enough to override any Presidential veto. They passed Reconstruction acts which declared existing state governments (except that of Tennessee) illegal and which divided the South into five military districts, each under the jurisdiction of a general. To qualify for readmission to the Union, these acts required states to elect delegates to new constitutional conventions on the basis of universal manhood suffrage. The conventions had to guarantee black suffrage and to ratify the Fourteenth Amendment. This amendment had originally been proposed in June 1866. But Tennessee, already under Radical control, was the only southern state to ratify it. Tennessee was restored to the Union on July 24, 1866.

The South refused to organize governments under these conditions. So Congress passed additional legislation requiring military commanders to enroll voters. About 700,000 blacks and 600,000 whites were registered in this way. The great majority of them were prepared to cooperate with the Radicals. The Radicals dominated the state conventions which met in 1868. But blacks also played an active role.

The new constitutions drawn up by the conventions guaranteed civil rights for blacks and disenfranchised ex-rebels. By 1870, all Confederate states were back in the Union. The Radicals were in control in all except Tennessee, Virginia, and North Carolina where the whites were in the majority. And the Democrats were able to regain control. In the same year, the Fifteenth Amendment went into effect.

Meanwhile, the struggle within the government between Congress and the President became critical. In order to gather a case for impeachment and to curb the powers of the executive, Congress passed, over Johnson's veto, a Tenure of Office Act. It forbade the President from dismissing any important civil official without the approval of the Senate. Johnson decided to test the constitutionality of the law. He dismissed Secretary of War Edwin M. Stanton, who had cooperated frequently with the Radicals. The House of Representatives, by a vote of 126 to 47, impeached Johnson on eleven counts. These counts included violation of the Tenure Act and trying to discredit Congress. The Senate tried the President. The vote to convict him was thirty-five to nineteen. This was one vote short of the two-thirds majority which the Constitution requires for conviction.

President Grant Supports the Radicals

The Radicals controlled Congress. But their hold on the public opinion of the country became less secure. In the Presidential election of 1868, the Republicans nominated Ulysses S. Grant. They endorsed Radical Reconstruction and condemned Johnson. The Democrats nominated a former governor of New York, Horatio Seymour. They adopted a platform opposing Radical Reconstruction. Three southern states did not participate in the election. And six others were under Radical control. The Republicans won by less than a 10 percent majority of the popular vote. Republican political control in the South made Grant's victory possible.

During his first term, Grant supported Radical Reconstruction. Congress investigated the attempt to restore white supremacy to the South through the terrorist activities of the secret Ku Klux Klan. And in 1870 and 1871 Congress passed legislation to enforce the Fourteenth and Fifteenth Amendments. By 1872, however, the Republicans themselves fell apart over the Reconstruction issue. A group of "liberal" Republicans split from the rest of the party. They nominated Horace Greeley for President. Their platform opposed the corruption being uncovered in the Grant administration and favored a more conciliatory policy toward the South. The party regulars renominated Grant, who won re-election. By the time he took office for a second term, however, the balance of power in the southern state governments had begun to slip back into the hands of southern whites.

In a number of northern states, blacks voted for the first time after the ratification of the Fifteenth Amendment.

The Ku Klux Klan was formed by southern extremists. They used terrorist tactics against blacks to win political control in the South.

326

The Compromise of 1877

The election of 1876 marked the official end of Reconstruction. The two major Presidential candidates were Rutherford B. Hayes, a Republican, and Samuel J. Tilden, a Democrat. Tilden won the popular vote. But Republican-controlled election boards in Florida, South Carolina, and Louisiana claimed victory—despite higher Democratic votes. They claimed that blacks had been prevented from voting. Without the electoral votes of these states, Tilden had 184 undisputed votes—1 short of the majority he needed. If the disputed votes all went to Hayes, he would have the 185 to win. Congress appointed an Electoral Commission consisting of fifteen men selected from the House, Senate, and Supreme Court. By an 8-7 vote, the election was awarded to Hayes, with the understanding that federal troops would be withdrawn from the South. This so-called "Compromise of 1877" formally marked the reconciliation of North and South. The South had been "redeemed." This meant that political leadership reverted largely to members of the old planter class.

Reconstruction: Progress and Problems

Was Reconstruction a failure? The answer depends on what is meant by the question. Reconstruction succeeded in that the Union was restored without slavery. Reconstruction failed in that blacks were not taken into the mainstream of American life on an equal basis with other citizens. And southerners continued to feel bitter toward the North.

What accounted for the failure of blacks to gain equality? Belief in equal rights for minorities was not popular in the 1860's and 1870's. Many of the Republicans who voted for civil rights legislation did so more because they wanted blacks to vote Republican than because they were concerned with the black as a person. In addition, many Americans associated the evidence of graft and corruption in the Reconstruction governments with uneducated blacks. They questioned whether blacks were prepared for all of the responsibilities of full citizenship.

There is no question that profit and corruption played a role in Radical Reconstruction. State taxes skyrocketed throughout the South. All too often, substantial revenues ended up in the pockets of unscrupulous legislators. Many black legislators in the South shared in the loot. But it does not appear that they were any more guilty than their white colleagues.

Graft and corruption were not peculiar to the South during the period. Scandals riddled Grant's administration. His Secretary of War resigned when it was disclosed that he had accepted bribes. During the same period, the infamous Tweed Ring swindled millions of dollars

William Marcy Tweed was the boss of Tammany Hall, the Democratic political organization in New York City.

The owners of the Union Pacific Railroad Company organized the Credit Mobilier to construct the railroad. They awarded contracts to the Credit Mobilier so as to guarantee themselves huge profits. When threatened with a congressional investigation of their dishonest dealings, they sold Credit Mobilier stock at a low price to influential congressmen.

from the people of New York City. At about the same time, prominent congressmen were selling their political influence to the Credit Mobilier Construction Company.

Blacks never dominated Reconstruction government. They never elected a governor. And they held a legislative majority only in South Carolina. Blacks who did hold office seem on the whole to have been as qualified as white officeholders. And the governments which they helped to shape made lasting accomplishments. For example, they helped to bring progressive welfare legislation and free public education to the South. Some of the black lawmakers, such as Jonathan Gibbs in Florida and Francis Cardozo in South Carolina, were better educated than their white colleagues. Most of the blacks active in southern politics during this period were moderate people. They tried to find a way to live together in peace and cooperation with whites.

Did Reconstruction fail? Students of American history must sift the evidence for themselves. Americans restored the Union without slavery. But in 1877, the American ideal of liberty, equality, and the pursuit of happiness for all was still a long way from reality.

The Growth of Industry

STATING THE ISSUE

At the end of the ninteenth century, people looked back on the years since the Civil War with amazement. The nation seemed to have changed completely in their lifetimes. All around them were huge new cities, hosts of immigrants from Europe, new machinery, a vast railroad network, and thousands of new factories, mills, and farms each whirring with machines.

These dramatic changes began well before the Civil War. The textile industry had developed in New England early in the nineteenth century. In most northern states, factories, mines, and mills developed along with the railroad boom of the 1840's and 1850's. After the Civil War, however, the entire economy, even in the defeated South, spurted ahead. New ways of doing things began to affect everyone, including the men and women who lived on isolated farms or in small country towns.

The new society made a deep impression on American writers. In 1889, a prominent writer on economic affairs wrote proudly: "The economic changes that have occurred during the last quarter of a century, or during the present generation, have unquestionably been more important and varied than during any former corresponding period of the world's history."

A few years later, John Dewey, America's foremost educator, told an audience: "One can hardly believe there has been a revolution in all history so rapid, so extensive, so complete." Hundreds of other observers made similar statements. Industry was changing America. Chapter 13 introduces the story of this postwar revolution through three readings and a historical essay.

1400 1500 1600 1700 1800 1900 2000

1859 The first successful oil well is drilled near Titusville, Pennsylvania
1866 First transatlantic telegraph cable is laid
1866 Plans are made to establish the Bessemer method of making steel in United States' industry
1868 Open-hearth process of making steel is introduced in Trenton, New Jersey
1869 First transcontinental railroad is completed
1869 John D. Rockefeller organizes Standard Oil Company
1887 Congress passes Interstate Commerce Act establishing "just and reasonable" rates on railroad shipping lines

1890 Congress passes Sherman Antitrust Act
1893 Business failures cause major depression
1894 First hydroelectric plant is built at Niagara Falls
1899 Andrew Carnegie forms Carnegie Steel Corporation
1901 United States Steel Corporation is formed
1914 Henry Ford introduces electric conveyor belt to automobile production
1920 Census reports that half the population lives in cities
1929 Stock market crash is followed by the Great Depression

48 COLD STATISTICS AND PEOPLE

The revolution Dewey wrote about surrounded Americans in 1900. New steel mills lined river valleys, filling the air with thick clouds of smoke and dust. American cities smelled of industry. Kerosene lamps and electric lights brightened long winter evenings. Immigrants from all parts of the world mixed with each other and with native Americans on streetcars, at work, and in polling places. People sensed that America was changing.

Yet impressions can be misleading. Observations can provide only a partial picture of the changes which were affecting America. People who study contemporary societies supplement their observations with other forms of data.

Many of the changes that had the greatest impact on the new America resulted from industrialism. These changes can be shown with statistics. But statistics are only numbers. They have meaning only when a person who uses them looks beyond the numbers to learn their significance for men and women.

Reading 48 contains statistics about various aspects of the American economy from the end of the Civil War to the onset of the great depression of the 1930's. Study questions accompany each figure.

Measuring Change: Some Data

FIGURE 48 A   **TOTAL POPULATION AND URBAN POPULATION, 1860-1930**

Which appeared to be growing faster, total population or urban population?

U.S. Bureau of the Census, Historical Statistics of the United States, Colonial Times to 1957 (Washington, D.C.: Government Printing Office, 1960), pp. 7, 14.

Year	Total Population	Population in Cities of 25,000 or More	% of Population in Urban Areas (2500 or More)	% of Population in Cities of 25,000 or More
1860	31,400,000	3,800,000	20%	12%
1870	39,800,000	5,800,000	25%	15%
1880	50,200,000	8,700,000	28%	17%
1890	63,900,000	14,000,000	35%	22%
1900	76,000,000	19,800,000	40%	26%
1910	92,000,000	28,500,000	46%	31%
1920	105,800,000	37,800,000	51%	36%
1930	122,800,000	49,200,000	56%	40%

FIGURE 48B   **GROSS NATIONAL PRODUCT, 1869-1929**

It is difficult to measure the value of all the goods and services produced in the United States. Figure 48B gives one way to measure this value. It is called the gross national product or GNP. The figures are expressed in constant 1929 dollars—the worth of the goods and services at prices charged in 1929. When more than one year is indicated, the estimate is the average annual GNP for the period.

How can you use this figure and Figure 48A to estimate the real increase in the wealth of the nation?

U.S. Bureau of the Census, Historical Statistics, p. 139.

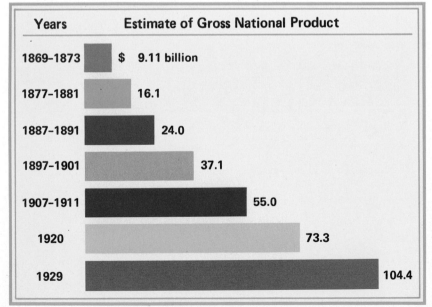

Years	Estimate of Gross National Product
1869–1873	$ 9.11 billion
1877–1881	16.1
1887–1891	24.0
1897–1901	37.1
1907–1911	55.0
1920	73.3
1929	104.4

►Which do you value more, increased production or efforts to save the environment? Why?

FIGURE 48C   NUMBER OF WORKERS IN SELECTED INDUSTRIES, 1870-1930

What appear to be the major trends described here?

U.S. Bureau of the Census, Historical Statistics, p. 74.

Industry	1870	1890	1910	1930
Total Workers°	12,920,000	23,740,000	36,730,000	47,400,000
Agriculture	6,430,000	9,990,000	11,340,000	10,180,000
Manufacturing	2,250,000	4,750,000	8,230,000	10,770,000
Construction	750,000	1,440,000	2,300,000	3,030,000
Education	190,000	510,000	900,000	1,630,000
Professional services	140,000	350,000	770,000	1,720,000
Government	100,000	190,000	540,000	1,130,000

°Totals include workers of industries not shown here.

FIGURE 48D   OUTPUT PER HOUR WORKED, 1869-1930

To compile these statistics, the author divided the value of all the goods and services produced in the United States in 1899 by an estimate of all the hours worked by Americans to produce the goods and services of this value. For convenience sake, his answer is described as an index figure of 100. Changes in the output per hour worked before or after 1899 can be described as more or less than the index figure.

1. What does this chart show you?
2. What are the limitations of expressing the increase in productivity solely in relation to hours worked?

American Economic History, Seymour E. Harris, ed. (New York: McGraw-Hill Book Company, Inc., 1961), p. 72.

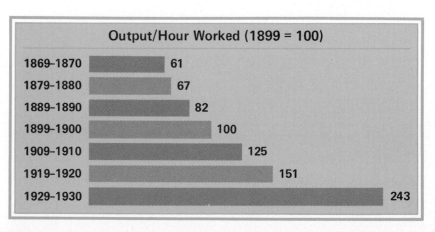

Output/Hour Worked (1899 = 100)

1869-1870	61
1879-1880	67
1889-1890	82
1899-1900	100
1909-1910	125
1919-1920	151
1929-1930	243

FIGURE 48E FAMILY EXPENDITURES ON CONSUMER GOODS, 1888-1918

By consumer goods, economists mean goods, such as food and clothing, which people use to satisfy their wants.

Figure 48E describes the results of three studies of the income and spending habits of industrial and clerical workers in American cities between 1888 and 1918. As in Figure 48B, the dollar amounts are expressed in constant dollars, in this case, constant 1950 dollars.

1. Was the standard of living in America improving between 1888 and 1918?
2. What did people do with their additional income?

	1888-1891	1901	1917-1918
Number of families surveyed	2,562	11,156	12,096
Average family size	3.9 persons	4.0 persons	4.9 persons
Average money income	$1793	$1914	$2408
Average total expenditure for goods and services	$1671	$1817	$2163
Average expenditure for food and drink	$ 797	$ 952	$ 854

U.S. Bureau of the Census, Historical Statistics, p. 181.

FIGURE 48F NUMBER OF BUSINESS FAILURES, 1870-1930

The growth of an economy is not always smooth. The "ups and downs" of an economy are called the business cycle. Figure 48F measures one dimension of the cycle. It describes the rate at which business firms have gone out of business because they could not make a profit and pay their bills.

How uneven was economic growth during this period?

U.S. Bureau of the Census, Historical Statistics, p. 570.

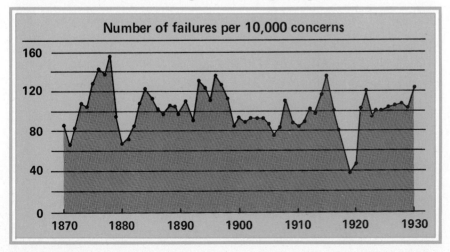

Number of failures per 10,000 concerns

▶Should the federal government give financial support to businesses that are failing?

49 TWO BUSINESSMEN EXPLAIN ECONOMIC GROWTH

Americans saw that their world was changing, and they struggled to explain why. The burden of explanation fell most heavily upon the leaders of giant business concerns. They were the people who seemed to have profited most from the changes. They felt called upon both to explain the changes and to justify them. People with a great deal of new personal wealth felt they had to justify their right to be wealthy. In the same way, business leaders, particularly of large firms, had to explain why it was right for them to direct the working lives of laborers whom they hardly knew. As business people struggled with these issues, they tried to answer the question: Who made the economy grow?

John D. Rockefeller and Andrew Carnegie were two of America's most successful businessmen. Beginning in the 1860's, Rockefeller organized a giant combination of oil refineries. By 1900, this combination controlled roughly 80 percent of the refinery capacity in the United States. Rockefeller's enormous personal income and wealth exceeded the imagination of most citizens. At the time of his death in 1937, he had given almost $600 million to charity.

Carnegie was born in Scotland and came to the United States as a youth. He achieved considerable success working for the Pennsylvania Railroad. At the close of the Civil War, he invested his savings in ironmaking. In the 1870's, he turned to steel production. He was a major figure in changing this technologically backward American industry. In 1901 he sold his interest in the Carnegie Steel Corporation to J.P. Morgan for about $440 million. At the time of the sale, the new firm, the United States Steel Corporation, controlled half of the steel productive capacity in this country. Reading 49 gives Rockefeller's and Carnegie's explanations for the growth of the American economy. As you read, try to answer these questions:

1. What were the qualities of a successful businessman according to Rockefeller and Carnegie?
2. How much did these business leaders depend on other people to carry out their plans?

John D. Rockefeller
Explains Business Growth

Rockefeller recorded his thoughts and observations on his life and times in his Reminiscences. *This selection from his book gives his explanation for business success.*

It is always, I presume, a question in every business just how fast it is wise to go. We went pretty rapidly in those days, building and expanding in all directions. We were confronted with fresh emergencies constantly. A new oil field would be discovered, tanks for storage had to be built almost overnight, and this was going on when old fields were being exhausted. So we were often under the double strain of losing the facilities in one place where we were fully equipped, and having to build up a plant for storing and transporting in a new field where we were totally unprepared. These are some of the things which make the whole oil trade a perilous one. But we had with us a group of courageous men who recognized . . . that a business cannot be a great success that does not fully and efficiently accept and take advantage of its opportunities.

The part played by one of my earliest partners, Mr. H.M. Flagler, was always an inspiration to me. . . . He undertook, single handed, the task of building up the east coast of Florida. He was not satisfied to plan a railroad from St. Augustine to Key West . . . But in addition he has built a chain of superb hotels to induce tourists to go to this newly developed country.

This one man, by his own energy and capital, has opened up a vast stretch of country, so that the old inhabitants and the new settlers may have a market for their products. He has given work to thousands of these people. . . .

You hear a good many people say much about greed in American life. One would think to hear them talk that we were a race of misers in this country. . . . It is by no means for money alone that these active-minded men labor. They are engaged in a fascinating occupation. The zest of the work is maintained by something better than the mere accumulation of money. And, as I think I have said elsewhere, the standards of business are high and getting better all the time. . . .

In my early days men acted just as they do now, no doubt. When there was anything to be done for general trade betterment, almost every man had some good reason for believing that his case was a special one. . . . For every foolish thing he did, or wanted to do, for every unbusinesslike plan he had, he always pleaded that it was necessary in his case. He was the one man who had to sell at less than cost, to disrupt all the business plans of others in his trade, because his individual position was so absolutely different from all the rest.

John D. Rockefeller, **Random Reminiscences of Men and Events** (New York: Doubleday and Company, Inc., 1933), pp. 9-11, 71-75. Copyright 1909, Doubleday and Company, Inc. Copyright renewed 1936, John D. Rockefeller. Reprinted by permission of the trustees of the trust created for Margaret de Cuevas under the will of John D. Rockefeller. Language simplified.

It was often a heart-breaking undertaking to convince those men that the perfect occasion which would lead to the perfect opportunity would never come. Even if they waited until the crack o'doom.

Then again, we had the type of man who really never knew all the facts about his own affairs. Many of the brightest kept their books in such a way that they did not actually know when they were making money on a certain operation and when they were losing. . . . When a man's affairs are not going well, he hates to study the books and face the truth. From the first, the men who managed the Standard Oil Company kept their books intelligently as well as correctly. We knew how much we made and where we gained or lost. At least, we tried not to deceive ourselves.

My ideas of business are no doubt old-fashioned. But the fundamental principles do not change from generation to generation. Sometimes I think that our quick-witted American businessmen, whose spirit and energy are so splendid, do not always sufficiently study the real underlying foundations of business management. . . . Many people assume that they can get away from the truth by avoiding thinking about it. But the natural law is inevitable, and the sooner it is recognized, the better.

One hears a great deal about wages and why they must be maintained at a high level, by the railroads, for example. A laborer is worthy of his hire, no less, but no more. And in the long run he must contribute an equivalent for what he is paid. If he does not do this, he is probably [made very poor] and you at once throw out the balance of things. You can't hold up conditions artificially, and you can't change the underlying laws of trade. If you try, you must inevitably fail. All this may be trite and obvious, but it is remarkable how many men overlook what should be the obvious. These are facts we can't get away from. A businessman must adapt himself to the natural conditions as they exist from month to month and year to year. . . . Real efficiency in work comes from knowing your facts and building upon that sure foundation.

Andrew Carnegie
Explains Business Growth

Andrew Carnegie wrote several books describing his views of life, money-making, democracy, and the responsibilities of wealth. The following selection if from his Autobiography. *It was published in 1920, a year after his death.*

Both Carnegie and Rockefeller were entrepreneurs—people who organized, managed, and assumed the risks of a business. The three people pictured on this page were also late nineteenth century entrepreneurs. How were their roles like those of Carnegie and Rockefeller? How were they different? Who is the entrepreneur in a modern corporation?

Andrew Carnegie, **Autobiography of Andrew Carnegie** (Boston: Houghton Mifflin Company, 1920), pp. 135-136, 202, 204. Copyright renewed 1948 by Margaret Carnegie Miller. Reprinted by permission. Language simplified.

As I became acquainted with the manufacture of iron I was greatly surprised to find that the cost of each of the various processes was unknown. Inquiries made of the leading manufacturers of Pittsburgh proved this. . . . Until stock was taken and the books balanced at the end of the year, the manufacturers were in total ignorance of results. . . . I felt as if we were moles burrowing in the dark. This to me was intolerable. I insisted upon such a system of weighing and accounting . . . as would enable us to know what our cost was for each process. [It would also tell us] what each man was doing, who saved material, who wasted it, and also who produced the best results.

To arrive at this was a much more difficult task than one would imagine. Every manager in the mills was naturally against the new system. Years were required before an accurate system was obtained. But eventually, by the aid of many clerks and the introduction of weighing scales at various points in the mill, we began to know what every department was doing. [We also knew] what each one of the many men working at the furnaces was doing, and thus [could] compare one with another. One of the chief sources of success in manufacturing is the introduction and strict maintenance of a perfect system of accounting. [In this way] responsibility for money or materials can be brought home to every man. Owners . . . were supplying tons of material daily to men in the mills without exacting an account . . . by weighing what each returned in the finished form.

▶ Should employers keep such a close accounting of their employees or should they trust them to do their best?

The Siemens Gas Furnace had been used to some extent in Great Britain for heating steel and iron. But it was supposed to be too expensive. I well remember the criticisms made by older heads among the Pittsburgh manufacturers about the extravagant expenditure we were making upon these new-fangled furnaces. But in the heating of great masses of materials, almost half the waste could sometimes be saved by using the new furnaces. The expenditure would have been justified, even if it had been doubled. Yet it was many years before we were followed in this new departure. And in some of those years the margin of profit was so small that most of it was made up from the savings derived from the adoption of the improved furnaces.

The Siemens Gas Furnace, introduced in 1868 by Karl Wilhelm Siemens, was used in the open-hearth method of making steel. The high temperatures reached by the open-hearth furnace break down the elements of the iron so thoroughly that low-grade ore and scrap can be used.

The mills were at last about ready to begin [1874]. An organization the auditor proposed was laid before me for approval. I found he had divided the works into two departments. [He] had given control of one to Mr. Stevenson, a Scotsman who afterwards made a fine record as a manufacturer, and control of the other to a Mr. Jones. Nothing, I am certain, ever affected the success of the steel company more than the decision which I gave upon that proposal. Upon no account could two men be in the same works with equal authority. . . . I said:

An auditor is a person who examines and verifies financial accounts and records.

338

"This will not do. I do not know Mr. Stevenson, nor do I know Mr. Jones, but one or the other must be made captain and he alone must report to you."

The decision fell upon Mr. Jones. In this way we obtained "The Captain," who afterward made his name famous wherever the manufacture of Bessemer steel is known.

Our competitors in steel at first [ignored] us. Knowing the difficulties they had in starting their own steel works, they could not believe we would be ready to deliver rails for another year. . . . The price of steel rails when we began was about seventy dollars per ton. We sent our agent through the country with instructions to take orders at the best prices he could obtain. Before our competitors knew it, we had obtained a large number—quite sufficient to justify us in making a start.

So perfect was the machinery, so admirable the plans, so skillful were the men selected by Captain Jones, and so great a manager was he himself, that our success was phenomenal. . . . The result of the month's operations left a margin of profit of $11,000. . . . So perfect was our system of accounts that we knew the exact amount of the profit. We had learned from experience in our iron works what exact accounting meant. There is nothing more profitable than clerks to check up each transfer of material from one department to another in process of manufacture.

FOR THOUGHT:

How does the information you learned from the writings of Rockefeller and Carnegie relate to the statistics you studied in Reading 48?

The Bessemer process for producing steel cheaply was invented independently by a Kentuckian, William Kelly, and an Englishman, Henry Bessemer, in the middle of the nineteenth century. A blast of hot air forced through the molten iron removed impurities. The open-hearth method of steel manufacture replaced the Bessemer process.

▶Are large profits justified? Should producers sacrifice higher profits in order to make less expensive goods?

50 AN INNOVATING PEOPLE

Both Rockefeller and Carnegie credited business leaders for the rate at which American industry grew. Business leaders assembled natural, capital, and human resources in efficient ways based on the latest knowledge. They built a new transportation system, assembled money to build mills and factories, pioneered new ways to market goods, and used the latest technology. No one denies the key role which business leaders played in industrialization.

But the few hundred business leaders who owned and ran major companies, such as Standard Oil and Carnegie Steel, could not have succeeded alone. If American customers had been wedded to the past, they would have refused to buy new products or try new ways. If the sons and daughters of farmers had remained on the farm, no one would have been available to work the new machines. And if American mechanics had been satisfied with old ways to do things, new machines would never have been invented.

Reading 50 contains three excerpts from foreigners who wrote about the United States. Each of these commentators was struck by characteristics of Americans which seemed to set them off from their European contemporaries. As you read, think about the following questions:

1. What characteristics of Americans made the most impression on these European visitors?
2. How did the size of the market influence the economic trends which these three writers described?

Judges of the London World's Fair View American Manufactures

In 1862, a great international exhibition, a world's fair, was held in London. Judges compared machines, tools, and products from many different nations, and then awarded prizes. There were no entries from the United States in Class XXXI, "Manufactures in Iron, Copper, and General Hardware." The judges, nevertheless, made the following comment.

International Exhibition, 1862, **Reports by the Juries** (London: William Clowes and Sons, 1863), Class XXXI, p. 3. Language simplified and modernized.

In the early nineteenth century, some skilled workers had organized local craft unions. In 1834, trade-union members organized the National Trades' Union which grew rapidly for a few years. Membership declined sharply after the Panic of 1837, and the trade-union movement was not revived until after the Civil War.

Unfortunately we cannot compare the European manufactures of Class XXXI with those of the United States, because there are no American exhibitors at the present time. Yet it is only just to state that those articles which find their way across the Atlantic are often copied and reproduced in Europe. They exhibit great ingenuity and successful effort on the part of the inventors to provide machines to replace manual labor for every purpose of domestic life. They are also constructed so as to be produced by labor-saving machinery. They are sure, as soon as they are invented, to be recieved favorably and adopted by the American public.

In the North American states, public feeling is the reverse of ours. There is little desire for trade-unions, and change and novelty seem to be the desire of all classes. Manufacturing companies are in great favor. They provide an abundance of capital for the trial of new projects. Many of these have failed, but many others have proved profitable to the shareholders.

The willingness of the American public to buy what is offered them, if it answers the purpose, has given a great advantage to the North American manufacturer. His European competitor has to contend with centuries-old habits and prejudices. The demand in the states during the last few years for hardware has been enormous. An American manufacturer can choose the best shapes and sizes of goods in large demand. He erects machinery to produce them cheaply and quickly, by special workmen and tools. By doing this, he can sell very large quantities of one kind or shape. He is sure to beat the European manufacturer. The European employs general workmen and has to contend with a heavy import duty and with competitors who are right on the spot where the consumption of the article takes place.

In every country useful inventions are first made to supply the wants of its own population. On proof of their utility, they are then adopted elsewhere. The United States has long been recognized by inventors as the place for the birth and manufacture of labor-saving machines that could supply enormous local wants. Artisans from all countries have taken their new ideas and technical skill to America to reap the rich harvest jointly with the natives. Newly invented goods are crude, when first brought before the public. They are only perfected by successive changes, suggested by experience. They are also generally expensive at first. They become gradually cheaper, as better methods of manufacture are discovered, and they are produced in larger quantities.

Americans overlook defects more than Europeans do. They are satisfied if a machine intended to replace domestic labor will work even imperfectly. However, we insist upon its being thoroughly well made and efficient.

It is difficult to introduce new articles into families in England and other countries where domestic servants and workpeople are abundant and trained to supply every want. Inventions are not well received. And manufacturers—only meeting with a small demand—must ask a high price, which limits consumption. In the United States, the manufacturer of a new article is listened to at once. Encouraged by a brisk demand for his goods, he at once erects labor-saving machinery.

▶ Under what conditions is it better to do things yourself, to hire somebody to do them for you, or to buy machines to do them? Explain.

An Englishman Views
American Growth

This selection comes from an Englishman's attempt to understand the sources of American economic growth.

Sidney J. Chapman, **Work and Wages** (London: Longmans, Green, and Company, 1904), Part I, pp. 175-178. Language simplified and modernized.

The keenness and originality of the American captains of industry have caused a steady advance in the productive capacity of American industry. The American working people have secured their share of the gains in production. Even in industries in which no improved methods have been introduced, wages have tended to rise. The employer has therefore had to save labor by devising labor-saving methods.

It is not astonishing that a comparatively new country should exhibit dash in economic affairs. American energy has, in addition, been stimulated by a growing market. When the market grows rapidly and steadily, an employer considers expanding his operation. In thinking of change, he thinks of possible improvements. Further, there is always room for new businesses. New businesses use the newest machines and methods. In beginning a business, men seek the best plans and appliances available. Wherever the proportion of new businesses to old ones is large, the industry of which they are parts will tend to develop fast.

The market for American textiles has grown faster than ours. America has had, and in some degree still has, her home market to win, and in addition her international trade to develop. And her home demand has been expanding rapidly. This is due partly to the natural increase of the American people, partly to immigration and the expansion of the country, and partly to increasing wealth.

The employer in the United States is less hampered than his English rival by interference from his workers. The apparent ease with which experiments can be conducted and changes made in factory organization in the United States suggests this. The American workman is readier to face new situations. He expects less permanence in the nature of his economic surroundings. If he is an immigrant, this is understandable. He is probably enterprising and he has already made a change. If he is an American, he has lived in an atmosphere of change. As things move faster in a rapidly developing country, every American has learned to take the ups and downs of life as normal. The new experience is upon him before the old is forgotten. Therefore, the thought of resisting or impeding advance is seldom so seriously entertained in America as in England. Besides, the American cotton workers are not so strongly organized as the English. And, in addition, there seems to be little doubt that the American workman's experience has not led him to fear new conditions. An English workman cannot imagine that the adoption of labor-saving methods could result in higher wages and more employment. But the American knows that an increased demand for labor has followed the recent improvements in the cotton industry in his own country. Some 85,000 automatic looms have been set running in the United States in the last few years. Yet the demand for weavers and all cotton workers is greater than ever. Wages in the northeastern states have risen fast.

In the cotton industry, most American wages are now much higher than English wages. As an immigrant weaver put it, "This is the right side of the water . . . better for making money."

▶ Today several unions try to prevent the use of new machinery that will eliminate people's jobs. Should unions be able to use their power in this way?

342

pocket TV.

Gifts for the Conspicuous Consumer

...monds comes ...drawstring. The ...ber and quality of the ...ment shown costs ...-Marcus.

This is expected to be a merry Christmas who traditionally make more than 15 pe sales in December. Department-stor FORTUNE's Business Roundup expe climb an average of 10 percent a levels. Specialty stores caterin of an increase. Stores like Marcus, and Abercro more willing tha

Each year American industry spends billions of dollars to advertise its wares, such as these. Some ads seem designed to stimulate demand for products that people could easily do without or that are clearly harmful to them. How do you weigh the harm that advertising does against the economic benefits which it brings?

A Russian Views
American Growth

Peter A. Demens left Russia for America in the late 1870's. In the United States, he established a number of businesses and wrote a book, Sketches of the North American United States. *In the following selection from his book, he explains some of the ways Americans expanded their businesses.*

Peter A. Demens [Tverskoy, pseud.], **Sketches of the North American United States** (St. Petersburg: I.N. Skorokhdov, 1895) as cited in **This Was America**, Oscar Handlin, ed. (Cambridge, Mass.: Harvard University Press, 1949), pp. 351-352, 361-362. Copyright © 1949 President and Fellows of Harvard College.

In 1867, Colonel Charles T. Harvey built an experimental one-track elevated line on the outskirts of New York. The elevated tracks are held up by strong steel beams. The railroad gets its power from a third rail running parallel to the track via a metal plate which slides along the rail and connects to the motor.

Huge sums are spent in advertising of every kind. Nowhere in the world is there such a mass of newspapers. In the majority of cases these hold almost nothing but advertisements. There are also many other methods [of advertising]. All the fences, the sides of buildings, and often the roofs are inscribed with signs. Many commercial houses have specially organized publicity departments which spend tens of thousands of dollars annually. The mails are choked with the circulars, throw-aways, and brochures of these enterprising men of letters. Frequently visited public places are equipped with billboards which command a high price. In buses, trolleys, and at railroad stations, the ceilings and walls are written over with these advertisements....About two months ago an enterprising soap dealer paid $17,000 at an auction sale for the right to advertise one year on the wall of the main entrance of the suspension bridge across the East River [in New York]. The New York elevated trains annually receive more than $100,000 for the [advertising] rights to their stations. And, most recently, shrewd speculators have reached the point where they hire special railroad cars, cover the outside walls with praises of their goods, and send them traveling over the whole Union.

But the most expensive, the most widespread, and the most unpleasant means of advertising is the dispatch of special people, called "drummers." These are clever, brash, nimble-tongued young gentlemen, usually [flashily] dressed, uninhibited in manners, and supplied with an inexhaustible fund of shrewdness and impudence. The drummer is provided with great trunks of samples of the goods he sells. Sometimes he works for a commission, but more often for a fixed salary, and his boss pays all expenses. Such a migratory young man costs a commercial house no less than $3000 a year. The smart ones may even cost $5000 and especially good ones get up to $15,000. I myself know many firms which support as many as ten or fifteen such traveling salesmen, and know dozens of companies the advertising costs of which exceed $100,000 a year.

The unusual mobility of the American people and their passion for changes of residence also foster...both the diffusion of knowledge and the spirit of general equality. Tens of thousands of people, artisans

344

for the most part, constantly move around over the whole Union....They constantly come in contact with new people, new ideas, and new impressions, which they assimilate very rapidly. I have often been amazed at the many-sidedness and knowledge of my own workers. Where have they not been, what have they not done, in what positions have they not found themselves? It would seem that there is nothing in the world of which they have not heard, nothing they have not seen.

Several Germans and Englishmen always worked for me. Although they were excellent workmen and perhaps in cleanliness and fineness of work surpassed the Americans, they were inferior to the latter in every other way. [They were] difficult at making a beginning, extremely conservative in their mode of work, and always exceedingly specialized. The Europeans knew a certain part of the job. Nothing else interested them. In the great majority of cases they learned nothing else. As they left their training, so will they die.

FOR THOUGHT:

How do the three excerpts in this reading relate to the statistics in Reading 48 and to the excerpts from Rockefeller and Carnegie in Reading 49?

51 A RECIPE FOR ECONOMIC GROWTH

HISTORICAL ESSAY

What must an inventive people do to generate steady economic growth? This essay examines the steps that innovating Americans took to promote the growth shown in the statistics in Reading 48.

Goods (such as food, clothing, or tools) and services (such as medical care or education) come from a combination of natural, capital, and human resources. Any careful investigation of economic growth must begin with an analysis of each of these components.

The Importance of Natural Resources

In the years after the Civil War, American industry tapped vast new deposits of precious raw materials. As iron ore mines in Pennsylvania began to run out in the 1870's, new fields near Lake Superior were exploited. Earlier in the 1800's, the iron-and-steel industry had opened rich iron ore deposits stretching from Birmingham, Alabama, to Chattanooga, Tennessee. Steelmakers had also begun to exploit a vast coalfield extending from northern Alabama to Lake Erie. In 1859, speculators drilled the first oil well near Titusville, Pennsylvania. Drilling rapidly expanded to new fields as they were discovered. Year after year, fresh deposits of minerals came to light. Great timberlands supplied a variety of woods. All the natural resources essential to a modern economy were available to Americans.

Until 1898, when the United States acquired Hawaii, the resource base of the American economy increased as the nation acquired new land. Since then, the total amount of resources available to the nation has not increased. Newly developed techniques to find deposits of raw materials, to extract them, and to process them, have, however, increased the quantity of many minerals. In addition, fertilizers and irrigation have improved crop yields and brought more land under cultivation. For example, Mexican farmers introduced irrigation methods which turned dry areas of the Southwest into fertile farmlands. New technology has also made it possible to turn uranium into energy in atomic reactors. These examples illustrate the application of capital and human resources to the natural resource base. Without capital and human effort and knowledge, minerals would remain in the ground, streams would continue to flow in their ancient paths, and forests would remain standing.

The Growth of Capital Resources

Capital resources, however, can be increased. In fact, the long-run growth rates of most major countries roughly parallel the percentage of their gross national product invested in capital goods. Throughout the nineteenth century, the United States was a high-saving and high-investing economy. Since the Civil War, about 12 percent of the gross national product has been saved and invested every year. This statement does not mean that the rate of savings has been 12 percent every year. In some years, savings have been higher, and in other years lower. In addition, there has been one small but significant general shift from the 12 percent figure. The rate of saving was probably highest in the few decades after the Civil War. Since then it has shown a slight tendency to decrease. Since the 1890's, Americans have saved less and invested a smaller percentage of their income in machines.

In the late 1800's, industrialists financed capital expansion in three ways. First, dozens of large businesses grew through reinvested profits. The income tax levied during the Civil War was repealed in 1871. Business people contributed little to support either their local or national governments. Special conditions permitted them to keep costs

To invest means to use money for the purchase of properties, stocks, or a business with the expectation of making a profit. To save means to set aside money for future use. Hence, money can be saved which is not invested. However, people typically save money by investing it.

Capital means any type of wealth that is used to produce more wealth, including factories, machines, tools, etc. Capital expansion is thus an attempt to increase the amount of property a business already has.

346

low. Since few unions existed, employers could fire workers when times were bad without contributing to their support. When a boom developed, both former farmhands and immigrants from Europe lined up before employment offices. They willingly worked overtime at regular hourly rates. In addition, new technical developments often gave an individual a temporary economic advantage which he could exploit. Men such as Carnegie and Rockefeller financed most of their expansion programs from reinvested profits.

A second way of financing capital expansion involved the growth of large financial institutions. For example, the banking house of J.P. Morgan made loans to finance new ventures or to expand going concerns. These financial firms also negotiated large sales of stocks or bonds to smaller investors. In this way, the savings of people all over the nation could be used to expand industry. In addition, many foreigners bought shares in American industry. Increasingly, business people formed corporations in order to raise capital and to protect themselves from the risks of single ownership.

Finally, government helped to finance some business ventures. The federal government gave millions of acres of land along rights-of-way to railroads. This policy encouraged them to build tracks into areas where business might not have developed for many years. In some cases, local governments bought bonds or shares of stock from railroads in order to persuade them to build through their towns. The government played a vital role in taking the risk out of large transportation ventures.

Although the rate of saving and investment declined from the 12 percent figure, the rate of production increased. Every year, as the figures in Reading 48 suggested, Americans produced more and more goods for every hour of labor. The rate of increase accelerated after World War I. What accounts for this increase when the natural resource base did not change and the rate at which Americans invested in machines tended to slow?

Corporations, unlike individually owned businesses and partnerships, are considered to be separate "beings" having independent legal existence. Shareholders who have invested in corporations are not personally responsible for the corporation's debts whereas individual owners and business partners are. Investors in corporations can lose only their initial investment. Corporations have an additional advantage over individual proprietorships or partnerships because they do not dissolve when the original founders or owners die.

The Nation's Human Resources

The answer to this question probably lies in the way accounts are kept of what is saved and what is invested. If Americans put their money in a bank and the bank then invests this money in a machine, it is counted as investment. If instead of putting money in a bank, they spend it to educate themselves or their children or to improve their health, it is counted as consumption. In other words, the wealth is used rather than saved. This accounting procedure can be deceptive. It labels investment in human resources as consumption. But investment in human resources has become the major ingredient of economic growth. Looked at another way, better education and improved health are investments in human resources which pay dividends later.

Four factors affect the quality of human resources: numbers, education, health, and attitude. Clearly, the more people an economy has, the larger the pool of human resources available for work. So long as the number of people does not become too great for the natural and capital resource base, numbers increase growth. From 1860 to 1930, as Figure 48A indicates, the population of the United States increased roughly four times. Part of the growth was natural increase. The remainder resulted from immigration. During these seventy years, more than 30 million immigrants entered the United States. The labor of these new Americans contributed substantially to overall economic growth. Most of them came as adults who had already been educated through the unproductive years of childhood. During these same years, as Figure 48B indicates, the Gross National Product increased roughly eleven times. And during these years, Americans invested about 12 percent of their Gross National Product each year.

More and better education accounts for some of the growth. Of the children between 5 and 17 years old in 1870, 57 percent were enrolled in public schools. In 1900, schools enrolled 72.4 percent of the children in this age group. In 1920, they enrolled 77.8 percent. These figures do not include parochial schools which, although relatively few in 1870, educated many children after 1900. In 1870, only 2 percent of the 17-year-olds in the United States had graduated from high school. In 1900, 6.4 percent were graduates. In 1920, this figure had leaped to 16.8 percent. In 1870, only 1.68 percent of students between 18 and 21 years of age were enrolled in institutions of higher education. By 1920, this figure had reached 8.09 percent.

Improved schools are only one aspect of investment in human resources which helps to explain the growth of the American economy. Training programs in business firms are another. Unfortunately there are no good statistics about these training programs. They were probably increasing at least as rapidly as public expenditures for schools. Business people had to establish training programs to develop the skilled workers they needed. They also tended to support the development of public high schools with the hope that schools would help train workers.

Improved health also raised the quality of the nation's human resources. Between 1860 and 1900, the number of people who died each year was relatively constant compared to total population. After 1900, however, the rate of death dropped rapidly. There were two major reasons. First, infant mortality declined. For every 1000 children born in 1900, in the state of Massachusetts, 141 died. In 1920, only 78 died. By 1940, the figure had fallen to 34. Second, the death rate of adults declined. For every 1000 Americans in the age group 35 to 44 in 1900, there were 10.2 deaths. In 1920, this figure was down to 8.1. In 1940, it dropped to 5.2, and in 1950, it dropped again,

Figures are available for Massachusetts because it was the first state to establish a state board of health (1869) which, among other tasks, kept such statistics.

to 3.6. Moreover, adults had fewer illnesses. This improvement in American health meant that more people lived into their productive years. Resources invested in training them were not wasted either through an early death or through losing hours on the job because of sickness.

In addition to numbers, education, and health, the attitudes of people affect their quality as human resources. Americans were willing to work. They were also willing to use part of their income to purchase capital equipment. This practice helped to make a steady increase in productivity per person possible. Finally, Americans accepted change willingly. They believed in progress. They thought that every person should strive to get ahead. All of these attitudes contributed to a rapid growth rate.

▶ What is your attitude toward work? Should you develop attitudes that will contribute to a rapid growth rate?

A New Industrial Setting

During the last part of the nineteenth century, manufacturing took place in a new industrial setting. It was characterized by large-scale enterprises. A vast transportation and communication system grew up to link deposits of raw materials to factories and mills and to speed messages between them. The railroads also distributed finished products across the land. In 1869, the first transcontinental railroad was finished. Within thirty years after 1869, four additional transcontinental railroads spanned the continent. From the end of the Civil War to 1930, American railroad companies built 395,000 miles of track. The telegraph spread rapidly, too. So did cables across the Atlantic and the number of telephones, particularly in large cities. All these developments helped to spur economic growth by speeding goods around the country. They also made giant enterprise practical. Figure 51A on page 351 shows some key inventions which were the basis of many of the giant enterprises.

So long as inexpensive transportation was available, industrialists could locate factories in places where the supply of raw materials, the presence of a skilled labor force, or some other factor contributed to low unit costs. Hence, factories grew larger and larger. And the jobs within a factory became more and more subdivided. When one complex job was divided into a number of more simple operations, relatively unskilled people could learn them quickly, and do them well. They also commanded less pay than a skilled worker.

The idea of interchangeable parts and the assembly line became part of the new production methods. The assembly line became the most famous product of the division of labor. On an assembly line, a product moved on a continuous belt past rows of workers. Each worker performed one simple function. Assembly lines had been used extensively in meat packing even before the Civil War. Henry Ford

Eli Whitney, the inventor of the cotton gin, had introduced the concept of interchangeable parts during the American Revolution in manufacturing firearms. His system allowed any part to fit any gun. Replacements for broken parts could be made from stock items. The practice of making interchangeable parts made the assembly line possible.

In what ways can the school activities shown on this page improve your value as a human resource?

FIGURE 51A   INVENTIONS AND DISCOVERIES, 1859-1918

Inventor or Discoverer	Date	Contribution
Edwin Drake	1859	oil drilling
George Pullman	1864	railroad sleeping car
Cyrus Field	1866	transatlantic cable
Christopher Sholes	1867	typewriter
George Westinghouse	1872	air brake
Alexander Graham Bell	1876	telephone
Thomas Alva Edison	1878	phonograph
	1879	incandescent light bulb
	1891	radio
George B. Selden	1879	first automobile patent
Ottmar Mergenthaler	1884	Linotype printing machine
C. Francis Jenkin and		
Thomas Armat	1896	motion-picture projector
Orville and Wilbur Wright	1903	first powered flight
Adolphus Busch	1898	first diesel engine
Robert H. Goddard	1914	liquid fuel rocket
Peter C. Hewitt and		
F. B. Crocker	1918	helicopter

introduced them into the automobile industry just before World War I. Actually, assembly lines organized around a continuous belt affected only a relatively small group of American workers. Still, most industrial laborers felt the effects of division of labor throughout the late nineteenth and earlier twentieth centuries. And the economy benefited through increased productivity per person.

Particularly after 1900, the quality of American machines improved. Large-scale factories and subdivision of labor encouraged technical improvements. When technology improves, the quality of capital resources goes up. Since World War II, technical change has been particularly rapid.

One additional factor which may help to account for rapid economic growth remains to be considered. America's economic, social, political, and religious atmosphere clearly favored individual initiative, the pursuit of material rewards, and hard work. Society placed a premium on economic success. It stamped its approval on a person who would make substantial contributions to economic growth.

At the same time, government was friendly to business and promoted economic growth. The constitutional protection of patents encouraged inventors. High tariffs protected American industry from foreign

▶Would you want to work on an assembly line? Why or why not?

Article 1, Section 8, Clause 8 gives Congress the power to issue copyrights and patents.

competition. Grants of land helped finance many railroads. Government support of agricultural experiment stations and of land-grant colleges contributed to improved technology and better human resources. In addition, government maintained peace and order, protected property rights, and provided essential services such as roads and schools. All these activities provided a firm base for economic growth.

The Transformation of Agriculture
and Rural Society

STATING THE ISSUE

In 1820, America was a land of farms and rural villages. More than 90 percent of the population was directly involved in agriculture. Farmers planted and harvested, saw animals born, and later butchered them for food. Today, the statistics are nearly reversed; less than 10 percent of the people are farmers. Most people's daily routines have little to do with nature directly. Canning, freezing, and the movement of fresh fruits and vegetables across continents have even freed the diets of city dwellers from the rhythm of agricultural seasons.

The shift from farm to city, from an intimate to a detached relationship with nature, may be examined from two points of view. On the one side, the shift is part of the history of industrialization and urbanization. On the other side, it is part of the continuous process of change on the farm itself and in rural society.

Chapter 14 focuses on the farm and on rural life. The earliest document dates from 1822. At that time, the techniques of agricultural production were much the same from one farm to another. They had not changed dramatically as far back as anyone could remember. By 1920, when this chapter closes, agriculture had been transformed. Production for the market was the rule rather than the exception. Farmers chose new seeds, fertilizers, and machines from catalogs and magazines. Sales people and government agents called on them. Farmers anxiously watched the movement of prices on national and international commodity exchanges. Those who could not afford to invest in change and who barely made a living were labeled a national problem. The selections in this chapter ask you to analyze the ways farmers related to each other and to the larger social worlds around them.

353

1400 | 1500 | 1600 | 1700 | 1800 | 1900 | 2000

1862 Congress creates the Department of Agriculture

1862 Congress passes the Morrill Land Grant Act

1867 The National Grange is formed

1877 In **Munn vs. Illinois** the Supreme Court allows the state to regulate storage rates for grain

1886 In the Wabash Case, the Supreme Court rules that states cannot regulate interstate railroad rates

1887 Congress passes Interstate Commerce Act

1887 Congress passes Hatch Act

1892 The Populist party is formed

1893 Business failures cause major depression

1896 Postal service is extended to include free delivery of mail to rural areas

1896 William McKinley wins Presidential election

1908 President Theodore Roosevelt creates Country Life Commission

1914 World War I begins

1916 Congress passes Federal Farm Loan Act and Warehouse Act

1917 The United States enters World War I

1917 Congress passes the Smith-Hughes Act

1919 Farmers organize the Farm Bureau Federation

52 PROMOTERS OF CHANGE

In the first fifty years of the nineteenth century, the American population increased four times. Most of the new Americans lived in rural areas. But a significant number were city dwellers. Furthermore, the city population grew nearly three times as fast as the rural population.

As the population grew, so did the demand for food. The demand was greatest in the growing cities. Sometimes food was scarce there. Food shortages often led to riots. For a while, some Americans feared that the failure to produce enough food for city dwellers on a regular basis would threaten the stability of American society.

However, these fears were groundless. Agricultural production kept pace with the increase in population. For example, between 1800 and 1840, the number of work hours required to produce a bushel of wheat declined by nearly a third. The average weight of hogs and cattle increased dramatically. By 1850, vast fields of wheat and corn had been sown across the prairies of the Middle West. These developments were both the result of and the cause of changes in rural life. The selections in this reading describe the views of three promoters of agricultural change in the years before the Civil War. As you read, think about these questions:

1. What problems did promoters of change encounter in trying to alter the behavior of farmers?
2. What were the major elements in the process of change as promoters described it?

Resistance to Innovation

This selection is from a speech made before the Fredericksburgh, Virginia Agricultural Society in 1822. The occasion was a prize contest for new farm implements.

We all well know the slow progress made by agricultural improvements and the delays before they get into general use. We believe nothing that we hear. We want to see and feel every improvement for ourselves. Even when we can see the evidence for ourselves, we are often slow to change. The history of new and better plows is a good example of our slowness to change. The first two of a

New England Farmer, Vol. I, No. 21 (December 21, 1882), pp. 164-165. Language simplified.

The American Agriculturist *on page 357 describes agricultural fairs held during the mid-1800's. The pictures on this page show two shows held in the United States during the 1970's. What are the purposes of these shows? How similar or different are they from the fairs described in the reading?*

particularly fine new type were brought to this town and remained in the stable yard of the Indian Queen Tavern nearly a year before anyone would even try them. During this time, there were a great many jokes about them. And many men were scared off, afraid that they would appear foolish. They probably would have stayed in the stable yard for many more years if an enterprising Yankee who used to live here had not been bold enough to try his luck with one of them. Even after he had demonstrated the merit of this plow, it was nearly ten years before it was generally used throughout this area.

One reason we are so slow may be because of the way we do business. Instead of going directly to the manufacturer to buy a new tool, we depend on local blacksmiths to copy it. We pay the blacksmiths in produce and think, therefore, that we are getting the new tool for almost nothing. In fact, however, the copies are terrible and work badly. They turn out to be very expensive in practice. We would be better off if we sold our crops for cash and used the money to buy the best made and most up-to-date tools.

Agricultural fairs of the sort we are at today are the best way of breaking the grip of this old way of doing business. At these fairs, we can see most of those inventions which mechanical skill and ingenuity have devised for our use. If there were no fairs we might never hear of these inventions, particularly if we never got to talk to any farmers other than those who are our neighbors. No one can grow if he doesn't pay attention to the broad world beyond his immediate neighborhood.

▶ Do you learn more new things from your friends or from "outside your neighborhood" by watching films on television, reading, attending lectures and concerts, and so forth?

The Virtues of Change at Home

Also in 1822, a speaker before the Worcester County Agricultural Society in Massachusetts described the virtues of changing at home.

New England Farmer, Vol. I, No. 23 (January 4, 1823), pp. 180-181. Language simplified.

In many of the most fertile parts of our country, farmers have no one nearby to whom to sell their produce. They must ship their produce to distant markets, relying on transportation companies and special agents. Here in Massachusetts, however, markets are close at hand. A farmer can bring his own produce in his own wagons to the capital of the state.

Strange that so obvious an advantage should not be more highly appreciated. Of what use is it that the boasted land of the West will produce its hundred-fold to labor, in comparison with the stubborn soil of our home, if the farmer has nothing to do with his crops other than to eat them himself? How much can a single family eat? I don't understand why so many people have been lured into leaving New England for distant areas. Those areas may be fertile, but their fertility doesn't benefit the farmer at all. There is no purchaser for his production. Moreover, life in the West is lonely. Ask the returning emigrant from the West or the South what he most highly appreciates now. Does he prefer the rough and hard, but vigorous soil of the East with the pleasures of company? Or does he like the large farms, and useless fertility in areas where neighborhood is unknown, the means for the education of children are denied, and opportunities for moral instruction and the public worship of God unenjoyed?

The cultivation of the earth is a practical lesson taught to the farmer in earliest life. He is instructed in the ways of his father and the safe ways of doing things. He is not easily persuaded to experiment with these ways. Hence, from generation to generation, men pass on in the track of their predecessors. They believe that the path they follow is the only wise path. Those who stray risk destruction. To conquer this stubborn way of thinking is the greatest effort and best result of agricultural associations. The practical man of conservative habits has to be shown results for his own eyes. We are ready to show him.

▶ Under what circumstances, if any, would you consider moving to an area in which schools and churches were located some distance from your home?

The Miracle of a Generation

The following selection is from an 1857 editorial in the American Agriculturist, *a farm journal published in New York and distributed across the country.*

The Latin poet Virgil describes a state of agriculture among the Romans in which the farmer is his own mechanic. He shapes his plow beam by anticipating his wants and forcing the young sapling to grow into a shape suitable for a plow beam. The present generation can remember that there was almost as little division of labor upon our own farms.

Now, labor has been so far divided that a farmer can find ready-made nearly every tool he wants to use upon his soil. He can also find a great variety of tools that were unthought of fifty years ago. The plow is no longer a rude tool. It is the combined result of the highest scientific knowledge and practical skill. Years of patient study and investigation of the laws of mechanical force have been spent upon it. It now produces its results with the least expenditure of animal strength. It is so constructed that it is easily guided. The holder can plow narrow or wide, deep or shallow, as suits his convenience. We have plows for various kinds of work—for the sward and for the stubble, for the surface and for the sub-soil, for the hill and for the plain, those turning a single furrow and those turning two.

In looking at the changes which have come over our agriculture none is more striking than the change in the farmer himself. He looks

American Agriculturist, Vol. XVI, No. 7 (July, 1857), pp. 145-146. Language simplified.

The sward is the grassy surface of the land. Stubble is the rough surface.

at his business from a new standpoint. It is no longer a stereotyped routine in which man uses as little mind as the cattle he drives over his fields. Among the more intelligent farmers, agriculture is no longer considered a perfected art. Its methods are not so well established that it is deemed a waste of time and labor to try anything new. It is a developing art in which every man feels that he has much more to learn. Experiments in new tools, crops, fertilizers, and methods of tillage are everywhere the order of the day. The practice of those who apply mind to farming is gradually influencing that very large class who apply only muscle. They see the results of deep plowing and high manuring. And, to some extent, they imitate their thinking neighbors. This experimenting is everywhere practiced among the readers of our agricultural journals. We regard this change in the farmer himself as the most important change brought about by agricultural reform. In it lies the germ of all future improvement. It is a work that is certain to go forward until the scientific principles of cultivation are everywhere recognized and practiced.

The crops, too, that are cultivated have felt the influence of this change. What a great variety of roots, grains, grasses, and fruits have been introduced within the last twenty years. We have new kinds of corn, potatoes, oats, rye, wheat, apples, pears, and other fruits. Even the national government has become interested in the distribution of seeds. And the results of the improvements in European agriculture are now put within the reach of many of our best farmers in all parts of the country. A single company has even gone beyond the government in the number of packages of seeds distributed, if not in the total amount. So wide is the distribution of these valuable seeds that it is very difficult for grasping men to get control of anything valuable for the purpose of speculation. There is much less chance than before for speculators to take advantage of the ignorance of farmers.

Another sign of progress is the increased attention paid to the fertilizing of the soil. It is felt, as never before, that this is the one thing necessary for the farm. With fertile acres, the tiller of the soil is master of his position and can do what he likes. The machine will work and turn out goods to order and enrich its owner. Without fertility, the soil is his master and he is but a slave. The more of it he owns the poorer he is. It is but a millstone to drag him down into the depths of poverty. The poor cultivation of his poor acres makes him a poor man. Fertility has become a prime necessity. Better methods are used to save what falls from the stock and to increase these by all the vegetable and animal waste of the farm. Art has done what it always ought to do. It has improved upon nature.

These are some of the things that cheer us in our work as journalists, the co-laborers of the tillers of the soil.

FOR THOUGHT:

What are the major values of the people who are trying to promote agricultural change?

53 A CRITIC'S VOICE

The areas where major crops were grown were established by 1850. Some new land outside these areas was added during the next seventy years. But the vast explosion of agricultural production occurred, by and large, within the established boundaries. Cotton crops in the South increased four times between 1860 and 1914. Production in the corn belt increased three times in the same period. Fruit and vegetable producers in California, Florida, and many other areas expanded their farms and orchards. The enormous growth of commercial canning and the introduction of refrigerated railroad cars enabled them to enter nationwide markets.

This expanding production far exceeded the country's internal needs. Prior to 1850, only American cotton and tobacco sold much abroad. After mid-century, however, great shiploads of grain and meat traveled from the United States across the world. American wheat farmers undersold Hungarian competitors in the markets of the Adriatic. American pork and beef were mainstays of western European diets.

Throughout the nineteenth century and into the twentieth change continued to be promoted by advocates of machinery, artificial fertilizers, advanced methods of cultivation, and selective breeding. There were, however, some skeptical voices who doubted either the value of the changes in rural life or the opportunities available to farmers. Reading 53 is drawn from the work of one such critic, William A. Peffer. Peffer was born in Pennsylvania and farmed in Indiana, Missouri, and Illinois. After the Civil War he edited local newspapers and a farm journal in Kansas. He was active in Kansas politics. Think about the following questions as you read:

1. How does Peffer explain the processes of farm change?
2. What problems does he see in adapting the behavior of farmers to economic and political changes?

The Farmer's Side

In 1891, the year he was elected to the United States Senate, *William Peffer published* The Farmer's Side, His Troubles and Their Remedy. *This selection is taken from that publication.*

William Peffer, **The Farmer's Side, His Troubles and Their Remedy** (New York: D. Appleton and Company, 1891), pp. 56-60, 64, 67. Language simplified.

Sashes are the movable frameworks of windows in which panes of glass are set. A molding is a decorative outline made of strips of wood and placed around doors and windows and between the walls and floors. A cornice is a molding placed between walls and ceiling.

A smokehouse is a small building in which meats are preserved by exposing them to smoke.

▶ Have you ever made jelly, canned or frozen foods, or picked your own berries or fruit? Do you—or would you—enjoy the contacts with nature that growing or preparing part of your own food involves?

Exorbitant means excessively high. Money lenders charged interest rates as high as 20 percent. They justified charging farmers higher rates than they charged other borrowers on the grounds that farming was riskier than business or industry.

The American farmer of today is altogether a different sort of a man from his ancestor of fifty or a hundred years ago. A great many men and women now living remember when farmers were largely manufacturers. That is to say, they made a great many implements for their own use. During the winter season wheat and flour and cornmeal were carried in large wagons drawn by teams of six to eight horses a hundred or two hundred miles to market. There they were traded for farm supplies for the next year—groceries and dry goods.

Besides this, skilled workers were scattered among the farmers. During winter time the neighborhood carpenter prepared sashes, blinds, doors, molding and cornices for the next season's building. When the frosts of autumn came, the shoemaker went to the farmers' dwellings. There, in a corner set apart to him, he made up shoes for the family during the winter.

When winter approached, the butchering season was at hand. Meat for family use during the next year was prepared and preserved in the smokehouse. The orchards supplied fruit for cider, apple butter, and preserves of different kinds, more than enough to supply the wants of the family during the year, with some to spare.

As a result of that sort of economy, farmers required a very small amount of money to conduct their business. Much was paid for in produce. A hundred dollars probably was as much as the largest farmers of that day needed in the way of cash to meet the demands of farm work.

Coming from that time to the present, we find that everything nearly has been changed. All over the West particularly, the farmer thrashes his wheat all at one time. He disposes of it all at one time. He sells his hogs, and buys bacon and pork. He sells his cattle, and buys fresh beef and canned beef or corned beef, as the case may be. He sells his fruit, and buys it back in cans. Indeed, he buys nearly everything now that he produced at one time himself. And these things all cost money.

Besides all this, and what seems stranger than anything else, in the earlier time Americans owned their own homes. Not one in a thousand homes was mortgaged to secure the payment of borrowed money. But a small amount of money was then needed for actual use in conducting the business of farming. And there was always enough of it among the farmers to supply the demand. Now, when at least ten times as much money is needed, there is little or none to be obtained. Nearly half the farms are mortgaged for as much as they are worth. And interest rates are exorbitant.

As to the cause of such wonderful changes in the condition of farmers, nothing more need be said than that the railroad builder, the banker, the money changer, and the manufacturer undermined the farmer. The manufacturer came with his woolen mill, carding mill, broom factory, rope factory, wooden-ware factory, cotton factory,

360

pork-packing establishment, canning factory, and fruit-preserving houses. The little shop on the farm has given place to the large shop in town. The wagon-maker's shop in the neighborhood has given way to the large establishment in the city. There men by the thousand work, and a hundred or two hundred wagons are made in a week. The shoemaker's shop has given way to large establishments in the cities where most of the work is done by machines. The old smokehouse has given way to the packing house. And the fruit cellars have been displaced by preserving factories.

The farmer now is forced to go to town for nearly everything that he wants. Even a hand rake to clean up the dooryard must be purchased at the city store. And what is worst of all, if he needs a little more money than he has about him, he is forced to go to town to borrow it. But he does not find the money there. He finds instead an agent who will "negotiate" a loan for him. The money is in the East, a thousand or three thousand or five thousand miles away. He pays the agent his commission, pays all the expenses of looking through the records and furnishing abstracts, and pays for every postage stamp used in the transaction. Finally he receives a draft for the amount of money required, minus these expenses. In this way the farmers of the country today are maintaining an army of middlemen, loan agents, bankers, and others. They are absolutely worthless for all good purposes in the community. Their services ought to be, and very easily could be, dispensed with. But by reason of the changed condition of things, they have placed themselves between the farmer and the money owner. In this way they absorb a livelihood from the people.

It will be urged that the farmers themselves are at fault in this matter. It will be said that they are responsible for many of the changes which have worked against them. This is doubtless true. Seamen might have continued the use of old-fashioned wooden ships. And we might all be traveling in stagecoaches. So might farmers still use steel and flint to start their fires with. They might be using sickle to cut their grain, and have the wheat kernels trodden from the straw by horses' hoofs. So, too, farmers might be spinning yarn, weaving cloth, tanning leather, and making ropes and rakes. But does anybody believe such things either desirable or practicable? What would be the common opinion of a man whose farm is conducted like that of his grandfather before the age of railroads?

Like other men, the farmer was moved ahead by a current which was moving all men. His habits and his methods have changed, not because he desired it or worked for it, but because conditions forced it. Whether for better or worse, the whole business world has changed. And methods, like machines, have changed in all departments of industry. It is apparent that if farmers had been less progressive, and had not adopted labor-saving devices, they would be still farther behind than they are.

▶ What does a corner grocery offer that a supermarket does not? Why do many people value the small merchants with whom they deal?

A fruit cellar is an underground room used for storing fruit.

A commission is a sum of money, usually determined on a percentage basis, allowed to an agent for his or her services. Farmers had to pay the agent's commission, as well as the interest on the loan.

Abstracts are legal documents which give a condensed history of the title to land. They contain summaries of all transfers of the property from one owner to another and of any liens or charges against the property. A bank draft is a written order that authorizes a bank to give money to someone.

Tanning is the process of converting hides or skins into leather.

▶These pictures show families of the nineteenth century doing farm chores. Most farm children of that period expected to become farmers. They learned this occupation by working with their parents. What similarities do you see in families today? What do young people learn from their parents? How do they learn?

3

4

5

It is expensive to supply a farm with improved utensils and machinery. But that is not a good reason why we should go back to the old tools. The truth is, farmers can and do produce vastly more now than they did or could produce under the old regime with an equal amount of labor.

Transportation brings the farm and the factory close together. Transportation makes it possible for men of different callings to serve one another, no matter how far apart they may be. The manufacturer supplies the tools, the machinery, and the oil to keep the farm and the railroad moving. In truth, the farmer, the carrier, and the manufacturer are natural allies. And some day they will so understand it. One reason why the farmer is behind in the race is because his forces are scattered while theirs are consolidated.

The railroad employs large numbers of men. So does the factory. These men, in political matters, are largely under the influence of their employers. This gives great social influence to the millionaires — enough, when combined with the power of the money they control, to dictate legislation in their favor. They are close to the governing agencies of the people. Lawmakers listen to the men that speak. And these are they who do the talking. Farmers have ceased to be congressmen and senators. Lawyers, bankers, railroad officers—they compose our legislative bodies largely now. It is men of their classes that ask and obtain laws to further or protect their interests.

FOR THOUGHT:

Compare Peffer's views with those of the promoters of agricultural change. Do they differ either in values or in perceptions of the realities of rural life?

54 A NEW RURAL LIFE

Peffer was deeply suspicious of many urban institutions. He understood, however, that the national networks of transportation and communication were closing the distance between city and country life. Trade in farm produce and farm machinery was followed by the exchange of more general goods and information. Influences moved in both directions. Until the twentieth century, city populations could barely reproduce themselves. Their growth depended upon a constant influx of farmers. Their social character was shaped by rural ways of living. Influencing country life were mail order catalog sales and five- and ten-cent chain stores that brought urban gadgetry and copies of the latest styles to rural America. In the twentieth century, automobiles, telephones, and radios drew the farmer and city dweller even closer together.

►Have you ever adopted a point of view—political or otherwise—because it was held by someone in power? Why?

Reading 54 is taken from an early attempt to study the impact of urban connections upon rural life. In 1908, President Theodore Roosevelt asked a group of men to report to him "upon the present conditions of country life, upon what means are now available for supplying the deficiencies which now exist, and upon the best methods of organized permanent effort in investigation and actual work along lines I have indicated." These men, organized as the Country Life Commission, submitted a report. It revealed many widely shared assumptions about the value of the farm and the differences between farm and city. As you read these selections from the report, keep these questions in mind:

1. What did the commission mean by the "social barrenness" of the open country?
2. What sort of rural community did the commission imagine building?

A Missouri Farmer's View of Country Life

This selection is from President Theodore Roosevelt's introduction to the Report of the Country Life Commission.

One of the most illuminating—and incidentally one of the most interesting and amusing—series of answers sent to the commission was from a farmer in Missouri. He stated that he had a wife and eleven living children. He and his wife were each 52 years old. They owned 520 acres of land without any mortgage hanging over their heads. He had himself done well, and his views as to why many of his neighbors had done less well deserve consideration. These views are expressed in terse and vigorous English; they cannot always be quoted in full. He states that the farm homes in his neighborhood are not as good as they should be because too many of them are mortgaged; that the schools do not train boys and girls satisfactorily for life on the farm, because they allow them to get an idea in their heads that city life is better. To remedy this he thinks practical farming should be taught.

To the question whether the farmers and their wives in his neighborhood are satisfactorily organized, he answers: "Oh, there is a little one-horse grange gang in our locality, and every darned one thinks they ought to be a king." To the question, "Are the renters of farms in your neighborhood making a satisfactory living?" he answers: "No; because they move about so much hunting a better job." To the question, "Is the supply of farm labor in your neighborhood satisfactory?" the answer is: "No; because the people have gone out of the

Report of the Country Life Commission, Senate Document No. 705, 60th Congress, 2nd Session (Washington, D.C.: United States Government Printing Office, 1909), pp. 10-11. Language simplified.

2

The pictures on these two pages show a number of late nineteenth- and early twentieth-century innovations. How could each one help to break down the isolation of rural life?

baby business"; and when asked as to the remedy he answers, "Give a pension to every mother who gives birth to seven living boys on American soil." To the question, "Are the conditions surrounding hired labor on the farm in your neighborhood satisfactory to the hired men?" he answers: "Yes, unless he is a drunken cuss," adding that he would like to blow up the stillhouses and root out whisky and beer. To the question, "Are the sanitary conditions on the farms in your neighborhood satisfactory?" he answers: "No; too careless about chicken yards (and the like) and poorly covered wells. In one well on a neighbor's farm I counted seven snakes in the wall of the well, and they used the water daily. His wife is dead now and he is looking for another." He ends by stating that the most important single thing to be done for the betterment of country life is "good roads."

Report of the Country Life Commission

It should be noted that this report was prepared at a time of generally rising farm prices.

Report of the Country Life Commission, Senate Document No. 705, 60th Congress, 2nd Session (Washington, D.C.: United States Government Printing Office, 1909), pp. 19-21, 48-65. Language simplified.

▶ Do you think that life in the open country produces better citizens than life in the city? Why or why not?

Many things rest upon the development of a new rural civilization. Our ability to continue to feed and clothe the hungry nations depends on it. Our ability to supply the city with fresh blood, clean bodies, and clear brains that can endure the strain of modern urban life depends on it as well. Furthermore, a race of people in the open country will be the strength of the nation in time of war and its guiding and controlling spirit in time of peace.

Broadly speaking, agriculture in the United States is prosperous. And the conditions in many of the great farming regions are improving. There has never been a time when the American farmers were as well off as they are today, when we consider not only their earning power, but the comforts and advantages they may have. Yet there is a widespread tendency for farmers to move to town. It is not advisable, of course, that all country persons remain in the country. But this general desire to move is evidence that the open country is not satisfying as a permanent home. In difficult farming regions and where competition with other farming sections is most severe, young people may go to town to better their condition.

Nearly everywhere there is a townward movement in order to win a better education for the children. This movement tends to destroy the open country and to lower its social status.

Social disorder is usually unrecognized. If the farms are financially profitable, the rural condition is usually pronounced good. But country life must be made attractive and satisfying, as well as profitable. It must be able to hold people's interest throughout their lifetime. With most persons this condition can come only with the development of a strong sense of community feeling.

The community feeling that is so marked among farm folk in older countries cannot be expected to develop at this period in American history. We are still a new country with undeveloped resources. We have many far away pastures which are always green and inviting. Our farmers have been moving. Numbers of them have not yet become so well settled as to speak of their farm as "home."

The middle-aged farmers of the central states sell the old homestead without much hesitation or regret. They then move westward to find greater acreage for their sons and daughters. The farmers of the Middle West sell the old home and move to the mountain states, to the Pacific coast, to the South, to Mexico, or to Canada.

Even when permanently settled, farmers do not easily unite with others for financial or social betterment. The training of generations has made them strong individualists. And they have been obliged to rely mainly on themselves.

They do not as a rule dream of a rural organization that can supply as completely as the city the four great requirements of human beings—health, education, occupation, and society. People in the city are moving out of the business section into the suburbs to get as much as possible of the country in the city. But farmers do not dream that it is possible to have the best of the city in the country.

Some ways to correct the social isolation and barrenness of farm life are already in existence or developing. Institutions such as the Grange are giving attention to the social and community questions. There is a widespread awakening, as a result of this work. This awakening is greatly aided by the rural free delivery of mails, and by telephones, the gradual improvement of highways, farmers' institutes, cooperative creameries, and other agencies.

In every part of the United States there seems to be agreement on the need to redirect the rural schools. The schools are held to be largely responsible for ineffective farming, lack of ideals, and the drift to town. It is probable that the farming population will willingly support better schools as soon as it becomes convinced that the schools will really be changed in such a way as to teach persons how to live.

The feeling that agriculture must influence rural public schools is beginning to express itself in the interest in nature study, in the introduction of agriculture classes in high schools, and in the establishment of separate or special schools to teach farm and home subjects. These agencies will help to bring about the complete reconstruction of rural life.

The people of the open country must learn to work together. This effort should be a genuinely cooperative one. All the members should have a voice in the management of organizations and share proportionately in their benefits. Many of the so-called "cooperative" organizations are really not such. They are likely to be controlled in the interest of a few persons rather than for all. Some of the societies that are cooperative in name are really strong centralized corporations or stock companies. They have no greater interest in the welfare of their patrons than other corporations have.

At present the cooperative spirit works itself out chiefly in business organizations devoted to selling and buying. The Commission has found many organizations that seem to be satisfactorily handling the transporting, distributing, and marketing of farm products. With some crops, particularly cotton and the grains, it is helpful to provide

▶ Do you agree with the authors of this report that the "four great requirements" of human beings are health, education, occupation, and society? Why, or why not?

Free delivery of letters and packages to mailboxes in rural areas was established in 1896. Before that, people in those areas had to go to the nearest post office—sometimes at a considerable distance—to get their mail. Pressure from the Grange influenced Congress to provide free rural delivery.

Groups of farmers organized cooperative associations to bypass dealers who served as intermediaries between the farmers and the consumers. Producer cooperatives processed farm products, such as milk, which was marketed directly to consumers. Farmers also organized consumer cooperatives. They were retail stores that sold such items as farm machinery and clothing at cost to the members of the cooperative.

▶ Do you think that it is the responsibility of schools "to teach persons how to live"? Why or why not?

With the Smith-Hughes Act of 1917, Congress provided money for vocational education in public schools, including courses in agriculture and home economics.

Patrons here refers to the members of cooperative associations.

cooperative warehouses. In these warehouses the growers may hold their products till prices rise, and scientific systems of grading of the products may be introduced.

Other kinds of organized cooperative efforts can be started. Cooperation to secure and to employ farm labor would be helpful. Or cooperatives might try to secure telephone service, extend electric lines, or improve highways.

It is, of course, necessary that farmers be well paid for their work. It is also true that money is frequently much emphasized in farm homes. Teachers of agriculture have placed too much emphasis on the income and production sides of country life. Money hunger is as strong in the open country as elsewhere. And as there are fewer opportunities and demands for spending this money for others and for society, hoarding and a lack of public spirit often develop.

The farming country by no means lacks leaders. It is not lost or incapable of helping itself. But it has been relatively overlooked by persons who are interested in making useful reforms. All of us should recognize the opportunity to do useful work in farm country.

FOR THOUGHT:

What were the values of the members of the Commission? How do they compare to Peffer's values? To the values of the authors of excerpts in Reading 52?

55 FARM COMPLAINTS AND FARM CHANGES

HISTORICAL ESSAY

People today are faced with the real possibility—and, in some areas, the actuality—of terrible famines in nations all over the world. Despite the fact that the United States is a great manufacturing nation, American farms are probably more important to the well-being of humanity than American factories.

Of course, both farm and factory play a part in the production of food. The link between them is suggested by the following four tables. They provide information on the use of land, labor, machinery, and commercial fertilizers in the period covered by this chapter. As you will see, the rise in agricultural production did not stem simply from an expansion of land in use or an increase in the number of men and women working on farms. The rise in total production and production per person was also due in large part to the role played by machines and chemicals.

370

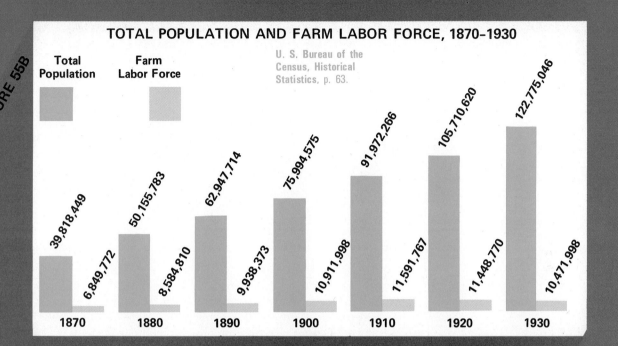

TOTAL POPULATION AND FARM LABOR FORCE, 1870–1930

Total Population

Farm Labor Force

U. S. Bureau of the Census, Historical Statistics, p. 63.

	1870	1880	1890	1900	1910	1920	1930
Total Population	39,818,449	50,155,783	62,947,714	75,994,575	91,972,266	105,710,620	122,775,046
Farm Labor Force	6,849,772	8,584,810	9,938,373	10,911,998	11,591,767	11,448,770	10,471,998

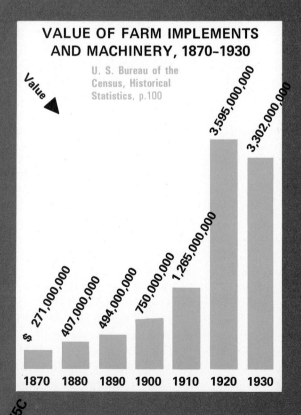

VALUE OF FARM IMPLEMENTS AND MACHINERY, 1870–1930

U. S. Bureau of the Census, Historical Statistics, p.100

Value

1870	1880	1890	1900	1910	1920	1930
$ 271,000,000	407,000,000	494,000,000	750,000,000	1,265,000,000	3,595,000,000	3,302,000,000

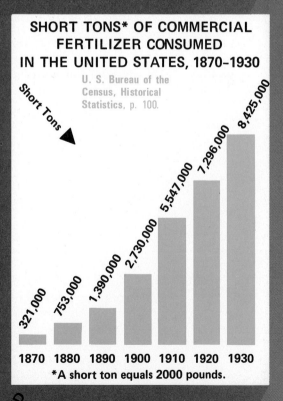

SHORT TONS* OF COMMERCIAL FERTILIZER CONSUMED IN THE UNITED STATES, 1870–1930

U. S. Bureau of the Census, Historical Statistics, p. 100.

Short Tons

1870	1880	1890	1900	1910	1920	1930
321,000	753,000	1,390,000	2,730,000	5,547,000	7,296,000	8,425,000

*A short ton equals 2000 pounds.

U. S. Bureau of the Census, Historical Statistics of the United States, 1789-1945 (Washington, D. C.: Government Printing Office, 1949), p. 95.

FIGURE 55D   NUMBER OF FARMS, FARM ACREAGE, AND VALUE OF FARMS, 1870-1930

Year	Number of Farms	Farm Acreage	Farm Lands and Buildings	
			Total Value	Average Value/Acre
1870	2,660,000	408,000,000	$ 7,444,000,000	$18.26
1880	4,009,000	536,000,000	10,197,000,000	19.02
1890	4,565,000	623,000,000	13,279,000,000	21.31
1900	5,737,000	839,000,000	16,615,000,000	19.81
1910	6,362,000	879,000,000	34,801,000,000	39.60
1920	6,448,000	956,000,000	66,316,000,000	69.38
1930	6,289,000	987,000,000	47,886,000,000	48.52

A Revolution in Agriculture

A combine is a harvesting machine that reaps, threshes, and cleans grain.

By 1870, mechanical reapers, binders, threshers, combines, gang plows, harrows, seeders, and cultivators were all widely used. After 1870, there was a new or improved machine on the market virtually every year. Until World War I, horses provided most of the power on farms. However, steam tractors pulled huge machines through large western wheat fields. In 1910, there were only about 1000 gasoline-powered tractors on American farms. By 1930, there were 920,000. Mechanization had taken command.

Education and research also contributed to farm productivity. In May 1862, President Abraham Lincoln had established the Department of Agriculture which had a budget of $64,000. Part of these funds were to be used to supply farmers with information about a number of practical subjects. Soon after this, Congress passed the Morrill Act. It granted every state then in the Union 30,000 acres of federal land for each senator and representative in Congress at the time. The money from the sale of the land was to be used to endow at least one college which would teach agriculture and the "mechanic arts" in every state. By 1916, the states had founded sixty-nine land-grant colleges. In 1887, the Hatch Act added agricultural experiment stations to the land-grant colleges. Both federal and state governments also developed extension work to educate farmers through lectures, county fairs, publications, and correspondence. All of these activities contributed to the agricultural revolution. They helped people develop excellent seeds, new fertilizers, and better machinery. And they educated farmers to use them well.

The Morrill Land Grant Act of 1862 granted public lands to the states and territories to be used to establish agricultural and mechanical colleges. Many of today's state universities began as land-grant colleges. The Hatch Act of 1887 provided federal money for agricultural experimental stations and farms. The Smith-Lever Act of 1914 provided federal money for county extension agents to act as intermediaries between the colleges and experimental stations and the farmers.

From 1870 on, many American farmers understood that the agricultural revolution of their times was an event of worldwide significance. They were particularly concerned that markets around the world would be open to American farm products. However, until very recently, farm issues were debated as if they were matters concerning only Americans. This situation may not surprise you since citizens

372

of other nations do not vote in American elections. Today, however, the situation is different. Agricultural policy is deeply involved in the foreign relations of the United States. Indirectly, hungry residents of other countries are represented in American elections. This change is the result of the increased international importance of the United States. However, it is also the result of shifts in the structure of American agriculture. In the decades surrounding the turn of the century, agriculture was a highly competitive industry. Today, American farm production is largely controlled by a small number of giant companies.

▶ Do you think that wealthy nations, such as the United States, should be responsible for helping poor nations in time of famine, or other natural disasters? Why or why not?

Competition and Agriculture

In order to be purely competitive, an industry must have: (1) a very large number of producers, each so small in relation to the total size of the market that his or her production will make no real difference in the market price or the quantity produced; (2) an identical product marketed by these producers so that the consumer has no preference about which one he or she buys; (3) easy entrance into this field of production and exit for those who fail in it; (4) an absence of any secret agreements among producers on the price, quantity, or quality of goods sold.

The wheat industry may serve as an example of pure competition. Throughout the entire period covered by this chapter, hundreds of thousands of farmers raised wheat. No single farmer raised as much as one tenth of one percent of a year's wheat crop. Hence, if an individual farmer refused to sell his wheat, the price would neither rise nor fall. Millers who bought wheat to make flour for bread had no reason to prefer grain from any particular farmer. It was easy to enter the wheat industry. A farmer who raised corn could quickly shift to wheat in many parts of the country. It was also easy to leave. A farmer could simply plant another crop or abandon farming. Finally, because farmers scattered all over the nation raised wheat, they could not get together to work out and enforce agreements to limit production or set prices.

Pure competition made the individual farmer helpless in an impersonal market. Again an example may help to clarify the problem. In 1867, farmers produced about 211 million bushels of wheat on almost 17 million acres. The average price per bushel was $2.01. Because prices were so high, farmers used savings or borrowed money to buy additional land and machinery. They harvested 246 million bushels on more than 19 million acres during 1868. The price fell to $1.46 per bushel. But instead of planting fewer acres the next year, farmers planted 2 million acres more and harvested almost 290 million bushels. The price fell to $.92 a bushel, less than half of what it had been two years before.

To understand what happened, take a look at the world from the point of view of the individual farmer. "Returns are high. I'll borrow $1000 to buy more land and some new machinery," a farmer might have said in 1867. "I grow about thirteen bushels an acre. Wheat sells for $2.00. If I plant ten more acres, I will harvest 130 additional bushels. And my income will increase by about $260 each year. In five years, I'll be able to repay the $1000, pay the interest on this money, and have some left over." When prices fell the next year and the loan still had to be repaid, the farmer persuaded himself to plant more wheat, not less. So, even though he received fewer dollars per bushel, his total income would remain constant.

Hundreds of other farmers thought the same way. Wheat flooded the market. And prices fell still further. Moreover, their fortunes were affected by international conditions since grains, cotton, meat, and many other products sold on a worldwide market. A bumper crop of wheat in the Ukraine or of cotton in India or Egypt could bankrupt American farmers. This competitive situation eventually forced inefficient farmers out of business, although it provided food and fibers to consumers at the lowest possible costs.

Farmers' Complaints

Since they could be hurt so easily by the ups and downs of the market, farmers were suspicious of anyone who seemed to be protected from losses. Railroad companies were particularly subject to this suspicion. In most areas of the country, farmers had to use the nearest railroad to transport their goods to market. This condition gave each company a local monopoly. It also generated an enormous demand for public regulation of railroad rates. This demand was first expressed in the program of the National Grange, formed in 1867. It was repeated in the platforms of the Farmers' Alliances formed in the 1880's and the People's or Populist party created in 1892. The demand might never have been successful, however, if it had been confined to farmers. Both small town and large city merchants and bankers frequently led the attack on the railroad rate structure. In the 1870's, many states passed rate regulations. In a series of decisions, the Supreme Court upheld these so-called Granger laws. In 1886, in the Wabash Case, the Court modified its position. It ruled that state legislatures could not regulate railroads which were engaged in interstate commerce. Congress assumed authority over these roads with the passage of the Interstate Commerce Act of 1887.

Aside from railroads and the warehousing and processing firms often linked to them, the greatest farm suspicion was directed to what was vaguely called, "the money power." Farmers were subject to the ups and downs of the market. But this money power was seen as somehow safe from these fluctuations. Indeed, the money power was seen as the source of change. "The hand of the money changer is upon

374

us," Peffer wrote. "Money dictates our financial policy. Money controls the business of the country. Money is plundering the people." The source of this image is not difficult to understand. Farming, unlike manufacturing, yields its product all at once. As the harvest is sold, the returns must be saved to support the farmer through the whole year and to finance next season's herds or crops. The difficulties of developing a steady cash flow were increased with the costly opening of new land and the introduction of expensive farm machinery. Farming was a risky business, competing for funds with a manufacturing sector which was also growing rapidly. Many farmers complained both that they had to borrow money—unlike the good old days when they owned farm and equipment outright—and that they could not borrow enough at low rates.

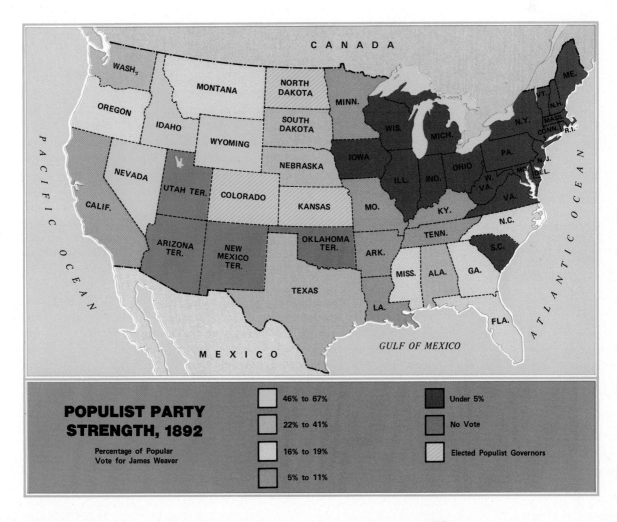

POPULIST PARTY STRENGTH, 1892

Percentage of Popular Vote for James Weaver

- 46% to 67%
- 22% to 41%
- 16% to 19%
- 5% to 11%
- Under 5%
- No Vote
- Elected Populist Governors

The issue of developing an adequate volume and method of farm financing was linked in the last three decades of the 1800's with a general complaint against the level of farm prices. People today are so used to living with inflation that it is hard to imagine a time when people assumed that prices would be lower next year. Between 1864 and 1900, the index of wholesale prices for all products fell 59 percent. The index for agricultural products dropped 65 percent. Farmers who had borrowed money when prices were high suffered during deflation. They had to repay the loan when the prices they received per bushel had fallen. Understandably, they often argued that a strategy to increase prices would not only improve their current income but would reduce the burden of their debts.

Even if every American farmer had agreed to a single position on railroad regulation, land reform, and inflation, it is unlikely that they would have voted for a single national party or Presidential candidate. Very rarely was a single issue, or set of issues, enough to change the feeling that a voter was a natural Democrat or Republican. Universal agreement among farmers was, moreover, extremely unlikely. Total farm income rose about 80 percent between 1870 and 1900. But the total farm population increased by only about 60 percent. Some farmers were obviously doing very well in the midst of the complaints of others. Most farm loans were not old legacies of a period of high prices but were taken on for a few months or years with the expectation that prices would decline. In both the South and on the western prairies many farmers tilled their land as sharecroppers. They paid for its use by turning a portion of their yield over to their landlords. Landlord and 'cropper, or owner and hired hand, often took opposing views of economic issues. Farmers in Illinois, Indiana, Michigan, Ohio, and Wisconsin did not fully share the complaints of farmers in Kansas and Nebraska against the railroads and the money power. Indeed, they often blamed their problems on the opening of the western prairies and plains and the reduction of transportation costs which allowed newcomers to steal their markets. The president of the Ohio Agricultural Society argued squarely in 1891: "It has been overproduction by the opening up of the great West . . . that has placed mortgages upon the farmers' homes of this state."

The result of this variety of views was that self-proclaimed agrarian candidates never attracted even a majority of farm voters. James Weaver, running for President on the People's party ticket in 1892, won only a million votes nationwide. In 1896, the Populists merged with the Democrats to nominate William Jennings Bryan for President. Bryan's appeal was directed to farmers. "The great cities," he told the nominating convention, "rest upon our broad and fertile prairies. Burn down your cities and leave our farms and your cities will spring up again as if by magic. But destroy our farms and the grass will

▶ Does ownership of property inevitably determine the way a person views economic issues? Why or why not?

376

grow in the streets of every city in the country." Bryan was decisively beaten.

The farm protest movements of the 1890's had an enormous political and emotional range. They ran the gamut from the economic issues of rural life to the general distribution of political power in American society. However, the most important question was always: How can farmers control the conditions of production so as to produce the greatest return on their investment?

After 1896, farm politics tended to change in tone. The Farm Bureau Federation formed in 1919 prided itself on its conservative tone and its interest in business methods. The organizations described by the Country Life Commission provided local groups of farmers with a concrete way of acting upon the general issues which had so troubled Peffer. The federal government took greater responsibility for farm policy in 1916. The Federal Farm Loan Act and the Warehouse Act permitted the government to store produce such as wheat and to offer loans to farmers until the price of their crops rose. In this way, many of the issues which were the subject of angry demands and confrontations in the 1890's were turned into subject for detailed negotiations between federal officials and farm groups.

The basic question of farm politics, however, remained the same. Farm income continued to be subject to dramatic changes in direction. The wholesale price index of all farm products rose almost 50 percent between 1900 and 1910. The index of products which farmers bought rose less than 20 percent. These trends continued to 1915, when the boom caused by World War I skyrocketed farm prices. Total farm production did not rise above the 1915 level, despite a substantial increase in acreage planted, until 1920. But as demand increased, prices shot up. Prices received by farmers more than doubled during these four years. However, the prices they paid for goods and services including interest and taxes rose less than 90 percent. Then the war ended.

In 1920, Europe's demands dropped. A temporary postwar slump that placed about 5 million Americans among the unemployed cut domestic demand. At the same time, total farm productivity rose 5 percent. Prices collapsed. The index of prices received by farmers fell from 215 in 1919, to 124 in 1921 while the prices of what they bought fell far less. Although conditions on the farm improved after 1923, farm income remained low throughout the 1920's. Farm organizations asked the government to support their prices in order to raise farm incomes. Congress approved several of these schemes, but they were vetoed by President Coolidge. In the 1930's, faced with a worldwide depression, these schemes were revived. Asking and answering the old question, the United States began a policy of reducing farm production in order to increase farm income.

American farmers supplied war-torn Europe with food for three years before America's entry into the war in 1917. Between 1914 and 1917 the value of wheat exported increased from $88 million to almost $300 million. When the war began, a bushel of wheat sold for less than $1.00. By 1918, the price had risen to $3.00.

Blacks and Whites in the Southern States

STATING THE ISSUE

Before the Civil War, blacks and whites had lived together as master and slave. Informal contacts between the two groups could not change this relationship. Therefore, whites did not hesitate to deal frequently and casually with blacks in daily life. Whites and blacks rode in the same railway cars or wagons. Sometimes they ate at the same table. They rarely formally married. But members of the two groups often had children together.

Emancipation and Reconstruction destroyed this system of race relations. However, for a time no clear substitute system emerged in its place. For twenty years, relations between blacks and whites remained in a state of flux. During that time, white and black southerners argued about the kind of system that should replace the one that had existed before the Civil War. Slavery could not be reimposed. But most white southerners were not willing to grant equality. Lacking white allies, blacks who demanded equality had little chance of success. The debate concluded at the end of the nineteenth century in a decision to suppress black rights and to legislate rigid inequality.

Chapter 15 focuses on the development of this new pattern of race relations in the South. It explores the debate, the decisions white southerners made about their relations with black citizens, and the social system that evolved from those decisions. It also examines the reactions of blacks—in the North and in the South—to these decisions.

378

1875 Tennessee adopts first "Jim Crow" laws

1877 Reconstruction period is officially ended

1881 Booker T. Washington organizes Tuskegee Institute

1889 Lewis Blair publishes **The Prosperity of the South Dependent Upon the Elevation of the Negro**

1890 Mississippi disenfranchises blacks with state constitutional amendment

1892 Populist Party is organized

1895 Booker T. Washington speaks at Atlanta Cotton States and Industrial Exposition

1896 William McKinley defeats William Jennings Bryan in Presidential election

1896 Supreme Court declares segregation constitutional in **Plessy vs. Ferguson**

1898 Louisiana becomes first state to include "grandfather clause" in state constitution

1901 President Theodore Roosevelt invites Booker T. Washington to White House

1901 Alabama Convention disenfranchises blacks

1901 Booker T. Washington publishes **Up From Slavery**

1903 W.E. DuBois publishes **Souls of Black Folk**

1915 Supreme Court declares "grandfather clause" unconstitutional

56 THE INDIVISIBLE SOUTH

The Civil War devastated the South. A quarter of a million people and hundreds of thousands of animals had died. Farm buildings and whole sections of cities were ruined. Railroad tracks were torn up. Locomotives were gutted. And factories were burned to the ground.

Destruction of physical resources remain intact. The South made an amazing recovery from the War. By 1875, southern agriculture had practically returned to its prewar level. In 1880, cotton production surpassed all prewar records. Before the War, merchants and bankers provided services only in a few large southern cities. After the War, they established businesses in smaller cities throughout the region. And, after the economic decline of the mid-1870's, northern financiers invested in southern railroads, iron and steel plants, and timber production.

The people who won political control in the South at the end of Reconstruction adopted the images of the old slaveholding elite. They boasted of their respect for southern traditions. Basically, however, they were interested in encouraging rapid economic growth. Through economic growth they hoped to transform southern life. They wanted a South dotted with new steel mills and tied together by railroads.

379

These people looked to the North for models of economic development. They felt that prosperity was to be achieved through mining and manufacturing. And they believed that economic development depended on cheap labor, freedom from government regulation of business, a stable society that supported property rights, and low taxes. In order to keep taxes low, political leaders in many states even cut the budgets of the public schools established during Reconstruction.

However, there were some southern leaders who believed that these policies were neither realistic nor wise. Lewis Blair was one of these leaders. He was a member of one of Virginia's most prominent political families. He challenged the idea that economic development could be achieved without a revolution in race relations. As you read this excerpt from his writings, consider the following questions:

1. What did Blair criticize about the South?
2. Why did he believe that white southerners would have to treat blacks better?

A Proposal for Southern Prosperity

In 1889, Lewis H. Blair published his proposal for southern prosperity. It was titled The Prosperity of the South Dependent Upon the Elevation of the Negro. *Here are some of Blair's arguments.*

Lewis Blair, **The Prosperity of the South Dependent Upon the Elevation of the Negro** (Richmond, Virginia: Everett Waddey, 1889), pp. 9-11, 28-29, 43-45, 50-51. Republished as **A Southern Prophecy** (Boston: Little, Brown and Company, 1964), pp. 25-27, 48-49, 67-68, 69, 75, 77. Language simplified.

There are many causes for the poverty of the South. The principal ones are widespread ignorance, a general disregard of human life, and a general lack of economy and self-denial. But great as these causes are, a greater and more far-reaching cause is the degradation of the Negro. Our principal source of labor, he is also our principal source of prosperity.

Each of these causes would greatly slow the prosperity of the South, or indeed of any country. But all of them combined are not as serious and as fatal as the last cause, namely: the degradation of the Negro. It is like a deadly cancer which poisons the whole system. It seems to intensify all the other drawbacks under which we labor. Thus general ignorance is increased by the gross ignorance of all the blacks and of the whites nearest them in social and financial condition. The general disregard of human life is intensified by the slight regard in which a Negro's life is held. The whites, regarding the Negro's life of little value, naturally regard all life as of little value. And therefore they freely take each other's life. The general lack of economy and self-denial is naturally increased by the careless, wasteful, and negligent manner in which the Negro, upon whom we depend for labor, does his work. The Negro is an extremely defective tool. No man,

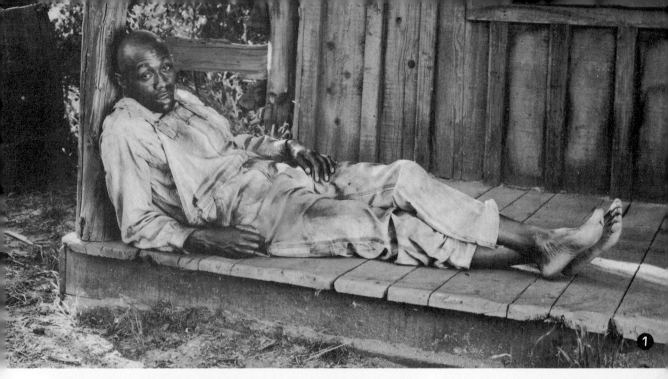

►These pictures show Stepin Fetchit, a black actor of the 1930's who played the part of a stereotyped southern black—shiftless, slow-speaking, and lazy. Should films and television portray people in ways which may help to maintain a false image such as the one which Blair described and Fetchit played?

whether planter, carpenter, or whatnot, can continue to use wretched tools without becoming wasteful and negligent himself. We would urge the South to improve its animals, tools, methods of planting, etc., so that it may derive more good from its labor and capital. We also urge the elevation of the Negroes. The better men and citizens they are, the more we, the whites, can in the end make out of them.

But the question will be very generally asked, Why elevate the Negro at all? Isn't it now good enough that he obeys us dutifully, and grows our corn, cotton, tobacco, rice, and sugar? What more do we want of him? But if the Negro is forever to remain simply the means of doing our menial and manual work, he is already too elevated. In his present condition he has some of the ideas and aspirations of a freeman, and some desires for education. He also has almost complete control of his personal life. He works when it suits him. But then he may loaf when we need him most in the fields. But since we cannot compel him with the lash to work, he is on the whole not a profitable laborer either for himself or for an employer. To make him efficient, and to make him work the crop at the proper time, the overseer with the lash must be ever before his eyes. To allow the Negro to remain as he is drags us down with him.

▶Do you learn more when teachers threaten to give you bad grades and parents threaten to punish you for them or when teachers and parents help you to learn? Why?

But if the Negro is to become an intelligent voter, a capable citizen, and a valuable co-worker, we have much to do in order to elevate him. To make him *our* assistant in the production of wealth, the Negro must be made to work. Or he must be persuaded, by the hope of enjoying in full the fruits of his labors, to work steadily and intelligently. If we are not willing to elevate him, we should set to work to chain both his mind and limbs, and to frighten him, so that a little white child can control a thousand. We will then at least get enough out of him to supply his few physical wants and to enable us to live in idleness and comparative comfort. But if there is no hope of our ever being able to do this, what is the next best thing for us to do for our own good? Make a man of him. But this can be done only by means of education, by cultivating his self-respect, by inspiring his hope, by letting him see that the land of his birth is as much his country as it is that of the richest and proudest white. Now he is not only an alien but an inferior—in reality a serf, in the land of his nativity.

Serfdom was a condition of most peasants under feudalism during the Middle Ages. Serfs were bound to the land and could not leave the land without their lord's permission. They held low status in the social structure.

We must trample, or we must elevate. To maintain the present situation is impossible. To trample is to keep and even make worse the poverty and stagnation under which we groan. To elevate is to make the South rich, happy, and strong. What are we going to do? Shall we oppose? Shall we drift and take chances? Or shall we promote the Negro's progress? Prejudice counsels the first; timidity, the second; common sense, the third. So what shall we do?

The majority will probably say, Wait. Why take any steps to correct any abuses? Evils, they say, will in time cure themselves. But history proves that evils do not always cure themselves. As often or oftener they ruin the patient. Yet we argue that time will happily bring about a solution to the Negro problem. But time is not only uncertain. It is also very long. And while we are waiting, we will suffer all the evils and disadvantages of actual poverty.

The measures necessary to elevate the Negro cannot be carried out quickly or by a simple act of legislation. They require time, care, wisdom, and patience. And they are impossible without the acceptance and cooperation of the whites. Great as is the power of the national government, it cannot elevate the Negroes itself. And it cannot force the whites to do so. The question is absolutely within control of the whites. They can keep the Negro in his present poor condition. But they cannot do so without at the same time laying the axe at the root of their own welfare. They can crush, but while crushing Negroes, they will be destroying themselves.

The whites cannot see this situation now for they are dominated by a great fear. They fear that raising the Negro means lowering the whites. This fear must be put to rest by showing them that little probable harm can come to them. Until then, it will be like appealing to the winds to urge them to take steps leading to Negro rights. In spite of all advice to love our neighbor as ourself, human nature will persist in loving itself better than its neighbor. And so, as long as the southern people believe that the complete elevation of the Negro will be an injury to them, they cannot be expected to take kindly to the idea. Show one that his interest lies in a certain direction, however, and there is little difficulty in getting him to go that way. So to elevate the Negro, we must show the whites that his elevation will be no disadvantage to them.

The South is truly a land of caste. Its chains hang heavily upon those of the lowest caste. Southern society is now virtually divided into two castes. In the first caste are merged gentleman, farmer, overseer, and poor white. Each and every one of these, regardless of education, worth, refinement, decency, or morality, belongs to this caste simply by reason of a white skin. The second caste is composed of all who have a black skin and all related to them, however remotely. All who are thus marked, however cultured and refined they may be, are confined as by fate to this caste. They are not permitted to throw off their chains. Society, by its verdict, decrees that the meanest, lowest, and most degraded of the first caste are the permanent superiors of the best, highest, and ablest of the second caste.

Hope cannot exist, certainly cannot flourish, under such a weight. If he is to remain forever a "nigger," an object of undisguised contempt, even to the lowest whites, the Negro will naturally say to himself, Why strive, why labor, why practice painful self-denial in order to rise, if I am to derive no good from my effort? On the contrary, he will not exert himself, but will sink into despondency.

▶Should members of minority groups be willing to wait for time to bring about equality? Or should they demand their rights immediately? Why?

A caste system rigidly divides members of society into groups on the basis of birth, wealth, or religion. No social mobility takes place within a caste system.

383

What changes in the attitudes of southern whites would have been
necessary for the success of Blair's program? What means might have
been used to bring about these changes?

57 THEY CANNOT BE EQUAL

Lewis Blair was not the only leader in the new South who
urged the elevation of blacks. Even if they did not advocate black
equality, many conservative leaders of the 1870's and 1880's believed
that blacks should not be barred from the political life of the region.
In fact, they looked to black voters to help defeat whites who
challenged their leadership. In return for their support, blacks received
minor offices in government and other jobs. Blacks often lived in fear
of reprisals from the terrorist Ku Klux Klan. But they were not
segregated legally from the white community.

This delicate balance in race relations was shattered in the last
decade of the nineteenth century. Beginning with Mississippi in 1890,
state after state passed laws to prevent blacks from voting. After taking
away the right to vote, southern states adopted policies to segregate
the races. Between 1900 and 1911, most states passed "Jim Crow"
laws. They required blacks and whites to sit separately in railroad
cars, trolleys, ferries, and steamboats. Many southern cities adopted
rules requiring whites and blacks to live in separate neighborhoods.
Southern reformers, fighting for progressive farm measures, urged
black and white farmers to take up segregated farmlands.

Many northerners, who had been friendly to blacks, consented to
this policy of segregation. Even the Supreme Court of the United
States endorsed it. In 1896, the Court decided in the case of *Plessy
vs. Ferguson* that a Louisiana law requiring blacks and whites to travel
in separate railroad cars did not violate the fourteenth Amendment.
The Court held that segregation did not mean discrimination. As long
as the railroad cars were of equal quality, it said, the constitutional
rights of blacks were not violated. The extension of the doctrine of
"separate but equal" to public schools allowed southerners to build
black schools and white schools. These schools, while separate, were
rarely equal.

Reading 57 consists of three parts. The first part is drawn from
the debates in the Alabama convention of 1901. The convention
deprived blacks of the vote. The second and third parts come from
the writings of two women who were prominent black activists. They
describe some of the conditions under which blacks lived in the South
after their rights were suppressed. As you read think about these
questions:

1. What role did the speakers at the Alabama convention want blacks to play in southern life? Why?
2. According to Barnett and Terrell, what was it like to be black in the South? Who, if anyone, do they feel was responsible for this situation?

The Alabama Convention Disfranchises Blacks

Attempts to take the vote away from black citizens often involved a proposal that only literate people could vote. But many white voters were also illiterate. Hence, Democrats in Alabama proposed that anyone whose grandfather had the right to vote could also vote whether or not he could read or write. This clause would enfranchise all white men but no blacks. The grandfathers of blacks living in 1901 had been slaves and could not have voted. The following selection presents arguments for the "grandfather clause" by delegates to the Alabama Democratic party convention in 1901.

MR. GRESNER WILLIAMS: How can you have a progressive and enlightened state unless white men rule it? It does not insult the white men of Alabama when you require the slave to have a qualification that the white man does not. Gentlemen of the Convention, God Almighty Himself put the seal on the white man. And He put it upon the negro. He has made the distinction and we only ask you to stand by your own people. I was fortunate when I was born in that my father had a good living after the dreadful Civil War. I know, however, young men whose fathers before the War were wealthy men who were my playfellows and those of my elder brothers. These young men today can scarcely write their names. And after it is written for them can scarcely read it, though printed in the boldest of letters. Would you disfranchise those men, or the children of those men, who were denied opportunities to get an education because of the scourges of war? Does not this section of the proposed law guarantee the right to vote to these men, grown to manhood and now having children of their own, who have not been able to attend school? Are you not willing to guarantee the ballot to those who will not be able to give to their children's children as much education as will be necessary to compete with the negro child whose blood has possibly mingled with the Caucasian? It is absurd that any man who has seen the changed conditions in this country cannot also see that our nation demands the enfranchisement of every man in this state with pure white blood in his veins.

Official Proceedings of the Constitutional Convention of the State of Alabama (May 21, 1901 to September 3, 1901), Vol. III, pp. 2839-2848. Language simplified.

Many southern states included a "grandfather clause" in their constitutions. This clause exempted from the literacy tests and poll taxes anyone who had been eligible to vote on January 1, 1867, or whose parents or grandparents had been eligible to vote at that time. This clause thus gave the vote to many uneducated, poor whites while denying it to blacks.

These pictures show stereotypes of five American groups—the Germans, the blacks, the Irish, the Chinese, and the Jews. To what degree, if any, have pictures such as these and verbal descriptions such as the ones you have been reading contributed to any stereotypes you might have?

386

CHINA·MAN.

OH GOLLY, BUT I'SE HAPPY!

▶Why do so many people reason from racial unity as a basis for accepting or rejecting a position on a public issue?

It has been said that a race war is possibly about to take place in Alabama. I don't believe it, but for the sake of argument I will admit it. Should a race war come, will not delegates to this Convention want the lowliest white men, whether they are able to read or write, to shoulder the musket and go out against the black? I say, put the test: white man against negro. And we ask you in this majority report to place the white man, be he ever so lowly, above the negro, be he ever so high and exalted among his own people. For we are tired . . .

THE PRESIDENT: The time of the gentleman has expired.

MR. WILLIAMS: And I am tired also.

MR. J. THOMAS HEFLIN: It was here in the United States, Mr. President, that the Caucasian race carved out a Republic. It was here that the representatives of the proudest race that ever lived established a government that will never fall. It was here that the white man drove the red man from his home in the forest, and took possession of this land. We find in the Bible that God gave His servants command, to go up and possess the land. I believe He reserved America, this section of the western world, for the permanent settlement of the Caucasian race. Here by mutual consent, the Caucasians came together. And by mutual consent they established a government for the good of all the people.

In the course of time, gentlemen of the Convention, slaves were hunted out in Africa. The negro wandered through the woods like a beast of the field, and was brought here to do what? To be put upon the block and sold to the highest bidder, to be the servant of his superior, the white man in this country. I believe as truly as I believe that I am standing here, that God Almighty intended the negro to be the servant of the white man. I believe that the Scripture will support my position on that question. I know he is inferior to the white man. And I believe that delegates of the Convention believe him to be inferior. He knows it himself.

Upon a question of state rights, and not on the question of slavery, the greatest civil conflict in human history was enacted in our country. Great men were arrayed upon opposing sides. For four years the undaunted sons of the South showed to the world the bravest spirit that has ever throbbed beneath God Almighty's sun. They fought for home rule, and for self-government, and what occurred? The President of the United States issued a proclamation freeing the slaves of the South. It took from the slaveowners that which they had bought and paid for with their own money. It snatched from them this property that they had bought in the market and which belonged to them. This was a military blow at the labor system of the South. Later on they said to this mass of ignorant slaves, "You may walk side by side with your master of yesterday and cast your vote." Unfit for the responsibilities of government, they were turned loose upon the

Here the speaker was in error. The Emancipation Proclamation freed those slaves living in states under Confederate control. In essence, President Lincoln had no jurisdiction over these states as they had seceded from the Union and had set up their own government. It was the Thirteenth Amendment that freed the slaves.

people of the South. Why, Mr. President, the striking from him of the title slave and placing in his hand the ballot was the most devilish piece of tyranny ever visited upon a proud though broken people.

Mr. President, this was the only instance in history where a race which you might say was physically prohibited from amalgamating or assimilating with another race was given equal rights and privileges by the law with that other race in the same community. You can't trace history back to a single recorded instance where two such opposite races were ever brought together under the same laws affecting both alike. There is nowhere a single recorded instance where African and Caucasian races were given the same political, legal, and social rights under the same government. Where two races are thrown together, the stronger will dominate. That is true, and the white man is going to dominate here.

The speaker is inaccurate here. For example, as far back as the eighteenth century B.C. in Egypt, both blacks and whites held positions of honor and influence in the government.

Mr. President, we have told the people of Alabama for years that we wanted to disfranchise the negro. He has been about the ballot box like sheep in the market for sale to the highest bidder. The white people who love the ballot, who love the sanctity of their fireside, who love the government of their homes and of their States, want to exercise that great weapon in the defense of things that are right and sacred. We want to take it out of the hands of men whom you can purchase for twenty-five cents and a drink of whisky. We want the white men who once voted in this State and controlled it to vote again. We want to see that old condition restored. Upon that theory we took the stump in Alabama. We pledge ourselves to the white people of Alabama, upon the platform that we would not disfranchise a single white man. It is our purpose to disfranchise every black in the State and not a single white man.

Mr. President, I love to think of how faithful the blacks were during the War. The gentleman from Montgomery spoke about how they protected our homes, and how they looked after our affairs. That, Mr. President, was the old-time slave of over thirty years ago. That, Mr. President, was the negro that had been brought up in the kitchen and in the backyard, and brought up to respect his master. There was a spirit of fear that went about him. Reverence for his superior, and a feeling of humility and obedience on occasions like that was inborn. And we are glad that they did so well. I am not an enemy to the negro. I am a friend to him in his place. My father owned more slaves than any man in Randolph County. I love the old-time southern negro. He was in his place as a slave and happy and contented as such. And, Mr. President, I love to think of the old black mammy. I believe the day will come when the South will erect a monument to the old black mammy for the lullabies she has sung. We like to think of all these things. We like to think of old Ephraim, sitting around the fireplace picking his banjo and eating roasted potatoes, and such. We love to go back and bring them back to memory.

But take the young blacks of today, and put them in the same position that their fathers were in. And, gentlemen, a quarter of a century from now you would not be on a floor like this singing their praises. I tell you that the old negroes are passing out and the young bucks that are coming on have got to be attended to. I like to think of the negro from the old-fashioned southern standpoint. I like to tell him you do this, or you do that John, and here is a quarter. You black my shoes, or catch my horse, and you go do this and that, and all is well. But I don't like it when I have to walk up to him and say, "John, come down off of that telegraph pole where you are setting telegraph wires through the city. Come down, I want to talk to you about the tariff question." We are equal in the light of the law. And I have got to sit down by you and ask you to vote my way, not because you are my equal, for God Almighty never made you so, but because a law that was born in hate and malice makes it so. Under it you are entitled to hear me and be persuaded by me to vote for me, or to vote against me. Is not that a sad state of affairs?

Why, Mr. President, I saw this morning a little fellow coming down the street as happy as could be with a piece of watermelon in one hand and a set of hollow reeds from the swamp tied together with a string, in the other, blowing "Boogoo Eyes." You see them now and then in a blacksmith shop, with a squeaking bellows, and with the hammer and anvil making music sweet. That is his home. That is where he ought to be. And that is where he must be.

Crimes Against Blacks

Many southerners held the attitudes expressed at the 1901 Alabama Democratic party convention. These attitudes often led to acts of violence. Ida Wells Barnett, a black educator, journalist, and leader of several black organizations, had been born to slave parents during the Civil War. In this excerpt from her writings, she describes crimes which whites committed against blacks during the three decades after the Civil War.

Not all or nearly all of the murders done by white men during the past thirty years in the South have come to light. But the statistics gathered and preserved by white men, and which have not been questioned, show that during these years more than ten thousand blacks have been killed in cold blood, without the formality of a judicial trial and legal execution. And yet, as evidence of the absolute freedom with which the white man dares to kill a black, the same record shows that during all these years, and for all these murders only three white men have been tried, convicted, and executed. Since no white

► Can you order anyone around? If so, how much do you respect him or her? Why?

A stereotype is a simple, standardized mental picture of a racial or nationality group or of an issue or event. This description of a black is an example of a stereotype formerly held by prejudiced white people.

A bellows is an accordion-like instrument that draws in air by expanding and contracting. It is used to fan fires.

Ida Wells Barnett, A Red Record (Chicago: Donohue and Henneberry, 1895), p. 8. Language simplified.

man has been lynched for the murder of black people, these three executions are the only instances of the death penalty being visited upon white men for murdering blacks.

▶Should people who hold positions of power and influence in a community receive special consideration from the police and the courts? Why or why not?

Being Black in the Nation's Capital

Mary Church Terrell was a leading black lecturer, writer, and activist. She was born during the Civil War, reared in Tennessee, and graduated at the head of her class from Oberlin College. In this excerpt, she describes the life of black people in Washington, D. C. during the late nineteenth and early twentieth centuries.

For fifteen years I have resided in Washington, D. C. And while it was far from being a paradise for black people when I first came here it has been doing its level best ever since to make conditions for us intolerable.

As a black woman I may walk from the Capitol to the White House, ravenously hungry and abundantly supplied with money with which to purchase a meal. But I would not be able to find a single restaurant in which I would be permitted to take a morsel of food, if it was patronized by white people, unless I was willing to sit behind a screen. As a black woman I cannot visit the tomb of the Father of this country without being forced to sit in the Jim Crow section of an electric car. If I refuse thus to be humiliated, I am cast into jail and forced to pay a fine for violating the laws.

Unless I am willing to engage in a few menial occupations, in which the pay would be very poor, there is no way for me to earn an honest living. It does not matter what my intellectual achievements may be or how great is the need for the services of a competent person. If I try to enter many of the numerous vocations in which my white sisters are allowed to engage, the door is shut in my face.

From one Washington theater I am excluded altogether. In the rest certain seats are set aside for black people. And it is almost impossible to get others.

With the exception of the Catholic University, there is not a single white college in the national capital to which black people are admitted. A few years ago the Columbian Law School admitted black students, but in deference to the southern white students the authorities have decided to exclude them altogether.

Mary Church Terrell, "What It Means to Be Colored in the Capital of the United States," **The Independent**, Vol. 62, No. 3034 (January 24, 1907), pp. 181-182. Language simplified.

▶Should privately owned schools, clubs, restaurants, and businesses have the right to determine whom they will admit and under what circumstances? Why or why not?

FOR THOUGHT:

To what degree, if any, had the attitudes of whites which Blair described changed between the Civil War and 1900?

Suppression of black rights spread quickly throughout the South. As time went on, more and more blacks saw the white southerner as an enemy. They had good reasons for this view. They were barred from the political life of the South. They were driven from skilled trades at which many had previously worked. Whites excluded them from jobs in new factories, except to use them as strikebreakers. In rural areas, blacks became tenant farmers or share-croppers, who owed large debts to farm owners.

When blacks protested or ran afoul of the law, they faced the threat of violence. Between 1884 and 1900, at least 2500 blacks were lynched in the South. The nineteenth century closed with a race riot against blacks in Wilmington, North Carolina. In 1906, white mobs pillaged and murdered in the black districts of Atlanta.

During this period of repression, black leadership faced serious difficulties. The largely illiterate black population, scattered through-out the rural South, was hard to reach and even harder to organize. Leadership depended largely upon the ability to mobilize relatively small black groups and often upon the consent and support of the white community.

Black leaders proposed two sharply different responses to the plight of blacks. Booker Taliaferro Washington represented the response that most whites preferred. Washington had been born a slave. He obtained an education after the Civil War by working as a school janitor. In 1881 he became the principal of an industrial training school for blacks in Tuskegee, Alabama. With the help of northern philanthropists, he made Tuskegee into a model institution. It combined formal education, self-help, and vocational training. President Theodore Roosevelt invit-ed him to dinner at the White House in 1901. This act confirmed Washington's status as the most celebrated black person in the United States. It also caused white racists to protest violently.

William Edward Burghardt Du Bois, who had been born free in Massachusetts, offered a different solution. W.E.B. Du Bois's academic success won him scholarships to Fisk and Harvard universities. He earned a Ph.D. from Harvard. He also studied in Germany. In the last years of the nineteenth century, he examined the sociological and economic life of black communities in both the North and the South. In 1905, he called for an organization of people who believed in "Negro freedom and growth." Twenty blacks responded and met at Niagara Falls. Later this group held several meetings and rallies in various cities. In 1909, they merged with an organization of white liberals to form the National Association for the Advancement of Colored People (NAACP). Du Bois became the Association's director of publicity and research. He also edited its magazine, *The Crisis*.

As you read the following excerpts from the writings of Washington and Du Bois, think about these questions:

1. What were the assumptions underlying Washington's proposal to "cast down your bucket"?
2. How did Du Bois regard these assumptions?

The Atlanta Exposition Address

In 1895, Booker T. Washington spoke at the Atlanta Cotton States and Industrial Exposition. Both northern and southern whites praised the speech. Portions of it are given here.

A ship lost at sea for many days suddenly sighted a friendly vessel. From the mast of the unfortunate vessel was seen the signal: "Water, water, we die of thirst." The answer from the friendly vessel at once came back, "Cast down your bucket where you are." A second time the signal, "Water, water, send us water," ran up from the distressed vessel and was answered, "Cast down your bucket where you are." A third and fourth signal for water was answered, "Cast down your bucket where you are." The captain of the distressed vessel, at last heeding the injunction, cast down his bucket and it came up full of fresh, sparkling water from the mouth of the Amazon River.

To those of my race who depend on bettering their condition in a foreign land or who underestimate the importance of cultivating friendly relations with the southern white man, who is their next-door neighbor, I would say: "Cast down your bucket where you are." Cast it down in making friends, in every manly way, of the people of all races by whom you are surrounded. Cast it down in agriculture, in mechanics, in commerce, in domestic service, and in the professions.

Our greatest danger is that in the great leap from slavery to freedom we may overlook the fact that the masses of us are to live by the production of our hands. We fail to keep in mind that we shall prosper in proportion as we learn to dignify and glorify common labor and put brains and skill into the common occupations of life. It is at the bottom of life we must begin, and not at the top. Nor should we permit our grievances to overshadow our opportunities.

To those of the white race who look to immigrants for the prosperity of the South, were I permitted, I would repeat what I say to my own race, "Cast down your bucket where you are." Cast it down among the eight millions of Negroes whose habits you know, whose fidelity and love you have tested. Cast down your bucket among these people who have, without strikes and labor wars, tilled your fields, cleared your forests, built your railroads and cities, and helped make

Booker T. Washington, **Up From Slavery, An Autobiography** (New York: Doubleday, Page and Company, 1902), pp. 219-224. Language simplified.

In 1822, the state of Liberia, in Africa, was bought as a home for freed slaves who wanted to relocate in Africa. Although some ex-slaves emigrated, the "back-to-Africa" movement declined. It was revived several times after the Civil War.

possible this magnificent progress of the South. Cast down your bucket among my people, helping and encouraging them as you are doing on these grounds. Give them education of head, hand, and heart, and you will find that they will buy your surplus land, make the waste places in your fields blossom, and run your factories. While doing this, you can be sure in the future, as in the past, that you and your families will be surrounded by the most patient, faithful, law-abiding, and unresentful people that the world has seen. In all things that are purely social we can be as separate as the fingers; yet we can be as one hand in all things essential to mutual progress.

The wisest among my race understand that the agitation of questions of social equality is the extremest folly. They understand that progress in the enjoyment of all the privileges that will come to us must be the result of severe and constant struggle rather than of artificial forcing. No race that has anything to contribute to the markets of the world is long excluded to any degree. It is important and right that all privileges of the law be ours. But it is vastly more important that we be prepared for the exercise of these privileges. The opportunity to earn a dollar in a factory just now is worth much more than the opportunity to spend a dollar in an opera house.

Up From Slavery

In 1901, Washington published his autobiography, Up From Slavery. *The following selection is taken from it.*

Washington, **Up From Slavery**, pp. 234-236. Language simplified.

I am often asked to express myself more freely than I do upon the political condition and the political future of my race. My own belief is that the time will come when the Negro in the South will be accorded all the political rights which his ability, character, and material possessions entitle him to. I think, though, that the opportunity to freely exercise such political rights will not come in any large degree through outside or artificial forcing. Southern white people will give the Negro such rights, and they will protect him in the exercise of those rights, as soon as the South gets over the old feeling that it is being forced by "foreigners," or "aliens," to do something which it does not want to do.

I believe it is the duty of the Negro—as the greater part of the race is already doing—to conduct himself modestly in regard to political claims. He should depend upon the slow but sure influences that proceed from the possession of property, intelligence, and high character for the full recognition of his political rights. I think that the full exercise of political rights is going to be a matter of natural, slow growth, not an overnight affair. I do not believe that the Negro should stop voting. A man cannot learn the exercise of self-government

▶ Should full political rights go only to people with "property, intelligence, and high character"? Why or why not?

by not voting, any more than a boy can learn to swim by keeping out of the water. But I do believe that in his voting he should more and more be influenced by those of intelligence and character who are his next-door neighbors.

In my opinion, the time will come when the South will encourage all of its citizens to vote. It will see that it pays better, from every standpoint, to have healthy, vigorous life than to have that political stagnation which always results when one half of the population has no share and no interest in the Government.

Du Bois Answers Washington

In 1903, W.E.B. Du Bois published a series of essays, The Souls of Black Folk. *In them he criticized Washington's philosophy.*

Mr. Washington represents in Negro thought the old attitude of adjustment and submission. He distinctly asks that black people give up, at least for the present, three things: political power, insistence on civil rights, and higher education of Negro youth. He asks Negroes to concentrate all their energies on industrial education, the accumulation of wealth, and the conciliation of the South.

In the fifteen years he has advocated this policy, these things have occurred: 1) the disfranchisement of the Negro, 2) the legal creation of a distinct status of civil inferiority for the Negro, and 3) the steady withdrawal of aid from institutions for the higher training of the Negro. These movements are not, to be sure, direct results of Mr. Washington's teachings. But his propaganda has, without a shadow of doubt, helped their speedier accomplishment.

Mr. Washington thus faces three contradictions: 1) He is striving nobly to make Negro craftsmen, businessmen, and property-owners. But it is utterly impossible, under modern competitive methods, for workingmen and property-owners to defend their rights and exist without the right to vote. 2) He insists on thrift and self-respect. But at the same time, he counsels a silent submission to civic inferiority, such as is bound to sap the manhood of any race in the long run. 3) He advocates public school and industrial training, and belittles institutions of higher learning. But neither the Negro common-schools, nor Tuskegee itself, could remain open a day were it not for teachers trained in Negro colleges, or trained by their graduates.

Two classes of colored Americans criticize Mr. Washington's position. One class hates the white South blindly. It thinks that the Negro's only hope lies in emigration beyond the borders of the United States. The other class of Negroes has hitherto said little aloud. Its members feel, in conscience, bound to ask three things of this nation: the right to vote, civic equality, and the education of youth according to ability.

W.E.B. Du Bois, **The Souls of Black Folk** (Chicago: A.C. McClurg & Company, 1904), pp. 50-58. Language simplified.

Civil rights means those freedoms and privileges given to all members of a community, state, or nation by law. They include freedom of press, religion and speech; equal protection of the laws; fair trial; and the right to own property and to vote. Since the Civil War; the term has referred especially to the extension of these rights to blacks.

▶Do you expect people in service jobs—sales people, waiters, gas station attendants, etc.—to act more deferentially toward you than people in other jobs? Why or why not?

In 1900, there were 99 black colleges in the United States and 2,624 blacks enrolled in schools of higher learning.

The pictures on these two pages show black Americans as farmers, cowboys, soldiers, and workers. Suppose that history books, films, television, and fiction had portrayed blacks mainly in these roles. What difference might this change have made in the ways that blacks think about themselves? What difference might it have made in the ways that whites think about blacks?

They acknowledge Mr. Washington's invaluable service in counseling patience and courtesy in such demands. They know that the low social level of the mass of the race is responsible for much discrimination against it. They also know, and the nation knows, that relentless color-prejudice is more often a cause than a result of the Negro's degradation.

This group of men honor Mr. Washington for his attitude of conciliation toward the white South. But they insist that the way to truth and right lies in straightforward honesty, not in flattery. They are absolutely certain that the way for a people to gain their reasonable rights is not by voluntarily throwing them away and insisting that they do not want them. The way for a people to gain respect is not by continually belittling and ridiculing themselves. On the contrary, Negroes must insist continually that voting is necessary to modern manhood, that color discrimination is barbarism, and that black boys need education as well as white boys.

▶Suppose that militant talk may offend many moderate people. Should leaders of a movement still state their stand in a militant way? Why or why not?

The growing spirit of kindliness and reconciliation between the North and South after the frightful differences of a generation ago ought to be a source of deep congratulation to all and especially to those whose mistreatment caused the War. But if that reconciliation is to be marked by the industrial slavery and civic death of those same black men, by permanently legislating them into a position of inferiority, then those black men are called upon to oppose such a course by all civilized methods, even though such opposition involves disagreement with Mr. Booker T. Washington. We have no right to sit silently by while the inevitable seeds are sown for a harvest of disaster to our children, black and white.

It is a great truth to say that the Negro must strive and strive mightily to help himself. It is equally true that unless his striving be aroused and encouraged by the initiative of the richer and wiser group, he cannot hope for great success.

In his failure to realize and impress this last point, Mr. Washington is especially to be criticized. His doctrine has tended to make the whites, North and South, shift the burden of the Negro problem to the Negro's shoulders and stand aside as critical and rather pessimistic spectators. In fact, the burden belongs to the nation. The hands of none of us are clean if we do not bend our energies to righting these great wrongs.

We cannot settle this problem by diplomacy and suaveness, by policy alone. If worse comes to worst, can the moral fiber of this country survive the slow throttling and murder of nine million men?

FOR THOUGHT:

Do the ideas of Washington and Du Bois reflect the conditions described by Blair and the members of the Alabama convention? If so, how?

59 "IN THE SAME DITCH"

HISTORICAL ESSAY

The readings in this chapter have concentrated heavily on the behavior of southern whites and the response of black leaders to that behavior. As you read Tom Heflin's speech to the Alabama convention, you may have wondered why blacks continued to stay in the South. Why didn't they leave the "house of bondage" to seek out freer areas of liberty in the North?

There is no simple answer to this question. In 1900, 90 percent of black Americans lived in the South. There had been some black migration to northern cities in the preceding decades. But most blacks migrated within their own region or into the border areas of Arkansas, Texas, and Oklahoma. The trickle northward grew into a small stream in the first decade of the twentieth century. But it did not become a substantial river of migrants until 1915. The beginning of World War I cut off migration to the United States from eastern and southern Europe. Blacks were recruited to fill the jobs which otherwise would have gone to newly arrived Poles, Italians, Slavs, or other immigrants. Blacks continued to move northward in the 1920's. But by 1930, they were still only 4 percent of the population of the Northeast. They were less than that in the Midwest. The exodus from the South had not even kept pace with the natural increase of the population. The total number of blacks in the South was greater in 1930 than it had been in 1900.

Why Blacks Stayed

Blacks stayed in the South for three reasons. First, they were not being pushed. Many European farmers who came to the United States in the nineteenth and twentieth centuries had been forced off the land by owners who wished to consolidate their holdings and reorganize production. Others were unable to purchase land as they married and tried to establish independent households. For many European immigrants, the trip to the United States was the second step in their movement from the farm. In the first step, they had moved into a European city to work for a while in a factory. This step reduced the felt distance from home to America.

In the South, on the other hand, land was relatively plentiful. And the technology of cotton production remained quite stable. New machines did not replace cheap field hands. Blacks were tied to this process of production by a complex pattern of obligations and debts. Three quarters of them were tenant farmers. More than a third sharecropped in the pattern discussed in Chapter 14. Many had promised crops years ahead in return for supplies from local merchants. Far from being pushed, blacks were often terrorized into staying. Sheriffs confiscated northern newspapers which promoted migration and hounded labor recruiters from small towns.

Second, the North offered few advantages for blacks for many years. Many northern localities had Jim Crow laws as severe as any in the South. Where the law did not impose segregation, local practices often did. There were black ghettoes, effectively separate school systems, and uncertain civil rights. A combination of employer and employee preferences kept blacks out of all but a few factories, warehouses, and docks. In the late nineteenth century, they were even forced out of haircutting and a few other favored service roles in which they had previously been dominant. The depth of northern racism became apparent as the number of blacks increased. A series of anti-black riots in smaller towns culminated in a week of shooting in Chicago in the summer of 1919.

Finally, life in the South was often rich and satisfying for black people. A large number of blacks adjusted well to life as free men and women. Many blacks established families and won places in the economy. Former field hands became sharecroppers or bought land of their own. By 1890, about 120,000 blacks were landowners. This was a remarkable achievement for a people who had been slaves twenty-five years before. To win a place in a market economy, they had had to learn how to buy and sell goods, make contracts, and work without supervision.

▶Which source of happiness plays a larger role in your life, day-to-day experiences or occasional public achievement? Why?

Life in the South was also satisfying because free blacks developed a rich community life built around churches and social clubs. In addition, despite racist ideas, blacks and whites often accommodated each other on terms close to equality. There were certainly more racially mixed work crews in southern cities, such as Atlanta or Birmingham, than there were in northern cities, such as Detroit or Pittsburgh. Heflin understood and feared these situations where whites and blacks worked as equals. His uppity, new-style black, you may remember, was a telegraph—or more probably, a telephone—lineman.

The Effects of Racism

What was the effect on both blacks and whites of life in a racist society? Significantly, it is easier to answer that question for whites than for blacks. For both groups, however, a great deal is still not known.

▶Do you think that a certain amount of conflict is good for a society? Why or why not?

The most obvious impact of racism on white southern society was the suppression of internal conflict. In the first half of the nineteenth century, there had been a vigorous two-party system in the South.

400

If you were black, how would you react if you came upon this scene?

The competition of Democrats and Whigs allowed rival groups to express their differences openly and to struggle for voter approval. The dispute over slavery killed the Whig organization. For a time during Reconstruction it appeared that a Republican party might develop in the South. Despite its genuine local roots, however, the party collapsed. Inevitably tainted by the charge of northern influence, it was left a mere shell of a few federal officeholders. After 1877, Republican national administrations even gave jobs and contracts to Democrats who supported them in Congress.

The absence of a Republican alternative forced all political controversy into the Democratic party. Issues were settled within party

401

meetings. While factions might compete for leadership within these meetings, issues tended to be resolved by private negotiation, rather than open discussion. This closed political system encouraged a narrow business domination of southern politics and the concept of development which Blair attacked.

During the 1890's, many southern farmers took what was to them an awesome step. They entered the new People's, or Populist party. This step broke the front of white solidarity and Democratic voting. The southern Populists achieved much greater success than their midwestern colleagues. Their strength was remarkable because their victories were achieved against tremendous obstacles. They were denied credit. If they succeeded in bringing voters to the polls, corrupt officials cheated them when the ballots were counted. Many Populists were thrown into jail on false charges. A few were even dragged from the jailor's hands by a mob and killed.

In response to this attack, the Populists sought an alliance with blacks. They were not willing to grant blacks full equality. "This is a white man's country and always will be controlled by the whites," a Virginia Populist wrote in an introduction to his essay urging increased rights for blacks. Nevertheless, the Populists did understand that black and white farmers had common interests and common problems. As one put it, "They are in the ditch just like we are." Tom Watson, the major Populist leader in Georgia, advised his fellows: "Let it once appear plainly that it is to the interest of a colored man to vote with the white man, and he will do it." He argued that "the accident of color can make no difference in the interest of farmers, croppers, and laborers." "You are kept apart," he lectured both races, "that you may be separately fleeced of your earnings."

The Populists proposed a comprehensive program for southern economic development. They recognized that new sources of credit, expanded educational opportunities, and tax reform were more important to them than inflation.

Southerners resisted the tendency in 1896 to focus the whole Populist program around the issue of money and to agree to a coalition with the Democrats. A national coalition of Populists and Democrats rankled them because they had invested so much effort in 1892 in their break with the local Democratic party. Nevertheless, the South voted strongly for William Jennings Bryan, the Democratic candidate, in 1896.

After the election of 1896 and Bryan's defeat, the Populist party was destroyed in the South. The few remaining southern Populists continued to insist that change would have to come about with a new comprehensive program for economic development. After the 1896 election, the Populists turned with vengeance on blacks. This happened because their attempt to unite white and black farmers had been used against them in local elections. Tom Watson reasoned that the only way to destroy racial equality as an issue in southern politics was to suppress blacks entirely. Men who in the early 1890's had reached out to blacks became the worst black-baiting politicians in the South. They hoped to prove their loyalty to the white race, remove the issue of black equality as a charge against them, and achieve political success. Therefore, their own political, economic, and social programs had to be implemented through the restrictive system of party management and private negotiation.

Beyond the suppression of conflict, it is likely that racism had a direct impact on the character of southern whites. The nature of these influences has been the subject of a great deal of analysis and speculation. Historians have described white southerners as uniquely aggressive and uniquely kind, as specially guilt-ridden and specially gallant. And they have linked all these traits to the structure of racial domination. You may want to judge these issues for yourself, either from personal knowledge or from the materials in this chapter. Knowing nothing other than what you have read here, how did Williams' or Helfin's racial ideas appear to affect their personal character?

Less is known about the impact of racism on blacks. There has been less research done on blacks than on whites. There have been relatively few black historians and social scientists who could bring a special sympathy to their subject. And the work of these few, until recently, was generally neglected by white scholars. Moreover, the position of blacks in American society, particularly before 1930, hardly encouraged open expression. Black novels frequently describe old men and women whose outward posture of submission would have delighted Heflin. Inwardly, however, and in the secret messages they conveyed to their children, their spirits were unbowed. Historical research has great difficulty in revealing such hidden feelings.

As with whites, the elements of open political behavior are easier to investigate. The black population of the South developed social classes and institutions which paralleled those of whites in many ways. At many points, however, respected black men and women such as teachers, ministers, and business people were dependent on the approval of whites. To violate this approval was to endanger their positions among whites. To seek it too eagerly was to threaten their respect in the black community. Caught in this dilemma, black leaders such as Booker T. Washington walked a tight line. They often managed to become the instrument of white racism. The willingness of blacks to control each other contributed to the stability and peace of southern society. There was no open race war. But the costs of this peace, as Du Bois noted, were borne mainly by blacks.

There are very few reliable guides to the influence of white racism on blacks. Until recently, little attempt was made to study the history of blacks. Their past was often dismissed as primitive or irrelevant.

▶ Do you act differently toward people in positions of power than you do toward people without power? Why or why not?

And their culture was seen as a variant or derivative of white southern culture. Characteristic patterns of black speech, for example, were long regarded as variations of white southern speech patterns. Recent studies have shown, however, that these patterns have African origins. Under these circumstances, it is impossible to understand adequately the impact on blacks of their interaction with the rest of American society.

The South as a Colonial Area

After the Civil War, southern political leaders hoped to copy the economic success of the North. They invited northern business people to invest money in industry and transportation in the South. The southern economy did make significant advances during the three decades after the Civil War. Railway mileage and the production of pig iron, for example, increased more rapidly in the South than in the North. The South developed new ways to manufacture tobacco which helped that industry to grow. Large numbers of cotton mills moved to the South where they could be close to their supplies of raw materials. Despite these advances, however, the South remained essentially an area that produced raw materials. Most final processing of such raw materials as cotton, sugar, forest products, and rice still took place in the North. The South remained essentially an outpost of the northern economy.

Throughout this period, southerners were poorer and less urbanized than northerners. In 1860, the income of the average southerner was roughly 72 percent of the national average. In 1880 and again in 1900, it was 51 percent. It rose to 62 percent by 1920 but fell again to 55 percent a decade later. In 1900, less than 10 percent of the people in the Atlantic states south of Maryland were classified as urban. In contrast, almost 60 percent of the people in the Atlantic states north of Pennsylvania lived in towns and cities.

The South also lost political power during this period. During the seventy-two years between Washington and Lincoln, southerners had sat in the White House for all but twenty-two of those years. In sixty of those years, the Chief Justice had been from the South. The South had also furnished about half of the Supreme Court justices and many diplomats and cabinet members. During the next half century, Andrew Johnson was the only southern President or Vice-President. In these fifty years, southerners made up only about 10 percent of the Supreme Court justices, diplomats, and cabinet members. The South did a little better after 1900. But well into the twentieth century, the South remained a satellite of both northern industry and northern politics.

404

The New Immigrants

STATING THE ISSUE

Between 1815 and 1920, roughly 35 million men, women, and children migrated from Europe, Asia, Canada, and Mexico into the United States. This enormous movement of people was part of an international process of development. It went beyond the history of any single nation. It was the human counterpart of the movement of capital and goods across oceans and continents.

Many of these migrants ultimately returned to their places of origin. In 1908, for example, nearly 750,000 people left the United States. For them, their stay in the United States was an episode in a family history. Its long-term effects were felt mainly in their native lands.

Most of the migrants stayed, however. There are two ways of looking at their history. In most textbooks, the process of migration is woven into the history of the nation. Immigrants had problems or made contributions to the nation. However, immigrant groups themselves often developed a different view of their histories. For them, the subject was not the nation, but the people. Some Italians lived in Naples. Some lived in New York. Some Chinese lived in Shanghai. Some lived in San Francisco. Some Poles lived in Warsaw. Some lived in Chicago. But the subject of the history was always the continuous people—Italians, Chinese, Poles, and others.

This chapter examines the experiences of those immigrants who came to the United States between 1880 and 1920. The documents ask you to switch back and forth between two perspectives—the national perspective and the perspective of the migrant people. In Chapter 1, you discussed the interaction between groups as processes of extermination, accommodation, assimilation, or amalgamation. Try looking at these processes first from one perspective and then from the other. Does the value you attach to each process vary from one perspective to another?

1882 Congress passes Chinese Exclusion Act

1885 Organized labor presses for restriction of immigration of foreign workers

1889 Jane Addams founds Hull House

1890 Jacob Riis publishes **How the Other Half Lives**

1897 Jane Addams addresses National Education Association

1904 Theodore Roosevelt is elected President

1907 Gentleman's Agreement limits number of Japanese entering United States

1910 Emily Balch publishes **Our Slavic Fellow Citizens**

1912 Woodrow Wilson is elected President

1917 United States enters World War I

1917 Congress imposes literacy test as basis for entry into United States

1921 First quota law restricting immigration goes into effect

1924 National Origins Act imposes a more restrictive quota

1965 Immigration Act eliminates national origins system

60 THE IMMIGRANT DILEMMA

Almost every immigrant group has gone through a process of asserting its true Americanism. In doing this, most have discovered a record of colonial settlers or revolutionary heroes. However, the first discovery made by the wave of nineteenth-century immigrants was very different. Opportunity and offers of jobs had encouraged many to emigrate. They were able to find work quickly at construction sites, on docks and farms, and in factories or mills. Nevertheless, most soon discovered that moving and becoming accepted in a new land could be very painful. The pain was greatest for those who seemed most different from native Americans. These included Orientals, and Europeans of the Catholic, Jewish, Greek Orthodox and Russian Orthodox faiths. Native Americans had difficulty understanding these people. And many had little sympathy for them. As a result, they tended to think of them in stereotyped and threatening terms. One nationality group had a hot temper, another was dull, another crafty, and so on.

Those Americans who reached out to the immigrants found that such stereotypes did not fit the people they came to know. They did not find a group of ignorant people bent on undermining American society. Instead, they discovered people wrestling with a series of deep dilemmas. What was America? Should they grasp it? Would they be allowed to grasp it? To how much of the old should they hold?

Reading 60 is drawn from the work of Emily Green Balch, one of the most expert and sympathetic American observers of immigrants. As you read, keep the following questions in mind:

1. How did the immigrants described by Emily Balch respond to America?
2. How did their children influence their responses?

What Are Americans?

Emily Balch taught economics at Wellesley College in Massachusetts at the time she wrote Our Slavic Fellow Citizens. *To collect data for her book, she traveled extensively in Austria-Hungary, the area of Europe from which most Slavs emigrated. In this excerpt she describes the immigrants' experiences in America.*

"My people do not live in America. They live underneath America. America goes over their heads. America does not begin till a man is a workingman, till he is earning two dollars a day. A laborer cannot afford to be an American."

Emily Balch, **Our Slavic Fellow Citizens** (New York: Charities Publication Committee, 1910), pp. 419, 424, 45, 58-60, 378-379, 381, 383-385, 412-415, 398-399. Language simplified.

These words were said to me by one of the wisest Slav leaders that I have ever met. They have rung in my mind during all the five years since he spoke them. Beginning at the bottom, "living not in America but underneath America," means living among the worst surroundings that the country has to show. They are often worse than the public would tolerate, except that "only foreigners" are affected.

Coming to America they are cut off from the life of their old country. But they cannot get into contact with the true life of their new home. They are shut off by language, by mutual prejudice, and by different ideas. To them, both parents are dead, the fatherland that begot them and the foster-mother that supports without cherishing them.

"Does the individual emigrant gain?" In the first place, emigration always involves pain. It involves pain to those who go, and, above all, pain to those who are left behind. Immigrants are inevitably to some extent exiles. They are separated from the old familiar scenes for which everyone sometimes yearns. And they are divided, even if the more immediate family has all been brought together, from some of those near and dear to them.

A person must experience what it means to be in a country where one cannot speak the language in order to understand it. People must even change their ways of expression. It seems as useless to gesture or smile as to speak. It is almost as if one could not even think, so pervasive and numbing is the sense that the channels of communication are blocked.

I get the impression that the women are more apt to be homesick than the men. As a matter of fact, I think that the women both lose more and gain less by the change than the men. They do not like the iron stoves, which do not bake such sweet bread as their old ovens. They miss, I think, the variety of work, employment within doors alternating with field work. Most of all they miss the familiar, sociable village life where everyone knows everyone else. And there are no superior Yankees to embarrass one. There the children do not grow up to be alien and contemptuous.

▶ If you were suddenly taken to a strange land where no natives knew your customs or spoke your language, how much would you miss life in the place you had left?

The men live more out in the world. They get more from America and perhaps had less to lose in the old conditions. Immigrants are often treated undemocratically in America. And this treatment sometimes makes one's blood boil. But they do get in America a sense of being regarded as equals that is new and dear to them. To the men it often means expansion.

One of the most surprising facts in the life of Slavs in America is the degree to which they are organized into societies. Many of their associations are small local groups of the most various sorts. In a New York Bohemian paper I found a list of 95 local societies among this group of perhaps 35,000 people.

Each of the main Slavic nationalities in the United States has one or more national societies. All are apparently organized on much the same plan. They have a central coordinating committee and numerous branches. The branches are founded primarily to provide mutual insurance, but they also serve many other purposes. The membership of these societies includes people of the same national or national-religious groups.

In addition to church-related societies, immigrants organized a wide variety of associations. These included loan societies, cooperative stores, patriotic organizations associated with political activities in their native countries, educational and cultural societies, and insurance organizations.

These scattered groups of poor and ignorant immigrants are totally unused to organization. And they are foreign to all ideas of parliamentary procedure. These societies must draw a large part of their membership from such people. Yet it is remarkable how rapidly they have grown and how highly developed and successful they are.

When people are scattered in a strange country, the "consciousness of kind" with fellow countrymen has a very special significance. To many an immigrant the idea of nationality first becomes real after he has left his native country. At home the contrast was between peasants as a class and landlords as a class. In America he finds a vast world of people. All speak strange tongues. For the first time he has a vivid sense of oneness with those who speak his own language, whether here or at home.

But it is not only common speech and ways, and in some cases common political aims that draw the different groups of immigrants together. The sense of economic weakness also draws them. The dangerous character of the work in the mines and foundries which employ so many Slavs helps them to appreciate the advantages of mutual aid.

A foundry is a plant where molten metal is cast or shaped in molds.

408

Closely connected with the societies are the newspapers. They also have attained a surprising development here. Among the Slovaks, and perhaps among some other nationalities, the circulation of papers in their own language is greater in America than it is at home.

The recent Slavic immigrants, Poles and others, have formed considerable colonies. Their hearts are set, with a strength of desire which we can hardly conceive, on having their children speak their own language as their proper tongue. I have heard of graduates of Polish schools in Chicago and Baltimore who do not understand English. I have seen a Polish "sister's" school where the children were singing Polish songs:

> "We are little exiles;
> Far from our dear home
> We weep night and day,"

or something like that, the little round-cheeked boys just in from play on a Chicago sidewalk were chanting.

A thousand more items to show the separateness of the foreign life in our midst might be piled together. In the end they would all be as nothing against the irresistible influence through which it comes about that the immigrants find themselves the parents of American children. They are surprised. They are proud. They are scandalized. They are stricken to the heart with regret. Whatever their emotions, they are powerless.

The prestige of America and the hatred of children for being different from their playmates is something the parents cannot stand against.

When they learn English, the children are apt to lose their parents' language. Against this the parents strive. It is very common, for instance, for the parents to try to have the children speak only the old language until they go to school. They foresee that after the children have entered school, they will speak English not only outside of the home but within it, too. They see that it will be impossible to keep English from becoming the family language. From then on, the parents must talk with their own children in a foreign tongue in which they are consciously at a disadvantage.

One of the great evils among the children of foreigners is the disastrous gulf between the older and the younger generation. Discipline, in this new freedom which both parents and children misunderstand, is almost impossible. The children have to act as interpreters for their parents and do business for them. So they are thrown into a position of unnatural importance. They feel only contempt for old-world ways, a feeling encouraged by the common American attitude. One hears stories of Italian children refusing to reply to their mother if spoken to in Italian.

► How would you feel about your parents if you knew more about living in your society than they did? Why might you feel that way?

409

The pictures on these two pages show a Slavic village in Europe and a Slavic settlement in the United States. How do you think it would feel to move from one to the other? Why would it feel that way?

The United States

The United States

Europe

One comes sometimes with a sense of shock to a realization of points of view strange to one's own. Take, for instance, a conversation that I once had with a Polish-American priest. I had said something about "Americans," that they were not apt to be interested in Polish history, or something of the sort. Instantly he was on fire.

"You mean English-Americans," he said. "You English constantly speak as if you were the only Americans, or more American than others." I remarked that if I went to Poland he would not consider me a Pole.

"No, that is different," was his reply. "America was empty, open to all comers alike. There is no reason for the English to seize the name of American. They should be called Yankees if anything. That is the name of English-Americans. There is no such thing as an American nation. Poles form a nation. But the United States is a country, under one government. It is inhabited by representatives of different nations. For myself, I do favor one language for the United States, either English or some other, to be used by everyone. But there is no reason why people should not also have another language. That is an advantage. For it opens more avenues to Europe and elsewhere."

The writer is dealing with two different meanings of "nation." According to one meaning, a nation is a group of people with a common language and tradition, not necessarily organized in a political state. The second concept of nation is of a politically united group under one government, which may contain several nations of the first type.

FOR THOUGHT:

Which one or more of the following terms—amalgamation, accommodation, or assimilation—would you use to summarize the experience of the immigrants described by Emily Balch? Why?

61 TRAINING IMMIGRANT CHILDREN

As immigrants wrestled with their dilemmas, they often changed in unexpected ways. In order to preserve their old way of life, they had to define it. And to do this the immigrants had to develop a new self-consciousness about their traditions. Organizing for self-protection also brought changes. Men and women who had barely thought beyond their own villages, suddenly began to think of themselves as Poles, Russians, or Italians. In the old country, the immigrants had been accustomed to small organizations in their local communities. In America, they learned to manage complex mutual aid organizations with large amounts of money, complicated finances, officers, and elections.

As Emily Balch emphasized, children were the most important agents of change. They stood between two worlds—the old world of their parents and the new world of their adopted home. The public schools tried, sometimes gently, sometimes forcibly, to bring immigrant children into what they defined as the American way of life. They trained them in English, citizenship, and "Americanism."

However, some Americans were not satisfied with the performance of the schools. Jane Addams was one of these. At the turn of the century, she was the most respected social worker in the United States. She was also an active participant in almost every major movement to benefit the disadvantaged and to promote international peace. She hoped that the public schools would promote both personal and community development. But she was disappointed with what she actually saw in them. Reading 61 presents Jane Addams' criticism of the public schools and her suggestions for their reform. As you read, consider the following questions:

1. What were the bases of Jane Addams' criticism of the schools she had visited?
2. What were Jane Addams' ideas for the reform of the schools?

American Schools and the Immigrant Child

In 1897 Jane Addams spoke to the National Education Association. She described the impact of the schools upon the immigrant children she knew in Chicago.

I have had unusual opportunities for seeing the children of immigrants during and after the period of their short school life. These observations are confined to the children of the Italian colony in the nineteenth ward of Chicago. What is said concerning them might be applied, however, to the children of Chicago's large Bohemian and Polish colonies.

The members of the nineteenth ward Italian colony have come to America with a distinct aim of earning money. They also seek more room for the energies of themselves and their children. In almost all cases they mean to go back again. Their imaginations cannot picture a continuous life away from the old surroundings. Their experiences in Italy have been that of simple, out-door activity.

And the ideas they have have come directly to them from their struggle with nature. Such a hand-to-hand struggle takes place when each man gets his living largely through his own cultivation of the soil, with tools simply fashioned by his own hands. The women, as in all primitive life, have had more diversified activities than the men. They have cooked, spun, and knitted, in addition to their almost equal work in the fields.

National Education Association, **Journal of Proceedings and Addresses of the Thirty-Sixth Annual Meeting Held at Milwaukee, Wisconsin, July 6-7, 1897** (Chicago: University of Chicago Press, 1897), pp. 104-112 passim. Language simplified.

413

The effect of immigration upon the women is that of idleness. All of those outdoor and domestic activities, which she would naturally have handed on to her daughters, have slipped away from her. The domestic arts are gone, with all their absorbing interests for the children, their educational value, and incentive to activity.

The child of these families has little or no opportunity to use his energies in domestic work, or, indeed, constructively, in any direction. No activity is supplied to take the place of that which, in Italy, he would naturally have found in his own home. No new contact with wholesome life is made for him.

Italian parents count upon the fact that their children learn the English language and American customs before they themselves do. The children act as interpreters of the language about them. And they also act as buffers between them and Chicago. This results in a certain, almost pathetic dependence of the family upon the child. When a member of the family, therefore, first goes to school, the event is filled with much significance to all the others.

Let us take one of these boys. Whatever interest has come to the minds of his ancestors has come through the use of their hands in the open air. Yet the first thing that the boy must do when he reaches school is to sit still, at least part of the time. And he must learn to listen to what is said to him, with all the perplexity of listening to a foreign tongue. The child is perfectly indifferent to showing off and making a good recitation.

▶What personal qualities do you think should be encouraged in students?

Too often the teacher's notion of her duty is to transform the child into a somewhat smug and comfortable type of American. She insists that the boy's powers must at once be developed in an abstract direction. And she ignores the fact that his parents have had to do only with tangible things. She has little idea of the development of Italian life. She fails, therefore, not only in knowledge of, but also in respect for, the child and his parents. She quite honestly judges the child by an American standard. The contempt for the experiences and languages of their parents which foreign children sometimes show is most damaging to their moral as well as intellectual life. It is doubtless due in part to the overemphasis which the school places upon speaking and reading in English. This cutting into his family loyalty takes away one of the most valuable traits of the Italian child.

In education it is necessary to begin with the experiences which the child already has through his spontaneous and social activity. The city street begins this education for him in a more natural way than does the school.

Some states had passed laws regulating child labor. In 1916, Congress passed the Keating-Owen Act. It forbade interstate shipping of products from factories employing children under 14 or from mines employing children under 16. The Supreme Court declared the law unconstitutional.

Let us leave the child who does not stay in school. And let us now consider the child who does faithfully remain until he reaches the age of factory work. In the most advanced of our factory states this means fourteen years. Has anything been done up to this time to make him conscious of his social value? Has the outcome of the

414

processes to which he has been subjected adapted him to deal more effectively with his present life? Has the public school given this child a knowledge of the social meaning of his work?

He finds himself in the drudgery of a factory. He is using his hands for unknown ends, and his head not at all. During his years in school he has used his head mostly, and his hands very little. Hence, nothing bewilders him so much as the suggestion that the school was intended as a preparation for his work in life.

Foreign-born children have all the drudgery of learning to listen to, and read and write an alien tongue. Many never get beyond this first drudgery. I have questioned dozens of these children who have left school from the third, fourth, and fifth grades. And I have met very few who ever read for pleasure.

From one point of view the school itself summarizes the competitive system of the factory. Certain standards are held up and worked for. Even in the school, the child does little work with real joy and spontaneity. The pleasure which comes from creative effort, the thrill of production, is only occasional. It is not the sustaining motive which keeps it going. The child in school often acquires the habit of expecting to do his work in certain hours, and to take his pleasure in certain other hours. Later, in the same spirit, he earns his money by ten hours of dull factory work. And he spends it in three hours of lurid and unprofitable pleasure in the evening. Both in the school and the factory, his work has been dull and growing duller. And his pleasure must constantly grow more stimulating. Only occasionally has he had the real joy of doing a thing for its own sake.

Some of us are looking forward to a time when work shall not be senseless drudgery, but shall contain some self-expression of the worker. But we sometimes feel the hopelessness of adding evening classes and social entertainments as a mere frill to a day filled with drudgery. We sometimes feel that we have a right to expect more help from the public schools than they now give us.

We have a curious notion. Our notion is that it is not possible for the mass of mankind to have interests and experiences of themselves which are worth anything. We transmit to the children of working people our own view that they will not find joy or profit in their work. We practically encourage them to get out of it as soon as possible.

I am quite sure that no one can possibly mistake this paper as a plea for the trade schools, or as a desire to fit the boy for any given industry. Such a specializing would indeed be stupid when our industrial methods are developing and changing, almost day by day. But it does contend that life as seen from the standpoint of the handworker, should not be emptied of all social consciousness and value. The school could make the boy infinitely more flexible and alive than he is now to the materials and forces of nature which, in spite of all man's activities, are unchangeable.

Addams is referring to the effects of the division of labor. Workers found that they were making one part repeatedly, rather than an entire finished product in which they could take pride.

▶ Is it unrealistic for people to expect the work they do for a living to be enjoyable and interesting?

Evening classes in subjects such as English, history, and government helped immigrants to adjust to American life. They also helped them to prepare for their naturalization tests. In order to become citizens, immigrants had to read and write English and to demonstrate a knowledge of American history and government.

Trade schools train students for a skilled trade, such as carpentry or mechanics.

School is now isolated from life. It fails to make life of more interest, and show it in its larger aspects. And this certainly tends to defeat the very purpose of education.

FOR THOUGHT:

How do you think the situation described by Jane Addams might have affected the interaction of immigrant and native Americans?

62 THE WORTH OF AMERICA

The immigrants confronted many difficult personal dilemmas. And they responded to them in a variety of ways. No group was able to impose a single pattern of adaptation on its members. As a result, there is no way of describing a single and unified Jewish, Polish, Italian, or Chinese answer to the challenge of immigration.

The two selections in this reading describe responses to the dilemmas faced by immigrants. These responses are widely separated in time. They are also very different, on the surface, in their evaluation of the worth of America and the costs of being an American. However, you may find that the insights offered by both responses complement one another.

The first selection is from the autobiography of Mary Antin, published in 1912. Mary Antin's father emigrated to America from their native village of Polotzk in Poland. He established himself in Boston and then sent for his wife and children after a wait of three years. The second selection is by Michael Novak, the grandchild of Polish Catholic immigrants. It was written in the 1970's. As you read, think about these questions:

1. What do Antin and Novak tell you about their parents' goals and methods?
2. Do Antin and Novak completely disagree in their evaluation of America and the immigrant experience?

The Promised Land

Apart from any other qualities, Mary Antin's autobiography is remarkable because it was written before she was thirty.

Mary Antin, **The Promised Land** (Boston: Houghton Mifflin Company, 1912), pp. 244-249. Language simplified.

My father, in his ambition to make Americans of us, was rather headlong and strenuous in his methods. To my mother, on the eve of departure for the New World, he wrote boldly that progressive Jews in America did not spend their days in praying. And he urged her to leave her wig in Polotzk, as a first step of progress. My mother,

416

like the majority of the women in the Pale, had all her life taken her religion on authority. So she was only fulfilling her duty to her husband when she took his hint and set out upon her journey in her own hair. Not that it was done without reluctance. The Jewish faith in her was deeply rooted, as in the best of Jews it always is. The law of the Fathers was binding to her. And the outward symbols of obedience were inseparable from the spirit. But the breath of revolt against orthodox externals was at this time beginning to reach us in Polotzk from the greater world, notably from America . . . Even within our town limits young women of education were beginning to reject the wig after marriage. A notorious example was the beautiful daughter of Lozhe the Rav. She was not restrained by her father's position in Judaism from exhibiting her lovely black curls like a maiden. And it was a further sign of the times that the Rav did not disown his daughter. What wonder, then, that my poor mother, shaken by these foreshadowings of revolution in our midst, and by the express authority of her husband, gave up the emblem of matrimonial chastity with but a passing struggle? The heavy burdens which she had borne from childhood had never allowed her time to think for herself at all.

They had obliged her always to tread blindly in the beaten paths. So I think it greatly to her credit that in her puzzling situation she did not lose her poise entirely. Bred to submission, submit she must. And when she saw a conflict of authorities, she prepared to accept the new order of things under which her children's future was to be formed.

My father gave my mother very little time to adjust herself. He was only three years away from the Old World with its settled prejudices. Considering his education, he had thought out a good deal for himself. But his line of thinking had not as yet brought him to include woman in the intellectual emancipation for which he himself had been so eager even in Russia. He held it to be a wife's duty to follow her husband in all things. He could do all the thinking for the family, he believed. And he was convinced that to hold to the outward forms of orthodox Judaism was to be hampered in the race for Americanization. So, he did not hesitate to order our family life on unorthodox lines. There was no conscious tyranny in this. It was only making haste to realize an ideal the nobility of which there was no one to dispute.

My mother, therefore, gradually divested herself, at my father's bidding, of the mantle of orthodox observance. But the process cost her many a pang. The fabric of that venerable garment was interwoven with the fabric of her soul.

My father did not attempt to touch the fundamentals of her faith. He allowed her to keep a Jewish kitchen as long as she pleased. But he did not want us children to refuse invitations to the table of our Gentile neighbors. He would have no bar to our social intercourse

The Pale was a section of Russian-ruled Poland to which Jews were confined by order of the Russian government.

In traditional Jewish communities, married women covered their hair with a wig as an act of modesty. Men, following rabbinic interpretation of a biblical statement, did not cut their forelocks with a razor.

▶ Suppose you were married and both you and your mate were looking for work. If you were each offered jobs in different towns, how would you decide which to take? Why?

Jewish dietary laws forbid the consumption of certain foods and the mixing of milk and meat dishes. Even approved foods may not be eaten if they have been prepared or served in utensils which have been used in prohibited ways. Jews who observe these rules find it difficult to eat freely at the homes of even close Gentile friends.

with the world around us. For only by freely sharing the life of our neighbors could we come into our full inheritance of American freedom and opportunity. On the holy days he bought my mother a ticket for the synagogue. But the children he sent to school. On Sabbath eve my mother might light the consecrated candles. But he kept the store open until Sunday morning. My mother might believe and worship as she pleased, up to the point where her orthodoxy began to interfere with the American progress of the family.

The price that all of us paid for this disorganization of our family life has been levied on every immigrant Jewish household where the first generation clings to the traditions of the Old World, while the second generation leads the life of the New.

That part of my life which contains the climax of my personal drama I must leave to my grandchildren to record. My father might speak and tell how, in time, he discovered that in his first violent rejection of everything old and established he cast from him much that he afterwards missed. He might tell to what extent he later retraced his steps, seeking to recover what he had learned to value anew. He might tell how it fared with his avowed irreligion when put to the extreme test. He might say to what, in short, his emancipation amounted. And he, like myself, would speak for thousands. My grandchildren, for all I know, may have a graver task than I have set them. Perhaps they may have to testify that the faith of Israel is a heritage that no heir in the direct line has the power to take away from his successors. Even I, with my limited perspective, think it doubtful if the conversion of the Jew to any alien belief or disbelief is ever thoroughly accomplished. What positive affirmation of the persistence of Judaism in the blood my descendants may have to make, I may not be present to hear.

It would be superfluous to state that none of these hints and prophecies troubled me at the time. I considered myself absolutely, eternally, delightfully emancipated from the yoke of indefensible superstitions.

Unmeltable Ethnics

Michael Novak's The Rise of the Unmeltable Ethnics *expresses many of the values that emerged from a recent movement to reassert pride in one's ethnic background. This movement rejected the idea that group differences should or could be lost in a single American cultural melting pot.*

All four of my grandparents, unknown to one another, arrived in America from the same country in Slovakia. My grandfather had a small farm in Pennsylvania. His wife died in a wagon accident.

Michael Novak, **The Rise of the Unmeltable Ethnics: Politics and Culture in the Seventies** (New York: Macmillan Publishing Company, Inc., 1973), pp. 64-66, xxxiii-xxxv. Copyright © 1971, 1972, 1973 by Michael Novak. Used by permission.

418

Meanwhile, Johanna, fifteen, arrived on Ellis Island, dizzy from witnessing births and deaths and illness aboard the crowded ship. She had a sign around her neck lettered Passaic. There an aunt told her of a man who had lost his wife in Pennsylvania. She went. They were married. She inherited his three children.

Ellis Island was the immigrant reception center in the port of New York.

Each year for five years Grandma had a child of her own. She was among the lucky. Only one died. When she was twenty-two and the mother of seven . . . her husband died. "Grandma Novak," as I came to know her many years later, resumed the work she had begun in Slovakia at the town home of a man known to my father only as "the Professor." She housecleaned and she laundered.

I heard this story only weeks ago. Strange that I had not asked insistently before. Odd that I should have such shallow knowledge of my roots. Amazing to me that I do not know what my family suffered, endured, learned, and hoped these last six or seven generations. It is as if there were no project in which we all have been involved, as if history in some way began with my father and with me.

▶How much have you questioned your parents and grandparents about their youth? Should you have inquired more?

The estrangement I have come to feel derives not only from lack of family history. Early in life, I was made to feel a slight uneasiness when I said my name.

. . . . When I was very young, the "American" kids still made something out of names unlike their own. And their earnest, ambitious mothers thought long thoughts when I introduced myself.

Under challenge in grammar school concerning my nationality, I had been instructed by my father to announce proudly: "American." When my family moved from the Slovak ghetto to Johnstown to the WASP suburb on the hill, my mother impressed upon us how well we must be dressed, and show good manners, and behave. People think of us as "different" and we mustn't give them any cause. "Whatever you do, marry a Slovak girl," was other advice to a similar end: "They cook. They clean. They take good care of you. For your own good." I was taught to be proud of being Slovak, but to recognize that others wouldn't know what it meant, or care. . . .

The acronym WASP is used to refer to white Anglo-Saxon Protestant Americans whose ancestors emigrated from western Europe.

Nowhere in my schooling do I recall any attempt to put me in touch with my own history. The strategy was clearly to make an American of me. English literature, American literature, and even the history books, as I recall them, were peopled mainly by Anglo-Saxons from Boston (where most historians seemed to live). Not even my native Pennsylvania, let alone my Slovak forebears counted for very many paragraphs. . . . I don't remember feeling envy or regret: a feeling, perhaps, of unimportance, of remoteness, of not having heft enough to count.

The fact that I was born a Catholic also complicated life. What is a Catholic but what everybody else is in reaction against?. . . .

It is hard to grow up Catholic in America without becoming defensive, perhaps a little paranoid, feeling forced to divide the world between "us" and "them."

The Price
Of Being Americanized

My grandparents, I am sure, never guessed what it would cost them and their children to become "Americanized."

In their eyes, no doubt, almost everything was gain. From the oppression experienced by Slovaks at the hands of the Austro-Hungarian empire, the gain was liberty; from relative poverty, opportunity; from an old world, new hope. . . .

They were injured, to be sure, by nativist American prejudices against foreigners, by a white Anglo-Saxon Protestant culture, and even by an Irish church. . . .

What price is exacted by America when . . . it sucks [in] other cultures of the world and processes them? What do people have to lose before they can qualify as true Americans?

For one thing, a lot of blue stars—and silver and gold ones—must hang in the window. You proved you loved America by dying for it in its wars. . . .

One is also expected to give up one's native language. My parents decided never to teach us Slovak. They hoped that thereby we would gain a generation in the process of becoming full Americans.

They kept up a few traditions: Christmas Eve holy bread, candlelight, mushroom soup, fish, and poppyseed. My mother baked kolacky. Pirohi, however, more or less died with my grandmother, who used to work all day making huge, steaming pots of potato dumplings and prune dumplings for her grandchildren. No other foods shall ever taste so sweet. . . .

What has happened to my people since they came to this land nearly a century ago? Where are they now, that long-awaited fully Americanized third generation? Are we living the dream our grandparents dreamed when on creaking decks they stood silent, afraid, hopeful at the sight of the Statue of Liberty? Will we ever find that secret relief, that door, that hidden entrance? Did our grandparents choose for us, and our posterity, what they should have chosen?

Now the dice lie cold in our own uncertain hands.

FOR THOUGHT:

How do Antin and Novak modify Emily Balch's description of the process of Americanization?

63 IMMIGRATION AND AMERICAN LIFE

HISTORICAL ESSAY

Ethnic background remains one of the most powerful factors in American life. It continues to influence the daily lives of many Americans—whom they marry, vote for, invite to dinner, or worship with. The day when all Americans will amalgamate into one indistinguishable people has not yet come to pass. In the last half of the twentieth century, most Americans still identify themselves by their ethnic origins. And many first and second generation Americans continue to retire to the cities, towns, and villages of their ancestors. The reasons why ethnic background continues to have such a strong hold on American life can be found in the history of the immigrants who have flocked to the United States from every nation.

American Population Growth

Before the Civil War, the population of the United States grew rapidly. Each year 103 Americans lived where only 100 had been twelve months before. Every twenty-five years the population doubled. This high growth rate is understandable. Since food was plentiful, Americans survived childhood better and lived a little longer than most people in other parts of the world. Also, during that period, the United States was primarily an agricultural nation. Large families helped farmers wrestle with a shortage of labor. So, the birth rate remained high.

After 1850, however, the birth rate began to fall. By that time, the United States was well on its way to becoming an industrialized, urbanized country. Larger families became a burden rather than a help, particularly in cities. Farm children were easy to house. And they did a lot of work around the farm. But in the city, children crowded small apartments. Moreover, they strained their parents' slender income. They were seldom able to find useful work. And preparing them for life in an urban industrial society required years of expensive education. So, many parents decided to limit their families. The decline in the birth rate may also have been one result of the movement to improve the status of American women, begun in the mid-nineteenth century. A great deal of research suggests that the size of families generally falls when women have more control of their own lives.

The decline in the birth rate contributed to a slow but dramatic change in the age level of the American people. In 1800, the median age of Americans was about sixteen years. It rose steadily for the

A median is a number exactly in the middle. In this case, it means that there were just as many people under the age of 16 as there were people over the age of 16 in the United States in 1800.

421

next century and a half. By 1950, the median age had passed thirty, almost double the 1800 figure. During most of the nineteenth and twentieth centuries, this rise in the median age resulted in a decrease in the "dependency ratio" in the population. In other words, more Americans than ever before were old enough to work. Fewer and fewer had to depend on parents or other adults for support. A greater supply of workers improved the productivity of the whole population. It decreased the labor shortage, too. But it did not do this fast enough to make up for the decline in the birth rate and the increased demand for workers in industry. As a result, the nation depended more and more on immigration to fill in the gap.

Who came and from where depended upon several factors. A major change in the social and economic structure of Europe played the most important role. European agriculture and industry were being transformed. Farms were subdivided among several sons. And they eventually became too small to support a family. Furthermore, European farmers were being forced to compete with American grain and livestock. Millions could not do this. So, many farm families moved to nearby cities. Or, they risked a new life abroad. At the same time, village artisans were being forced to compete with machine-made products. They, too, eventually gave up the struggle and left their homes. They sought better opportunities either in European factories or in the industries of the New World. People were also encouraged to emigrate by relatives and friends who had already braved the Atlantic crossing and established themselves in the United States. In addition, improvements in land and ocean transportation reduced the time and hardships of the long voyage. Occasionally, immigration was triggered by such factors as religious persecution or the desire to escape military service.

Finally, conditions within the United States helped stimulate immigration. During the mid-nineteenth century, the construction of railroads from northeastern cities to the Middle West opened large areas of the nation to development. Many companies had received land grants to stimulate expansion into unsettled areas. And, consequently, they set up immigration agencies to advertise the potential of these lands. Often, companies discounted all or part of the expense of transportation from the cost of land purchased by the immigrants. And through tickets and group rates were provided from remote parts of Europe to newly settled sections of the country. Several of the states also set up agencies to promote rapid settlement. Certainly, the information available in Europe about opportunities in the New World encouraged many immigrants to move directly from their original homes to newly opened regions of the United States.

Through the 1860's, these factors attracted immigrants mostly from England, Germany, Ireland, and Scandinavia. Between 1850 and 1859, around 2,750,000 immigrants arrived in the United States. Immigration slowed down during the Civil War. But the pace increased rapidly in the late 1860's. It reached a new peak in 1873 when more than 400,000 people arrived in one year. The pace slackened again in the mid-1870's when the United States suffered economic problems. However, immigration reached an unprecedented volume in the 1880's as more than 5.3 million newcomers entered the United States, primarily from southern and eastern Europe. The 1900 census revealed that a third of the nation was either foreign born or the children of the foreign born. The largest wave of immigration came between 1901 and 1924. In 1907, the peak year of this wave, 1.3 million immigrants entered the country. Figures 62A and 62B present the story of immigration statistically from 1861 to 1930.

FIGURE 62A   THE SOURCE OF EUROPEAN IMMIGRATION, 1861-1930

U.S. Bureau of the Census, Historical Statistics of the United States, Colonial Times to 1957 (Washington, D.C.: Government Printing Office, 1960), pp. 56-58.

Period	Total Immigrants Admitted	Northern and Western Europe		Southern and Eastern Europe	
1861-70	2,314,824	2,031,624	87.8%	33,628	1.4%
1871-80	2,812,191	2,070,373	73.6	201,889	7.2
1881-90	5,246,613	3,778,633	72.0	958,413	18.3
1891-1900	3,687,564	1,643,492	44.6	1,915,486	51.9
1901-10	8,795,386	1,910,035	21.7	6,225,981	70.8
1911-20	5,735,811	997,438	17.4	3,379,126	58.9
1921-30	4,107,209	1,284,023	31.3	1,193,830	29.0

U.S. Bureau of the Census, Historical Statistics, pp. 58-59.

FIGURE 62B   IMMIGRANTS FROM CHINA, JAPAN, CANADA, AND MEXICO, 1861–1930

Period	China	Japan	Canada	Mexico
1861-70	64,301	186	153,878	2,191
1871-80	123,201	149	383,640	5,162
1881-90	61,711	2,270	393,304	1,913 [2]
1891-1900	14,799	25,942	3,311 [1]	971 [2]
1901-1910	20,605	129,797	179,226	49,642
1911-1920	21,278	83,837	742,185	219,004
1921-1930	29,907	33,462	924,515	459,287

[1] The actual figure is higher because good records are not available for 1892 and 1893.
[2] The actual figure is higher because no figures are available from 1886-1893.

Between 1854 and 1883, substantial numbers of Chinese came to the United States. They sought better economic opportunities. In 1882, almost 40,000 Chinese entered the country. Many took jobs building railroads in the West. In 1882, Congress barred further immigration of Chinese for ten years. This prohibition was renewed every ten years until the close of World War II.

After 1883, Japanese began to emigrate in larger numbers. In order to prohibit Japanese immigration, the United States government persuaded the government of Japan to prohibit the emigration of laborers to the United States. The measures taken against the Chinese and the Japanese had been promoted by western states, particularly by labor unions in the West. They feared competition from Oriental workers and claimed that the Chinese and Japanese were an alien race in a land peopled mainly by Caucasians.

After 1900, both Canadians and Mexicans began to arrive in the United States in large numbers. In the decade after 1910, about 1 million English-speaking and 500,000 French-speaking Canadians crossed the border. However, this population traffic went both ways. Between 1890 and 1914, almost a million Americans emigrated to Canada. They moved primarily into the provinces bordering the states from Minnesota to Montana. In addition, the census revealed that in 1930, about 750,000 Mexicans lived in the United States. They were concentrated in Texas, New Mexico, Arizona, and California where they worked primarily as farm laborers.

The Characteristics of the Immigrants

At the time of entry, officials asked each immigrant to state his or her occupation. Figure 62C was compiled from immigrants' answers.

FIGURE 62C   THE OCCUPATIONS OF IMMIGRANTS TO THE UNITED STATES AT ENTRY, 1860–1910

Decade	Agri-culture	Skilled labor	Unskilled labor	Domestic service	Profes-sional	Misc.
1861-70	17.6%	24.0%	42.4%	7.2%	0.8%	8.0%
1871-80	18.2%	23.1%	41.9%	7.7%	1.4%	7.7%
1881-90	14.0%	20.4%	50.2%	9.4%	1.1%	9.4%
1891-1900	11.4%	20.1%	47.0%	15.1%	0.9%	15.1%
1901-10	24.3%	20.2%	34.8%	14.1%	1.5%	14.1%

Adjusting to American Society

Once within the United States, the changes in immigrants described by Emily Balch seem to have been almost universal. The experience of emigration weakened attachments to the villages and towns in which immigrants had been born. It also increased identification with the national state. Groups whose life had focused around the family developed a wide range of community organizations. A vigorous press grew up among people who had hardly seen a newspaper before. In every group, children confronted parents with conflict between old and new cultures.

This experience was not exactly the same for every immigrant group. For each, it involved slightly different opportunities, choices, and difficulties. The eastern Europeans, for example, included approximately 1½ million Jews. Jews had been forbidden by law to own land in eastern Europe. And they had not been permitted to participate fully in society. They lived differently from eastern European peasants. Most of them earned their livings as artisans or merchants. They were accustomed to being treated as aliens in a strange and often hostile land. Jews valued knowledge and achievement as measures of individual worth. In addition, their own traditional culture had been changing for several centuries. Young Jews had become excited by ideas of "enlightenment" and nationalism. Released from the constraints of their native villages when they emigrated to Vienna or New York, Jews moved rapidly into the mainstream of modern life.

On the American side of the Atlantic, Jews quickly developed strong community institutions. They gave them mutual protection and helped them accommodate to American society. They achieved unusual personal successes. By the first decade of the twentieth century, children of Jewish immigrants who entered the United States in 1890 were protesting against discrimination in college admission procedures. This personal success had a twofold effect upon the institutions which first-generation immigrants had set up. On the one hand, successful men and women provided a large fund of capital and of trained personnel for community purposes. On the other hand, success by American standards challenged, more rapidly than in other groups, the adequacy of group identification and pride as a way of participating in American life. Jews have, at one and the same time, spoken vigorously for "cultural pluralism"—the idea that there are many American cultures, each to be represented—and for full assimilation into America.

Jews have not been entirely unique. The Oriental communities of the west coast showed many of the same traits of enterprise and emphasis upon achievement and intellectual accomplishment. Both Orientals and Jews met greater discrimination as they became more successful by American standards. For example, California tried to

▶ What criteria do you use to measure your worth or that of another individual?

Enlightenment refers to a belief in progress, natural law and natural rights, and reason. Young enlightened people scorned tradition and believed that each generation would, by its efforts, contribute a better life for the next generation. The eighteenth century is often called the Age of Enlightenment.

restrict Japanese land ownership at a time (1913) when Japanese immigrants threatened to take over large stretches of land, such as the San Joaquin Valley. And, like Jews, Orientals have contributed a disproportionately large number of intellectuals and professional people to the society.

The differences which developed among immigrant groups between the early twentieth century and today did not grow exclusively from the values which immigrants brought with them to this country. Differences also stemmed from the American experience. Each group tended to cluster in a special set of industries or occupations. The initial concentration was in part accidental. It depended upon the most active employers at the time when a particular immigrant group first entered the country. Later, clustering was not so accidental. The first entrants, with the support of their employers, encouraged their friends and relatives to move to the firm or industry with which they were familiar. Several of these industries, particularly in individual cities, were dominated by single groups such as Irish in construction, Jews in clothing manufacturing, and Slavs and Magyars in steel.

A Magyar is a person who speaks the main language of what is now Hungary.

Immigration Restriction

The era of mass immigration closed during the 1920's. Since the first onset of heavy Irish immigration in the 1840's, "native" Americans had responded ambiguously to the newcomers. Some welcomed them. Others feared for American values and greeted the newcomers with hostility. In the 1840's and 1850's this hostility, combined with anti-Catholicism, was probably the most important political issue through most of the northeastern United States. Anti-Catholic riots broke out in most major cities. And the Know-Nothing Party became a major political force. If there had been a public opinion poll at the time, the number one issue on people's minds would probably have been "nativism" rather than slavery.

The Know-Nothing, or American, party began as a secret organization opposed to immigrants, particularly Catholics. With the disintegration of the established parties, the Know-Nothings won substantial victories in 1854 and elected several governors, state legislators, and representatives to Congress.

Nativism did not die after the Civil War. But for a time, other issues seemed more important. In the 1880's and 1890's, however, three events helped it gain strength. The first was the increase in the proportion of eastern and southern European immigrants. Native-born Americans—whose ancestors came from northern and western Europe—claimed that the newcomers came from less desirable backgrounds. Second, the old immigrants were beginning to take part in American political life. Several eastern cities elected their first mayors of Irish descent. Germans insisted that public schools should teach German and that beer gardens should be allowed to remain open on Sunday. Many older groups resented the new power of recent immigrants. Third, the increasing economic growth and urbanization of the country threatened the self-images and traditions of many people. The immigrants, so much a part of the new age, became scapegoats for the problems they created.

This renewed nativism showed its first important fruits in the 1890's. Local communities throughout the country redoubled their efforts to make everyone more patriotic. They passed laws insisting upon English as the only language of instruction in the schools. Such laws also prohibited some of the "immoral" practices associated with immigrants, especially in matters such as gambling and liquor sales that conflicted with religious attitudes of native groups.

Nativists also led a movement to restrict immigration. During the first three quarters of the nineteenth century, states that were the ports-of-entry for a large number of immigrants had attempted through the police power to keep out diseased persons, paupers, and criminals. In 1882, Congress excluded convicts, idiots, and persons likely to become public charges. It also imposed a head tax of fifty cents on each immigrant admitted. In a series of later acts, Congress excluded additional groups, increased the head tax, and forbade contract labor. These acts were based on the principle that the government should select the types of persons to be admitted. They did not noticeably decrease the total flow of immigrants. A demand for stricter selection and for restricting the total to be admitted built up steadily, particularly among union members.

A bill providing for a literacy test in any language as a basis of admission passed one house of Congress thirty-two times and on four occasions passed both houses, only to be vetoed by the President. In 1917, however, the bill passed over President Wilson's veto. This act was restrictive because a large proportion of the immigrants from southern and eastern Europe could not read. Fearing a flood of immigrants in the years following World War I despite the literacy test, Congress passed another restrictive law in 1921. This law limited annual immigration to 357,802 and set a quota for each nation. The quota was arrived at by taking 3 percent of the total number of persons of that nationality residing in the United States in 1910. The quota favored northern and western Europe.

In 1924, the law was toughened. It provided that after 1927 total immigration in any one year would be limited to 150,000. To make up this total, a quota was allocated to each country according to the proportion of its natives in the population of the United States in 1920. The quota allocated to each group had no relationship to the number of people who actually wanted to come to the United States. The quota for England, which was very large, was unused while the quotas for eastern and southern European nations were small in comparison to the number who wanted to emigrate. This quota system implied that the newer immigrants were less desirable than those from northern and western Europe.

▶ Should a national government have the right to prohibit entry of immigrants with physical or mental disabilities? Why or why not?

In 1864, Congress had passed a Contract Labor Law which allowed employers to recruit laborers from Europe. Workers signed contracts agreeing to work for one employer for a specified period of time for specified wages. Workers could not legally leave the job during the contract term. American laborers objected to the law, and Congress repealed it in 1885.

The "Literacy Test Act" required aliens over 16 to read "not less than 30 nor more than 80 words in ordinary use" in English or some other language.

Since 1968, the United States admits 120,000 immigrants from the Western Hemisphere and 170,000 from elsewhere each year. Preference is given to those who are scientists, professionals, or victims of political oppression, and to those having relatives in the United States. There are no longer any strict national quotas.

427

The Contributions of Immigrants

Textbooks often contain long lists of immigrants who made important contributions to American society. The lists are usually filled with names of famous men and women: political leaders, authors, musicians, inventors, athletes, soldiers, and so forth. Without exception, every immigrant group has distinguished candidates for such a list. But a list of people who became successful does not begin to indicate the major contributions of immigrants to American life. A walk through any major city offers far richer data.

Look at the New York subways, built largely by the labor of Irish and Italians. Look at the restaurants, with food whose recipes came in the holds of ships from ports around the world. Observe the architecture, reminiscent of Europe, Asia, or the Middle East, of churches, stores, and houses. Enter the shops of importers who travel to their homelands each year to buy fresh stock. Watch the billboards advertising dance troupes and orchestras filled with foreign-born artists. Most of all, look at the people. All Americans are immigrants and the offspring of immigrants. And all have contributed to the infinite variety and richness of the nation.

Work and Community

STATING THE ISSUE

The last four chapters only mentioned the concept of industrialization. But they left it largely undefined. The concept appears
to have two different meanings. Some historians describe industrialization as a process which increases human productivity by supplying tools to increase the work done by human muscles. They also
stress the ability of human beings to release and control energy
from such resources as coal, petroleum, or natural gas. These
scholars rank societies as more or less industrialized by measuring
productivity, energy, and the use of resources.

Other scholars are more interested in the forms of work itself.
Industrialization, in their view, is a change in the way people relate
to each other as they engage in the production of goods and services.
They also see it as a change in the way people relate to the means
of production, such as tools and factories, and to the other people
with whom they work.

This chapter adopts this second view. In the last century, the
processes of work have been cut off from the rest of life. Unlike
any time in the past, a majority of the American population does
not live within walking distance of the places where it works. Children
see their parents doing housework. But they have very little image
of them in factory, shop, or office. School is commonly described
as preparation for work. But most academic high school programs
give only a vague image of work, production, and careers. Television
hardly remedies the vagueness. It portrays only a very narrow
segment of the world's occupations.

So it is not surprising then that we have almost no ordinary
vocabulary for describing work—an activity which occupies a third
or more of people's lives. The readings in this chapter deal with
a dramatic change in the patterns of work in the iron and steel
industry between 1880 and 1920. They are intended to remove
some of the mystery which surrounds work. The essay at the end
of the chapter analyzes the role of work and describes the history
of labor unions during this period.

CHAPTER
17

429

1869 Uriah Stephens organizes Knights of Labor

1877 Federal troops suppress strikes in several cities

1886 Violence erupts during labor demonstration in Haymarket Square, Chicago

1886 American Federation of Labor is organized

1892 Steelworkers strike against Carnegie Steel Company

1894 Eugene V. Debs leads Pullman railway strike

1901 J. P. Morgan finances United States Steel Corporation

1905 Industrial Workers of the World (IWW) is organized in Chicago

1913 Congress creates Department of Labor

1914 Congress passes Clayton Antitrust Act, legalizing strikes, peaceful picketing, and boycotts

1917 United States enters World War I

1919 Steelworkers organize nationwide strike

1935 The Committee for Industrial Organization (C.I.O.) is formed

64 WORK AND PARTICIPATION

In 1880, observers who compared the American with British, German, and French iron industries recognized that American methods for producing iron and steel had fallen behind. American mill owners had failed to take advantage of new manufacturing techniques discovered in the previous twenty years. American manufacturers still heated pig iron in large crucibles. Men called "puddlers" then stirred cinders into the molten metal until it formed crystallized balls which could be squeezed and rolled. The process required physically strong workers who could make judgments about the properties of metal as it passed from one stage to another. Moving great batches of metal manually within the mill also required strong men.

The American iron and steel industry soon caught up with its European competitors. In rapid succession, manufacturers switched from the crucible to the Bessemer and then to the open-hearth process for making steel. The Bessemer converter blew hot air rapidly through molten pig iron to burn out major impurities. The open-hearth system involved huge furnaces which heated the metal to extremely high temperatures. It allowed for better control of the quality of the metal.

Both methods reduced the hot back-breaking work men had performed previously in iron and steel production. But as these new methods replaced the old, fewer skilled workers were needed. Semiskilled and unskilled workers entered the industry in increasing numbers.

Reading 64 describes the processes of work in a steel mill in 1919. It is taken from the diary of Charles Walker. As you read his account, think about the following questions:

1. How did the workers relate to one another?
2. What were the general characteristics of the work process as Walker described it?

The Diary of a Furnace Worker

In the summer of 1919, Charles Walker, a Yale graduate who had recently resigned his commission as an army lieutenant, decided to learn the steel business. He bought some second-hand clothes and went to work on an open-hearth furnace near Pittsburgh. Walker later became a well-known analyst and critic of industrial work processes.

I stood behind the furnace near the spout, which still spread a wave of heat about it, and Nick, the second-helper, beside me yelling things in Anglo-Serbian, into my face. . . .

Charles Rumford Walker, **Steel: The Diary of a Furnace Worker** (Boston: The Atlantic Monthly Press, 1922), pp. 38-41, 50-54, 92-94. Copyright © 1922 by Charles Rumford Walker. Reprinted by permission. Language simplified.

"What you think. Get me"—a long blur of Serbian, here—"spout, quick mak a"—more Serbian with tremendous volume of voice—"furnace, see? You get that mud!"

When a man says that to you with profound emotion, it seems insulting, to say, "What" to it. But that was what I did.

"All right, all right," he said. "Me get myself, all the work"—blurred here—third-helper—wheelbarrow, why don' you—*quick now when I say!*"

"All right, all right, I'll do it," I said, and went away. I was never in my life so much impressed with the necessity of *doing it*. His language and gesture had been profoundly expressive—of what? I tried to concentrate on the phrases that seeped through emotion and Serbian into English. "Wheelbarrow"—hang on to that; "mud"—that's easy: a wheelbarrow of mud. Good!

I wheeled back . . . and found Nick coming out at me. When he saw that hard-won mud of mine, I thought he was going to snap the cords in his throat.

When speech returned, he said, "I tell you, get wheelbarrow dolomite, and half-wheelbarrow clay, and pail of water, and look what you bring."

So that was it—he probably said pail of water with his feet.

Dolomite is a form of limestone rich in certain minerals.

431

▶Many steel workers
labored twelve hours a day
and seven days a week at
furnaces such as this one.
Was a rising GNP worth
such human costs? Why or
why not?

"Hunky" was a derogatory
term applied to unskilled
workers of foreign birth,
especially those from
Hungary. Walker uses it here
with a sympathetic familiarity
and without any disrespect.

▶Have you ever felt
completely beaten like this
because you didn't
understand your school work
or couldn't meet someone's
standards? What should a
person do in these
circumstances?

"Oh, all right," I said. "I thought you said mud. I'll get it, I'll get it."

This is amusing enough on the first day. You can go off and laugh in a superior way to yourself about the queer words the foreigners use. But after seven days of it, fourteen hours each, it gets under the skin, it burns along the nerves, as the furnace heat burns along the arms. . . . It suddenly occurred to me one day, after someone had bawled me out for not knowing where something was that I had never heard of, that this was what every immigrant Hunky endured. It was a matter of language largely, of understanding, of knowing the names of things, the uses of things, the language of the boss. Here was this Serbian second-helper bossing his third-helper largely in an unknown tongue, and the latter getting the full emotional experience of the immigrant. I thought of Bill, the pit boss, telling a Hunky to do a clean-up job for him. And when the Hunky said, "What?" he turned to me and said: "Lord! but these Hunkies are dumb." . . .

One day I met Jack. He was an old regular-army sergeant, a man about thirty. He had come back from fixing a bad spout. . . .

"Do you ever feel low?" he said, sitting down on the back of a shovel. "Every once'n while I feel like telling 'em to take their job. You strain your guts out, and then they swear at you."

"I sometimes feel like a worm," I said, "with no right to be living any way, or so mad I want to lick the bosses and the president."

"If you were first-helper, it wouldn't be so bad," he mused. "You wouldn't have to bring up that manganese in a wheelbarrow—and they wouldn't kick you around so much.". . .

432

I found out that everyone hid his shovel at the end of the shift, beside piles of brick in the cellar of the mill, under dark stairways, and so forth. I hadn't yet acquired one, but used mostly a fork, which isn't so personal an instrument, and of which there seemed to be a common supply. I felt keen to "acquire" though.

After supper, I wrote in my diary and thought a bit before going to bed. There's a genuine technique of the shovel, the pick, and especially of the wheelbarrow, I thought. That plank from the ground to the cinder-box! It takes all I can muster to teeter the wheelbarrow up, dump without losing the thing quite, and bring it down backward without barking my shins. There's a bit of technique, too, in pairing off properly for a job, selecting your lick of work promptly and not getting left jobless to the eyes of the boss, capturing your shovel and hiding it at the end of the turn, keeping the good will of the men you're with on teamwork, distinguishing scrap from cinder and putting them into the proper boxes, not digging for slag too deeply in the pit floor, and so forth and so on. . . .

Another day went by, hewing cinders in the pit. . . . At twenty minutes to five I went upstairs to my locker. Dick Reber, senior melter, stopped me.

"Need a man to-night. Want to work?" he said. "Always short, you know, on this—long turn."

"Sure," I said.

That was one way to get promoted, I thought, and wondered how I'd stand fourteen more hours on top of the ten I had had.

"Beat it," yelled the melter.

Jack and I got our flat manganese shovels, and went on the run. . . . This furnaceful had cooled twenty-two hours. Nick was kneeling on water-soaked bagging, on the edge of the hot spout. He dug out the mud in the tap-hole with a pointed rod and sputtered oaths at the heat. Every few minutes the spout would burn through the bagging to his knees. He would get up, refold the bagging, and kneel again to the job. . . .

There was something queer about this heat. The soles of my feet—why should [they] burn so! There was a blazing gas in the air—my nostrils seemed to flame as they took it in. This was different from most manganese shoveling. My face glowed all over in single concentrated pain. What was it? I saw Jack shoveling wildly in the middle of that second pile. We finished it in a panic.

"What was the matter with that ladle?" I asked as we got our breath in the opening between the furnaces.

"Spout had a hole in the middle," he said.

The fire-clay of the spout had given way, and a hole forming in the middle let the metal through. That made it necessary, in order to catch the steel, to bring the ladle close, till part of it was under the platform on which we worked. The heat and gas from the hot

▶ "Common" labor often requires real skills such as these, as well as pride in one's work. Have you ever admired the work done by cleaning people or clerks?

433

steel in the ladle had been warming the soles of our feet, and rising into our faces.

"Here's a funny thing," I said, looking down. One of the sparks which had struck my pants burned around, very neatly taking off the cuff and an inch or two of the pant-leg. The thing might have been done with a pair of shears.

I came out of the mill whistling and feeling pretty much "on the crest." I'd worked their "long turn," and stood it. It wasn't so bad, all except that ladle that got under the manganese. I ate a huge breakfast, with a calm sense of virtue rewarded, and climbed into bed with a smile on my lips.

The alarm clock had been ringing several minutes before I realized what it was up to. I turned over to shut if off, and found needles running into all the muscles of my back. I struggled up on an elbow. The alarm was still going.

I fought myself out of bed and shut it off; stood up and tried to think. . . . I sat down again on the bed, and prepared to lift my feet back in.

Then I got up, and washed fiercely, threw on my clothes, and went downstairs, and out into the afternoon sun.

Down by the restaurant, I met the third-helper.

"Long turn wouldn't be so bad, if there weren't no next day," he said, with a sort of smile.

In the mill was a gang of men. Things all went wrong. Everybody was angry and tired. Their nerves made mistakes for them.

"I only wish it were next Sunday!" I said to someone.

"There aren't any Sundays in this place," he returned. "Twenty-four hours off between two working days ain't Sunday.". . .

I became a part of an exclusive group of seven men, who had worked together for about two years. There is a cohesiveness and a structure of tradition about a semipermanent mill-group of this sort that marks it off from the casual-labor gang. The physical surroundings remain unaltered. And methods and ways of thought grow up upon them. I was struck by the amount of character a man laid bare in twelve hours of common labor. There are habits of temper, of cunning and strength, of generosity and comradeship, of indifference. It begins by being extensively intimate in personal and physical ways. You know every man's idiosyncrasies in handling a sledge or a bar or a shovel, and the expression of his face under all phases of a week's work. You know naturally the various garments he wears on all parts of his body. You proceed to acquaint yourself . . . with the mannerisms and qualities of his spirit. It is astonishing . . . how little is ultimately concealed or kept out of the common understanding.

I was impressed by the precise practices established in doing the work. Every motion and every interval of the job had been selected by long trial. If you didn't think the formula best, try it out. Many

Steelworkers worked days for two weeks and then nights for two weeks. They worked without interruption for twenty-four hours when they moved from the day to the night shift and had twenty-four hours free two weeks later.

▶Have you ever had a similar feeling as part of an athletic team or other group? What does that feeling contribute to your life?

434

considerations went into its selection—to-day's fatigue, to-morrow's, and next month's. . . .

When the flue dust had been removed from the blast-stoves, I found wheeling and dumping it an easy and congenial set of movements, and consequently took off my loads at a great speed.

At once I became a target. "Tak'it eas'—What's the matter with you; tak' it eas'."

John put in an explanation: "Me work on this job two year, me know; take it easy. You have plenty work to do."

"Take it easy," I said, "and no get tired, eh? feel good every day?"

"You no can feel good every day," he amended quickly. "Gas bad, make your stomach bad."

So I slowed up on my wheelbarrow loads, sat on the handles, and spat and talked, till I found I was going too slow. There was a work-rhythm that was neither a dawdle nor a drive. If you expected any comfort in your gang life of twelve hours daily, you had best discover and obey its laws. It might be, from several points of view, an incorrect rhythm, but, at all events, it was a part of the gang mores. And some of its inward reasonableness often appeared before the day was out, or the month, or the year.

Mores mean the customs of a group.

FOR THOUGHT:

Would work in the steel mills have been any different if all the workers spoke English and were descendants of the immigrants who had come over on the *Mayflower?*

65 THE LIMITS OF WELFARE

In the 1880's, many American steelworkers belonged to unions. By 1892, members of the Amalgamated Association of Iron and Steel Workers held about half the jobs in the industry. The Amalgamated bargained with employers about wages and rules of employment and work.

In 1892, at the Homestead mills just outside of Pittsburgh, the Carnegie Corporation gave the union an ultimatum—accept the company wage offer or be totally excluded from the mills. The union refused to accept terms that made negotiations with the company impossible. It called a strike and occupied the plant to support its claim that workers had "property" rights in their jobs. They believed these rights could not be taken away without compensation.

The company denied this claim. "The question at issue is a very grave one," one of the company officers argued. "It is whether the Carnegie Company or the Amalgamated Association shall have absolute control of our plant." The strike collapsed after five months.

435

Suppose you worked for twelve hours a day under the conditions shown in pictures 1, 5, and 6. How would you feel, knowing that you and your family had to live in the surroundings shown in pictures 2, 3, and 4?

In the decade following the Homestead strike, Carnegie and the owners of other companies asserted the right to "absolute" control of their "property."

In order to be successful, however, such a policy could not be confined to the industrial plant itself. In 1892, the union was a power in the local community of Homestead as well as in the mills. The police and a large part of the clergy sympathized with the workers. Business people extended credit to the striking workers. And the local newspapers reported favorably on the workers' activities. In order to gain control of its plants, the company had to revolutionize community life.

The new forms of work, employer-employee relations, and community life in industrial society disturbed social critics. Many of them realized that these new aspects of society had to be understood if they were to be altered. Others realized that a thorough knowledge of that complex society was required in order to change it. Reading 65 comes from a volume in *The Pittsburgh Survey*. It was a comprehensive attempt to analyze the ways in which the changes in work and employer-employee relations affected community life. As you read, think about these questions:

1. What sorts of communities were the companies, notably United States Steel, trying to establish?
2. How did the workers regard their communities?

Life in Steelworkers' Communities

Shortly after 1900, a group of Pittsburgh charitable organizations realized that to work effectively they had to know more about their communities. With the support of the Russell Sage Foundation of New York, they commissioned an intensive investigation of the life of industrial workers in Pittsburgh and its suburbs. Portions of the findings follow.

John A. Fitch, **The Steel Workers** (New York: Charities Publication Committee, 1910), pp. 192-194, 196, 198-204, 207, 210, 212-214, 216; 219. Language simplified.

Entirely apart from unionism or non-unionism are certain arrangements which may be termed employees' benefit policies. The arrangement has become general in the Carnegie mills of delivering coal to employees at cost. The company also loans money to employees for the purpose of building homes. It is an advantage to a mill-town employer to have property-owning employees. The labor force is more stable and there is less likelihood of a strike. The employees do not wish to take a chance of losing their jobs after a house has been acquired, lest they have to move.

438

In Homestead and Munhall the Carnegie Company owns a number of houses. It has proved itself a good landlord in comparison with some of the small owners of rented properties in these boroughs. The company charges 30 to 40 percent less for these houses than other landlords charge.

This year [1910] the United States Steel Corporation has announced two important developments in the way of a relief plan and a pension system. As long as a man remains an employee, the company will help protect his family against the dangers of industry. It will also make some provision toward his old age. A man will think twice before giving up a job which will give him a pension if he loses that pension by taking another job that pays a little more. He will be reluctant, especially as he stays for many years with a company, to risk discharge. He will not join a union if joining means discharge.

These plans illustrate the administrative and, to a degree, the human advantages which have come with consolidating the ownership of the steel industry. In the first place, inventions and changes begun in one plant may at once be introduced in many. An expert staff can be set to study difficult problems with all of the corporation's mills as their laboratory. Standards once adopted, whether of safety inspection, accident compensation, or surgical service, may be enforced by executive act so as to affect 200,000 men instead of waiting for such programs to be introduced by a hundred independent managers. Again, the private owners of the 1890's faced severe competition. But profits went wholly into their own pockets. The directors and executive officials of the Steel Corporation bear a different relation to the year's profits. Their personal incomes are not affected by starting a relief fund, for example.

The break with unionism had no direct bearing on the policies which have thus far been cited. Some of them were begun by the employers during the times of greatest union strength. But there are other conditions which have come into being that would certainly have been opposed if the men had retained their collective power.

One of these is the internal organization of the industry. In eliminating waste of all kinds and introducing mechanical changes, it has also put the entire control of the mills back into the hands of foremen and superintendents. In this way the labor force is coordinated so as to make it most easy to control and most difficult to unionize. Another is the wage policy. While advancing the wages of common labor, it has brought down the earnings of men of highest skill. Cuts in pay have accompanied increased output. The whole wage movement, unprodded by union demands, lags behind the rise in prices of family necessities.

Let us look at the situation as it is reflected in the everyday life of the men. The immediate effect of such a working schedule is on

Dangers of industry refers to accident compensation which involves payment for injuries received on the job.

▶ Is it better to have pension plans set up by each company, or to have one plan, such as the Social Security System, for everyone? Why?

A director of a corporation is usually a large stockholder and receives a fee for attending Board of Directors' meetings. Officials of the company who carry out the day-to-day business are salaried. Therefore, their annual salaries would not be affected by setting up a relief fund, nor would any one stockholder's earnings. Individual owners of companies do receive the profits that are not reinvested. If a relief fund were set up, profits would be lower.

439

the home. Many a steelworker has said to me with grim bitterness, "Home is just the place where I eat and sleep. I live in the mills." The steelworkers are united in saying that "on the night shift you can't do anything but work, eat, and sleep anyhow." So home pleasures and social pleasures alike are entirely lacking during a full half of the time. Whatever opportunity for enjoyment of the home there may be, must come in the alternate weeks on day shift.

Steel workers worked nights one week and days the following week.

The wife of the steelworker, too, has a hard day, and even a longer one than her husband's. To prepare a breakfast by six in the morning she must rise not later than half past five. The family cannot sit down at the supper table until seven or later. And after that the dishes must be washed. There is little time for husband and wife to have each other's company. It is only by making an extra effort that they can spend an evening out together. And the evening at home is robbed of much of its charm by prolonging the domestic duties, such as dishwashing, beyond the time that would be required if the meal were served earlier. The father, too, has little time with his children. If they are quite small, he may go for weeks without seeing them except in their cribs.

▶How could children get to know their fathers under such conditions? How might this lack of knowledge affect a child's life?

Not only is home life threatened, but other healthy influences in the mill towns feel the blighting effect of the twelve-hour day. Opportunity for mental culture would seem to be ample in the mill towns. Each has its Carnegie Library. Each has its auditorium and music hall with a fine pipe organ, where lectures and concerts of high grade are held. But the steelworkers seldom make use of these privileges. The trouble is the same as that which has already spoiled half of the home life. There is not enough energy left at the end of a twelve-hour day.

Andrew Carnegie believed that millionaires should use their surplus wealth for the benefit of the public. Before his death, Carnegie had given away over $350 million to set up libraries, schools, colleges, research institutes, and foundations for the advancement of peace.

It now becomes necessary to discuss the reasons for the apparent agreement of the steelworkers to existing conditions. The obvious obstacle to collective action on their part is the fact that they are non-union. But that merely suggests the question: Why don't they organize? To understand the absence of united action and resistance to the policies of the companies one must understand the obstacles that stand in the way.

In the first place, there is the so-called profit-sharing system of the United States Steel Corporation. Beginning in 1903, the corporation has set aside shares of stock. Each employee can buy as many shares as he wishes within limits depending upon his annual salary.

The stock-issue system brings those employees who invest in stock more surely under the domination of the corporation. The bonus paid each year for five years is to go to those who have shown "a proper interest in the welfare and progress" of the corporation. The extra dividends at the end of the five-year period are awarded to those whom the corporation finds "deserving thereof." There is nothing to prevent an employee of the corporation from purchasing stock on the same basis as the outsider. But in that case he will receive only ordinary dividends. The extraordinary return received by the holder of employees' stock is based on his acquiescence as an employee.

The steel companies also employ a system of espionage, or spying. I doubt whether you could find a more suspicious body of men than the employees of the United States Steel Corporation. They are suspicious of one another, of their neighbors, and of their friends. I was repeatedly suspected of being an agent of the corporation, sent out to sound out the men's attitudes toward the corporation and toward unionism. The fact is, the steelworkers do not dare openly express their convictions. They do not dare assemble and talk over affairs pertaining to their welfare as mill men. They feel that they are living always in the presence of a hostile critic.

All of the steel companies have effective methods of learning what is going on among the workmen. The Jones and Laughlin Company has an organization that keeps it informed about the likelihood of disorder breaking out. The United States Steel Corporation has regular secret-service departments. Its agents are thought by the men to be scattered through all of the mills of the corporation. They believe that these agents work shoulder to shoulder at the rolls or furnaces with honest workmen, ready to record any "disloyal" utterances or to enter into any movement among their fellows. The workmen feel this espionage. They believe it exists, but they do not know who the traitors are. It may be that the friend of long standing who works at the next furnace is one of them, or, possibly, the next-door neighbor at home. They do not know. Is it any wonder, therefore, that they suspect each other and guard their tongues?

FOR THOUGHT:

Some native Americans also worked under these conditions. Do you suppose that their lives were very different from the lives of the immigrants?

66 STRIKE!

In 1917, the United States entered World War I. President Woodrow Wilson told the American people that they were involved in a great international struggle to preserve democracy. American steelworkers expected to benefit from this struggle. They hoped at war's end to find a new democratic atmosphere in their communities. Workers had derived many benefits from company welfare policies before the war. But they had been denied participation in all company and many community decisions. Wilson's words seemed to signal a new day.

On September 22, 1919, nearly a year after the war had ended, the steelworkers struck. The steel strike of 1919 was a complex affair. But the real issue focused on the workers' demand that the steel companies deal with them collectively. The officers of the companies agreed to talk to any individual worker who wanted to complain about his wages or his conditions of work. The workers insisted, however, that the companies must deal with them through a few leaders chosen by the workers to discuss terms for all. This is what "collective bargaining" meant.

The American Federation of Labor, an alliance of established trade unions, aided the steelworkers in their struggle. Despite this assistance, the strike required strenuous efforts and sacrifices from the steelworkers themselves. In many ways, they had to readjust their own picture of themselves. Unskilled immigrant workers and skilled, often native-born, workers had to cooperate.

The steel companies also faced a readjustment. To accept collective bargaining meant to accept a powerful, rival voice in deciding wages and in determining the organization of work and community life. The companies resisted this adjustment. With the help of the federal, state, and local governments, the press, and many of the churches, the companies were finally able to defeat the workers' efforts to unionize the industry.

After the strike, a group of Protestant clergymen investigated the causes of the strike and the reasons for its failure. Reading 66 is taken from their report. As you read, think about these questions:

1. What means were used to break the strike?
2. What did Judge Gary mean by American institutions?

The Immigrants
Assert Themselves

The Interchurch World Movement represented several Protestant denominations working together to help solve the social problems of industrial society. During the strike, the leaders of the movement worked to arrive at a peaceful solution. After it was over, they investigated the strike. This portion of their report analyzes some of the sources of strikers' discontent.

The Commission of Inquiry of the Interchurch World Movement, **Public Opinion and the Steel Strike** (New York: Harcourt Brace Jovanovich, Inc., 1921), pp. 239-241. Abridged. Language simplified. Reprinted by permission.

The determination of immigrant workers to assert themselves was the chief reason why the foreign and the English press, and especially the "American" [native-born] elements of society, considered the strike as having deeper motives than mere demands of ordinary trade unionism. Not only the mill managers, but all the governing classes in steel towns were accustomed to seeing immigrants docile and

442

submissive. To them any strike was indeed a revolution. Formerly the immigrants obeyed orders without questioning. They did the unpleasant work, the heavy and exhausting work, and never asked the reason why.

They had submitted for years to militaristic mill discipline. In the community they had acted in the same way. They had lived their lives away from the others, at first purposely keeping out of their way. Then as they became "Americanized," they began in recent years to assert themselves as members of the community. As one "American" minister explained it, "The foreigners want too much. They own the largest churches in the community, are buying up the property, and are now even running their own candidates for political office."

Most important, the immigrants in the steel mills had tasted better conditions during the war. They had had an opportunity to earn more by working on the better-paying jobs. For the first time they had been treated considerately by the foreman, etc. In the community, they had also been looked upon differently, that is either as "Americans" or as worthy allies.

The immigrant workers took these new developments seriously. And they were very much disillusioned after the signing of the armistice when the employers and the dominant elements in the community took the attitude that, now the war was over, it was time to return to all the old conditions. The immigrants were again "Hunkies." This was the last straw. Thereafter they waited for anybody to lead them into the promised land.

▶ Some people think it is acceptable to refer jokingly to members of ethnic, racial, or religious minorities by terms such as "Hunky" as long as no insult is intended. Do you think this practice is all right? Why, or why not?

It was because the immigrants deepest emotions and instincts were stirred that this huge and unprecedented strike was possible. The immigrants wanted not only better wages and shorter hours. They resented being treated as a possession or a "Hunky."

Not Unionism, but Americanism

One portion of the clergymen's report contained an interview between Bishop J. McConnell and Dr. Daniel A. Poling, who represented the Interchurch World Movement and Judge Elbert H. Gary, Chairman of the Executive Committee of the United States Steel Corporation. Selections from that interview follow.

Mr. Gary insisted that the point at issue was not now unionism as such, but whether the American government should be supported and American institutions upheld. He insisted that the whole movement of the steel strike was a movement of Communists. He repeatedly

Public Opinion and the Steel Strike, pp. 336-338. Language simplified.

▶In the late nineteenth and early twentieth centuries, immigrant women often paraded and picketed when strikes took place. Do you think that housewives and mothers ought to take part in such activities? Why or why not?

▶Why do people sometimes make appeals to principles such as these when they are under attack?

Sovietism refers to the system of government in the Union of Soviet Socialist Republics.

avowed his belief that the only outcome of a victory for unionism would be Sovietism in the United States "and forcible distribution of property." "And, therefore," he said, "my positive word is a refusal to arbitrate."

The Chairman then said, "Judge Gary, you are on record in your own testimony as being in favor of collective bargaining. Would you look with favor upon an organization in your shops in which the workers should choose their own representatives to state any grievances to the authorities that they might have?"

Judge Gary replied that he was heartily in favor of such an organization, "provided it be the right kind of organization."

The Chairman then called attention to the fact that the testimony gathered by our investigators and by the members of the Commission themselves showed that, while Mr. Gary's statement might favor collective bargaining, as a matter of fact the men could not get their grievances beyond the foremen.

Mr. Gary then rather closely cross-questioned the Chairman and Mr. Poling on the type of men whom the Commission had interviewed. He insisted that it could only have been men to whom we were directed by Communists.

The Chairman then asked Judge Gary this question: "Supposing all the men have gone back and the strike has failed in the sense that the men have returned to work with a consciousness of failure, with the feeling that they have been beaten, what kind of a situation is produced by the presence of men in such a temper in the mills?"

444

Mr. Gary replied that this statement was not adequate to the real situation. He said that the men were contented and had been frightened into going out. As soon as adequate police force and United States soldiers arrived on the scene they voluntarily returned. And they returned all the more willingly because Mr. Gary himself had stated to his officials that the strike was not voluntary and that they must see that the families even of the strikers suffered no lack of food or other necessities while they were out. Mr. Gary stated positively, "We fed the families of strikers."

Mr. Gary insisted that the issue was not unionism but fundamental devotion to American institutions. He spoke quite strongly that "there had been red organizations in Pittsburgh known to the officers of the government which the government had not broken up."

Mr. Gary said that of course this Commission could make any public statement that it pleased. But he warned us "to bear in mind that the very foundations of the American government were involved in the matter."

Breaking the Strike

This selection, also from the Interchurch World Movement, describes the companies' strike-breaking efforts.

Great numbers of workers came to believe: that local mayors, magistrates, and police officials try to break strikes; that state and Federal officials, particularly the Federal Department of Justice, help to break strikes, and that armed forces are used for this purpose; that most newspapers actively and promptly exert a strikebreaking influence; that most churches do so passively.

The steel strike made tens of thousands of citizens believe that our American institutions are not democratic or not democratically administered.

The basis of such beliefs will be hastily summarized here.

Local magistrates, police authorities, etc., around Pittsburgh were very frequently steel mill officials or relatives of mill officials. Therefore, when a striker was taken before public-officials, he was likely to suspect connections between his fate and the steel company's desires. In many other cases officials of mills personally gave the orders for arrests. And they made decisions as to whether arrested workers should be jailed, generally after learning whether or not the striker would return to work.

The charges on which strikers were arraigned before local magistrates, then imprisoned or fined, were often never recorded and never learned by the prisoners.

The Commission of Inquiry of the Interchurch World Movement, **Report on the Steel Strike of 1919** (New York: Harcourt Brace Jovanovich, Inc., 1920) pp. 238-244. Abridged. Reprinted by permission.

Arraigned means that a person has been called before a court to answer a charge or an accusation.

Arrested men were frequently taken, not to jail, but inside the steel mill and held there. The charges of beatings, and clubbings, often substantiated by doctors' and eye-witnesses' sworn statements, were endless and monotonous. In most communities the only public official to appeal to turned out to be a mill official.

The feeling of the steelworkers, then, might be summed up thus: Local and national government not only was not their government but was government in behalf of interests opposing theirs. In strike times government activities tended to break strikes.

FOR THOUGHT:

Suppose the steel companies had hired you after the strike as a consultant on employee relations. What advice would you have offered?

67 THE POLITICS OF WORK

HISTORICAL ESSAY

During the nineteenth century, the social setting of industrial work was changed by several major developments. This essay begins by discussing them.

First, the maximum efficient size of individual manufacturing plants increased. At any given stage of technology, there is a point of maximum efficiency. Beyond this point, the production process often ceases to be efficient. For example, an extra assembly area for automobiles increases the cost of producing additional units. In the first half of the nineteenth century, this point of maximum efficiency was such that most individual factories were very small. The average plant had around five to ten employees. The largest plant had a few hundred. Through the rest of the century, technological innovations changed this point of maximum efficiency dramatically. Many small shops remained in business. But the largest factories were enormous. Homestead, where Charles Walker worked, employed about four thousand workers.

Second, the number of functions performed by individual firms also increased. During most of the nineteenth century, typical American manufacturing firms performed one process upon one product. A foundry turned coal, iron ore, and limestone into pig iron which it then sold. Even the marketing of the product was often left to another firm.

In the last third of the century, this pattern began to change. Many innovative business people decided that they could increase company profits by performing additional functions. For example, Andrew Carnegie's company began by building bridges. It grew by acquiring the foundries which produced the iron and steel used in bridge construction. Carnegie then acquired coal and iron mines and the railroad cars and ships needed to transport these raw materials. As steel beams rather than rails became the firm's major product, the marketing department took a leading role.

Third, in major industries, a few large firms developed monopoly power. Industry may be described on a scale from pure competition to monopoly. A competitive industry is one in which no single producer can significantly influence the price at which his or her products are sold. At the opposite economic extreme is monopoly. In a monopolistic situation, a single producer has complete control of the production, and thus the price of a good or service. The producer cannot force consumers to buy its product. But, if they wish to purchase it, they must pay the monopolist's price.

▶Should producers of goods and services be able to charge whatever they wish for their goods and services as long as people will pay it? Why, or why not?

▶The people who work on this assembly line do the same small task over and over again each day. Although they are well paid, there is a high turnover rate and a high absentee rate because the work is so boring. How willing are you to study hard in order to prepare yourself for work offering greater psychological rewards?

By the end of the nineteenth century, several major manufacturing and food processing industries came close to exercising monopoly power in their particular area. For example, there were many steel companies. But they all tended to follow the price leadership of Carnegie and then of United States Steel. They tended to act as if they were a single company. As early as 1880, the Standard Oil Company, organized by John D. Rockefeller, refined more than 90 percent of the nation's oil. This gave the firm monopoly power over the prices charged to consumers, the money paid to owners of oil wells, and the payments to railroads.

Monopoly power could be gained in several different ways. An individual firm might grow very large, or competitive firms might merge. According to British and American law, such tactics were not illegal. But groups of firms acting together to control markets broke age-old prohibitions against "conspiracies in restraint of trade." The best example of this kind of control is a *pool*, in which a group of producers agreed to limit production or to set prices. For example, in 1887 the manufacturers of rail set up a pool giving a quota to each manufacturer and giving financial penalties if the quota were exceeded. Fines were also distributed to those producers who had not fulfilled their quotas. Thus the pool was able to fix prices.

Pools had certain defects. They could be successfully operated only during good times. When business was good, the members of the pools followed their agreements. But during times of depression, when there was not enough work to go around, some manufacturers broke their agreements and lowered their prices. Pools proved to be unworkable.

Another method of controlling markets was the *trust*, in which one board of trustees ran several companies in related industries. One example of a trust was the Standard Oil Company. In 1882, the stockholders of this company gave control of the company to a group of nine "trustees." They were empowered to set prices and control production. Within a few years, these same nine men acquired control of most of the other refining companies in the nation. They could run these companies without being accountable to the public since they were not legally the owners. The stockholders still owned them. For a while, trusts dominated whole industries.

The creation of monopolies allowed individual plants and firms to grow beyond the point of maximum efficiency. In a competitive industry, an owner would be penalized for going beyond this point. As the growth of a plant led to higher prices for its products, competing plants would be able to undersell it. But, in a monopoly setting, inefficient production could still lead to higher profits, for there would be no competitors.

Fourth, the characteristic forms of business were changed to accumulate capital more efficiently. For centuries, business people in

448

western Europe and America had joined in complex partnerships to finance trading expeditions and transportation projects. By the mid-1800's, a type of corporation in which the partners were simply shareholders with little influence on the business as well as little responsibility for it were common. These corporations were used to organize banks and for canal and railroad ventures. In the late 1800's, corporations spread rapidly into manufacturing. The shares of manufacturing companies were bought and sold freely on stock exchanges.

Change Brings Problems

Each of these developments was shaped by conscious decisions of business people. Together these developments increased both the size and complexity of industrial work. They also brought problems. An individual employing forty or fifty workers could know each of them by name. Such personal involvement was impossible in larger firms. Size also brought new problems involved in controlling production. For example, no one person could supervise the four thousand people employed at the Homestead plant of Carnegie Steel.

Size created other problems, too. The technology which made large and efficient factories and mills possible reduced the number of places in the productive process requiring human labor. Hence, the pace of factory life came to be set by the machines, not by the workers. This pace has come to be symbolized by the assembly line. (See page 349.) By 1914, Henry Ford had perfected the assembly line process at his automobile factory to the point where he could produce more than a thousand cars a day. The assembly line cut down the need for skilled craft workers. It made mass production of an item more efficient. But it also cut down the amount of a worker's personal involvement in his or her work. And this development began to generate boredom and discontent in the factory.

▶ How do you feel about a teacher or a counselor who does not learn your name for several weeks or even months? Why do you feel that way?

The Response of Management and Workers

The first management response to these problems was a crude form of decentralization. Managers gave more power to foremen. Foremen were told how much to produce and given raw materials, a budget, and the authority to hire and fire workers. If they could meet their goal below the estimated costs, they could keep all or some of the savings for themselves. For many individual workers, these foremen loomed as petty tyrants. They were more important to the workers than central management because they had virtually absolute control over their workers' lives. However, this first response became inadequate to the central managers.

449

The second management response was, therefore, a set of strategies which came to be called "scientific management." Researchers were hired to analyze each step in the process of production. They then established work norms—how many shovelfuls per hour, or how many lathe operations per minute. The analysts would often recommend that a step in the production process be further subdivided in order to increase efficiency. They recommended, too, that workers who did not meet these norms should be fired.

Another response of management was to turn to welfare capitalism. Many managers offered a number of welfare programs such as those described in Reading 65. Some owners even formed company unions dominated by men sympathetic to management in order to make their workers feel that they shared in important decisions.

The full history of the worker response to the developments which changed the nature of work has yet to be written. Many historians have commented on the readiness with which Americans accepted industrial discipline. There was very little machine-breaking or factory-burning. Until the twentieth century, employees did not—or were not able—to insist that they "owned" their jobs and that employers should compensate them for changes in work patterns. However, workers did attempt, though not always successfully, to respond forcefully to the problems they faced at work. The creation of unions was part of this response.

Figure 67A provides information on labor union membership between 1870 and 1930. As you can see, the union movement grew slowly during this period. And the number of union members represented only a small proportion of the total number of industrial workers. However, the figures are not a measure of the workers' desire for unions. They are only a measure of actual union membership.

▶ Ask your parents if they have ever felt as if they "owned" some part of a job. Why did they feel that way?

U.S. Bureau of the Census, Historical Statistics of the United States, Colonial Times to 1957 (Washington, D.C.: Government Printing Office, 1960), pp. 72, 98.

FIGURE 67A   UNION MEMBERSHIP, 1870-1930

Year	Average annual union membership	Number of workers, 10 years and over, excluding agricultural workers	Union membership as a percentage of the total number of workers outside agriculture
1870	300,000°	6,075,000	4.9%
1880	200,000°	8,807,000	2.3%
1890	372,000°	13,380,000	2.7%
1900	868,000	18,161,000	4.8%
1910	2,140,000	25,779,000	8.3%
1920	5,048,000	30,985,000	16.3%
1930	3,393,000	38,358,000	8.8%

° Figures for 1870, 1880, and 1890 are estimates.

Governmental attitudes were largely responsible for low union membership. Both state and national laws had long been hostile to labor unions. Early in the nineteenth century, the courts frequently treated unions as if they were criminal conspiracies organized to raise wages "unnaturally." The courts often held unions responsible for harm to the property of their employers during strikes. They accused unions of encouraging employees to break their contracts. They also held unions responsible for encouraging consumers to boycott the products of anti-union employers. Judges frequently issued injunctions that forbade strikes or boycotts. Police, militia, and the regular army enforced these court orders.

An injunction is a court order issued by a judge without a jury trial. It requires that a certain party refrain from taking a certain action.

With minor exceptions, the national government had not had to express any view of labor disputes until the last third of the nineteenth century. Unionization of the interstate railroad network in the 1870's repeatedly forced the national hand. Federal troops intervened to suppress strikes in Baltimore, Pittsburgh, Toledo, Chicago, St. Louis, and San Francisco in 1877. In 1894, a strike in the Pullman works, where sleeping cars were built, spread to the railway workers themselves. It was suppressed by a combination of a United States federal court order and federal troops. During World War I, the government attitude softened. In order to avoid disruption of production, President Woodrow Wilson established administrative boards to regulate industrial relations. The result of this change in government attitude is apparent in the union membership figures for 1920. The steel strike of 1919 brought an end to this era of good feeling. And the return to the normal pattern is apparent in the 1930 membership figures.

George Pullman was the first person to build a railroad sleeping car. He also developed the idea of dining and parlor cars to make rail travel more comfortable.

This hostile atmosphere generated three different responses among active union members. The first response centered in an organization called the Noble and Holy Order of the Knights of Labor. It was founded by Uriah Stephens and began to recruit members in 1869. The Knights tried to appeal to "all who toiled." It concentrated, however, on local assemblies composed primarily of already organized skilled workers and semiskilled workers with little previous union experience. At first, strikes were discouraged. And long platform statements marshalled support for a host of political measures. These included paper money, the eight-hour day, a national income tax, the abolition of child labor, prohibition of alcoholic beverages, cooperatives, and so on. In the mid 1880's the Knights prospered, rising to 700,000 members in 1886. And they struck more frequently. The national leadership, dominated by Terence V. Powderly, remained convinced, however, that only minor advantages could be obtained directly by wresting concessions from individual employers. To reach labor's goals, Powderly supported political activity and the development of cooperatives.

The people who belong to a cooperative factory or store own it together and share the profits.

The Knights collapsed after the Haymarket Affair. At a labor demonstration in Haymarket Square, Chicago, in May 1886, a bomb

Eight men were arrested. Seven men were sentenced to death. The eighth was given a 15-year sentence. Four were hanged, one committed suicide, and the other three were pardoned by Governor Altgeld in 1893. The actual bomb thrower was never identified.

thrown into the crowd killed seven persons. The public hysteria against labor militants which followed was in many places directed against the Knights. By 1890, they had barely 100,000 members.

The second response came from a varied group of men and women working in the socialist tradition. Today, a great many measures advocated by socialists at the beginning of the century have become accepted public policy. Yet few Americans now describe themselves as socialists. In 1900, however, large groups of native Americans and immigrants proudly wore the socialist label. They urged a wide range of programs. They advocated public ownership of the means of production, regulation of industry, redistribution of wealth through an income tax, and many similar proposals. In 1912, the Socialist party offered Eugene Debs as its candidate for President. He received 897,000 votes, 6 percent of those cast.

The most important union in the socialist tradition was the Industrial Workers of the World, popularly known as the "Wobblies." The IWW had its principal base among migratory workers in lumber, mining, and agriculture. Cut off from their families and often unable to vote, these men worked long hours at dangerous jobs for low pay. They became convinced that they would have to win complete control of industry through worker ownership in order to make fundamental improvements in their working lives. They became revolutionaries advocating forcible overthrow of the government and sabotage. When conditions became desperate in industries such as textiles, the IWW often led dramatic strikes, largely of unskilled immigrants. The immigrants, alarmed at talk of revolution, usually did not become permanent IWW members. The IWW collapsed during World War I when government repression deprived it of its leaders and relative prosperity turned the minds of workers away from thoughts of radical change.

The third and most effective response was the American Federation of Labor. It was a national alliance of skilled workers formed in 1886. The A. F. of L. was led by Samuel Gompers. Gompers thought that labor should work primarily for higher wages, shorter hours, and better working conditions. He did not believe that labor should align itself with a particular political party. Instead, Gompers felt, workers should reward friendly legislators of all parties with votes and punish the enemies of labor, no matter what their party affiliation, by working against them. He opposed talk of revolution or the use of violence. Most of the A. F. of L. unions were composed of skilled workers. Thus, they had the power to stop production in an industry because it could not run without the skills of union members.

A federation of industrial unions, the Committee for Industrial Organization (C.I.O.), was formed in 1935.

The A. F. of L. approach was successful for its members. But it could not easily be extended, as Gompers discovered in the steel strike of 1919, to large national corporations employing masses of relatively unskilled workers. Until there was a shift in both union strategies and government support, the history of the 1919 steel strike would be repeated over and over.

452

Wild West and Wild Cities

STATING THE ISSUE

During the late nineteenth century, the United States expanded on two frontiers. Cattle ranchers, farmers, lumberjacks, and miners opened one frontier on the vast stretch of land west of Kansas and Nebraska. American and European ex-farmers with a few European city dwellers opened the other on the streets of the nation's rapidly growing cities. On the surface, the western and the urban frontiers seem different. Yet their problems had much in common.

Settlers on both frontiers had to make new rules for owning and controlling land, for example. In medieval Europe, land ownership had involved an elaborate network of social privileges and responsibilities. In the centuries that followed, the concept of property had become restricted to mean primarily the owner's right to use a piece of real estate freely. In every new situation, however, the rights and privileges of owners had to be redefined as new questions arose. In the West, did ownership of land imply a right of access to water, a right to build a fence across a cattle trail, or a right to cultivate soil freely, even if cultivation led to erosion? In the new cities, could property owners do anything they wanted to on their lands—slaughter animals, throw clouds of smoke and soot into the air, crowd tenants into a room, dump sewage in their yards?

A second important question the men and women of both frontiers confronted involved maintaining law and order in their societies. In the new West, for example, who would stand for law and order in an area where everyone was a stranger and where settlements were too sparse to support elaborate law enforcement and judicial systems? In the cities, rapid growth and crowding strained the traditional patterns and institutions of justice even more severely. Chicago was probably a more dangerous place in the late nineteenth century than Cheyenne or Dodge City.

Chapter 18 examines the responses of western and urban frontier people to these and other problems. The essay at the end of the chapter analyzes the history of the western frontier during this period.

1836 President Andrew Jackson establishes Bureau of Indian Affairs

1848 Gold is discovered at Sutter's Fort in California

1849 Congress creates Department of the Interior

1859 Prospectors discover gold near Pike's Peak in California

1859 Comstock Lode is discovered in Nevada

1862 Congress passes Homestead Act

1867 "Long Drive" from Texas to Kansas is established

1869 The Central Pacific and the Union Pacific railroads are joined together at Promontory Point, Utah

1872 The first national park, Yellowstone, is established

1874 J. F. Glidden invents barbed wire

1875 The refrigerator car comes into common use

1886 United States troops capture the Apache chief, Geronimo

1887 Congress passes the Dawes Act

1893 Western Federation of Miners is organized

1895 Congress passes the Carey Act

1896 Gold is discovered in the Klondike

1902 Newlands Reclamation Act gives federal government authority to regulate irrigation

1924 Congress grants full citizenship to all Indians

68 PLANNING THE LAND AND WATER

Americans who moved beyond western Kansas took with them laws and patterns of behavior which had been developed in the settled areas of the East. Under the Homestead Act of 1862, the federal government offered to give farmers 160 acres of public land if they would live on the land and raise crops for five years. As a result, small farms spread across the countryside where there was adequate water for crops and enough timber for houses, barns, and fences.

The Great Plains beyond western Kansas lacked both adequate water and timber. This fertile but arid area challenged traditional methods of farming. Breaking up the tough sod of the plains demanded new, expensive plows. Acquiring water for animals and crops required complicated equipment to drill wells two or three hundred feet deep. Without wood, settlers built sod houses which they heated with dried buffalo dung. Or they imported lumber and fuel from the East.

Wheat farmers and cattle ranchers who moved into the area had to adapt their ways to these new conditions. The expense of breaking up the soil, drilling wells, irrigating and fencing the land, and constructing homes and farm buildings kept poor settlers from farming the plains profitably. Farmers with larger amounts of capital found 160 acres too little to justify investing in tools and machines. Ranchers required larger grazing areas for their animals.

On the frontiers of Montana and Wyoming, cattle grazers allowed enormous herds to roam freely over public lands. They often tried to fence off their own private preserves. Faced with an unsatisfactory land system, they resorted to evasion, fraud, and often violence. In 1885, William Andrew Jackson Sparks, a Federal Land Commissioner, attempted to enforce the laws and to safeguard millions of acres of public land from what he considered to be greedy cattle ranchers and lumberjacks. Westerners responded bitterly. They attacked "King" Sparks, who, they argued, dealt ignorantly with a complex situation. Reading 68 examines the controversy between Sparks and Governor Warren of Wyoming. As you read, consider these questions:

1. According to Sparks, how were federal laws violated? What evidence was there that the laws had not been made wisely?
2. Why did Governor Warren believe that the development of the new territory should proceed rapidly?

A Federal Land Commissioner's Report

William Andrew Jackson Sparks investigated the ways in which some individuals acquired public lands. Sparks believed that the practices he found prevented genuine settlers from getting land. Parts of his report to the Secretary of the Interior follow.

Report of the Secretary of the Interior (Washington, D.C.: Government Printing Office, 1885), Vol. 1, pp. 205-215 passim. Language simplified.

A public land entry was the application a settler made to secure legal title to public lands.

A meridian is half of a circle passing through the north and south poles. On a map the meridian is represented by lines of longitude running north and south.

In preparing this report, I had before me many documents. They included the records of special agents and various inspectors, communications from United States attorneys and other officials, and letters from public men and private citizens throughout the country. All pointed to a common story of widespread, persistent land robbery committed under the mask of various forms of public land entry.

In many sections of the country, the investigations showed public land entries were chiefly fictitious and fraudulent. (This is especially true of regions west of the ninety-ninth meridian. These regions are dominated by cattle-raising interests.) The entries were made largely through methods adopted by organizations that parceled out land among themselves. They maintained possession of unentered lands with armed riders. By using systems of espionage and intimidation, they kept out settlers.

In farming regions near the cattle belt, speculation by individuals was covering whole townships of agricultural land. Entries were made for the purpose of selling the claims to others or for acquiring large parcels of land.

In timbered regions, the forests were being seized by domestic and foreign corporations through fraudulent entries that evaded the law. Newly discovered coal fields were seized and possessed in a similar way.

The following extracts are from general reports of officers of this department. They disclose the usual methods of fraudulent appropriation of land. And they indicate the extent to which it is carried on.

From A. R. Greene, Inspector, November 3, 1884

Generally speaking, I believe that fraudulent entries of the public lands include a large percent of the whole number.

▶ Should people get away with what they can? Or should everyone always abide by the letter of the law? Why do you think as you do?

The idea prevails almost universally that strict compliance with the conditions imposed is not essential. People do this because they believe that the government has generously given public lands to its citizens. Men who would scorn to commit a dishonest act toward an individual, even a total stranger, eagerly listen to every scheme for evading the settlement laws. In a majority of instances, I believe they practice such schemes.

Our land officers share this feeling in many instances. This is especially true with entries made under the Timber-Culture Law. At the very best, this law was a doubtful experiment at the start. Most of the lands upon which planted groves of trees could be grown without irrigation had passed from the government before it was enacted. Climate and neglect together have made its success by this time impossible.

The Timber-Culture Law passed in 1873 offered an additional quarter section (160 acres) to a settler who would plant 40 acres of it in timber.

The problem is not to encourage greater productivity from a climate and soil favorable to forest growth. Rather it is a question of trying to make forests grow on unfriendly soil amid blighting winds. The experiment had about as much chance of success as an effort to make water flow uphill. I doubt if the trees standing on any timber-culture entry west of the one hundredth meridian would stop a mild breeze.

I have seen small patches of land, possibly five acres, where the prairie had been furrowed and an occasional sickly cottonwood sprout stands two or three feet high. In other cases, the land had evidently been honestly plowed at some time. But through neglect it had grown up again to grass. The trees were holding up their tiny branches in silent protest against the absurdity of the law.

A more vicious system of fraudulent entries has been practiced successfully by and in the interests of cattlemen and stock corporations.

The pictures on this page show two scenes from films about the American West.
How do these scenes relate to the report of William Andrew Jackson Sparks?

If the law had been enacted solely for their benefit it could scarcely have been more successful. A "cattle king" employs a number of cowboys. The herd is located on a favorable portion of the public lands where grass, water, and shelter are convenient. Each cowboy is required to make a timber-culture entry of lands along the stream. These entries often very nearly, if not quite, occupy all the watered lands in a township. They make the remaining lands undesirable for actual settlement for farming purposes. Settlers avoid such places as they would districts stricken with a plague.

From Special Agent T. H. Cavenaugh, Olympia, Washington Territory, November 8, 1884

The country lying west of the Cascade Range of mountains and north of the Columbia River in Washington Territory is a vast and almost impenetrable forest. The frauds attempted in this district are prompted solely by a desire to secure the valuable timber lands for lumbering purposes.

The way to secure lands under the Act of 1878, is for a party interested in acquiring timber to be appointed a notary public for Washington Territory. This authorizes him to act in any county in the territory. He then establishes himself close to the lands which he intends to secure. All papers pertaining in any way to entries are made before him. All the papers, acts, and facts concerning the entries are in his possession. Notaries public in this territory are not by law required to keep a record of their official acts. Therefore, there can be no inspection to prove or to determine the rate of the entry, acknowledgment of deeds, mortgages, etc.

The Timber and Stone Act of 1878 offered for sale 160 acres of timber land in California, Nevada, Oregon, and Washington at $2.50 an acre.

A notary public is an official authorized to notarize, or certify, legal documents.

A deed is a notarized document that records a transfer of property from one owner to another.

Report of the Secretary of the Interior, Vol. II, pp. 1007-1009. Language simplified.

A Governor's Protest

In 1886, Wyoming was not yet a state. The President appointed the governor, who closely represented the interests of the area's ranchers. Portions of Governor Francis E. Warren's protest to Sparks's report follow.

Efforts of the General Land Office to protect the public domain of the United States for actual settlers and to prevent frauds are commendable. But if an overenthusiastic course is pursued and the acquisition of land by genuine entrymen is made too difficult, very great injury is done to the people whom such efforts are intended to benefit.

The public lands of the United States should pass as rapidly as possible into the hands of private owners. However, this should always be done through lawful settlement and improvement. The growth and success of our country largely depend upon the development of new territory.

From close observation, it is estimated that more than three fourths of the rejected land proofs today affect the poorer classes. The entries are made in good faith. And they are entirely free from fraud or double dealing. But, in many cases, people are unable on this arid land to support their families. They cannot make necessary improvements on their homesteads. And they cannot live entirely off their land as the law requires. Settlers frequently must leave their land to work for wages in order to secure food and the necessary means to make improvements.

If this is so, should not the Land Office display greater leniency and liberality? It must be remembered that Wyoming is not a natural garden spot. In Iowa, Nebraska, Kansas, and other states, every acre requires but to turn the sod to grow abundant crops. In this territory agricultural products, aside from the sparse native grasses—fit only for grazing—cannot be produced except through expensive, long-term irrigation. In fact, months of patient labor must be expended in getting water upon the land. Perhaps years must then pass before agricultural crops can be produced, if at all.

It should be kept in mind that the laws made to cover the fertile lands of the older eastern states are not applicable to the arid lands of Wyoming. They should be made more generous to the settler. And they should be applicable to the arid condition of this country.

It is true that settlers are not forced to settle on public lands. And the government can afford to hold these lands. But it is nevertheless true that the government is of the people and for the people. And these lands belong to the settler under traditional rights, subject only to legal and proper rules and regulations. On principle, a person should receive the benefit of a doubt in making final proof of his or her land claim. He should not be subject to the arbitrary rule that all doubts shall be held against him and that he shall be considered dishonest until he proves himself honest.

FOR THOUGHT:

How were the issues described in this reading the product of a different environment?

69 PLANNING THE SEWERS

Cities grew in all regions of the United States during the late nineteenth century. New cities developed close to established urban areas in the East. Marketing towns sprang up across the countryside with the increase of crops raised to be sold. From the beginning, the mining industries of the Rocky Mountain states were centered in cities. By 1910, every region of the country, except the

Land proofs were evidence that the applicant for public lands had complied fully with the requirement for obtaining title to the land. Such requirements might include improvement of or settlement on the land or the payment of legal fees or purchase money.

▶ Do you agree that laws should be adapted to the needs of a particular area of the country? of a particular group of people? Why or why not?

Southwest, included a city with more than 100,000 people. The urban giants—New York, Chicago, and Philadelphia— had grown at a rate unknown in all previous history.

The enormous concentration of people in the new cities posed a number of interrelated problems. In large mid-nineteenth-century cities, for example, men and women moved about either on foot or in horse-drawn buses. Only a very small percentage of the population enjoyed the privilege of private, horse-drawn transportation. As urban population mushroomed, limited transportation systems required changes in land use and patterns of life. For cities to support large-scale industry, people had to be housed densely near centrally located factories. Or industry had to spread throughout the city so that people could get to work easily.

As each city grew, a balance was struck between these solutions. In Philadelphia, small, privately owned row houses spread across the metropolis. And industrial centers spread with them. In Boston, four-story houses concentrated the labor force. And in New York, five-story tenements became the main form of workers' housing.

The housing patterns in each city changed with the introduction of new methods of transportation. The largest cities built elevated railroads, and in a few cases, subways. These allowed the population to spread out. Electric streetcars were even more common. By 1895, there were ten thousand miles of trolley lines operating in American cities. Settlements stretched along the trolley tracks.

A city is a complex system of interrelated parts. Almost any urban problem involves complex relationships with other problems. Reading 69 focuses on the problem of water and waste removal in two cities. As you read, try to answer these questions:

1. How were sewage problems related to housing patterns? to transportation systems? to the use of the land?
2. Why weren't the sewer systems better planned and maintained?

Sewer Systems in
Two American Cities

These selections are drawn from the first comprehensive survey of American cities. It was prepared as part of the 1880 census.

San Francisco, California

The total length of sewers constructed up to 1880 is about 126 miles. Of these, about 75 miles had been constructed at the time of the preparation of a complete sewer plan (1876) by William P. Humphreys, city and county surveyor. Mr. Humphreys describes the condition of the sewers existing at that time as follows:

Department of the Interior Census Office, **Report on the Social Statistics of Cities,** compiled by George E. Waring, Jr. (Washington, D.C.: Government Printing Office, 1887) Vol. I, pp. 823, 825, 830, and Vol. II, p. 807. Language simplified.

"Most of these sewers are of brick. But their cost has been too high, because, among other reasons, they have been unnecessarily large. Most of the streets in the older portion of the city have brick sewers. They extend up the hillsides to irregular distances. In the lower portions of the city, the foundation is not sufficiently solid to sustain a brick sewer without pilings. There the sewers are of wood. And they are generally level, or nearly level. Being down, or nearly down, to low water, the tide rises and falls in them. It so checks their outflow that most of them are today nothing more than long cesspools badly choked with offensive sewage matter. This evil must go on increasing from year to year until some change is made.

"In fact, the existing sewers in the city have been built without regard to a system for the general drainage of the city. Each sewer appears to have been built independent of all others and without regard to the duty it has to perform. Some of the alleys and short streets in the city, for instance, where there are only a few houses, have sewers of the same size as those in the larger streets.

"San Francisco Bay with its great size and its strong tidal currents, affords great facilities for getting rid of the city's sewage. But to make the Bay useful the sewers must be carried out to points where there are strong currents. If they stop short, the lower parts of the city must always remain in an offensive and unhealthy condition.

"Along the busy waterfront of the city some of the sewers do not extend out into the Bay. They stop short, ending inside of the rubble-stone bulkhead. There the offensive solid matter is deposited. The liquid matter is allowed to escape as best it can. This makes the slips between the wharves at times offensive to the last degree of endurance. All of these sewers should be carried out to the ends of the wharves. There they should discharge their contents through a bent hood, leading from the outer end of the sewer down below the level of low water. The tide will then speedily remove the sewage matter away from the city. And there will be no offensive smell about the wharves."

Philadelphia, Pennsylvania

There is no system of inspection of sewers in Philadelphia. Few persons have ever been in them except workmen to make the necessary repairs. These people enter the sewers only at rare intervals, for repairs and connections are almost invariably made from the outside. Hence the condition of the inside of sewers is unknown. Moreover, it appears to be uncared for, so long as water turned into them gets away and does not come back to the surface or flow into cellars or basements. When, therefore, anybody proposes to go into a sewer to find out its sanitary defects and condition, he is met with expressions of genuine astonishment and surprise on the part of the city officials.

The first indication that a sewer is out of order is that the street caves in. The break is mended and the street and pavement are

Pilings are heavy timbers or beams driven into the ground to support bridges, docks, buildings, or sewers.

A cesspool is an underground pit or basin that collects drainage and other household filth.

A bulkhead in a harbor is a wall or embankment built to hold back the water. A slip is a place between piers for a ship to enter.

▶ Should cities pay people who do unpleasant work such as maintaining sewers more than they pay people with similar skills who do more pleasant work? Why or why not?

461

restored. But nobody knows or cares what becomes of the rubbish, bricks, and paving stones that have fallen into the sewer. It is supposed that these are washed away by the water. But when one walks through a sewer he learns better. Even in large main pipes where there is a great rush of storm-water, the heavier rubbish, such as loose bricks and paving stones, are met farthest down stream. And behind these accumulate the different grades of pebble, gravel, sand, and mud. The slackwater backed up behind all shows the deposits still to be in progress.

Several things impress themselves very strongly on the mind of any person who goes into the sewers of Philadelphia.

First. The city needs a system of maintenance and repairs to keep the interior clear of the rubbish, bricks, paving-stones, and debris falling in from the many breaks which recur constantly. It may be assumed that any system of public works worth building is worth maintaining in repair when it is built. If it is worthwhile to expend $14,000 to $15,000 a mile to build branch sewers, it is also worthwhile to pick up and remove the building refuse and rubbish left in them by the masons and workmen. Then the water may have some chance to flow through when they are done. There are about 200 miles of public sewers in Philadelphia. In them about 400 to 500 breaks occur every year. On the average this is not far from one break per year for every half mile of sewer. Hence it seems quite essential that the rubbish and debris from so many places should be taken out before the whole system of underground work gets filled up.

Second. The sewers of Philadelphia are obliged to carry almost everything which a great population wants to get rid of. Probably it is quite unavoidable that much kitchen waste, garbage, and liquid garbage should find its way into the sewers. But there seems to be no good reason why they should be filled up with ashes and cinders, cast-off clothing, boots and shoes, broken dishes and glass, the waste products from slaughter-houses and markets, or the steam and hot water from factories and machine shops.

The Philadelphia sewer system presents many serious difficulties. At present the sewage is discharged at different points along the river front, mainly into the Delaware River. The river cannot be expected to dispose completely and properly of the sewage of the enormous population. The area of the city is being greatly extended. Hundreds of acres are being covered by small houses occupied by single families. This presents difficulties when we consider gathering together and transporting to a proper outlet the immense volume of foul sewage. The working classes of New York and other large cities are concentrated in limited areas. Tenement houses of five and six stories, with four families on each floor, are not as satisfactory as the houses occupied by the same class of people in Philadelphia. There each family has its own house, open both front and rear to the light and air. However,

Masons are skilled workers who build structures with bricks or stones.

▶ Should the national or state governments have power to force cities, industries, or individuals to stop polluting water? Why or why not?

462

Third Annual Conference

1973 COMPOSTING and WASTE RECYCLING CONFERENCE

May 3 – 4, 1973   St. Louis, Missouri

Theme: USING MUNICIPAL WASTES IN AGRICULTURE

AGENDA:

Latest Developments in Composting: Equipment and Methods

Composting Sewage Sludge

The Role of Haulers and the Secondary Materials Industry in Resource Recovery Projects

European Experiences with Applying Sludge to Land

United States Studies in Sludge Application to Land

Landfill and Composting--Differences and Similarities

Nitrogen Fertilization, City Wastes and Farming Methods

The pictures on this page show some of the problems which modern cities face as they try to dispose of waste products. How are these problems like those which San Francisco and Philadelphia faced in 1887?

PRO   Should Primary Control Of Anti-Pollution Efforts Rest With The Federal Government?   CON

by HON. CHARLES E. GOODELL
United States Senator, New York, Republican

by HON. BENJAMIN B. BLACKBURN.
United States Representative, Georgia, Republican

the removal of liquid wastes is a simple proposition in New York compared with the problem of providing all of Philadelphia's thousands of scattered houses with proper connections with a proper sewer system.

The work done on Philadelphia's sewers includes some well-planned and well-constructed main sewers. The system as a whole, however, is totally and inexcusably bad. It violates nearly every accepted principle of sanitary engineering. And it inevitably counteracts those natural influences which are so favorable to the health of a population.

The question of the universal sanitary improvement of the city is one of the greatest importance. There are about 2000 miles of streets in the city. Population is rapidly extending in every direction. There are at this time (1880) less than 200 miles of sewers, all told. A very large proportion are entirely unsuited for the use for which they were intended.

To construct proper sewers throughout the city, to secure the needed remodeling of house-drainage, and to provide for the permanent unobjectionable disposal of the city's filth, would involve an expenditure of money and an application of engineering skill hardly called for in any other city of the civilized world.

FOR THOUGHT:

How were the problems described in this reading the product of a different environment? How do these problems compare to land and water problems in the West?

70 LAW AND VIOLENCE IN THE CITIES AND THE WEST

From the very beginnings of American history, violence has been associated with frontier settlements. The image of frontier violence, however, is a combination of a realistic appraisal of the facts with myths created in people's minds. People back in the old settlement wanted to believe that the frontier was an exciting place where the rules of civilization were relaxed. In their minds, people and nature were both magnificent and untamed.

Each frontier has enjoyed a reputation for rough-hewn violence. In the popular imagination of today, only the cattle frontiers retain the image. It is an image magnified by movies and television into the major violent American experience.

Since the eighteenth century, large cities throughout Europe and America have also had a reputation for danger. This reputation, however, did not have the same exciting overtones that the West enjoyed. Medieval European cities had symbolized personal safety. But few people thought of eighteenth-century Paris or London as places of personal security. When Thomas Jefferson warned Americans of the dangers inherent in the growth of cities, he was, among other things, warning of riots, robberies, and murders. Alexis de Tocqueville's account of the United States in the early 1830's indicated his fear that New York and Philadelphia might be overtaken by unruly mobs. Violence was common in American cities around 1900.

The historical image of cities as centers of violence and danger has been largely forgotten. As a result, discussions of today's high crime rates or riots confuse people's view of the present. Superficial commentators on the American scene report that Americans were once secure, but are now sliding into an abyss of urban violence. However, the crime rate in the nineteenth century was probably higher than it is today.

Reading 70 looks at nineteenth-century cities from two perspectives. It examines the police as a source of violence in New York City in the 1890's. And it examines labor disputes as sources of violence on the western frontier. As you read, try to answer these questions:

1. What were the causes of the violence described in each selection?
2. Why did some Americans believe that police departments and courts were taking sides in a war between social groups rather than acting as fair exponents of justice?

Police Brutality, 1895

The Democratic party usually controlled New York City government. The Republicans normally held a majority of the seats in the New York State Legislature. Every once in a while, Republicans in the legislature decided to show "just how badly" the city Democrats were doing. This selection is from a report of a legislative committee on New York City police, prepared in 1895.

Persons in the humbler walks of life were subjected to horrible outrages. They were abused, clubbed, and imprisoned. They were even convicted of crime on false testimony by policemen and their accomplices. People in business were harassed and annoyed in their affairs. They, too, were forced to bend their necks to the police yoke so that they might share that so-called protection which seemed necessary to their affairs. People from all walks of life seemed to feel that to antagonize the police was to call down upon themselves the swift judgment and persecution of an invulnerable force. The Police Department is so thoroughly entrenched in the municipal government as to defy ordinary attacks. It is strong in itself. And it is united by self-interest and the common goal of unlawful gain.

Report and Proceedings of the Senate Committee Appointed to Investigate the Police Department of the City of New York (Albany: James B. Lyon, 1895), Vol. I, pp. 25-32. Language simplified.

The poor, ignorant foreigner residing on the great east side of the city has been especially subjected to a brutal and infamous rule by the police. In the lower criminal courts, it is beyond a doubt that innocent people who have refused to yield to criminal extortion, have been clubbed and harassed and confined in jail.

It is generally agreed that the municipal police are unsurpassed in efficiency and desire to protect life and property upon New York streets.

It is a significant fact that little corruption has been traced into the pockets of the ordinary patrolman. His sins are mainly abuse of physical force, infringement upon the rights and privileges of private citizens, and failure to reveal the criminal conduct of his superiors.

▶ Should private citizens bring charges against officials, such as police officers, who treat them badly? Why or why not?

A stream of witnesses poured continuously into the sessions of the committee. Their testimony proved that many of the members of the force, and even superior officers, have abused the physical power which has been given to them. In making arrests and in restraining disorder, they gratify personal spite and brutal instincts by reducing their victims to a servile condition. Even in the eyes of our foreign-born residents our institutions have been degraded. Those who have fled from oppression abroad have come here to be oppressed in a professedly free and liberal country.

It appears, therefore, that the police formed a separate and highly privileged class. They are armed with the authority and the machinery for oppression and punishment. But they are practically free themselves from the workings of the criminal law.

We emphasize finding police brutality because it affects every citizen, whatever his or her condition. It shows an invasion of constitutional liberty by one of the departments of government, whose supreme duty is to enforce the law. And it establishes a condition gravely endangering safety and welfare.

Violence on the Mining Frontier

In many places on the timber and mining frontiers of the West, a small number of employers dominated local business and government. Workers in these areas often felt that they had little control over either their working lives or their political fortunes. The labor unions formed by miners and loggers frequently expressed the idea that democracy was a sham, cloaking the power of a few rich people. Meetings between angry union members and powerful employers often led to violence. This selection is from a report on a bitter strike in Idaho Springs, Colorado.

466

In the spring of 1903, there was a strike of gold miners at Idaho Springs in Clear Creek County. They struck for a working day of eight hours, with no reduction of wages.

The Sun and Moon mine had employed about 125 men before the strike. It resumed operations, on June 8, with a small non-union force. By July 1 it had about 70 employees.

Shortly after 11 o'clock on the night of July 28 there was a terrific explosion at the Sun and Moon mine. It was caused by kegs of dynamite. They were rolled down the hillside and wrecked the transformer house. As it happened, the only loss of life was one of the dynamiters, a union man.

Deputy sheriffs began scouring the hills for the dynamiter or dynamiters. Meanwhile other deputy sheriffs visited the homes of officers and members of the miners' union. They placed them under arrest, and confined them in jail. Thirteen were arrested during the night and others the next day.

A meeting to denounce the crime was called by the Citizens' Protective League. This was an association of mine owners and businessmen. It had been organized at the beginning of the strike at Idaho Springs.

Lafayette Hanchette, manager of the Lamartine mine and president of the First National Bank of Idaho Springs, said: "Don't do anything unlawful. But we can't have bad citizens among good ones. We must get rid of them. I now move that it is the sentiment of this meeting that we go to the jail and there take the prisoners and escort them to the edge of the city limits and tell them firmly to go and never return."

The chairman then put the motion. It was carried with a shout. The meeting broke up and the people started for the county jail. The crowd was composed of about five hundred citizens, including many business and professional people. On reaching the jail they demanded the prisoners. The three guards were required to give up the keys and the door was unlocked. Fourteen of the twenty-three men in the jail were ordered out. All of these men were members of the Western Federation of Miners.

With the fourteen union men in front the crowd moved down the main street to the extreme eastern end of the city, more than a mile away. At that point Lafayette Hanchette told the fourteen men that the citizens of Idaho Springs would not condone violence. He said that they were convinced that at least some of the men had instigated the plot to dynamite the Sun and Moon mine, and also planned to assassinate certain mine managers. He said that the citizens had decided that these men must leave and never return. "Never show your faces in Clear Creek County again," he said. "If you do we will not be responsible for what may happen to you. A very considerable element here has been for hanging you men. But the conservative

A Report on Labor Disturbances in the State of Colorado, From 1880 to 1904, Inclusive, Senate Document No. 122, 58th Congress, 3rd Session (Washington, D.C.: Government Printing Office, 1905), pp. 151-159. Language simplified.

A transformer is an apparatus used in telephones, radios, and common electrical appliances, for the purpose of increasing or decreasing the voltage of an electric current.

The Western Federation of Miners was organized in 1893 in the Rocky Mountain area. Its goals were higher wages, an eight-hour day, and laws establishing safety regulations for the mines. From the start, the union became involved in a long series of strikes. Leaders of the Western Federation of Miners helped to organize the Industrial Workers of the World (Wobblies).

citizens have prevailed. They expect you to keep moving until you get out of the state. Don't stop in Denver except long enough to get aid from your Federation."

On July 30, the executive committee of the Citizens' Protective League issued the following statement: "The members of the union were given to understand from the first that so long as they were supporters of socialistic principles we would hold them responsible for any damage done to any property in the district. The people of Idaho Springs had reached the limit of endurance. This has never been a union stronghold. Our people believe that they would rather give up their homes and businesses than submit to policies of tyranny. The action of last night shows that the people will not submit to the dictation of a few imported union agitators. There may be some people who believe that the action was too radical. But for each of them, there are two others who believe that it was not radical enough."

On July 31, four additional union men were deported from Idaho Springs, and on the next day one more. On August 4, there was a meeting of the Citizens' Alliance at Denver with about five hundred present. Resolutions were adopted and the following is quoted from the preamble:

> Our attention has been called to the recent action of the Citizens' Protective League of Idaho Springs. Technically speaking, it was without due process of law. Yet, from the standpoint of expediency and self-defense, it was calculated to save lives, liberty, and property.
>
> Now, therefore, we, the Citizens' Alliance of Denver, believe that the business men of Idaho Springs acted within that higher and unwritten code of self-preservation to which resort must always be had by men when there is no speedy and adequate remedy at law.

The attorney of the deported men complained to the court about these actions. On August 10, 1903, Judge Frank W. Owers, sitting in the district court at Georgetown, granted an injunction. It restrained each and every member of the Citizens' Protective League from interfering with the deported men or preventing their return to their homes and business.

Eight of the deported men returned to Idaho Springs on August 11. On the complaint of Manager H. N. Sims, of the Sun and Moon mine, a police officer issued warrants for the arrest of the eight men. They were charged with destroying the transformer house. On the same day, they were confined in the city jail.

On complaint of the attorney of the deported men, Judge Owers issued bench warrants for 129 citizens of Idaho Springs. He charged them with rioting, making threats, and assault. Most of these men

▶ Under what conditions, if any, are private groups justified in taking physical action against people whose principles and actions they disapprove?

The Fifth Amendment guarantees that no person shall be "deprived of life, liberty, or property without due process of law." The Fourteenth Amendment contains a similar clause, binding on the states.

468

were arrested. They gave bond for their appearance in the sum of $500 each. The deported men who had been reimprisoned were also released on bail.

In December 1903, John E. Chandler, financial secretary and business agent of the Federation in Idaho Springs, Foster Milburn, Ralph Sanborn, Frank Napoli, and Joseph Carbonetti were tried at Georgetown, Clear Creek County. They were charged with conspiracy to blow up the transformer house of the Sun and Moon mine. They were acquitted. But they were rearrested immediately, and brought to Central City, Gilpin County. They were charged with malicious mischief in blowing up the transformer house. In the trial at Central City, Chandler was acquitted in June 1904. And Milburn was acquitted in July 1904. After this the district attorney dropped the cases against Sanborn, Napoli, and Carbonetti.

In the district court at Georgetown on February 8, 1904, District Attorney H. G. Thurman entered a *nolle prosequi* in each of the cases against the citizens charged with rioting and making threats and assaults when they drove union miners away from Idaho Springs. F. F. Richardson had been engaged to aid in the prosecution. He severely criticized the action of the district attorney. Mr. Richardson said that it seemed that pressure had been brought to bear. He said it seemed as though there was one law for influential citizens and another for poor people. He further declared that in his whole experience at the bar he had never known a case to be dropped with the evidence so clear and convincing.

After the union miners were deported from Idaho Springs only non-union men were able to secure employment in the mines there.

FOR THOUGHT:

In what ways are the issues described in the reading the result of trying to adjust to new environments?

71 TAMING THE FRONTIER

HISTORICAL ESSAY

During the period between 1860 and 1890, the most important American frontier lay in the West. Miners, cattle ranchers, and farmers closed in from both the East and from California on the Great Plains and the Rocky Mountain region. By 1890, the Bureau of the Census proclaimed that a clear frontier line no longer existed. Isolated spots of settlement now dotted every area of the nation. Settlement of the West continued for several decades after 1890. During these

To give bond means to pledge money or property as bail. This pledge releases an arrested person temporarily on assurance that he or she will appear in court at an appointed time for a trial.

Acquitted means to be found not guilty of the crime for which one has been brought to trial.

A district attorney is a lawyer elected or appointed in a specified district who serves as the prosecutor for the state in criminal cases.

A **nolle prosequi** is a formal notice made by a prosecutor that he or she will proceed no further in the prosecution of a criminal case.

Two of the Pacific coast states—California and Oregon—became states before the Civil War. The "last West," or last frontier, was the remaining area west of the states forming a line from Louisiana to Minnesota. The Census Bureau defined a frontier as any area having more than two persons but less than six persons per square mile.

decades, however, a larger number of people moved from the country-side to the city than from the settled areas into the West. The cities became America's most important frontier. This essay, however, concentrates on the events that took place on the western frontier. Reading 75 will trace the development of the modern urban frontier in greater detail.

The Native Americans

In the 1840's, farmers reached the eastern edge of the Great Plains, roughly at the ninety-ninth meridian. (See map, page 471.) Then, instead of moving steadily westward, the line of settlement jumped to the Pacific Coast. There tales of gold and rich lands drew settlers by the thousands. Fifteen hundred miles of plains and mountains stretched between these two settled areas. This territory included roughly one fifth of the total land area of the United States. On this land lived about 225,000 native Americans, a formidable obstacle to white settlement.

The Spanish explorer Francisco Vásquez de Coronado had first described the Indians of the plains in the sixteenth century. According to his account, they dressed in leather, lived in tepees, ate buffalo meat, and followed the buffalo herds on which their livelihood depended. Coronado admired these fearless people who could creep close to a buffalo herd on their hands and knees, covered with a wolf skin as a disguise, and bring down a giant animal with a single shot from a bow and arrow.

White settlers considered all the Indians of the plains as one group. The Indians, however, considered themselves Cheyenne, or Sioux, or Apache, and not part of a large group called Indians. They spoke different languages. They had separate ancestries. And, until the mid-eighteenth century, they shared no substantial common culture. The various tribes often fought each other. Thus, it was unlikely that they would unite against a common enemy.

But even in small numbers, the plains Indians were worthy foes. Their fearlessness, their determination to maintain their way of life, and their aroused anger when whites broke treaties and sent hunters and settlers to slaughter the buffalo upon which their livelihood depended all inspired them to resist. They battled bravely for their homelands against a ruthless enemy with a superior technology who was determined to exterminate them or to shut them up in reservations.

▶ If Indians lived on valuable mining sites, should whites have left them there and left the minerals undeveloped? If not, what should whites have done? Why?

The first serious invasions of Indian areas in the West came in California. In 1850, about 100,000 native Americans lived in California. Ten years later, only about 35,000 remained. White miners pushed the Indians from one valuable mining site after another. Penniless, starving, and homeless, they died off. The Commissioner of Indian

470

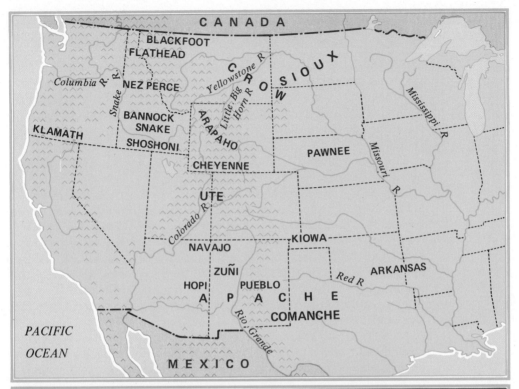

THE INDIAN FRONTIER, 1870

Affairs described the process: "They have been robbed by irresistible forces of the land of their fathers. There is no country on earth to which they can migrate. They live in the midst of a people with whom they cannot assimilate. They have no recognized claims upon the government and are compelled to become vagabonds—to steal or to starve." As miners pushed into the mountains and cattle ranchers and settlers invaded the Great Plains, this process was often repeated.

Before the Civil War, the Indians had fought intermittently with white settlers. Skirmishes increased in number during the war itself. In 1862, the Sioux tribes in the Dakotas went on the warpath. They killed almost a thousand settlers in Minnesota. Revenge fell swiftly upon innocent and guilty alike. Whites exacted a similar vengeance for attacks by the Cheyenne in Colorado in 1864. When the Civil War ended, the government sent 25,000 veteran troops to the frontier. During the next twenty or so years, warfare raged constantly. Occasionally, Indians would win an engagement. But numbers and superior technology eventually won out. The capture of the Apache chief, Geronimo (1886) marked the virtual end of Indian resistance.

471

Treaties that the American
government made with the
various tribes were often
complicated by cultural
differences. For example,
many tribes did not
understand the concept of
owning land, and not all
chiefs had the right to make
treaties for their people.

A Century of Dishonor was
written to protest the
government's injustices
toward the Indians.

The native American was
considered to be a "ward"
of the federal government
and a citizen of his or her
reservation. The Fourteenth
Amendment, which defined
citizenship, was never
interpreted to include native
Americans.

The Bureau of Indian Affairs
was set up in 1836 by
President Andrew Jackson. In
1849, the Department of the
Interior was created. The
Indian Bureau then became
part of that department.

A lode is a mineral deposit
that fills a vein or a crack in
a rock.

The entire process by which the native Americans were deprived of their lands or killed if they resisted invasion was filled with deceit and trickery. Treating each Indian tribe as if it were a sovereign nation like Great Britain or Germany was clearly unrealistic. Indians often did not understand the terms of treaties they signed. And men who negotiated these treaties often failed to explain them clearly. Railroads cheated tribes of their lands. Frontier people and soldiers subscribed widely to the notion that the only good Indian was a dead Indian.

The conscience of the nation, or at least of easterners who were not actively involved in the advancing frontier, was at last aroused. Stirred partly by Helen Hunt Jackson's book, *A Century of Dishonor*, Congress passed the Dawes Act in 1887. It established policy toward the native Americans for a half century. The Dawes Act dissolved the tribes as legal units and divided a tribe's land among its members. For twenty-five years, native Americans were forbidden to sell the land they had acquired in this way. Then they were to receive full legal rights to their land as well as citizenship. In 1924, Congress finally granted full citizenship to all native Americans, whether they had land or not.

Hailed as the Indian Emancipation Act, the Dawes Act instead proved to be a disaster for native Americans. Within fifty years after its passage, lands owned by native Americans decreased from 138 to 48 million acres. Many of these lands were virtually worthless. Rather than protect its charges, the Indian Bureau sometimes helped to rob them of their heritage. The low point may have been reached in the 1920's when Secretary of the Interior Albert B. Fall tried to take away oil lands belonging to the Navajos. The Indians were finally pushed onto reservations where they lived on government handouts while their culture crumbled around them. What a fate for the offspring of a proud and free people.

The Mining Frontier

Miners opened the first frontier of the last West. The map on page 474 shows the most important mining areas. The discovery of gold at Sutter's Fort in 1848 pulled a throng of miners to California. In 1859, a new strike near Pikes Peak in Colorado started a rush to the eastern edge of the Rockies. By 1860, the Territory of Jefferson, whose name was later changed to Colorado, had a population of 35,000. In that same year, Nevada was carved out of Utah after the discovery of the Comstock Lode, the world's richest vein of silver, in the mountains near Lake Tahoe. Within twenty years, the Comstock Lode alone yielded more than $300 million in silver. Gold was also discovered in 1860 in eastern Washington and in Idaho and Montana. This discovery led to the settlement of a few thousand miners who took $100 million in gold from Montana alone within a decade. In the

1880's, William Clark opened the Anaconda Mine near Butte, Montana. Miners extracted more than $2 billion in copper from this mine during the next fifty years. The last gold rush within the continental United States took place in the mid 1870's when miners rushed into the Black Hills of the Dakotas. Finally, a strike in the Klondike region of Alaska in 1896 brought miners who in two years numbered 30,000.

The miners' frontier had a short history—about forty years in all. But the miners played a vital role in the settlement of the West. They advertised the area's magnificent resources. They forced the government to do something about the native Americans. Thus, they opened the way for the cattle ranchers and farmers who were to follow. Between 1860 and 1890, they mined about $2 billion in gold and silver. And they added to the lore of the West. They produced a number of the characters who have become the stock in trade of western novelists and moviemakers.

The Cattle Frontier

The cattle frontier was opened in 1867. In that year the "long drive" north from Texas became established. And the town of Abilene, Kansas, shipped its first herd of cattle over the Kansas Pacific Railroad. The map on page 475 shows the main trails and the cattle towns. The cattle industry suffered in the two terrible winters of 1885-1886 and 1886-1887. Thousands of cattle died on the open range. But the twenty years between 1867 and 1887 marked the development of America's most romanticized industry. It was recorded in songs, films, and novels as the age when cowboys, rustlers, cattle barons, Indians, "peace officers," and soldiers wrestled to dominate raw towns.

A number of developments combined to make the cattle frontier possible. The government opened the public domain after the Civil War. The army relentlessly killed off native Americans. Soldiers, settlers, and professional hunters annihilated the buffalo which had long fed on the vast grasslands. Railroads stretched out onto the prairies. Meat-packing centers grew up in Kansas City, Chicago, and elsewhere. They shipped meat all over the nation by the newly developed refrigerator car, which came into common use about 1875. Finally, the consumption of meat increased in the East at the same time that production of cattle and sheep declined there.

Longhorn cattle, the descendants of Spanish herds, had grazed for centuries on the rich prairie grasses of Texas. In 1846, cowboys drove the first herd of these semi-wild creatures to Ohio. Ten years later, a herd of Texas cattle reached Chicago. By the end of the Civil War, the "long drive" had ceased to be only an experiment. In such towns as Abilene and Dodge City in Kansas, cowboys loaded hundreds of thousands of cattle onto railroad cars bound for slaughtering centers such as Chicago. Later, the long drive extended farther north, to the Union Pacific and Northern Pacific railroads. They crossed northern

Texas cattle ranchers and cowboys used to drive the cattle northward over a thousand miles of plains to the nearest railroad towns, usually in Kansas. There the cattle would be shipped to the stockyards of Kansas City and Chicago. A head of cattle was worth about $4 in Texas and $40 in Chicago.

The Union Pacific and the Central Pacific were joined together at Promontory Point, Utah, in 1869. The Atchison, Topeka and Santa Fe reached Colorado by 1872 and Los Angeles by 1883. The Southern Pacific Railroad reached El Paso by 1881.

The cattle kingdom originated on the Spanish, later Mexican, ranches of southeast Texas. The first cowboys were Mexican vaqueros. They were riders of the western range whose costume, equipment, vocabulary, and life-style were taken over by American cowboys in the years after the Mexican War. Moreover, pioneer ranchers in border areas depended almost exclusively on Mexican vaqueros to do their work.

473

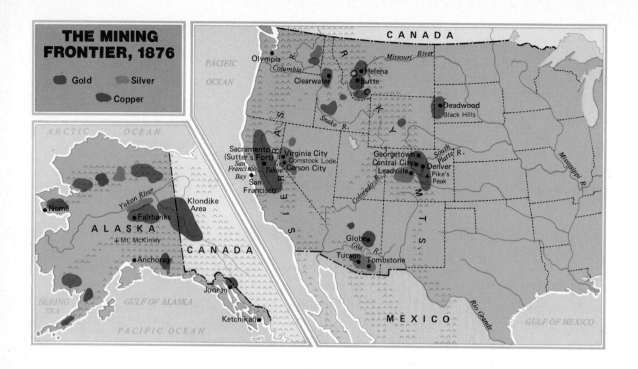

THE MINING FRONTIER, 1876

Gold   Silver

Copper

grasslands where cattle fattened at the end of their long trip north. Between 1866 and 1888, about 6 million head of cattle were driven from Texas to winter in Colorado, Wyoming, or Montana.

This new industry challenged the settled institutions imported from the East. What good was a 160-acre homestead to a cattle rancher? What good was land to anyone if a rancher owned the banks of streams that determined people's access to water? What could a farmer do when a huge herd of wild cattle driven by tough cowboys trampled through his wheat field? And who would settle disputes when two or more cattle barons vied for the same land or when cattle ranchers and sheepherders tried to pasture their animals on the same range?

A state like Wyoming, whose vast acres were unsuited for farming but superb for large-scale ranching, typified some of the problems of this new way of life. Cattle barons seized both Indian lands and public lands there. For almost two decades, the Wyoming Stock Growers' Association practically ran the state. It wrote laws as it saw fit. When sheepherders moved into the territory in the 1870's, the cattle ranchers wiped out entire flocks. Only the intervention of the United States Army blocked the outbreak of a full-scale war. Hence, the recommendations of men like Sparks.

The cattle boom reached its peak in 1885. The two terrible winters that followed wiped out thousands of head of cattle on the northern

The railroads that brought cattle to market also brought sheep to the Great Plains. Sheepherders would break up the "open range," where the cattle fed, into farms surrounded by barbed wire. Sheep eat the grass much closer to the ground than cattle do. Therefore, the two animals could not pasture together.

ranges. But even without bad weather, the long drive was falling victim to the advance of settlement. Railroads blocked the trails. So did the barbed-wire fences of people who established settled ranches and farmers who tried to protect their fields from the cattle herds. Cattle diseases had led to state quarantine laws which complicated interstate drives. Cattle ranchers began to fence off their lands. The ranch replaced the long drive across the public domain. The cowboys lingered on, domesticated on ranches. The glamorous days of the cattle frontier faded into history.

The Farmers' Last Frontier

More than any other factor, the rush of farmers into the West ended the picturesque days of the mining and cattle frontiers. A number of factors accounted for this movement. Tales of rich lands and fantastic yields per acre whetted the appetites of easterners. Immigrants from Europe were willing to purchase farms in more settled areas. The railroads provided transportation to the West and a way to market crops. Furthermore, they encouraged settlement through offers of their land at cheap prices. The invention of barbed wire by J. F. Glidden, in 1874, solved the fencing problem in a land where trees were scarce. Deep wells and windmills provided a supply of fresh water on the

Immigrants did not know how to farm on the frontier where they had to cope with either a dense forest or the thick sod of the prairie. Hence, they moved in behind frontier farmers.

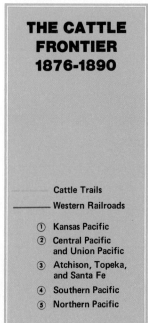

THE CATTLE FRONTIER 1876-1890

- - - - Cattle Trails
———— Western Railroads
① Kansas Pacific
② Central Pacific and Union Pacific
③ Atchison, Topeka, and Santa Fe
④ Southern Pacific
⑤ Northern Pacific

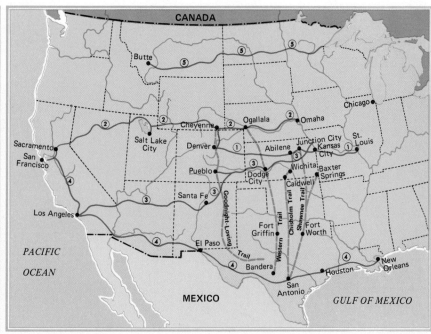

semi-arid plains. Dry-farming techniques permitted farmers to grow grains in semi-arid regions. Finally, the growth of new markets in eastern cities and in Europe provided an outlet for the rich harvests of the new West.

Men and women came by the millions. The population of the area west of the Mississippi rose from 6,877,000 in 1870 to 16,775,000 in 1890. The center of the corn and wheat belts shifted from the old Granger states of the 1870's to the Populist states—Kansas, Nebraska, the Dakotas, and western Minnesota—in the 1890's. The agricultural revolution traced in Chapter 14 followed. A million new farms opened in the decade of the 1890's. However, there was no longer an identifiable frontier line. If farmers were to increase productivity during the twentieth century, they had to do so by using additional tools and better farming techniques, not by moving onto new soil.

Millions of acres of arid lands could be made productive with irrigation, however. Congress passed the Carey Act in 1895 and the Newlands Reclamation Act in 1902 to open these acres. By 1910, about 14 million acres of western land were being irrigated mainly with waters impounded behind government-owned dams. By 1930, more than 5 million additional acres had been added.

Political Organization

Figure 71A shows the political results of this last surge of settlement. Fifteen new states, all except West Virginia from beyond the Mississippi, were added to the Union between the admission of Kansas in 1861 and of New Mexico and Arizona in 1912. They embraced more than a third of the territory of the nation.

FIGURE 71A The Formation of New States, 1861-1959

State	Date of Admission	Area in Square Miles
Kansas	1861	82,276
West Virginia	1863	24,181
Nevada	1864	110,540
Nebraska	1867	77,237
Colorado	1876	104,247
North Dakota	1889	70,665
South Dakota	1889	77,047
Montana	1889	147,138
Washington	1889	68,192
Idaho	1890	83,557
Wyoming	1890	97,914
Utah	1896	84,916
Oklahoma	1907	69,919
New Mexico	1912	121,666
Arizona	1912	113,909
Alaska	1959	586,400
Hawaii	1959	6,435

The Carey Act authorized the President to cede to any state up to 1 million acres of land owned by the federal government for the purposes of cultivation, irrigation, and settlement. The Newlands Reclamation Act authorized the federal government to use the money raised from the sale of land in 16 western states to build irrigation projects such as dams.

Utah was denied statehood several times because it permitted men to have more than one wife (polygyny). Congress had passed laws in 1862, 1882, and 1887 forbidding this practice. In 1890, the Mormon Church ratified an edict advising its members to refrain from practicing polygyny.

The constitutions of these new states were much like those of the older ones. Wyoming and Utah permitted women to vote in their constitutions. And other western states imitated this precedent by law a few years later. Most of the new states provided for regulation of railroads in their constitutions. Some had provisions for direct democracy, such as the initiative, referendum, and recall. But on the whole, they wrote constitutions much like those of the more established eastern states. That American democracy is a product of the unsettled frontier is one of the myths which Americans cling to despite evidence to the contrary. The vigilantes of frontier towns; the summary justice of the sheriffs, their posses, and ropes; the cruel slaughter of the Indians; and the gunshot justice of cattle barons contributed more to the American tradition of violence than they did to justice and free choice.

Adjusting Institutions on the Last Frontier

The American people were forced to adjust their institutions to the demands of the new environment in the West. Three conditions affected this adaptation. First, the federal government maintained considerable control over both land and natural resources, such as water. Figure 71B shows what had happened to the public domain by 1904.

FIGURE 71B The Disposal of the Public Domain by 1904

Disposition	Number of Acres
Purchased by individuals	278,000,000
Granted to states or railroads	273,000,000
Acquired by or available to individuals free of charge	147,000,000
Unappropriated	474,000,000
Reserved explicitly to the government	209,000,000

Between 1904 and 1920, an additional 175 million acres were reserved to the government, primarily in new or expanded national parks. About 200 million acres available to citizens still lay vacant. The government was by far the largest landowner in the West.

Second, policies that were poorly adapted to the new environment often brought disaster. Cattle died by the thousands in the blizzards of the 1880's in Wyoming. Thousands of acres of semi-arid lands in western Kansas, Nebraska, and Oklahoma blew away in the dust storms of the 1930's. Careless disposal of wastes from mines ruined hundreds of streams in the West.

Finally, scientific knowledge developed rapidly to cope with the challenges of the new environment. Scientists, many of whom worked for state or national governments, developed new methods of dry farming, irrigation, and animal husbandry. Engineers built new dams

A vigilante is a member of a self-appointed group that makes itself responsible for interpreting and enforcing the law and preventing crime. Law-enforcement agencies as they exist today generally were not found in the West.

Only Congress can designate national parks. It usually chooses sites that are distinguished for their scenic beauty, scientific interest, or historic significance. The National Parks System in the Department of Interior administers these parks. The first national park was Yellowstone, established in 1872.

The story of these "Okies" and their trek from the Dust Bowl to California is realistically described in John Steinbeck's novel, **The Grapes of Wrath**, written in 1936.

and developed new techniques to irrigate vast areas of semi-arid soil. The refrigerator car, the windmill, and barbed wire made farming and ranching on the Great Plains possible.

American cities between 1870 and 1930 faced similar problems of adjusting institutions to a new environment. Unlike the federal government in the West, however, cities controlled little land. They had given most of it to private individuals early in the century. They had to buy it back at high prices to build parks, streets, or other public facilities. Moreover, the taxation system required owners of adjoining property to pay special assessments for sewers, streets, sidewalks, and so forth. This system made centralized planning almost impossible. Most developmental decisions were made by private citizens.

Just as they did in the West, policies poorly adapted to the environment brought disaster in the cities. Like westerners, citizens in cities turned to scientists to help them solve their problems. With their engineering allies, scientists developed streetcars, subways, elevated lines, automobiles, and trucks to attack the transportation problem. The cable, telegraph, and telephone helped to speed communications. Scientific knowledge and engineering skill provided the means to purify water and dispose of waste. But scientists and engineers also perfected skyscrapers and built four- and five-story tenements, concentrating urban dwellers in crowded slums. No one could solve all the problems of modern cities with governments designed for simple farming and trading communities. Chapter 19 describes the attempts of Americans during the first decades of the twentieth century to cope with the problems of the new urban environment.

The Progressives and the New City

STATING THE ISSUE

During the last decades of the nineteenth century, the United States became steadily more urban. Towns and cities had played important roles in American life since the first settlers landed along the Atlantic coast. But the majority of American citizens had lived in rural areas and made their living from the soil. The census of 1900, however, revealed that 40 percent of the nation's people lived in towns or cities of more than 2500 people. In 1920, more than half of the nation's population was urban. The problems of these urban areas, and particularly of the great cities, drew the attention of critics and reformers.

Ordinary citizens also called for change. Some residents of cities wanted parks. Others demanded tree-lined boulevards. Still others asked for changes in the way in which members of boards of education or city councils were chosen. Some demanded regulation of public transportation or public ownership of utilities. Others concerned themselves with aid to working people struck down by industrial accidents. A few insisted that the most pressing issue was the control of housing to reduce overcrowding. Other reformers called for regulating the labor of women and children. A few people were actively concerned with all these great issues. Many more pressed for only one or two of them but identified themselves as progressive people of action. They saw themselves linked to others by their common interest in reform.

Many historians have argued that a great progressive movement for reform developed during the late nineteenth and early twentieth centuries. Chapters 19, 20, and 22 examine this argument and raise some serious questions about it. They raise a key issue: whether or not the efforts to plan and control the environment were too complex to be brought together in a single social movement. Chapter 19 focuses on progressivism in the new city.

479

1863 Free delivery of mail is begun in a number of cities
1871 **The New York Times** exposes the corrupt Tweed Ring
1873 Andrew Hallidie invents the cable car
1874 Stephen Dudley Field invents the first electrically powered streetcar
1879 Thomas Alva Edison invents the first practical incandescent bulb
1882 First central electric-power plant is established in New York City
1898 South Dakota becomes first state to adopt initiative and referendum
1900 Galveston, Texas, becomes the first city to adopt the commission form of government

1901 President McKinley is assassinated; Theodore Roosevelt becomes President
1903 Wisconsin becomes first state to adopt direct primary
1904 Lincoln Steffins publishes **The Shame of the Cities**
1908 William Howard Taft is elected President
1912 The Progressive Party is formed
1912 Woodrow Wilson is elected President
1920 Census reports that half the population lives in cities

72 DEMANDS
OF INTERDEPENDENCE

During the middle and late nineteenth century, American cities suffered from decentralized government. Sewers were built bit by bit with little centralized direction or control. Local police captains administered the law with little regard for either police commissioners or constitutional guarantees. Boards elected at the neighborhood level often ran public school systems. Yet the control of waste, the protection of lives and property, and educational needs affected the entire city.

Observers of the American scene claimed that cities were run by all-powerful bosses who controlled all aspects of city life. Although many bosses did exploit people, none of them exercised universal power. Nineteenth-century cities suffered from too little government, not too much.

Toward the end of the nineteenth century, people demanded more central control of urban development. In one city after another, public commissions recommended public control, regulation, and planning of vital services such as transportation, public utilities, waste disposal, or schools. Countless plans for broad, tree-lined boulevards or for regulating bodies to control the distribution of electricity or gas emerged.

The need for coordinated planning seemed particularly acute in Los Angeles, a new city which sprouted from a tiny town in 1870. In 1880, the population was only 11,000. But by 1900, the metropolitan area housed 190,000 persons and by 1910, almost 500,000 people lived there. A metropolitan area contains a central city and the area surrounding it. By 1910, Los Angeles was already sprawling over a vast land area. A number of independent municipal governments were set up.

In 1911, Los Angeles asked a traffic expert, Bion J. Arnold, to recommend plans for a coordinated transportation system for the city. As you read parts of his report, think about these questions:

1. What problems did Arnold analyze?
2. What recommendations did he make?

An Expert Analyzes Transportation Problems in Los Angeles

When he was asked to study the transportation problems of Los Angeles, Bion J. Arnold was Chief Engineer of the Chicago transportation system. He had helped to plan the street railways of Chicago and Pittsburgh and the subway system of New York. His study of Los Angeles began when a group of business people became concerned about transportation to the harbor. They expected the harbor to grow rapidly with the scheduled completion of the Panama Canal in 1914.

The transportation of both passengers and freight is the very life blood of the Los Angeles district. Unless passengers and freight flow freely to every part of the community, the city's growth will be restricted. On the other hand, we cannot provide transportation facilities too far in advance of actual needs. If we do, we will invest large sums of money without adequate financial returns. Ideally we should be able to find a halfway point which will meet the increasing demands for transportation without providing too much in one year and not enough in others. The development of transportation must go forward steadily. Nothing more directly affects the cost of living than transportation. The welfare of the people of any district depends largely on their ability to obtain adequate transportation at minimal cost.

"The Transportation Problem of Los Angeles," The California Outlook, A Progressive Weekly, Vol. XI, no. 19 (November 4, 1911). Language simplified.

The pictures on these two pages show six types of transportation used during the late nineteenth and early twentieth centuries. What were the advantages and disadvantages of each type of transportation in American cities?

Municipal Railroad

The city needs a municipal railroad to connect the main business section of Los Angeles, which is twenty miles inland from the Pacific Ocean, with the new city-owned harbors at Wilmington and San Pedro. Such a railroad will be easy to locate and construct. The terrain between Los Angeles and the sea presents no significant engineering difficulties. The right-of-way for the railroad should be at least 250 feet wide in order to provide for eight railroad tracks and two highways. In fact, the entire enterprise appeals strongly because of the possibilities for highways.

Automobile trucks are now being developed rapidly. A large part of the tonnage between the harbor and local delivery and collection points may soon be handled by means of trucks. When the distance is comparatively short, the largest part of the cost of transportation comes in the cost of handling freight at terminals. Trucks will make it possible to deliver goods from wharf or warehouse directly to stores or factories. This procedure eliminates the expense of intermediate transfers. The already extensive use of trucks in the Los Angeles area proves the practicality of this suggestion.

Local Street Railways

A large part of the streetcar system in Los Angeles and its immediate vicinity operates independently of the streetcar lines which serve the surrounding towns and communities. The city and between-cities systems use different gauges of track. In the city proper, Mr. H. E. Huntington, who controls the streetcar lines, uses a narrow gauge system. He supplies a liberal amount of up-to-date and well-maintained equipment. As a result, travel upon the city tracks reaches nearly one ride for each inhabitant per day. Other cities of a similar size have a ratio of about one ride to two inhabitants. Los Angeles street railways have already introduced a system of universal transfers. People can travel over the entire city for one fare and often follow "through routes." Many cities do not have these benefits.

Three problems concerning transportation requirements face the city: to do away with present and future congestion in the business district; to plan future extensions including the building of crosstown and outside circuit lines; and to provide better pavement between and next to the rails.

The street railway system lacks crosstown and circuit lines. This is particularly true inside the four-mile circle at the center of the city. Lines which radiate out from the center of the city have been built liberally. Even extensions into the outlying districts have been built, although the long haul and the small amount of business has

▶ Suppose a few people had built houses where the tracks and roads were to be built. Should government give them more than their property is worth to pay them for building a new house and moving? Why or why not?

Gauge is the distance between rails in a railroad track. The standard gauge in the United States is now 4 feet, 8½ inches.

484

meant a loss to the company. However, the cross connecting lines have been neglected. These lines could join two outlying districts to each other and are usually considered as desirable parts of a system of this size.

Two results should be sought in planning these circuit routes. First, the city should try to get a route—and eventually more than one route—entirely around the city outside the downtown congested district. Second, the city should try to use crosstown lines to connect lines which radiate out from the city center. Eventually, crosstown lines could form a series of outside loops. These loops will make it possible to get around the city without returning each time to the center of town.

This inter-urban system should be laid on level ground. It should eliminate almost all city stops. If these plans are carried out, high-powered cars should reach the circle five miles out from the center of the city in from ten to twelve minutes. In thirty minutes cars should reach centers twelve to fifteen miles from the business district. Beyond a certain distance from the city's center, it is clear that the territory can be best served by a high-speed system.

An inter-urban system is one that runs between cities.

Development of high-speed terminals in the inter-urban systems will affect the business center of Los Angeles. Good rapid transit will enable the thirty-five thousand people living in Pasadena to get to the shopping centers of Los Angeles as rapidly as residents of the city who live between three and four miles from the center. There is no other way for Los Angeles to extend the area it serves than to have an excellent inter-urban system. The rides per capita of people in this district are already very high. Every improvement will make it still easier to travel from one center to other centers. Improvements will further increase the riding habit. Towns and cities have been built up in this district at remarkable speed. The prosperity of the community paralleled the activity of its people which was made possible by electric-car service. These conclusions can only point to still greater extensions of the service. Of all possible improvements, building a comprehensive Los Angeles city terminal for the inter-urban system would be the most important.

Pasadena is a suburban residential city, 8 miles northeast of Los Angeles.

Immediate Relief from Main Street Congestion

The first step to be taken to improve transit conditions in Los Angeles and vicinity involves the relief of congested traffic. This congestion is due to the operation of both inter-urban and local surface cars on Main Street. During rush hours each day, as many as forty thousand riders on both systems are delayed for between five and forty minutes. As many more riders are inconvenienced in non-rush hours because of crowding along Main Street.

The first electric streetcar began to operate in Richmond, Virginia, in 1888. The current, generated from a power house, passes through copper wires. The streetcar is attached to the overhead line by a long trolley pole which conducts the current to the motors under the car.

485

City and District Planning

Greater Los Angeles can grow by unifying the present city with its satellite communities. These communities lie within a radius of perhaps twenty-five miles from the present center. An enlarged district such as this, however, could not reach its greatest potential for civic development under the present form of city government. The city needs some form of consolidation such as a borough system. Such a system would unite the present metropolitan center with surrounding communities so that common problems of transportation, water supply, sewage, and street plans could be coordinated and centrally controlled. In this way, the more strictly local problems, such as street cleaning and lighting, fire and police protection, can be administered by each individual locality.

This report is not a city plan. It would be better for both transportation and city planning, however, if the city could solve both problems—that is, transportation and governmental reform—at once.

Every community naturally tends to develop around centers. Every city has its business center. Even within the business center, certain kinds of businesses are to be found together. City planning should recognize this tendency toward centralization. It should establish centers of amusement and recreation, of art, of education, of conventions and assemblies, and so forth. Once this development has taken place, the transportation system can be built to carry people most effectively between their homes and these common meeting points.

City and district planning, therefore, should start by adopting this principle of centers. It should also recognize that the development about any center—even the original one—may become too large. For this reason, subcenters will develop. The location and the character of such subcenters should be controlled by natural influences. Transportation will play the key role in developing the district and its subcenters by providing a rapid, comfortable, and economic system of communication among them. Citizens should be able to reach each center, to pass through it, or to avoid it entirely by a convenient by-pass. As centers grow, each will need an individual collecting and distributing streetcar system. Such a system will contribute to the effectiveness of main rapid-transit lines by providing additional cars which make local stops. Thus the inter-urban lines can confine service to the stops at centers.

FOR THOUGHT:

What sort of governmental structure would be required to carry out Arnold's recommendations? Could a decentralized system of government do the job?

Satellite communities grow up around a larger city, such as Los Angeles, and become secondary centers of industrial activity.

A borough is a unit of local government. It is chartered by the state and usually has its own police force, fire department, school system, and governing board.

▶How do you feel about central planning to solve such problems as transportation or waste disposal? Why do you feel as you do?

73 THE MACHINE: AN ABC OF POLITICS

Many other reformers argued, like Arnold in Reading 72, that America's cities needed efficient, centralized, "scientific" government if they were to solve basic problems. At the same time, many denounced the corrupt alliance of business people and city bosses. They claimed that city bosses ruled America's metropolitan areas with iron hands. Throughout the first decade of the twentieth century, newspapers and magazines were filled with articles that denounced this alliance. Lincoln Steffens, the most famous urban journalist of the time, called toleration of this corrupt coalition "the shame of the cities." What chance would centralization have unless corruption could be eliminated? Hence, reformers attacked corrupt bosses. They urged a return to freedom, honesty, and democratic government.

The reformers seemed to be urging contradictory policies. On the one hand, they demanded centralization to solve problems involving a large geographic area. On the other, they denounced the existing central governments as corrupt. They demanded that control of the government be returned to the people. Much of their attack on existing governments centered on the political boss.

Reading 73 examines the role of the boss in municipal government. Around 1900, George Washington Plunkitt, a local political leader in New York, discussed municipal government with a reporter named William Riordan. Plunkitt was an official in Tammany Hall, New York's Democratic party machine. Since he was neither a party leader nor a mayor, he saw politics from the bottom up. He knew the base of politics at the ward level as well as any person in the country. Many reformers recognized the valuable functions that people like Plunkitt performed. The second excerpt, written by a Boston settlement worker, indicates this point. As you read these two excerpts, think about these questions:

1. What services did Plunkitt provide for the voters who lived in the district he controlled? Where did he get the money to provide these services?
2. Why did Woods think that opposition to a local boss was futile? What did reformers lack that people like Plunkitt had?

Plunkitt of Tammany Hall

In the first part of this selection, Riordan tries to capture the flavor of Plunkitt's speech. The second part of the selection contains

William L. Riordan, **Plunkitt of Tammany Hall** (New York: Alfred A. Knopf, Inc., 1948), pp. 22, 25-27, 121, 123-126, 131-132.

This chapter is based on extracts from Plunkitt's diary and on my daily observation of the work of the district leader.

—W.L. Riordan

Tammany Hall, named after an Indian chief, was formed in 1789 as a patriotic and social club. After 1854 and until the inauguration of Mayor Fiorello LaGuardia, a Republican, in 1934, it controlled New York City politics most of the time. The bosses in Tammany Hall nominated candidates, got them elected, and handed out city jobs and contracts.

▶ Suppose you wanted to be a leader of your organization. Are you willing to hustle at menial jobs for a year or so to build up a reputation as a person who works for the organization? Why do you feel as you do?

In boxing, the timekeeper rings a gong to start and end rounds of fighting. A rest period occurs between rounds. A fighter loses if he cannot "answer the gong" at the end of a rest period.

his observations of a typical day in Plunkitt's busy life. The third section contains Plunkitt's analysis of "honest graft."

Reformers Only Mornin' Glories

College professors and philosophers who go up in a balloon to think are always discussin' the question: "Why Reform Administrations Never Succeed Themselves!" The reason is plain to anybody who has learned the ABC of politics.

The fact is that a reformer can't last in politics. He can make a show for a while, but he always comes down like a rocket. Politics is as much a regular business as the grocery or the dry-goods or the drug business. You've got to be trained up to it or you're sure to fall. Suppose a man who knew nothing about the grocery trade suddenly went into the business and tried to conduct it according to his own ideas. Wouldn't he make a mess of it? He might make a splurge for a while, as long as his money lasted, but his store would soon be empty. It's just the same with a reformer. He hasn't been brought up in the difficult business of politics, and he makes a mess of it every time.

You can't begin too early in politics if you want to succeed at the game. I began several years before I could vote, and so did every successful leader in Tammany Hall. When I was twelve years old, I made myself useful around the district headquarters and did work at the polls on election day. Later on, I hustled about gettin' out voters who were drunk or who were too lazy to come to the polls. There's a hundred ways that boys can help, and they get an experience that's the first real step in statesmanship. Show me a boy that hustles for the organization on election day, and I'll show you a comin' statesman.

That's the ABC of politics. It ain't easy work to get up to Y and Z. You have to give nearly all your time and attention to it. Of course, you may have some business or occupation on the side, but the great business of your life must be politics if you want to succeed in it.

Do you understand now, why it is that a reformer goes down and out in the first or second round, while a politician answers to the gong every time? It is because the one has gone into the fight without trainin', while the other trains all the time and knows every fine point of the game.

Strenuous Life of the Tammany District Leader

This is a record of a day's work by Plunkitt:

2 A.M. Aroused from sleep by the ringing of his door bell. Went to the door and found a bartender, who asked him to go to the police

How did this cartoonist picture the roles of city bosses? How do these versions differ from Plunkitt's view of his role?

"WHAT ARE YOU GOING TO DO ABOUT IT?"

WHO STOLE THE PEOPLE'S MONEY? "—DO TELL. NY.TIMES   'TWAS HIM.

1871 "RING OUT THE OLD"   RING IN THE NEW (?) 1872

STEALING IS THE BEST POLICY. TAMMANY

HONESTY IS THE BEST POLICY. TAMMANY

CAN THE BODY CAST OFF ITS SHADOW?

"You have the liberty of voting for anyone you please; but we have the liberty of counting . . .

station and bail out a saloon-keeper who had been arrested for violating the excise law. Furnished bail and returned to bed at three o'clock.

6 A.M. Awakened by fire engines passing his house. Hastened to the scene of the fire, according to the custom of the Tammany district leaders, to give assistance to the fire sufferers, if needed. Met several of his election district captains who are always under orders to look out for fires, which are considered great vote-getters. Found several tenants who had been burned out, took them to a hotel, supplied them with clothes, fed them, and arranged temporary quarters for them until they could rent and furnish new apartments.

8:30 A.M. Went to the police court to look after his constituents. Found six "drunks." Secured the discharge of four by a timely word with the judge, and paid the fines of two.

9 A.M. Appeared in the Municipal District Court. . . . Paid the rent of a poor family about to be dispossessed and gave them a dollar for food.

11 A.M. At home again. Found four men waiting for him. One had been discharged by the Metropolitan Railway Company for neglect of duty, and wanted the district leader to fix things. Another wanted a job on the road. The third sought a place on the subway and the fourth, a plumber, was looking for work with the Consolidated Gas Company. The district leader spent nearly three hours fixing things for the four men, and succeeded in each case.

3 P.M. Attended the funeral of an Italian. Hurried back to make his appearance at the funeral of a Hebrew constitutent. Went conspicuously to the front both in the Catholic church and the synagogue. . . .

7 P.M. Went to district headquarters and presided over a meeting of election-district captains. Each captain submitted a list of all the voters in his district, reported on their attitude toward Tammany, suggested who might be won over and how they could be won, told who were in need, and who were in trouble of any kind and the best way to reach them. District leader took notes and gave orders.

8 P.M. Went to church fair. Took chances on everything, bought ice cream for the young girls and the children. Kissed the little ones. . . .

9 P.M. At the club house again. Spent $10 on tickets for a church excursion and promised a subscription for a new church bell. . . . Listened to the complaints of a dozen pushcart peddlers who said they were persecuted by the police and assured them he would go to Police Headquarters in the morning and see about it.

10:30 P.M. Attended a Hebrew wedding reception and dance. Had previously sent a handsome wedding present to the bride.

12 P.M. In bed.

That is the actual record of one day in the life of Plunkitt. He does some of the same things every day, but his life is not so monotonous as to be wearisome.

490

Constituents refer to the voters who live in the district Plunkitt controlled.

Between 1900 and 1914, the cost of food increased greatly. Eggs went from 21¢ to 35¢ a dozen, milk from 7 to 9¢ a quart, steak from 13 to 24¢ a pound. At these prices, a dollar could feed a family for a day or two.

▶How willing are you to work hard and to watch out for the welfare of people who belong to organizations you may lead?

By these means the Tammany district leader reaches out into the homes of his district. . . . Is it any wonder that scandals do not permanently disable Tammany and that it speedily recovers from what seems to be crushing defeat?

Honest Graft and Dishonest Graft

Everybody is talkin' these days about Tammany men growin' rich on graft. But nobody thinks of drawin' the distinction between honest graft and dishonest graft. There's all the difference in the world between the two. Yes, many of our men have grown rich in politics. I have myself. I've made a big fortune out of the game, and I'm gettin' richer every day. But I've not gone in for dishonest graft—blackmailin' gamblers, saloon-keepers, disorderly people, etc.—and neither has any of the men who have made big fortunes in politics.

There's an honest graft, and I'm an example of how it works. I might sum up the whole thing by sayin': "I seen my opportunities and I took 'em."

Just let me explain by examples. My party's in power in the city, and it's goin' to undertake a lot of public improvements. Well, I'm tipped off, say, that they're going to lay out a new park at a certain place.

I see my opportunity and I take it. I go to that place and I buy up all the land I can in the neighborhood. Then the board of this or that makes its plan public, and there is a rush to get my land, which nobody cared particular for before.

Ain't it perfectly honest to charge a good price and make a profit on my investment and foresight? Of course, it is. Well, that's honest graft.

Or supposin' it's a new bridge they're going to build. I get tipped off and I buy as much property as I can that has to be taken for approaches. I sell at my own price later on and drop some more money in the bank.

Wouldn't you? It's just like lookin' ahead in Wall Street or in the coffee or cotton market. It's honest graft, and I'm lookin' for it every day in the year. I will tell you frankly that I've got a good lot of it, too.

I'll tell you of one case. They were goin' to fix up a big park, no matter where. I got on to it, and went lookin' about for land in that neighborhood.

I could get nothin' at a bargain but a big piece of swamp, but I took it fast enough and held on to it. What turned out was just what I counted on. They couldn't make the park complete without Plunkitt's swamp, and they had to pay a good price for it. Anything dishonest in that?

▶ Do you think it is dishonest to use inside information obtained as a public official to make a private profit?

An approach is a small road by which a main roadway or bridge can be reached.

491

A watershed is that area of land from which water drains into a river, lake, or city water supply.

Up in the watershed I made some money, too. I bought up several bits of land there some years ago and made a pretty good guess that they would be bought up for water purposes later by the city.

Somehow, I always guessed about right, and shouldn't I enjoy the profit of my foresight? . . . The answer is—I seen my opportunity and I took it. I haven't confined myself to land. Anything that pays is in my line.

A Settlement-House Worker
Analyzes the Role of the Local Boss

Robert Woods found he could work comfortably with the local leader in the south end of Boston, "Honorable Jim" Donovan. Together, they gained a series of public improvements for their district. The settlement-house worker was a useful ally in a battle against Donovan's political opponents. He encouraged the "better elements" of the district to support Donovan.

Robert Woods, "Settlement Houses and City Politics," **Municipal Affairs**, Vol. IV (June 1900), pp. 396-397. Language simplified.

In nearly all cases it is idle for the settlement to attempt to win away the following of local politicians. To make such an attempt is to ignore the loyalties of class, race, and religion which bind the people of the crowded wards to their political leaders. The young university man cannot, by living in such a ward a few years and dispensing kindness around, become political master of the situation. This notion belongs to the story books. The successful political leader is the man born to the local manner. He enters instinctively into the ambitions and passions of his people. They return to him even after he has been untrue to them, as one does to a blood relation. No ready-made attachment can take the place of such a bond as this.

The method of the boss in organizing his local power, however, has two fatal defects. The awarding of his favors has the uncertainty of a game of chance. After election he may not have favors to award. It has in addition a great deal of unfairness and partiality. The strength of the method lies in the fact that the boss supplies tangible benefits to meet keenly felt human needs characteristic of his constituency. He controls some of the best avenues to livelihood. The winning of a job or a license depends on him. A man in need may through him reach the resources of charity. A wrongdoer may through him find immunity from punishment.

FOR THOUGHT:

What sort of government providing what sorts of services would have been required to replace bosses such as Plunkitt?

492

74 THE REFORM
OF URBAN POLITICS

Many people agreed that major political changes had to precede the reforms that people like Bion Arnold described for Los Angeles. Reformers urged many different proposals. They suggested that people be permitted to vote directly upon many public issues in a popular referendum. They proposed rules which would make it possible to recall public officials who had betrayed their trust. They suggested that a large group of citizens could require officials to stand for re-election before their normal term of office was over. They urged the adoption of commission governments or the appointment of city managers who reported to elected boards.

All these plans seemed to provide ways to undercut the power of the bosses. With the initiative and referendum, citizens could pass legislation which could not be vetoed by a boss-controlled council. Recall provided a method to remove a dishonest boss from power. Professional managers or commissions elected at large deprived a local boss like Plunkitt of his base of operations.

Reading 74 contrasts two progressive views of the needs of urban government. The first selection comes from a speech given by the mayor of Oakland, California, to a citizens' group in Los Angeles. The speech was made in 1911, the same year as the Arnold report. The second excerpt describes Jane Addams' justification for political activity. Jane Addams was one of the leading figures in the establishment of Chicago's Hull House. Hull House was one of the first and most famous settlement houses. As you read the excerpts, think about these questions:

1. Why did Mayor Mott want to change municipal government? Who would benefit from the changes he proposed?
2. Why did Jane Addams disagree with Robert Woods? Did she have the same interests as Mayor Mott?

Mayor Mott Discusses
Commission Government

In the summer of 1911, Oakland, California, adopted a commission form of government. Mayor Frank K. Mott traveled to Los Angeles in October to discuss the new system with a group of business people.

Mayor Frank K. Mott, "Suggestions for Municipal Government," **The California Outlook,** Vol. XI, no. 19 (November 4, 1911), pp. 11-12, 15-16. Language simplified.

Widespread unrest has spread through American cities. Everyone deplores the lack of business methods in government. No one seems confident that taxes have been spent wisely and economically in the public interest. As a result, we see numerous attempts to break away from old forms of municipal government in the name of greater democracy and more efficiency. Greater democracy leads to demands for the recall, the initiative, and the referendum. To get more efficiency, citizens recommend the so-called commission form of government.

Politicians should be the leaders and teachers of the people. We must no longer shut our eyes to the hideousness of much of our architecture, to our haphazard care of streets, to the absence of parks and playgrounds, to the lack of shade trees along our thoroughfares, to the unsightly and dangerous array of poles which shut out the sky by networks of wires. At the same time we must strive for better

▶ Mayor Mott argued that politicians should be both leaders and teachers of the people. How does this newspaper story demonstrate qualities of leadership in a politician?

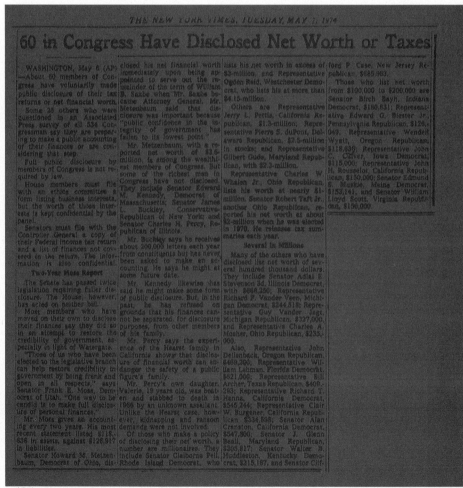

sanitary conditions, for better transportation, for purer and more abundant water, for better gas and electric service for domestic and industrial uses, for more and better schools, and for the development of business interests.

One of the most obvious characteristics of German cities is the administrative body called the magistracy. The burgomaster is the head of this body. It is an administrative body, responsible to the municipal council. In reality these German cities have a commission form of government similar to that proposed for American cities. The magistracy is a body of immense authority and dignity. It is always ready for action. It has both paid and unpaid members. The former, experts in their fields, are chosen for their technical skill or their previous experience. The unpaid members are required to be men of general experience in public affairs. The German system is not a government by experts nor a government of experts. The system makes use of experts very well. But every group within the society takes an active part in controlling the work of the experts.

▶ Do you trust experts more than you trust elected officials to make decisions? Why do you feel this way?

In all lands experts are usually specialists who can be carried away by professional zeal for their specialty. They can allow other interests to suffer in their pursuit of things dear to their own hearts. In America, several conditions seem to prevent anything like a government in which experts play the principal part.

No doubt it would be best if citizens elected men who have had experience and who would employ men with high technical skills in administration. But we cannot count on the electorate to choose experts. Personal popularity is still the major criterion for election to office. Surely citizens should see the advantages of having experienced and trained men at the head of their municipal governments, but unless only trained candidates become eligible for office, we cannot expect this outcome. Reason, judgment and principle influence only a minority of the electorate. In addition, a good specialist or expert would seldom be a good vote getter. He would usually be unwilling to spend his time in a strenuous campaign for an office which lasted only a short term. A long term of office is unpopular in America. How then shall the situation be met?

The spirit of the German system may be captured by the hoped-for efficiency of the commission form of government to which some of our cities are now committed. Let us have an official council drawn from voluntary bodies such as the Chamber of Commerce, taxpayers' associations, improvement clubs, and so forth, as well as representatives from among citizens at large.

A body like this would be non-partisan and representative of the varied interests of the city. It would serve as a sensitive medium to test public opinion. Members could carry discussion of every question into the homes of the people. Their approval would strengthen the administration and leave it free to carry on important works for the public good. Under such conditions it would be safe to enlarge the tasks which city governments might do. The city charter might become a true constitution for the city government, a statement of broad principles. If citizens chose for elective office only people who had served a year on the citizens' council, a degree of expertness would come to the administrative body. The commission should appoint no one but experts to important positions. It should make fitness for office the criterion for appointment or promotion in all cases.

Jane Addams Attacks a Boss

Unlike Robert Woods, Jane Addams was unable to work successfully with her local councilman, Johnny Powers. This selection is an attack on Powers and his system. Powers, in turn, insisted that "the trouble with Miss Addams is that she is just jealous of my charitable work in the ward." He promised that Hull House would be driven from his territory.

Jane Addams, "Ethical Survivals in Municipal Corruption," **International Journal of Ethics**, Vol. VIII (April 1898), pp. 278-279, 288-289.

An alderman is a member of the governing council of a ward, district, or city.

Padrones were men who contracted employment for Italian immigrants. They also handled their money for them as well as advanced them loans, usually at a large profit. Civil service jobs were a threat to their income.

The alderman's action in standing by an Italian *padrone* of the ward when he was indicted for violating the Civil Service law had a bad effect on public morals. The Commissioners had sent out notices to certain Italian day laborers who were upon the eligible list. They were told to report for work at a given day and hour. One of the *padrones* intercepted these notices and sold them to the men for five dollars apiece. He also made the usual bargain for a share of the wages. The *padrone's* entire arrangement followed the custom which had prevailed before the Civil Service law. Ten of the laborers swore out warrants against the *padrone*. He was convicted and fined seventy-five dollars. This sum was promptly paid by the alderman. The *padrone*, assured that he would be protected from any further trouble, returned triumphant to the colony. The Italians were bewildered by this show of a power stronger than that of the Civil Service law which they had trusted. This was one of the first violations of its authority, and various sinister acts have followed. No Nineteenth-Ward Italian feels quite secure in holding his job unless he is backed by the friendship of the alderman. According to the Civil Service law, a laborer has no right to a trial. Many are discharged by the foreman, and find that they can be reinstated only upon the recommendation of the alderman. The alderman thus practically holds his old power over the laborers working for the city. The popular mind is convinced that an honest administration of the Civil Service is impossible, and that it is but one more instrument in the hands of the powerful. It will be difficult to establish genuine Civil Service among these men who learn only by experience. To their minds it is "no good."

The positive evils of corrupt government are bound to fall heaviest upon the poorest and least capable. When the water of Chicago is foul, the prosperous buy water bottled at distant springs. The poor have no alternative but the typhoid fever which comes from using the city's supply. When the garbage contracts are not enforced, the well-to-do pay for private service. The poor suffer the discomfort and illness which are inevitable from a foul atmosphere. Prosperous business people have a certain choice as to whether they will deal with the boss politician or preserve their independence on a smaller income. But to an Italian day laborer it is a choice between obeying the commands of a political boss or practical starvation. Slowly the conviction enters his mind that politics is a matter of favors and positions, that self-government means pleasing the boss and standing in with the gang. He hands this slowly acquired knowledge on to his family. During the month of February, his boy may come home from school with tales about Washington and Lincoln. The father may for the moment be fired to tell of Garibaldi, but such talk is only periodic. The fortunes of the entire family, even to the opportunity to earn food and shelter, depend upon the boss.

This lowering of standards, this setting of an ideal, is perhaps the worst of the situation. Our daily actions and decisions not only determine ideals for ourselves, but largely for each other. We are all involved in this political corruption, and as members of the community stand indicted. This is the penalty of a democracy—that we are bound to move forward or backward together. None of us can stand aside, for our feet are mired in the same soil, and our lungs breathe the same air.

▶ Realistically, why should prosperous people care about the day-by-day welfare of the "poorest and least capable"?

Giuseppe Garibaldi (1807-1882) was an Italian nationalist and military leader who helped to bring about the unification of Italy.

FOR THOUGHT:

Given the problems of the cities and the nature of boss politics, how realistic were the reforms recommended by Mott and Addams?

75 THE AMERICAN CITY

HISTORICAL ESSAY

By far the greatest growth period for urban areas in the United States was the fifty years between 1860 and 1910. In 1860, four times as many people lived in rural as in urban areas. By 1910 urban and rural populations were almost equal. The 1920 census indicated that the balance had swung to cities and towns. This shift from rural areas to towns and cities had an enormous impact on the lives of the American people.

The Development of Cities

Figure 75A describes the development of urban population between 1860 and 1930.

U.S. Bureau of the Census, Historical Statistics of the United States, Colonial Times to 1957 (Washington, D.C.: Government Printing Office, 1960), p. 14.

FIGURE 75A   Number of Cities, by Population, 1860-1930

Year	Rural Population	Urban Population	Number of Urban Places	100,000 or more No.	100,000 or more Population
1860	25,226,803	6,216,518	392	9	2,638,781
1870	28,656,010	9,902,361	663	14	4,129,989
1880	36,026,048	14,129,735	939	20	6,210,909
1890	40,841,449	22,106,265	1,348	28	9,697,960
1900	45,834,654	30,159,921	1,737	38	14,208,347
1910	49,973,334	41,998,932	2,262	50	20,302,138
1920	51,552,647	54,157,973	2,722	68	27,429,326
1930	53,820,223	68,954,823	3,165	93	36,325,736

Year	50,000 to 100,000 No.	50,000 to 100,000 Population	5,000 to 50,000 No.	5,000 to 50,000 Population	2,500 to 5,000 No.	2,500 to 5,000 Population
1860	7	452,060	213	2,531,162	163	594,515
1870	11	768,238	329	3,917,805	309	1,086,239
1880	15	947,918	437	5,352,959	467	1,617,949
1890	30	2,027,569	636	8,103,729	654	2,277,007
1900	40	2,709,338	827	10,343,072	832	2,899,164
1910	59	4,178,915	1,093	13,789,685	1,060	3,728,194
1920	76	5,265,408	1,323	17,077,334	1,255	4,385,905
1930	98	6,491,448	1,642	21,420,409	1,332	4,717,590

Cities of all sizes grew rapidly throughout the nation except in the South, which remained primarily rural. In 1900, only 15.2 percent of the South's population was urban. The national figure for the percentage of people in urban areas had been 15.3 percent in 1850.

Fundamental economic changes spurred city growth. Specialization of labor in factories and mills resulted in the development of trade and manufacturing centers to make and exchange goods. Cities grew in several different types of locations. Many developed around ports which also became centers of manufacturing, such as New York City, Boston, San Francisco, Baltimore, or Philadelphia. Some grew where special technological or economic developments took place. For example, Schenectady, New York, became the home of the General Electric Company; Hershey, Pennsylvania, manufactured chocolate; and Memphis, Tennessee, processed cottonseed oil. Some towns and cities, such as Butte, Montana, Scranton, Pennsylvania, or Tulsa, Oklahoma, grew up around mines or near oil wells. Dozens of cities developed along, or in anticipation of, railroad lines. A few—Washington, D.C. and several state capitals—grew primarily because they were governmental centers. The location of American towns and cities at places like these indicates the close ties between city growth and economic change.

Promoters played a key role in the development of most nineteenth-century cities. They often stressed the prosperity which would come to a town after a mining strike or completion or a railroad. Promoters advertised the advantages of townsites so widely that they drew investors from as far away as Europe. The rapid development of cities such as Los Angeles, California, Seattle, Washington, and Wichita, Kansas, were all spurred by the work of promoters.

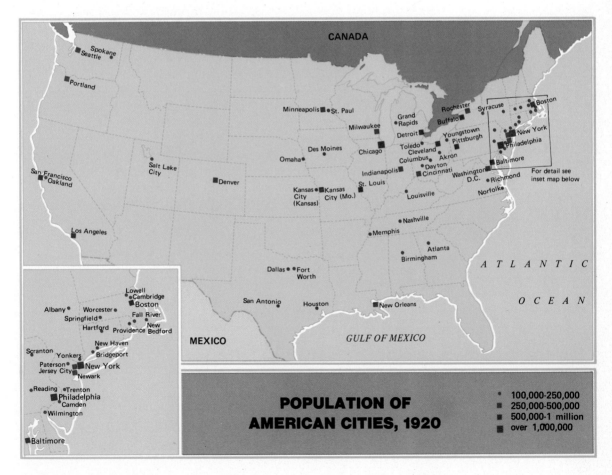

POPULATION OF
AMERICAN CITIES, 1920

• 100,000-250,000
■ 250,000-500,000
■ 500,000-1 million
■ over 1,000,000

More People, More Problems

City dwellers came from four major sources. Almost 12 million people who lived in cities in 1910 were not living there in 1900. Of course 12 million people, about 41 percent, were immigrants from abroad. About 29.8 percent had come from American rural areas. Another 21.6 percent had been born in cities since the 1900 census. And 7.6 percent had lived in towns which cities had incorporated within their boundaries during the decade. These figures indicate that high birth rates in rural areas in both Europe and the United States sustained the growth of American cities. American migrants often moved first to a nearby town, then to a larger regional city, and finally to one of the giants, such as Chicago or New York. Immigrants from abroad frequently moved immediately to large cities.

The growth of urban areas demanded a new technology to cope with problems such as transportation, communication, water supply, waste disposal, housing, roads, lighting, and sewage. Before the Civil War, the horse-drawn bus, the steam railroad, and the horse-drawn railway car provided movement through cities. New York built an elevated line for steam railroads just after the Civil War. A few years later, a number of cities, including New York, Philadelphia, and San Francisco, pioneered the use of cable cars. The most important innovation, however, took place in the 1880's and 1890's. The electric-powered railway, or streetcar, made its appearance at that time. The development of streetcars made the use of the subway possible. Experiments in both Boston and New York City around 1900 proved the practicality of this new development. New ideas for building bridges were developed during the 1870's. Bridges helped to link parts of the new cities, many of which were located on rivers or harbors. Automobiles and buses began to appear in cities in large numbers around World War I.

Better communication systems accompanied improvements in transportation. In 1863, free urban mail delivery was established in New York City. It spread rapidly to other metropolitan centers. The telephone eventually revolutionized urban communication. In 1880, 148 telephone companies in 85 cities had fewer than 50,000 subscribers. By 1900, nearly 800,000 telephones were in use. Their numbers continued to increase rapidly.

Additional technological developments helped to make life in the cities more attractive. Experiments with bricks, stone blocks, and wood eventually led to the use of inexpensive asphalt paving. This development solved the problem of an efficient road-building material. In the 1880's, the electric carbon arc lamp began to replace less satisfactory gas and kerosene lamps. The incandescent electric light and the first central power system (1882) revolutionized lighting and paved

The cable car was invented in 1873 by Andrew Hallidie to travel the steep hills of San Francisco. A cable running through a trench in the ground pulls the car. A gripping device attaches the car to the cable.

One new idea was that of the suspension bridge which hangs on parallel cables made of twisted steel wire, fastened to high towers. This type of bridge is not as expensive as others. The idea was perfected by John Roebling, who designed the Brooklyn Bridge.

Light is produced in an electric carbon arc lamp when a current of electricity leaps from one end of an electrode to another. The current causes the electrode, usually a pointed rod made of carbon, to turn to glowing vapor and waste away.

the way for the development of the electric motor. This invention caused dramatic changes in industry. New ways to filter water and to dispose of sewage were developed between 1890 and 1910. Finally, the invention of the steel skeleton and the elevator made it possible to erect tall buildings.

All these developments helped to crowd more people into less and less space. The four- and five-story tenements in which workers in New York lived in the late nineteenth century were unbelievably crowded. Many were windowless except in the front and rear, and without plumbing or heat. Some packed as many as 800 people into a building erected on a lot that measured 245 feet by 35 feet. In the 1880's, builders developed the dumbbell tenement. It at least provided interior ventilation. The dumbbell tenement was built five or six stories high with fourteen rooms to a floor. It covered most of a standardized 25 foot by 100 foot New York City lot. The dumbbell had a narrow indentation on both sides at the center of the building which permitted windows to open on an air shaft. Four families lived on one floor. Ten dumbbells on one block often housed as many as 4000 people. Imagine how a farm family from either a European village or an American farm would feel, packed into three or four rooms in one of these buildings. And how could people live in them unless everyone spoke the same language and shared the same outlook? The buildings themselves helped to create the patchwork of immigrant colonies, each containing its own stores, banks, clubs, and churches.

Municipal Government

The rapid growth of cities made it difficult to achieve any public consensus on policy. The very organization of city government made action difficult. City charters called for divided and extremely limited powers. Cities had to appeal constantly to state legislatures for additional powers or to call on states to provide essential services. Budgets were surprisingly small. In 1810, New York City's budget was only $100,000—one dollar for each citizen. Voluntary associations took care of the poor, and volunteer fire companies served without pay. There were no uniformed policemen in most cities until about 1850.

Government became more complicated as new functions and powers were added. At one time, Philadelphia's city government included thirty boards. Each board was responsible for a separate function, such as supervising health or running the schools. In the meantime, state governments interfered constantly to amend city charters or pass laws for cities. Many of these laws were requested by special interest groups. The New York State Legislature, for example, passed thirty-nine laws for the city of Brooklyn in 1870.

The incandescent electric light, developed by Thomas Edison, gives off light when an electric current flows through a metal filament such as one made of tungsten. It lasts much longer than a carbon arch light.

▶ How important are privacy and adequate living space to your happiness?

In 1898, Brooklyn became a borough of New York City. Brooklyn now has three different forms of local government. It has its own borough president with local responsibilities. He sits with nine other representatives from Brooklyn on the New York City Council. As a county, Brooklyn elects its own district attorney, county clerk, and county judges.

501

Although city governments became more complicated and more subject to interference from states, they also became more important. By mid-century, large cities had started municipally owned water works to replace private wells. By 1870, all major cities had a board of education. Around the 1870's, cities began to set up boards of health. These boards gave inspectors the power to enforce laws, clean up the slums, and require that tenements have windows in every bedroom. A modern, uniformed police force was organized in New York in 1845. The practice spread to other cities. In the 1850's, paid firemen began to replace volunteer companies. Between 1850 and 1870, most cities began to build public sewers, to collect garbage and trash, and to sweep the streets. At about the same time, they began to purchase land for public parks. All these developments cost money. In New York City, per capita expense for government quadrupled between 1850 and 1900. Many cities went heavily into debt to finance municipal improvements.

The Rise of the Bosses

Political organizations of the sort described by George Washington Plunkitt played an important role in city development. At the level of the neighborhood, Plunkitt and men like him provided a variety of services. At the city-wide level, political parties provided a chain across the maze of government agencies and contending publics. The links in the chain were the combined power of jobs and money. Government jobs were distributed by party leaders. Companies holding city franchises graciously provided jobs for the machine's supporters. Many companies that won contracts of franchises from the city also kicked back a portion of their fee to the city leaders.

Reform groups occasionally ousted bosses, as New York reformers did to William Marcy Tweed in 1871. But they or their heirs often won control again within a few years. Many bosses sprang from the poor who gave them votes. The poor looked to them as if they were Robin Hoods, caring for the poverty-stricken with money taken from the rich and well born.

Reform in City Governments

Agitation for the reform of city governments grew in the 1870's. By the end of the 1880's, reform talk was in the air in every American city. During the next few decades, a number of key reform demands turned up in one city after another.

The proposal for commission government, which Mayor Mott of Oakland described in Reading 74, flourished after it was first adopted in Galveston, Texas in 1900. A hurricane and tidal wave had devastated the city. Responding to this disaster, the state legislature temporarily

A franchise is the right or privilege granted to a company by the city government to carry on a business with little or no competition. Cities often granted franchises to utility or transportation companies. Franchises often lasted for 50 or 100 years.

Instead of paying a bribe beforehand to a boss, companies that received contracts would give the boss a certain percentage of the fees they charged the city.

In 1871, **The New York Times** began an expose of the corrupt regime of Boss William Marcy Tweed. The cartoons of Thomas Nast in **Harper's Weekly** did much to enrage public opinion. In 1872, Tweed was convicted of having robbed New York City of $75-200 million.

In recent years many cities have elected centralized school boards. Lately citizens in many cities have tried to win control of local schools away from these centralized boards. What advantages do you see in centralization? in local control?

The teachers' strike in New York hit at the very heart of the city's agonized attempt to deal with the problem of urban education. Aided by grants from the Ford Foundation, three experimental school districts were set up last year as the start of citywide school decentralization. This program would shift some of the authority from the city's cumbersome Board of Education and give neighborhood boards a share of the responsibility. Under the best of circumstances, such a revolutionary move would be a tough proposition. Under the stress of the urban crisis, paired with the opposition of many school administrators and teachers and the impatience and militance of black communities, it has at times become a monster.

When Ocean Hill-Brownsville, one of the Negro-controlled experimental districts, dismissed a group of white teachers and refused to take them back, the United Federation of Teachers saw a threat to job security and called a strike. But —and this was a bright sign for the future—some schools within districts where local control had begun to work ran smoothly and at full capacity despite the strike.

After two days, the Ocean Hill-Brownsville governing board did agree to take back the dismissed teachers and a strike settlement was reached. But militants within the Ocean Hill-Brownsville community still refused to receive the teachers. Another strike was threatened, and the delicate problems of local control forebode a long series of bitter confrontations.

replaced the city government with a five-man commission. The group worked so well that it was made a permanent government in 1903. By 1917, about five hundred small and medium-size cities had adopted commission governments.

Another group of cities adopted a variation of the commission plan. They hired city managers to coordinate all of the administrative work of the city. The managers reported to elected officials. At least in theory, the manager was an expert in municipal affairs who was free of political ties. By the mid 1920's, more than three hundred cities had hired managers.

Most large cities, however, did not adopt an entirely new form of government. But many did take steps to centralize authority, usually in the hands of the mayor. They also tried to make public service more professional. By the end of the 1920's, most cities had adopted some form of municipal civil service. They employed engineers in many departments and retained professional planners to develop comprehensive programs. Even local school boards were replaced by city-wide boards elected from the city at large. Each district no longer had its own representative. In many cities, all members of the city council were also chosen at large rather than on a district-by-district basis.

▶ So long as government runs well, what difference does it make that lower classes do not play an active role in it?

These developments tended to exclude the lower classes from an active role in municipal politics. People with high social and business status led many municipal reform movements. They tended to emphasize the importance of expert knowledge. In Pittsburgh, for example, the Voters' League argued that "small shopkeepers, clerks, and workmen at many trades could not, however honest, be expected to administer properly the affairs of an educational system, requiring special knowledge, and where millions are spent each year."

Some of the products of these reforms have been unusually praised. Others are more controversial. On the one hand, expenditures for public health increased six or seven times between 1900 and 1910. Infant mortality began to drop rapidly as a result. New parks and boulevards began to grace many urban landscapes. In several large cities, fire and sanitation departments were among the best in the world. By the end of the 1920's most cities had established minimal standards for housing and for controlling the use of land through zoning ordinances.

Zoning is the practice of dividing a city into districts or zones, specifying what each district may be used for. Zoning provides for industrial districts, local buisness districts, and residential districts. It also restricts the height of buildings, and segregates different types of residences (one-family houses, apartments) or industries (factories, stores).

On the other hand, the new governments devoted more attention and more money to transportation than to housing. Within the housing field, more effort was expended on middle-class accommodations than on the housing of the poor. Zoning laws often kept poor people out of neighborhoods by requiring that houses there use more land than the poor could afford. As a result, segregation of poor from well-to-do groups increased. Realtors often supported new zoning laws because

504

many middle-class citizens wished to separate themselves from the poor, particularly if the poor were also black or immigrants. Finally, although the health of all classes improved, that of richer people improved more rapidly than that of the poor.

One unexpected result of the progressive reforms in cities was the alienation of many citizens from their municipal governments. Lower-class urbanites, in particular, complained in the 1920's and 1930's that the new experts and commissions were not as approachable as the old politicians. Not until the 1960's, however, was the basic premise of the progressive period challenged. In the early part of this century it seemed clear that professionalism and expertise were ways for urban dwellers to gain control of their destinies. Recently, however, political conflicts over the organization of schools, police, and social welfare agencies have raised a set of new questions: Have expert professionals exaggerated their expertise and isolated themselves from the public they serve? What new forms of political control and public service are necessary to re-establish the connection between urban governments and their citizens?

In February 1968, the New York City Board of Education gave communities the right to control their own schools. The school boards dismissed several white teachers. According to established city law, these teachers had passed the qualifying tests and had taught long enough to be permanent employees who could not be dismissed without due process. The city board had failed to establish clearly what power local boards did and did not have. The local boards claimed they did have the right to dismiss teachers they considered unsuitable for local students. All city teachers went on strike the following fall to protest the threat they saw to their jobs. Some local boards hired outside teachers. The strike was not settled until the city set up clear rules that protected both the teachers' rights and the rights of the local boards.

National Politics, 1876-1920

STATING THE ISSUE

In the 1970's the various units of the national government spent between one fifth and one quarter of the gross national product or GNP. They outspent state and local government units by proportions of nearly two to one. The national government is, by far, the dominant public partner. It has assumed a vital role in financing and regulating even such traditionally local concerns as education. Several major firms are so dependent on public contracts and research that they are, for many purposes, nationally owned businesses. Washington carefully watches the level of economic activity, interest rates, and prices. Even in periods when there is no particular crisis, federal agencies are daily involved in the minor adjustments which are part of the process of managing the economy.

In the years between 1876 and 1920, nearly the complete reverse of this situation existed. Until the outbreak of World War I, the national government spent around one twentieth of the gross national product. State and local governments outspent the national government by proportions of more than three to one. The telegraph, telephone, and electric power networks grew without support from Washington. The national government virtually ignored the growth of public high schools, the most important educational development of the period. The abuses of railroad magnates and the officers of trusts went on with only an occasional slap on the wrist from Washington. Most administrations during the last three decades of the nineteenth century were content to keep down civil disorder at home and negotiate with representatives of foreign nations. They interfered as little as possible with the ''natural laws'' which were thought to govern the economy.

Chapter 20 examines some of the reasons for the relative inactivity of the national government during this period. It explores the major political issues that occupied the time of officials in the American government. And it asks you to consider what the nature of national politics reveals about American society during this period.

1877 Electoral Commission awards Presidency to Rutherford B. Hayes
1878 Greenback-Labor party is formed
1880 James A. Garfield is elected President
1881 President Garfield is assassinated; Chester A. Arthur becomes President
1884 Grover Cleveland is elected President
1887 Benjamin Harrison is elected President
1890 Congress passes Sherman Antitrust Act
1892 Populist Party is formed
1892 Grover Cleveland is elected President
1894 Decline in business results in major depression

1896 William McKinley is elected President
1901 President McKinley is assassinated; Theodore Roosevelt becomes President
1902 The Bureau of the Census is established
1912 Woodrow Wilson becomes President
1913 States Ratify Sixteenth and Seventeenth amendments
1914 Congress passes Federal Trade Commission Act and Clayton Antitrust Act
1917 United States enters World War I
1920 Nineteenth Amendment provides for woman suffrage

76 POLITICS: A STATISTICAL ACCOUNT

Traditional accounts of national politics in the United States move from one election campaign to another. They describe the issues debated by the candidates and then the results of each election. These accounts suggest that in each two- or four-year period, American voters make up their minds on a number of issues, most of them economic, and decide who shall be their President or representatives in Congress. The votes of citizens determine which candidate and party control the country.

Accounts like these have never been accurate, no matter what period of American history is concerned. The great Democratic party majority of the first half of the nineteenth century was composed of many smaller groups. It contained such diverse people as northern abolitionists and southerners who defended slavery. Even after leading the nation to victory in the Civil War, the new Republican party was

507

so torn internally that it maintained control through Reconstruction only with the votes of southern representatives and senators. A majority of members of one party in the Senate and the House has never guaranteed effective control of Congress unless the majority was substantial and the party united.

Reading 76 carries the story of American Presidential elections for the years 1876-1920. These were years during which the Granger and the Populist movements agitated farmers. At the same time, American industry grew rapidly with all the new problems that industrialization brought in its wake. One of these problems, for example, was a serious depression that struck the nation in 1894. This occurred shortly before Grover Cleveland entered office for his second term. Estimates of the proportion of unemployed ran as high as one out of five. "Armies" of unemployed workers marched on Washington to demand relief. These demonstrators were generally peaceful. But President Cleveland warned of the danger of mob rule and anarchy. This long serious depression, together with the agitation of the Populists, eventually began to have an effect on national politics. So did World War I, which America entered in 1917.

Reading 76 consists of four tables and an excerpt from the Inaugural Address of President Grover Cleveland. Specific questions accompany each section of the reading.

Figure 76A
Presidential Elections,
1876-1920

This figure lists the major candidates for President in every election from 1876 through 1920. The winner's name appears first in each group and in capital letters. In some instances, the total is less than 100 percent because some small political parties have been omitted.

1. How close were these elections? Is there any difference in the margin of victory between the first five and next four elections?
2. What difference would it make in the ability to pass sweeping legislation if margins of victory had been larger? smaller?

Year	Candidates	Party	% of Popular Vote
1876	RUTHERFORD B. HAYES	Republican	48.0
	Samuel J. Tilden	Democratic	51.0
1880	JAMES A. GARFIELD	Republican	48.5
	Winfield S. Hancock	Democratic	48.1
	James B. Weaver	Greenback-Labor	3.4
1884	GROVER CLEVELAND	Democratic	48.5
	James G. Blaine	Republican	48.2
	Benjamin F. Butler	Greenback-Labor	1.8
	John P. St. John	Prohibition	1.5
1888	BENJAMIN HARRISON	Republican	47.9
	Grover Cleveland	Democratic	48.6
	Clinton B. Fisk	Prohibition	2.2
	Alson J. Streeter	Union Labor	1.3
1892	GROVER CLEVELAND	Democratic	46.1
	Benjamin Harrison	Republican	43.0
	James B. Weaver	Populist	8.5
	John Bidwell	Prohibition	2.2
1896	WILLIAM McKINLEY	Republican	51.1
	William J. Bryan	Democratic	47.7
1900	WILLIAM McKINLEY	Republican	51.7
	William J. Bryan	Democratic; Populist	45.5
	John G. Woolley	Prohibition	1.5
1904	THEODORE ROOSEVELT	Republican	57.4
	Alton B. Parker	Democratic	37.6
	Eugene V. Debs	Socialist	3.0
	Silas C. Swallow	Prohibition	1.9
1908	WILLIAM H. TAFT	Republican	51.6
	William J. Bryan	Democratic	43.1
	Eugene V. Debs	Socialist	2.8
	Eugene W. Chafin	Prohibition	1.7
1912	WOODROW WILSON	Democratic	41.9
	Theodore Roosevelt	Progressive	27.4
	William H. Taft	Republican	23.2
	Eugene V. Debs	Socialist	6.0
	Eugene W. Chafin	Prohibition	1.4
1916	WOODROW WILSON	Democratic	49.4
	Charles E. Hughes	Republican	46.2
	A. L. Benson	Socialist	3.2
	J. Frank Hanly	Prohibition	1.2
1920	WARREN G. HARDING	Republican	60.4
	James M. Cox	Democratic	34.2
	Eugene V. Debs	Socialist	3.4
	P. P. Christensen	Farmer-Labor	1.0

U.S. Bureau of the Census, **Historical Statistics of the United States, Colonial Times to 1957** (Washington, D.C.: Government Printing Office, 1960), p. 682.

The Greenback-Labor party, formed in 1878, supported the unlimited coinage of silver, minimum hours for workers, an end to immigration of Chinese workers, women's suffrage, a graduated income tax, and federal regulation of interstate commerce.

The Prohibition party was organized in 1869, when the Democratic and Republican parties refused to support prohibition.

The Union Labor party was organized in 1887 by Grangers, Greenbackers, and members of the Knights of Labor.

In 1896, the Populist party supported the Democratic candidate, William Jennings Bryan, an advocate of free silver.

The Progressive party, the liberal wing of the Republican party, was also referred to as the "Bull Moose" party.

The Farmer-Labor party, founded in 1920, called for government ownership of railroads, mines, and natural resources, and advocated social security legislation and laws to protect farmers and union members.

Figure 76B
Votes for President in Four
New York Counties,
1888-1900

This figure presents the votes for President in two urban and two rural New York counties for the four Presidential elections between 1888 and 1900. The two rural counties had the highest percentage of Democratic votes of all the rural counties in the state.

1. Where did support for Republicans seem to come from, urban areas, rural areas, or both?
2. How do you account for the rise in Republican strength in cities in the 1896 election?

Lee Benson, "Research Problems in American Political Historiography," in **Common Frontiers of the Social Sciences**, Mirra Komarousny, ed. (Glencoe, Illinois: The Free Press, 1957), p. 168.

	New York County (urban)		Kings County (urban)		Schoharie County (rural)		Seneca County (rural)	
	Dem.	Rep.	Dem.	Rep.	Dem.	Rep.	Dem.	Rep.
1888	60.1	39.9	53.7	45.6	56.1	41.4	49.8	48.1
1892	61.5	34.7	56.8	40.0	55.3	39.5	47.7	46.4
1896	44.0	50.8	39.7	56.3	51.0	46.6	44.6	53.5
1900	52.2	43.9	48.3	49.6	51.6	46.2	46.8	51.2

Figure 76C
Party Control of
the Executive
and Legislative Branches,
1875-1921

Voters in national elections also elected representatives. Until 1916, they elected senators indirectly. State legislatures chose senators until the Seventeenth Amendment provided for their election directly by voters. Figure 76C shows the results of these decisions by voters.

1. Which party controlled the Presidency, the House, and the Senate from 1875 to 1895? from 1895 to 1911? from 1911 to 1920?
2. What effect would these alignments have on the ability of a President to push through an imaginative program of legislation?

Year	President's Party Affiliation	Majority Party and Margin House of Rep.	Senate
1875-1877	R	D (60)	R (16)
1877-1879	R	D (13)	R (3)
1879-1881	R	D (19)	D (9)
1881-1883	R	R (12)	even
1883-1885	R	D (79)	R (2)
1885-1887	D	D (43)	R (9)
1887-1889	D	D (17)	R (2)
1889-1891	R	R (7)	R (2)
1891-1893	R	D (147)	R (8)
1893-1895	D	D (91)	D (6)
1895-1897	D	R (139)	R (4)
1897-1899	R	R (91)	R (13)
1899-1901	R	R (22)	R (27)
1901-1903	R	R (46)	R (24)
1903-1905	R	R (30)	R (22)
1905-1907	R	R (114)	R (22)
1907-1909	R	R (58)	R (30)
1909-1911	R	R (47)	R (29)
1911-1913	R	D (67)	R (10)
1913-1915	D	D (164)	D (7)
1915-1917	D	D (34)	D (16)
1917-1919	D	D (6)	D (11)
1919-1921	D	R (50)	R (2)

U.S. Bureau of the Census, Historical Statistics of the United States, Colonial Times to 1957 (Washington, D.C.: Government Printing Office, 1960), p. 691.

Figure 76D
Federal Government Finances, 1876-1920

Figure 76D shows the receipts, expenditures, quantity of surplus or deficit, and total gross debt of the federal government for every fifth year from 1876 to 1920. You may gain perspective on this budget when you realize that the 1973 budget for the federal government was $246.6 billion, the deficit was $14.4 billion, and the total estimated national debt was $458.4 billion.

A surplus is the amount that remains of something when use or need is satisfied. A deficit is the amount of something that is lacking.

1. Did government expenditures from 1876 to 1920 follow any set trend? What evidently happened to expenditures during the World War I period (1915-1920)?
2. What does the size of the budget indicate about the attitudes of government officials toward the federal government?

U.S. Bureau of the Census, Historical Statistics, p. 711.

Year	Receipts	Expenditures	Surplus or Deficit	Total Gross Debt	Estimated Population
1876	$ 294,096,000	$ 265,101,000	$ 28,995,000	$ 2,130,846,000	46,107,000
1880	333,527,000	267,643,000	65,884,000	2,090,909,000	50,262,000
1885	323,691,000	260,227,000	63,464,000	1,578,551,000	56,658,000
1890	403,081,000	318,041,000	85,040,000	1,122,397,000	63,056,000
1895	324,729,000	356,195,000	−31,466,000	1,096,913,000	69,580,000
1900	567,241,000	520,861,000	46,380,000	1,263,417,000	76,094,000
1905	544,275,000	567,279,000	−23,004,000	1,132,357,000	83,820,000
1910	675,512,000	693,617,000	−18,105,000	1,146,940,000	92,407,000
1915	697,911,000	760,587,000	−62,676,000	1,191,264,000	100,549,000
1920	6,694,565,000	6,403,344,000	291,222,000	24,299,321,000	106,466,000

The Political Philosophy of Grover Cleveland

Of the nineteenth-century Presidents after Abraham Lincoln, only Grover Cleveland has won a good reputation. He did not pioneer new ways to do things. But he was honest and purposeful. This excerpt from his Second Inaugural Address illustrates Cleveland's political philosophy.

1. What was Cleveland's view of the role of the federal government in relationship to the economy?
2. What relationship do you see between Cleveland's philosophy and the budget figures in Figure 76D?

Inaugural Addresses of the Presidents of the United States from George Washington 1789 to Harry S Truman 1949, House Document No. 540, 82nd Congress, 2nd Session (Washington, D.C.: Government Printing Office, 1950), pp. 153-157. Language simplified.

Every American citizen must look with utmost pride and enthusiasm upon the growth and expansion of our country, the ability of our institutions to withstand violence, the wonderful thrift and enterprise of our people, and the demonstrated superiority of our free government. Nevertheless, we must constantly watch for every symptom of weakness that threatens our national vigor.

512

Paternalism ruins republican institutions and imperils government by the people. It degrades the plan of rule of fathers established and handed on to us. It corrupts the patriotic sentiments of our countrymen. And it tempts them to try to find ways to get the government to support them. It undermines self-reliance and substitutes in its place dependence upon governmental favors. It stifles the spirit of true Americanism. The people should patriotically and cheerfully support their government. But the government should not support the people.

Under our scheme of government, wasting public money is a crime against citizens. The contempt of our people for economy and thrift in personal affairs saps the strength of our national character. It is a plain principle of good government that public expendures should be limited by public necessity. Necessity, in turn, should be measured by the rules of strict economy. It is equally clear that thrift among the people will best guarantee support of free institutions.

One way to avoid misappropriation of public funds is to appoint good and efficient workers to government jobs instead of appointing people whose major claim to office is that they have been the political supporters of the official who appoints them. To get better people appointed to office, civil service reform has found a place in our public policy.

The growth of trusts formed to limit production and fix prices is inconsistent with a free enterprise system. Competition in business should not be replaced by trusts that have the power to destroy competition. Nor should the people lose the benefit of lower prices which usually results from wholesome competition. These combinations of business firms frequently constitute conspiracies against the interests of the people. They are unnatural and opposed to our American sense of fairness. To the extent that they can be restrained by federal power, the government should relieve our citizens from their interference with competition.

The people of the United States have decreed that on this day, the control of their government shall be given to a political party pledged in the most positive terms to the accomplishment of tariff reform. They have thus spoken in favor of a more just and fair system of federal taxation. This Administration is, therefore, determined to devote itself to tariff reform.

Above all, I know there is a Supreme Being who rules the affairs of men and whose goodness and mercy have always supported the American people. I know He will not turn from us now if we humbly and reverently seek His powerful aid.

FOR THOUGHT:

Why did the national government play a relatively small role in American life between the Civil War and 1900?

Paternalism refers to a system in which persons in authority treat those under them in a fatherly way by regulating their conduct and supplying their needs.

▶Under what circumstances, if any, should the government support the people? Why?

Cleveland referred here to the passage of the Pendleton Civil Service Act in 1883.

In his campaign, Cleveland pledged to lower the McKinley tariff passed by the Republicans in 1890. The Wilson-Gorman tariff, passed in 1894, although lower, was still thoroughly protective. Therefore, Cleveland allowed it to become law without his signature.

77 ROOSEVELT AND WILSON DISCUSS THE ROLE OF GOVERNMENT

Throughout the closing decades of the nineteenth century, most political leaders, like President Grover Cleveland, advocated limited governmental intervention in the economy. At the same time, they supported special subsidies for particular interests such as railroads. These interests received large grants of land from the government. Belief in limited government, however, caused politicians to look skeptically at suggestions that the government should try to control unemployment, develop national resources in a comprehensive way, or pass extensive social-welfare legislation.

Support of restricting the amount of government intervention—sometimes loosely called laissez-faire—had many roots. In part, it came from the desire of business people to be left alone, free of what they felt was government incompetence. This desire received support from the works of many nineteenth-century economists who believed in the principles of a competitive economy.

Late in the nineteenth century, philosophers called Social Darwinists began to combine economic ideas with biological concepts. Charles Darwin, the famous English naturalist, had argued that some individual organisms are better fitted to the conditions of their environment than others. And the fittest will be most likely to survive and pass their characteristics on to the next generation. This process, Darwin thought, improved the species because the better-adapted creatures survived. Darwin, however, never applied his theory to human society. Social Darwinists made this application. Government or even private organizations, they said, should not interfere with "natural laws." If government provided jobs, passed laws to regulate working conditions, or gave the poor relief, some of the "less fit" might survive and drag down the rest of the society. For this reason, they said, government should not interfere with the economy. It should permit the "natural laws" to operate. The new forces of an urban-industrial society, however, demanded government action.

Presidents Theodore Roosevelt (1901-1909) and Woodrow Wilson (1913-1921) represent people of change. Neither broke completely with the past, but both tried new ways. As you read excerpts from their speeches, think about the following questions:

1. What did Roosevelt and Wilson think was the responsibility of the federal government in relationship to the welfare of the American people? Why did they take their particular stands?
2. What were the origins of the problems each man discussed?

514

Theodore Roosevelt
on the New Nationalism

After two terms as President, Theodore Roosevelt took a long hunting trip to Africa. On his return, he broke with his hand-picked successor, William Howard Taft. He gave the speech which follows before veterans of the Grand Army of the Republic gathered at Osawatomie, Kansas, in 1910.

One of the main objectives in every wise struggle for human betterment has been to achieve equality. In the struggle for this goal, nations rise from barbarism to civilization. Through it people press forward from one stage of enlightenment to the next. The destruction of special privilege is one of the chief factors in progress. The essence of any struggle for liberty has always been, and must always be, to take from some people the right to enjoy power, wealth, position, or immunity which has not been earned by service to their fellows.

When we achieve it, equality of opportunity for all citizens will have two great results. First, all people will have a fair chance to reach the highest point to which their capacities can carry them. In this, they will be unassisted by special privilege and unrestricted by special privileges of others. Second, the society will get from all citizens the highest service they are able to contribute.

I stand for the square deal. However, I do not mean merely that I stand for fair play under the present rules of the game. I stand for having those rules changed to work for greater equality of opportunity and reward.

This philosophy means that our national and state governments must be freed from the sinister influence or control of special interests. Every special interest is entitled to justice—full, fair, and complete. If there were any attempt by mob-violence to do harm to a special interest or a wealthy man, I would fight for him. And you would fight, too, if you were worth your salt, even if you disliked him. He should have justice. Every special interest is entitled to justice. But no person or interest is entitled to a vote in Congress, to a voice on the bench, or to representation in any public office. The Constitution guarantees protection to property. And we must make that promise good. It does not, however, give the right of suffrage to any corporation.

The absence of effective state and national controls over unfair money-getting has tended to create a small class of enormously wealthy and powerful men. Their chief object is to hold and increase their power. We must change the conditions which enable these men to accumulate power which they can use against the general welfare. They should have power only so long as it benefits the community.

Theodore Roosevelt, **The New Nationalism** (New York: Outlook Company, 1911), pp. 30-33. Language simplified.

▶What must a society do to such institutions as schools and welfare organizations in order to achieve full equality of opportunity? Should society make such changes?

515

by HON. EDWARD M. KENNEDY
United States Senator, Massachusetts, Democrat

From an address given on the floor of the United States Senate on April 2, 1974, on the occasion of his introducing the proposed Comprehensive National Health Insurance Act of 1974, a measure jointly sponsored by House Ways and Means Committee Chairman Wilbur Mills, Ark., D., and introduced by Rep. Mills in the House of Representatives at the same time.

FIVE YEARS AGO, I introduced the Health Security Act, a far-reaching proposal for national health insurance, into the Senate. Since that time, I have reintroduced this proposal in both the 92d and 93d Congresses, with broadening support from America's labor movement, from numerous national organizations, and from millions of Americans at the grass roots level in communities across the Nation. I am proud to be associated with this movement begun by Walter Reuther and his Committee of 100 for National Health Insurance—and continued today under the chairmanship of Leonard Woodcock, and with the strong support of the AFL-CIO.

I will continue to work for the principles of health security that have made this movement great. I believe we will fulfill these principles in our Nation. Good health care must be guaranteed to all Americans as a matter of right. We must eliminate financial barriers to health care by enacting a universal program of comprehensive health insurance that is paid for equitably according to a family's income. We must improve and expand our health care system to control costs and assure that high quality care is available to every American in every community across our Nation. To obtain these objectives, we must make the Social Security Administration the health insurer for all Americans.

The program of national health insurance that I have introduced in the Senate

by HON. CASPAR W. WEINBERGER
United States Secretary of Health, Education and Welfare

From testimony presented on April 24, 1974, before the Committee on Ways and Means of the U.S. House of Representatives in the course of hearings on national health insurance proposals.

COMPREHENSIVE health insurance is a long-debated idea whose time for enactment has arrived.

This can and should be the year in which we move decisively to protect every American against the high costs of health care. This can and should be the year in which we install new incentives for our health care system to become even better than it is. And this can and should be the year in which we succeed in getting fair but effective controls on the health care cost inflation that has plagued us for the better part of the past 20 years.

That last consideration, cost control, adds an additional critical urgency to the Committee's deliberations. Without the kind of comprehensive cost controls that are proposed in the Administration bill, the American people appear to be in for a very rough period indeed as far as health care costs are concerned. For example, the March Consumer Price Index for physicians' services registered the largest single monthly increase in recent history of 1.7 per cent. If continued, this would mean an annual increase in excess of 22 per cent. I think this points up the inability of a voluntary constraint program.

Further, the Cost of Living Council estimates that, with no controls in effect the cost of health care will rise by an additional $4-$5 billion in the next fiscal year and perhaps by another $9 billion in the following year. This extra spending, let me emphasize, would be in addition to the normal 12-13 per cent increase in

▶This newspaper story refers to a proposal for universal health insurance. It would work something like the social security system. Do you think that the national government should sponsor and run such a system? Why or why not?

▶For centuries, the word "man" has been used when a speaker or writer wishes to refer to human beings in general. Until recently, this usage was both common and accepted. Do you think it should be followed in the future? Or, should speakers and writers use words such as person which can refer to both males and females?

This conclusion implies more active governmental interference with social and economic conditions in this country than we have yet had. I think we must face the fact that such an increase in governmental control is now necessary.

I think we may go still further. Everyone admits that government has the right to regulate the use of wealth in the public interest. Let us also concede that government has the right to regulate the conditions of labor in the interest of the common good. Every man should have a chance to reach a position in which he will make the greatest possible contribution to the public welfare. Give him a chance. Don't push him up if he will not be pushed. Help any man who stumbles. No man can be a good citizen unless he earns more money than he requires to cover the bare cost of living. He must have hours of labor short enough so that he will have time and energy to bear his share in the management of the community after his day's work is done. We prevent many men from being good citizens by the conditions of life under which we force them to live. We need comprehensive workmen's compensation acts. We need both state and national laws to regulate child labor and the work of women. And we need practical training for daily life and work to supplement book-learning in public schools. We need to provide better sanitary conditions for our workers. And we need to extend the use of safety appliances in industry and commerce. In the interest of the working man himself, we need to set our faces like flint against mob-violence just as we do against corporate greed. We need to set our faces against violence and injustice and lawlessness by wage-workers, just as much as against lawless cunning, greed, and selfish arrogance by employers.

I do not ask for too much power for the central government. But I do ask that we work in a spirit of broad and far-reaching nationalism. We are all Americans. Our common interests are as broad as the continent. The National Government belongs to the whole American people. Where the whole American people are interested, that interest can be guarded effectively only by the National Government.

The American people rightfully demand a New Nationalism. Without it we cannot hope to deal with new problems. The New Nationalism puts the national need before sectional or personal advantage. It is not patient with the confusion which comes when local legislatures attempt to treat national issues as local issues. It is still more impatient of the lack of power which springs from dividing governmental powers widely, making it possible for local selfishness or legal cunning, hired by wealthy special interests, to bring national activities to a deadlock. This New Nationalism regards the executive power as the guardian of the public welfare. It demands that the courts shall be interested primarily in human welfare rather than in property. It demands that legislatures shall represent all the people rather than any one class or section of the people.

Woodrow Wilson
on the New Freedom

The Republican party split in 1912 over the rival candidacies of William Howard Taft and Theodore Roosevelt. And Woodrow Wilson won the Presidency. His Inaugural Address opened a remarkable period of legislative activity in Congress. Major legislation followed quickly in the three fields he mentioned in his Address: banking, tariff reduction, and the regulation of business activity.

There has been a change of government. What does the change mean? That is the question which is uppermost in our minds today.

A Compilation of the Messages and Papers of the Presidents Prepared Under the Direction of the Joint Committee on Printing, of the House and Senate (New York: Bureau of National Literature, Inc.), Vol. XVII, pp. 7868-7870. Language simplified.

It means much more than the mere success of a party. The success of a party means little except when the nation is using that party for a large and definite purpose. No one can mistake the purpose for which the nation now seeks to use the Democratic party. It seeks to use it to interpret a change in its own plans and point of view.

Nowhere else in the world have noble men and women shown more sympathy and helpfulness in their efforts to right wrong, ease suffering, and give the weak strength and hope. We have built up a great system of government. It has become a model for those who seek to set liberty upon foundations that will endure. Our life contains every great thing. And it contains it in rich abundance. But evil has come with the good. And much fine gold has been corroded. With riches has come inexcusable waste. We have wasted a great part of what we might have used. And we have not stopped to conserve the bounty of nature, without which our genius for enterprise would have been worthless and powerless. We have been proud of our industrial achievements. But we have not stopped thoughtfully enough to count the human cost. It is the cost of lives snuffed out, energies overtaxed and broken, a fearful physical and spiritual cost to men, women, and children upon whom the burden has fallen. The groans and agony of it all has not yet reached our ears. The great government we loved has too often been used for private and selfish purposes. And those who used it had forgotten the people.

▶Should society take care of people who are "broken" by industrialization, or should that responsibility fall to the individuals or the firms for which people work? Why?

At last we have a vision of our life as a whole. We see the bad with the good. With this vision we approach new problems. Our duty is to cleanse, to reconsider, to restore, to correct evil without harming the good, to purify and humanize every part of our life without weakening or sentimentalizing it. There has been something crude, heartless, and unfeeling in our haste to succeed and be great. We said, "Let every man look out for himself, let every generation look out for itself," while we built giant machinery which made it impossible for anyone except those who stood at the controls to have a chance to look out for themselves. We had not forgotten our morals. But we were very heedless and in a hurry to be great.

We have come now to a sober second thought. We have made up our minds to measure every process of our national life against the standards we so proudly set up at the beginning and have always carried in our hearts. Our work is a work of restoration.

We have listed the things that ought to be altered and here are some of the chief items. We must alter a tariff which cuts us off from our proper part in the commerce of the world, violates just principles of taxation, and makes the government an instrument in the hands of private interest. We must change a banking and currency system based upon outmoded financial principles which result in concentrating cash improperly and restricting loans. We must alter an industrial system which holds capital in check, restricts the liberties

518

and limits the opportunities of labor, and exploits the natural resources of the country. We must change a body of agricultural activities less efficient than big business, handicapped because science has not served the farmer directly enough, and crippled because the system of credit does not serve it well. We have watercourses undeveloped, waste places unreclaimed, forests untended, fast disappearing without plan or prospect of renewal, unregarded waste heaps at every mine. We have studied as perhaps no other nation has the most effective means of production. But we have not studied cost or economy as we should.

Nor have we studied and perfected the means by which government may be put at the service of humanity to safeguard the health of the nation. This is no sentimental duty. The basis of government is justice, not pity. These are matters of justice. There can be no equality of opportunity, the first essential of justice, if men and women and children are not shielded from the consequences of great industrial and social processes which they cannot alter, control, or cope with by themselves. Society must not crush, weaken, or damage its own parts. Law must keep sound the society it serves. Sanitary laws, pure food laws, and laws setting up conditions of labor which individuals are powerless to determine for themselves are intimate parts of the business of justice and legal efficiency.

These are some of the things we ought to do. We must not, however, leave the others undone, the old-fashioned, never-to-be-neglected, fundamental safeguarding of property and of individual rights. This is the high enterprise of the new day. We must lift everything that concerns our life as a nation to the light that shines from every person's conscience and vision of the right.

FOR THOUGHT:

What new roles did Theodore Roosevelt and Woodrow Wilson propose for the government to play in American life?

78 WAR AND THE IMAGE OF GOVERNMENT

Neither the hopes of Roosevelt's New Nationalism nor those of Wilson's New Freedom were wholly fulfilled. Neither President was able to push his entire program through Congress. Neither conceived of a role for government in a peacetime setting of the sort that exists today. The beginning of World War I, however, altered the framework of national politics and dramatized a new image of government's role.

Following the defeat of Napoleon in 1814, Europe enjoyed a century of peace. No general war involved all the great powers. No single power threatened to dominate the entire European continent. So American interests were safeguarded with little expenditure of funds. Americans enjoyed what one historican has called "free security." This condition encouraged people to think that they did not have to worry about military preparedness or foreign warfare. The beginning of World War I in 1914 and American entrance in 1917 shattered this confidence.

In the first months at war, lack of experience with major governmental enterprise yielded disastrous results. The production of heavy guns was completely confused. The first vessels did not emerge from the largest government shipyard until after the war was over. The railroad lines were totally disorganized, freight cars were scarce, and the government finally took over the roads.

Thousands of regulations flowed out of Washington. Elevator operators were told that they could make so many stops and no more. Traveling salesmen were restricted to two trunks. Everyone in the nation was given just so much coal and oil and no more. The railroad administration ran the railroads as a single system. The National War Labor Board guaranteed that the rights of industrial workers would be safeguarded if they promised not to strike. Collective bargaining was introduced into many industries where it had been unknown. Food prices were manipulated to encourage additional production. Shark steak and whale meat appeared on restaurant menus to enlarge the sources of protein. The United States shipped three times as much food to the allied countries during the war as it had before the beginning of hostilities.

The documents in Reading 78 describe the ways in which two contemporaries imagined that the war would change American political assumptions and structures. As you read, think about the following questions:

1. How did Baruch and Dewey reevaluate industrial competition and cooperation in the light of their war experiences?
2. Why did they believe that some wartime governmental activities should be continued after the peace settlement?

Bernard Baruch on the Peacetime Implications of the War

As a young man, Bernard M. Baruch (1870-1965) made a fortune in the stock market. In later life, he became an adviser to a number of American Presidents. The selection that follows has been taken from the Final Report of the War Industries Board. It was the central planning agency responsible for mobilizing the civilian war effort. Baruch was the chairman of the W. I. B.

The experience of the War Industries Board in controlling American industry leads its members to make a further suggestion. This suggestion has less to do with war than with the normal practices of business during peacetime.

Bernard M. Baruch, American Industry in the War—A Report of the War Industries Board (Washington, D.C.: Government Printing Office, 1921), pp. 98-100. Abridged and language simplified.

During the past few decades, American businessmen and technical experts have made extraordinary strides in converting the natural resources of this country into goods useful for human comfort and satisfaction. In the process, the older and simpler relations of government to business have been gradually forced to give way. We have been compelled to drift away from two old doctrines of Anglo-American law. The first is that government activity should be limited to preventing breach of contract, fraud, physical injury, and injury to property. The second is that government should protect only non-competent persons. Modern industry has made it necessary for the government to reach out its arm to protect competent individuals against the practices of mass industrial power. We have already evolved a system of government control over our railroads and over our merchant fleet. We continue to argue, however, that competition can be preserved in all other industries so that the interests of the public will be served and efficiency and wholesome growth in the development of natural wealth will take place. With this end in view, the Sherman and Clayton Acts have forbidden combinations in restraint of trade, monopolies, and many other vices which develop where individuals control great masses of capital. This legislation represents little more than a moderately ambitious effort by the government to make business conform to the simpler principles which worked satisfactorily in the past.

A breach of contract occurs when a party to an agreement violates the terms of that agreement or contract. Contracts are enforceable by law.

The war introduced a new element into this situation. The Sherman Act had broken many large companies into smaller ones. Many of these smaller companies grew during the war until some of them have become larger than the original parent company. The conditions of war made developments like these desirable. The war brought an absolute demand for goods, no matter what they cost or how difficult they were to acquire. A shortage of some goods developed. And most goods were in short supply for a time, at least. Group action, industry by industry, accompanied by government control of prices and distribution, was the only solution.

The Sherman Anti-Trust Act of 1900 and the Clayton Act of 1914 will be discussed in the historical essay of this chapter.

During the war, hundreds of trades were organized for the first time into national associations. Each was responsible for its component companies. They were organized on the suggestion and under the

SAVING DAYLIGHT!

"SET THE CLOCK AHEAD ONE HOUR AND WIN THE WAR!"

UNCLE SAM, YOUR ENEMIES HAVE BEEN UP AND ARE AT WORK ON THE EXTRA HOUR OF DAYLIGHT — WHEN WILL YOU WAKE UP?

United Cigar Stores Company

UNCLE SAM NEEDS THAT EXTRA SHOVELFUL

Help Uncle Sam to Win the War
by following these Directions:

1. Fire small amounts of coal often.
2. Keep fuel bed even by putting coal on thin spots. Avoid raking and slicing.
3. Keep fuel bed about six inches thick.
4. Look out for air leaks in brickwork.
5. Increase or decrease steam pressure by opening or closing draft damper in uptake.
6. Clean fires when the demand for steam is small, and while cleaning have the draft damper partly closed.

UNITED STATES FUEL ADMINISTRATION

STOP

SAVE
Prune pits
Plum pits
Cherry pits
Date seeds
Olive pits

Peach Stones
Apricot pits
the shells of
Hickory nuts
Butternuts and
Walnuts

The carbon produced from these materials when placed in respirators will
SAVE SOLDIERS' LIVES
by absorbing
GERMAN POISON GAS
DRY MATERIALS THOROUGHLY AND DELIVER TO POINTS DESIGNATED BY
THE AMERICAN RED CROSS
DO YOUR BIT — SAVE THE PIT

►Hundreds of posters such as these three called for sacrifice to achieve victory during World War I. Similar posters made similar pleas during later wars. Why are most people willing to sacrifice more in a war against another nation than they are in a "war" against poverty or against people who violate the civil rights of other citizens?

522

supervision of the government. Practices aimed at efficient production, price control, conservation of scarce materials, control of the quantity of production, and so forth began everywhere. As a result, many businessmen experienced the tremendous advantages to themselves and the general public of combination, cooperation, and common action with their natural competitors. To restore through new legislation the competitive situation which immediately preceded the war will be very difficult. On the other hand, to leave business combinations without adequate supervision and attention by the Government will tempt businessmen to run businesses for private gain with little reference to public welfare.

These associations can be beneficial to the general public. They can eliminate wasteful practices which result from producing a larger number of different brands or types of the same articles. They can help to cultivate the public taste for excellent goods. They can exchange information to eliminate wasteful methods of production and distribution. They can localize production in places where goods can be produced most economically. By exchanging information about purchases and goods, they can balance supply and demand more economically. In an emergency, these associations would be of invaluable aid to the government.

These combinations are also capable of doing great harm to the public. They can keep production just short of current demand and thus cause prices to rise steadily. They can set up agreements about prices to keep them abnormally high. They can favor one buyer over another. Nearly every businessman in the country learned during the war that a slight shortage of his product helped him. He could then charge more for it and make larger profits. Trade associations can influence management to produce just enough goods to keep prices high.

The question, then, is what kind of government organization can be devised to safeguard the public interest while these associations continue to carry on the good work of which they are capable. The country will quite properly demand the vigorous enforcement of all proper measures for the suppression of unfair competition and unreasonable restraint of trade. But this essentially negative policy of curbing vicious practices should, in the public interest, be supplemented by a positive program. To this end the experience of the War Industries Board points to the desirability of giving some government agency the power to create programs as well as the power to investigate abuses. This agency should encourage, under strict government supervision, cooperation and coordination in industry to increase production, eliminate waste, conserve natural resources, improve the quality of products, promote efficiency in operation, and thus reduce costs to the ultimate consumer.

▶Do you like to be able to choose among twenty brands of toothpaste or ten kinds of aspirin tablets? Or, does making a choice depend only on habit or an advertising gimmick?

John Dewey Reflects upon
the Wartime Experiences

John Dewey was one of America's best-known philosophers and educators. Unlike many intellectuals, he supported the war effort. In the article that follows, he predicted what some of the consequences of the war would probably be.

John Dewey, **Characters and Events—Popular Essays in Social and Political Philosophy** (New York: Holt, Rinehart and Winston, Inc., 1929), Vol. II, Book 4, Section 1, pp. 551-557. Abridged and adapted. Copyright © 1957 by John Dewey. Reprinted by permission of Holt, Rinehart and Winston, Inc.

▶Should "production for profit" be subordinated to "production for the public good" in peacetime as well as in wartime? Why or why not?

The first result of the war which I see is the more conscious and extensive use of science for community purposes in the postwar world. Changes produced by new mechanical inventions and appliances endure. The transformation brought about first in industry and then in general social and political life by the steam engine, the locomotive, and the gasoline engine have remained with us. Matters which in their day absorbed much more conscious attention have disappeared. Mechanically speaking, the greatest achievements of the year have been the submarine and airplane. Is it not likely that the combined effects of the two will do more to displace war than all the moralizing in existence?

The war has made it customary to utilize the collective knowledge and skill of scientific experts in all lines, organizing them for community ends. We shall probably never return wholly to the old divorce of knowledge from the conduct of public life. This divorce made knowledge abstract and left public affairs in the hands of men who ruled by routine, vested interest, and skilled manipulation. Used for the ends of a democratic society, the social mobilization of science should bring about changes in the practice of government. And these may eventually develop into a new type of democracy. With respect to this development, as with respect to the airplane, we are more likely to underestimate than to exaggerate the consequences which will follow.

In every warring country, people have demanded that production for profit should be subordinated to production for the public good. Legal restrictions and individual property rights have had to give way before the good of the society. The old idea of the absoluteness of private property has received a blow from which it will never wholly recover. The control of an individual or group over their "own" property has become relative to public needs. Public requirements may at any time be given precedence over private desires by public machinery created for that purpose.

Ways have been developed to regulate or control every part of our national life. Banking, finance, and new corporations have been affected by regulations to various degrees in all countries. The demand for food during the war has made clear to everyone the social meaning of all the occupations related to the food industry. Consequently, the question of the control of our land for use instead of for speculation has become acute. Regulations have also been passed to control the transportation and distribution of food, fuel, and metals such as steel and copper which play a vital role in war.

Not every agency developed during the war to protect the public interest will last. Many of them will melt away when the war comes to an end. But it must be borne in mind that the war did not create the inter-dependent interests which have given social significance to enterprises which were once private and limited in scope. The war only revealed the state of affairs which the application of steam and electricity to industry and transportation has already brought about. It offered an impressive object lesson about what had occurred. And it made it impossible for men to proceed any longer by ignoring the revolution which has taken place.

FOR THOUGHT:

To what degree did Baruch and Dewey call for the same types of reforms that Roosevelt and Wilson demanded?

79 FIFTY YEARS OF NATIONAL POLITICS

HISTORICAL ESSAY

Although many of the political issues that arose between 1789 and 1860 had national implications, the activities of the national government had relatively little effect on the daily lives of American citizens during this period. The national capital seemed far away. Men and women worked hard to make a living from the soil, from trade, or from manufacturing. Local and state governments built roads, educated children, and passed the majority of laws. And officials of these governments frequently came into direct contact with citizens.

This situation changed during the Civil War. But from the death of Lincoln in 1865 to the inauguration of Franklin D. Roosevelt in 1933 the national government was again relatively inactive.

Why the National Government Was Inactive

Six major factors help to explain this inactivity. First, most Presidents during the period from Grant through Hoover had a narrow view of the role of the Presidency. Many of them believed that the

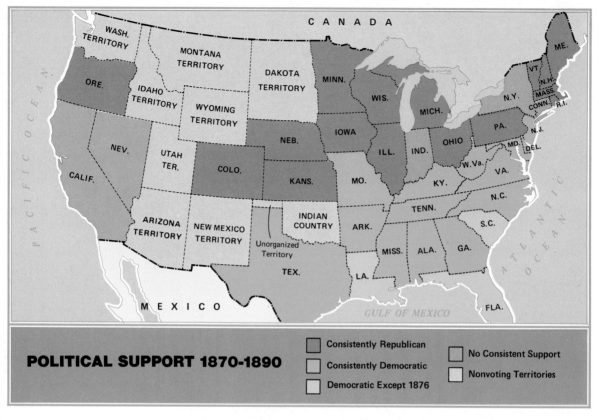

POLITICAL SUPPORT 1870-1890

- ■ Consistently Republican
- □ Consistently Democratic
- □ Democratic Except 1876
- ■ No Consistent Support
- ■ Nonvoting Territories

government was best which governed least. A number had been influenced by the ideas that the national government should not interfere with the workings of the economy. Only Theodore Roosevelt and Woodrow Wilson attempted to exercise active national leadership.

Nevertheless, interest in politics remained high. Torchlight parades and flamboyant oratory attracted crowds to political rallies. Local bosses in both urban and rural areas kept in close contact with voters whose vital interests they served. And the percentage of people who voted in elections kept pace with the rise in population through the last decades of the nineteenth century. A base for dramatic political action on a national scale did exist. But no one managed to put together a firm coalition of voters willing to support an active national government.

Second, during the late nineteenth century, the two major parties received roughly the same number of votes at national elections. Of all the Presidents between Hayes and Roosevelt, only McKinley received more than 50 percent of the popular vote. Two Presidents (Hayes and Benjamin Harrison) received fewer popular votes—although more electoral votes—than one of their rivals. Democrats

▶ If you were forced to choose, would you work on building a strong, active political organization in your locality or on the national level? Why?

526

usually held a majority in the House of Representatives. And Republicans usually controlled the Senate. The Republicans controlled both houses of Congress between 1896 and 1911, usually by generous margins. But the Republican party was divided into opposing factions. The progressive wing was led by Theodore Roosevelt. The conservative wing was dominated by many prominent senators. So, while the Republicans controlled both the Congress and the Presidency during this period, their internal difficulties made it virtually impossible for the federal government to provide united, consistent national leadership for the nation.

Third, the lack of national consensus on major political issues also hampered political action. Local political leaders rallied voters to their own banners. They tried through the use of patronage and other devices to weave a web of personal loyalty. But they did not try to develop bonds that tied voters to a national party. Thus, voters tended to focus their attention on local issues which affected their lives directly rather than on less personal problems on the national level. To achieve any sweeping reforms of American institutions the federal government would have to find some way of shifting the voters' attention from local to national issues.

Except for such momentous national issues as wars, however, citizens of the United States did not yet have enough in common to support comprehesive national political action. Early in the twentieth century, large daily newspapers and magazines began to reach a substantial national audience. Journalists, whom President Theodore Roosevelt called "muckrakers," used these newspapers and magazines to inform readers of the "harsh reality" of the new industrial society. However, journalists could not create a political revolution alone. Illiteracy had been reduced to 10 percent by 1910. But most Americans had never been within the walls of a high school. Reforming magazines such as *The Saturday Evening Post*, which had a circulation of about 2 million in 1914, served the enlarged middle class. But they hardly touched the minds of most Americans. Only great events like war or the Depression of the 1930's sharply affected the lives of most citizens. By the 1930's, the radio helped President Franklin D. Roosevelt to rally support directly from voters for his programs. After World War II, television began to play a similar and far more important role. But in the era of Theodore Roosevelt and Woodrow Wilson, a national constituency was only beginning to form. And its members were largely middle-class people.

A fourth reason for the relative inactivity of the national government was the active part played by state and local governments in dealing with the major political issues of the day. The first important laws to regulate railroads were passed by state legislatures in the 1870's. The early progressives made their most significant gains on the local and state levels. These efforts succeeded far more rapidly than any similar movement on the national scale. Eventually, these reformers learned that many of the issues with which they were concerned, such as railroad regulation, the control of trusts, or the regulation of child labor, could only be settled on a national level. But in the meantime, they drew attention from Washington to mayors' and governors' offices.

In the fifth place, the national government needed more money to do effective work. The federal government's expenditures amounted to about 5 percent of the gross national product. (By comparison, in the 1970's, the federal government was spending about 20 percent of the gross national product.) Citizens asked government to take on a host of new tasks. But they did not provide the money. Lack of money helps to explain both the failure to start new programs and the inability to enforce ones which were already on the books. In September 1914, for example, Congress passed the Federal Trade Commission Act. It was followed one month later by the Clayton Antitrust Act. The Federal Trade Commission was empowered to gather information on business activities and to ". . . prevent persons, partnerships, or corporations . . . from using unfair methods of competition." The Clayton Antitrust Act listed many activities which were to be considered restraints of trade under the original antitrust legislation, the Sherman Act (1890). But the FTC never got enough funds to do its job. The Antitrust Division of the Justice Department never included more than eighteen lawyers during Wilson's Administration. Experience during the 1930's indicated that the department required a staff at least ten times that large to check abuses adequately.

Funds for thorough investigations were not provided and staffs were small. So, government officials often had to depend on information provided by the industries they were regulating as a basis for action. Naturally, they did not always learn what they needed for effective control. By controlling the flow of information, businesses were subtly able to shape regulations to their own liking. Aroused by muckraking books such as Upton Sinclair's *The Jungle* (1906), an exposure of abuses in the meat-packing industry, Congress moved to regulate packing houses. Big packers were anxious to establish standards high enough to protect them against the competition of small, local packers. The Pure Food and Drug Act and the Meat Inspection Act passed easily for two reasons. The major packers supplied data in support of regulation. And Roosevelt avoided a battle with these industrialists by taking money for inspection out of general tax funds instead of asking for a special fee to be paid by packers themselves. No acts, no matter how excellent their intention, could serve the public effectively without strong provisions for enforcement backed by congressional appropriations. Not until 1913, when the adoption of the

Sixteenth Amendment legalized the income tax, did the government have a practical way to raise the huge funds that expanded federal services would require.

The last major factor that helps to account for the relative inactivity of the federal government was lack of reliable knowledge about the nation. Late in the nineteenth century, the executive branch began to improve its facilities for gathering data. The census of 1880 had been a massive attempt to gather a huge amount of information. The result of this effort filled twenty-five volumes. But when the census was finished, the staff was dispersed. It had to be gathered anew in both 1890 and 1900. In 1902, the Bureau of the Census was finally established with a permanent staff which worked constantly instead of once every ten years. New series of statistics, begun during the first decades of the twentieth century, later played a vital part in guiding legislation. In the meantime, social scientists developed new theoretical models of the social and economic structure of the nation. In the 1920's and 1930's, the concept of the gross national product became important among some economists. They began to develop techniques by which the government might control inflation and depression and insure steady economic growth. Even if they had wanted to do something to stabilize the economy, American Presidents as late as the 1920's lacked both the theoretical knowledge and the statistical data on which a full-scale attack on a depression could have been based.

In 1894, as part of the Wilson-Gorman tariff, Congress passed a 2 percent tax on incomes over $4000. The following year, the Supreme Court ruled the tax unconstitutional on the grounds that it was a direct tax not apportioned among the states according to population as specified in Article 1, Section 2, Clause 3.

National Legislation

Four issues dominated national politics between 1872 and 1920. They were the regulation of business, the control of the money supply, the regulation of the tariff, and the development of ways to eliminate corruption in government and to make government more directly responsive to the wishes of voters. Occasionally other issues occupied the attention of legislators. Congress set up land-grant colleges, agricultural experiment stations, and county extension programs. Particularly under President Theodore Roosevelt, the federal government established irrigation projects and set aside land for national parks. Under Woodrow Wilson, the government established the Department of Labor. It passed such measures as the following: La Follette Seaman's Act (1915) established minimal working conditions on steamships; the Adamson Act (1916) established the eight-hour day on interstate railroads; a Child Labor Act (which was later declared unconstitutional) established minimal working standards for children; the Federal Farm Loan Act set up flexible ways for farmers to get credit; and the Rural Post Roads Act established a precedent for federal aid to highway construction. But legislation like this was unusual.

FIGURE 79A   FEDERAL LEGISLATION REGULATING INDUSTRY, 1887-1920

Name of Act	Date	Provisions
Interstate Commerce Act	1887	Created Interstate Commerce Commission (I.C.C.) of five members to regulate and investigate railroads. Required railroads to charge "reasonable and just rates" and give 10-day notice and public posting of new rates. Forbade pooling, charging more for a short haul than a long haul, and discriminating by allowing special favors or rebates.
Sherman Antitrust Act	1890	Declared all combinations in the form of trusts or conspiracies "in restraint of trade" illegal.
Elkins Act	1903	Forbade shippers, railway officials, and agents from giving or receiving rebates. Made railroads charge only the published rates.
Hepburn Act	1906	Forbade railroads from granting free passes. Increased I.C.C. to seven members and gave it authority to fix maximum rates and to regulate express and sleeping-car companies, oil pipelines, ferries, bridges, and railroad terminals.
Pure Food and Drug Act	1906	Prohibited the manufacture, sale, and transportation of adulterated or mislabeled goods and drugs. Required manufacturers of patent medicines to label containers indicating contents.
Meat Inspection Act	1906	Provided for federal inspection of all companies selling meat between states.
Mann-Elkins Act	1910	Authorized I.C.C. to regulate telephones, telegraphs, and cables.
Clayton Antitrust Act	1914	Prohibited price discrimination, interlocking directorates over $1 million, and the acquisition of another company's stock in order to create a monopoly.
Federal Trade Commission Act	1914	Set up Federal Trade Commission (F.T.C.) of five members to investigate companies and prevent unfair business practices such as false advertising and mislabeling.
Esch-Cummins Act	1920	Authorized I.C.C. to fix minimum and maximum rates and to approve railroad consolidations.

Figure 79A shows the major laws which regulated business. The growth of industry made these laws necessary. Many of them were directed at the abuses of railroads against which farmers had protested so vigorously for decades. Others tried to assure competition in industry by controlling the activities of pools, trusts, and giant corporations which threatened to win monopolistic control of many industries. These laws were minimally successful. In many cases, the Supreme Court undermined them by decisions that limited the power of administrators to do what legislators had seemingly wished them to do. Because government agencies were underfinanced and understaffed, they were unable to prosecute business as vigorously as they should have done. Finally, a number of proposals which might have led to more effective legislation were defeated or watered down in Congress by legislators who were firm believers in laissez-faire and beholden to business.

Until the passage of the Federal Reserve Act under Woodrow Wilson in 1913, debate over the money supply and banking regulations occupied an enormous amount of attention. Farmers in particular pressed for an expanded money supply in order to combat the long-run deflationary trend which extended through most of the 1870's, 1880's, and 1890's. During the Populist campaign of 1892 and the 1896 Presidential contest, the proposal to coin silver in unlimited amounts in order to expand the money supply dominated political debate. An influx of gold from Alaska and South Africa halted the inflationary spiral and drove the issue of an expanded currency out of politics. But the Federal Reserve Act was still needed, as the list of legislation in Figure 79B explains, to keep currency flexible.

FIGURE 79B   MONEY AND BANKING LEGISLATION, 1863-1913

Name of Act	Date	Provisions
National Banking Act	1863	Permitted five or more people with capital of $50,000 to secure charter and set up national bank. Required banks to invest one third of capital in government bonds and to issue bank notes up to 90% of face value of bonds.
Coinage Act	1873	Ended coinage of silver dollars.
Resumption Act	1875	Agreed to redeem greenback dollars in gold if presented to Treasury on or after January 1, 1879.
Bland-Allison Act	1879	Required Treasury to buy and mint $2—4 million silver a month.
Sherman Silver Purchase Act (repealed 1893)	1890	Required Treasury to purchase 4.5 million ounces of silver each month at the market price and to pay for it with paper money redeemable in either gold or silver.
Gold Standard (Currency) Act	1900	Made gold the standard unit of value backing the dollar. Provided gold reserve of $150 million for redemption of paper money.
Aldrich-Vreeland Act	1908	Authorized national banks to issue emergency money to be backed by commercial paper and state and local bonds.
Federal Reserve Act	1913	Divided United States into 12 districts, each to be served by a federal reserve bank, all supervised by Board of Governors appointed by President for 14 years. Required federal reserve banks to serve district banks by clearing checks, lending money, rediscounting loans, issuing paper money (federal reserve notes) backed by gold and commercial paper, and transferring money between districts in emergencies. Required all national banks to join, keep a certain percentage of deposits in reserve bank, and buy a percentage of bank's stock.

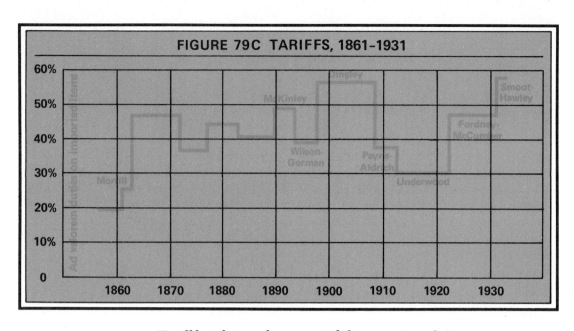

FIGURE 79C TARIFFS, 1861–1931

Ad valorem duties on imported items

60%
50%
40%
30%
20%
10%
0

1860   1870   1880   1890   1900   1910   1920   1930

(Chart labels: Morrill, McKinley, Wilson-Gorman, Dingley, Payne-Aldrich, Underwood, Fordney-McCumber, Smoot-Hawley)

Secretary of the Treasury, Benjamin H. Bristow, discovered that a "whiskey ring," which included the Supervisor of Internal Revenue, was robbing the federal government of $1 million annually by not turning over revenue taxes collected on distilled liquors and fines place on tax-evading distillers. Secretary of War, William E. Belknap, was forced to resign when it was revealed that he had accepted $24,000 in bribes from a trader in Oklahoma. The Secretary of the Navy "sold" contracts to shipbuilders. And the Secretary of the Interior was found to be working closely with land speculators.

Tariff legislation also occupied the attention of almost every administration. Figure 79-C traces the history of the major laws. Advocates of high tariffs won support from industry. Managers argued that high tariffs protected American employers and workers from the competition of foreign goods produced by workers earning lower wages than Americans. Foes of the tariff pointed out that high tariff rates permitted inefficient producers to charge higher prices because tariff walls protected them from competition by efficient foreign firms. Tariffs also hurt farmers, they argued, by raising prices on manufactured goods with no compensating increase in the price of foodstuffs which farmers raised. Business exerted an enormous influence over large numbers of senators and representatives. So tariffs tended to be high despite the barrage of excellent arguments leveled by economists against them.

The final issue that occupied the attention of the President and Congress concerned corruption in government and government responsiveness to the demands of citizens. During the Grant Administration, corruption ran rampant through a number of administrative departments. It led eventually to the discharge of a number of Grant's appointees. In later administrations the spoils system led to a wholesale turnover of federal appointees whenever the Presidency changed hands from one party to another. Several Presidents complained that most of their time was spent in the tiresome task of interviewing applicants for federal jobs. Finally, after a disappointed office-seeker assassinated President James A. Garfield in 1881, Chester Alan Arthur, who succeeded him, pushed through the Pendleton Civil Service Act. Its provisions can be found in Figure 79D. The other major developments on the national scene were the passage of two important amendments. The Seventeenth Amendment (1913) provided that United States senators should be elected directly by voters instead of by the members of state legislatures who had chosen senators since 1789. The Nineteenth Amendment extended the franchise to women.

FIGURE 79D		MAKING GOVERNMENT MORE DEMOCRATIC, 1880-1920
Name of Act	Date	Provisions
Pendleton Civil Service Act	1883	Set up three-man Civil Service Commission to draw up and administer competitive examinations for certain federal jobs. Forbade political party in power from asking for campaign contributions
Publicity Act	1910	Required congressional representatives to file statements of campaign contributions.
Seventeenth Amendment	1913	Called for popular election of senators.
Nineteenth Amendment	1920	Provided for woman suffrage.

The Place of National Politics in History

"History is past politics," a famous historian once said. This point of view seems narrow—even inaccurate—to most contemporary historians. The history of the United States involves all its people and all their lives—where they came from, what they thought, how they made a living, and how they got along with each other and with people from other nations.

Most people view their lives differently than they view the history of their nation. Personal lives involve the cycle of birth, growth, work, aging, and death. Occasionally an event in national politics affects someone personally. A war breaks out and families are disrupted. Congress passes a new tax, and paychecks are smaller. But most of the days of people's lives, even in an age when television fills the airwaves with news from Washington, pass by without direct, personal knowledge of the way in which national politics have affected them.

Yet national politics reveal a great deal about the past. In a way, they reflect a people's collective conscience. What troubles the nation greatly eventually troubles Congress. People can learn much about themselves and about their ancestors by watching what their representatives have done. But this conclusion does not indicate that a history book ought to be organized around national politics. Thomas Edison probably had a more significant impact on American society than any nineteenth-century senator. Most high school and college history textbooks are still organized around a "Presidential synthesis," that is, the events of American history have been related to various administrations as if Presidents bound the past together. During the period between the end of the Civil War and the first administration of Franklin D. Roosevelt, this tie was not nearly so important to the future of the nation as many others: the development of American industry, the dramatic changes taking place in agriculture, the shift of people from rural areas in Europe and the United States to great new cities, the development of new frontiers in the West and on the streets of urban areas, and even the events which took place in the council chambers of city governments. After 1933, however, the federal government began to sponsor a series of new programs which eventually touched the life of every American virtually every day.

The United States
Becomes a World Power, 1898-1920

STATING THE ISSUE

Throughout most of the nineteenth century, Americans were concerned with extending the frontier, settling a vast new land area, developing agriculture and industry, building roads, canals, and railroads, and dealing with sectional conflicts sharpened by the Civil War. Following the War of 1812, most Americans had paid little attention to their nation's role in the world. Then between 1898 and 1920, the United States became one of the strongest and most influential nations in world affairs. This change took both Americans and citizens of other countries by surprise. It also had a great influence on international relationships.

In 1898, the United States felt frustrated with a long, bloody revolution in Cuba. It declared war on Spain in order to end the revolt. The three-month war left Cuba independent. It also left the United States in control of Puerto Rico and the Philippine Islands.

During World War I, the United States helped Great Britain, France, and their allies to defeat Germany and its supporters. American influence was so great at the end of the war that President Woodrow Wilson played the leading part in the conference that wrote the peace treaty and created an international organization to keep peace.

Many Americans cheered the advance of the flag into the far Pacific and the Caribbean, and many acclaimed the League of Nations. But others disapproved strongly of the nation's expanded role abroad. Because Americans themselves differed over their national goals, other countries often did not know what to expect of the United States in international affairs.

The readings in Chapter 21 analyze the motives and attitudes of Americans toward overseas expansion at the time of the Spanish-American War. They also examine American policies in the Philippine Islands. The historical essay which closes the chapter traces American foreign policy through World War I.

1400 1500 1600 1700 **1800** **1900** 2000

1885 Reverend Josiah Strong publishes book **Our Country**	**1904** United States assumes control of Dominican Republic's economic affairs
1893 American businessmen attempt to overthrow Hawaiian Queen Liliuokalani	**1906** Algeciras Conference convenes to settle Moroccan crisis
1898 Battleship **Maine** is sunk in Havana harbor; United States declares war on Spain	**1912** Woodrow Wilson is elected President
1898 Commodore Dewey defeats Spanish fleet in Manila Bay	**1914** World War I begins in Europe
1899 United States sends delegates to international peace conference at the Hague	**1915** Germans sink British liner **Lusitania**
1900 American troops aid in putting down rebellion in China	**1916** General John J. Pershing goes into Mexico to capture Pancho Villa
1901 McKinley is assassinated; Theodore Roosevelt becomes President	**1917** United States enters World War I
1902 The Philippine Islands become a United States territory	**1918** Armistice is called
1903 United States gains right to build canal in Panama	**1919** United States Congress rejects Treaty of Versailles
	1921 United States Congress declares war with Germany officially over

80 THE IDEOLOGY OF EXPANSION

Several times during the 1890's Americans had to decide whether to extend the nation's power into weak foreign lands. During the nineteenth century, European countries had carved up Africa. Together with Japan, they had taken control of rich or strategic parts of China. In the Middle East and in Southeast Asia, European rivals competed for territory and influence.

The United States showed some interest in the competition. In 1867, it purchased Alaska from Russia. In 1879, it joined England and Germany in an agreement to provide military protection for the Samoan Islands in the South Pacific. In return, Samoa permitted England, Germany, and the United States to control its trade and relations with other nations. Later, the United States acquired a naval base at Pearl Harbor in Hawaii.

But the relationship between the United States and Latin American countries is more typical of American attitudes toward overseas

536

expansion. The United States had many chances to take advantage of the political instability of Latin America. Except during the Mexican War, however, the United States sent neither armies nor navies to try to gain territory or win influence in Latin America. Most Americans did not want their country to expand south of the border nor did they want to take away other American republics' independence.

Yet the pull of imperialism was strong. The force of imperialism owed much to nationalism. During the nineteenth century, nationalism grew rapidly in many countries, including the United States. Nationalism usually celebrated the unique qualities of a people, including their culture, history, and virtues. It always produced an upsurge of national pride. This feeling of pride often contributed to aggressive behavior toward other nations. The Social Darwinism of the times also helped the growth of imperialism. (See Chapter 20.) It persuaded many people that the behavior of nations differed little from that of animals preying on each other in nature. Thus strong nations could excuse their domination of the weak by saying it was "survival of the fittest."

You can begin to understand the American version of imperialism by examining the ideas used to justify it. As you will see, nationalism and Social Darwinism played significant parts in those ideas. But since imperialism, like any major social development, was complex, the ideology of imperialism was also complex. As you read, try to answer these questions:

1. What basic ideas appear in the Strong and Mahan arguments for expansion? Why might they appeal to Americans?
2. What other ideas supporting expansion appear in the editorials favoring annexation of Hawaii in 1893? Do any of Strong's and Mahan's ideas reappear there?

The Anglo-Saxon Mission

The Reverend Josiah Strong (1847-1916), a Congregational minister, was a leader in the movement to convert people in non-Christian parts of the world to Christianity. This movement was especially strong among American Protestants at this time. In his book, Our Country, *published in 1885, Strong offered his vision of the future of the world.*

Josiah Strong, **Our Country: Its Possible Future and Its Present Crisis** (New York: The Baker and Taylor Company, 1891), pp. 205-216.

The two great needs of mankind are, first, a pure, spiritual Christianity, and second, civil liberty. It follows, then, that the Anglo-Saxon, as the great representative of these two ideas, is divinely commissioned to be his brother's keeper. Add to this the fact of his rapidly increasing strength in modern times, and we have well-nigh a demonstration of his destiny.

INFORMATION WANTED.

HE WOULDN'T TAKE IT ANY OTHER WAY.

How did these cartoonists picture some of the results of expansion? Do you agree or disagree with their views?

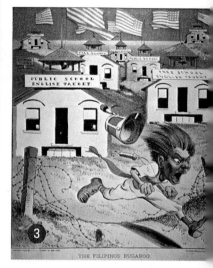

THE FILIPINOS BUGABOO.

During these two hundred years, our population has increased 250 times. In one century the United States has increased its territory ten times. The enormous acquisition of foreign territory by Great Britain—and chiefly within the last hundred years—is wholly unparalleled in history. This mighty Anglo-Saxon race comprises only one thirteenth of mankind. But it now rules more than one third of the earth's surface, and more than one fourth of its people.

It seems to me that God, with infinite wisdom and skill, is training the Anglo-Saxon race for an hour sure to come in the world's future. Before, there has always been in the history of the world a comparatively unoccupied land westward. The crowded countries of the East have poured their surplus populations into these lands. But the widening waves of migration meet today on our Pacific coast. There are no more new worlds. The unoccupied arable lands of the earth are limited, and will soon be taken. The time is coming when the pressure of population on the means of making a living will be felt here as it is now felt in Europe and Asia. Then will the world enter upon a new stage of its history—*the final competition of races, for which the Anglo-Saxon is being schooled.* If I read correctly, this powerful race will move down upon Mexico, down upon Central and South America, out upon the islands of the sea, over upon Africa and beyond. And can anyone doubt that the result of this competition of races will be the "survival of the fittest"?

Sea Power and American Strength

Alfred Thayer Mahan (1840-1914) was an officer in the United States Navy and a noted historian. He developed theories about the role of sea power in the rise and fall of nations. His theories influenced American politicians, like Theodore Roosevelt, and foreign governments, like that of Germany. In the following article, written in 1890, Mahan looked forward to the impact of the building of a Central American canal on international relations. The canal would connect the Atlantic and Pacific oceans. The first result, he thought, would be the end of American isolation from European affairs.

When the Isthmus of Panama is pierced this isolation will pass away, and with it the indifference of foreign nations. All ships that use the canal will pass through the Caribbean. Large commercial and political interests will center around such a focus of trade. To protect and develop its own, each nation will seek points of support and means of influence in a place where the United States has always been jealously sensitive to the intrusion of European powers. Already France and England are giving to ports held by them a degree of strength uncalled for by their present importance. They look to the near future. There are now many positions of great importance, held by weak or unstable states, among the Caribbean islands and on the Central American mainland. Is the United States willing to see them sold to a powerful rival? But what right will she invoke against the transfer? She can allege but one,—that of her reasonable policy supported by her might.

Whether they will or not, Americans must now begin to look outward. The growing production of the country demands it. An increasing volume of public sentiment demands it. The position of the United States, between the two Old Worlds and the two great oceans, makes the same claim. This claim will soon be strengthened by the creation of the new link joining the Atlantic and Pacific. The tendency will be increased by the growth of European colonies in the Pacific, by the advancing civilization of Japan, and by the settling of our Pacific states with people who have the aggressive spirit of national progress. Nowhere does a vigorous foreign policy find more favor than among the people west of the Rocky Mountains.

Alfred Thayer Mahan, "The United States Looking Outward," **The Atlantic Monthly**, Vol. LXVI (1890), pp. 821-823.

▶ Under what conditions, if any, should a nation force a "reasonable policy" on other countries by using its might?

Ideas in Action:
The Movement to Annex Hawaii

By 1893 Americans had gained a dominant commercial position in the Hawaiian Islands. Hawaii was a monarchy headed by Queen Liliuokalani. In 1893 American sugar planters and business people staged a revolt to overthrow the queen. The bloodless revolt was a success due to the fact that the American minister to Hawaii, John L. Stevens, conspired with the rebels. He ordered Marines and artillery ashore from an American warship to overawe the queen and her government. The rebels promptly asked the United States to annex Hawaii as a territory. But because of Stevens' flagrant interference, President Grover Cleveland refused in late 1893 to consider annexation. Americans, and the American press, differed over annexation. Editorials from early 1893, before the details of the plot became known, provide insight into the views of those who favored expansion.

NEW YORK COMMERCIAL ADVERTISER (INDEPENDENT), FEBRUARY 18, 1893

▶ Under what conditions does one people have the duty or right to force law and order on another people?

In dealing with a partly barbarous country, the United States need not follow the same demands of justice which a civilized country might properly make of us. The native population is entitled to humane treatment. But the underlying principle in the negotiations is that law and order must be insisted upon by the nations of the earth. When a people proves itself unable to maintain a stable government, it is the province of a higher civilized nation to step in and supply the need. The Hawaiians are to be treated kindly, firmly as children. The time has passed for seriously regarding them as competent to govern themselves, or to tell others how to govern them. President Benjamin Harrison has more wisely taken his counsel from superior, trustworthy Anglo-Saxons. Then, his duty clear, he ceased to talk, and acted. The Anglo-Saxons are the nation-builders of the world.

WASHINGTON POST (INDEPENDENT), FEBRUARY 1, 1893

The Hawaiian question is a national question. It is one of patriotic feeling and plain common sense. Shall we take Hawaii, and thereby prosper and magnify ourselves? Or shall we let England take it, and thereby enfeeble and humiliate us? If we be a great nation, with pride and purpose and intelligence, we shall seize the opportunity. If we are inert, cowardly, and stupid, we'll keep quiet and let England complete the chain of her hostile environment.

This is an affair for us to settle for ourselves. Hawaii is the natural and logical outpost of the United States in the Pacific. Its possession would mean the saving of millions in coast defense and the control of the commercial pathways of more than half the salt water on the globe. The Hawaiians have come to us for protection and help. In responding to their petition we shall immeasurably strengthen and enrich ourselves. Shall we do it? That is the only question. England's protests are not to be considered.

DENVER NEWS (DEMOCRAT), JANUARY 29, 1893

There can be little doubt of the great importance which the acquisition of the Hawaiian Islands will prove to the Pacific coast cities. Their ownership would at once give strength to the naval force of this government and a most commanding position in the event of a naval war between the United States and France, England, or Germany.

BOSTON TRAVELLER (REPUBLICAN), FEBRUARY 13, 1893

Is Hawaii worth annexing, or should the United States abandon it to itself and leave it to work out its own destiny? There are facts and figures worthy of consideration. In the fiscal year ending June 30, 1892, the United States alone received Hawaiian products, chiefly sugar, to the value of $8,075,881. That is an astonishing amount of merchandise for 85,000 people, many of them hampered by the laziness common to natives of tropical countries. Of course, the surplus products of Hawaii were not all marketed in the United States. The total exports were about $9 million, or over $100 for every man, woman, or child in the Hawaiian Islands. Such a foreign commerce, maintained by a country with only a semi-civilized system of government, is at once a proof of almost phenomenal natural resources.

A fiscal year is a full year for keeping financial records. The federal government's fiscal year runs from July 1 of one year to June 30 of the following year. States, big companies, and other organizations establish their own fiscal years to suit their particular financial patterns.

FOR THOUGHT:

Why might Americans find the ideas in Reading 80 appealing?

81 THE ISSUE OF IMPERIALISM, 1898–1900

In 1898 Commodore George Dewey's ships blasted a rickety Spanish fleet out of the water in Manila Bay in the Philippines. With this event, the most perlexing question to grow out of the Spanish-American War became apparent: Should the United States rule a distant land that contained people with an alien culture? This, of course, was the same question that had been raised by the Hawaiian issue earlier. But the Philippine question was more complicated.

Not since the United States had won the Southwest from Mexico in 1848 had territorial expansion generated such controversy among the American people. The anti-imperialist movement lacked effective organization and leadership. But it did include social reformers, such as Jane Addams, political reformers, such as Carl Schurz, two former Presidents, Republican Benjamin Harrison and Democrat Grover

Cleveland, industrialist Andrew Carnegie, and some of America's most distinguished college professors and literary artists. But President McKinley studied American opinion closely. He consulted his own judgment and decided to annex the Philippine Islands. At the time, his diplomats were discussing a peace treaty with Spain in Paris. He instructed them to insist upon American ownership of not only the Philippines, but of Guam in the Pacific and Puerto Rico in the Caribbean.

Americans never voted directly on the issue of keeping the Philippines. But President McKinley won reelection easily in 1900, in a campaign in which his Democratic opponent, William Jennings Bryan, strongly opposed imperialism. In spite of vocal opposition to annexation, most Americans probably approved of the President's decision.

Reading 81 gives the major arguments used by those who supported and those who opposed annexation of the Philippines. As you read them, consider these questions:

1. Why was McKinley not sure about what to do with the Philippines?
2. How did Beveridge's and Mason's views of American democracy differ?

President McKinley Decides to Annex the Philippines

This selection is taken from a biography of President McKinley. It describes his thoughts about annexing the Philippine Islands. He was discussing them with a committee of men interested in Christian missionary work.

Charles S. Olcott, **The Life of William McKinley** (Boston: Houghton Mifflin Company, 1916), Vol. II, pp. 110-111.

Manila is the largest city of the Philippine Islands. It is situated on the largest island, Luzon.

When I realized that the Philippines had dropped into our laps, I confess I did not know what to do with them. I sought counsel from all sides—Democrats as well as Republicans. But I got little help. I thought first we would take only Manila; then Luzon, then other islands, perhaps, also. I walked the floor of the White House night after night until midnight. And I am not ashamed to tell you, gentlemen, that I went down on my knees and prayed Almighty God for light and guidance more than one night. And one night late it came to me this way. I don't know how it was, but it came: (1) That we could not give them back to Spain—that would be cowardly and dishonorable; (2) that we could not turn them over to France or Germany—our commercial rivals in the Orient—that would be bad business and discreditable; (3) that we could not leave them to themselves—they were unfit for self-government—and they would

PHILIPPINE-A !!!

JUST RETURNED FROM
THE PHILIPPINES.
"And what was your greatest difficulty
in your missionary work?"
"Lack of ammunition."

How did these cartoonists
picture the cause of American
expansion into the Philippines?

THE CAUSE OF IT ALL.

soon have anarchy and misrule over there worse than Spain's was; and (4) that there was nothing left for us to do but to take them all, and to educate the Filipinos, and uplift and civilize and Christianize them, and by God's grace do the very best we could by them as our fellow-men for whom Christ also died.

▶ Does religious duty ever require that you impose benefits on other people if they do not want you to? Why do you feel as you do?

"The March of the Flag"

Albert J. Beveridge, an Indiana Republican, was elected to the Senate in 1899. This selection comes from a speech he made on the Philippine issue in 1898.

Albert J. Beveridge, **The Meaning of the Times and Other Speeches** (New York: The Bobbs Merrill Co., 1908), pp. 359-363.

In this campaign, the question is larger than a party question. It is an American question. It is a world question. Shall the American people continue their resistless march toward the commercial supremacy of the world? Shall free institutions broaden their blessed reign until the empire of our principles is established over the hearts of all mankind? And shall we reap the reward that waits on our discharge of our high duty as the sovereign power of earth? Shall we occupy new markets for what our farmers raise, new markets for what our factories make, new markets for what our merchants sell—aye, and, please God, new markets for what our ships shall carry?

The opposition tells us that we ought not to govern a people without their consent. I answer: The rule of liberty is that all just government derives its authority from the consent of the governed. It applies only to those who are capable of self-government. I answer: We govern the Indians without their consent, we govern our territories without their consent, we govern our children without their consent. I answer: How do you assume that our government would be without their consent? Would not the people of the Philippines prefer the just, humane, civilizing government of this republic to the savage, bloody rule of looting and extortion from which we have rescued them?

▶ Was it fair of Beveridge and other Americans to consider commercial advantages to the United States when deciding whether to annex the Philippines? Why or why not?

The opposition asks us how we will govern these new possessions. I answer: Out of local conditions and the necessities of the case, methods of government will grow. If England can govern foreign lands, so can America. If Germany can govern foreign lands, so can America. If they can supervise protectorates, so can America. Why is it more difficult to administer Hawaii than New Mexico or California? Both had a savage and alien population. Both were more remote from the seat of government when they came under our dominion than Hawaii is today.

Will you say by your vote that American ability to govern has decayed? Will you say that a century's experience in self-rule has failed? Will you affirm by your vote that you are a nonbeliever in American vigor and power and practical sense? Or, that we are of the ruling race of the world; that ours is the blood of government; ours the heart of dominion; ours the brain and genius of administration? Will you remember that we do but what our fathers did. We but pitch the tents of liberty farther westward, farther southward—we only continue the march of the flag.

Fellow Americans, we are God's chosen people. Yonder at Bunker Hill and Yorktown His providence was above us. At New Orleans and on blood-covered seas His hand sustained us. Abraham Lincoln was His minister, and His was the Altar of Freedom the boys in blue set on a hundred battlefields. His power directed Dewey in the East, and delivered the Spanish fleet into our hands on the eve of Liberty's birthday. We cannot fly from our world duties. It is ours to execute the purpose of a fate that has driven us to be greater than our small intentions. We cannot retreat from any soil where Providence has unfurled our banner. It is ours to save that soil for liberty and civilization. For liberty and civilization and God's promise fulfilled, the flag must henceforth be the symbol and the sign to all mankind—the flag!

"I Ask Only an Endorsement of the Declaration of Independence"

Senator William E. Mason of Illinois was a leader in the Senate in the fight against annexation of the Philippines. He offered the following resolution and supporting argument.

Whereas all just powers of government are derived from the consent of the governed: Therefore, be it

Resolved by the Senate of the United States, That the Government of the United States of America will not attempt to govern the people of any other country in the world without the consent of the people themselves, or subject them by force against their will.

Mr. President, I ask only an endorsement of the Declaration of Independence. Surely American gentlemen will not sneer at my simplicity. Surely American gentlemen have not outgrown this document. And if they have, they will have to pardon me that I have not mentally, morally, and loyally kept pace with them in their wonderful growth.

I am for the independence of the people of the Philippine Islands, as I am for independence of the people of Cuba. Mr. President, let us say to them, as we have said to Cuba, "Go on your way; learn by evolution." That is the only way. Give them the independence

Beveridge was referring to sites of battles in the American Revolution (Bunker Hill and Yorktown), the War of 1812 (New Orleans), the Civil War, and the Spanish-American War.

Congressional Record, 55th Congress, 3rd Session, Vol. 32, Part 1, pp. 528-529, 531, 533 passim.

Mason was addressing the President pro tempore of the Senate. President McKinley's death had made Theodore Roosevelt President and had left the country without a Vice-President.

The last clause of the war resolution against Cuba stated that the United States had no intention of ruling Cuba and that, after the war, the Cubans could govern themselves. The statement, known as the Teller Amendment, denied any imperialist motive on the part of the United States.

they plead for, and we shall have kept our promise with the people of the world.

Our government was built right. The just powers of the government have been derived from the consent of the people. It is built on a rock that cannot wash away. It has within itself the well-spring of eternal youth.

Mr. President, who wants to govern the Philippines, let me ask in conclusion? Where is the ambitious senator who wants to make laws at this desk to govern people ten thousand miles away? Who is the kindhearted statesman? You cannot speak their language. You cannot read their newspapers. You do not know their schools. You do not know their religion. I never even saw one of their papers.

I have an idea that their homes are sacred, that their children are beloved, that they love their soil, and that they have their songs and prayer. Who wants to govern them here? In the name of God, who wants to do it? Who craves the power to make laws for men ten thousand miles away whom you never saw?

Ah, Mr. President, the fever has run high, the temperature has been almost beyond our power to withstand. The war made heroes of all of us—some of us in our minds, some of us on the field. In the contemplation of the heroic work of Dewey and the army and navy we have grown so heroic that we know not where to stop. In love of power we have forgotten the high purpose and the lofty plan upon which the declaration of war was founded.

FOR THOUGHT:

What relationships do you see between the origins of overseas expansion discussed in Reading 80 and the way in which expansion was conducted which you studied in today's reading?

82 AMERICAN RULE IN THE PHILIPPINES

In the Philippines, as in Cuba, rebels had been fighting for years to win independence from Spain. When Commodore George Dewey defeated the Spanish fleet in Manila Bay in 1898, Filipino nationalists helped him to raise a native army to attack Spanish land forces. The army raised by Emilio Aguinaldo, the chief Filipino nationalist, and his fellow nationalists helped to convince the Spanish to surrender.

At the time of the Filipino nationalists' aid to Dewey, no one knew that the United States would be interested in owning the Philippines. But as part of the treaty of peace with Spain, the United States

THE HEATHEN YIELDS TO CHRISTIAN INFLUENCE.

WHO SAID "NOBODY LOVES A FAT MAN?"

How did these cartoonists interpret the role of religion in American expansion? Whose point of view do they probably represent?

ACCORDING TO THE IDEAS OF OUR MISSIONARY MANIACS.

THE CHINAMAN MUST BE CONVERTED, EVEN IF IT TAKES THE WHOLE MILITARY AND NAVAL FORCES OF THE TWO GREATEST NATIONS OF THE WORLD TO DO IT.

demanded possession of the islands. Aguinaldo viewed this as a betrayal. He maintained that American officials had promised to grant the Philippines independence. But there was no written agreement. So the Filipino nationalists took to the forests, hills, and villages to carry on their war of independence—this time against the United States.

Eventually, Congress investigated some of the consequences of American acquisition of the Philippines. The following excerpts are taken from testimony given to a committee of the United States Senate. The committee began its hearings in early 1902, when the Philippine insurrection against the Americans had been going on for three years. As you read, try to answer these questions:

1. What was Governor William Howard Taft's attitude toward the Filipinos as people? as potential citizens of a democracy?
2. How did the guerrilla warfare of the Philippine insurrection affect the Filipinos? the Americans?

The Creation of
a Civil Government

William Howard Taft (1857-1930), who later became President of the United States, served as American governor of the Philippines from 1900 to 1904. He administered skillfully the transition from military to civil government. He also established excellent relations with Filipino leaders. Some of his testimony follows.

Hearings Before the Committee on the Philippines, United States Senate, 57th Congress, 1st Session (Washington, D.C.: Government Printing Office, 1902), Document #331, Part I, pp. 333-342.

GOV. TAFT: The effect of giving the people independence now would be, in my judgment, to commit the 90 percent of uneducated people largely to the same condition that they occupied under Spanish rule. They would never learn individual liberty nor would they learn the power of asserting it.

One of our great hopes in elevating these people is to give them a common language and that language should be English. By reading English literature, by becoming aware of the history of the English race, they will breathe in the spirit of Anglo-Saxon individualism.

SEN. RAWLINS: If we proceed to deal with them and legislate for them as if they were a dependent colony, would it not be a constant source of trouble?

GOV. TAFT: I think not. If you show by your legislation, as I hope you may, that you are really extending to them the means of self-government. What they desire as I understand it, is a declaration that

548

Congress expects to establish a civil government. They also desire to know what kind of a civil government it will be.

I think it would be well to repeat in a law like this, the rights already set forth. These rights include everything secured by the bill of rights except the right to bear arms and the right to a trial by jury.

My objection to extending those personal rights contained in the Constitution is chiefly based on the fact that I do not think they are ready for trial by jury. Educated in an entirely different system of law and having the defects which I have already pointed out, they are not ready for trial by jury. And then I do not think that the Filipinos themselves would ask to have the right to bear arms. The right to bear arms given to a people in which thievery is so chronic would lead to oppression of the Filipinos. The Filipinos would be the last to desire to have it.

I wish to impress this fact: If the government were turned over to those who profess to be the leaders in the insurrection today, civil liberty would be the last idea which would be carried into effect.

SEN. RAWLINS: This race of people, like other Asiatic races, have never established and perhaps never will establish a civil republican form of self-government and maintain it. That being true, are we not attempting to fly in the face of human nature? Will not our efforts to uplift them and civilize them end, if we turn over the government to them, in a government that will result in absolutism?

GOV. TAFT: After we have educated them?

SEN. RAWLINS: After our efforts?

GOV. TAFT: We feel this way about the people. They are unlike other Malay races. For three hundred years they have been educated in the Christian religion. That is one bond of sympathy which we have with them. They tend—where they are very ignorant and where the priesthood is also ignorant—towards fetishism. But, nevertheless, they have churches all over the island. And the doctrines of the Christian religion have been taught there for three hundred years.

We hope that with the imitative character of the people, their anxiety to learn English, and their desire to be educated, we can justify our course. We hope to carry out this experiment even though history has offered no example of the establishment of a popular government by a Malay race.

SEN. RAWLINS: Do you not think we will have constant trouble in the islands in the future?

GOV. TAFT: If I may say it, personally I did not favor going into the Philippine Islands. I was sorry at the time that we got into it. But we are there. I see no other possible means of discharging that duty which chance has put upon us than to carry out the plan I suggest. Any other plan, Senator, would lead us back to the same place where we now are or were two years ago.

Agricultural societies with weak civil governments often suffer from organized banditry.

Fetishism means the worship of material objects which are thought to have magical powers.

549

The Army Contends
with Guerrilla Warfare

On July 1, 1902, Congress passed the Philippine Government Act. It adopted Taft's recommendations and made the Philippines a territory of the United States. On July 4, President Theodore Roosevelt proclaimed the Philippine insurrection officially ended and extended amnesty to the rebels. But three and a half years of war had brought great destruction and suffering, and death to about four thousand Americans and twenty thousand Filipinos. The following testimony was given to the Senate investigating committee by two Americans who had served as soldiers in the Philippines.

TESTIMONY OF SEIWARD J. MORTON

Hearings Before the Committee on the Philippines, Part III, pp. 2060-2069, 2895-2906.

SEN. CULBERSON: Did you witness the burning of any towns by United States soldiers?

ANSWER: Oh, yes.

QUESTION: Just state what towns you saw burned.

ANSWER: Well, we started one morning at three o'clock and rode around the country to the north of Jaro to San Miguel. We came back down this road. It was not the town of San Miguel, but houses built along the road side by side—barrios. We burned that old string of houses there, it is my impression. Brown was my scout leader, and I was his squad. I was the only one in the squad present. Brown was acting corporal in the scouts and was ordered to go out with his squad and burn houses. He obeyed the order.

Barrio means a district. When used in the United States, barrio usually refers to a Spanish-speaking community.

QUESTION: How many houses did you burn at that time and place?

ANSWER: I could not say how many houses we burned. We burned a great many of them and doubtless a great many we left we did not burn. The troop was traveling right along. We did not make any observation after we lighted a house.

QUESTION: Why was that barrio burned?

ANSWER: I think to intimidate the natives. I know after we got through our burning, coming back to San Miguel, we came across the bodies of two American horses. They were carcasses of horses that had been ridden by the soldiers that were fired upon.

SEN. BEVERIDGE: Oh, they had been firing from these barrios?

THE WITNESS: They must have been.

SEN. CULBERSON: What other barrios and towns were burned besides these you have mentioned, within your knowledge?

ANSWER: We burned a great many barrios which I did not know the names of. We burned a good deal of the country as we were fired upon. If a column was marching along and was fired upon, it was the practice to burn the buildings in that neighborhood. That

▶ Do soldiers have the right to destroy houses in this way if they cannot tell which specific houses are being used by hostile forces? Why or why not?

550

impressed the natives with the fact that they could not fire upon us, although they often did not do very great damage.

QUESTION: Were the people in the houses warned to get out before setting fire to them?

ANSWER: Oh, yes.

QUESTION: You have stated that with the exception of isolated cases the treatment of Filipinos by American soldiers was humane?

ANSWER: Yes, sir; very much so.

TESTIMONY OF FORMER CORPORAL DANIEL J. EVANS

THE CHAIRMAN: The committee would like to hear from you concerning the conduct of the war. Did you witness any cruelties inflicted upon the natives in the Philippine Islands, and if so, under what circumstances?

ANSWER: The case I had reference to was where they gave the water cure to a native in the Ilicano Province at Ilocos Norte.

QUESTION: That is in the extreme northern part of Luzon?

ANSWER: Yes, sir. There were two native scouts that were with the American forces. They went out and brought in a couple of insurgents. They were known to be insurgents by their own confession. Besides that, they had the mark that most insurgents in that part of the country carry. It is a little brand on the left breast, generally inflicted with a nail or head of a cartridge. They tried to find out from this native—

QUESTION: What kind of a brand did you say it was?

ANSWER: A small brand put on with a nail head or cartridge.

SEN. BEVERIDGE: A scar on the flesh?

THE WITNESS: Yes, sir. They tried to get him to tell where the rest of the insurgents were at that time. We knew about where they were, but we did not know how to get at them. They were in the hills, and it happened that there was only one path that could get to them. They refused to tell this one path and they commenced this so-called "water cure." The first thing one of the Americans did—I mean one of the scouts for the Americans—was to grab one of the men by the head and jerk his head back. Then they took a tomato can and poured water down his throat until he could hold no more. During this time one of the natives had a rattan whip, about as large as my finger. He struck him on the face and on the bare back. Every time they would strike him it would raise a large welt, and some blood would come. When this native could hold no more water, they forced a gag into his mouth. They stood him up and tied his hands behind him. They stood him up against a post and fastened him so he could not move. Then one man, an American soldier, who was over six feet tall, and who was very strong, too, struck this native in the pit of the stomach. He hit him as hard as he could strike him, just as

Rattan here refers to the stem of a palm leaf from which wicker furniture is often made.

551

rapidly as he could. It seemed as if he didn't get tired of striking him.

SEN. ALLISON: With his hand?

ANSWER: With his clenched fist. He struck him right in the pit of the stomach and it made the native very sick. They kept that operation up for quite a time. I thought the fellow was about to die, but I don't believe he was as bad as that, because finally he told them he would tell. He was taken away, and I saw no more of him.

QUESTION: Did he tell?

ANSWER: I believe he did, because I didn't hear of any more water cure inflicted on him.

SEN. RAWLINS: Was there any effort to conceal it?

ANSWER: Not in the least.

QUESTION: Was it a matter of common knowledge?

ANSWER: Yes, sir, it has been the talk of almost the whole army. They do not try to conceal it.

QUESTION: How long has that been the case?

ANSWER: Well, it has been practiced, to my knowledge, from along in July 1900 until the time I left the islands. Of course, after that time I knew nothing about it. I left the islands about February 1901.

FOR THOUGHT:

Was there anything in the motives and attitudes of Americans involved in overseas expansion that accounts for the occasional use of the sort of brutality described in this reading? Or does war inevitably result in such brutality from time to time?

83 THE USES OF AMERICAN POWER AND INFLUENCE

HISTORICAL ESSAY

Between 1815 and 1875, Americans played a minor role in international politics. The United States formed neither diplomatic nor military alliances with other nations. It fought its only foreign war against an American neighbor, Mexico. It sought no territory outside North America.

Yet lack of political involvement did not mean isolation. American business people, ships, and seamen expanded the nation's foreign trade. American diplomats served in distant places of the world. And when the United States chose to act, it commanded some respect. In 1853 an American naval squadron under Commodore Matthew C. Perry

> Would torture of this kind be justified if it resulted in the saving of American lives? Why or why not?

visited Japan. This visit combined diplomacy, commerce, and a show of strength. Japan, which had been isolated by choice, was persuaded to open its ports to foreign traders.

The Monroe Doctrine

Concerned with their own national security, Americans had always tried to keep European powers from establishing new footholds in the Western Hemisphere. As the nineteenth century passed, the United States held European influence in the Americas to a minimum. In 1864, during the Civil War, for example, France sent troops to Mexico. The French wanted to establish an empire headed by an Austrian archduke, Maximilian. In 1865, when Union armies finally defeated the Confederacy, Secretary of State William Seward warned France against maintaining its puppet state. French soldiers withdrew, and the empire of Maximilian collapsed in 1867. By 1900, the United States dominated the New World so completely that no European nation willingly risked challenging American wishes in the area.

As the power of the United States grew, relationships with its old enemy, Great Britain, improved. Fortunately, Britain chose to support independent Latin American republics rather than compete for territory and influence in Latin America. Both the United States and Great Britain wanted to avoid war. They were each others' best customers. And the British had invested heavily in the development of American agriculture and industry. The British knew that Canada would be hard to defend. In turn the United States knew that the British navy could ruin American ocean commerce in the event of war.

The Monroe Doctrine was enforceable in 1823, when it was issued, only because Great Britain stood behind it. As the United States grew, it found that its own power would deter European nations from interfering in the New World. In return, the United States kept out of European affairs as much as possible.

In 1861, Great Britain, Spain, and France sent an expedition to Mexico to collect a debt. After payment, both Britain and Spain withdrew. Napoleon III, of France, however, refused to remove his troops. He hoped that by creating a Mexican Empire, he could restore France's prestige and regain favor with his people.

Treaties Between Great Britain and United States		
Name	Date	Provisions
Rush-Bagot	1817	Agreed to naval disarmament of the Great Lakes
Webster-Ashburton	1842	Settled the boundary between Maine and New Brunswick
Aberdeen Proposal	1846	Fixed boundary between United States and British territory in the Northwest at the 49th parallel
Clayton-Bulwer	1850	Agreed to a joint control of any canal built across Central America and guaranteed that such a canal would be unfortified and neutral
Treaty of Washington	1871	Agreed to arbitration by an international tribune of damages claimed by United States against British shipbuilders for Civil War losses
Hay-Pauncefote	1901	Cancelled Clayton-Bulwer Treaty; United States could build and control the canal but canal was to be open to all nations

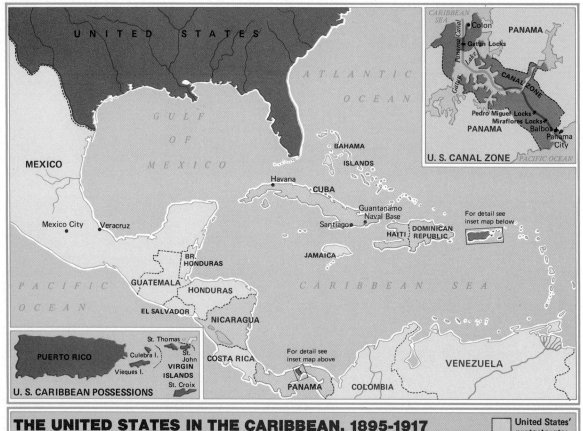

MEXICO

Mexico City • Veracruz

UNITED STATES

GULF OF MEXICO

ATLANTIC OCEAN

BAHAMA ISLANDS

Havana • CUBA

Guantanamo Naval Base

Santiago • HAITI DOMINICAN REPUBLIC

For detail see inset map below

JAMAICA

BR. HONDURAS

GUATEMALA

HONDURAS

EL SALVADOR

NICARAGUA

PACIFIC OCEAN

CARIBBEAN SEA

COSTA RICA

For detail see inset map above

PANAMA COLOMBIA

VENEZUELA

CARIBBEAN SEA

Colon • PANAMA

Gatun Locks

Gatun Lake

CANAL ZONE

Pedro Miguel Locks
Miraflores Locks

PANAMA

Balboa • Panama City

U. S. CANAL ZONE

PACIFIC OCEAN

PUERTO RICO

St. Thomas

Culebra I. St. John

Vieques I. VIRGIN ISLANDS

St. Croix

U. S. CARIBBEAN POSSESSIONS

THE UNITED STATES IN THE CARIBBEAN, 1895-1917

United States' protectorates

Dominance in the Caribbean

▶ Is destruction or seizure of private property ever a sufficient reason for going to war? Why or why not?

The publisher William R. Hearst sent the artist Frederic Remington to Cuba to sketch the atrocities taking place there for publication in the **New York World**. When Remington reported that conditions were not so bad, Hearst is alleged to have answered, "You furnish the pictures and I'll furnish the war."

The United States moved toward further control of the Caribbean and involvement in world affairs when it declared war against Spain in 1898. In some ways Americans reached this decision reluctantly. They disapproved of harsh Spanish attempts to repress rebellions in Cuba. They were concerned about the destruction of sugar plantations owned by Americans. But neither President Grover Cleveland nor his successor, William McKinley, wanted to intervene. American business people, too, generally opposed intervention. They feared Spanish attacks on American shipping and ports.

Then the unexplained sinking of the American battleship *Maine* occurred in Havana harbor in February 1898. This sinking, with the loss of 260 lives, aroused American indignation. The resulting furor in metropolitan newspapers helped to inflame public opinion. Some newspapers even manufactured stories of Spanish atrocities to attract readers. By April both President McKinley and Congress sensed that

554

the public wanted war. They overlooked the concessions to American demands made by the Spanish government in early April. These concessions amounted to sweeping changes in Spanish policies in Cuba. McKinley asked Congress for intervention in Cuba on April 11. Congress declared war on April 20.

The fighting lasted only three months. On May 1 Commodore George Dewey's squadron destroyed Spanish naval power in the Philippines. American ships destroyed a Spanish fleet at Santiago, Cuba on July 3. Spanish land forces surrendered by mid-August, and the two nations agreed to discuss peace terms. The treaty gave Cuba independence as Congress had promised in the Teller Amendment. It also granted the Philippines, the islands of Guam and Midway in the Pacific, and Puerto Rico to the United States.

During the treaty negotiations ending the Spanish-American War, Spain agreed to cede the Philippines to the United States in return for $20 million.

Theodore Roosevelt became famous during the war. Roosevelt resigned as Assistant Secretary of the Navy to organize a group of volunteer cavalrymen called the Rough Riders to fight in Cuba. The publicity given his courageous leadership helped him to win the governorship of New York in 1898 and the Vice Presidency of the United States in 1900. He succeeded to the Presidency in September 1901, when an anarchist assassinated McKinley. He came to symbolize American expansion and a vigorous foreign policy.

Two episodes concerning the Dominican Republic and the Panama Canal reveal Roosevelt's approach to Latin America. The Dominican Republic owed money to European creditors. In 1904, the creditors threatened that their governments would intervene to collect the debts. Roosevelt responded by promising to intervene in Latin American countries in order to preserve order and to provide for the payment of such debts. Under this "Roosevelt Corollary" to the Monroe Doctrine, the United States ran the Dominican Republic's customs service for two years.

A deranged anarchist assassinated President McKinley at a reception at the Pan American Exposition in Buffalo. Leon Czolgosz, the assassin, had concealed the gun in his bandaged hand.

Roosevelt recognized the importance of navies in international politics. He and other leaders also realized that a canal connecting the Caribbean and the Pacific would give a tremendous advantage to the United States in war or peace. It would reduce the time and risk of shipping between the east and west coasts. It would also eliminate the need for separate American fleets in the Atlantic and Pacific. But unless the canal were American-owned, it could put shipping at the mercy of unstable or unfriendly governments.

The United States and Britain signed the Hay-Pauncefote Treaty in 1901. In it, Britain agreed to yield any control over building a canal. A French company had attempted to build a canal across the Isthmus of Panama—then part of Colombia. But it had failed financially. The United States agreed to buy the French rights for $40 million. Colombia stalled, however, hoping to get more money if it waited until the French time limit was up. Then in November 1903,

Several attempts had been made earlier by the United States to build a canal through Nicaragua, which many engineers think would have provided a better route. American investors in the Panama Canal, however, helped convince the government to favor Panama.

a revolt broke out in Panama. A group of Panamanians, supported by the canal company, declared Panama's independence.

Roosevelt, who knew of the likelihood of a revolt, took full advantage of it. He sent an American warship, the *Nashville*, to Colon, Panama. The *Nashville* appeared on November 2. The insurrection broke out on November 3. The *Nashville* kept Colombian troops from reaching the fighting. The United States recognized the independence of Panama only three days after the revolt began and signed the Hay-Bunau-Varilla Treaty twelve days later. It guaranteed Panama's independence. It also gave the United States the right to build a canal and a ninety-nine year lease on a ten-mile-wide strip of land. Colombia's protests were ignored; the canal was built.

Thrust into the Pacific

The American decisions to take Hawaii and the Philippines obligated the United States to use its army and navy to protect its new interests in the far Pacific. Following suppression of the Philippine independence movement, the United States also had to embark upon policies to increase literacy, build roads, and promote self-government. The Philippines gained independence in 1946 after going through several stages of gaining increased control over their own government.

China suffered a military defeat by Japan in 1894-1895. As a result, the Chinese could not resist the imperialist demands of European powers for political and economic concessions. In its new international role, the United States tried to prevent the breakup of China. In 1899, Secretary of State John Hay sent a letter to six great powers asking them to agree to preserve free trade in China. He asked them not to assume special privileges over trade in spheres of influence they controlled. Although the answers to his letters were vague, Hay announced in 1900 that the powers had agreed. This so-called "open door policy" did little, however, to maintain China's territorial integrity. In 1900, American troops took part in an international force which helped China put down a rebellion. The rebellion was launched by a militant band of anti-foreigners, known as the Boxers. Hay took this chance to notify the great powers that the United States desired to maintain Chinese independence. Nobody paid much attention. Russia seized part of the Chinese province of Manchuria shortly afterward. And the United States itself tried unsuccessfully to obtain territory for a naval base on the coast of China.

America's China policy showed little more than unrealistic good intentions. But American policy towards Japan revealed a somewhat more realistic attitude. Presidents Roosevelt, Taft, and Wilson understood that the American people would not exert military force in the far Pacific in order to impose American ideas about territorial changes there. In 1904-1905, Japan defeated Russian forces and seized Manchuria and other parts of China controlled by Russia. The United

States and Japan then made the secret Taft-Katsura Agreement that gave Japan a free hand in Korea. In return the Japanese promised to keep out of activities in the Philippines. The Root-Takahira Agreement of 1908 furthered the two nations' policies of respecting each others' possessions in the Pacific.

American Power and Europe

The United States had departed from the Monroe Doctrine's pledge of non-intervention in European affairs in minor ways only. The United States had cooperated in submitting disputes with other powers to the arbitration of international commissions, such as the Hague Tribunal. Theodore Roosevelt, acting at the request of Germany, had helped to bring about an international conference at Algeciras, Spain, in 1906. Its purpose was to settle a crisis which had arisen over French-German competition in Morocco, a country in North Africa.

An international conference was called in 1899 at the Hague, a city in the Netherlands. The conference set up a Permanent Court of Arbitration, sometimes called the Hague Tribunal, to encourage nations to settle their disputes through mediation.

This tradition of non-intervention ended when America entered World War I in 1917. The war in Europe had begun in 1914, after a Serbian nationalist assassinated an Austrian archduke. European countries were so deeply involved in alliances that Britain, France, Russia, and Italy found themselves fighting on the side of Serbia. Germany, Austria, and the Ottoman Empire opposed them. Since America considered it a European war, it maintained neutrality. But American companies did sell supplies and make loans to both sides. However, most business was done with Britain and its allies.

Serbia is now part of Yugoslavia. Turkey was the heart of the Ottoman Empire.

Britain and Germany struggled desperately for control of the seas. Both interfered with American commerce. Britain blockaded ports supplying Germany. In 1915, Germany announced it would sink any boats carrying supplies into the war zone it proclaimed around Britain. To attack ships, Germany used its new war vessel, the submarine, also called a U-boat. Americans were shocked when a U-boat sank a British liner, the *Lusitania*. Nearly twelve hundred passengers died, including over a hundred Americans. President Wilson sent Germany a strongly worded note. After several exchanges of notes and the sinking of another British liner, the *Arabic*, Germany agreed to suspend submarine warfare against passenger ships. In 1916, Wilson attempted in vain to negotiate a peace in Europe.

Germany claimed that the **Lusitania** was carrying rifles and ammunition.

Then early in 1917, Germany, threatened by loss of the war, announced it would resume submarine warfare. American opinion, already hostile to Germany, grew more hostile. It was further influenced by the Zimmermann note. The British had intercepted a coded note from the German Foreign Secretary Zimmermann to the German minister in Mexico. Zimmermann suggested that if the United States entered the war on the side of the Allies, Mexico, in turn, could enter on Germany's side. He promised that if Mexico entered the war, Germany would help reconquer Texas and the territories lost in 1848. The telegram was made public on March 1, 1917.

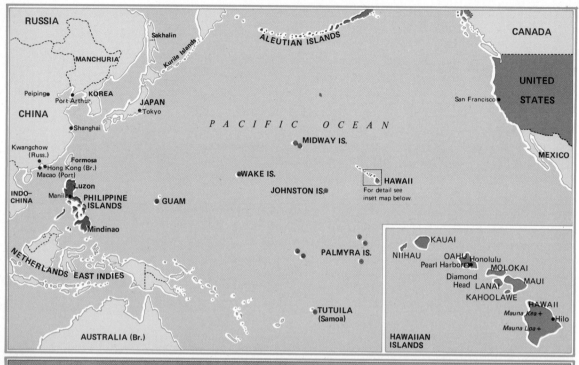

THE UNITED STATES IN THE PACIFIC, 1895-1917

The last hope of avoiding war lay in German restraints on their U-boats. But in March the submarines sank four unarmed American merchant ships. On April 2, President Wilson asked Congress to declare war. After two days of debate, Congress complied.

Other factors had caused the United States to sympathize with Britain, France, and their allies. Americans remembered France as an invaluable friend during the American Revolution. Anglo-American friendship was at its highest point since 1815. Germany, on the other hand, had invaded Belgium ruthlessly. British propaganda, some of it false or exaggerated, helped to convince many Americans that German troops committed atrocities there. The United States also discovered that Germany and Austria were trying to sabotage arms production in the United States. Finally between 1914 and 1917, the American economy became more and more committed to an Allied victory.

American soldiers arrived in Europe at a crucial time in the spring of 1918. German armies were pushing back weary French and British forces. Within months fresh American troops, who eventually numbered 2 million, helped to stop and drive back the Germans. At the same time, the American navy organized an effective convoy system.

558

This practice cut losses of ships to German submarines. The fighting ended with an armistice on November 11, 1918.

The Allied victory marked the peak of American power and influence. But were Americans willing to continue such influence in European affairs? President Wilson had denounced the system of alliances that had led to war. He knew that few Americans wanted to commit their nation to further military alliances. He worked desperately for his ideal which was an international peace-keeping organization.

The peace treaty that the President submitted to the Senate in 1919 disappointed Americans in some ways. In his declaration of war aims, called the Fourteen Points, Wilson had promised that the United States would not fight for territorial gains. Obviously, however, Germany had lost its colonies to the European Allies. And Japan had encroached further upon China in taking over German holdings there. The goal of freedom of the seas was also not ensured.

Wilson had also called for the establishment of an international peace-keeping organization. He succeeded in having the League of Nations included as part of the treaty. The League suited American

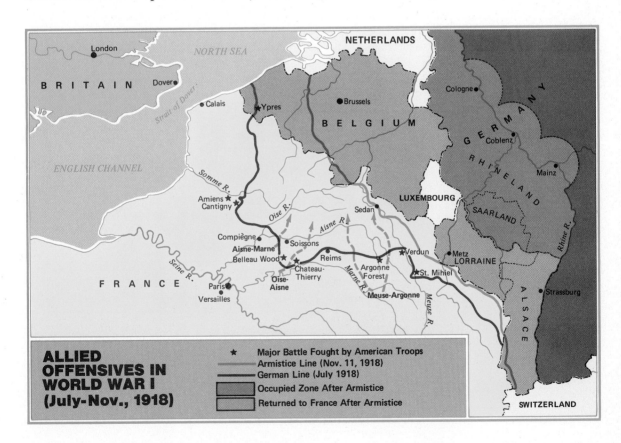

ALLIED OFFENSIVES IN WORLD WAR I (July–Nov., 1918)

★ Major Battle Fought by American Troops
Armistice Line (Nov. 11, 1918)
German Line (July 1918)
Occupied Zone After Armistice
Returned to France After Armistice

The Senate refused to ratify the Treaty of Versailles. The treaty required Germany to admit guilt for the war, give up colonies, pay reparations (which amounted to $56 billion), and maintain disarmament. Instead of signing the treaty, Congress passed a joint resolution in 1921 declaring that the war between the United States and Germany was over.

ideals about an impartial way to keep order in the world. Yet, it was the issue of the League that prevented Senate ratification of the treaty. Led by Henry Cabot Lodge of Massachusetts, senators opposed to the treaty offered amendments which would restrict American participation in the League. They thought Wilson would not accept such restrictions. They were right. The President, embittered by their opposition, refused to accept any important amendments. The treaty did not receive the necessary two-thirds vote in the Senate. By a margin of seven votes, the United States failed to join the League of Nations. In the Presidential election of 1920, the Republican party swept the Democrats out of office. President Warren G. Harding took the election results as an American rejection of League membership. The issue never again arose seriously.

Thus in the early twentieth century the United States extended its power vigorously but uncertainly. Its ventures into Latin America gave it an unprecedented amount of control over its neighbors. But aside from a naval base in Cuba, its control of the ten-mile-wide Panama Canal Zone, and its purchase of the Virgin Islands from Denmark in 1917, it obtained no territory. It continued to refuse to make alliances with Latin American as well as other nations. In the Pacific, the United States obtained no further territory after 1898. Instead it used its influence, without much effect, to maintain the situation as it was in Asia. And in Europe the United States withdrew its forces at the end of World War I. It refused to make either military or political commitments to guarantee the peace it had helped to establish.

The 1920's: Values and Behavior

STATING THE ISSUE

CHAPTER
22

Suppose you had been able to survey American patterns of communication in 1870. It is likely that you would have discovered a definite localism. Most people spoke only with friends and family who lived close-by. Newspapers, which were widely read, were local. National magazines published in remote cities had only a small number of readers. Outside of the largest cities, plays were produced either by local amateur companies or by touring companies. All performances were subject to the approval or jeers of the local audiences.

A similar survey in 1930 would have revealed a different pattern. Each day, network radio linked millions of listeners together. Mass transportation, the telephone, and the automobile made it possible for friends and family to communicate while living greater distances from each other. In many urban centers, a few large newspapers belonging to national chains had replaced the variety of small journals of the nineteenth century. National magazines attracted millions of readers, who poured over the same photographs and stories each week. In darkened movie houses, screens were filled with images produced far-away. The players did not have to contend with the applause or the groans of the audience.

The shift from a local to a cosmopolitan pattern of communication was not felt immediately by everyone, everywhere. By the 1920's, however, most Americans were aware of the shift. Movies and radio allowed almost no one to escape the outside world. Journalists and social scientists reported on both new national images and the impact of the new media. The documents in this chapter take you back to the 1920's. They ask you to estimate the impact of the cosmopolitan pattern of communication upon American society.

561

1913 Congress passes the Underwood Tariff

1915 The Ku Klux Klan is reorganized

1918 An Armistice is signed; World War I ends

1919 A "Red Scare" breaks out in the United States

1919 The Eighteenth Amendment is ratified

1920 Census reports that half the United States' population lives in cities

1920 Congress passes the Volstead Act

1920 The Nineteenth Amendment is ratified

1920 KDKA, the first commercial radio station, begins broadcasting in Pittsburgh

1922 Congress passes Fordney-McCumber Tariff

1923 The Senate orders investigation of leasing of Teapot Dome oil reserves

1923 President Warren G. Harding dies; Calvin Coolidge becomes President

1924 National Origins Act puts quota on immigration

1925 John T. Scopes is tried and convicted for teaching evolution in a public high school

1927 Warner Brothers releases **The Jazz Singer**, the first "talkie"

1929 The stock market crashes; the Great Depression begins

1929 Robert and Helen Lynd publish **Middletown**

1930 Congress passes Hawley–Smoot Tariff

84 PARENTS AND CHILDREN IN A MIDWESTERN CITY

In the middle of the 1920's, two young sociologists, Robert and Helen Lynd, decided to study a city as representative as possible of contemporary American life. They chose a city of 35,000 people. It was small enough for them to analyze it in what they called a "total situation study." They called their town "Middletown." It was, in fact, Muncie, Indiana, a town that had grown from 11,000 inhabitants in 1890. Most of its citizens were white native Americans.

The Lynds did not claim that Middletown was typical of America. But they did select a place with many of the characteristics which a typical town might have. Muncie had a temperate climate. Since its population had more than tripled in thirty-five years, it had many of the growing pains that accompanied social change all over the United States. Muncie had a number of factories. But no single one was large enough to make the city a "company town." Modern, high-speed machine production had brought many aspects of an industrial culture to the city. This industrial culture, however, was balanced by an abundant artistic life. Moreover, Muncie had no outstanding peculiarities or severe local problems to set it off from other American towns.

Assisted by a staff of three researchers, the Lynds moved to Muncie for more than a year. They investigated every phase of the city's life. Using 1890 as a base line, they assessed the changes that had been taking place in the culture. The Lynds finished gathering data in 1925. They published the results of their study in 1929.

The three readings in Chapter 22 have all been taken from *Middletown*. As you study the excerpts in this first reading, think about the following questions:

1. What social forces had been influencing family life in Middletown?
2. How did parents and children try to cope with the new problems that came with changing conditions?

Child-Rearing in Middletown

Families of six to fourteen children, upon which the grandparents of the present generation prided themselves, are considered as somehow not as "nice" as families of two, three, or four children. With increasing regulation of the size of the family, emphasis has shifted somewhat from child-bearing to child-rearing.

Middletown parents are [accustomed] to speak of many of their "problems" as new to this generation. . . . Even from the earliest years of the child's life, the former dominance of the home is challenged. The small child spends less time in the home than in the ample days of the nineties. Shrinkage in the size of the yard affords less play space. "Mother, where can I play?" wailed a small boy of six, as he was protestingly hauled into a tiny front yard from the enchanting sport of throwing ice at passing autos. The community has recently begun to institute public playgrounds, thereby hastening the passing of the time when a mother could "keep an eye on" the children in the home yard. The taking over of the kindergarten by the public schools in 1924 offers to children of four and five an alternative to the home. "Why, even my youngster in kindergarten is telling us where to get off," exclaimed one bewildered father. "He won't eat white bread because he says they tell him at kindergarten that brown is more healthful". . .

With entry into high school, the agencies drawing the child away from home multiply. Athletics, dramatics, committee meetings after school hours demand his support. Y.M.C.A., Y.W.C.A., Boy Scouts,

Robert S. Lynd and Helen Merrell Lynd, **Middletown: A Study in American Culture** (New York: Harcourt Brace Jovanovich, Inc., 1929), pp. 131-152. Abridged. Copyright © 1929 by Harcourt Brace Jovanovich, Inc. Copyright renewed 1957 by Robert S. and Helen M. Lynd. Reprinted by permission of the publishers.

Girl Reserves, the movies, auto-riding—all extra-neighborhood concerns unknown to his parents in their youth—are centers of interest. Club meetings, parties or dances, often held in public buildings, compete for his every evening.

"I've never been criticized by my children until these last couple of years since they have been in high school," said one business-class mother. "But now both my daughter and older son keep saying, 'But, Mother, you're so old-fashioned.'" "My daughter of fourteen thinks I am 'cruel' if I don't let her stay at a dance until after eleven," said another young mother. "I tell her that when I was her age I had to be in at nine, and she says, 'Yes, Mother, but that was fifty years ago.'"

The first four sources of disagreement with their parents indicated by the boys were: 1) the hours they must come home, 2) the number of evenings they may stay out late, 3) school grades, and 4) the amount of spending money.

▶What issues, if any, bring you into conflict with your parents? How can you resolve these conflicts?

Use of the automobile ranks fifth among the boys and fourth among the girls as a source of disagreement. The extensive use of this new tool by the young has extended their mobility and the range of alternatives before them. Joining a crowd motoring over to a dance in a town twenty miles away may be a matter of a moment's decision, with no one's permission asked. Furthermore, among the high school set, ownership of a car by one's family has become an important criterion of social fitness. A boy almost never takes a girl to a dance except in a car. There are persistent rumors of the buying of a car by local families to help their children's social standing in high school.

The more sophisticated social life of today has brought with it another "problem" much discussed by Middletown parents. [This problem is] the apparently increasing relaxation of some of the traditional prohibitions upon the approaches of boys and girls to each other's persons. Here again new inventions of the last thirty-five years have played a part. In 1890 a "well-brought-up" boy and girl were commonly forbidden to sit together in the dark. But motion pictures and the automobile have lifted this taboo, and, once lifted, it is easy for the practice to become widely extended. Buggy-riding in 1890 allowed only a narrow range of mobility. Three to eight were generally accepted hours for riding, and being out after eight-thirty without a chaperon was largely forbidden. In an auto, however, a party may go to a city halfway across the state in an afternoon or evening. And unchaperoned automobile parties as late as midnight, while subject to criticism, are not exceptional.

The relaxing of parental control combines with the decrease in group parties to further the greater exclusiveness of an individual couple. In the nineties, according to those who were in high school then, "We all went to parties together and came home together. If any couple did pair off, they were considered rather a joke." Today the press accounts of high school club dances emphasize the escort of each girl attending. The number of separate dances at a dance is smaller and there is much more tendency for each individual to

▶What are the advantages of pairing off? of group parties?

564

dance with fewer partners, in some cases to dance the entire evening with one person. "When you spend four or five dollars to drag a girl to a dance," as one boy put it, "you don't want her to spend the evening dancing with everyone else."

Mothers of both working and business class, whether they lament the greater frankness between the sexes or welcome it as a healthy sign, agree that it exists. [They] mention the dress and greater aggressiveness of girls today as factors in the change. Such comments as the following from the mothers of both groups are characteristic:

"Girls aren't so modest nowadays. They dress differently." "It's the girls' clothing. We can't keep our boys decent when girls dress that way." "Girls have more nerve nowadays—look at their clothes!" "Girls are far more aggressive today. They call the boys up to try to make dates with them as they never would have when I was a girl."

A natural reaction to these various encroachments upon parental dominance . . . is the vigorous reassertion of established standards. And in Middletown the traditional view that the dependence of the child carries with it the right and duty of the parents to enforce "discipline" and "obedience" still prevails.

And yet not only are parents finding it increasingly difficult to secure adherence to established group sanctions, but the sanctions themselves are changing. Many parents are becoming puzzled and unsure as to what they would hold their children to if they could. As one anxious business-class mother said:

Sanctions are rewards or punishments a group uses to obtain conformity to its standards.

"You see other people being more lenient and you think perhaps that it is the best way. But you are afraid to do anything very different from what your mother did for fear you may leave out something essential or do something wrong. I would give anything to know what is wisest, but I don't know what to do."

A more democratic system of relationships with frank exchange of ideas is growing up in many homes. "My mother was a splendid mother in many ways, but I could not be that kind of mother now. I have to be a pal and listen to my children's ideas," said one of these mothers.

Not all of the currents in the community are set in the direction of widening the gap between parents and children. It is the mother who has the chief responsibility in child-rearing. Many Middletown mothers, particularly among the business class, are devoting a part of their increasing leisure to their children. Such comments as the following represent many of the business-class wives interviewed:

565

"I accommodate my entire life to my little girl. She takes three music lessons a week and I practice with her forty minutes a day. I help her with her school work and go to dancing school with her."

The attitude that child-rearing is something not to be taken for granted but to be studied appears in parents of both groups. . . . Yet a prevalent mood among Middletown parents is bewilderment, a feeling that their difficulties outrun their best efforts to cope with them:

By both groups, the author means working-class and business-class parents.

"Life was simpler for my mother," said a thoughtful mother. "In those days one did not realize that there was so much to be known about the care of children. I realize that I ought to be half a dozen experts. But I am afraid of making mistakes and usually do not know where to go for advice." . . .

One shrewd businessman summarized the situation: "These kids aren't pulling the wool over their parents' eyes as much as you may think. The parents are wise to a lot that goes on, but they just don't know what to do, and try to turn their back on it."

▶Is it a good idea for parents to turn their backs if they think that their children did something of which they do not approve? Or should they talk the issue out with their children?

FOR THOUGHT:

Were the problems of Middletown's parents and children similar to those in your life? How modern was Middletown in the 1920's?

85 THE HIGH SCHOOL COMES OF AGE

In many contemporary high schools, more than half the graduating class enrolls in college or some other form of post-high school education. College is becoming expected of millions of young people. In the 1920's, high schools were in the position that colleges are today. High schools were becoming a part of the educational experience of most young people. This new trend marked a major revolution. In no other nation did such a large percentage of teen-aged youth go to school, instead of work for a living.

The Lynds were impressed by the change in the role of the school in Middletown's society between 1890 and 1925. The curriculum had been expanded to meet the needs of a new day. More and more children went to school for longer and longer periods of time. The school became an important center of town life. Considerable local pride was involved in the triumphs of its students both in the classroom and on the athletic field.

566

The following selection from *Middletown* describes these changes. As you read, think about the following questions:

1. What roles did the schools play in the life of Middletown?
2. What subjects did the school stress?

Schooling in Middletown

Robert S. Lynd and Helen Merrell Lynd, **Middletown: A Study in American Culture,** pp. 181-220. Abridged.

In the culture of thirty-five years ago it was deemed sufficient to teach during the first seven years of this extra-home training the following skills and facts, in rough order of importance:

a. The various uses of language. (This was overwhelmingly first in importance.)

b. The accurate manipulation of numerical symbols.

c. Familiarity with the physical surroundings of peoples.

d. A miscellaneous group of facts about familiar physical objects about the child—trees, sun, ice, food, and so on.

e. The leisure-time skills of singing and drawing.

Today the things for which all children are sent to school fall into the following rough order:

▶ What do you think should be learned in school?

a. The same uses of language.

b. The same uses of numerical figures.

c. Training in patriotic citizenship.

d. The same familiarity with the physical surroundings of peoples.

e. Facts about how to keep well and some physical exercise.

f. The same leisure-time skills of singing and drawing.

g. Knowledge and skills useful in sewing, cooking and using tools about the home for the girls, and, for the boys, an introductory acquaintance with some of the manual skills by which the working-class members get their living.

The school training of a generation ago appears to have been a more casual adjunct of the. . ."bringing up" that went on day by day in the home. Today, however, the school is relied upon to carry a more direct, if at most points still vaguely defined, responsibility.

The high school has been more adaptable than the lower school. Here group training no longer means the same set of facts learned on the same days by all children of a given grade. The freshman entering high school may [follow] any one of twelve different "courses of study."

The most pronounced region of movement appears in the rush of courses that. . .seek to train for specific tool and skill activities in factory, office, and home. A generation ago, a solitary optional senior course in bookkeeping was the thin entering wedge of the trend that today controls eight of the twelve courses of the high school. [This trend also claimed] 17 percent of the total student hours during the first semester of 1923-1924 and 21 percent during the second. At no point has the training . . . of children . . . approached more nearly actual preparation for the dominant concerns in the daily lives of the people of Middletown. This [practical] commandeering of education is frankly stated by the president of the School Board: "For a long time all boys were trained to be President. Then for a while we trained them all to be professional men. Now we are training them to get jobs."

Second only in importance to the rise of these courses addressed to practical vocational activities is the new emphasis upon courses in history and civics. These represent yet another point at which Middletown is bending its schools to the immediate service of its institutions—in this case, bolstering community solidarity against [various] divisive tendencies. A generation ago a course in American history was given to those who survived until the eighth grade. Today, separate courses in civic training and in history and civics begin with the first grade for all children and continue throughout the elementary school. [In] high school the third-year course in American history and the fourth-year course in civics and sociology are, with the exception of the second-year English course, the only courses required of all students after the completion of the first year.

▶What do you think of these reasons to study history? Why do you think history should be studied?

Evidently Middletown has become concerned that no child shall be without this pattern of the group. Precisely what this stamp is appears clearly in instructions to teachers:

> "History furnishes no parallel of national growth, national prosperity and national achievement like ours," asserts the State Manual for Secondary Schools for 1923. "Practically all of this has been accomplished since we adopted our present form of government, and we are justified in believing that our political philosophy is right, and that those who are today assailing it are wrong. To properly grasp the philosophy of this government of ours, requires a knowledge of its history."

Further insight into the stamp of the group with which Middletown children complete their social studies courses is gained through the following summary of answers. [A questionnaire was completed by] 241 boys and 315 girls, comprising the social science classes of the last two years of the high school. [See page 569 for summary.]

Accompanying the formal training afforded by courses of study is another and informal kind of training, particularly during the high school years. The high school, with its athletics, clubs, sororities and fraternities, dances and parties, and other "extracurricular activities," is a fairly complete social [world] in itself. This informal training is not a preparation for a vague future that must be taken on trust,

568

Statement	Percentage Answering True		Percentage Answering False		Percentage Answering Uncertain		Percentage Not Answering	
	Boys	Girls	Boys	Girls	Boys	Girls	Boys	Girls
The white race is the best race on earth.	66	75	19	17	14	6	1	2
The United States is unquestionably the best country in the world	77	88	10	6	11	5	2	1
Every good citizen should act according to the following statement: "My country—right or wrong!"	47	56	40	29	9	10	4	5
A citizen of the United States should be allowed to say anything he pleases, even to advocate violent revolution, if he does no violent act himself	20	16	70	75	7	7	3	2
A pacifist in war time is a "slacker" and should be prosecuted by the government	40	36	34	28	22	28	4	8
The fact that some men have so much more money than others shows that there is an unjust condition in this country which ought to be changed.	25	31	70	62	4	5	1	2

as is the case with so much of the academic work. To many of the boys and girls in high school this is "the life," the thing they personally like best about going to school.

This whole spontaneous life of the school becomes important in the eyes of adults through the medium of the school athletic teams—the "Bearcats." The businessman may "lay down the law" to his adolescent son or daughter at home and patronize their friends, but in the basketball grandstand he is if anything a little less important than these youngsters of his who actually mingle daily with those five boys who wear the colors of "Magic Middletown."

The relative disregard of most people in Middletown for teachers and for the content of books, on the one hand, and the exalted position of the social and athletic activities of the schools, on the other, offer an interesting commentary of Middletown's attitude toward education. And yet Middletown places large faith in going to school. The heated opposition to compulsory education in the nineties has virtually disappeared. And yet when one looks more closely at this dominant belief in the magic of formal schooling, it appears that it is not what actually goes on in the schoolroom that these many voices [praise].

Literacy, yes, they want their children to be able to "read the newspapers, write a letter, and perform the ordinary operations of arithmetic." But, beyond that, many of them are little interested in what the schools teach. This thing, education, appears to be desired frequently not for its specific content but as a symbol. [It is desired] by the working class as an open sesame that will mysteriously admit their children to a world closed to them, and by the business class as a heavily sanctioned aid in getting on further economically or socially in the world.

►Which seems more important to you, the "open" curriculum learned in courses or the "hidden" curriculum designed to teach industry, friendship, individualism, and obedience to authority?

Rarely does one hear a talk addressed to school children by a Middletown citizen that does not contain in some form the idea, "Of course, you won't remember much of the history or other things they teach you here. Why, I haven't thought of Latin or algebra in thirty years! But . . ." And here the speaker goes on to enumerate what *are* to his mind the enduring values of education which every child should seize as his great opportunity: "habits of industry," "friendships formed," "the great ideals of our nation." Almost never is the essential of education defined in terms of the subjects that are taught in the classroom. . . .

FOR THOUGHT:

How has education changed since 1925?

86 THE REACH OF TECHNOLOGY

The Lynds had sought a town relatively independent of a nearby metropolis. But once on the scene, they learned that the city had made itself felt through modern transportation and communication. No longer could most American parents raise their children in cultural isolation. Through technology, Chicago and Indianapolis, New York and Hollywood became a part of the lives of young people in Middletown.

The following selection focuses on the impact of the car, motion pictures, and radio on the people of Middletown. As you read, think about these questions:

1. What did the automobile, the movies, and the radio do to the culture of Middletown?
2. How did these inventions affect parents' ability to control the experiences of young people?

Technology's Effect.
on Middletown

"Why on earth do you need to study what's changing this country?" said a lifelong resident and shrewd observer of the Middle West. "I can tell you what's happening in just four letters: A-U-T-O!"

The first real automobile appeared in Middletown in 1900. About 1906 it was estimated that "there are probably 200 in the city and county." At the close of 1923 there were 6,221 passenger cars in the city, one for every 6.1 persons, or roughly two for every three families. As, at the turn of the century, business-class people began to feel apologetic if they did not have a telephone, so ownership of an automobile has now reached the point of being an accepted essential of normal living.

No one questions the use of the auto for transporting groceries, getting to one's place of work or to the golf course, or in place of the porch for "cooling off after supper" on a hot summer evening. [No matter how] much the activities concerned with getting a living may be altered by the fact that a factory can draw from workmen within a radius of forty-five miles, or [no matter how] much old labor-union men resent the intrusion of this new alternate way of spending an evening, these things are hardly major issues. But when auto riding tends to replace the traditional call in the family parlor as a way of approach between the unmarried, "the home is endangered," and all-day Sunday motor trips are a "threat against the church." It is in the activities concerned with the home and religion that the automobile occasions the greatest emotional conflicts.

Group-sanctioned values are disturbed by the inroads of the automobile upon the family budget. A case in point is the not uncommon practice of mortgaging a home to buy an automobile. According to an officer of a Middletown automobile financing company, 75 to 90 percent of the cars purchased locally are bought on time payments. A working man earning $35.00 a week frequently plans to use one week's pay each month as payment for his car.

Many families feel that an automobile is justified as an agency holding the family group together. "I never feel as close to my family as when we are all together in the car," said one business-class mother. And one or two spoke of giving up Country Club membership or other recreations to get a car for this reason. "We don't spend anything on recreation except for the car. We save every place we can and put the money into the car. It keeps the family together," was an opinion voiced more than once. Sixty-one percent of 337 boys and 60 percent of 423 girls in the three upper years of the high school say that they motor more often with their parents than without them.

Robert S. Lynd and Helen Merrell Lynd, **Middletown: A Study in American Culture,** pp. 251-271. Abridged.

In borrowing money to buy a car, a person would transfer the mortgage or ownership of his house to the lender with the condition that the transfer would not be effective if the borrower paid back the money.

▶Do television programs sometimes bring your family together? Does anything else give your family a common experience on a regular basis?

571

COLLEGE IN THE 1920'S: A PORTFOLIO

The three readings from Middletown describe the life of high school students and their families during the 1920's. Many of these students later went to college. This portfolio illustrates some aspects of college life during the 1920's. How was it similar to or different from the life of high school students which you read about in Middletown?

The girls' basketball team at Cornell

"Do you fellows wash your own
    clothes at the house?"
"Heck, no."
"Well, what's that washing machine
    for?"
"That's no washing machine. That's
    our cocktail shaker."

CORNELL WIDOW

A chemistry class at Cornell

Mud-slinging at Cornell

The Columbia Class of 1920 at Commencement

"Whiskey kills more people than bullets."
"That's because bullets don't drink."
WASHINGTON AND LEE MINK

A football game at University of Minnesota, 1926

Theta: What's your brother like?
Beta: Wine, women and song.
WASHINGTON DIRGE

She: I want that car in the window.
He: Well, it's in the window.
VANDERBILT MASQUERADER

"Will your people be surprised when you graduate?"
"No, they've been expecting it for several years."
AMHERST LORD JEFF

A dance at University of Minnesota

A 1924 Lincoln at the University of Minnesota

A JASS AGE GLOSSARY

ALL WET—wrong; arguing a mistaken notion or belief.

APPLESAUCE—a term of derogation; nonsense; same as baloney, bunk, banana oil, hokum and horsefeathers.

BEE'S KNEES—a superb person or thing.

BELLY LAUGH—a loud, uninhibited laugh.

BERRIES—anything wonderful; similar to bee's knees.

BIG CHEESE—an important person.

BULL SESSION—an informal group discussion.

BUMP OFF—to murder.

CARRY A TORCH—to suffer from unrequited love.

CAT'S MEOW—anything wonderful; similar to bee's knees, berries.

CHEATERS—eyeglasses.

COPACETIC—excellent.

CRUSH—an infatuation with a person of the opposite sex.

DOGS—human feet.

FALL GUY—a scapegoat.

FLAPPER—a typical young girl of the '20's typically with bobbed hair, short skirts and silk stockings.

GIGGLE WATER—an alcoholic drink.

GIN MILL—a speak-easy.

GOOFY—silly.

HARD-BOILED—tough; without sentiment.

HEEBIE-JEEBIES—the jitters.

HEP—wise.

HOOCH—bootleg liquor.

LOUSY—bad; contemptible.

MAIN DRAG—the most important street in a town or city.

NERTS (NUTS)—an interjection expressing the speaker's disgust.

OSSIFIED—drunk.

PEPPY—full of vitality.

PINCH—to arrest.

PUSHOVER—a person or thing easily overcome.

RITZY—elegant (from *Ritz*, the Paris hotel).

SMELLER—the nose.

SPEAK-EASY—a saloon or bar selling bootleg whiskey.

SPIFFY—having an elegantly fashionable appearance.

SPIFFLICATED—drunk.

STUCK ON—having a crush on.

SWANKY—ritzy.

SWELL—marvelous.

574

But this centralizing tendency of the automobile may be only a passing phase. Sets in the other direction are almost equally prominent. "Our daughters [eighteen and fifteen] don't use our car much because they are always with somebody else in their car when we go out motoring," lamented one business-class mother. And another said, "The two older children [eighteen and sixteen] never go out when the family motors. They always have something else on." "In the nineties we were all much more together," said another wife. "People brought chairs and cushions out of the house and sat on the lawn evenings. We rolled out a strip of carpet and put cushions on the porch step to take care of the unlimited overflow of neighbors that dropped by. We'd sit out so all evening. The younger couples perhaps would wander off for half an hour to get a soda but come back to join in the informal singing or listen while somebody strummed a mandolin or guitar." "What on earth *do* you want me to do? Just sit around all evening!" retorted a popular high school girl of today when her father discouraged her going out motoring for the evening with a young blade in a [sporty] car waiting at the curb. "The desire of youth to step on the gas when it has no machine of its own," said the local press, "is considered responsible for the theft of the greater part of the [154] automobiles stolen from [Middletown] during the past year."

Sharp, also, is the resentment aroused by the elbowing new device when it interferes with old-established religious habits. The minister must compete against the strong pull of the open road. . . . Preaching to 200 people on a hot, sunny Sunday in midsummer on "The Supreme Need of Today," a leading Middletown minister denounced "automobilitis—the thing those people have who go off motoring on Sunday instead of going to church. If you want to use your car on Sunday, take it out Sunday morning and bring some shut-ins to church and Sunday School. Then in the afternoon, if you choose, go out and worship God in the beauty of nature—but don't neglect to worship Him indoors too."

But if the automobile touches the rest of Middletown's living at many points, it has revolutionized its leisure. More, perhaps than the movies or any other intrusion new to Middletown since the nineties, it is making leisure-time enjoyment a regularly expected part of every day and week rather than an occasional event. The readily available leisure-time options of even the working class have been multiplied many-fold. As one working-class housewife remarked, "We just go to lots of things we couldn't go to if we didn't have a car." Beefsteak and watermelon picnics in a park or a nearby wood can be a matter of a moment's decision on a hot afternoon.

Use of the automobile has apparently been influential in spreading the "vacation" habit. The custom of having each summer a [rest],

▶ How important to your life is the freedom of choice which modern technology has brought? What are the costs of this technology in human and psychological terms?

575

usually of two weeks, . . . is increasingly common among the business class, but it is as yet very uncommon among the workers. "Vacations in 1890?" echoed one substantial citizen. "Why, the word wasn't in the dictionary!"

Like the automobile, the motion picture is more to Middletown than simply a new way of doing an old thing. It has added new dimensions to the city's leisure. To be sure, the spectacle-watching habit was strong upon Middletown in the nineties. Whenever they had a chance people turned out to a "show." But chances were relatively fewer. Fourteen times during January 1890, for instance, the Opera House was opened for performances ranging from *Uncle Tom's Cabin* to *The Black Crook*, before the paper announced that "there will not be any more attractions at the Opera House for nearly two weeks." In July there were no "attractions." A half dozen were scattered through August and September. There were twelve in October.

Today nine motion-picture theaters operate from 1 to 11 P.M. seven days a week summer and winter. . . .

"Go to a motion picture . . . and let yourself go," Middletown reads in a *Saturday Evening Post* advertisement. "Before you know it you are *living* the story—laughing, loving, hating, struggling, winning! All the adventure, all the romance, all the excitement you lack in your daily life are in—Pictures. They take you completely out of yourself into a wonderful new world. . . . Out of the cage of everyday existence! If only for an afternoon or an evening—escape!

▶ Is the ability to "let yourself go," and to "escape," an increase in freedom?

As in the case of the books it reads, comedy, heart interest, and adventure compose the great bulk of what Middletown enjoys in the movies. "Middletown is amusement hungry," says the opening sentence in a local editorial. At the comedies Middletown lives for an hour in a happy sophisticated make-believe world that leaves it, according to the advertisement of one film, "happily convinced that Life is very well worth living."

Actual changes of habits resulting from the week-after-week witnessing of these films can only be inferred. Young Middletown is finding discussion of problems of mating in this new agency. . . . Large illustrated advertisements [boast,] "Girls! You will learn how to handle 'em!" and "Is it true that marriage kills love? If you want to know what love really means, its exquisite torture, its overwhelming raptures, see_____."

▶ How much do films influence your ideas of proper behavior? Are films a good guide to the considered life?

"Sheiks and their 'shebas'," according to the press account of the Sunday opening of one film, ". . . sat without a movement or a whisper through the presentation. . . . It was a real exhibition of love-making and the youths and maidens of [Middletown] who thought that they knew something about the art found that they still had a great deal to learn."

576

Some high school teachers are convinced that the movies are a powerful factor in bringing about the "early sophistication" of the young and the relaxing of social taboos. One working-class mother frankly welcomes the movies as an aid in child-rearing, saying, "I send my daughter because a girl has to learn the ways of the world somehow and the movies are a good safe way." The judge of the juvenile court lists the movies as one of the "big four" causes of local juvenile delinquency. [He believes] that the disregard of group [moral attitudes] by the young is definitely related to witnessing . . . fictitious behavior sequences that habitually link the taking of long chances and the happy ending.

Though less widely [spread] than automobile owning or movie attendance, the radio nevertheless is rapidly crowding its way in among the necessities in the family standard of living. Not the least remarkable feature of this new invention is its accessibility. Here skill and ingenuity can in part offset money as an open sesame to swift sharing of the enjoyments of the wealthy. With but little equipment one can call the life of the rest of the world from the air. And this equipment can be purchased piecemeal at the ten-cent store. . . .

[As people sit] at home listening to a Philharmonic concert or a sermon by Dr. Fosdick, or to President Coolidge bidding his father good night on the eve of election, and as [the radio wedges] its way with the movie, the automobile, and other new tools into the . . . habits [of] the 35,000 people of Middletown, readjustments necessarily occur.

The place of the radio in relation to Middletown's other leisure habits is not wholly clear. As it becomes more perfected, cheaper, and a more accepted part of life, it may cease to call forth so much active, constructive ingenuity and become one more form of passive enjoyment. Doubtless it will continue to play a mighty role in lifting Middletown out of the humdrum of every day. It is beginning to take over that function of the great political rallies or the trips . . . to the state capital to hear a noted speaker . . . that a generation ago helped to set the average man in a wide place. . . . Indeed, at no point is one brought up more sharply against the impossibility of studying Middletown as a self-contained, self-starting community than when one watches these space-binding leisure-time inventions imported from without—automobile, motion picture, and radio—reshaping the city.

Dr. Harry Emerson Fosdick (born 1878), a clergyman, was a spokesman in the 1920's for liberal theology. His sermons were impressive and practical and were nationally broadcast until his retirement in 1946.

FOR THOUGHT:

What technological developments have played a role in the lives of teenagers today similar to the role played by the automobile, movies, and radio in the 1920's?

Three trends marked the decade of the 1920's. First, except in agriculture and a scattering of depressed industries, the economy pushed steadily ahead to new heights of prosperity. Second, politics saw little constructive legislation. Three lackluster Presidents, all from small towns or rural areas, presided over an urban-industrial society which they did not understand. Beneath the surface, however, people laid the foundations of a political realignment which was to result in a new majority for the Democratic party. Finally, the new prosperity contributed to changing patterns of behavior. Some of these patterns were described in the three readings from Middletown. In addition, the 1920's marked a new step in female emancipation, saw the deterioration of the family accompanied by a wave of delinquency and crime, and witnessed militant attacks against foreigners, Catholics, Jews, blacks, and radicals.

The Economy

After World War I ended in November 1918, a postwar boom set in. This boom collapsed in 1920. As many as 5 million workers may have been unemployed in 1921 during the depths of the depression. Almost half a million farmers lost their farms, and bankruptcies in business topped the 100,000 mark. By the middle of 1923, however, the economy had recovered completely. For the next seven years, a constantly expanding boom pushed production to new heights.

The boom grew primarily through two sources: investments in a number of new industries and purchases of large quantities of new consumer durable goods. A housing boom supported expansion in the construction industry until the middle of 1927. The rise of the automobile industry created huge investments in new plants and equipment. Other industries, such as electric power, aluminum, radios, and refrigerators, also spurred growth. Only a few industries, such as textiles (in New England) or coal mining, lagged behind. But agriculture was in decline as worldwide competition flooded the market with foodstuffs after the war. Farm population dropped by a million persons during the decade. And 13 million acres of farmland were abandoned. Nor did labor prosper as much as the owners of capital. Under constant attack from industry, the American Federation of Labor lost about 1 million members during the decade while wages generally rose more slowly than rents, interest, and dividends. In the meantime, a boom in stock prices pushed the market to unprecedented heights. During

Durable goods are items such as cars, machines, and household appliances, that may be used for several years.

578

an eighteen month period, for example, United States Steel doubled in price. General Electric and Westinghouse tripled.

Local Politics

On local and state levels, reform activities continued on a reduced scale throughout the 1920's. The reformers of the first decade of the century had called for a change in the entire society. In the 1920's, reformers were more likely to work for changes in individuals rather than for full-scale reform of society. They expected the poor to adjust to their condition and to learn to solve personal emotional problems. Professional social workers stuck to their tasks. They left overall social reform to amateurs, or to professional politicians.

Many of the reform measures pioneered in the early 1900's spread rapidly in the 1920's, however. The city manager and commission forms of government were adopted in hundreds of cities. Many cities used zoning ordinances to control the use of land for public purpose. More and more states adopted industrial insurance. But, despite these reforms, the pace of change in the cities declined during the 1920's. Between 1900 and 1930, the number of people who lived in the central cities of thirteen large metropolitan areas declined from 69.1 percent to 63.7 percent. It is easy to understand what happened. First the streetcar and then the automobile made it easier for people to move out of central cities. In 1911, manufacturers sold 199,000 automobiles in the United States. In 1917, they sold 1,746,000; in 1923, 3,624,717; in 1929, 4,587,400. The ability to move to the suburbs allowed many Americans to leave the problems of central cities behind them. These people poured their energy into suburban schools, suburban libraries, suburban social services, and suburban police. Gradually, the quality of life in the central city and its suburbs grew apart.

See readings 74 and 75.

Particularly during the 1960's, Americans began to realize that people who had moved to the suburbs had not left urban problems behind them. A metropolitan region makes up an interdependent unit. People who live in central cities and the suburbs which surround them must work together to solve their common problems. Dwellers in suburbia can no more ignore the problems of the city than the United States can live isolated from the rest of the world. But during the 1920's, flight to the suburbs seemed to be an escape from an entanglement of problems.

National Politics

Three Republicans won the Presidency during the 1920's. The Republican party also maintained substantial majorities in both the Senate and the House of Representatives. Figure 87A shows the popular vote in Presidential elections between 1920 and 1928. Figure 87B demonstrates Republican dominance in the House and Senate during this period.

U.S. Bureau of the Census, **Historical Statistics of the United States, Colonial Times to 1957** (Washington, D.C.: Government Printing Office, 1960), p. 682.

FIGURE 87A	THE ELECTIONS FOR PRESIDENT, 1920-1928		
Year	Candidates	Party	% of Popular Vote
1920	WARREN G. HARDING	Republican	60.4
	James M. Cox	Democratic	36.2
	Eugene V. Debs	Socialist	3.4
	P. P. Christensen	Farmer-Labor	1.0
1924	CALVIN COOLIDGE	Republican	54.0
	John W. Davis	Democratic	24.5
	Robert La Follette	Progressive	16.6
1928	HERBERT HOOVER	Republican	58.2
	Alfred E. Smith	Democratic	40.9

Historical Statistics, p. 691.

FIGURE 87B   PARTY CONTROL OF THE EXECUTIVE AND LEGISLATIVE BRANCHES OF GOVERNMENT, 1921-1931

Year	President's Party	Majority Party and Margin	
		House of Rep.	Senate
1921-1923	R	R (172)	R (22)
1923-1925	R	R (20)	R (8)
1925-1927	R	R (64)	R (17)
1927-1929	R	R (42)	R (3)
1929-1931	R	R (100)	R (17)

The issues which had dominated national legislation for fifty years—money and banking, the tariff, business regulation, and efficiency in government—continued into the 1920's. But they no longer occupied the center of the stage. No significant banking legislation was passed. The Fordney-McCumber Tariff (1922) and the Hawley-Smoot Tariff (1930) reversed the trend set by the Underwood Tariff (1913). These two tariffs raised rates substantially and placed new ones on many agricultural products. Trusts and holding companies grew at a rapid rate, but Congress failed to pass significant legislation to control them. Scandals during the Harding administration failed to arouse the nation sufficiently to bring a change in administration. Rather than these traditional issues, immigration restriction, already discussed in Chapter 16, and prohibition occupied the center of the political stage during the 1920's.

Twenty-six states had already adopted prohibition laws by 1917. During World War I, Congress first prohibited the manufacture or sale of intoxicating liquors. It then passed the Eighteenth Amendment, which placed this prohibition in the Constitution. Ratified in 1919, the amendment went into effect in 1920 together with the Volstead Act. This act provided the means to enforce prohibition. Americans,

President Harding, although not involved in any scandals, appointed dishonest, undeserving men to office. Harry Daugherty, Attorney General, used his office to protect violators of the prohibition law. Charles F. Forbes, Director of Veteran's Bureau, robbed his agency of about $250 million. Thomas W. Miller obtained $50,000 by fraudulently selling foreign-owned properties seized by the United States government during World War I.

580

by the millions, however, violated the prohibition laws. Prohibition agents tried in vain to enforce a law which a large number of citizens broke willingly.

Conventional political histories of the 1920's often emphasize the defeat of progressivism and the new dominance of big business. In 1920, President Warren G. Harding spoke of a "return to normalcy" and an end to "wild experiments." He died in 1923, as scandals were erupting in his administration. His successor, Calvin Coolidge, was an even more determined advocate of the American business system. "The business of the country is business," he once said. His successor, Herbert Hoover, returned to an early Wilsonian idea of the role of government in the economy. During his second term, Woodrow Wilson had turned to government aid to agriculture, the regulation of the length of the working day, and similar positive governmental measures. Hoover, however, attacked relief programs for the farmer, public ownership or control of electric power facilities, and even the development of a state liquor monopoly. He saw them as measures which "would impair the very basis of liberty and freedom."

Emphasizing Republican dominance and support of business in national politics during the 1920's obscures a more vital matter. The 1920's saw a number of conflicts arise over the fundamental nature of American society and American politics. A whole set of conflicting images became compressed under the labels "wet" and "dry"; Protestant or Catholic; country town and farms, or big city; old immigrants long removed from Europe or new immigrants still caught up in European values.

Because it contained roughly equal representation of people favoring both images, the Democratic party became the center of this conflict. A resolution attacking the Ku Klux Klan as un-American divided the Democratic Convention in 1924. The resolution lost by a narrow vote (546-541). It was replaced by a compromise plank in the platform condemning religious and racial antagonisms. The battle over the platform carried over into the nominating procedure. The South supported W.G. McAdoo, formerly Wilson's Secretary of the Treasury. The North supported Governor Alfred E. Smith of New York, a second-generation Irish Catholic who advocated repeal of prohibition. Supporters of the two men battled stubbornly through 102 ballots. Finally, an exhausted convention settled on a compromise candidate, John W. Davis, a New York corporation lawyer who had been raised in West Virginia.

Smith won the nomination more easily in 1928, only to have normally Democratic voters turn against him. The contrasts between Smith from New York and Hoover, once an Iowa farm boy, stood out vividly. Most Americans still identified with Iowa farms. Hoover broke the Democratic dominance of the South, capturing Florida, North Carolina, Tennessee, Texas, and Virginia. Smith carried only the remaining

The Volstead Act defined an alcoholic beverage as one containing ½ of 1 percent alchohol. It placed the enforcement of the law under the Bureau of Internal Revenue. Any person manufacturing or selling liquor was to be fined not more than $1000 or imprisoned not more than 6 months for a first offense and receive more severe punishments for succeeding offenses.

The most famous scandal was the Teapot Dome scandal. Secretary of the Interior, Albert B. Fall, had persuaded Secretary of the Navy, Edwin C. Denby, to transfer his department's jurisdiction of certain oil reserves to the Interior Department. In 1922, Fall secretly leased the reserve at Teapot Dome, Wyoming, to Harry F. Sinclair, and the reserve at Elk Hills, California, to Edward L. Doheny. A Senate investigation revealed that the two oil speculators had "loaned" Fall about $350,000. All three men were indicted for conspiracy and bribery, but only Fall was convicted.

The old Ku Klux Klan, defunct for many years after the Civil War, was revitalized in 1915. By 1925, the Klan was operating in the North and South and numbered between 4 and 5 million members.

states of the old Confederacy and two New England states, Massachusetts and Rhode Island.

Beneath this massive Republican victory lay an important shift in the electorate. This shift was not immediately clear. The Republican majority had been fashioned in the 1890's around a coalition of farmers and small- and big-city voters who joined in a common image of the good life. In the 1920's, this coalition was breaking apart. Figures 87C and 87D tell much of the story.

Ethnic identification and urban residence lay at the center of political shifts in the 1920's. In the election of 1928, Smith did make impressive gains in cities with large Catholic and immigrant populations. These results suggested that the Democrats could crack the Republican coalition if they could hold the South and sweep the large cities of the Northeast and Midwest.

As long as the country was prosperous, Hoover's image remained attractive to many voters. It was not, however, an image that could capture the imagination of the urban masses. Nor could it retain the allegiance of poor blacks. Many blacks did continue to vote Republican into the 1930's out of loyalty to the party that had freed the slaves.

Hoover's image and the policies of the Republican party could not even hold the farm vote once the Depression struck after 1929. Hoover described a rural America of a bygone day. Throughout the 1920's, American farmers suffered a sharp reversal in their fortunes. Between 1921 and 1924, the farm bloc in Congress, which represented mainly large and relatively prosperous farmers, pushed through measures to restore farm prosperity. When these measures failed, the farm bloc pushed for expanded government aid in the form of a price support plan called the McNary-Haugen Bill. Coolidge vetoed the measure. Hoover echoed Coolidge's policies. Farmers stirred restlessly. Then the collapse of farm prices at the onset of the Depression in 1929 added this farm discontent to the urban and ethnic unrest which were building a new political coalition for the Democratic candidate, whoever he might be.

The Society

To a marked degree, the people described in *Middletown* shared many of the trends taking place in American society during the 1920's. Industry, the radio, the movies, and the automobile were slowly forging a national culture.

The shift from a rural to an urban society and from agriculture to industry changed the American family. For every five marriages during the 1920's there was almost one divorce. Women had become far more independent. The number of female wage earners had been rising steadily. And it continued to rise during the 1920's. With the

The McNary-Haugen Bill of 1924 proposed a federal farm board to buy farm surpluses and either store them until prices rose or sell them abroad at the international price. The bill suffered successive defeats in both houses, was finally passed in 1927, only to be vetoed by President Coolidge.

The first commercial radio station—KDKA—began broadcasting in Pittsburgh in 1920. Radio broadcasting grew rapidly in the 1920's. Until 1927, movies had all been silent films. *The Jazz Singer* was the first motion picture to use sound.

FIGURE 87C PRESIDENTIAL VOTES IN
CITIES WITH FIFTY PERCENT OR MORE IMMIGRANT STOCK

City	Democratic Vote in Nearest Thousand		Percent Change	Republican Vote in Nearest Thousand		Percent Change	
	1920	1928		1920	1928		
Boston	68	205	202	108	99	—7.7	Carl N. Degler, "American
Buffalo	40	126	215	100	145	45.0	Political Parties and the Rise
Chicago	197	716	266	635	812	27.8	of the City: An
Cleveland	71	166	132	149	195	30.7	Interpretation," *Journal of*
Detroit	52	157	201	221	265	19.9	*American History*, Vol. LI
Jersey City	63	153	143	102	100	—1.9	(June 1964), pp. 53-56.
Los Angeles	56	210	275	178	514	189.0	
Milwaukee	25	111	344	73	82	12.2	
Minneapolis	143	396	178	519	561	8.1	
Newark	41	118	188	116	169	45.6	
New York	345	1,168	239	786	715	—9.1	
Oakland	21	61	190	73	119	63.2	
Philadelphia	90	276	209	308	420	36.5	
Pittsburgh	40	161	301	139	216	55.5	
Providence	46	97	112	80	86	7.5	
Rochester	29	74	156	74	100	35.2	
St. Paul	21	57	171	40	53	32.5	
San Francisco	33	97	195	96	96	0.0	
Seattle	17	47	176	59	96	62.9	

FIGURE 87D   PRESIDENTIAL VOTES IN
CITIES WITH LESS THAN FIFTY PERCENT OF IMMIGRANT STOCK

City	Democratic Vote in Nearest Thousand		Percent Change	Republican Vote in Nearest Thousand		Percent Change	
	1920	1928		1920	1928		
Akron	28	32	14.3	44	79	79.5	Degler, pp. 53-56.
Atlanta	9	7	—22.5	3	6	100.0	
Baltimore	87	126	44.8	126	135	7.3	
Birmingham	25	17	—32.0	7	18	157.0	
Cincinnati	78	110	41.0	113	148	31.0	
Columbus	48	47	—2.3	60	92	53.2	
Dallas	14	17	21.4	5	27	440.0	
Denver	23	41	78.5	44	74	68.1	
Houston	15	22	47.7	8	27	237.0	
Indianapolis	61	73	19.7	80	110	37.4	
Kansas City, Mo.	77	97	26.0	80	127	58.6	
Louisville	56	64	14.3	68	98	44.3	
Memphis	16	18	12.5	9	12	33.3	
New Orleans	33	56	70.0	18	14	—22.2	
Portland, Ore.	28	45	60.5	45	76	68.8	
St. Louis	106	176	66.0	163	162	—0.68	
Toledo	30	45	50.0	52	78	50.0	

passage of the Nineteenth Amendment in 1920, women won the vote. A new attitude to sex developed, spurred by the automobile, the glamor of illegal liquor, a knowledge of psychology, and a higher educational level.

Children also tended to drift from home. Movies and the radio gave them new models to imitate. The automobile freed them from the restraints of their parents and opened a new and exciting world. New courses taught in the schools also gave many children a glimpse of a new culture. Large numbers of them revolted, particularly during the college years.

In response to these trends, another segment of the public reasserted the value of old-time morality. Prohibition was one indication of this counterattack. So was fundamentalism. Revivalists such as the former major-league baseball player, Billy Sunday, appeared before enormous crowds. They preached the virtues of religion and strict moral standards. A Tennessee court convicted a high school biology teacher, John T. Scopes, of disobeying a law which forbade the teaching of Darwinism in the public schools. The law had been passed overwhelmingly by the state legislature. And then there were the attacks on radicals, real and pretended.

In 1919, a full-scale Red Scare broke out led by A. Mitchell Palmer, Attorney General under Woodrow Wilson. The hysteria came in the wake of the Communist revolution in Russia. The government jailed thousands of men and women on trumped-up charges and deported hundreds of them. After 1920, the modern Ku Klux Klan, which had been reorganized in 1915, began to grow rapidly. It attacked radicals, Catholics, Jews, and blacks, particularly in the midwestern states. The Klan advocated racist doctrines and claimed to protect "Americanism." Its power declined around the middle of the decade, particularly after the corruption of some of its officers was exposed. In the meantime, the entire country had become involved in the trial of two anarchists, Nicola Sacco and Bartolomeo Vanzetti. They were accused of murdering a payroll guard in Braintree, Massachusetts. Although the two men were convicted in 1921, they were not executed until 1927 while appeals crept through the courts.

The 1920's tumbled new and old America together in bewildering combinations. Families drove to old-time revival meetings in their new Model T Fords. Republican Presidents used the magic of radio to appeal to classic virtues, such as thrift and individualism. In politics, prohibition and immigration restriction looked back to days long past while measures to support agricultural prices anticipated the reforms of the New Deal. Then in October 1929, came the stockmarket crash, which heralded the advent of the Great Depression.

Fundamentalism is a conservative Protestant movement that emphasizes the belief in the literal truth of the Bible.

Tennessee law prohibited the teaching of evolution because of the fundamentalist claim that it contradicted the Bible. Scopes's trial attracted national attention, largely because William Jennings Bryan, the former Presidential candidate, argued for the prosecution and Clarence Darrow, a lawyer of national prominence, defended Scopes.

The trial of Sacco and Vanzetti attracted national attention. Many people believed that anti-immigrant and anti-radical feelings were primarily responsible for their conviction. Many felt their trial had been grossly unfair.

584

The New Deal

STATING THE ISSUE

A one-page essay entitled "Stating the Issue" has introduced most of the chapters in this book. In Chapter 23, however, you are asked to find an issue for yourself. Reading 88 consists of pictures, lyrics to songs, a Depression shopping list, and some graphs. What historical problem do you find in these materials?

1929 Stock market crash launches Great Depression

1931 Congress establishes Reconstruction Finance Corporation

1932 Franklin Delano Roosevelt is elected President

1933 President Roosevelt declares a bank holiday

1933 Tennessee Valley Authority begins reclamation of farmland

1933 Civilian Conservation Corps is established to provide work for unemployed

1933 Congress passes Agricultural Adjustment Act

1934 Congress passes National Industrial Recovery Act

1935 President Roosevelt establishes Works Progress Administration, creating more jobs

1935 Congress passes the Social Security Act, insuring workers against unemployment and old age

1935 Supreme Court declares National Industrial Recovery Act unconstitutional

1936 President Roosevelt wins reelection

1936 President Roosevelt tries to increase number of judges in Supreme Court

1938 Economic recession spurs the passage of more New Deal legislation

1938 Congress of Industrial Organization is established

1939 World War II begins, and international affairs assume greater importance

WORK-IS-WHAT-I
WANT-AND-NOT-CHARITY
WHO-WILL-HELP-ME-
GET-A-JOB-7 YEARS-
IN-DETROIT-NO-MONEY
SENT-AWAY-FURNISH-
BEST-OF-REFERENCES
PHONE RANDOLPH 83 #59.

BUY
APPLES
5

U.S. Bureau of the Census,
**Historical Statistics of the
United States: Colonial
Times to 1957**
(Washington, D.C.:
Government Printing Office,
1961), p. 73.

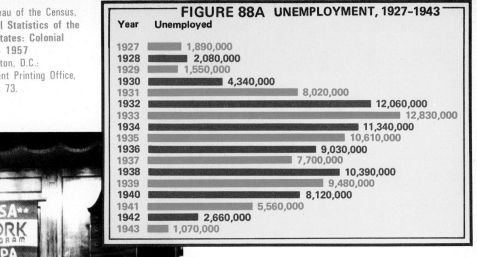

FIGURE 88A   UNEMPLOYMENT, 1927–1943

Year	Unemployed
1927	1,890,000
1928	2,080,000
1929	1,550,000
1930	4,340,000
1931	8,020,000
1932	12,060,000
1933	12,830,000
1934	11,340,000
1935	10,610,000
1936	9,030,000
1937	7,700,000
1938	10,390,000
1939	9,480,000
1940	8,120,000
1941	5,560,000
1942	2,660,000
1943	1,070,000

U.S. Bureau of the Census,
Historical Statistics, p. 73.

FIGURE 88B   UNEMPLOYED AS A PERCENTAGE OF THE CIVILIAN LABOR FORCE

Year	Percentage of Civilian Labor Force Unemployed
1927	4.1
1928	4.4
1929	3.2
1930	8.7
1931	15.9
1932	23.6
1933	24.9
1934	21.7
1935	20.1
1936	16.9
1937	14.3
1938	19.0
1939	17.2
1940	14.6
1941	9.9
1942	4.7
1943	1.9

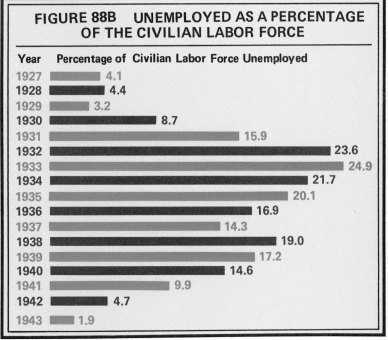

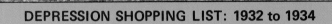

DEPRESSION SHOPPING LIST: 1932 to 1934

AUTOMOBILES
NEW
Pontiac coupé	$585.00
Chrysler sedan	995.00
Packard	2,150.00
USED	
Studebaker '30	200.00
Ford '29	57.50

CLOTHING
WOMEN'S
Mink coat	585.00
Cloth coat	6.98
Raincoat	2.69
Wool dress	1.95
Wool suit	3.98
Wool sweater	1.69
Silk stockings	.69
Leather shoes	1.79
MEN'S	
Overcoat	11.00
Wool suit	10.50
Trousers	2.00
Shirt	.47
Pullover sweater	1.95
Shoes	3.85

HOUSEHOLD ITEMS
Silverplate flatware, 26 piece	$4.98
Double-bed sheets	.67
Bath towel	.24
Wool blanket	1.00
Linen table cloth	1.00
Wool rug (9'x12')	5.85

APPLIANCES
Electric iron	$2.00
Electric coffee percolator	1.39
Electric mixer	9.95
Vacuum cleaner	18.75
Electric washing machine	47.95
Gas stove	23.95

MISCELLANEOUS
Dental filling	$1.00
Tooth paste (large)	.25
Razor blades (10)	.49
Cigarettes	.15
Cigarette lighter	.39
Fountain pen	1.00
Desk typewriter	19.75
Kodak Box Brownie	2.50
Automobile tire	6.20
Gasoline (per gallon)	.18

FOOD
Sirloin steak (per lb.)	$0.29
Bacon (per lb.)	.22
Ham (per lb.)	.31
Leg of lamb (per lb.)	.22
Milk (per qt.)	.10
Butter (per lb.)	.28
Margarine (per lb.)	.13
Eggs (per dozen)	.29
Cheese (per lb.)	.29
Bread (20 oz. loaf)	.05
Coffee (per lb.)	.26
Sugar (per lb.)	.05
Rice (per lb.)	.06
Potatoes (per lb.)	.02
Oranges (per doz.)	.27
Bananas (per lb.)	.07
Onions (per lb.)	.03
Cornflakes (8 oz. package)	.08

6

7

8

BEANS, BACON AND GRAVY

I was born long a-go,— in eight-een-nine-ty-four, and I've
seen man-y a pan-ic I will own, I've been hun-gry, I've been cold, and
now I'm grow-ing old, but the worst I've seen is nine-teen thir-ty-two.

Chorus:
Oh those beans, ba-con and grav-y,— They al-most drive me cra-zy,— I
eat them till I see them in my dreams. (in my dreams) When I
wake up in the morn-ing— and an-oth-er day is dawn-ing,— I
know I'll have an-oth-er mess of beans.

We congregate each morning
At the country barn at dawning
And everybody is happy, so it seems;
But when our work is done
We file in one by one,
And thank the Lord for one more mess of beans.

REFRAIN

We have Hooverized on butter,
For milk we've only water,
And I haven't seen a steak in many a day;
As for pies, cakes, and jellies,
We substitute sow-bellies,
For which we work the country road each day.

REFRAIN

If there ever comes a time
When I have more than a dime
They will have to put me under lock and key,
For they've had me broke so long
I can only sing this song,
Of the workers and their misery.

REFRAIN

The owner of this farm went bankrupt in the early 1930's. The bank that owned the mortgage held an auction to raise the money to pay the farmers' debt.

U.S. Bureau of the Census, Historical Statistics, p. 144.

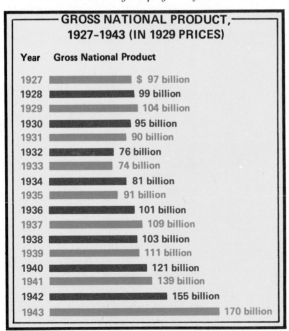

GROSS NATIONAL PRODUCT, 1927-1943 (IN 1929 PRICES)

Year	Gross National Product
1927	$ 97 billion
1928	99 billion
1929	104 billion
1930	95 billion
1931	90 billion
1932	76 billion
1933	74 billion
1934	81 billion
1935	91 billion
1936	101 billion
1937	109 billion
1938	103 billion
1939	111 billion
1940	121 billion
1941	139 billion
1942	155 billion
1943	170 billion

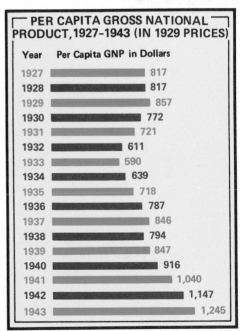

PER CAPITA GROSS NATIONAL PRODUCT, 1927-1943 (IN 1929 PRICES)

Year	Per Capita GNP in Dollars
1927	817
1928	817
1929	857
1930	772
1931	721
1932	611
1933	590
1934	639
1935	718
1936	787
1937	846
1938	794
1939	847
1940	916
1941	1,040
1942	1,147
1943	1,245

U.S. Bureau of the Census, Historical Statistics, p. 144.

89 AMERICAN PEOPLE FACE THE DEPRESSION CRISIS

Herbert Hoover had been in office only seven months when the stock market crash echoed down the narrow canyons of Wall Street. Hoover told the public that the Depression would soon end. He met with leaders of business, labor, and the farmers, asking each group to support voluntary methods to restore prosperity. But economic conditions only got worse.

The Democrats won control of the House of Representatives in the congressional election in 1930. Democrats and a few progressive Republicans also had a majority in the Senate. These people passed several bills to deal with the worst aspects of the Depression crisis. The federal government even appropriated $300 million for direct relief payments to the unemployed. But conditions did not improve. Only after Franklin D. Roosevelt was elected in 1932 did the government begin to intervene to end the Depression on a large scale.

Throughout the decade after 1929, the Depression was the major fact of life for many American families. The pictures and statistics in Reading 88 gave a vivid picture of the crises these people faced. In 1934 about one family out of every four in the labor force was unemployed. Many millions of people lived on handouts from private charity or from local, state, or national governments. Men and women spent all of their savings. And they saw their possessions fall under the hammer of the auctioneer to the highest bidder. Reading 89 contains five accounts of ways in which Americans reacted to the Depression crisis. As you read, keep the following questions in mind:

1. How did each of the people described in this reading try to meet the Depression crisis?
2. What were the human costs of the Depression?

An Incident of the Depression

People who lived through the Depression have many stories to tell. Studs Terkel interviewed hundreds of Americans and printed their stories. The following selection is an interview with Emma Tiller, whose family had a small farm in western Texas.

In 1934, in this Texas town, the farmers was all out of food. The government gave us a slip, where you could pick up food. For a week, they had people who would come and stand in line, and they couldn't

Studs Terkel, **Hard Times: An Oral History of the Great Depression** (New York: Pantheon Books, 1970), pp. 232-233. Copyright © 1970 by Studs Terkel. Reprinted by permission.

get waited on. This was a small town, mostly white. Only five of us in that line were Negroes. The rest was white. We would stand all day and wait and wait and wait. And get nothin' or if you did, it was spoiled meat.

We'd been standin' there two days, when these three men walked in. They had three shotguns and a belt of shells. They said, lookin' up and down that line, "You all just take it easy. Today we'll see that everybody goes home, they have food." Three white men.

One of 'em goes to the counter, lays his slip down and says he wants meat. He had brought some back that was spoiled. He said to the boss, "Would you give this meat for your dog?" So he got good meat. He just stood there. So the next person gets waited on. It was a Negro man. He picked up the meat the white man brought back. So the white guy said, "Don't take that. I'm gonna take it for my dog." So the boss said, "I'm gonna call the police."

So the other reaches across the counter and catches this guy by the tie and chokes him. The Negro man had to cut the tie so the man wouldn't choke to death. When he got up his eyes was leakin' water. The other two with guns was standin' there quietly. So he said, "Can I wait on you gentlemen?" And they said, "We've been here for three days. And we've watched these people fall like flies in the hot sun, and they go home and come back the next day and no food. Today we purpose to see that everybody in line gets their food and then we gonna get out." They didn't point the guns directly at him. They just pointed them at the ceiling. They said, "No foolin' around, no reachin' for the telephone. Wait on the people. We're gonna stand here until every person out there is waited on. When you gets them all served, serve us."

The man tried to get the phone off the counter. One of the guys said, "I hope you don't force me to use the gun, because we have no intentions of getting nobody but you. And I wouldn't miss you. It wouldn't do you any good to call the police, because we stop 'em at the door. Everybody's gonna get food today." And everybody did.

▶If government officials do not carry out their duties, do private citizens have the right to use force in order to make them do so? Why or why not?

Another Incident of the Depression

Harry Terrell, who had lived for seventy-seven years in and around Des Moines, Iowa, told Terkel the following story.

This was at the time that mortgaging of farms was getting home to us. So they was having ten cent sales. They'd put up a farmer's property and have a sale and all the neighbors'd come in, and they got the idea of spending twenty-five cents for a horse. They was paying

Studs Terkel, **Hard Times**, pp. 214-215. Reprinted by permission.

ten cents for a plow. And when it was all over, they'd all give it back to him. It was legal and anybody that bid against that thing, that was trying to get that man's land, they would be dealt with seriously, as it were.

Private elevator refers to a grain elevator used to store wheat or other grain.

That infuriated all the people that wanted to carry on business as usual. It might be a bank or an implement dealer or a private elevator or something like that. They had their investments in this. The implement dealer, he was on the line, too. The only place he had of getting it was from the fellow who owed him. And they'd have a sheriff's sale.

The people were desperate. They came very near hanging that judge. Because they caught this judge foreclosing farm mortgages, and they had no other way of stopping it. He had issued the whole bunch of foreclosures on his docket.

A docket is a list of legal cases to be tried.

It all happened in Le Mars. They took the judge out of his court and took him to the fairgrounds and they had a rope around his neck, and they had the rope over the limb of a tree. They were gonna string him up in the old horse thief fashion. But somebody had sense enough to stop the thing before it got too far.

They had marches, just like we have the marches nowadays. They came from all over the state. That was the time of the Farm Holiday. There was a picket line. The Farm Holiday movement was to hold the stuff off the market, to increase the price. It saw violence, too.

▶ Do any economic conditions justify illegal acts such as these? Why or why not?

They stopped milk wagons, dumped milk. They stopped farmers hauling their hay to market. They undertook to stop the whole agriculture process. They thought if they could block the highways and access to the packing plants, they couldn't buy these hogs at two cents a pound.

They'd say: we're gonna meet, just east of Cherokee, at the fork of the road, and so on. Now they spread it around the country that they were gonna stop everything from going through. And believe me, they stopped it. They had whatever was necessary to stop them with. Some of 'em had pitchforks. (Laughs.) You can fix the auto tire good with a pitchfork. There were blockades.

The country was getting up in arms about taking a man's property away from him. It was his livelihood. When you took a man's horses and his plow away, you denied him food, you just convicted his family to starvation. It was just that real.

I remember one man, as devout a man as I ever met, a Catholic. He was mixed up in it too—the violence. His priest tried to cool him down. He says, "My God, Father, we're desperate. We don't know what to do." He was the most old, established man you could find. He was in the state legislature.

I remember in court when they were going to indict a Norwegian Quaker, when they were offering them lighter sentences if they'd plead guilty, his wife said, "Simon, thee must go to jail."

594

Two Families Face Starvation

Some families, too proud to beg or go on relief, preferred to starve. Although people such as these were exceptions, their stories indicate one response to the Depression.

Middletown, N.Y., Dec. 24 Attracted by smoke from the chimney of a supposedly empty summer cottage near Anwana Lake in Sullivan County, Constable Simon Glaser found a young couple starving. Three days without food, the wife, who is twenty-three years old, was hardly able to walk.

The couple, Mr. and Mrs. Wilfred Wild of New York, had been unemployed since their formerly wealthy employer lost his money. And several days ago they invested all they had, except 25 cents for food, in bus fare to this region in search of work. Finding none, they went into the cottage, preferring to starve rather than beg. They said they had resigned themselves to dying together.

An effort is being made to obtain employment for them. But if this fails they will be sent back to New York.

Danbury, Conn., Sept. 6 Found starving under a rude canvas shelter in a patch of woods on Flatboard Ridge, where they had lived for five days on wild berries and apples, a woman and her sixteen-year-old daughter were fed and clothed today by the police and placed in the city almshouse.

▶In 1974, members of the Symbionese Liberation Army, a small group of revolutionaries in California, kidnapped Patricia Hearst, the daughter of a rich newspaper publisher. The Hearsts gave away $2 million in food at the demand of the kidnappers. Were the members of the SLA justified in using force to help feed poor people? Were people in the Depression justified in using force for the same purpose? Why or why not?

The woman is Mrs. John Moll, 33, and her daughter Helen, of White Plains, N.Y. They have been going from city to city looking for work since July 1931, when Mrs. Moll's husband left her.

When the police found them, they were huddled beneath a strip of canvas stretched from a boulder to the ground. Rain was dripping from the improvised shelter, which had no sides.

College Graduates Help Each Other

Unemployment was no respecter of education. The following short article indicates what graduates of one group of distinguished colleges did in the midst of the Depression crisis.

The New York Times (July 27, 1932). Copyright © 1932 by The New York Times Company.

The League for Industrial Democracy was founded in 1905. It is made up of educators, labor union officials, journalists, and students. It sponsors lectures, radio broadcasts, and public affairs conferences.

Organization of the Association of Unemployed College Alumni was announced yesterday after a meeting of graduates of nine eastern colleges at the offices of the League for Industrial Democracy. Estimating the number of unemployed alumni in this city alone at more than ten thousand, the association made public a plan of action designed to enlist members throughout the country.

In a statement prepared at the meeting, the group pointed out that since June 1929, it had become increasingly difficult for university graduates to obtain positions. Distress consequent upon unemployment was more acute among college-trained men and women, according to the announcement, because of their relatively high standards of living and education. . . .

Colleges represented at the meeting included Columbia, Harvard, New York University, Vassar, Hunter, City College, Swarthmore, Columbia Law School, and New York Dental School.

An Unemployed Seaman
Looks for a Place to Sleep

Rather than move into the shantytowns which grew up in every city, some people preferred a more individualistic solution to the problem of living.

The New York Times (July 9, 1932). Copyright © 1932 by The New York Times Company. Reprinted by permission.

Somewhere in Tin Mountain, the four-acre jungle on the Red Hook waterfront in Brooklyn, Louis Bringmann put down his old sea chest last night and looked about him for a place to sleep. He was sixty years old, penniless, friendless, and jobless.

Up to 9 A.M. yesterday, Louis Bringmann had had a home on the top landing of the Atlantic Theatre, at Flatbush Avenue and Dean Street. But the Fire Department inspector on his monthly round discovered it.

Patrolman Richard Palmay of the Bergen Street police station climbed the fire-escape stairs at 8 A.M. with orders to "remove the fire hazard." At the top landing he peered over the walls of corrugated cardboard which Bringmann had built around the grillwork. The tenant was fast asleep.

On the cardboard wall was a neat sign, done in old-school flourishes and shading:

NOTICE

Please be kind enough not to destroy or take anything from this resting place. I am out of work and this is all I have. I have no money and I can't find a job, so please leave me alone. I'll appreciate your kind consideration and

THANK YOU.

Patrolman Palmay looked down on the tired old face, the slight figure outlined beneath the worn but clean-looking blankets, at the socks and spotless shirt fluttering in the breeze on the short clothes-line overhead. He had his orders, but—

An hour later, doubling back on his post, Palmay saw Louis Bringmann leaving his cardboard shelter. He watched him as he dipped into the rain barrel he had fixed under the copper leader, to make his morning ablutions. Then he walked over.

Ablutions means washing.

"You'll have to move, old man." He hated the job.

"I can't stay? I'm not bothering anyone. And they don't use the theatre in the summertime. I keep everything clean. I—"

"They gave me orders," replied Palmay, "It's against the fire laws."

The snow-white head nodded. Louis Bringmann was too patient a man to vent his bitterness in vain argument.

He rolled his blankets carefully and dressed. He took his little sea chest under one thin arm. The other meager chattels dangled from his white fingers. He started to move.

Chattels are a person's possessions.

Palmay thrust a half dollar into the free hand and walked away. . . .

The white-haired Bringmann plodded up the avenue, immaculate in his worn brown trousers and blue jacket, heading toward the river.

He had known of Tin Mountain before, but he was proud. In Tin Mountain, a sprawling village of tin huts and makeshift dugouts at the foot of Henry Street, are all types of men—brawny Scandinavian seamen, husky Irish longshoremen—good men, but a bit rough. One of its streets has the bitter legend on a placard, "Prosperity Boulevard."

Late in the afternoon he was still sitting on the little chest that contains the meager souvenirs of better days—a few faded menus he had made up when he was head chef of one of the big Manhattan hotels. He wouldn't tell which one.

"The past," said Louis Bringmann, "is a turned-over page. When I read it I read it alone. They tell me now that I'm even too old for dishwashing—that's the whole story. I have no friends and my money is gone."

FOR THOUGHT:

What obligation, if any, did the government have to help the people described in this reading? Why do you think as you do?

90 A CASE HISTORY OF A DEPRESSION FAMILY

No typical experience can capture the effect of the Depression on American families. Some families lived through the entire Depression decade with their pattern of living relatively unchanged. Others found their entire way of life disrupted. For the majority of families, the Depression meant a reduced standard of living, but no drastic change in accustomed patterns of life.

Cases of extreme want have become part of American folklore. The Okies were farmers from the Great Plains who were driven off their lands by a series of dust storms. They became famous through John Steinbeck's novel, *The Grapes of Wrath*. Unemployed people who left their homes to seek work elsewhere often lived in shantytowns on the edges of cities. By calling these temporary communities Hoovervilles, they added a new word to the language. Everyone who lived through the 1930's remembers the breadlines outside soup kitchens and the proud people who sold apples on street corners rather than beg or go on relief.

State, local, and federal governments all sponsored relief projects. The two most famous were the Works Progress Administration (WPA) and the Public Works Administration (PWA). These two programs kept millions of Americans alive during the worst days of the Depression. With one person in four unemployed, projects sponsored by these agencies often enlisted unskilled laborers, skilled mechanics, and college graduates. They worked side by side and were united by a common bond of misfortune.

Reading 90 traces the history of one family through the Depression crisis. As you read it, think about the following questions:

1. What did the Park family do to live through the Depression years? How do you think these experiences may have affected their image of themselves? their attitude toward the role of the government in the economy?
2. How much money did the Parks have in a typical Depression year? What did the organization of the federally supported public works projects mean to them?

The Claud Park Family
Faces the Depression

During 1938-1939, the Works Progress Administration made a survey in Dubuque, Iowa, of 103 Depression families. The WPA published 45 case histories in mimeographed form. The Claud Park family was as typical as any of the others. The history of the Parks indicates the impact of the Depression on one working-class family.

PARK

Mr. Claud Park	32
Mrs. Martha Park	31
Claud, Jr.	11
Mary	9
Dorothy	4

The Personal Side, Jessie A. Bloodworth, ed. (Washington, D.C.: Works Progress Administration, Division of Research, 1939), pp. 13-18. Language simplified.

Interviewing completed January 2, 1938

Claud Park was granted a pay raise a year ago at the Mississippi Milling Company, where he had been hired in August 1935 after four years of unemployment. The Parks thought the Depression was ended for them. Now, however, with working hours reduced to twenty-five hours a week, the Park family fear that they are "getting right back" where they were five or six years ago.

At 32, Claud is weatherbeaten in appearance and shows the effects of worry and anxiety. Though frank and spontaneous, he is slow of speech and drawls out his words as he discusses the family's Depression experiences. After the long siege of unemployment and dependency on either direct relief or work projects, Claud considers himself an "authority on the Depression."

The Parks live in a rented five-room brick house in a neighborhood of small homes in the north end of town. Martha Park, the mother of three children, has struggled desperately to make ends meet on a limited budget. However, she has found time to take an active part in the Parent Teachers Association and the Mothers Club of the church. She considers that her high school courses, especially home economics,

►This picture shows a scene from a famous musical of the 1930's, **The Great Ziegfeld**. Musicals were popular throughout the decade. How do you explain this popularity? What kinds of films do you like to see? Why?

have stood her in good stead in managing her household on a limited budget. She believes that the family's depressed circumstances should not be permitted to interfere with the proper rearing of the children. So she has always taken advantage of anything that would help her to become a more understanding mother and homemaker. Claud Jr., 11 years old, is in the sixth grade, and Mary, 9, is a fourth-grader. Dorothy, 4, a "Depression baby," is the pet of the family.

Claud and Martha Park "grew up" in a small town in southern Minnesota. But they have lived in Dubuque during most of the thirteen years of their marriage. Claud's education was cut short. He had to leave school after completing the eighth grade to help his father support a large family.

The Parks moved to Dubuque immediately after their marriage in 1924, when Claud, through a relative, got a job as a spray painter at the Iowa Foundry. His entrance rate was 45¢ an hour and he worked 54 hours a week. After two years, Claud was advanced to the position of foreman of the paint department. His rate of pay was increased to 50¢ an hour. The paint did not agree with him, however. He lost considerable weight and suffered from ulcers of the throat. So he decided to quit early in 1927 and go to Chicago. There he had heard of a chance to "get on" as a janitor in a new building at $200 a month. Soon after the Parks arrived in Chicago, they both came down with typhoid fever. By the time Claud had recovered, all jobs in the new building had been filled. He found a janitorial job in another building. But it paid only $100 a month. He worked at this job for about two years. Then he decided that with the higher cost of living in Chicago, he would be better off working at the foundry in Dubuque.

On his return to Dubuque, he worked at the Iowa Foundry for a year. He was laid off during the general reduction in force in February 1931. From February 1931 to the fall of 1932 he worked irregularly for a barge line and at an insulating plant. He averaged from $5 to $25 a week, depending on the amount of work available. The family began running into debt and it was necessary for Claud to borrow $200 from his "folks." When this was exhausted, $80 was borrowed on a $1,000 insurance policy, which was later allowed to lapse. Claud regrets very much losing his only insurance policy. On their return from Chicago, the Parks lived in a five-room house for which the rent was $18 a month. But as circumstances became more strained, they moved to a small four-room house for which they paid only $10.

By December 1932, the situation had become desperate. The temperature was below zero, and there was little fuel or food left. The Parks owed a coal bill of $40 and a grocery bill of $25. And they expected credit to be discontinued at any time. To add to the seriousness of their plight, Mrs. Park was pregnant. After talking things over one night, they could see no alternative except to apply for relief. Yet they both felt that they would be "disgraced." Mrs. Park bitterly opposed going on relief. But during the night Claud got "scared about the kids." He thought "we can't let the kids starve just because we are proud." The next morning, without telling his wife his intentions, he went to the courthouse to make application for relief. When he arrived at the courthouse, he couldn't go in. "I must have walked around the block over a dozen times—it was 10 below zero, but I didn't know it." Finally he got up sufficient courage to make his application.

The family was "investigated" and after about two weeks "a lady brought out a grocery and coal order." This was just in the "nick of time" as they were completely out of provisions. Mr. Park considered that they got along very nicely on the weekly grocery order. Part of the time they were also allowed milk from the milk fund and "this helped a lot." The Parks feel that they were well treated by the relief office and did not find the routine investigations obnoxious. "It's part of the system and when you ask for relief, of course you have to cooperate. The questions didn't bother us so much as the idea of being on charity."

During the Depression, it was common for individuals to borrow money from their insurance companies, using the insurance policy as security for the loan. One could usually borrow up to the cash value of the policy and still remain insured while the loan was outstanding.

▶ Would you feel ashamed if your family went on relief or welfare? Why or why not?

During the winter of 1934, the Civilian Works Administration (CWA) created for 4 million people such jobs as resurfacing highways, painting, and building or repairing playgrounds, schools, and airports. When President Roosevelt saw how much the program cost ($1 billion), he discontinued it.

Claud Park "never felt right about accepting the relief slip." He says, "Later, when they let me do some work for it, I felt better." The relief office allowed only $7.50 a month for rent and Claud did odds jobs for the landlord to make up the difference. In the fall of 1933 he was placed on a CWA road construction project at $80 a month. He was delighted to be paid in cash and didn't feel that he was getting "something for nothing." At the close of CWA in the spring of 1934, he was placed by the public employment office on the lock and dam project. And his wages were cut to $50 a month and later to $48. He was intermittently employed on emergency work projects until August 31, 1936. At that time, he got a job as a benchman finishing sashes at the Mississippi Milling Company. Claud had made application at all the factories in town. But he feels that he would never have been taken on at the Mississippi Milling Company had not an old employee there spoken for him.

The Parks kept a detailed monthly account of their income from all sources, including work relief, direct relief, and odd jobs, from 1933 through 1935. The total income in 1933 was $450.96, and for 1935 it was $698.64. Included in these amounts is work for back rent totaling $85.15 in 1933 and $107.25 in 1935. The Parks feel that 1932 and 1933 were their "hardest years." After Claud started to work on emergency projects, the family had "a little more to live on."

During the lean years of the Depression, the Parks barely "subsisted." And Claud feels that it would be impossible "even to subsist" on this low income over an extended period as clothing and furniture would have to be replaced. The Parks thought they were very economical in 1926. In that year their total expenditures were $1,095.15, including payments on furniture, medical bills, insurance, and a move to Chicago. At that time, there were only three in the family. But in 1933, there were five. The Parks are keeping the calendars on which they marked every item of income for the Depression years as "relics" to look at when they are old, and Claud hopes, "better off."

At the Mississippi Milling Company, Claud had worked 9 hours a day, 5½ days a week, for about 7 months. The time was then reduced to 35 hours a week, and about two months ago, a 25-hour week went into effect. His entrance rate was 45¢ an hour, but when he requested a raise a few months after starting work, his rate was increased to 47¢ an hour. At present, the weekly paycheck amounts to only $11.75. And the family is again getting behind with the bills. Because of the uncertainty of the working hours at the mill, it is impossible for Claud to "fill in" with odd jobs. He feels that there is no use to look for more regular work in other factories. In most of them work is just as irregular as at the Mississippi Milling Company. Then, too, if he quits to take another job, he might never be able to get on again at the Mississippi Milling Company.

▶ Do you feel that Mr. Park should go on relief rather than accept such low wages? Why or why not?

602

After Claud's pay raise, "things began to look bright again." The family moved to their present home where the rent is $17 a month. Mrs. Park felt that the overcrowding in the other house was bad for the children. After paying up back bills, she had even started some long-needed dental work. But she discontinued it before completion when Claud went on short hours. She told the dentist he could keep the bridge he had finished in his safe. But he said that it was of no use to him and he was willing to trust the Parks.

In an attempt to make ends meet with the reduced income, the Parks now take one quart of milk for the children instead of two, and buy meat only once a week. They have enough canned and dried vegetables from their garden on "the island" to last through the winter. The biggest problem is warm clothing for the children. Claud Jr. and Mary both need shoes, overshoes, and winter underwear. But so far it has been impossible for the Parks to do more than buy food and pay the rent, gas, and electric bills. In bad weather "the children will have to be kept home from school." And Mrs. Park "feels terrible" about that. She thinks "employers don't begin to realize how much hardship they cause by reducing the paychecks of the workers."

In order to have enough to eat during the Depression, many families supplemented their meager groceries by keeping fruit and vegetable gardens.

FOR THOUGHT:

In addition to providing relief payments, in what other ways might the government have helped the Park family?

91 FDR AND THE NEW DEAL

HISTORICAL ESSAY

The Onset of the Depression

October 1929 dramatized the end of the prosperity of the 1920's. Through September, prices in the stock market had wavered up and down. Then on October 24 and again on October 29, a deluge of sell orders sent prices tumbling. The stock market crash accentuated weaknesses throughout the economy. The long, dismal spiral into the Depression had begun.

The crash wiped out the savings of small investors who had had hopes of quick and easy gains. Their confidence gone, they clung to the rest of their money rather than spend it on consumer goods. Sales, and hence production, fell off rapidly. The industrial depression aggravated an already serious agricultural situation. And prices of farm products continued to fall. In the whole economy, investment in factories and tools fell from $10 billion in 1929 to $1 billion in 1932. By 1932, about one in every four workers was unemployed.

Breaking the Jam

To Keep This Deal a Fair Deal!

The six cartoons on these two pages portray Roosevelt during the early days of the New Deal. How do they picture the President? How do you respond to them?

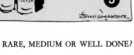

RARE, MEDIUM OR WELL DONE?

Herbert Hoover made a poor Depression President. He offended politicians because he was rigid. He failed to attract public support because he seemed so indifferent to suffering. He placed faith in his powers to persuade Americans to accept policies he suggested and in the ability of state and local governments to deal with the Depression crisis. His overemphasis on a balanced budget, his refusal to permit the federal government to sponsor relief programs, and his support for the protective Smoot-Hawley Tariff cost the country dear and hurt his party. As the election drew near in November 1932, Hoover seemed pessimistic and defeated. And his occasional announcements that prosperity lurked around the corner rang hollow in the ears of hungry millions.

The Hundred Days

In November 1932, Franklin D. Roosevelt swept to an impressive victory. Hoover had won forty states in 1928. He now carried only six. During the months between the election and Roosevelt's inauguration on March 4, the economy reached low ebb. Then the banking system collapsed. As citizens rushed to withdraw money, one institution after another ran out of cash and turned depositors away. By March 4, four fifths of the states had suspended banking.

Roosevelt's inaugural speech, delivered on a bleak March day, captured the faith of the American people. For a hundred days, Congress passed measures that Roosevelt requested, as Figure 91A indicates.

Banks rarely keep much cash on hand. Most of the depositors' money is invested in mortgages, stocks, etc. When an unusually large number of people tried to withdraw money, the banks could not supply it. In addition, many investments had declined in value, leaving banks with little or no assets.

FIGURE 91A LEGISLATION AND AGENCIES OF THE NEW DEAL—FIRST HUNDRED DAYS

Name	Date	Provisions
Emergency Banking Relief Act	3/9/33	Authorized President to regulate banking transactions and foreign exchange. Forbade any bank to reopen until it proved solvency to Treasury Department.
Civilian Conservation Corps (CCC)	3/31/33	Set up work camps employing 18–25-year-olds in conservation tasks.
Federal Emergency Relief Act (FERA)	5/12/33	Authorized federal money to be given to states for direct relief.
Agricultural Adjustment Act (AAA)	5/12/33	Limited farm surplus by curtailing production. Provided farm subsidies raised by taxing food processors. Set up Federal Land Banks to lend money at low interest rates.
Tennessee Valley Authority (TVA)	5/18/33	Set up publicly owned corporation to develop resources of the area.
Federal Securities Act (Truth-in-Securities Act)	5/27/33	Compelled promoters to give investors complete and truthful information about new securities.
Home Owners' Loan Corporation (HOLC)	6/13/33	Provided mortgage loans at low interest to refinance mortgages on non-farm homes.
National Recovery Administration (NRA)	6/16/33	Suspended antitrust laws. Helped industry set up fair codes of cooperation. Gave to labor the right of collective bargaining.
Public Works Administration (PWA)	6/16/33	Set up public-works projects to provide employment and to increase business activity.

Four types of activities were particularly important. First came a series of measures to untangle the national financial mess. On the day after his inauguration, Roosevelt declared a national bank holiday. He forbade anyone to export gold. Supported by Congress, the Administration developed a plan to reopen banks after a Treasury Department inspection testified to their soundness. Congress established the Federal Deposit Insurance Corporation. It insured bank deposits against failure, established the Home Owners' Loan Corporation, and made other banking reforms. By the Federal Securities Act, Congress required promoters to give explicit information about new issues of stocks. And it gave the Federal Trade Commission the power to regulate stock issues. Finally, Roosevelt took the nation off the gold standard. He fixed the price of gold at $35 an ounce in an attempt to raise prices.

Second, the Administration pushed through measures designed to stimulate the economy. The practice of pumping federal funds into the economy to help business revive and employ more people was known as "pump priming." An appropriation of $500 million launched the Civilian Conservation Corps. Then the National Industrial Recovery Act opened a three-pronged attack on the Depression. It created the Public Works Administration with an appropriation of $3.5 billion to provide work such as building schools and roads. It also set up the National Recovery Administration to draw up industry-wide codes of fair business practices in order to limit production and raise prices. In addition, the codes established minimum wages and maximum hours. Finally, Section 7A of the act set up boards to conduct elections in order to determine whether or not workers wished to be represented by a union. As a result, the membership of labor unions spurted rapidly, especially the newly formed Committee for Industrial Organization.

Third, the Agricultural Adjustment Act of May 1933, launched the agricultural reforms of the New Deal era. The act aimed to raise farm prices to "parity" with the goods which farmers bought. Farmers who withdrew part of their acres from cultivation received cash payments from the government. Reduced acreage, combined with a drought, raised prices substantially within the next few years. Roosevelt chose Henry A. Wallace to administer this program.

Finally, the Administration launched the Tennessee Valley Authority. It was designed to develop hydroelectric power, establish fertilizer plants, inaugurate a system of flood control and improved navigation, and coordinate efforts at reforestation, soil conservation, and industrialization in a huge area covering all or part of seven states. The TVA was opposed by private power interests. But it forged steadily ahead, substantially improving the standard of living for millions of people.

No overall philosophy guided this emergency legislation. Some measures that Congress passed were contradictory or worked against

▶ Should government act as a patron of the arts only in emergencies such as the Depression? Or, should government always support artistic activities? Why?

In later years, Coughlin's pro-Fascist sympathies and anti-Semitic overtones alienated many of his followers.

each other. But despite vague pronouncements, contradictory measures, and all the things that remained to be done, it was obvious that a fresh spirit had entered American politics. The public seemed convinced that Roosevelt cared and that he wanted to improve people's lives.

Four million people remained unemployed. But the Democrats picked up seats in both the Senate and the House of Representatives in 1934. Two measures to fight unemployment may have rallied some of this support. In May 1933, Congress had appropriated $500 million to be given to state relief organizations through the Federal Emergency Relief Administration. Harry Hopkins, the Director of the FERA, insisted, however, that unemployed people needed jobs rather than handouts. He persuaded Roosevelt to establish the Civil Works Administration late in 1933. FDR permitted the CWA to die. But he continued a public works program during 1934 through the FERA.

In May 1935, Roosevelt put Hopkins in charge of a new federal agency, the Works Progress Administration. In eight years, the WPA employed about 8.5 million people and spent about $11 billion. In addition to public works, the WPA also sponsored projects to employ actors, writers, and artists. And it organized the National Youth Administration which created part-time jobs for about 2 million young people. But the WPA did not reach enough of the unemployed, pay high enough wages, or undertake large enough projects to provide the massive stimulus the economy needed.

Attacks from Right and Left

Three movements threatened the Democratic domination during these years. Senator Huey Long of Louisiana at first supported Roosevelt. Later, he broke with him and threatened to start a new party. He started the "Share-Our-Wealth" movement. It proposed to distribute money taken from the rich among the masses. Long's program had widespread appeal among the poor.

Father Charles E. Coughlin of Detroit had even wider influence. Coughlin was a Catholic priest who made nationwide radio broadcasts. He changed from an avid New Deal supporter to one of its staunchest opponents in 1935. Coughlin's National Union for social Justice appealed primarily to Catholics. However, many Americans of other faiths also joined.

The third movement formed behind a scheme to pay a monthly pension of $200 to people over sixty on the condition that they would spend the entire sum within thirty days. A retired California physician, Dr. Francis E. Townsend, spearheaded this movement. About half the national income would have been needed to make these payments. But Townsend and his followers pressed on.

608

These threats to his political base, the increasing alienation of the business community, and the influence of trusted advisors combined to push Roosevelt in a new direction. In May 1935, the Supreme Court declared the NIRA unconstitutional in the case of *Schecter vs. U.S.* A month later, Roosevelt called on Congress to pass a series of new laws, launching the "Second New Deal" in the process. (See Figure 91B below.)

Among these advisors were Louis D. Brandeis and Felix Frankfurter. Brandeis was appointed to the Supreme Court by President Wilson. Frankfurter was appointed to the Supreme Court in 1939 by President Roosevelt.

FIGURE 91B   LEGISLATION AND AGENCIES OF THE NEW DEAL, 1934-1938

Name	Date	Provisions
Gold Reserve Act	1/30/34	Gave federal government control over dollar devaluation.
Securities and Exchange Commission (SEC)	6/6/34	Set up commission to supervise issuance of new securities and to supervise stock exchanges.
Reciprocal Trade Agreements Act	6/12/34	Authorized President to raise or lower tariffs by as much as 50% without Senate's consent.
Federal Housing Administration (FHA)	6/28/34	Insured banks against commercial loans for construction and repair of houses and business properties.
Works Progress Administration (WPA)	4/8/35	Provided for large-scale national work programs.
Rural Electrification Administration (REA)	5/11/35	Set up to provide isolated rural areas with low-cost electricity.
National Youth Administration (NYA)	6/26/35	Provided part-time work for needy students.
National Labor Relations Act (Wagner-Connery Act)	7/5/35	Set up National Labor Relations Board (NLRB) to arbitrate employer-employee differences. Upheld labor's right of collective bargaining.
Social Security Act	8/14/35	Provided unemployment compensation, old-age security, and social services.
United States Housing Authority (USHA)	9/1/37	Authorized loans of federal funds to local agencies for slum clearance and housing projects.
Agricultural Adjustment Act (Second AAA)	2/16/38	Provided for production quotas through soil-conservation programs, marketing quotas, and parity payments.
Food, Drug, and Cosmetic Act	6/24/38	Prohibited misbranding and false advertising. Required manufacturers of foods, drugs, and cosmetics to list ingredients.
Fair Labor Standards Act	6/25/38	Set up minimum wages and maximum hours for workers in interstate trade. Prohibited child labor under 16.

The Second New Deal

Among the most important of these new laws was the National Labor Relations Act, often called the Wagner Act. It gave workers the right to bargain collectively and forbade employers from interfering when unions tried to organize workers. It established the National Labor Relations Board which was authorized to hold elections, indicate which union, if any, had a right to represent the workers, and investigate charges of unfair labor practices.

In August 1935, Congress passed the Social Security Act, which insured workers against unemployment and old age. Taxes on workers and their employers financed social security. Although many workers, particularly farmers and the self-employed, were not covered and the payments were small, this law marked a vital beginning.

Four additional laws also marked significant turning points. One law gave federal agencies increased powers to regulate public utilities. A new banking act reorganized the Federal Reserve System. Legislation establishing the Rural Electrification Administration brought electricity to farmers, only one in ten of whom had electricity in 1935. Finally, the Wealth Tax Act raised taxes on high incomes, gifts, and estates, shifting the burden of taxation toward those most able to pay.

Under the REA, farmers were encouraged to form associations, subsidized by low-interest loans from the REA, to erect light and power lines to furnish electricity to those people not receiving central-station service.

The End of an Era

Three candidates competed for public favor in 1936. The Democrats nominated Roosevelt by acclamation. The Republicans chose a moderately liberal governor, Alfred M. Landon of Kansas. Dissatisfied elements, such as those who followed Coughlin and Townsend, organized the Union party with Congressman William Lemke of North Dakota as its candidate. But the extremists were losing ground. Long had been assassinated in September 1935. And the legislation of the Second New Deal cut the ground from under the Townsendites. Roosevelt's Administration had been remarkably free of racial prejudice. And the economic reforms of the New Deal which had helped black voters shifted that block of votes to FDR. Farmers supported Roosevelt because of the AAA. Labor supported him because of the Wagner Act. The elderly appreciated Social Security. And the homeowners blessed him for HOLC. For all these reasons, Roosevelt carried every state except Maine and Vermont.

In September 1935, at the new state capitol building, Huey Long was assassinated by Dr. Carl A. Weiss, the son-in-law of one of his political opponents. Long's bodyguards immediately killed the assassin.

Noting in his inaugural address that a third of the nation remained "ill-housed, ill-clad, and ill-nourished," Roosevelt seemed set for a further wave of reforms. But the Supreme Court stood in his way. Four of the nine judges staunchly opposed his new trends. Two, including Chief Justice Charles Evans Hughes, wavered depending on the issue. The Court had invalidated the first AAA, the NIRA, and laws establishing minimum wages at both state and national levels. Some of its members seemed intent on destroying the entire New Deal.

The Constitution provides for a Supreme Court. But it does not specify the number of justices. Congress has varied the number of judges from five to ten. Since 1869, the figure has been set at nine. President Roosevelt asked Congress for the power to appoint an additional judge for each judge who did not retire upon reaching seventy years of age.

610

Roosevelt tried to increase the size of the Court. He asked for permission to appoint additional judges. A public outcry broke out. The balance among the three branches of government seemed threatened. After a long battle, Congress defeated the measure. But the justices began to interpret the Constitution less strictly. As justices retired, Roosevelt appointed men who shared his point of view. And the conservatives abandoned the fight.

Three developments, coming atop the Supreme Court fight, ended the New Deal. First, a rash of sit-down strikes which marked the organizing drives of the C.I.O. in 1937 frightened many middleclass people. Instead of leaving factories, workers in industries such as automobiles and rubber sat down at their machines in order to gain concessions from their employers. Afraid to resort to force, management conceded. In a few instances, violence did break out, particularly in the steel and automobile industries. These new tactics and reports of clashes between strikers and police cooled the ardor for reform.

In the midst of the Court fight and the sit-down strikes, economic recession set in. Roosevelt had cut the relief program sharply in June 1937. Within five months, unemployment rose by 2 million. Not until April 1938 did he urge Congress to pass a $3.75 billion public works program. He also sponsored a new AAA measure. Finally, he pushed through the Fair Labor Standards Act, which established a forty-hour week and minimum wage of 40¢ an hour. These three measures further alienated conservative voters. But they did not affect the economy.

Then Roosevelt committed a major political blunder. Southern congressmen had increasingly resisted reform measures. In the 1938 election, Roosevelt set out to get rid of them. He failed. His major targets won in the primaries and returned to Washington prepared for vengeance. In addition, Republicans picked up seats in the House and the Senate. Combined with conservative southern Democrats, they were able to effectively brake further reform.

The Meaning of the New Deal

The New Deal failed to overcome the Depression. Only a wave of war orders from the allied nations finally put the remainder of the unemployed back to work. But the New Deal left a vital legacy. It convinced Americans that their government should accept responsibility for the nation's economy and should protect its people from old age and unemployment. Farmers, industrial workers, bank depositors, stock buyers, homeowners, and others benefitted. TVA and REA made farm life far more pleasant. A serious endeavor to appoint blacks to public office started this long abused minority on the long road to equality in American society. Finally, the New Deal brought a new spirit into American life and helped to change a people defeated by economic catastrophe.

President Roosevelt appointed seven justices within the next four years. He appointed such people as Senator Hugo L. Black, Felix Frankfurter, and William O. Douglas. They appeared to be more sympathetic to New Deal legislation.

▶Are workers justified in "sitting-in" on private property in order to win their demands? Why or why not?

The Second AAA (1938) provided farmers with cash benefits proportionate to acreage withheld from production to use for plant-conserving crops. If two thirds of the farmers producing a certain commodity agreed, the government could assign marketing quotas limiting the amount that the farmers could sell. If surpluses still existed, the farmers could store them in government warehouses. With the crops as security, the government would grant the farmers "commodity loans." When the market price of the stored items rose, the farmers would sell the surplus and pay back the government.

Years of Peace and War, 1921-1945

STATING THE ISSUE

During the 1920's and most of the 1930's Americans concentrated on internal affairs. They were concerned in the beginning with what President Harding called a return to normalcy. After 1929 they became concerned with the "abnormal" but nevertheless grimly real Depression.

Meanwhile, fateful changes were taking place in the balance of power elsewhere in the world. Japan came under military rule and attacked China. And anti-democratic dictators took power in Italy and Germany. Then the Japanese, Italians, and Germans all launched attacks on other nations.

At first, most Americans believed that the rise of dictators in Europe and Asia should not directly concern the United States. As the 1930's continued, however, an increasing number of Americans came to believe that the nation had a moral stake in world affairs. They also felt it was very much involved in the struggle between democratic and totalitarian nations. Their disagreement as to what role America should take in that struggle was decisively resolved when Japan attacked Pearl Harbor on December 7, 1941.

Chapter 24 examines America's role in World War II from both an internal and an external point of view. The readings are concerned with the ways in which mobilization for total war changed the American way of life at home. The summary essay discusses the war as a part of the history of America's role in world affairs between 1921 and 1945.

612

1921–22 Representatives of major powers meet at Washington Naval Conference

1928 Sixty-two nations sign Kellogg-Briand Pact, outlawing war

1932 Stimson Doctrine declares United States will not recognize territory set up by force

1933 President Roosevelt announces Good Neighbor Policy toward Latin America

1935–37 Congress passes series of neutrality acts

1939 Nazis invade Poland; World War II begins

1939 Congress permits selling of arms to Allies on "cash and carry" basis

1941 Congress passes Lend-Lease Act

1941 Japanese attack Pearl Harbor; United States enters World War II

1942 United States forces begin "island-hopping" strategy in Pacific

1944 Allied troops land at Normandy to begin liberation of Europe

1945 Churchill, Roosevelt, and Stalin meet at Yalta

1945 Germany surrenders unconditionally

1945 United States drops atomic bombs on Hiroshima and Nagasaki

1945 Japan surrenders; World War II ends

92 MOBILIZING PUBLIC OPINION FOR WAR

Before the attack on Pearl Harbor, the American people were divided over the course of American foreign policy. Some of them supported President Roosevelt in aiding the allied forces in Europe. Others warned that any departure from a policy of strict neutrality might draw the United States into war. The attack on Pearl Harbor swept internal divisions aside. Four days later, Germany and Italy declared war against the United States. For the first time in their history, Americans found themselves facing attack from powerful enemies in two hemispheres.

From 1941 until 1945 America was engaged in the greatest war effort in its history. It was an effort requiring dramatic changes in the life-styles of those who served in the armed forces and of those who stayed home. The readings and advertising which follow suggest some of the ways in which Americans mobilized for the war effort at home. As you read them, try to answer the following questions:

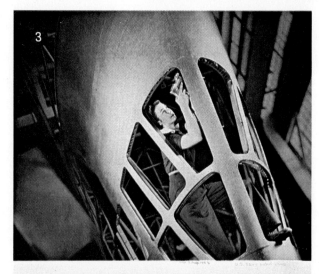

**THE MACHINES
BEHIND THE MEN
BEHIND THE GUNS . . .**

It's all out for victory now. Guns, tanks, planes and ships come first, and so does the figure work needed to make them, transport them and operate them. Monroe machines are in the thick of it, speeding up these essential figures.

Government as well as industries engaged in war production, are calling for—and getting—Monroe machines in ever increasing quantities. To fill this demand is naturally our first duty; nevertheless we are doing our utmost to meet the needs of general business as well. There are Monroe machines for every kind of figure work; and 150 Monroe-owned branches stand ready to assure uninterrupted figure production everywhere. Ask the nearest branch for facts about Monroe utility, speed, economy, or write Monroe Calculating Machine Co., Inc., Orange, N. J.

Invest in Victory and Your own Future—Buy Defense Bonds and Stamps

FOR VICTORY — Because of our long experience in building precision machines, Monroe has been selected to produce special munitions equipment, where extreme accuracy and dependability are vital.

MONROE
Machines for Calculating, Adding, Bookkeeping, Checkwriting

AROUND THE WORLD TODAY wherever American forces fight on land, sea, or in the air, there Goodyear rubber fights also. It serves in many forms—assault boats and life rafts—barrage balloons and blimps—gas masks and bullet-puncture-sealing gasoline tanks—tires for giant bombers and combat tires immune to machine gun fire. From tiny bomb-release gaskets to giant tank-carrying pontons, all are built to the same quality standard that has made Goodyear tires the world's first choice for more than a quarter-century. And because America's reserve of natural rubber is so scant today, we are now building many of these military essentials with Chemigum—Goodyear's own synthetic rubber which will provide the public with tires of our customary excellence, when its production can be stepped up beyond war's need.

GOOD YEAR

THE GREATEST NAME IN RUBBER

The advertisements on these two pages appeared in American newspapers and magazines during World War II. What were the objectives of these advertisements? What do they reveal about the ways in which the war affected the lives of typical American people?

1. How were American families expected to change their ways during the war?
2. What common themes do you find in the examples of wartime advertising?

Victory Homes

The following selections are taken from a widely circulated government pamphlet, What Can I Do?

What Can I Do? (Washington, D.C.: Office of Civilian Defense, 1942.)

This is your war—and your part in it is clear. You don't need spare time. You need imagination to see the connection between tasks which to you may seem small and unimportant—and winning the war.

You need understanding, resourcefulness, self-discipline, determination, and love of America.

Conservation is a war weapon in the hands of every man, woman, and child. And here are two simple rules for using your weapon.

1. *Get along with less.* Every time you decide *not* to buy something, you help to win the war. Be tough with yourself in making each decision. Luxuries are out. And lots of things we used to think of as necessities begin to look like luxuries as we get more and more war-minded.

2. *Take good care of the things you have.* Most of the comforts and conveniences you now enjoy will have to last you for the duration. It's only common sense to make them last as long as possible. But there is no need to become frantic about your possessions, or to attach too much importance to them. That kind of thinking leads to a wild scramble for possessions and then to hoarding. In wartime, hoarders are on the same level as spies. Both help the enemy.

▶ Suppose that someone you knew hoarded food when it was scarce and the public was rationing it. What would you think of that person? Why?

War production goes faster when home life runs smoothly. And so it is a good idea to keep our homes and personal possessions in good order and repair. Do it now. Don't wait until your things are past repairing. The more shipshape and tidy we keep our homes and personal possessions the less we will feel the need to buy new things.

Most people understand the *why* of conservation. But they want to know *how*—how to get on without, how to use less so as to contribute to the war supply, how to save, substitute, and salvage. Here are some of the "hows."

Consider, for example, a material so scarce that civilians will not get any more of it for the duration—rubber. Rubber is high up on the list of things we must contribute to the war.

Much of the rubber used in the United States came from Southeast Asia, which had been conquered by the Japanese.

We have been slow in changing our driving habits. Tollbridge receipts were higher in January 1942 than in January 1941. This news must have pleased Hitler. It is bad news for Americans—as bad as losing a battle.

We are beginning to do much better. Pleasure riding is out for the duration. As of today we must pool our cars for necessary use,

616

for driving to work, to school, to the shops. We must share necessary rides with our friends and neighbors so that no car goes on the road with even one empty seat. The empty seat is a gift to Hitler.

Make a thorough search of your closets, attic, cellar, and garage. You will be surprised at the amount of useless metal, rubber, rags, and paper that can be salvaged. Have a special place to put each kind of salvaged material. The children can help.

Millions of Americans are fighting this war in their homes every day in the week, every week in the year. They are doing millions of hard jobs, full chores, making millions of small sacrifices. They are saving and salvaging, conserving and converting. They are foregoing small pleasures, putting up with inconveniences and annoyances. They are doing these things freely and gladly because they understand the meaning of their fight for freedom: freedom for themselves, their children, and the America they love.

The Victory Home or V-Home award is a badge of honor to those families which have made themselves into a fighting unit on the home front. If you and your family have earned such an award, you are entitled to put the V-Home certificate in your window. You will receive the award from your local Defense Council. If you and your family have not yet enlisted on the home front you can join today—the greatest civilian army in American history.

The V-Home certificate means something: it has to be earned. This is what it says:

THIS IS A V-HOME!

We in this house are fighting. We know this war will be easy to lose and hard to win. We mean to win it. Therefore we solemnly pledge all our energies and all our resources to fight for freedom and against fascism. We serve notice to all that we are personally carrying the fight to the enemy, in these ways:

I. *This home follows the instructions of its air-raid warden*, in order to protect itself against attack by air.

II. This home *conserves* food, clothing, transportation, and health, in order to hasten an unceasing flow of war materials to our men at the front.

III. This home *salvages* essential materials, in order that they may be converted to immediate war uses.

IV. This home *refuses to spread rumors* designed to divide our nation.

V. This home *buys* War Savings Stamps and Bonds *regularly*.

We are doing these things because we know we must to *Win This War*.

FOR THOUGHT:

In what ways did the war change the everyday lives of typical people? Did the war emergency justify these changes?

V was a symbol for victory widely used during the war.

Defense Councils were organized in all towns and cities to coordinate the war effort.

During the war, cities had air alerts supervised by civilian air-raid wardens.

Many people bought war bonds and stamps each payday. The money went to finance the war effort.

93 CIVIL RIGHTS IN WARTIME: THE CASE OF THE JAPANESE-AMERICANS

During the early years of the war, a great deal of attention was given by the press to the alleged threat of "fifth column" activities in America. The fifth column was the name given to groups of people within the allied nations who actively worked for the cause of an enemy. It was widely believed that German victories in northern and eastern Europe had been aided by fifth column efforts. The existence of substantial populations of aliens and citizens of German, Italian, and Japanese descent in America encouraged the belief that what had happened in Europe might happen here.

The Japanese-Americans were the most vulnerable of these groups. On the eve of the war, there were about 126,000 Japanese-Americans living in the United States. Two thirds of these people were native-born citizens. The Japanese population was heavily concentrated on the west coast, especially in California. Under the direction of federal authorities in 1942, more than 100,000 of these people were taken from their homes and transferred to government camps. Later during the war, some of the evacuees were allowed to leave the camps in order to work or attend school. Eventually, Japanese-Americans served in the armed forces with great distinction.

The following selections are taken from congressional hearings held before the Japanese were placed in government camps. As you read them, try to answer the following questions:

1. Why did Attorney General Warren want the Japanese moved?
2. How did Japanese-Americans respond to the possibility of relocation to government camps?

Congress Hears Testimony About Relocating Japanese-Americans

In February 1942, President Roosevelt gave the army power to name military areas within the United States from which any person or group of people could be banned. A congressional committee heard testimony from officials in California and from Japanese-Americans regarding how that order should be carried out.

TESTIMONY OF THE ATTORNEY GENERAL FOR CALIFORNIA

ATTORNEY GENERAL WARREN: I believe that up to the present and perhaps for a long time to come the greatest danger to continental United States is that from well organized sabotage and fifth column activity.

California presents, perhaps, the most likely objective in the nation for such activities. There are many reasons why that is true. First, there are a number of large naval and military establishments in California. This would make it attractive to our enemies as a field of sabotage. Our geographical position with relation to our enemy and to the war in the Pacific is also a tremendous factor. The number and the variety of our war industries is extremely vital. The fire hazards due to our climate, our forest areas, and the type of building construction make us very susceptible to fire sabotage. We have a tremendous number of aliens residing here. This makes it almost an impossible problem from the standpoint of law enforcement.

A wave of organized sabotage in California accompanied by an actual air raid or even by a prolonged black-out could be more destructive to life and property. It could also result in holding back the entire war effort of this nation far more than the treacherous bombing of Pearl Harbor.

I hesitate to think what the result would be of the destruction of any of our big airplane factories in this state. It will interest you to know that some of our airplane factories in this state are entirely surrounded by Japanese land ownership or occupancy. It is a situation that is fraught with the greatest danger and under no circumstances should it ever be permitted to exist.

To assume that the enemy has not planned fifth column activities for us in a wave of sabotage is simply to live in a fool's paradise. These activities, whether you call them "fifth column activities" or "sabotage" or "war behind the lines upon civilians," or whatever you may call it, are just as much a part of Axis warfare as any of their military and naval operations. When I say that I refer to all of the Axis powers with which we are at war.

We believe that when we are dealing with the Caucasian race we have methods that will test the loyalty of them. And we believe that we can, in dealing with the Germans and the Italians, arrive at some fairly sound conclusions because of our knowledge of the way they live in the community and have lived for many years. But when we deal with the Japanese we are in an entirely different field. We cannot form any opinion that we believe to be sound. Their method of living,

Hearings Before the Select Committee Investigating National Defense Migration (Washington, D.C.: House of Representatives, 1942), XXLX, pp. 11010-11019, 11137, 11144-11149, 11229-11231. Language simplified.

Axis here refers to Germany, Italy, and Japan.

619

their language, make for this difficulty. Many of them who show you a birth certificate stating that they were born in this state, perhaps, or born in Honolulu, can hardly speak the English language. Although they were born here, when they were four or five years of age they were sent over to Japan to be educated. And they stayed over there through their adolescent period at least. Then they came back here thoroughly Japanese.

MR. ARNOLD: Let me ask you a question at this point.

ATTORNEY GENERAL WARREN: Yes, Congressman.

MR. ARNOLD: Do you have any way of knowing whether any one of this group that you mention is loyal to this country or loyal to Japan?

ATTORNEY GENERAL WARREN: It seems strange to us that airplane manufacturing plants should be entirely surrounded by Japanese land occupancies. It seems to us that it is more than circumstance that after certain government air bases were established Japanese undertook farming operations in close proximity to them. You can hardly grow a jackrabbit in some of the places where they presume to be carrying on farming operations close to an Army bombing base.

Many of our vital facilities, and most of our highways are just pocketed by Japanese ownerships that could be of untold danger to us in time of stress.

So we believe, gentlemen, that it would be wise for the military to take every protective measure that it believes is necessary to protect this state and this nation against the possible activities of these people.

MR. SPARKMAN: I do want to add a word to what the chairman said. I am sure you people out here know it, but your congressional delegation in both houses of Congress has been very much on the alert in discussing and making plans for the defense of this area. A week, ten days, or two weeks ago, this very recommendation was made to the President and, as I read the order, it follows out almost word for word the recommendation that was made by your congressional delegation.

I have noticed suggestions in newspaper stories. I noticed a telegram this morning with reference to the civil rights of these people. What do you have to say about that?

ATTORNEY GENERAL WARREN: I believe, sir, that in time of war every citizen must give up some of his normal rights.

TESTIMONY OF JAPANESE-AMERICANS

▶ Are there any rights which should not be given up in wartime? If so, what are they?

MR. SPARKMAN: First, will you give your name to the reporter?

MR. MASAOKA: Just to show you how Americanized we are, I have an English name and Japanese tag-end there. Mike Masaoka, I am the national secretary and field executive of the Japanese-American Citizens League. This gentleman is Mr. Dave Tatsuno, president of

620

The pictures and news articles on this page contain evidence about the military record of Japanese-Americans who fought in World War II. How do you feel about these men and their contribution to the war effort? Would you have fought as they did if your family had been sent to a government camp?

AMERICAN-JAPANESE WIN PRAISE IN ITALY

Lieut. Gen. Clark Commends Unit for Bravery Under Fire

Special to THE NEW YORK TIMES.

WASHINGTON, Oct. 14 — The combat record of the One Hundreth Infantry Battalion, composed of Americans of Japanese ancestry, which has been under fire in Italy, has been praised by Lieut. Gen. Mark W. Clark in a report to the War Department, Secretary of War Henry L. Stimson disclosed today.

The American-Japanese, mostly from the Hawaiian Islands, underwent thorough training in the United States, then went to North Africa and recently went into action in Italy.

"Their behavior under fire and their combat discipline have received the praise of General Clark," Mr. Stimson stated.

"On one occasion, this battalion acted as advance guard. The men of the unit displayed great coolness under fire and used their weapons with confidence and skill. They have been eager for combat and their morale is of the highest.

"General Clark remarks the

JAPANESE-AMERICANS HEROES AT BENEVENTO

One Squad Rescued 22 Paratroopers, Trapped for 16 Days

WITH THE FIFTH ARMY IN ITALY, Oct. 11 (U.P.) — The story now can be told of the heroism of Japanese-American soldiers fighting at Benevento and how one of them led a squad into no-man's land to rescue twenty-two American paratroopers cut off behind German lines for sixteen days.

Sergt. Yutaka Nezu, from Oahu in Hawaii, led a squad from his unit, which had been under almost constant enemy fire for four days, through German lines and brought back the paratroopers to the main American detachment.

Capt. Taro Suzuki, commander of a company, told how another Japanese-American soldier fulfilled his mission to report details on an enemy machine-gun nest despite a fatal head wound and then dropped dead at the feet of his platoon sergeant.

Captain Suzuki said he was trying to get a posthumous decoration for the soldier.

Although most of the soldiers of the Japanese-American battalion are from Hawaii, some of their officers are from the United States mainland. Lieut. Paul Froning, who is of German descent, is from New Bremen, Ohio; Lieut. Roy Peterson, of Swedish descent, is from Orange, N. J.; Lieut. Andrew Krivi, of Czechoslovak descent, is from Bridgeport, Conn., and Lieut. Young Ok Kim, of Korean descent, is from Los Angeles.

the San Francisco chapter of the Japanese-American Citizens League. And Mr. Henry Tani, the executive secretary of our group.

MR. SPARKMAN: Did you ever attend Japanese schools in this country?

MR. MASAOKA: Personally I did not, but frankly—

MR. SPARKMAN (*interposing*): A great many of your people do?

MR. MASAOKA: Oh, yes. But I did not.

MR. SPARKMAN: What about the membership of your organization? Could you say what percentage of them have received at least a part of their education in Japan?

MR. MASAOKA: Those figures are rather hard to get. We estimate approximately 20 to 30 percent, which I think is a rather generous estimate.

MR. SPARKMAN: I wonder if you could give us some estimate as to a portion of your membership who have received a part of their education in Japanese schools in this country.

MR. MASAOKA: That would be large; say 85 percent.

MR. SPARKMAN: That is more or less characteristic, is it not, of the Japanese to have these Japanese schools?

MR. MASAOKA: Yes. It is characteristic, but at the same time I think it is the same as any other immigrant group. I feel that I should make this statement at this time. Before Pearl Harbor many of us had been teaching, or at least attempts had been made to teach, concerning the honor of Japan as a nation. But I think the attack at Pearl Harbor demonstrated to those who were on the fence that there wasn't anything honorable in that. And I think most of us condemned more than Americans condemned the dastardly thing that was done there. And I think the first generation feel that.

MR. SPARKMAN: Do you think you could say with reference to the membership of your organization that there is not a feeling of a definite connection and loyalty to the Emperor of Japan?

MR. MASAOKA: No. I don't think our league subscribes to that. I don't think the great membership of our league subscribes to that. In fact, I am quite sure.

MR. SPARKMAN: Do you think you could truthfully and sincerely say that there is not in your membership a feeling of pride on the accomplishments of the Japanese Empire?

MR. MASAOKA: Well now, there are a lot of things that I think we ought to recognize that are fine about Japan, possibly courtesy, and so on. But I think that the Japan of our parents is certainly not the Japan of today. And I think there that we may have been misguided as to many things there, too.

MR. SPARKMAN: Let me ask you this. Of course, you appreciate that the feeling which you have heard expressed here does exist?

MR. MASAOKA: Yes, I do. I certainly do.

MR. SPARKMAN: You acknowledge that fact. Do I understand that it is your attitude that the Japanese-American citizens do not protest necessarily against an evacuation? They simply want to lodge their claims to consideration?

MR. MASAOKA: Yes.

MR. SPARKMAN: But in the event the evacuation is deemed necessary by those having charge of the defenses, as loyal Americans you are willing to prove your loyalty by cooperating?

MR. MASAOKA: Yes. I think it should be—

MR. SPARKMAN (*interposing*): Even at a sacrifice?

MR. MASAOKA: Oh, yes; definitely. I think that all of us are called upon to make sacrifices. I think that we will be called upon to make greater sacrifices than any others. But I think sincerely, if the military say "Move out," we will be glad to move. We recognize that even behind evacuation there is not just national security but also a thought as to our own welfare and security. We may be subject to mob violence and otherwise if we are permitted to remain.

MR. SPARKMAN: And it affords you, as a matter of fact, perhaps the best test of your own loyalty?

MR. MASAOKA: Provided that the military or the people charged with the responsibility are cognizant of all the facts.

MR. TANI: With reference to the line of questioning that you are asking Mr. Masaoka, about the influence of the Japanese culture in us. We don't walk around with our heads bowed because we are Japanese. But we can't help being Japanese in features. My mother left Japan over thirty years ago. And the Japan of which she speaks to us of thirty years ago is not the Japan of today. I feel it is different from that of my mother's day. And so is the culture that she instilled in us. By "culture" I mean courtesy, loyalty to the state and country in which we are, obedience to parents. Those are cultures of Japan with which most of us have been brought up. And I don't think those things are things of which we should be ashamed or things which we should ignore.

As for influences upon us today I, as an individual, or as a leader of a group, have never been approached officially, unofficially, directly, or indirectly in any respect in all my years.

MR. OMURA: I am strongly opposed to mass evacuation of American-born Japanese. It is my honest belief that such an action would not solve the question of Nisei loyalty. If any such action is taken I believe that we would be only procrastinating on the question of loyalty. I believe that we are afraid to deal with it. And I believe that at this, our first opportunity, we are trying to strip the Nisei of their opportunity to prove their loyalty.

I do not believe there has even been, or ever could be again, a situation of this kind where the Nisei can prove their loyalty.

It is doubtlessly rather difficult for Caucasian Americans to properly understand and believe in what we say. Our citizenship has even been attacked as an evil cloak under which we expect safety for the

American-born Japanese were called Nisei.

▶ Do you think that peoples' loyalties have anything to do with national background or the way they look and speak?

623

evil purpose of conspiring to destroy the American way of life. To us—who have been born, raised, and educated in American institutions and in our system of public schools, knowing and owing no other allegiance than to the United States—such a thought is clearly unfair.

I would like to ask the committee: Has the Gestapo come to America? Have we not risen in righteous anger at Hitler's mistreatment of the Jews? Then, is it not incongruous that citizen Americans of Japanese descent should be similarly mistreated and persecuted?

We cannot understand why General DeWitt can make exceptions for families of German and Italian soldiers in the armed forces of the United States while ignoring the civil rights of the Nisei Americans. Are we to be condemned merely on the basis of our racial origin? Is citizenship such a light and transient thing that that which is our inalienable right in normal times can be torn from us in times of war?

FOR THOUGHT:

How did the war affect the lives of Japanese-Americans? Did the war emergency justify these changes?

94 THE FAMILY IN WARTIME

The war required a massive effort on the part of almost every American. Over 12 million Americans served in the armed forces. The total of dead, wounded, captured, or missing came to more than 1 million. Those who stayed home had to adjust themselves to a strikingly different style of living. The economy was closely controlled by the government. Food, fuel, and other strategic materials were rationed. And prices and wages were regulated by federal agencies. Because of the many people who joined the military, there was an acute labor shortage. Men left peacetime occupations for defense jobs. And women and children were drawn into the work force in greater numbers than ever before. Americans had always been a mobile people. But during the war years, as new factories were built throughout the country, they were on the move more than ever.

Thus one of the most important effects of the war was the social dislocation it caused to the Americans who remained at home. The following selections suggest what this meant for the American family. As you read them, try to answer the following questions.

1. What were the advantages and disadvantages of living in a small American city with a big defense industry nearby?
2. How did war disturb the normal patterns of family life?

The Gestapo was the secret police of Nazi Germany.

General J.L. DeWitt was commanding officer in charge of the relocation of Japanese-Americans.

A Boomtown in the South

The American novelist John Dos Passos describes how the defense effort had changed Mobile, Alabama, in March 1943.

The mouldering old Gulf seaport with its ancient dusty elegance of tall shuttered windows under mansard roofs and iron lace overgrown with vines, and scaling colonnades shaded by great trees, looks trampled and battered like a city that's been taken by storm. Sidewalks are crowded. Gutters are stacked with litter that drifts back and forth in the brisk spring wind. Garbage cans are overflowing. Frame houses on treeshaded streets bulge with men in shirtsleeves who spill out onto the porches and trampled grassplots and stand in knots at the streetcorners. There's still talk of lodginghouses where they rent "hot beds." (Men work in three shifts. Why shouldn't they sleep in three shifts?) Queues wait outside of movies and lunchrooms. The trailer army has filled all the open lots with its regular ranks. In cluttered backyards people camp out in tents and chickenhouses and shelters tacked together out of packingcases.

In the outskirts in every direction you find acres and acres raw with new building, open fields skinned to the bare clay, elevations gashed with muddy roads and gnawed out by the powershovels and the bulldozers. There, long lines of small houses, some decently planned on the "American standard' model and some mere boxes with a square brick chimney in the center, miles of dormitories, great squares of temporary structures, are knocked together from day to day by a mob of construction workers in a smell of paint and fresh sawed pine lumber and tobacco juice and sweat. Along the river for miles has risen a confusion of new yards from which men, women, and boys ebb and flow three times a day. Here and there are whole city blocks piled with wreckage and junk as if ancient cranky warehouses and superannuated stores had caved in out of their own rottenness under the impact of the violence of the new effort. Over it all the Gulf mist, heavy with smoke of soft coal, hangs in streaks, and glittering the training planes endlessly circling above the airfields.

To be doing something towards winning the war, to be making some money, to learn a trade, men and women have been pouring into the city for more than a year now: tenants from dusty shacks set on stilts above the bare eroded earth in the midst of the cotton and the scraggly corn, small farmers and trappers from half cultivated patches in the piney woods, millhands from the industrial towns in the northern part of the state, garage men, filling station attendants, storekeepers, drug clerks from crossroads settlements, longshore fishermen and oystermen, Negroes off plantations who've never seen any town but the county seat on Saturday afternoon, white families who've

John Dos Passos, **State of the Nation** (Boston: Houghton Mifflin Company, Inc., 1943), pp. 92-94, 99. Copyright © 1972 by Elizabeth H. Dos Passos. Reprinted by permission.

Superannuated means that people or things can no longer function effectively because they are so old.

625

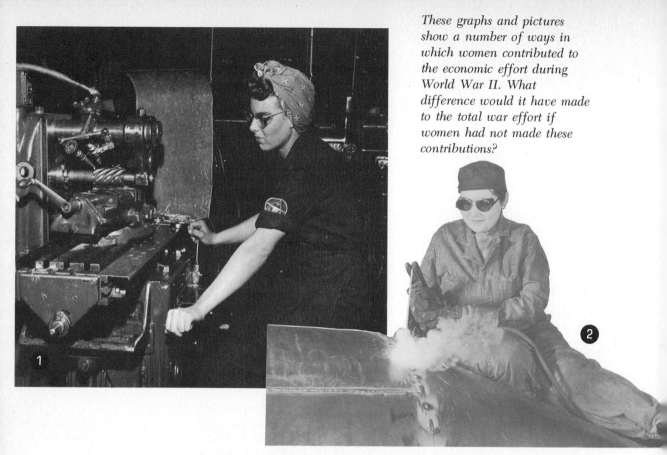

These graphs and pictures show a number of ways in which women contributed to the economic effort during World War II. What difference would it have made to the total war effort if women had not made these contributions?

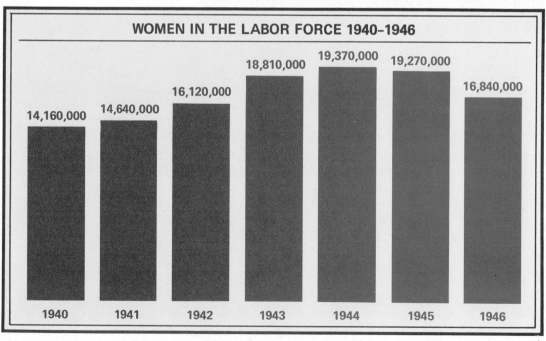

WOMEN IN THE LABOR FORCE 1940–1946

1940	1941	1942	1943	1944	1945	1946
14,160,000	14,640,000	16,120,000	18,810,000	19,370,000	19,270,000	16,840,000

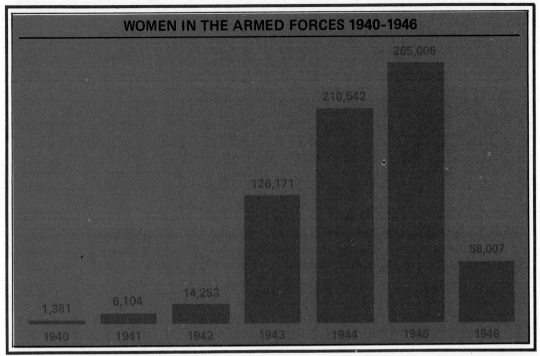

WOMEN IN THE ARMED FORCES 1940–1946

Year	Count
1940	1,381
1941	6,104
1942	14,253
1943	126,171
1944	210,542
1945	265,006
1946	58,007

3

White meat is a kind of bacon. Cornpone is a form of corn bread often made without milk or eggs.

lived all their lives off tobacco and 'white meat' and cornpone in cranky cabins forgotten in the hills.

For them everything is new and wonderful. They can make more spot cash in a month than they saw before in half a year. They can buy radios, they can go to the pictures, they can go to beer parlors, bowl, shoot craps, bet on the ponies. Everywhere they rub elbows with foreigners from every state in the Union. Housekeeping in a trailer with electric light and running water is a dazzling luxury to a woman who's lived all her life in a cabin with half-inch chinks between the splintered boards of the floor. There are street cars and busses to take you anywhere you want to go. At night the streets are bright with electric light. Girls can go to beauty parlors, get their nails manicured, buy readymade dresses.

And all the while, by every bus and train the new people, white and black, pour into the city. As fast as a new block of housing is finished, it's jampacked. As soon as a new bus is put into service, it's weighed down with passengers. The schools are too full of children. The restaurants are too full of eaters. If you try to go to see a doctor, you find the waitingroom full and a long line of people straggling down the hall. There's no room in the hospitals for the women who are going to have babies. "So far we've been lucky," the health officers say with terror in their voices, "not to have had an epidemic. But we've got our fingers crossed."

Children During the War

The following statement is taken from the testimony of Katherine F. Lenroot, Chief of the Children's Bureau in the Department of Labor. She was testifying before a Senate investigating committee in 1943.

Wartime Health and Recreation (Washington, D.C.: Hearings Before a Subcommittee of the Committee on Education and Labor, United States Senate, 1944), Part I, pp. 100-115. Language simplified.

▶ Has your father or your mother been away from home for periods of time? If so, how did their absence affect your family life?

Some of the wartime conditions mean that homes and communities are not meeting the needs of children as well as they formerly did. These conditions include the following:

Fathers are separated from their families because they are serving in the armed forces or working in distant war industries.

Mothers in large numbers are engaged in full-time employment. They are therefore absent from the home most of the day.

An increasing number of children are now employed. In many instances, they work under unwholesome conditions that impede their growth, limit their educational progress, or expose them to moral hazards.

The widespread migration of families to crowded centers of war industry has uprooted children from familiar surroundings. It has also subjected them to life in communities where resources are overtaxed by the increased population.

Dance halls, beer parlors, and other attractions flourish in industrial centers and near military establishments. Unless they are kept under community control, they frequently exert a harmful influence on youth.

A general spirit of excitement and adventure has been aroused by the war. And tension, anxiety, and apprehension are felt by parents or other adults. All these are reflected in restlessness, defiance, emotional disturbance, and other negative forms of behavior on the part of children and young people.

Conditions affecting children and young people in war-affected communities may bring about a lack of parental responsibility, neglect, and delinquency of children. In a report from a child-welfare worker in a southwestern state it was stated that several mothers who had followed their husbands to a military camp secured work as waitresses or taxi dancers in the night cafes. They left their children alone in hotel rooms without supervision. It is not surprising that such children, without protection of a secure home life, find it easy to drift into delinquency.

Taxi dancers charged a fee each time they danced with a man.

A typical situation reported by child-welfare workers as occurring in communities near Army camps is illustrated by the story of Julia, a fourteen-year-old girl found living with her girl friend aged fifteen, who was the wife of a soldier at the nearby camp. Both of the girls were having many soldiers visit them each night and were picked up by the police in one of the taverns near the camp. Julia told the child-welfare worker of her unhappy home situation in a dull little village in an adjoining state. She thought hitchhiking was fun and life around an Army camp exciting.

The type of community conditions which contribute to delinquency is pictured in the following excerpt from a special report made in a southern city located near a military camp:

"On either side of the road, a few feet apart, are gray framed structures, each indentical to the next, with three rooms in a row. Each houses at least two families. A bed is visible from each open, unscreened front door. Forty to fifty percent of the gross income of the inhabitants of these shacks goes to rent. The houses have never known paint. The yards have never been planted. There is evidently overcrowding because of the large number of people of all ages sitting on steps and in the yards. All are barefooted. The yards are filled with garbage and a few sprigs of grass. Ragged white laundry is slung over fences and porch rails. The children are sitting idly or playing among all this."

The above description is typical of many situations where thousands of children are living in trailer camps, in shacks, and in overcrowded homes. Families and young girls especially flock to communities to be near the servicemen. Often the war worker brings his family into already crowded areas. Two or three families live in one apartment and lack any privacy. Children live in trailer camps without adequate play space. And there is a lack of stores and other essential community resources. These conditions add to the general tensions of family life. Although war-housing projects have alleviated crowded housing conditions, community living also requires more than mere shelter. It includes indoor and outdoor play space, accessible schools, churches, and stores. When decent housing and adequate community services are present, the dangers of juvenile delinquency decrease.

The difficulties faced by school authorities in many war-affected communities, in making proper educational provision for increased numbers of children, should be mentioned as a factor closely related to the present delinquency problem. Reports from some of these communities show that school enrollment has increased out of all proportion to available buildings, teachers, and equipment. Such conditions obviously affect the adjustment of children. And they seriously limit the positive contribution which the school can make to prevention of delinquency. This is an important consideration in relation to the fact that most juvenile delinquents are of school age.

Employment of Mothers

► Does society have an obligation to care for the children of working mothers? Why or why not?

A factor of major proportion in the cause of delinquency is the employment of mothers outside the home. The number of children requiring child-care services because their mothers are employed is constantly mounting. Some 5½ million women with children under fourteen years of age were working outside their homes in April 1943. This was about 1 million more than the number so employed in 1942. It was estimated that at least a million more workers would be employed this year. Most of them will have to come from the ranks of housewives. This will increase the number of children for whom care will be needed.

Child Labor and Youth Employment

The great increase in both full-time and part-time employment of boys and girls has aspects which are significant in any consideration of delinquency problems.

A honky tonk was a cheap night club or dance hall.

Employment under proper controls and under satisfactory conditions may have constructive elements for some children. However, many are working in jobs, such as those in places where liquor is sold, cheap restaurants, dance halls, honky tonks, and juke joints in which conditions are harmful to young people and may be factors in leading some of them into delinquency. It was reported to the Children's Bureau that in a military camp area in a southern state, girls thirteen to fourteen years old have been found working from four in the afternoon to twelve at night in questionable places such as honky tonks.

Some types of employment in the refreshment and amusement industries such as bowling alleys constitute special social hazards to young people. In one large city in New York state, the school attendance officer stated that there were only three alleys in the city that did not sell liquor. Many boys and girls are working for long hours and late at night—sometimes until 2 or 3 A.M. When employed late at night, they often are released in groups. And in seeking recreation for themselves after work, they drift into situations that contribute to delinquency. An example of this is found in the report of three boys in an eastern city who went into a drinking place on the way home from work in a bowling alley and became intoxicated. In another state some twelve- and thirteen-year-old boys were brought before the court for stealing tires at 2 A.M. when on their way home from work in a bowling alley.

FOR THOUGHT:

How did the war affect American families? Did the war emergency justify these changes?

95 FROM ISOLATION TO TOTAL WAR

HISTORICAL ESSAY

America's refusal to join the League of Nations after World War I set the tone of American diplomacy in the 1920's. American hostility to the League declined somewhat as the decade passed. United States representatives eventually cooperated with several international commissions set up by the League. But American public opinion and Congress remained deeply suspicious of international organizations. Despite the urging of Presidents Coolidge and Hoover, for example, Congress refused to allow the United States to cooperate with the new World Court, set up to arbitrate international disputes.

As a dominant industrial power, however, the United States could not withdraw from world affairs. As a result, American diplomacy during this period reflected a curious blend of moralism and self-interest. Woodrow Wilson had interpreted World War I in moral terms. He saw it as a war to make the world safe for democracy. Most of the American people eventually rejected this interpretation. However, the United States continued to take a moralistic approach to world affairs. In 1921, the United States sponsored the Washington Naval Conference, which resulted in agreements by the major powers to limit naval armaments. In 1927, the United States played a leading role in drawing up the Kellogg-Briand Pact in which sixty-two nations agreed to outlaw war. But the participants in these agreements provided no way to enforce them.

From Isolation to Intervention

Isolationism dominated America's foreign policy in 1931. Ten years later, the nation willingly provided assistance just short of war to support the defense of Great Britain. This reversal of attitudes represented a dramatic response to the rise of Fascist governments in Germany, Italy, and Japan. The aggressive conquests of these nations forced Americans to reconsider their foreign policy.

Fascist aggression began in 1931 when Japan attacked China without provocation and converted Manchuria into a Japanese satellite. This action violated both the American Open Door Policy in China and the Kellogg-Briand Pact. But President Hoover refused to apply military or economic sanctions against Japan. However, Secretary of State Henry Stimson did announce, in the Stimson Doctrine, that the United States government would not recognize the validity of any Japanese actions taken in violation of existing treaty rights. A few months later, Japan withdrew from the League.

President Roosevelt was inaugurated in 1933, the same year that Japan left the League of Nations, and one year before Hitler assumed power in Germany. A former Assistant Secretary of the Navy under Wilson, Roosevelt had strong internationalist convictions. Problems of the Depression absorbed him during his first administration. Except for a more constructive approach to Latin America, the United States played a minor role in world affairs.

The high point in American isolationism came in the mid-1930's. In 1935, Hitler imposed a military draft on Germany. He began to raise an army and air force in clear violation of the Treaty of Versailles. During the same year, Italy attacked Ethiopia. As Fascist aggression and the possibility of general war increased, so did Americans' insistence that their nation should not become involved. Between 1934 and 1936, the Senate Munitions Investigating Committee, chaired by Senator Gerald P. Nye of North Dakota, investigated the reasons for United States' entrance into World War I. The Nye Committee suggested that America's entrance had really been plotted by greedy munitions manufacturers. This theme contributed to the tide of isolationist feeling. Congress passed neutrality legislation in 1935, 1936, and 1937 aimed at keeping the United States out of another war.

The Fascists were a political group that arose in Italy in 1919. The term fascist is also applied to other political groups who believe in strong central government, control of industry, and other totalitarian principles.

The United States tried to improve relations with Latin America by replacing its imperialistic policy with a Good Neighbor policy. The Roosevelt administration tried to improve trade, political, and cultural relations with the nations of the Western Hemisphere. It canceled the Platt Amendment, which had proclaimed the right of the United States to intervene in the affairs of Cuba. It also removed troops from Haiti.

632

In October 1937, President Roosevelt called for an international quarantine of aggressors. American isolationists protested this action vigorously.

Events in Europe from 1937 to 1939 played a vital role in changing American attitudes. Great Britain and France had stood by passively while Hitler rebuilt his army and air force, reoccupied the Rhineland, and annexed Austria. In the Munich Conference, they practically handed Czechoslovakia to Hitler in the interests of peace. Meanwhile, Mussolini invaded Albania. Britain and France finally acted when Hitler attacked Poland in September 1939. True to their treaty promises, England and France declared war on Germany. In less than a year Poland, the Netherlands, Belgium, Norway, and France had all fallen to Germany, now allied with Italy. German air raids left British cities in flames. If Britain fell, no friendly power would stand between the United States and the Fascist aggressors in Europe.

Between January and December 1941, the United States moved rapidly toward becoming a partner with England in the war against fascism. Congress passed the Lend-Lease Bill in March with an initial appropriation of a billion dollars. In May, President Roosevelt declared an unlimited national emergency. He closed all German and Italian consulates in the United States. In June Germany violated the Non-Aggression Pact and invaded the Soviet Union. Roosevelt promised American aid to the Soviets. By autumn, the United States Navy convoyed supply ships as far as Iceland. And German submarines sank American destroyers and merchant ships.

As the United States became increasingly involved in the war in Europe, American-Japanese relations continued to deteriorate. Japan purchased oil from the United States to supply its military forces. But the United States government banned sales of scrap iron and machine tools. The United States, through Secretary of State Cordell Hull, sought to get Japan to withdraw from China. Hull also wanted Japan to promise not to attack unprotected French and Dutch colonies in Southeast Asia. Japan moved into French Indo-China in July 1941. The United States froze Japanese assets in the United States and placed a total embargo on oil. Japan offered to limit further expansion if the United States would lift the embargo and allow "a just peace" in China. The United States refused. And the military party in power in Tokyo prepared a coordinated assault on the Dutch East Indies, British Malaya, and the Philippines. But they decided first to immobilize the American Pacific Fleet with a surprise air attack on the United States naval base at Pearl Harbor.

American intelligence experts knew that Japan planned an attack somewhere. The government sent general alerts to Pacific forces. But the Hawaiian Islands lacked adequate protection. On December 7, 1941, Japanese planes reduced the American navy and air force at

In a speech delivered on October 5, 1937, in the isolationist city of Chicago, Roosevelt moved away from his position of isolation and neutrality. He came out against the aggressor nations, particularly Japan, which had just launched its attack against China.

The Treaty of Versailles (1919) provided for the demilitarization and allied occupation of the Rhineland, a region of West Germany located west of the Rhine River. Allied troops were withdrawn in 1930. In 1936, in violation of the Treaty, Germany began to remilitarize the Rhineland.

Hitler demanded that Czechoslovakia give him the Sudetan region, which contained many German-speaking people. In order to prevent war, British Prime Minister Neville Chamberlain, French Premier Edouard Daladier, Hitler, and Mussolini met at Munich and signed a pact on September 30, 1938. The pact gave Germany the Sudetan region and all important Czech fortresses.

Bank balances in the United States were frozen. And the Japanese could neither withdraw the money nor spend it here. Trade relations between the two countries were completely terminated. In order to get oil, iron, steel, and other vital war materials, Japan would either have to attack Southeast Asia and risk war, or induce the United States to resume trade.

Legend:
- Axis countries, 1939
- Countries allied with, and territories occupied by Axis powers
- Furthest extent of Axis control, 1942
- Allied nations and territories held by the allies
- Allied advances
- Neutral countries

EUROPEAN AND NORTH AFRICAN THEATER OF WAR

Pearl Harbor to flaming ruins. The next day, the United States Congress declared war on Japan. On December 11, Germany and Italy declared war on the United States.

War on Two Fronts—The Strategy of Victory, 1941-1944

The year 1942 was critical for the allied cause. In the Pacific, Japan rapidly overran almost all of Southeast Asia, the Philippines, and most of China. In Europe, Germany controlled western Europe and penetrated deep into the Soviet Union. Italian and German forces held most of North Africa. At the same time, German submarines threatened to break the Atlantic supply line.

In January 1942, Manila surrendered. Douglas MacArthur, the American general who was recalled from the area in March 1942, remarked, "I shall return." He did three years later. And, in February 1945, the Japanese were defeated.

634

Before 1942 ended, however, the Allies launched a counter-offensive. British and American military leaders agreed that Germany was the most powerful enemy and should be dealt with first. In November 1942, a combined British and American force landed in North Africa. They moved against German and Italian forces in the first phase of a campaign which, under General Dwight D. Eisenhower's leadership, eventually resulted in the first major allied victory of the war.

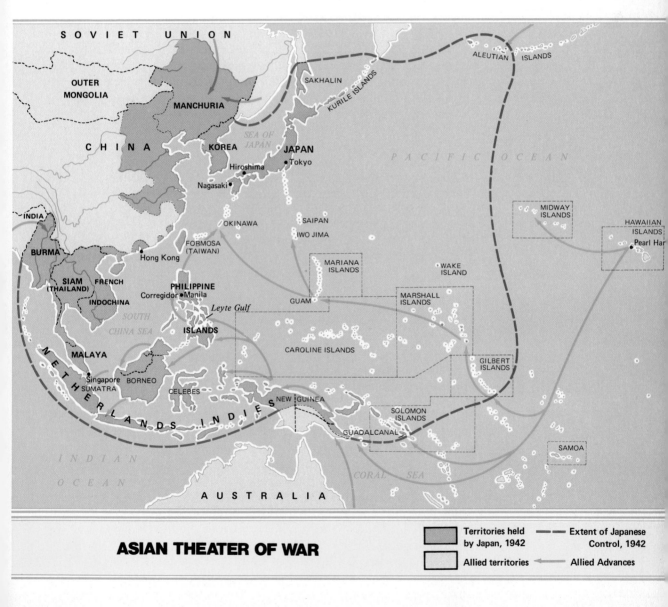

ASIAN THEATER OF WAR

Territories held by Japan, 1942
Allied territories
Extent of Japanese Control, 1942
Allied Advances

At the same time, the Soviet Union, after absorbing enormous losses, stalled the Nazi offensive on the northern front. In the Pacific, the American navy thwarted the Japanese threat against Australia in the Battle of the Coral Sea. The Japanese also lost a major naval engagement in their attempt to seize Midway Island. In August 1942, United States marines landed at Guadalcanal in the Solomon Islands. Under the leadership of General Douglas MacArthur and Admiral Chester Nimitz, American forces began the "island-hopping" strategy that would bring victory.

In the spring of 1943, the Allies crushed enemy resistance in North Africa. They captured 250,000 troops and invaded Italy. At about the same time, Soviet forces began to push back the German front in Russia. A year later, on June 6, 1944, Great Britain and the United States launched the Normandy invasion successfully. Under General Eisenhower's command, 176,000 troops initially moved across the English Channel. They were supported by 4,600 ships and 11,000 planes. British troops pushed the Germans from the south and west and the Soviets drove them from the east. Victory seemed assured.

In the Pacific, events moved somewhat more slowly. The Americans cut off the Japanese forces in the Solomons from their supply lines. At the same time, they landed in the Marshalls and the Marianas within effective bombing distance of Tokyo. In October 1944, MacArthur invaded the Philippines. And in the Battle of Leyte Gulf the American navy decisively crushed Japanese sea power. Victory in the Pacific was within sight. But American military strategists expected that a massive and costly offensive on the Japanese mainland would still be required to attain it.

Political Strategy

American political strategy during the war was neither as clearcut nor as successful as the military strategy. Most Americans believed they were fighting for survival. Beyond that, they pointed to a larger moral purpose in the Four Freedoms which Roosevelt had enunciated as world goals in 1941—freedom of speech, freedom of religion, freedom from want, and freedom from fear. Before the United States entered the war, Roosevelt had met Prime Minister Churchill to formulate the broad postwar principles of the United States and Great Britain. The Atlantic Charter, drawn up at this meeting, emphasized the principles of self-determination, respect for treaties, disarmament of aggressors, renunciation of territorial gain, freedom of the seas, and world economic and political cooperation.

Once the United States joined the war, Roosevelt and Churchill worked closely together, as did the military chiefs of the two countries. The alliance was probably the most successful in history, largely

The American strategy in the Pacific was to advance to Tokyo by "island hopping," destroying Japanese strongholds in the Pacific. Led by General MacArthur, allied troops won victories at Guadalcanal in the Solomon Islands, the Gilbert, Marshall, and Caroline Islands, Guam, and the Philippines. From these bases destructive raids were launched on the Japanese mainland.

because of the respect and admiration the two men had for each other.

The alliance with the U.S.S.R., however, involved formidable political problems. The Communist ideology of the U.S.S.R. rejected western values and anticipated their eventual destruction. Moreover, the events just prior to the war had left a heritage of ill will and suspicion between the Soviet Union and the western countries. Joseph Stalin, the Soviet leader, believed that England and France had compromised with Germany in the 1930's because they opposed communism more strongly than they opposed fascism. On the other hand, the Allies had watched the Soviet Union suddenly reverse an anti-Nazi policy and sign a Non-Aggression Pact with Germany in 1939, invade Poland from the east after Germany's attack on September 1, and launch an attack on Finland, October 1940.

Once Germany attacked the Soviet Union, however, public opinion among the Allies changed remarkably, especially in the United States. The people of the Soviet Union had to bear the brunt of the war until the United States could mobilize people and material to help Britain mount an offensive against Germany. The toughness of the Soviet army and the tenacity and heroism of the Soviet people during the darkest days of the war won the admiration of Americans. To help sustain their Soviet allies, the United States government supplied them with billions of dollars of lend-lease aid.

The Soviet Union professed a willingness to work with the Allies on military and postwar problems. In 1942, it signed the Declaration of the United Nations in which the Allies agreed to take no new territory after the war. In 1934, it dissolved the Comintern, the official agency for promoting world revolution. In November 1943, Roosevelt, Churchill, and Stalin met for the first time at Teheran, Iran. They agreed to coordinate the Normandy invasion with a Russian offensive against Germany. Stalin promised to enter the war against Japan after Germany's defeat. And the three heads of state formulated a general plan for a postwar international organization.

The most important and controversial wartime conference was held in the Crimea, in the southern part of the Soviet Union, in 1945. At the Yalta Conference, the three major powers made important agreements for ending the war and organizing the postwar world. They agreed that Germany would pay heavy reparations and, pending a peace treaty, be divided into American, Soviet, British, and French military zones. They decided that the Soviet Union would enter the war against Japan and in return would receive the Kurile Islands north of Japan, the southern part of the island of Sakhalin, and railroad and port concessions in Manchuria. New Polish borders were to be established giving Polish territory to the Soviet Union in the east and German territory to Poland in the west. And the Polish government

Roosevelt and Churchill had conferred at Washington, Casablanca, and Quebec to plan military strategy. Prior to the Teheran Conference, Churchill and Roosevelt met with Generalissimo Chiang Kai-shek, head of the Nationalist government of China, in Cairo to plan action against Japan.

would be set up by the U.S.S.R. temporarily while preparations were made for democratic elections.

After the war, when the U.S.S.R. and the United States had become more enemies than allies, many Americans severely criticized the Yalta agreements. They accused Roosevelt of "selling out" to Stalin. The Soviet's most flagrant violation of the Yalta agreements came in Poland where democratic elections were never held. Poland became a Soviet satellite after the war, thus thrusting Soviet power to the heart of Europe. The criticisms of the commitments made at Yalta, however, came after the Cold War had already begun. In 1945, allied victory was made possible because the three great powers had cooperated in war. Roosevelt, far more than Churchill, believed that they could cooperate in peace, as well. The Yalta agreements were based on the assumption that the U.S.S.R. would live up to its obligations. To Roosevelt and his advisors, and to most Americans, this seemed possible in 1945.

Victory and the Bomb

In April 1945, American and Soviet troops met each other at the Elbe River. By the end of the month, the Soviets reached Berlin. Italian partisans captured and killed Mussolini. And Hitler committed suicide in a Berlin bomb shelter. Germany surrendered unconditionally, as the Allies had demanded, May 8, 1945.

President Roosevelt did not live to see Germany's surrender. He died of a cerebral hemorrhage on April 12, after having led the nation through a longer and more perilous period than any other American President.

Roosevelt's successor, Harry S Truman, had to carry the war against Japan to a conclusion. To do this, he had to make the most momentous decision of the war. In 1939, President Roosevelt, in response to information that Germany was working on a similar project, authorized the government to launch a program of atomic research. In July 1945, government scientists succeeded in exploding the first atomic bomb in the New Mexico desert. The United States now possessed the most terrible weapon in history. Should it be employed against the Japanese to end the war in the Pacific?

Truman based his decision to use the bomb on the assumption that Japan would fight to the end and that thousands of American lives would be lost in an invasion of the Japanese mainland. American military leaders predicted at least eighteen more months of fighting before final victory. On July 26, Truman and Churchill demanded that Japan surrender or face "utter destruction." Japan refused on July 29.

One week later, on August 6, an American superfortress airplane dropped an atomic bomb on Hiroshima, killing 75,000 people and

Partisans are resistance fighters working behind enemy lines, performing reconnaissance and sabotage, and upsetting enemy movements as much as possible. They do not belong to the regular army but usually operate under orders from a professional military commander.

▶Was Truman justified in his decision to use the atom bomb against civilians rather than risk the lives of American soldiers? Why or why not?

injuring 100,000 out of a total population of 344,000. The Soviet Union declared war on Japan two days later. On August 15, 1945, after a second atomic bomb had hit Nagasaki, Japan surrendered.

The United States emerged victorious from the most devastating war in history. Over 12 million Americans had served in the armed forces. More than 300,000 had died. The totalitarian aggressors had been destroyed. But a large part of the world lay in ruins. The United States moved into a postwar world, searching for lasting peace, but armed with a weapon that could destroy humankind.

The Cold War, 1945-1974

STATING THE ISSUE

Although World War II was not the longest war in history, it was the most destructive. By the end of the war, political and economic systems in many countries in Europe and Asia had collapsed. Millions of people on both continents faced hunger and homelessness.

For a time, hope for a better world seemed well founded. The enemy nations had been thoroughly defeated. Moreover, the United Nations Organization, founded by fifty nations in the spring of 1945, promised a new era of international peace and order. The world soon recognized, however, that the United States and the Soviet Union would not easily settle their differences over the conference table. The Soviet Union wanted a postwar world which would protect its boundaries and favor the expansion of communism. The United States sought a democratic world in which American interests would be secure. The rivalry between these two nations became so intense that people began to refer to it as the ''Cold War.''

It soon appeared that the Soviet Union would turn eastern Europe into a Soviet sphere of influence and that Communists would take control in China. American leaders quickly proposed policies designed to check the expansion of Communist influence. Billions of dollars in military and economic aid were given to nations friendly to the United States. And thousands of Americans died on distant battlefields in ''limited wars'' defending these policies.

By the mid 1970's the Cold War seemed to be moving into a more hopeful phase. The United States and the Communist world powers began to cooperate with each other in peaceful undertakings. This chapter begins with a historical essay on the Cold War. It ends with three readings designed to help you understand ways in which the United States and the Communist powers have tried to come to terms with each other.

1945 Germany and Japan surrender; World War II ends

1945 Fifty nations sign charter for the United Nations

1945 General George C. Marshall is sent to China to reconcile Chinese leaders

1947 President Truman announces Truman Doctrine pledging United States' aid to Greece and Turkey

1947 Marshall Plan provides for the post-war economic recovery of Europe

1948 Soviet Union blockades roads to Berlin; Berlin airlift begins

1949 Twelve nations sign pact for North Atlantic Treaty Organization

1949 Congress passes National Defense Assistance Act

1950 General Douglas MacArthur leads United Nations forces to aid South Korea after invasion by North Korea

1951 United States and Japan sign peace treaty

1954 North and South Vietnam are divided at the seventeenth parallel

1961 The Berlin wall is built to divide East and West Berlin

1962 United States supports group of Cuban exiles in unsuccessful attempt to overthrow Fidel Castro

1962 President John F. Kennedy orders Premier Khrushchev to dismantle Soviet missile bases in Cuba

1965 President Lyndon Johnson orders bombing of military sites in North Vietnam

1972 President Richard M. Nixon visits China; formal diplomatic relations reestablished between China and the United States

1973 United States and North Vietnam sign cease-fire agreement; United States' troops leave South Vietnam

96 AMERICAN INVOLVEMENT IN A DIVIDED WORLD

HISTORICAL ESSAY

Since 1945, the United States government has become increasingly involved with other nations. Some nations, such as Great Britain and France, are old allies. Others, such as Pakistan and South Vietnam, are new nations which did not exist before World War II. In Europe, American foreign policy has been relatively successful.

641

In non-western countries and in Latin America, it has been less successful. Despite an enormous expenditure of money, lives, and natural resources, Americans continue to live in an unstable world.

A high point in Soviet-American cooperation came on June 26, 1945. On that day Vyacheslav Molotov, the Soviet foreign minister, signed the charter for the United Nations in San Francisco. Agreement had been reached on an international organization divided into two major parts: a General Assembly and a Security Council. All member nations had one vote in the Assembly. Members discussed issues in the Assembly and then recommended action to the Security Council. The Security Council consisted of five permanent members—the United States, the Soviet Union, Great Britain, France, and China. Six other nations were elected for two-year terms. The United Nations Charter authorized the Council to apply diplomatic, economic, or military sanctions against nations that threatened world peace. The charter stated, however, that the Council could not take any action without the approval of all five permanent members. Therefore, any of the five could veto a proposed United Nations action.

Divisions and Alliances in Europe

The years immediately following World War II showed clearly that the nations of the world were united in name only. Stalin seemed determined to turn his wartime territorial gains into permanent political gains. The Soviet Union emerged from the war with its troops in Poland, the eastern half of Germany, all the Balkan states (Hungary, Romania, Bulgaria, Yugoslavia, Albania), and the Baltic states (Latvia, Lithuania, Estonia). By 1948, the Soviet Union had incorporated the Baltic states into its own government. It had also installed Communist governments in East Germany, Poland, Czechoslovakia, and the Balkan countries.

In March 1946, Winston Churchill, the British prime minister, visited the United States. In a famous speech at Clayton, Missouri, he told his listeners that Stalin had lowered an "Iron Curtain" over Europe and had split the continent in half. Churchill's speech met with a mixed reception. Many Americans still hoped that the Soviet Union would cooperate in peace as it had in war. The United States government, however, took Churchill's warning seriously. In March 1947, President Truman announced that the United States would provide economic and military aid to the government of Greece. It was threatened by Communist guerrillas. The United States later expanded this so-called Truman Doctrine by promising to support any nation threatened by outside military pressure or armed aggression. Later in 1947, Secretary of State Marshall announced the Marshall Plan. It was designed to support the non-Communist nations of Europe with economic aid. The United States government made these commitments in order to prevent the Soviet Union and later the People's Republic of China from extending their power. These commitments became known collectively as the "containment policy."

▶Why, if for any reason, should the United States try to stop other nations from expanding?

The Soviet Union denounced the Marshall Plan as a capitalist plot. But non-Communist countries in Europe agreed to it eagerly. Congress appropriated $13 billion for the program. The Marshall Plan quickly brought nations such as Britain, France, Belgium, and the Netherlands closer together politically. These nations also realized that their economic recovery depended to a large extent upon the political and economic fate of Germany.

Germany was still split between the allied zones in the west and the Soviet zone in the east. Allied attempts to get Soviet agreement on a peace treaty to unify Germany failed. So in 1948 the western nations announced plans for creating the Republic of West Germany. The Soviets reacted to this announcement and to the success of the Marshall Plan by blockading the roads to Berlin in June 1948. When the Soviets refused to let allied convoys into Berlin, the citizens of West Berlin faced starvation. Any allied attempt to break through the blockade might mean war with the Soviet Union. The Allies solved the crisis by bringing in supplies by air. In May 1949, the U.S.S.R. lifted the blockade. But Berlin continued to play a potentially explosive role in the Cold War. Thousands of refugees from the Soviet zone of the city fled to the allied zone. In order to halt the flow of refugees, Soviet Premier Nikita Khrushchev had a wall built in 1961 along the line dividing the city.

Berlin is located within East Germany. All communication and transportation lines from West Germany must go through 100 miles of East German territory before reaching the city. Before 1949, when East Germany proclaimed itself the German Democratic Republic, the city of Berlin had been jointly occupied by France, Britain, the U.S.S.R., and the United States.

The United States depended upon military power to support its containment policy. In April 1949, it signed—with eleven other nations—a mutual defense pact that set up the North Atlantic Treaty Organization (NATO). The twelve nations agreed to consider an attack on any treaty member "an attack against them all." They pledged themselves to support treaty members with whatever action might be necessary "including the use of armed force." The United States Senate ratified the North Atlantic Treaty. Congress also passed the Mutual Defense Assistance Act to provide military aid largely to other NATO members.

Involvement in Asia

The policy of containment based on economic aid and a military alliance succeeded in Europe. No European nation came under Communist control after 1948. In the non-western world, however, the United States confronted three problems. It had to make peace with Japan, gain the friendship of the new non-western nations, and end Communist expansion.

President Truman successfully kept the Soviet Union from playing an important role in the occupation of Japan. Under the command of General Douglas MacArthur, American troops ran the country. The Japanese introduced a series of political and economic reforms. The old Japanese empire was dissolved, including Japan's claims in China and Korea. Meanwhile, stimulated by American aid, the Japanese economy recovered remarkably. In 1951, the Japanese Peace Treaty was signed. It formally ended American occupation, even though the United States continued to maintain troops in Japan.

American policies succeeded in Japan. But they failed hopelessly in China. At the end of the war, China was a divided nation. The nominal head of the government was Chiang Kai-shek, leader of the Nationalist party. Mao Tse-tung, leader of the Chinese Communist party, had opposed Chiang after the Communists and the Nationalists had split in 1927. By 1945, the Communists controlled most of the northern provinces of China and about one fourth of the total population. The Soviet Union formally recognized the Communists as the real rulers in China and gave them some aid. The United States supported Chiang Kai-shek. But it took the position that no Chinese government could succeed unless the Nationalists and the Communists cooperated. In 1945, President Truman sent General George Marshall to China to try to bring Chiang and Mao together. Marshall's attempt at mediation failed. In 1947, a full-scale civil war broke out in China. By 1949, the Communists had defeated the Nationalists. Chiang and his army took refuge on Formosa.

The failure of American policy in China provoked an intense political debate in the United States. President Truman's opponents accused him of betraying Chiang Kai-shek and the free world. Truman and his advisors probably underestimated the strength of the Chinese Communists. Their swift success surprised even Stalin who had given them only a modest amount of aid. Moreover, Truman felt that Chiang lacked strong support among the Chinese people. He believed that only massive American military assistance, which Congress probably would not have given, could have sustained him. The Communists had identified themselves with a revolutionary movement in China which had widespread popular support.

With a new Communist power dominating the Asian continent, how would the United States apply its containment policy in the Far East? The answer came in Korea. Korea was located on a narrow peninsula, close to Japan and bordering on both China and the Soviet Union. It had become a Japanese colony early in the twentieth century. After World War II, Korea was divided into two zones. Soviet troops occupied the north and American troops occupied the south. The United States tried to refer the question of Korean unity and independence to the United Nations. But the U.S.S.R. refused to allow such action. Finally, North and South Korea set up separate governments. Each claimed authority over the whole country. The Soviet Union

The Nationalist party or Kuomintang was founded by Dr. Sun Yat-sen (1866-1925). The Nationalists led by Dr. Sun overthrew the Manchu Dynasty and established the Republic of China in 1912. Thereafter, Sun Yat-sen and his party fought against the local warlords to unify China and establish a stable government based on the economic and political philosophy he described in **Three People's Principles**—democracy, nationalism, and socialism. In 1921, he was elected president of a national government proclaimed at Canton.

On August 5, 1949, the State Department issued a White Paper. It was a collection of documents which blamed the Nationalist government of China and not American foreign policy for the collapse of the Chiang government. This White Paper depicted the Nationalist government as inept, selfish, and shortsighted. It was favorably received by the American public and denounced by many Republicans.

and China backed North Korea. The United States supported South Korea.

On June 25, 1950, North Korean troops invaded South Korea. The United States immediately took the issue to the U.N. Security Council which the Soviets were boycotting at the time. Council members demanded that North Korea withdraw and urged the United Nations to aid South Korea.

Responding to the United Nations request, President Truman ordered American forces into the conflict under General Douglas MacArthur. Fifteen other nations sent troops to Korea. But Americans and South Koreans always made up at least 90 percent of MacArthur's United Nations army. During the first few months of fighting, the North Korean armies almost drove the U.N. forces off the peninsula and into the sea. Then MacArthur executed a brilliant amphibious landing behind the enemy lines at Inchon which turned the tide. The North Korean armies lost their momentum as they retreated.

MacArthur requested that he be permitted to pursue the North Koreans toward the Chinese border. President Truman consented. Then in November 1950, Chinese troops crossed the Yalu River in force. (See map, page 646.) They sent MacArthur's troops reeling toward the South. MacArthur demanded permission from President Truman to bomb Chinese bases. He suggested that a naval blockade be mounted on the China coast. President Truman rejected MacArthur's proposals. He feared that the Soviet Union might join the Chinese and thus create a third world war. When MacArthur objected to this decision publicly, Truman removed him from command. MacArthur returned to a hero's welcome in the United States. During the congressional investigation that followed, the Joint Chiefs of Staff supported Truman's decision not to extend the war.

United Nations troops finally stabilized the Korean front close to the old North-South Korea border. In June 1951, agreement was reached to negotiate an armistice. The crisis subsided. But some fighting continued for two years before the armistice was finally signed in July 1953.

The Korean crisis eased. But the United States soon became embroiled in a similar crisis in Vietnam. Throughout its long history, Vietnam had been invaded repeatedly by foreigners. For centuries, it was under the sway of China. In the nineteenth century, it came under French rule along with Cambodia and Laos. At the end of World War II, most Cambodians, Laotians, and Vietnamese wished to be free of French rule. Many groups worked for independence for Vietnam. The most important of these groups was the Vietminh League. It was led by Ho Chi Minh, a Vietnamese nationalist. In 1945, the Vietminh League proclaimed the establishment of the Democratic Republic of Vietnam. Hanoi was to be its capital.

The U.S.S.R. was boycotting the U.N. in protest against the decision not to admit the People's Republic of China.

Within the Department of Defense, Congress set up an agency called the Joint Chiefs of Staff in 1949. It consists of the military advisers to the President, the National Security Council, and the Secretary of Defense. The four permanent members are the chairman, appointed by the President, and the chiefs of staff for the army, navy, and air force.

Fighting was fierce during negotiations, particularly the air war between Russian-built MIGS and American Sabre Jets.

Cambodia, Laos, and Vietnam form part of the area westerners call Indochina.

645

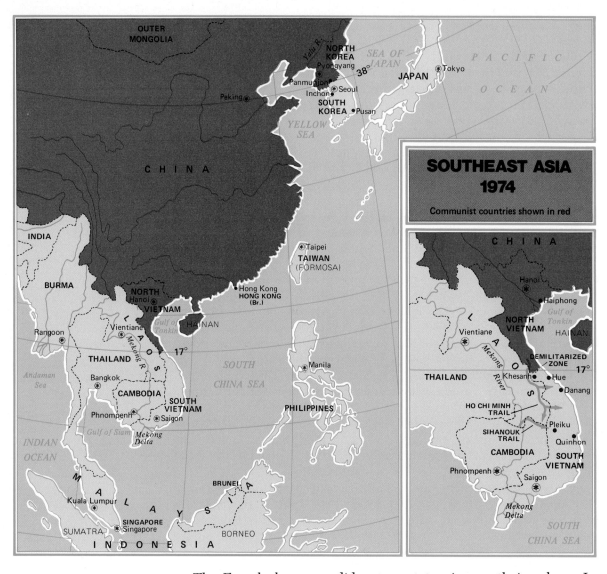

SOUTHEAST ASIA
1974

Communist countries shown in red

French troops withdrew in 1956.

The French, however, did not want to give up their colony. In 1946, war broke out between the French and the Vietnamese nationalists. It lasted until 1954 when agreements were signed at Geneva ending the war. The agreements, known as the Geneva Accords, divided Vietnam into two zones. The northern zone was placed under the government of the Vietminh League. The southern zone was placed under the control of the French army and a provisional South Vietnamese government. The French agreed to withdraw their troops when asked to do so by the government of the southern zone. The Geneva Accords also stated that elections to decide the future government of Vietnam were to take place in 1956.

646

In 1955, Ngo Dinh Diem, the French-educated leader of the southern zone, proclaimed it a republic. He became its first president. He ignored the part of the Geneva Accords which called for elections in 1956. He imposed a dictatorship on the Republic of South Vietnam. He declared that this action was necessary because free elections could not be held in North Vietnam. Actually, Diem and other South Vietnamese politicians feared that Ho Chi Minh, the popular nationalist leader, would win if any elections were held. Diem's actions were backed by the United States. The French army withdrew in 1956. By 1958, civil war had erupted in Vietnam.

The United States had been training the South Vietnamese army since 1956. When civil war broke out, it supplied military aid to Diem's forces. These forces were opposed in the south by the National Liberation Front. The NLF was a group of Vietnamese nationalists and pro-Communists, supported by the government of North Vietnam. The military wing of this group was known as the Vietcong.

Diem failed to cope successfully with the civil war. He lacked popular support and his army was filled with corruption. The campaign begun by the National Liberation Front, on the other hand, won support from many of the peasants—the majority of Vietnam's population. Moreover, its troops were efficient, well-disciplined, and had a higher morale than Diem's.

In 1962, United States aid to South Vietnam was increased as the National Liberation Front took over large sections of the south. In 1963, Diem's government was overthrown by a group of Saigon generals. Diem was murdered and his family were forced to flee South Vietnam. The murder of Diem and the change in the government did not hasten the end of the war, however. Ho Chi Minh increased North Vietnamese aid to the National Liberation Front. And, in 1965, the United States intervened actively on the side of the South Vietnamese government. President Lyndon Johnson ordered the air force to bomb military sites in North Vietnam. And United States troops fought against the NLF and North Vietnamese troops in the south. By 1968, there were more than half a million American military personnel in Vietnam. And 29,000 Americans had been killed in action.

Saigon is the capital city of South Vietnam.

Relations with Latin America

America's difficulty in finding any final solution for the expansion of Communist power in Asia has been matched by its inability to prevent the rise of hostile governments in Latin America. Immediately after World War II, the United States concentrated on European and Asian problems to the neglect of Latin America. Many South American countries were beset with serious social and economic problems. They often blamed the United States for not giving enough aid to them or for supporting corrupt political leaders. Resentment against the

United States reached a high point in 1958. Vice-President Richard Nixon received such a hostile reception on his goodwill tour of South America that he was forced to cancel his trip and return to the United States.

American leaders sought a Latin American policy that would promote reforms in these countries. They wanted to gain the friendship of the Latin American people. And at the same time, they wanted to inhibit the growth of communism. With painful clarity, Cuba illustrated the difficulties of making such a policy work.

In 1959, Fidel Castro led a successful revolution to overthrow the government of Fulgencio Batista. The Batista government was one of the most corrupt and dictatorial regimes in the Western Hemisphere. President Eisenhower quickly granted diplomatic recognition to the Castro government. Castro, however, was violently anti-American. He harangued the United States in long speeches. He seized American-owned property without adequate compensation. And he openly courted the support of the Soviet Union as he set up a Communist state in Cuba.

The prospect of an unfriendly Communist power so close to the United States infuriated the American government. It tried to meet the threat Castro posed to the hemisphere. On April 17, 1961, a band of anti-Castro exiles trained by the Central Intelligence Agency of the United States unsuccessfully invaded Cuba at the Bay of Pigs. They intended to dislodge Castro. Castro, in turn, established even closer relationships with the Soviet Union. In 1962, American planes took aerial reconnaissance photographs over Cuba. The photographs showed that Soviet technicians were installing intermediate range missile sites. A dangerous encounter between the United States and the Soviet Union followed. President John F. Kennedy demanded that Premier Khrushchev dismantle the bases. And he ordered the United States Navy to turn back any Soviet ships en route to Cuba with offensive weapons. At the same time, he warned that any nuclear attack on the United States from Cuba would result in "a full retaliatory response upon the Soviet Union." The world trembled, apparently at the brink of war, until Khrushchev withdrew his missiles.

Toward an End of the Cold War?

The Vietnam war gradually became unpopular in the United States. Largely because of this development, President Lyndon B. Johnson decided not to run for re-election in 1968. His successor, Richard Nixon, promised to "Vietnamize" the war. He said that he would withdraw American troops and train the South Vietnamese to fight their own war under the protective cover of American weapons. From 1969 until a cease fire agreement was reached in January 1973, American troops and casualties in Vietnam steadily declined. Organized opposition to the war also declined. However, a wave of violent demonstrations on many college campuses followed Nixon's decision to broaden the war temporarily by sending troops into Cambodia in the spring of 1971.

The winding down of the Vietnam war seemed to mark a decisive change in the Cold War. It took place at the same time that the United States was entering into closer relationships with China and the Soviet Union. Henry Kissinger, first as Mr. Nixon's advisor and then as Secretary of State, pushed for détente. In February 1972, Mr. Nixon paid a goodwill visit to China. The public ceremonies associated with the visit were viewed on television all over the world. It appeared that the two great powers of the East and West were prepared to develop closer cultural and economic relationships for the future.

Two months later Mr. Nixon visited the Soviet Union. He concluded a series of agreements with Soviet leaders. The agreements covered arms limitation, trade, and technical and scientific cooperation. Before leaving for Peking the American President had said that the world could not afford to have two great powers such as China and the United States existing in hostile isolation from each other. When he was in the Soviet Union he said, "The United States and the Soviet Union are both great powers. . . . In the long history of both our nations we have never fought one another in war. Let us make decisions now which will help ensure that we shall never so do in the future."

▶ Should the United States cooperate in these ways with nations whose ideology it opposes? Why or why not?

As the 1970's moved toward the halfway mark some Americans thought that the President was being dangerously optimistic. But public opinion polls showed that most Americans wanted the easing of old tensions to continue. For the first time in more than a quarter of a century they were beginning to speculate about a possible end to the Cold War.

97 THE NEW BALANCE OF POWER

War often creates more problems than it solves. It is one thing to gain victory in the field. But it is something else again to turn that victory into a realization of long term national goals. The history of American foreign relations since World War II illustrates this point.

After the war the American people believed they had fought a war in the interests of democracy. But they found themselves confronting a world of expanding Communist power. What had gone wrong? Were American leaders to blame? Or, had the war created a new kind of world which they were just beginning to understand? Should

America rely on military strength and force the Communists to retreat? Or, should it learn how to live in a world in which the great powers were divided by deep ideological differences?

The excerpts in Reading 97 are intended to put the big problems of the postwar period into historical perspective. They were also intended to provide you with two ways of explaining the difficulties encountered by American policy makers during that period. As you read them, try to answer the following questions:

1. Why does Kennan say that World War II was "not fully winnable" from the American point of view?
2. What is Kissinger's criticism of American Cold War policy?

George Kennan:
Consequences of World War II

George F. Kennan, American Diplomacy 1900-1950: Charles R. Walgreen Foundation Lectures (Chicago: University of Chicago Press, 1952), pp. 74-75. Reprinted by permission.

Here Kennan refers to World War II.

George Kennan is a distinguished historian and former ambassador to the Soviet Union. He was largely responsible for the containment policy discussed in the historical essay. In the following selection he explains how the war changed the balance of power in the world.

It occurs to me that perhaps the most helpful thing to understand about this recent war is the extent to which it was prejudiced, as a military encounter, before it was begun—the extent to which, you might say, it was not fully winnable.

Let me explain how this was. Before the war began the overwhelming portion of the world's armed strength in land forces and air forces had accumulated in the hands of three political [groups] —Nazi Germany, Soviet Russia, and Imperial Japan. All were deeply and dangerously hostile to the western democracies. As things stood in the late thirties, if these three powers were to combine their efforts and stick together in a military enterprise, the remaining western nations plainly had no hope of defeating them on the land mass of Europe and Asia. . . . In Europe and Asia, western democracy had become militarily outclassed. The world balance of power had turned decisively against it.

I am not claiming that this was perceived, or would have been easy to perceive, by western statesmen. But I believe it was a reality. And, as such, it plainly limited the actual prospects for the West, if war were to come. Of the three totalitarian powers, Japan was the only one which could conceivably be defeated by the democracies without [asking] for this purpose the aid of one of the other totalitarian powers. In the case of Germany and Russia, circumstances were bitter.

650

Together, they could not be defeated at all. Individually, either of them could be defeated only if the democracies had the [assistance] of the other.

But such [assistance], if permitted to proceed to the point of complete victory, would mean the relative strengthening of the [assisting] power and its eventual appearance as a greedy . . . claimant at the peace table. Not only that: Any war in which one of these two powers was fighting on the side of the democracies could scarcely be fought to a complete and successful finish without placing the [assisting] totalitarian power in occupation of large parts of eastern Europe simply by virtue of the sweep of military operations.

As things stood in 1939, therefore, the western democracies were already under the handicap of being militarily the weaker party. They could hardly have expected to avoid paying the price. Theirs were no longer the choices of strength. The cards were so stacked against them that any complete . . . democratic victory in a new world war was practically impossible to foresee.

Henry Kissinger Criticizes American Cold War Policy

Henry Kissinger is a former political scientist and historian at Harvard University. He became foreign affairs advisor and then Secretary of State under President Nixon. The following selection reflects his criticism of American foreign policy as it was carried on under President Eisenhower.

The notion that war and peace were separate and successive phases of policy has been at the root of much of our postwar policy. It came to expression in the dominant western policy of the postwar period: the policy of containment. This was based on the assumption that a substantial effort to rebuild western strength had to *precede* any serious negotiation with the Soviet Union. Conferences would be futile until the Communist countries found themselves confronted by [overwhelming] strength all around their [border]. "What we must do," said Secretary Acheson, "is to create situations of strength; we must build strength; and if we create that strength then I think the whole situation in the world begins to change. . . . With that change there comes a difference in the negotiating position of the various parties and out of that I should hope that there would be a willingness on the part of the Kremlin to recognize the facts . . . and to begin to solve at least some of the difficulties between East and West."

In the context of 1951, these statements were highly plausible. After three years of Communist provocation, after the Berlin blockade and

► War involves huge losses in lives and money. Given this fact, should a nation be willing to end a war short of victory?

Henry A. Kissinger, **The Necessity for Choice: Prospects of American Foreign Policy** (New York: Harper & Row, Publishers, Inc., 1961), pp. 200-203. Copyright © 1960, © 1961 by Henry Kissinger. Reprinted by permission.

► Why should a nation negotiate with a country which has a philosophy of life opposed to its own?

Dean Acheson was Secretary of State in the administration of President Harry S Truman.

The Kremlin in Moscow is the headquarters of the Soviet government.

Pierre in Aux Ecoutes, Paris

FRENCH: "Isn't it touching to see two sisters so inseparable?"

Tarantel Press, Berlin

"I shall set you free."

The cartoons on this page comment on various ways in which the United States tried to contain the Soviet Union. What point does each cartoon make? Do you agree with each point?

the invasion of Korea, it was understandable that we should have given priority to achieving security against Soviet invasion. How the strength we were building was to be conveyed to the Communist leaders, and how precisely one went about negotiating from strength seemed then questions not worth considering. Expansionism was believed inherent in Stalinist communism. Thwarted in the possibility of foreign adventures, communism would have to transform itself. At that point fruitful negotiations would be possible.

Here Kissinger refers to the interpretation of Communist principles developed by Josef Stalin, leader of the Soviet Union from 1929 to 1953.

[Now however] our concern with the transformations of Soviet society causes us to be either too rigid or too accommodating. It makes us overlook that we have to deal in the first instance with Soviet foreign and not with its domestic policy. From the notion that a settlement depends on a change in Soviet society, it is not a big step to the view that liberalization of Soviet society is equivalent to a settlement. In such an atmosphere, it is not surprising that a controversy should have raged about the desirability of relaxing tensions but not about the conditions which would make such a relaxation meaningful, about the need for peace but not about the elements of stability, about the level at which we should talk but not what we should discuss once we get there.

A responsible approach to negotiations must be quite different. We should make no unjustified concessions to a Soviet leader simply because we consider him to be liberal. We should not refuse to make concessions, which are otherwise desirable, simply because we consider a Soviet leader Stalinist. The ultimate test in either case is whether a given measure enhances stability or detracts from it.

A lasting settlement is possible only if the Soviet leaders become convinced that they will not be able to use the West's desire for peace to demoralize it. If they are serious about their desire to avoid war, they must realize that negotiations can be used for purely tactical purposes only so often and that, measured against the dangers of such a course, the gains they may score are paltry. We in turn should strive to demonstrate to the Soviet leaders that they have a real policy decision to make which we will do everything possible to ease. They must face the fact that the policy of applying relentless pressures on the West creates untold perils for all the peoples of the world. On the other hand, they must be convinced that they can increase their security through negotiation. Should they seriously seek a settlement, they would find us flexible and conciliatory.

Negotiations are important. But it is essential to conduct them without illusions. We do not need to postulate a basic Soviet transformation in order to believe in the possibility of a settlement. Nor is it a prerequisite to successful negotiation to pretend that a relaxation of tensions is primarily within western control. The West must have much more positive goals than to divine Soviet intent. We do ourselves an injustice if we make an issue of the desirability of relaxing tensions

Conciliatory means acting in such a way as to bring individuals or groups together, or to win an individual's or group's goodwill.

To postulate means to assume or presuppose something.

or of ending the Cold War. The test of conciliatoriness does not reside in interpreting Soviet trends in the most favorable manner. Nor does it consist of proving the desirability of peace—which should be taken for granted. Rather, the challenge which confronts the West is to determine what are the possibilities of a settlement which does not hazard our security and is consistent with our values. Only in the purposeful is flexibility a virtue.

FOR THOUGHT:

What do you think were the biggest problems which the postwar period posed for American policy makers?

98 CONFRONTATION BETWEEN THE SUPERPOWERS

The basic policies of the Cold War were set forth in the late 1940's. They were later followed by both Republican and Democratic administrations. American policy makers tended to think of the world as divided into three parts. The Free World included those countries in Europe, Asia, and Latin America independent of Communist control and opposed to Communist ideology. The Communist World included the Soviet Union, Communist countries in eastern Europe, China, and North Korea. Third World countries consisted of the underdeveloped nations, mostly in Africa, Asia, and the Middle East, which had not yet committed themselves to communism or democracy.

The objectives of American policy were to keep Communist powers from expanding and to develop cooperative relationships with Third World nations. This policy was ultimately tested in costly wars in Korea and South Vietnam. But direct confrontations between the United States and the Soviet Union were generally avoided. The great exception to this pattern came in 1962. The United States discovered that Cuba, a country which had traditionally been considered within the Free World, was allowing Soviet missile sites to be built on Cuban soil. The following documents deal with the Cuban missile crisis of 1962. As you read them, try to answer these questions:

1. How did Kennedy and Khrushchev justify the policies and actions of their nations?
2. How did Kennedy distinguish between the people of Cuba and Castro?

President Kennedy Alerts the Nation

Fidel Castro came to power in Cuba in 1959. For the first time, the United States had to cope with a neighboring nation sympathetic to communism. Both the Eisenhower and Kennedy administrations denounced Castro. In the spring of 1961 the United States government even supported an unsuccessful attempt by Cuban refugees to oust the Cuban leader. Relations between Cuba and the United States grew progressively worse. Finally, on October 22, 1962, President Kennedy made the following announcement to the American people.

Department of State Bulletin, Vol. XLVII (November 12, 1962), pp. 715-720. Language simplified.

"That imprisoned island" refers to Cuba.

Within the past week unmistakable evidence has established the fact that a series of offensive missile sites is now in preparation on that imprisoned island. The purpose of these bases can be none other than to provide a nuclear strike capability against the Western Hemisphere.

This urgent transformation of Cuba into an important strategic base—by the presence of these large, long-range, and clearly offensive weapons of sudden mass destruction—constitutes a clear threat to the peace and security of all the Americans.

Neither the United States of America nor the world community of nations can tolerate deliberate deception and offensive threats on the part of any nation, large or small. We no longer live in a world where only the actual firing of weapons represents a sufficient challenge to a nation's security to constitute grave danger. Nuclear weapons are so destructive and ballistic missiles are so swift that any greatly increased possibility of their use or any sudden change in their position may well be regarded as a definite threat to peace.

Acting, therefore, in the defense of our own security and of the entire Western Hemisphere, and under the authority entrusted to me by the Constitution as endorsed by the resolution of the Congress, I have directed that the following *initial* steps be taken immediately:

First: To halt this offensive buildup, a strict quarantine on all offensive military equipment under shipment to Cuba is being initiated. All ships of any kind bound for Cuba from whatever nation or port will, if found to contain cargoes of offensive weapons, be turned back. This quarantine will be extended, if needed, to other types of cargo and carriers. We are not at this time, however, denying the necessities of life as the Soviets attempted to do in their Berlin blockade of 1948.

Second: I have directed the continued and increased close surveillance of Cuba and its military buildup. The Foreign Ministers of the OAS in their message of October 3 rejected secrecy on such matters

▶ Should a President have the power to take steps such as these which might lead to war. Why or why not?

See Reading 96 for a discussion of the Berlin blockade.

The OAS is the Organization of American States. Its membership is made up of nations in North and South America.

The United States still maintains a heavily fortified military base at Guantanomo on the island of Cuba.

A consultation takes place when two or more people meet to share their views on a problem or issue.

Nikita S. Khrushchev was the leader of the Soviet government at this time.

▶ Should your country give up all offensive nuclear weapons if other countries are willing to do the same thing? Why or why not?

in this hemisphere. Should these offensive military preparations continue, thus increasing the threat to the hemisphere, further action will be justified. I have directed the Armed Forces to prepare for any eventualities. And I trust that, in the interest of both the Cuban people and the Soviet technicians at the sites, the dangers to all concerned of continuing this threat will be recognized.

Third: It shall be the policy of this nation to regard any nuclear missile launched from Cuba against any nation in the Western Hemisphere as an attack by the Soviet Union on the United States, requiring a full retaliatory response upon the Soviet Union.

Fourth: As a necessary military precaution I have reinforced our base at Guantanamo. I evacuated the dependents of our personnel there. And I ordered additional military units to be on a standby alert basis.

Fifth: We are calling tonight for an immediate meeting of the Organ of Consultation, under the Organization of American States. Our other allies around the world have also been alerted.

Sixth: Under the Charter of the United Nations, we are asking tonight that an emergency meeting of the Security Council be convoked without delay to take action against this latest Soviet threat to world peace. Our resolution will call for the prompt dismantling and withdrawal of all offensive weapons in Cuba, under the supervision of U.N. observers, before the quarantine can be lifted.

Seventh and finally: I call upon Chairman Khrushchev to halt and eliminate this underhanded, reckless, and provocative threat to world peace and to stabilize relations between our two nations. I call upon him further to abandon this course of world domination and to join in an historic effort to end the perilous arms race and transform human history. He has an opportunity now to move the world back from the abyss of destruction—by returning to his Government's own words that it had no need to station missiles outside its own territory, and withdrawing these weapons from Cuba—by refraining from any action which will widen or deepen the present crisis—and then by participating in a search for peaceful and permanent solutions.

Finally, I want to say a few words to the captive people of Cuba, to whom this speech is being directly carried by special radio facilities. I speak to you as a friend, as one who knows of your deep attachment to your homeland, as one who shares your hopes for liberty and justice for all. And I have watched and the American people have watched with deep sorrow how your nationalist revolution was betrayed and how your homeland fell under foreign domination. How your leaders are no longer Cuban leaders inspired by Cuban ideals. They are puppets and agents of an international conspiracy which has turned Cuba against your friends and neighbors in the Americas—and turned it into the first Latin American country to become a target for nuclear

Green in The Providence Journal

"Concern for the rest of the barrel."

❷

"Manana!"

Pratt in The Sacramento Bee

❸

These cartoons comment on Cuban-American relations. What point does each cartoonist make? Do you agree with each point?

war and also the first Latin American country to have these weapons placed on its soil.

Premier Khrushchev Replies

Following President Kennedy's speech, the United States put a naval blockade around Cuba. The Soviet Union was unwilling to test the blockade. So, Soviet ships turned around and headed back towards their home ports. Meanwhile Soviet technicians refused to dismantle missiles already in place. The United States responded by threatening to bomb the missile sites. It was in this situation that Khrushchev sent the following note to Kennedy on October 27.

Department of State Bulletin, Vol. XLVII (November 12, 1962), pp. 741-746.

Our purpose has been and is to help Cuba. And no one can challenge the humanity of our motives aimed at allowing Cuba to live peacefully and develop as its people desire. You want to relieve your country from danger and this is understandable. However, Cuba also wants this. All countries want to relieve themselves from danger. But how can we, the Soviet Union and our government, measure your actions? In effect, your actions mean that you have surrounded the Soviet Union with military bases, surrounded our allies with military bases, set up military bases literally around our country, and stationed your rocket weapons at them. This is no secret. High-placed American officials declare this. Your rockets are stationed in Britain and in Italy and pointed at us. Your rockets are stationed in Turkey.

You are worried over Cuba. You say that it worries you because it lies at a distance of 90 miles across the sea from the shores of the United States. However, Turkey lies next to us. Our sentinels are pacing up and down and watching each other. Do you believe that you have the right to demand security for your country and the removal of such weapons that you feel are offensive, while not recognizing this right for us?

You have stationed devastating rocket weapons, which you call offensive, in Turkey literally right next to us. How then does recognition of our equal military possibilities tally with such unequal relations between our great states? This does not tally at all.

This is why I make this proposal. We agree to remove those weapons from Cuba which you regard as offensive weapons. We agree to do this and to state this commitment in the United Nations. Your representatives will make a statement to the effect that the United States, on its part, bearing in mind the anxiety and concern of the Soviet state, will evacuate similar weapons from Turkey. Let us reach an understanding on what time you and we need to put this into effect.

658

The Crisis Is Averted

Kennedy replied to Khrushchev on the same day.

The first thing that needs to be done is for work to cease on offensive missile bases in Cuba [and for all weapons systems in Cuba] capable of offensive use to be made unworkable under effective United Nations arrangements.

As I read your letter, the key elements of your proposals—which seem generally acceptable as I understand them—are as follows:

(1) You would agree to remove these weapons systems from Cuba under appropriate United Nations observation and supervision. And you would undertake, with suitable safeguards, to halt the further introduction of such weapons systems into Cuba.

(2) We, on our part, would agree—upon the establishment of adequate arrangements through the United Nations to ensure the carrying out and continuation of these commitments—(a) to remove promptly the quarantine measures now in effect and (b) to give assurances against an invasion of Cuba. I am confident that other nations of the Western Hemisphere would be prepared to do likewise.

I would like to say again that the United States is very much interested in reducing tensions and halting the arms race. And we are quite prepared to consider with our allies any useful proposals.

FOR THOUGHT:

How do you think confrontations like the Cuban missile crisis can be best avoided in the future?

99 A THAW IN THE COLD WAR

By the early 1970's it seemed that the Cold War might be entering a new phase. In January 1973, a cease-fire was successfully negotiated in Vietnam. This event seemed to symbolize important changes in attitude and policy on the part of the United States toward the Communist world. The principal American policy maker during this period was Henry Kissinger. As you read in the first reading of this chapter, he had been a critic of early Cold War policy. Dr. Kissinger's and President Nixon's concern for reaching some kind of long range accommodation with the Communist world was dramatized by the reestablishment of formal diplomatic relations between China and the United States in 1972. This concern was also shown by President Nixon's visits to China and the Soviet Union that year.

The emergence of a Communist regime in China in the late 1940's had been difficult for most Americans to accept. Most Americans were unwilling to believe that Communists really controlled China. This disbelief was reflected in official American policy. It continued to recognize the Chinese Nationalist government on Formosa as the legitimate government of China. The hostile attitude of mainland China toward the United States during the Korean and Vietnam wars intensified feelings of distrust between the two nations. By 1972, however, the Soviet Union and China had fallen into open and bitter disagreement over many issues. Moreover, the public mood in America began to change. People saw that it might be possible to bring the Cold War to an end. President Nixon attested to this change in mood in his widely acclaimed trips to China and the Soviet Union in February and May of that year.

The first document in Reading 99 reports what the heads of state in China and the United States were able to achieve at their meeting. The second document is taken from an American news story describing Mr. Nixon's trip to Moscow. In your reading, try to answer the following questions:

1. What major areas of agreement were achieved and what areas of disagreement remained after the two conferences?
2. In what ways does United States participation in the China and Moscow conferences represent a change in the American attitude toward Communist nations?

A Joint Declaration by the United States and China

President Nixon visited China from February 21 to February 28. He was accompanied by Mrs. Nixon, Secretary of State William Rogers, special Presidential advisor Henry Kissinger, and a large staff of American officials. The President's party included many American journalists. The visit was viewed on television in America and elsewhere in the world. The following document is taken from an official joint statement issued at the conclusion of the visit.

Weekly Compilation of Presidential Documents (February 28, 1972), pp. 473-476.

The U.S. side stated the following. Peace in Asia and peace in the world requires efforts both to reduce immediate tensions and to eliminate the basic causes of conflict. The United States will work for a just and secure peace. It will be just because it fulfills the hopes of peoples and nations for freedom and progress. It will be secure because it removes the danger of foreign aggression. The United States supports individual freedom and social progress for all the peoples of the world. The United States believes that the effort to reduce tensions is served by improving communication between countries that have different ideologies. This policy will lessen the risks of confrontation through accident, miscalculation, or misunderstanding. Countries should treat each other with mutual respect and be willing to compete peacefully. They should let performance be the ultimate judge. No country should claim infallibility. And each country should be prepared to re-examine its own attitudes for the common good.

The Chinese side stated the following. Wherever there is oppression, there is resistance. Countries want independence. Nations want liberation and the people want revolution. This has become the irresistible trend of history. All nations, big or small, should be equal. Big nations should not bully the small. And strong nations should not bully the weak. China will never be a superpower. It opposes power politics of any kind. The Chinese side stated that it firmly supports the struggles of all the oppressed people and nations for freedom and liberation. China believes that the people of all countries have the right to choose their social systems according to their own wishes. They also have the right to safeguard the independence, sovereignty, and territorial integrity of their own countries. They can oppose foreign aggression, interference, control, and subversion. All foreign troops should be withdrawn to their own countries.

There are essential differences between China and the United States in their social systems and foreign policies. However, the two sides agreed that countries, regardless of their social systems, should conduct their relations on the following principles: respect for the sovereignty and territorial integrity of all states, non-aggression against other states, non-interference in the internal affairs of other states, equality and mutual benefit, and peaceful coexistence. International disputes should be settled on this basis, without resorting to the use or threat of force. The United States and the People's Republic of China are prepared to apply these principles to their mutual relations.

With these principles of international relations in mind the two sides stated the following:

Progress toward the normalization of relations between China and the United States is in the interests of all countries.

Both wish to reduce the danger of international military conflict.

Neither should seek a preponderant influence in the Asia-Pacific region. And each is opposed to efforts by any other country or group of countries to establish such an influence.

And neither is prepared to negotiate on behalf of any third party or to enter into agreements or understandings with the other directed at other states.

Both sides agreed that it would be against the interests of the peoples of the world for any major country to conspire with another against other countries, or for major countries to divide up the world into spheres of interest.

►The two pictures on this page show American ping pong players in China and a parade at the Olympic Games. Do sports events such as these bring greater understanding among nations? Why or why not?

The two sides agreed that it is desirable to broaden the understanding between the two peoples. To this end, they discussed specific areas in such fields as science, technology, culture, sports and journalism, in which people-to-people contacts and exchanges would be mutually beneficial.

An American Interpretation of Détente

After President Nixon's visits to China and the Soviet Union, American newspaper readers went to their dictionaries to look up the meaning of "détente." They found it defined as a relaxing of tensions between nations. The following selection shows how one widely read American magazine interpreted what many Americans were calling the détente between the United States and the Soviet Union.

Down a red-carpeted stairway came the two men, walking to a simple table beneath the giant gilt chandelier of the Kremlin's St. Vladimir Hall. Aides laid blue and red leather folders before them. One of the men joked about the number of times he had to sign the documents. Then Richard Nixon and Leonid Brezhnev rose. Handshakes, champagne, toasts. With some variations, the scene had become familiar, even repetitive, by the time the summit ended.

Time (June 5, 1972), pp. 13-18.

The particular document signed and sealed with such pomp was the most notable in a series of agreements that the President brings back from the Soviet Union this week: the long-expected undertaking to limit nuclear weapons, not an end to the costly arms race but still a sign of hope and good sense. Other, lesser agreements had come with similar ceremony almost every day. It had all been stage-managed carefully and the accords had been worked on for months or even years. Theoretically, they could have been revealed to the world without the Kremlin spectacular. Yet the way in which they were signed and sealed gave them special import.

Many of those who watched the week unfold in Moscow concluded that this summit—the most important since Potsdam in 1945 and probably the most important Soviet political event since Stalin's death—could change world diplomacy. It was all the more impressive because it seemed not so much a single cataclysmic event but part of a process, part of a world on the move.

The summit certainly has not transformed the Soviet Union, or wiped out the problems and animosities between the U.S. and Russia. But when Richard Nixon returns home this week after visits to Teheran and Warsaw, he will bring back a set of significant new facts—or a confirmation of facts that are gradually emerging.

The meeting underscored the drive toward détente based on mutual self-interest—especially economic self-interest on the part of the Soviets, who want trade and technology from the West. None of the agreements are shatterproof, and some will lead only to future bargaining. But the fact that they touched so many areas suggested Nixon's strategy: he wanted to involve all of the Soviet leadership across the board—trade, health, science—in ways that would make it difficult later to reverse the trends set at the summit.

For better or for worse, the meeting reaffirmed that there are still only two superpowers, despite all the recent talk of a multipolar world. The Russians seemed bent on showing that Moscow is the joint capital of world power, sharing superpower status equally—and only—with Washington. They wanted to demonstrate that Richard Nixon's phenomenal week in Peking was simply that—a phenomenon, while in Moscow the hard realities of arms, technology and billions of dollars were being settled or shaped. To say that Nixon had succeeded in playing China off against Russia and vice versa would be putting it far too crudely, and would be premature at that. But U.S. policy has more room for balance and maneuver—a situation of some risk but considerable opportunities.

In domestic policy Brezhnev himself is a hard-liner. He will probably still deal harshly with dissenters: on the eve of the summit, five Jewish leaders were arrested, and writer Alexander Solzhenitsyn was once again denounced as an "opponent of Soviet reality." Many Americans have long hoped that an opening to the West and a better life for the Soviet consumer would bring about a more liberal political climate in Russia. But détente with the West does not necessarily mean détente within Russia. In fact, in cooperating with the West, the Soviets will have to face the problem of how to keep ideological infections from seeping in along with western technology and taste.

The summit has not brought the millennium, peace, but it had brought some tremendously significant new conditions in the world. Reports TIME Correspondent John Shaw from Moscow: "A move from the 'absence of war' toward something not only safe but fruitful cannot be achieved easily and certainly not by remote control or through ambassadors and technicians, no matter how able. It requires the eyes, hours of talking that reveal leaders and their motives to one another."

FOR THOUGHT:

What do you think were the most important things which contributed to the relaxation of tensions among the United States, the Soviet Union, and China?

Equal Opportunity in a Democratic Society

STATING THE ISSUE

As Americans entered the 1970's, they were acutely aware that the relationships of certain minority groups to American society had recently changed dramatically. The changes grew largely out of a rising concern for equality of opportunity for black Americans. The campaign for black equality produced new educational and job opportunities. But its by-products included riots and assassinations. The fate of the campaign appeared uncertain. What did seem certain was that the success or failure of the quest for equal opportunity would help to determine the meaning and future of democracy for all Americans.

The black Americans' search for equality in civil rights and equal access to jobs, education, and housing stretched back to the Revolutionary War. Their battle overlapped the struggles, past and present, of other minority groups for equality in American society. It resembled the struggles of other minority groups in some ways but differed significantly in others.

Immigrant groups arriving in the nineteenth century often met the same sorts of prejudice and discrimination faced by blacks. They often worked as laborers or at menial jobs, clustered in slums under dismal conditions. And they struggled to deal with unfamiliar customs and language. Women, who constituted more than half of Americans, also suffered legal and political discrimination. The native Americans who survived the loss of their land to the dominant whites were treated as separate and inferior dependents by an indifferent American society. Even recent arrivals like the Mexican-Americans in the Southwest and the Puerto Ricans of the cities on the east coast encountered discrimination of many kinds.

Each of these groups can tell a story that reveals much about the history of American democracy. The first three readings of this chapter focus on the struggle to achieve equality by the 11 percent of Americans who are identified as black. The historical essay, the last reading in the chapter, will relate the experience of blacks to those of other minority groups in recent American history.

1400 1500 1600 1700 1800 1900 2000

1890 Over two hundred Indians are massacred at Wounded Knee, South Dakota
1909 National Association for the Advancement of Colored People is formed
1911 National Urban League is founded
1916 Marcus Garvey organizes Universal Negro Improvement Association
1925 A. Philip Randolph organizes the Brotherhood of Sleeping Car Porters and Maids
1934 Elijah Muhammed assumes leadership of the Black Muslim movement
1941 President Roosevelt passes law to prevent discrimination in hiring in defense plants
1942 James Farmer organizes Congress of Racial Equality (CORE)
1954 In **Brown vs. The Board of Education,** Supreme Court rules against segregation in public schools
1957 President Eisenhower sends National Guard to Little Rock, Arkansas

1957 Martin Luther King founds Southern Christian Leadership Conference
1960 Student Non-Violent Coordinating Committee (SNCC) is founded
1964 Malcolm X forms Organization for Afro-American Unity
1964 Martin Luther King wins Nobel Peace Prize
1964 Congress passes Civil Rights Act outlawing discrimination in voting and in public accommodations
1965 Congress passes Voting Rights Act
1966 Betty Friedan founds National Organization for Women (NOW)
1966 United Farm Workers Organizing Committee is formed
1968 Martin Luther King is assassinated
1973 Indians seize control of Wounded Knee, South Dakota

100 PROTESTS AND PROGRAMS AFTER WORLD WAR I

In 1900, there were 10 million black heirs of the slave system. They occupied the bottom of the ladder of achievement in American life. As a group they were poorer by far than whites. Their children died younger, as did their adults. They were more often hungry and ill.

Yet there was hope. Literacy was increasing rapidly among blacks. Despite some coercion by whites who depended on their labor in the South, blacks moved fairly freely and sought economic opportunity where they could find it. One of their leaders, Booker T. Washington, urged them to work hard in order to take advantage of American life. He pledged his faith in American democracy.

As Washington was speaking in the early 1900's, however, racial segregation was increasing rapidly in the South and border states. In public facilities such as railroads and streetcars, restaurants and theaters, and in private businesses and organizations, blacks were rigidly segregated or excluded. It reached the point, as one historian has remarked, where whites and blacks took oaths on separate Bibles in some southern courtrooms. In the North and West, informal segregation of neighborhoods was common. The process resulted in virtually segregated schools. But laws enforcing segregation were rapidly being eliminated in the North and West at the same time that they were spreading in the South.

Other black leaders argued that Washington's protests against segregation were too weak. They felt that they amounted to passive acceptance. And they believed that his emphasis on vocational education was shortsighted. W.E.B. Du Bois declared that Washington's program betrayed the "talented tenth"—those blacks who should be admitted to higher education for training as leaders.

Two related events of great significance helped change the basis of this controversy. They gave the eventual victory to Du Bois's more militant point of view. In 1909, a group of whites and blacks formed the National Association for the Advancement of Colored People. Its purpose was to fight segregation and illegal violence against blacks. The organization quickly became the most effective agency working for equal rights for blacks. And between 1910 and 1920, southern blacks by the hundreds of thousands poured northward to seek employment. They found jobs in industries and in service occupations during a labor shortage created by the reduction in immigration and the booming of production during World War I. The shape of the future became visible. American blacks, traditionally southern and rural, were on the way to becoming a predominantly northern and urban people.

Immediately after the war a new militancy and a new consciousness of racial identity became apparent among American blacks. The two excerpts in Reading 100, written by W.E.B. Du Bois and Marcus Garvey, illustrate these trends. As you read them, think about the following questions:

1. What did Du Bois and Garvey demand?
2. What is the tone of these two articles? Were the authors submissive? militant? moderate? radical?

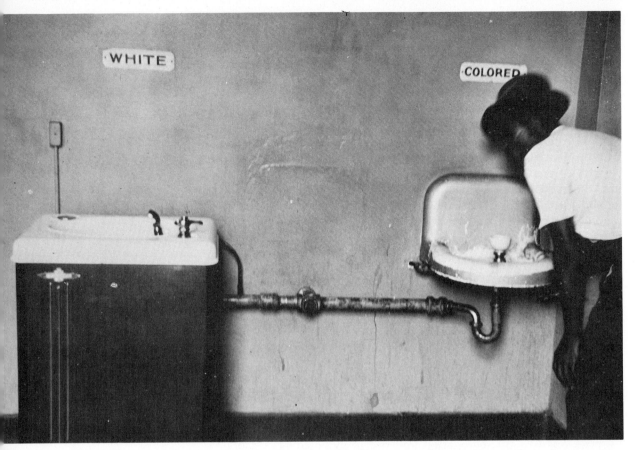

Suppose you were a black citizen and saw a sign such as this one. How would you feel? Why would you feel this way?

A Call for Justice and for Militancy

As they had in every previous war, blacks served valiantly in segregated troops in World War I. Nearly 400,000 blacks answered the call to the colors in 1917 and 1918. The return of black troops from France in 1919 prompted W.E.B. Du Bois, the editor of the NAACP organ The Crisis, *to ask some searching questions about the future of blacks in America.*

W.E.B. Du Bois, "A Call for Democracy After the War," **The Crisis**, XVIII (May 1919), pp. 13-14. Reprinted by permission of The Crisis Publishing Company, Inc. Language simplified.

We are returning from War! *The Crisis* and tens of thousands of black men were drafted into a great struggle. For bleeding France and what she means and has meant and will mean to us and humanity and against the threat of German race arrogance, we fought gladly and to the last drop of blood. For America and her highest ideals, we fought in far-off hope. For the dominant southern oligarchy entrenched in Washington, we fought in bitter resignation. For the America that represents and gloats in lynching, disfranchisement, caste, brutality and devilish insult—for this, in the hateful upturning and mixing of things, we were forced by vindictive fate to fight also.

But today we return! We return from the slavery of uniform which the world's madness demanded us to don, to the freedom of civil garb. We stand again to look America squarely in the face and call a spade a spade. We sing. This country of ours, despite all its better souls have done and dreamed, is yet a shameful land.

It *lynches.*

And lynching is barbarism of a degree of contemptible nastiness unparalleled in human history. Yet for fifty years we have lynched two Negroes a week. And we have kept this up right through the war.

It *disfranchises* its own citizens.

Disfranchisement is the deliberate theft and robbery of the only protection of poor against rich and black against white. The land that disfranchises its citizens and calls itself a democracy lies and knows it lies.

It encourages *ignorance.*

It has never really tried to educate the Negro. A dominant minority does not want Negroes to be educated. It wants servants, dogs, and monkeys . . . .

It *steals* from us.

It organizes industry to cheat us. It cheats us out of our land. It cheats us out of our labor. It confiscates our savings. It reduces our wages. It raises our rent. It steals our profit. It taxes us without representation. It keeps us consistently and universally poor. And then it feeds us on charity and derides our poverty.

It *insults* us.

It has organized a nation-wide and lately a world-wide propaganda of deliberate and continuous insult and defamation of black blood wherever found. It decrees that it shall not be possible . . . for a black man to exist without silent or open acknowledgement of his inferiority to the dirtiest white dog . . . .

This is the country to which we Soldiers of Democracy return. This the fatherland for which we fought! But it is *our* fatherland. It was right for us to fight. The faults of *our* country are *our* faults. Under similar circumstances, we would fight again. But . . . now that the war is over, we [must] marshal every ounce of our brain and brawn to fight a sterner, longer, more unbending battle . . . .

We return. We return from fighting. We return fighting.

Make way for Democracy! We saved it in France. And by the Great Jehovah, we will save it in the United States of America, or know the reason why.

An oligarchy is a select, elite governing group. Du Bois was probably referring to the control of key congressional committees by white, southern congressmen.

▶Would a person who has been discriminated against by society be justified if he or she refused to serve in the armed forces? Why or why not?

Marcus Garvey Proposes
an African Homeland

Marcus Garvey was a black leader born in the West Indies. He organized a mass movement in the United States in the 1920's to procure an African homeland to which American blacks might emigrate.

Marcus Garvey, **Philosophy and Opinions of Marcus Garvey,** compiled by Amy Jacques-Garvey (New York: Universal Publishing House, 1926), Vol. II, pp. 34-36.

Hue and cry is a loud outcry used in pursuit of criminals.

During the war, Marcus Garvey organized the Universal Negro Improvement Association. It offered a nationalistic solution for the plight of American blacks.

Garvey is referring to the provisions of the Versailles Treaty which ended World War I and disabled Germany.

▶To what degree do you value your identity as an American? What, if anything, would be missing from your life if you did not feel an attachment to your nation?

On every side we hear the cry of white supremacy—in America, Canada, Australia, Europe, and even South America. There is no white supremacy beyond the power and strength of the white man to hold himself against the others. The supremacy of any race is not permanent. It is a thing only of the time in which the race finds itself powerful. The whole world of white men is becoming nervous about its own future and that of other races. With the desire of self-preservation, they raise the hue and cry that the white race must be first in government and in control. In the face of such a universal attitude the Negro must marshal all his forces to protect himself from the threatened disaster of race domination and ultimate extermination.

The Universal Negro Improvement Association feels that the Negro should appeal to the same spirit of racial pride and love as the great white race is doing for its own preservation. While others are raising the cry of a white America, a white Canada, a white Australia, we also without reservation raise the cry of a "Black Africa." The critic asks, "Is this possible?" And the 400 million courageous Negroes of the world answer, "Yes."

Out of this very reconstruction of world affairs will come the glorious opportunity for Africa's freedom. Out of the present chaos and European confusion will come an opportunity for the Negro. He will have the opportunity to expand himself and consolidate his manhood in the direction of building himself a national power in Africa.

No one believes in the permanent disablement of Germany. But all thoughtful minds realize that France is laying the foundation through revenge for a greater conflict than has as yet been seen. With such another upheaval, there is no reason why organized Negro opinion could not be directed in the channel of their own independence in Africa.

To fight for African redemption does not mean that we must give up our domestic fights for political justice and industrial rights. It does not mean that we must become disloyal to any government or to any country where we were born. Each and every race outside of its domestic national loyalty has a loyalty to itself. Therefore, it is foolish for the Negro to talk about not being interested in his own racial, political, social and industrial destiny. We can be as loyal American citizens or British subjects as the Irishman or the Jew. And yet we can fight for the redemption of Africa, a complete emancipation of the race.

Fighting for the establishment of Palestine does not make the American Jew disloyal. Fighting for the independence of Ireland does not make the Irish-American a bad citizen. Why should fighting for the freedom of Africa make the Afro-American disloyal or a bad citizen?

The Universal Negro Improvement Association teaches loyalty to all governments outside of Africa. But when it comes to Africa, we feel that the Negro has absolutely no obligation to anyone but himself.

FOR THOUGHT:

In what ways did Du Bois and Garvey want the same thing? In what ways did they want something different?

101 BREAKTHROUGH IN CIVIL RIGHTS: LAWS AND REACTIONS

Led by the NAACP, civil rights groups made slow and painstaking efforts to strike down laws requiring or permitting segregation in public facilities and discrimination in other civil rights. These efforts achieved success in the years after World War II. Both the United States Supreme Court and lower courts declared all segregation laws illegal. And governmental agencies began enforcing desegregation in public facilities. By the 1960's, also, an increasing number of blacks had won election to public offices. They included, for example, the first blacks to sit in the Georgia legislature since Reconstruction, the first southern black sheriffs since that era, the first black United States senator ever elected from a northern state, and the first black mayors of large northern cities.

As far back as 1915, the Supreme Court had begun striking down segregation laws. Among the first of these laws were Maryland and Oklahoma constitutional provisions that discriminated against black voting and a Louisville, Kentucky, city law that tried to enforce racial segregation by neighborhoods. In the years between the two world wars, the Supreme Court cut down little by little the areas in which segregation could legally operate. For example, it prohibited political parties from holding primary elections restricted to white voters. And it ordered states to admit blacks to university graduate schools where no separate but equal facilities were available for them. The resulting changes were significant. But they came slowly and affected only a few people.

Many American Jews had supported the creation of a new state in Palestine as a Jewish homeland. Irish Americans had supported Ireland's independence from Britain. When the state of Israel was eventually carved out of Palestine, and when part of Ireland was established as the independent state of Eire, American Jews and Irish Americans continued to consider themselves Americans.

World War II marked a dividing line. In the years immediately after the war many states, led by New York, adopted Fair Employment Practice Acts. These acts were designed to prohibit discrimination in employment. The federal government also moved to integrate the armed forces. And the Supreme Court struck down a variety of segregation laws in the vast area of the use of public facilities. The most crucial and controversial of the Court's decisions came on May 17, 1954. On that day, in *Brown vs. the Board of Education*, the Court declared that segregation in the public schools was illegal. This decision reversed the *Plessy vs. Ferguson* decision of 1896, in which the Court said that "separate but equal" facilities were acceptable. In a subsequent ruling, the Court added that segregated schools had to desegregate "with all deliberate speed." Many whites, especially from the South, protested this decision strongly. But there was relatively little open conflict over it. Most school districts in border states moved gradually to comply with the law. Most of those in the deep South maintained segregation.

Reading 101 contains two excerpts related to subsequent events. The first describes the Federal government's reaction to the local and state governments' opposition to the desegregation of Central High School in Little Rock, Arkansas. In the second excerpt, Dr. Martin Luther King, Jr. explains why he could no longer accept a "go slow" strategy in the pursuit of blacks' rights. As you read, think about the following questions:

1. What did President Eisenhower do in the Little Rock crisis? Why was this action significant?
2. Why did Martin Luther King reject the advice to "go slow"?

President Eisenhower Intervenes at Little Rock

In the fall of 1957, trouble erupted in Little Rock, Arkansas. The Supreme Court had ordered the city to admit a few black children to Central High School. Governor Orval Faubus of Arkansas intervened by calling out National Guardsmen who prevented blacks from entering the school. When he later withdrew the Guard, mobs of whites blocked the school entrance without interference by police and threatened the children. At this point, President Dwight Eisenhower acted to uphold the authority of the federal courts. He ordered army troops to Little Rock to guarantee the black children safe access to Central High. Excerpts from Eisenhower's radio message to the nation explaining his action follow.

Vital Speeches of the Day, Vol. XXIV, No. 1 (October 15, 1957), pp. 11-12. Language simplified.

For a few minutes this evening I want to talk to you about the serious situation that has arisen in Little Rock. To make this talk I have come to the President's office in the White House. I could have spoken from Rhode Island, where I have been staying recently. But I felt that, in speaking from the house of Lincoln, of Jackson, and of Wilson, my words would better convey both the sadness I feel in the action I was forced to take today and the firmness with which I intend to pursue this course until the orders of the Federal Court at Little Rock can be executed without unlawful interference.

In that city, under the leadership of extremists, disorderly mobs have deliberately prevented the carrying out of proper orders from a Federal Court. Local authorities have not eliminated that violent opposition. And, under the law, I yesterday issued a Proclamation calling upon the mob to disperse.

This morning the mob again gathered in front of the Central High School of Little Rock. Obviously they gathered for the purpose of again preventing the carrying out of the Court's order relating to the admission of Negro children to that school.

Whenever normal agencies prove inadequate to the task and it becomes necessary for the Executive Branch of the Federal Government to use its powers and authority to uphold Federal Courts, the President's responsibility is inescapable.

In accordance with that responsibility, I have today issued an Executive Order. It directs the use of troops under federal authority to aid in the execution of federal law at Little Rock, Arkansas. This became necessary when my Proclamation of yesterday was not observed. And the obstruction of justice still continues.

▶ Under what conditions, if any, should the federal government use troops to enforce a court order?

It is important that the reasons for my action be understood by all our citizens.

As you know, the Supreme Court of the United States had decided that separate public educational facilities for the races are unequal. Therefore, compulsory school segregation laws are unconstitutional.

Our personal opinions about the decision have no bearing on the matter of enforcement. The responsibility and authority of the Supreme Court to interpret the Constitution are very clear. Local Federal Courts were instructed by the Supreme Court to issue such orders and decrees as might be necessary to achieve admission to public schools without regard to race—and with all deliberate speed.

The very basis of our individual rights and freedoms rests upon the certainty that the President and the Executive Branch of Government will support and insure the carrying out of the decisions of the Federal Courts, even, when necessary, with all the means at the President's command.

Unless the President did so, anarchy would result.

There would be no security for any except that which each one of us could provide for himself.

In August 1963 several hundred thousand Americans, both black and white, staged a march on Washington to demand federal enforcement of civil rights. Dr. Martin Luther King led that march. What can you do to help your fellow citizens win their rights?

The interest of the nation in the proper fulfillment of the law's requirements cannot yield to opposition and demonstrations by some few persons. Mob rule cannot be allowed to override the decisions of our courts.

Martin Luther King
Explains His Philosophy

The Rev. Dr. Martin Luther King, Jr., acted as a spokesman for the Montgomery, Alabama, blacks. In 1955 they carried on a year-long successful boycott against the city transit system because it insisted on segregated seating in buses. King later led the Southern Christian Leadership Conference (SCLC) into protest marches, boycotts, and other kinds of direct action for equal opportunity. He won the Nobel Peace Prize in 1964 for the support of the principle and practice of nonviolence. He was assassinated in 1968 while preparing to assist in demonstrations for higher wages by sanitation workers in Memphis, Tennessee. The excerpts below are from a letter he wrote from jail where he was being held after a demonstration. It was addressed to a group of southern white clergymen.

The Southern Christian Leadership Conference is an agency with headquarters in Atlanta. It was founded in 1957 as an extension of the Montgomery Improvement Association, headed by Martin Luther King, Jr. It advocates nonviolent demonstrations.

674

I must make two honest confessions to you. . . . First, I must confess that over the past few years I have been gravely disappointed with the white moderate. I have almost reached the . . . conclusion that the Negro's great stumbling block in his stride toward freedom is not the White Citizens' Councilers or the Ku Klux Klanner, but the white moderate, who is more devoted to "order" than to justice; who prefers a negative peace which is the absence of tension to a positive peace which is the presence of justice; who constantly says: "I agree with you in the goal you seek, but I cannot agree with your methods of direct action"; who . . . believes he can set the timetable for another man's freedom . . . and who constantly advises the Negro to wait for a "more convenient season." Shallow understanding from people of good will is more frustrating than absolute misunderstanding from people of ill will. Lukewarm acceptance is much more bewildering than outright rejection.

You speak of our activity in Birmingham as extreme. At first I was . . . disappointed that fellow clergymen would see my nonviolent efforts as those of an extremist. I began thinking about the fact that I stand in the middle of two opposing forces in the Negro community. One is a force of complacency. [It is] made up in part of Negroes who, as a result of long years of oppression, are so drained of self-respect and a sense of "somebodiness" that they have adjusted to segregation. [It is also made up of] a few middle-class Negroes who, because of a degree of academic and economic security and because in some ways they profit by segregation, have become insensitive to the problems of the masses. The other force is one of bitterness and hatred, and it comes dangerously close to advocating violence. It is expressed in the various black nationalist groups that are springing up across the nation, the largest and best-known being Elijah Muhammad's Muslim movement. Nourished by the Negro's frustration over the continued existence of racial discrimination, this movement is made up of people who have lost faith in America, who have absolutely repudiated Christianity, and who have concluded that the white man is an incorrigible "devil."

I have tried to stand between these two forces, saying that we need [imitate] neither the "do-nothingism" of the complacent nor the hatred and despair of the black nationalist. For there is the more excellent way of love and nonviolent protest. I am grateful to God that, through the influence of the Negro church, the way of nonviolence became an integral part of our struggle.

Excerpts from "Letter from Birmingham Jail" (April 16, 1963) in Martin Luther King, Jr., **Why We Can't Wait** (New York: Harper & Row, Publishers, Inc., 1963), pp. 87, 90. Copyright © 1963 by Martin Luther King, Jr. Reprinted by permission of Harper & Row, Publishers.

White Citizens' Councils began to appear in the South after the **Brown vs. the Board of Education** decision. Their aim was to maintain segregation through threats, economic pressure, and occasional violence.

▶ Does a commitment to nonviolent action mean that a person must never resist violence on the part of others? Why?

The Nation of Islam, usually known as the "Black Muslim" movement, was organized in 1930 by Wali Farad. His followers believed him to be an incarnation of Allah and that he had come to America to rescue all blacks from bondage. In 1934, he was succeeded by Elijah Muhammad. The group is opposed to integration. It has renounced Christianity. And it seldom cooperates with other black groups.

FOR THOUGHT:

To what degree did Du Bois, Garvey, Esienhower, and King argue from similar principles?

102 THE NEW
BLACK MILITANCY

To most black leaders, the ideal of black separatism embraced by Marcus Garvey in the 1920's seemed for many years an undesirable or impossible solution. Their hope of gaining the equal opportunity that was promised by the American democratic political system still seemed a brighter and more genuine possibility. But in the years after 1950 new developments caused many persons to doubt that integration into a color-blind American society was possible.

The achievement of the principle of desegregation in public schools meant little in practice for most blacks. Ten years after the Supreme Court's famous decision in 1954, fewer than 11 percent of the black pupils in southern and border states were enrolled in desegregated school districts. In the deep South, the figure was lower than 1 percent. In the North, most black pupils attended schools that were nearly all black. They lived in segregated areas because of poverty, prejudice, and sometimes preference.

As the big cities of the North took in more and more black migrants from the South, more and more whites left for the suburbs. The most extreme case of such transfer of populations was Washington, D.C. Its population rose from 35.4 percent black in 1950 to 54.8 percent black in 1960. Its public school enrollment rose from 45.2 percent black in 1960 to 88 percent black in 1965. A disproportionately large amount of funds was spent on ghetto schools in such cities as New York. However, heavy turnovers of both teacher and student populations in such schools contributed to educational difficulties there.

A far more powerful source of black dissatisfaction was inequality of opportunity in employment and in housing. Some progress was made in overcoming discrimination in hiring practices and in admission to unions. But unemployment among blacks remained far higher than among whites. Housing conditions in the black ghettos of American cities were often miserable. And discrimination in housing—which by 1975 was usually illegal—prevented many blacks from obtaining living quarters elsewhere.

The continuing vast difference between the living and working conditions of whites and blacks prompted a new sense of militancy among blacks. This spirit affected the older protest and welfare groups, such as the NAACP and the Urban League, to some extent. But it was most evident in newer organizations. Reading 102 offers two selections. The first is from an article by Stokely Carmichael, a black militant. The second selection is from a recent survey which tried to measure the goals and expectations of black Americans. As you read, consider these questions:

676

1. Why did Carmichael believe that blacks had to achieve their goals through their own efforts and their own organizations?
2. Can the attitudes of black Americans, as seen through the *Ebony* poll, be described as optimistic or pessimistic?

Stokely Carmichael Explains "Black Power"

Like Marcus Garvey, Stokely Carmichael was born in the West Indies. But he was educated in the United States. He first won national prominence as chairman of the Student Nonviolent Coordinating Committee (SNCC). SNCC engaged in many direct action projects, notably in voter registration drives among blacks in the deep South. He wrote the following explanation of the term "black power" in 1966.

One of the tragedies of the struggle against racism is that up to now there has been no national organization which could speak to the growing militancy of young black people in the urban ghetto. There has been only a civil rights movement, whose tone of voice was adapted to an audience of liberal whites. It served as a sort of buffer zone between them and angry young blacks. None of its so-called leaders could go into a rioting community and be listened to. In a sense, I blame ourselves—together with the mass media—for what has happened in Watts, Harlem, Chicago, Cleveland, Omaha. Each time the people in those cities saw Martin Luther King get slapped, they became angry. When they saw four little black girls bombed to death, they were angrier. And when nothing happened, they were steaming. We had nothing to offer that they could see, except to go in and be beaten again. We helped to build their frustration. . . .

An organization which claims to speak for the needs of a community—as does the Student Nonviolent Coordinating Committee—must speak in the tone of that community, not as somebody else's buffer zone. This is the significance of black power as a slogan. For once, black people are going to use the words they want to use—not just the words whites want to hear. And they will do this no matter how often the press tries to stop the use of the slogan by equating it with racism or separatism.

. . . The concept of "black power" is not a recent or isolated phenomenon. It has grown out of the ferment of agitation and activity by different people and organizations in many black communities over the years. Our last year of work in Alabama added a new concrete possibility. In Lowndes county, for example, black power will mean that if a Negro is elected sheriff, he can end police brutality. If a

Stokeley Carmichael, "What We Want," **The New York Review of Books**, Vol. VII, No. 4 (September 22, 1966), pp. 5-7 passim.

Watts is a section of Los Angeles. Harlem is a section of Manhattan. The five places mentioned were scenes of black riots during the 1960's.

In 1963, a church bombing in Birmingham, Alabama, killed four black girls attending Sunday school.

677

black man is elected tax assessor, he can collect and channel funds for the building of better roads and schools serving black people—thus advancing the move from political power into the economic arena. In such areas as Lowndes, where black men have a majority, they will attempt to use it to exercise control. This is what they seek: control. Where Negroes lack a majority, black power means proper representation and sharing of control. It means the creation of power bases from which black people can work to change statewide or nationwide patterns of oppression through pressure from strength—instead of weakness . . .

▶ Does a black person who becomes successful have an obligation to continue to live in a ghetto? Should a successful white slum dweller stay in a slum?

Integration speaks not at all to the problem of poverty, only to the problem of blackness. Integration today means the man who "makes it," leaving his black brothers behind in the ghetto as fast as his new sports car will take him. It has no relevance to the Harlem wino or the cottonpicker making three dollars a day. . . . As a goal, it has been based on complete acceptance of the fact that *in order to have* a decent house or education, blacks must move into a white neighborhood or send their children to a white school. This reinforces, among both black and white, the idea that "white" is automatically better and "black" by definition inferior. This is why integration is a subterfuge for the maintenance of white supremacy. It allows the nation to focus on a handful of southern children who get into white schools, at great price, and to ignore the 94 percent who are left behind in unimproved all-black schools. Such situations will not change until black people have power—to control their own school boards, in this case. Then Negroes become equal in a way that means something, and integration ceases to be a one-way street. . . .

The need for psychological equality is the reason why SNCC today believes that blacks must organize in the black community. Only black people can convey the revolutionary idea that black people are able to do things themselves. They must get poverty money they will control and spend themselves. They must conduct tutorial programs themselves so that black children can identify with black people. This is one reason Africa has such importance. The reality of black men ruling their own natives gives blacks elsewhere a sense of possibility, of power, which they do not now have.

This does not mean we don't welcome help, or friends. But we want the right to decide whether anyone is, in fact, our friend. In the past, black Americans have been almost the only people whom everybody and his momma could jump up and call their friends. We have been tokens, symbols, objects—as I was in high school to many young whites, who liked having "a Negro friend." We want to decide who is our friend, and we will not accept someone who comes to us and says: "If you do X, Y, and Z, then I'll help you." We will not be told whom we should choose as allies. We will not be isolated from any group or nation except by our own choice. We cannot have

▶ What conditions, if any, should you place on an offer of friendship?

678

the oppressors telling the oppressed how to rid themselves of the oppressor. . . .

But our vision is not merely of a society in which all black men have enough to buy the good things of life. When we urge that black money go into black pockets, we mean the communal pocket. We want to see the cooperative concept applied in business and banking. We want to see black ghetto residents demand that an exploiting landlord or storekeeper sell them, at minimal cost, a building or shop that they will own and improve cooperatively. They can back their demand with a rent strike, or a boycott, and a community so unified behind them that no one else will move into the building or buy at the store. The society we seek to build among black people, then, is not a capitalist one. It is a society in which the spirit of the community and humanistic love prevail. . . . The love we seek to encourage is within the black community, the only American community where men call each other "brother" when they meet. We can build a community of love only where we have the ability and power to do so: among blacks.

A rent strike occurs when building residents hold back their rent until the landlord makes substantial improvements.

Do you think that taking pride in your heritage, such as this woman is doing by wearing African dress, is important? Why? What is your heritage? How can you show pride in it?

Opinion Poll Reveals Mood
of Black Americans

The civil rights movement of the early 1950's touched off the most active phase of black Americans' search for equal opportunity. Twenty years later, after both successes and disappointments, Ebony magazine commissioned Daniel Yankelovich, Inc., to conduct a national poll to sample blacks' opinions on a variety of subjects. The results follow.

Four Major Themes

"A New Portrait of Black America," **Ebony** (September, 1973), p. 122. Reprinted by permission.

Dominating Yankelovich's social-political portrait of black America are four major themes: 1) black pride and identification; 2) mounting frustration with the inequities of the American system; 3) a readiness for radical change— but a simultaneous rejection of violence; and 4) a new kind of integration.

The single strongest theme in black America is its fixation on black identification. Blacks neither think of themselves as, nor aspire to be, "just Americans." Instead, they emphasize at least equally the word "black" and pride in being black. Only a handful of blacks (12 percent) think of themselves as American first and then black, while the vast majority (62 percent) regard themselves as "equally black and American." And a sizable group (24 percent) go considerably beyond even this view and say forthrightly that they are blacks first and then Americans.

Yankelovich finds the second major theme within black America to be deep despair, frustration and impatience about the inequities of American society. For blacks share the same uneasy feeling of most Americans that things are not going well. They differ from whites in their estimate of the social system and opportunities for change within it. Four out of ten blacks believe the American system is no longer viable and that radical alternatives are necessary. Most blacks (62 percent) reject outright the concept of violence. Another 30 percent believe that violence is only justified when all else has failed. Only 8 percent believe that violent means are often necessary.

Fewer Than Half Want Integration

Not surprisingly, Yankelovich finds black America divided on the subject of integration. Fewer than half (47 percent) support the traditional concept that integration is the best method for overcoming racial inequities. The majority—surprisingly—hold differing views. One small sector (16 percent) stands squarely behind separatism as the solution to black problems. A much larger group (36 percent)

680

favors what might be called a modified formula for integration. Their solution calls for first ending present inequities by giving the black community equal rights in housing and education and then encouraging integration among equals.

These four themes cut across every segment of black America—young, old, employed, unemployed, educated, uneducated. . . . Furthermore, they help define and explain four major groupings ranging all the way from a small group of really satisfied blacks to an even smaller group of radical revolutionaries. For most blacks, however, the choice swings between moderate hope and moderate pessimism about the future. Yankelovich identifies: 1) *The satisfieds*: Only about 10 percent of blacks are firmly committed to the American way of life, strongly favor integration and are firmly opposed to violence. They include primarily older, less well-educated and low-income blacks. 2) *The optimistic moderates*: Four out of ten blacks are as concerned as other blacks about the inequities of present society but still view the American system as basically sound and able to resolve these problems. They hope for change within the system, support integration and are opposed to violence. 3) *The troubled and unhopeful*: This is the single largest sector—43 percent—in the black community. These are blacks beginning to despair of the system but who are not yet certain about how to change it or resolve the problems. Essentially tolerant of, but still unsure about, violence and black separatism, they include many young men and women, since 37 percent are under 30. Half have less than a high school education. 4) *The Radicals*: This is the smallest group with a membership of only 7 percent. Also the most militant and extremist, they are almost totally dissatisfied with the American system and see violence and/or separatism as a viable means of resolving the black community's problems. About 52 percent are under 30 years of age; 28 percent have attended college; 30 percent are earning more than $10,000. As a result of its composition, the Radical group probably has disproportionate influence and impact.

Blacks Support "Protestant Ethic"

When Yankelovich examines personal life style values in black America he finds that support for traditional "Protestant Ethic" values runs deep within the black community. Blacks share with other Americans belief in the family as a social unit, in economic self-sufficiency, in the importance of planning and in personal integrity. Blacks also tend to be even more conformist than other Americans. They lag behind only in their stress on achievement and advancement—with their values in this instance, undoubtedly reflecting their perception of social realities. On other more personal values, blacks indicate an even stronger sense of commitment than other people. These include such personal fulfillment values as the importance of sophistication and cultivation, physical attractiveness, and self-improvement. Similarly, blacks express even greater concern than other Americans about the importance of self-expression and an enriched quality of life. . . .

FOR THOUGHT:

To what degree do the attitudes of the black Americans questioned in this poll reflect the ideas of the black leaders you have been reading?

103 THE UNCERTAIN QUEST FOR EQUALITY

HISTORICAL ESSAY

▶What difference might it make if all of us thought of prejudice and discrimination as problems of the white majority rather than problems produced by the presence of minority groups?

Although the terms "black" or "Negro" refer to a member of one of the three major races, in the United States, they are often applied to people of mixed racial background who have any African ancestry.

In 1944 a distinguished Swedish economist, Gunnar Myrdal, wrote a book about blacks and whites in the United States called *An American Dilemma*. Whites had created a deep dilemma, Myrdal thought, by denying equality to blacks while they themselves preached equality as a central part of the American democratic system. Thus eighty years after the end of slavery, blacks remained victims of prejudice, limited opportunity, poverty, and segregation in the midst of the world's greatest democracy. At the same time, whites were troubled by the contradiction between their principles and their practices.

Even in 1944, however, the groundwork for change had been established. Industrialization and urbanization had shifted blacks out of the rural South. Political action by both whites and blacks had begun to make an impact on discrimination. Since World War II, the contest between those who have sought to end the dilemma and those who have tried to evade it has created a dramatic story. Part of that story has appeared in the first three readings in this chapter. Before resuming the account of the black experience, however, let us consider the experiences of four other groups. Each experience will give perspective to the story of the others.

Four Groups Battle Discrimination

The first of these groups is the one that became a minority first: the original native Americans. Whites herded most Indians who survived the white occupation of the country into reservations. There they lived almost entirely separate from the rest of American society. Their lands were often cramped and infertile. However, they remained apart in order to preserve tribal life. But despite tribalism, native

Americans suffered a sharp cultural shock. Hunting and fishing were the basis of many Indian cultures. Now the restrictions of reservation life made it virtually impossible to live by hunting and fishing. Many Indians on reservations came to depend increasingly on government rations of food and clothing to keep alive. Both tribal and individual morale declined sharply. Dominant American values, as taught in the white-run schools on the reservations, did little to foster a favorable self-concept among Indian youth. Children learned, in effect, that whites regarded them and their traditional cultures as inferior. In order to adjust to the world outside they had to abandon tribal culture completely. American society has still not solved the problem of the separateness of Indian life.

Americans from Spanish-speaking countries constitute a loosely related set of minority groups. Their experiences have been influenced both by length of residence in the United States and by ethnic identity. The original Indian population of Mexico and the West Indies became intermixed with both Spanish and African peoples. The earliest Spanish-speaking peoples in the American Southwest came from this mixed group. They increased in number gradually, then rapidly. Since 1924, when large-scale European immigration to the United States was cut off, Mexico has been the chief source of immigrants to this country. More than 5 million Mexican-Americans now live in the United States, most of them in the Southwest and the West.

Most Mexican immigrants have been agricultural workers. They encountered widespread prejudice and discrimination from native-born Americans. They also suffered from educational handicaps and lacked political power. Yet they have begun to achieve a higher economic, social, and political place fairly rapidly in recent years. About 250,000 Mexican-Americans served in the armed forces during World War II. Thus, they took a step towards merging with American society. The election to Congress after World War II of its first Mexican-Americans, Edward Roybal of California and Henry Gonzalez of Texas, suggests growing political participation and strength. School segregation of Mexican-Americans has begun to weaken recently. The conditions of agricultural labor in the Southwest, especially those of the "braceros" who migrated to the United States each year to work at harvesting crops, have been improved. This improvement is due partly to government action and also to the efforts of such organizations as the Alianza Hispana-Americana.

In 1970, more than 1,500,000 Puerto Ricans lived in the continental United States. Most of them came to the mainland after World War II. All Puerto Ricans are American citizens. But the Spanish-speaking arrivals constituted a clearly defined minority. They were set off from both white and black native Americans by their language and customs. They concentrated in eastern cities, especially in New York City. There they reached a strength of more than 800,000 in 1970.

About half of the 920,000 Indians in the United States still live on reservations.

Rising resentment about the inadequacy of reservation life and other instances of discrimination led to the formation of the American Indian Movement (AIM) and other protest groups. Indian demonstrators seized and held Wounded Knee, South Dakota, for more than two months during 1973. The town was the site of a notorious massacre of Indians in 1890.

Many Spanish-speaking Americans use the term "chicano" in describing themselves.

One Mexican-American laborer, Cesar Chavez, organized the grape-pickers of California into a union, the United Farm Workers Organizing Committee. It is affiliated with the AFL-CIO. Chavez launched a campaign against those vineyards that did not recognize his union. His boycott won support in the East. And the United Farm Workers spread to cover other agricultural workers.

Herman Badillo, a
Congressman and influential
political leader in New York
City, became one of the
most widely known Puerto
Ricans in the United States
in the early 1970's.

Many Cubans left their
country for the United States
in the 1960's. They were
fleeing the revolution brought
about by Fidel Castro and
his followers. Nearly half a
million Spanish-speaking
people live in and around
Miami, Florida, the principal
center for refugee Cubans.

The best known of the new
women's organizations was
the National Organization for
Women (NOW). It was
founded in 1966.

Puerto Ricans, too, encountered discrimination and segregation. Typically they were poor, lacked skills needed for urban industrial or commercial jobs, and often had little education. Yet in the relatively few years after they became a sizeable minority, Puerto Ricans adapted rapidly to their new circumstances. Like Mexican-Americans, they began to make their political weight felt. And they benefited from activities of their social and religious organizations. Unlike the Indians, both Spanish-speaking groups came from westernized cultures which gave them a base from which to adapt to American society.

The attempts of blacks, Indians, and Spanish-speaking Americans to make the democratic system work in their behalf influenced strongly the activities of another group. Women in American society actually number more than half the population. But traditional discrimination against them, mainly economic and social, gave them grievances similar to those of minorities. In the 1960's women founded a number of organizations dedicated to eliminating discrimination against them. They pushed vigorously for the adoption of an amendment to the Constitution which would guarantee equal rights for women. They also exercised strong influence in getting the federal and some state governments to help women obtain employment opportunities equal to those given to men. Perhaps the movement's greatest success in the early 1970's, however, was less easy to observe. This was the persuasion of an increasing number of men—and women—that real problems of discrimination against women did actually exist.

In some ways, the experiences of these four groups, though different, resembled those of blacks. For example, most Indians and Spanish-speaking Americans and all women were visibly different from the dominant group—males of northern European background. Hence, they could be discriminated against more easily than those who looked like the dominant group. However, none of the four had quite the same problem as blacks. Only blacks carried the visible marks of a past in slavery. It was a past that had been followed by a century of discrimination. In the twentieth century this mistreatment changed for the better. Yet the remains of this deep-rooted prejudice and discrimination increased uncertainty among blacks about the American ideal of assimilation.

The Black Experience and Assimilation

Until recent years, most blacks have probably wanted to assimilate with the white community. The barriers to assimilation did not at first seem to be of major importance. In the late nineteenth and early twentieth centuries, blacks were far more interested in getting equal treatment before the law and winning a chance at jobs and education than in gaining full acceptance by whites. The issue of assimilation was not then important. And blacks started from a position of severe disadvantage. So black leaders sought white aid and accepted it gladly in organizing protest and welfare movements. But they maintained the ideal of integration as a goal.

The industrial training programs of such institutions as Booker T. Washington's Tuskegee Institute depended heavily on the gifts of white philanthropists. Both the NAACP and the National Urban League were joint black-white organizations. Most of the direct-action organizations that grew up after World War II, were also interracial in membership and control when founded.

Racism prevailed in the early years of the twentieth century. More than 100 blacks suffered death by lynching in some years. Between 1900 and World War II, riots aimed at blacks broke out periodically in cities in both South and North. These developments were only the most extreme signs of a prejudice that could be found in almost every aspect of life.

Between the two world wars a minority of blacks emerged as a middle class. They were still largely separate from white society. Their higher education was obtained mainly in predominantly black colleges. Their businesses, usually small, often provided services mainly for blacks. But they acquired the economic power and position which made them leaders of their communities. Black workers were still denied entry by most unions. But they made significant gains during the 1930's when newly organized industrial unions like the United Automobile Workers and the United Steel Workers admitted them as members. State and national politics provided openings for a few black leaders. But in the 1930's civil service jobs provided many more.

Perhaps the greatest opportunities for blacks to establish equality of economic opportunity came in two widely separated areas. The massive public works and welfare programs of the New Deal served in many places to set a minimum to the income of both black and white unemployed. This meant that private employers of labor were obliged to offer them at least a subsistence wage. However, the greatest rewards for a few, in combined money and prestige, came in the fields of sports and entertainment.

Much more substantial gains, however, have come in the years since 1945. Most of the million black Americans serving in World War II were placed in segregated units. After the war, by order of President Harry S Truman, all branches of the armed services eliminated segregation. The success of integration in the services can be judged by both the achievements of the fighting men and the decline in the number of objections to integration.

On the home front, A. Philip Randolph, a union leader, threatened to march on Washington in 1942 to protest job discrimination. President Franklin D. Roosevelt then issued an executive order prohibiting discrimination in industries with government war contracts. After the war, other executive orders and congressional legislation broadened

These organizations included the Congress of Racial Equality (CORE) and the Student Non-Violent Coordinating Committee (SNCC). CORE was originally a local group set up to fight discrimination in Chicago. It was organized by James Farmer on a national level in 1942. SNCC was organized in 1960. It drew its support primarily from college students. Like CORE, it engaged in such direct action protests as "freedom rides" and "sit-ins." After 1966, CORE and SNCC became more militant. They favored the "black power" philosophy of Stokely Carmichael. By 1967, SNCC numbered only a few hundred members.

▶ Should government forbid discrimination in all public organizations such as labor unions? in private organizations such as clubs? Why or why not?

A. Philip Randolph, born in 1889, organized the Brotherhood of Sleeping Car Porters. In 1957, he became a vice-president of the AFL-CIO. He was one of the organizers and principal speakers at the "March on Washington" on August 28, 1963.

685

1

2

The pictures on these two pages show demonstrations on behalf of several minorities. What do these groups have in common? How do they differ from each other?

the guarantees of equal opportunities in employment and in business dealings with the federal government.

Congress took even more significant actions in 1964 and 1965. It adopted laws which guaranteed equal access to public facilities. It also provided for ways to register citizens who were being kept from voting on account of race. The latter law led to the registration of numbers of black voters in some parts of the deep South for the first time in more than half a century. Blacks had been playing an increasingly important part in local and national politics for a long time before then, however. Heavy black support had helped to reelect President Truman in a close election in 1948. And blacks helped elect President John F. Kennedy in a closer election in 1960. In subsequent national elections blacks continued to show overwhelming support for Democratic candidates.

The most striking political advances made by blacks as a group were in those localities where they were either a majority or close to a majority of the population. In the 1960's Newark, New Jersey, Cleveland, Ohio, and Gary, Indiana, elected blacks as mayors. In 1973 Los Angeles, California, and Atlanta, Georgia, followed suit. Blacks also established political control of a few counties in the South. In Fayette County, Mississippi, Charles Evers, brother of the murdered NAACP leader Medgar Evers, became mayor of the town of Fayette. In the 1972 elections, blacks won 1,144 political offices in southern states. This was ten times the number they had held as recently as 1965.

Perhaps the most crucial role in the movement to guarantee equal opportunity fell to the Supreme Court. The Court, led by Chief Justice Earl Warren, rendered literally dozens of decisions striking down segregation laws and upholding legal guarantees of equal rights in the years after 1952. Critics of the Court argued that the judges were making political decisions that properly belonged to legislators. Defenders of the Court argued in return that it was responsible for interpreting the Constitution when constitutional questions were raised. Moreover, they said, the critics were usually defenders of a racial status quo which the Court was not obliged to maintain.

By no means all action taken to secure equality of opportunity came through the federal government. State and local legislatures and agencies throughout the North and West also took a variety of actions to suppress discrimination in the years after World War II. Among the most important laws they passed were ones that forbade discrimination in employment and housing.

Blacks made substantial gains in employment after World War II. This was partly the result of legislation and of increasing acceptance of blacks by whites. But it was also the result of threats of boycotts and other economic and political pressures. The number of black union members rose steadily. They were concentrated in big industrial

688

unions. But they also entered some craft unions that had traditionally barred blacks. For the first time, large businesses and industries began seeking black employees actively. They also began recruiting them to serve in lower management positions. The upper levels were still reserved for whites.

Blacks cracked the wall of segregation in professional baseball, football, basketball, and other sports. They also began to appear in movie, television, and stage roles in parts different from the stereotyped character parts to which they had been restricted. In the field of law and government, blacks made distinguished contributions. The most notable were those of Thurgood Marshall, Edward Brooke, Shirley Chisholm, Constance Baker Motley, and Ralph Bunche. The person who won the greatest international recognition, however, was Martin Luther King, Jr. He was awarded the Nobel Prize for Peace for his efforts to maintain nonviolent processes in seeking equality.

While these notable gains were being made, the question of ultimate assimilation occasionally emerged. The attitudes of many whites made it increasingly clear to blacks that assimilation was an unrealistic goal in the near future. Hence, some blacks turned to the development of all-black organizations. The goals of these organizations often emphasized separatism. Blacks also turned to the development of an identification with African traditions and modern Africans. In the 1920's, Marcus Garvey's Universal Negro Improvement Association drew members by the hundreds of thousands from the black masses.

In the years after World War II, black nationalism and separatism both grew rapidly. They were spurred by the independence achieved by dozens of former European colonies in Africa. The successes of the Southern Christian Leadership Conference, of sit-in demonstrations by black groups to obtain the use of public facilities, and of boycotts to persuade businesses to hire more blacks, helped stimulate the growth of all black movements. Of these one of the most striking all black groups was the Muslim religious organization. Its size was undetermined. But it possessed societies, buildings, and other property in dozens of cities, mostly in the North. The Muslims preached a doctrine of black racism which portrayed whites as creatures of the devil. The assassination of black leaders like King and Medgar Evers strengthened the militancy of blacks engaged in civil rights movements. Such tragic resorts to violence probably weakened the spirit of non-violence so successfully fostered by King and others. They also encouraged blacks in urban ghettos toward violence and destruction of property when riots broke out.

The emergence of black nationalism and separatism puzzled many Americans, including some blacks. This trend seemed to reject the ideal of integration in American life at the very time when blacks were making significant gains toward equality of opportunity. Many persons were also puzzled by the rise of black militancy at the very

In 1947, Jackie Robinson was signed by the Brooklyn Dodgers and became the first black player in the major leagues.

Thurgood Marshall became the first black justice of the Supreme Court. Edward Brooke was elected to the Senate from Massachusetts. Shirley Chisholm was the first black woman elected to the House of Representatives. Constance Baker Motley was the first black woman to become a federal judge. And Ralph Bunche served as Undersecretary of State and then as Undersecretary of the United Nations.

In 1963, one of Elijah Muhammad's followers, Malcolm X, broke from the Nation of Islam and formed the Organization of Afro-American Unity. After his assassination in 1965, he became a hero for many black militants.

time when white cooperation in interracial ventures reached its height. Perhaps one answer to these ironies lies in the depth and extent of black resentment and suspicion. They were always there but seldom were revealed because of the danger of violent repression. Perhaps another answer lies in the deeply felt need of many blacks for a group identity which does not depend in any way on the favor or support of white society. Perhaps black power will become a permanent ideology. On the other hand, strong feelings of racial pride may eventually make genuine assimilation possible among white and black citizens. Each will be proud of his or her heritage and insistent upon his or her full rights in a democratic society. No more vital issue faces modern Americans.

The Present and the Future

STATING THE ISSUE

Many historians refuse to make predictions about the future. They do not believe that history repeats itself. Nor do they believe that history provides adequate guides to what will happen next. Historians, they think, should interpret past events and leave the future to others.

Nor will some historians attempt to write contemporary history. The events of our own day involve all of us. As thinking people, we take sides, get involved in controversies, and become partisan. Hence we lack the sort of historical detachment and perspective which we can gain on events that happened a century or more ago. Without that perspective, some historians argue, people cannot write good history.

On the other hand, no person ever approaches a historical problem from a neutral position. All of us are products of our life experiences. The hypotheses we pose to explain both present and past events grow partly out of these experiences. Our frames of reference also influence the way we interpret data. Historical perspective cannot guarantee neutrality. The argument that we lack historical perspective on present events, other historians argue, should therefore not keep us from examining the history of our own times.

Chapter 27 provides an exercise in writing and learning about contemporary history. It opens with a brief essay about the next twenty-five years. A group of individual and small group activities follow this essay. These activities invite you to write histories of various environmental problems in your community. The final two readings in the chapter—and in this book—contain accounts of the administrations of Lyndon B. Johnson and Richard M. Nixon.

CHAPTER
27

691

1400 1500 1600 1700 1800 1900 2000

1963 President John F. Kennedy is assassinated; Lyndon B. Johnson becomes President
1964 President Johnson announces plans for a "war on poverty"
1964 Office of Economic Opportunity is established
1964 Congress passes Urban Mass Transportation Act providing funds for study of urban transportation problems
1964 Congress passes Civil Rights Act
1965 Congress passes Medicare legislation
1965 President Johnson creates Department of Housing and Urban Development
1965 Civil Rights Act outlaws use of literacy tests to prove qualification for voting
1965 Congress passes Elementary and Secondary Education Act
1965 Immigration Act abolishes use of national origins and quota systems

1966 President Johnson creates Department of Transportation
1965-67 Riots break out in many of the nation's cities
1967-70 Students hold demonstrations on campuses across the country
1968 Martin Luther King is assassinated in Memphis, Tennessee
1968 Senator Robert F. Kennedy is assassinated in Los Angeles, California
1968 Richard M. Nixon becomes President
1972 President Nixon wins re-election
1973 Spiro T. Agnew resigns from the Vice-Presidency
1974 House of Representatives orders impeachment proceedings against President Nixon
1974 Richard M. Nixon resigns; Gerald R. Ford becomes President

104 THE PRESENT AND THE FUTURE

The agriculture revolution marked humankind's first dramatic turning point. The ability to grow food freed people from ceaseless wandering over the face of the earth in pursuit of game or wild plants. It made civilization possible. Scientific knowledge and industrialization began to mark a second great turning point about two or three hundred years ago. In the twentieth century the long-run effects of these two developments is becoming clear. The present era may well be a watershed as significant to humankind as the domestication of plants and animals.

The Twentieth Century as a Turning Point

Twenty-five percent of all people who have ever lived are now alive. In the near future, the percentage may reach fifty. World population now increases at a rate of 2.2 per second, 132 per minute, 190,000 per day, more than 1.3 million per week, about 72 million a year, or about 1 billion in fifteen years. World population reached 1 billion about 1800 and 2 billion about 1930. In 1975, it will probably pass the 4 billion mark. This fantastic explosion of people may well be the most significant development of the late twentieth century.

Knowledge grows at a similar rate. About every ten years, the total amount of knowledge doubles. About a million significant articles now appear each year, in more than fifteen thousand learned journals printed in hundreds of languages. Like population growth, the increase in knowledge will transform the modern world.

During this century, the world's population has shifted from rural to urban areas. Experts predict that by the year 2000, one quarter of the world's population will live in cities whose population exceeds 100,000. By 2050, half the world's people will live in such cities. The 1970 United States census indicated that 73.5 percent of Americans already lived in urban areas. This great transition has become possible because scientific knowledge and mechanization have made farmers so productive. About 5 percent of the population of the United States can now feed the entire nation.

Two sets of figures may help to indicate the growth of technology in the twentieth century. About half of all the energy used by humankind throughout history has been consumed within the last hundred years. And about half of the metals mined from the earth have been removed since about 1910, a period within the lifetime of most grandparents of today's high school students. No wonder that change tumbles upon change with bewildering rapidity.

The twentieth century has seen a host of new developments. Movies, radio, and television have revolutionized communications. Airplanes have linked every corner of the world. New 490-passenger jets fly from New York to London in five hours. Rockets now link the earth to the moon and to planets far in space. Scientists use nuclear energy to power ships and manufacture electricity. The computer is working an electronic revolution in industry. With the discovery of DNA, scientists may be able to control evolution. They have already transplanted hearts and fitted plastic organs into human bodies. The list is endless.

The Next Twenty-Five Years

Prediction is risky, particularly in a world where one scientific advance can change a whole era. Still some trends seem certain. Take the nature of the American people, for example. By the year 2000,

▶Should people limit their families voluntarily to two children in order to curb this population growth? Why do you feel as you do about this question?

▶What responsibility do you feel to recycle materials made of these metals rather than throw them away?

DNA is a complex compound, a nucleic acid. It is the chief material found in chromosomes, the cell bodies that determine the heredity of plants and animals. In 1957, Dr. Arthur Kornberg, an American biochemist, demonstrated that DNA could reproduce outside a cell.

despite a declining birth rate, the present 200 million population will have grown to 300 million. Many Americans will live well beyond retirement age. Medical advances will permit more and more people to reach their eighties. A greater proportion of all these people will live in the western states. They will have moved increasingly to metropolitan areas. They will be incredibly wealthy by the standards of any past society unless inflation and scarce natural and agricultural resources bring on a worldwide depression. Pockets of poverty may still exist, however, particularly among the aged and among minority groups. Wealth and mass communications will probably turn most Americans more and more toward middle-class standards. Whether or not the society moves in the direction of a melting pot or continues to marry primarily within religious and racial groups remains to be seen.

There is no question, however, about the progress of industrialization. The computer is changing mass-production industries into vast, automated complexes of machinery. A few people control entire manufacturing processes. This process will continue. New energy sources and machines will enable a far smaller percentage of the labor force to produce an enormously increased output of goods. GNP will continue to rise. In 1968, it was $860 billion. By 1973, it had risen to $1.1 trillion. What will the nation do with all these goods and services?

The United States may have to use most of them to help people of other lands. The population explosion threatens life itself in much of the non-western world. Outside the United States, the world spends about $80 million each year for population control. The world's military budget totals $154 billion. The United States and the Soviet Union spend two thirds of this amount. Money taken from guns and given to population control might possibly stem the tide of people which seems inevitably destined to overwhelm the world's food resources.

People in developing lands, recently freed from colonial rule, demand a better life. They will not sit quiet and hungry as they watch American families buy their second home, their third automobile, and their fourth television set. They need capital goods and skilled people to help them start the difficult process of economic growth. In the near future, many of them will control nuclear bombs. More can raise enormous armed forces. As the world's richest nation, the United States will face the responsibilities of power in a world where other nations, disturbed by our dominance, will grasp every opportunity to force us to face our human responsibilities, to provoke us, and to make us share our wealth. If we become impatient, we can set off an atomic war. A few strategically placed cobalt bombs can kill everyone on earth.

In January 1968, the North Koreans seized the U.S. Navy ship **Pueblo**. In April 1969, they shot down a Navy reconnaissance plane. Both times the United States protested, but did not retaliate. "The weak can be rash. The powerful must be restrained," said Secretary of State William Rogers.

A cobalt bomb is an atomic bomb to which cobalt, a silver-white metallic element, is added. Scientists have not yet produced a cobalt bomb because it would produce large quantities of radiation fallout.

694

The pictures on this page show ways in which young people can make their opinions known on vital issues such as those discussed in this reading. Which of the activities shown would you feel able to take part in?

In the near future, living and working patterns of Americans will change drastically. The exodus from American farms to cities is almost at an end. But metropolitan areas will continue to grow. And people will become even more crowded. More of them will live in apartments rather than houses. Suburbs will sprawl over what is now open countryside. Traffic congestion, already of frightening proportions, will become infinitely worse. People will have more leisure—the twenty-hour work week seems quite possible twenty-five years hence. Moreover, with the society in such rapid transition, people may hold several different jobs in a lifetime. New machines or new techniques may eliminate the job they originally trained for. Unless they have learned how to learn, and unless education becomes a continuous process extending throughout a lifetime, people in their early thirties may well find themselves unemployable.

Sooner or later, governments must deal with problems like these. Governments can reallocate resources among the great variety of needs in a modern society. Governments can raise enough money for significant economic aid to foreign nations. Governments can make urban life attractive. Governments can develop an educational system which can help a person keep pace with a society in rapid flux. And if government assumes these tasks, the taxpayer must foot the bill.

Citizens may be caught in competition between private and public wants. Americans demand steadily increasing real wages. But if private incomes rise too rapidly, there may not be enough public money to end poverty, make the cities livable, revolutionize education, expand foreign aid enormously, and perform all the other tasks which government must do in an international, urbanized, industrialized society. The cost of providing vital public services may well be reducing private expenditures, or seeing them rise slowly. The battle over which sector of the economy gets what will take place in the political arena. Its outcome may well determine the quality of life for the entire world.

Many of these political battles will focus on problems of the environment. Chapter 11 discussed attitudes toward the environment during the nineteenth century. Americans were then faced with such issues as the disappearance of the wilderness, the destruction of animals such as passenger pigeons, the steady depletion of our soils, and the beginnings of pollution. Today, spurred by fantastic worldwide population growth, environmental problems threaten the very existence of humans on the earth.

The energy crisis of 1973-74 began to make many Americans aware that the world's stock of non-renewable natural resources was limited and would eventually become exhausted. Mass starvation in sub-Saharan Africa and inflation of food prices in the United States has brought the coming worldwide shortage of food into people's awareness. Polluted air and water, and even the crowds of people in parks and on beaches, remind us of the severe environmental problems which we face and which will inevitably grow worse.

The remainder of Reading 104 invites you to investigate some of these environmental problems in your own community. Many of the activities which follow require you to write history, much of it contemporary history. Taken together, the activities could form the basis of a history of your community's environment, its problems, and your attempts to cope with them.

You should select an activity which appeals to you from the list which follows. Some activities are suitable for individual work. In most cases, however, two, three, or more people can work on an activity together. Your teacher will keep a record of who is doing what and arrange to receive your papers and reports.

ACTIVITY 1: FINDING OUT ABOUT RECYCLING CANS AND BOTTLES

In 1973 Americans threw away billions of disposable bottles and billions of disposable cans. Society spends many millions of dollars each year to dispose of these containers. Particularly in urban areas, we are rapidly running out of space to put them. In addition, throwing away cans and bottles wastes precious non-renewable natural resources. They include bauxite from which aluminum is made, iron ore, nickel, and the coal and oil required to make electricity used to manufacture cans and bottles.

This project requires one or more of three related activities involved in the problem of disposable cans and bottles. They are:

A. Keep a record of the number of bottles and cans your family uses in a week. Record glass bottles, aluminum cans, and tin cans separately. You may also wish to record paper milk containers which use up forest products. Then estimate the number of disposable glass, metal, and paper containers which your family uses in a year. Remember that you may drink more beverages in the summer than in the winter. Report in an interesting way, perhaps by an illustrated chart, about the "contribution" your family makes annually to the disposable container problem.

B. Find out how and where to purchase products in containers which can be reused. Make a list of the firms that package or sell products in reusable containers. A trip to a beverage store or dairy store may get this information for you.

C. Make a report about what your town or city does with solid waste. The sanitation department of the city government can provide information. What is its budget? What does it do with the trash? What percentage of trash could be recycled?

ACTIVITY 2: SURVEYING ELECTRIC APPLIANCES IN YOUR HOME

Indirectly, electricity contributes to environmental problems. In many areas, fossil fuels such as coal and oil are used to make electricity. These fuels throw off gases into the air and use up precious nonrenewable natural resources. Many nuclear power plants use water from lakes or rivers to cool installations. Thus, the electricity made in such plants often contributes to thermal pollution.

Most of us can cut down on the amount of electricity we use. For example, many people use frivolous electric appliances such as electric can openers or toothbrushes. We run dishwashers, washing machines, or dryers with part loads. Or we run them at peak use hours (between 5:00 P.M. and 7:00 P.M.). We leave lights on in rooms which are not being used. In the winter, we leave the heat on during the day when some houses are empty. In the summer, we keep air conditioners running when we are not at home or out of a room.

This activity asks you to survey the use of electric appliances in your home. Make a list of all the ways in which your family uses electricity. Perhaps your parents can help you. For each use, chart ways in which you can save power—and reduce the family electric bill. As you make your survey, ask your parents and grandparents—if they are around—how they managed the household chores before some modern appliances were available.

Report the results of your survey in some imaginative way. Some students, for example, may wish to make illustrated charts or bulletin board displays. Try to include some information about what members of your family did before so many electric gadgets came along.

ACTIVITY 3: A REPORT ON WATER POLLUTION

Each community keeps records of the quality of its water and of any problems it may have with water pollution. The water department of your city makes these reports available to the public. The city sanitary engineer will be able to tell you more about your local water supply and its history.

This activity asks you to find out about any water problems which your city now has. Are your supplies adequate? Will they be adequate if water use continues to rise? What does the city do to make sure that water is not polluted? What does the water system cost to users? Have these costs increased in recent years? Who started the water system in your city and when?

You could present a report in a number of interesting ways. You might take photographs of the water system to form the basis of a bulletin board display or poster. You may choose to write a brief history of the water system in your community. Or you may describe a particular crisis in the city's water supply.

ACTIVITY 4: SURVEYING THE WAY THINGS YOU BUY ARE PACKAGED

Packaging costs money and sometimes wastes resources. Much packaging is unnecessary. It has been designed as part of an advertising plan rather than to preserve products or make them better. Some stores prepack products such as meat. Then they place them in a special bag, and then place this bag inside a still larger bag with other purchases. These practices waste millions of trees—the ultimate source of paper in packaging—each year. Using plastic wrap wastes petroleum, the source of many plastics, in a similar way.

This activity asks you to find out about how the merchants your family patronizes package their goods. Find an ingenious way to keep a record of all the packaging that comes into your home in a week. What is the material made of? Is it really necessary? What happens to it after you throw it away? What problems does this solid waste material present to your community? Find an original way to present your findings. Include suggestions about what you and your family can do to reduce the amount of unnecessary packaging. For example, what would happen if every family bought two or three reusable inexpensive string bags, like those commonly used in Europe, instead of accepting paper bags at the supermarket? What did people do before the "packaging revolution" struck American society after World War II?

ACTIVITY 5: LEARNING HOW TO MAKE A COMPOST HEAP

Even people who live in apartments in the city often have use for a little fertile soil for house plants or a roof-top garden. Those of you who have lawns and flower or vegetable gardens need much more good soil. You can make it yourself out of waste organic materials by starting a compost heap.

Compost heaps are made from five kinds of materials: organic wastes, such as leaves or grass clippings; animal wastes, such as fresh or dried manure; soil; lime; and water. Compost heaps may be large or small. Some people make compost in an old trash barrel from which the bottom has been cut out while the sides have been buried a few inches in the soil. Get a book about organic gardening from the library or look up compost in your encyclopedia. Find out how to turn your organic wastes into rich soil. You will make something useful at the same time that you reduce the amount of solid waste in the society.

When you have finished your work, write directions about how to build a compost heap suitable to your family's needs. In your directions, you might tell a little about the history of compost-making in this country and of the organic farming movement of which it is a part. Turn in this report. But save a copy to refresh your memory as you make your own compost heap according to your own directions.

ACTIVITY 6: ORGANIZING A CLEAN-UP CAMPAIGN

Litter mars the beauty of many streams, lakes, vacant lots, and other public areas. Most of this litter is a by-product of our throwaway society. People carelessly discard paper, cans, bottles, and other rubbish rather than dispose of it properly. Only a changed public attitude can solve this problem.

This activity invites you to record an attempt to change this basic public attitude through a clean-up project. First, organize a clean-up campaign, perhaps for a Saturday. Select an area such as a stream, a beach, or a vacant lot. Persuade a number of your friends to pitch in. They should bring containers in which to place the trash they gather. Sometimes you can persuade the city to send a truck to pick up all the litter you collect. Perhaps a parent or the school board will be willing to provide a truck.

You should record the entire activity with your camera. Take pictures of the area before you begin to clean it, of the workers who are doing the cleaning, of the place where you take the trash for disposal, and of the newly cleaned area. Then organize this record into a display. You might write the story of this event for publication in your school newspaper, or in a newspaper in your community.

ACTIVITY 7: A HISTORY OF THE SEWAGE SYSTEM OF YOUR TOWN OR CITY

It might be more interesting than you think. Remember the readings about sewers in the 1880's which appeared in Chapter 18. All communities keep records in the form of reports about their sewers. In many cities, it took public officials decades to get good sewers built. Histories of campaigns for public improvements such as sanitary sewers can make fascinating reading.

Consult the reports of your community's sanitary engineer in the local library or in the appropriate offices in city hall. Then write an account of how the sewers in your community were built. You may choose to narrow your subject, writing an account of sewers in a particular decade or describing one campaign to get an adequate sewage treatment plant built. You may be able to find photographs to illustrate your history.

ACTIVITY 8: A SURVEY ABOUT ATTITUDES TOWARD POPULATION GROWTH

The rapid growth of population throughout the world presents a serious long-run threat to the future of humankind. World population now doubles in about thirty-five years. We must either curb this runaway growth. Or we must face the prospect of mass starvation and the utter depletion of stocks of non-renewable natural resources, such as petroleum. In recent years, population growth in the United States has slowed down. But our population is still increasing. And our attitudes and activities in the field of population control still influence people in other nations.

In this activity you will try to find out what attitudes your classmates and their parents have toward population growth. First, draw up a questionnaire containing about ten questions, each with three possible answers. Here is an example of an introduction to such a questionnaire and a couple of questions:

A Questionnaire About Population Growth

This questionnaire has been written by members of a social studies class at West High School. We are trying to find out what the attitudes of high school students and their parents are toward controlling population growth throughout the world. Will you please take a few moments to complete this questionnaire? Your replies will be kept in confidence. After each statement on the questionnaire, check the space under Agree, Disagree, or Don't Know which most clearly expresses your feelings about the statement.

1. Every family should voluntarily limit itself to two children.

2. The United States should not export food to countries with rapidly growing populations even if people are starving there.

Agree   Disagree   Don't Know

Have all members of the class fill in the questionnaire. Then ask the members to have their parents fill it in and return it to you. Compile the answers to the questions by all respondents, students only, and parents only. Present your results in an interesting way, perhaps in a line graph. Beneath your graph, you may want to write one or more paragraphs hypothesizing about any differences you may find in attitudes between the two generations of respondents.

ACTIVITY 9: MAPPING RECREATIONAL AREAS IN YOUR COMMUNITY

Every community has a number of public recreational areas such as parks, mini-parks, or playgrounds. They add to the quality of life by providing open spaces where people can gather to play, picnic, or enjoy themselves in some other way. Yet many of us do not know where all these areas are or how they came into being.

This activity asks you to map the major recreational areas of your community, or of some part of it. Then you will write a brief history of one recreational area you identify. Get a map of your community from a service station. Either on this map or on an outline map traced from it, show all of the recreational areas in some distinctive way. You may wish to include a key with your map. Then arrange an interview with the recreational director of your community or with his or her representative. Tell this person that you want to write a brief history of one park. Find out where to go for information. Complete your project by writing a history in a few hundred words.

ACTIVITY 10: MAKING A COLLAGE, POSTER, OR SCRAP-BOOK ABOUT ENVIRONMENTAL STORIES

Newspapers and magazines are full of stories about the environment. For this activity, cut the environment related stories from your local newspapers and from national magazines for a week or two. Then present your clippings creatively, perhaps in a collage, a poster, or a scrapbook. You may find some creative way to group your stories so that they make up a slice of the history of the environment in your area.

ACTIVITY 11: COLLECTING ADVERTISEMENTS ABOUT THE ENVIRONMENT

Many companies now run advertisements in magazines or newspapers about their contributions to a good environment. This activity requires you to collect a number of these ads from magazines which you can find at home or in the homes of friends. Cut them out and find out what they have in common. Then think of an interesting way to present them, perhaps in a collage, poster, or scrapbook.

Choose the publication in which you found the most ads. Go to the library and look through an issue of that publication five years ago and one ten years ago. Make a record of the number of environmental ads you found during those years to compare to the current issue which you used. In a paragraph or so, tell what you found out and hypothesize about the cause of these developments.

ACTIVITY 12: KEEPING A RECORD OF AUTOMOBILE USE

Your family must agree to cooperate in this activity. It involves keeping a complete record of the uses of your family's automobile or automobiles for an entire week. Keep a pad of paper in the car. On the pad all drivers must agree to keep a log in the same way that a captain keeps a log of happenings on shipboard. Enter on the log every trip you make, the destination, the purpose of the trip, the number of passengers, and the number of miles traveled. Keep a record of how much gasoline you use during the week and the cost of this fuel. Then find a way to present this information. You may wish to organize it by family member, by the purposes for which the car was used, or in some other way. You could then present the information in a table or chart.

Beneath your table or chart, indicate how you could have lived your life while reducing the use of the automobile. What trips were least necessary? Could several people rather than one have used the car on a particular trip? Were alternative means of transportation available? Or could people have walked or used a bicycle on some occasions? The energy crisis will inevitably get worse. This exercise may reveal one of the causes of the shortage of petroleum and suggest a cure or two.

ACTIVITY 13: CHARTING THE POPULATION OF YOUR COMMUNITY

The United States Census Bureau gathers figures on the population of each community every ten years. You can find these figures in your local public library. This activity asks you to go to the library, get the figures for your community's population at each census from 1900 through 1970, and present them in a chart. The geographic boundaries of your community may have changed during these seventy years. Your librarian can help you to find out if this development took place. If it did, you must find a way to indicate geographical changes on your chart.

Beneath the chart, write a summary of the population changes in your community. If you live in a metropolitan area, you may find that most population growth has taken place in the suburbs rather than in the central city. Indicate such findings in your paragraph. You may also wish to speculate about what your part of the world will look like if population growth there goes on in the future at the rate it has taken place in recent decades.

ACTIVITY 14: A HISTORY OF THE ENERGY CRISIS OF THE EARLY 1970'S

Environmentalists had known for years that the nation would sooner or later face a severe energy crisis. The general public, however, seemed unaware of the problem. Then, in 1973, war broke out between Israel and the Arab states. In order to discourage the United States from helping Israel, the Arabs, who control about half of the world's known oil resources, placed an embargo on petroleum exports to the United States. This embargo touched off an energy crisis which lasted for most of a year.

This activity asks you to write a report of that incident. Find out through magazine articles or books how much petroleum Americans consumed. Why did the embargo from the Arab nations, from which we bought only a small proportion of our petroleum, produce such a crisis? What did the American government do? How did Americans react to the crisis? What role did the world petroleum industry play in the crisis? What impact did the crisis have on Americans? What caused it to end? Write your report in the form of a historical essay.

ACTIVITY 15: A SOUND-SLIDE SHOW ABOUT AN ENVIRON-MENTAL TOPIC

This activity requires you to take photographs, make a recording on a tape recorder, and synchronize the slides with the recording for a presentation. Choose an interesting environmental topic. You may want to concentrate on a particularly flagrant act of pollution. On the other hand, you may want to show a particularly attractive aspect of your local environment.

Plan carefully what you want to say and what pictures you will need. Then shoot the pictures as you develop a script. Record the script. And indicate by inserting numbers at the appropriate places when you wish to change pictures. Then present the slide tape show to your classmates.

ACTIVITY 16: THE ADVANTAGES AND DISADVANTAGES OF STRIP MINING

Strip mining takes place when huge machines strip earth from the surface to expose minerals which are then mined. Sometimes mining companies do not fill in the holes they have dug. These holes often fill up with water which becomes polluted with acid and minerals. Many states require that companies fill in abandoned strip mines and replant the land, a procedure which raises costs.

Experimental strip mines have recently been opened in the West to obtain petroleum from deposits of shale rock. After the oil has been extracted, processed shale swells in volume and cannot fit into the area from which it came. Hence, it causes an environmental problem at the same time that shale mining helps to relieve the energy crisis.

This activity invites you to make a report about strip mining. You may want to narrow the topic—only coal, or only other minerals, or only petroleum. You may choose to narrow the subject in another way. You can tell the story of one successful effort to combat pollution caused by strip mining or the story of one case of pollution. You may be able to find pictures from which you can make a bulletin board display or a poster. If not, you may choose to write a report. In either case, be sure to tell how strip mining began, what benefits it offers, and what environmental problems result. Pay particular attention to any strip mining which goes on near your home.

ACTIVITY 17: AN ACCOUNT OF A LOCAL ENVIRONMENTAL ORGANIZATION

Almost every town or city has one or more environmental organizations. Some of them are branches of national organizations such as the Sierra Club or Friends of the Earth. Others are local groups such as the Western Pennsylvania Conservancy or the Berkeley (California) Ecology Action. Many of these groups have a fascinating history.

Get in touch with officers or members of one of these groups and arrange for an interview. Find out how the group got started, who belongs to it, what its aims are, and what it has done in the past. Perhaps you will be able to attend a meeting. Then present this history in an interesting way. You might edit interviews recorded on a tape recorder, write a brief history, or make a bulletin board display if the group can provide photographs. Be sure to tell your readers how to join the organization or how to participate in its projects.

ACTIVITY 18: A SURVEY OF BILLBOARDS

This activity requires you to have a camera and film. Use them to take pictures of billboards in your neighborhood. Make a display of these pictures to show how they either do or do not contribute to the beauty of their surroundings. What are they for? Do you think that they function well? Should society control the use of billboards in any way?

Then arrange an interview with a person who knows something about billboards. You can find references to outdoor advertising companies in the yellow pages of most telephone directories. Most city governments have an official who must enforce any rules which may exist for billboards. In addition, some environmental organizations have members who have taken a particular interest in billboards and their effect on the environment. From one or more of these people, find out what you can about billboards. Then combine the pictures and your information in a report, perhaps in the form of a collage, a bulletin board display, a poster, or a sound slide show.

ACTIVITY 19: A HISTORY OF A LOCAL RECREATIONAL AREA

Many recreational areas have fascinating histories. The system of national parks extends throughout the nation. Every state has established a number of state parks. And most towns, cities, and counties have parks, some of which are very old.

This activity asks you to write a brief history, or present information in a visual form, about one of these areas. When was it set aside as a park? Who founded it, and why? Park officials will be happy to help you find this information. Most of them are required by law

These pictures are typical of the kinds of photographs that appeared in American newspapers and magazines during the second Johnson administration. Why might they alarm typical Americans?

to turn in annual reports which you can obtain. You may wish to make a visual display with pictures provided by park officials or with pictures you take yourself.

ACTIVITY 20: REPORTING ABOUT WATER USE IN YOUR CITY

How much water does your community use in a year? Where does this water come from? What does your community do to assure a clean and sanitary supply of water? Who uses the water, and for what purposes?

This activity invites you to answer these and other questions about your community's water system. You might begin by consulting reports from your water department. They can be found in the public library or in the appropriate city department. Then develop an imaginative way to present the information you have found. You might photograph every step in the process of getting water from its original source in a lake, stream, or wells to its disposal through the sewer system. These pictures could make the basis of an excellent display or poster. As an alternative you might simply write a report about the water system. Those of you who choose to write reports might focus on one or two key events in the history of the water system of your city.

105 JOHNSON'S SECOND TERM

HISTORICAL ESSAY

Many of the trends which seem likely to dominate the next twenty-five years became noticeable during Lyndon B. Johnson's two terms. Chapters 25 and 26 touched upon various events during the Johnson administration. The following analysis traces these events. And it explains others which have not been mentioned.

President Kennedy had worked hard to combat poverty and to bring justice to America's minorities. But Congress had balked. His death, Johnson's ability to work with Congress, and a sweeping electoral victory in 1964 produced new legislation. Johnson sponsored a series of measures in the tradition of Roosevelt's Second New Deal. The Eighty-Ninth Congress passed more reform and welfare legislation than any Congress in the previous thirty years.

During Johnson's first term, a tax cut helped maintain spending. This, in turn reduced unemployment and increased GNP, which grew from $681 billion in 1965 to $860 billion in 1968. Through the 1960's, this growth rate averaged more than 5 percent a year. It was one of the highest in American history and in the contemporary world. This growth widened the gap between the wealth of a typical American and of the poverty-stricken citizens of developing nations.

▶ Should we try to narrow this gap? Why?

Soon after assuming office, Johnson launched a War on Poverty. The Economic Opportunity Bill set up the Office of Economic Opportunity. It sponsored activities to benefit America's poor. The OEO developed the Job Corps. This agency set up training programs for young people who had been unable to find jobs in modern industry. It also organized programs such as Head Start, Upward Bound, VISTA, and the Neighborhood Youth Corps. However, bills to assist the poor in the Appalachian region, to set up health insurance for the aged, and to increase social security benefits failed to pass Congress.

The Urban Mass Transportation Act (1964) appropriated $375 million to study ways to improve mass transportation. Urban areas had been increasingly choked with traffic. Workers and shoppers drove automobiles into central cities rather than rely upon inadequate public transportation. With cities increasing both in number and size, this legislation clearly looked to the future.

Head Start, composed of professional teachers and volunteer aids, sought to broaden the experiences of preschool children from low-income families and prepare them for formal schooling. Volunteers in Service to America (VISTA) was often referred to as the Domestic Peace Corps. Men and women over 18 lived and worked in poor communities throughout the country. The Neighborhood Youth Corps was sponsored by local sanitation departments. Young residents were employed to clean up their neighborhoods. Many of the programs described here were phased out by the Nixon administration.

Finally, Congress passed a Civil Rights Act in June 1964. The act required identical voting requirements for whites and blacks. It prohibited discrimination in most public accommodations. It gave the attorney general powers to speed school desegregation. It assisted school districts that were desegregating. And it prohibited discrimination in employment in firms whose products entered interstate commerce. Some states and some private citizens continued to drag their feet. But the new law steadily added to the rights enjoyed by black citizens.

In 1964, Johnson soundly defeated Senator Barry Goldwater, the Republican nominee for President. The election swept Democratic senators and representatives into office with Johnson. He faced fewer conservative opponents in Congress than any President since the mid-1930's.

The Eighty-Ninth Congress passed a number of measures to aid the aged and the poor. Medicare, a health plan for people over sixty-five, finally got through Congress (1965). It had been rejected there frequently since World War II. Amendments to the Social Security Act provided larger pensions and extended coverage to millions of additional workers. Amendments to the Fair Labor Standards Act raised the minimum wage to $1.40 in 1967 and to $1.60 a year later. It also extended coverage to 8 million additional persons. In 1965, the War on Poverty received an appropriation of $1.5 billion, twice as much as the year before. Congress also passed a bill appropriating $1.1 billion to improve economic conditions in Appalachia. It is one of the nations most depressed areas.

▶ Should the government set minimum wages at all? Or, should we let the market set wages?

708

To make the cities more livable, Johnson created the Department of Housing and Urban Development. In 1966, he created another cabinet position, the Department of Transportation. It was authorized to attack the vital urban problem of transportation. The Demonstration Cities Act and the Metropolitan Development Act were passed in 1966. They provided federal funds to plan and develop model neighborhoods in some eighty cities across the nation. However, urban housing continued to deteriorate faster than society could clear slums and erect modern apartments.

Several measures helped to reform American education. The Elementary and Secondary Education Act appropriated $1.3 billion for a wide variety of programs in education. These programs were focused on improved teacher training, funds for books and equipment, and similar goals. The Higher Education Act provided scholarships for college students and money for books and laboratories. It also established the National Teacher Corps to prepare teachers for substandard schools. The Cold War GI Bill offered financial support to veterans who had served for more than six months in the armed services since 1955. The original GI Bill, passed during World War II, had expired then. Finally, Congress established the National Foundation of Arts and Humanities.

Two measures affected civil rights. The Voting Rights Act of 1965 removed barriers to black voting, particularly literacy tests. In addition, the Immigration Act of 1965 abolished both the national origins and the quota systems which had been in force since the 1920's. A new annual ceiling on immigration—120,000 from the Western Hemisphere, and 170,000 from elsewhere—went into effect.

Finally, Congress passed a number of minor measures which had to do with safety or with the pollution of the environment. A Truth-in-Packaging Act required manufacturers to state what their products contained. The Motor Safety Vehicle Act established safety standards for new cars. Highway beautification projects, supported strongly by Mrs. Johnson, and increased programs to prevent air and water pollution, made a start in these directions.

This significant legislative spurt ended in 1966. The Republicans made a comeback in Congress in the off-year elections. They gained forty-seven seats in the House and three in the Senate. Perhaps more important, however, were the influence of the Vietnamese war, the racial troubles which haunted American cities, and revolts by young people, particularly on college campuses. These issues divided American society more deeply than anything else since the 1930's.

Vietnam; The Black Revolt; The Student Protests

In 1964, about 25,000 American soldiers served in Vietnam. By 1968, this number had increased to more than a half million. American

President Johnson appointed Robert C. Weaver Secretary of the Department of Housing and Urban Development. He became the first black to hold a cabinet position.

Veterans serving after January 31, 1955, became eligible for benefits under the 1966 act. All who have served at least 180 days and received an honorable discharge are eligible for such benefits as education loans up to $17,500 and $100 a month grants for veterans without dependents.

The National Foundation of Arts and Humanities assists individuals, states, and non-profit organizations engaged in artistic endeavors. It also encourages training and research in the humanities by a program of fellowships and grants.

battle deaths rose steadily—1,728 in 1965; 6,053 in 1966; 11,048 in 1967; 14,592 in 1968. During 1967, the government spent about $67.5 billion on defense, largely on Vietnam. During 1968, it spent $80.5 billion. Little could be done about domestic issues so long as the war drained the attention, the energy, and the money of the American people. Toward the end of the Johnson period, federal spending decreased in most non-military areas.

The Kennedy administration had escalated the Vietnam war. Early in 1965 after the election was over, Johnson sent American bombers over North Vietnam in response to North Vietnamese ground raids. Although no one knew it at the time, the war was on—and it was very hot. During the next few months, the U.S. government mounted increasing air attacks. It sent more troops to Vietnam. And it began to take over more and more of the fighting.

The conflict between Doves and Hawks escalated in turn. At first a minority, the Doves steadily increased in number and influence. By late 1967, polls revealed that the majority of Americans considered the Vietnamese war a mistake. The Hawks lost ground when predictions of success from military leaders consistently proved false. The so-called Tet offensive, which began on January 31, 1968, proved that the Viet-Cong and their allies could launch attacks under the noses of American troops. This offensive brought the Vietnamese issue to a head.

As Chapter 26 has indicated, the momentum of the movement for black rights picked up steadily after World War II. Congress passed five Civil Rights Acts between 1957 and 1968. Blacks and whites worked closely together to obtain most of this legislation. They also organized the sit-ins and protest marches which dramatized the cause of black citizens. But in the 1960's, the black movement changed steadily toward a new emphasis on black power and black separatism. Black leaders more than forty years old had grown up in integrated organizations such as the NAACP and the Urban League. The younger generation, impatient of gradualism, began to found militant all-black organizations. They led the civil disturbances which swept the nation, beginning with the Watts riot in Los Angeles in 1965. During the next three years, riots broke out in dozens of cities, particularly after the murder of the Rev. Martin Luther King, Jr. in April 1968. The change in the black revolution, like the war in Vietnam, deeply divided the American people.

So did campus revolts. Throughout the 1950's, critics complained that college students wanted only a steady job, a suburban home, and future security. The few "beatniks" who opposed this complacent attitude were vastly outnumbered. But the 1960's saw a sharp generational conflict spring up. "You can't trust anyone over thirty," one student protestor proclaimed. The alienation represented by this slogan took both passive and active forms.

The Communist offensive was launched during the cease-fire called during the lunar New Year (Tet). During the offensive, an estimated 14,000 South Vietnamese soldiers and 13,000 civilians were killed or wounded. Two thousand Americans were killed. And an estimated 50,000 Communist troops were killed.

After the riots of 1965, President Johnson appointed an Advisory Commission on Civil Disorders. It was headed by Governor Otto Kerner of Illinois and Mayor John Lindsay of New York. The two black members of the group were Roy Wilkins, head of the NAACP, and Senator Edward Brooke of Massachusetts. The Commission, or Kerner Report, was issued in March 1968. It stated that the riots were not the result of a conspiracy but resulted from urban conditions caused by "white racism." The overall conclusion was that "our nation is moving toward two societies, one black, one white—separated and unequal."

The passive resisters often became hippies. They dropped out of "straight" society. And they made their way to hippie colonies such as those in the Haight-Ashbury district of San Francisco or New York City's East Village. But some of the activists were determined to destroy the society. Led by militants organized in the Students for a Democratic Society (SDS), they began to occupy college buildings and make demands of college presidents and deans. Turned off by the Vietnam war and by the conflicts over civil rights, they were convinced that American society was not worth saving. By 1967, some SDS leaders counseled violence. Their activities at Berkeley, Columbia, Harvard, and many other universities alarmed many Americans. Thousands of other students joined campus revolts. They acted partly in opposition to tactics by police against students and partly because America's universities had many abuses which had been ignored by trustees, administrators, and faculty members alike.

These developments—the war, the black revolt, and the campus uprisings—disturbed the body politic. In November 1967, Senator Eugene McCarthy of Minnesota announced that he would seek the Democratic nomination for President. He concentrated on opposition to the war as a campaign issue. Most voters refused to take his candidacy seriously. But he won the Democratic primary in New Hampshire in March, about five weeks after the Tet offensive had begun. Soon afterward, Senator Robert F. Kennedy of New York, brother of the late President, declared himself a candidate.

Two weeks later, Lyndon Johnson announced that he would halt bombing in North Vietnam and start movements for peace talks. In order to separate these peace moves from partisan politics, Johnson announced that he would not be a candidate for another term. Four days later, an assassin killed Martin Luther King, Jr. in Memphis, Tennessee. Riots swept through black ghettos all over the country. Shortly afterward, Vice-President Hubert H. Humphrey announced his candidacy. Then on June 4, after winning the California primary, Robert Kennedy was assassinated in Los Angeles. During this period, riots prompted by a student revolt broke out at Columbia University. The national consensus of 1966 had burst.

Richard M. Nixon moved steadily toward nomination by the Republicans. He was opposed by such liberals as Governors George Romney of Michigan and Nelson Rockefeller of New York, and by conservatives such as California's Governor Ronald Reagan. Nixon won the Republican nomination easily and chose Maryland's little-known governor, Spiro T. Agnew, as his running mate. In the South, ex-Governor George Wallace of Alabama started a third party movement. An avowed conservative, he promised to shoot looters and to suppress student rebels with clubs. He chose retired Air Force General Curtis LeMay as his Vice-Presidential candidate. In the meantime, the Democrats had nominated Humphrey with Maine's Senator Edmund S. Muskie

Hippies are young people, predominantly white, who have rejected the values and rewards of an affluent middle-class society. Although alienated by the work ethic, which often demands a 9-5 routine, many hippies will work on projects that do not violate their ideals. Several groups are known for their community activities. These activities include organizing schools, communes, camps, and neighborhood work details.

Martin Luther King's assassin, James Earl Ray, was tried, found guilty, and sentenced to life imprisonment.

Robert Kennedy's murderer, Sirhan Sirhan, was found guilty and sentenced to the death penalty. This sentence was later changed to life imprisonment.

711

filling out the ticket. But bitter debate at the Democratic Convention and the activities of Chicago police against student protesters provoked a cry of dissatisfaction.

Polls indicated that Nixon began the campaign with a generous lead. But he lost ground steadily. The vote was unusually close. Nixon polled only about a third of a million plurality in a total vote of 71 million. And the Democrats retained control of both the House and the Senate. With no clear mandate from the voters and with an opposing party in control of Congress, Nixon entered office with severe handicaps.

106 The Nixon Administrations and the Constitutional Crisis

HISTORICAL ESSAY

At 11:30 A.M. on Friday, August 9, 1974, Secretary of State Henry Kissinger received a short, formal letter. It said: "Dear Mr. Secretary: I hereby resign the office of the President of the United States. Sincerely, Richard Nixon." This single sentence brought to a dramatic conclusion the most serious crisis in the history of the American Presidency. This crisis had divided the American people and occupied much of their leaders' time for two years. But it ended with the government intact and with governmental institutions stronger than ever. Gerald R. Ford made the point well when he was sworn in as President to succeed Mr. Nixon. He said: ". . . our long nightmare is over. Our Constitution works. Our great republic is a government of laws, not men."

The people of the United States solved their constitutional crisis slowly, painfully, and in public. Democracies work that way. The deposing of Premier Nikita S. Khrushchev by a group of Soviet leaders in 1964 is a dramatic contrast to the way in which our democratic government functions. In October 1964 Khrushchev was vacationing at a Black Sea resort. In Moscow, leading members of the Communist party held a meeting without Khrushchev's knowledge. Two nights later, they announced that Khrushchev had resigned "at his own request." He returned to Moscow where he was placed under house arrest. Then he became a pensioner at $600 a month. Only a handful of people meeting in secret took part in this decision. Soviet media universally praised the development. The Central Committee of the Communist party endorsed it unanimously. To this day, no one outside the small group of powerful decision-makers knows the full story of what happened. Thus does a government of people—not of laws replace its political leaders.

What was Richard M. Nixon like? And what did he finally do that forced him—the 37th President of the United States—to resign his high office? The answer to the first question lies in Nixon's character. The answer to the second involves a series of actions which violated Article 2, Section 4 of the Constitution: "The President, Vice-President, and all civil officers of the United States, shall be removed from office on impeachment for, and conviction of, treason, bribery, or other high crimes and misdemeanors."

Nixon's personal characteristics both won and lost the Presidency for him. He was bright, graduating near the top of his class from high school, college, and the Duke University Law School. He was ambitious and hardworking, putting in long hours at whatever he did. Early in life, he showed a knack for politics by winning offices in high school, college, and law school. But with this political talent went a certain ruthlessness. He sometimes used questionable means to reach his goals. He was often described as secretive, suspicious, and a "loner" who surrounded himself with people of similar characteristics. He saw criticism as part of a plot aimed at him. He responded to it by "toughing it out" or "stonewalling" instead of making constructive responses.

For example, Nixon went out for football faithfully while in college although he always sat on the bench.

At the beginning of his political career, Nixon served two terms in the House of Representatives. In his first campaign, he charged that his opponent, Congressman Jerry Voorhees, had Communist support. The facts did not support this accusation. He used similar tactics against Helen Gahagan Douglas when he ran for and won a seat in the Senate in 1950. Nixon won national recognition as a member of a congressional committee investigating charges that Alger Hiss, a former state department official, had been a Communist during the 1930's. In 1952, Dwight Eisenhower chose Nixon as his Vice-Presidential running mate. Nixon held that office for eight years, spending much time abroad as an envoy for the President. He was defeated by John F. Kennedy in a race for the Presidency in 1960. In 1968, however, he won the Presidency in a close election against Hubert H. Humphrey. He chose a little-known Maryland politician, Spiro T. Agnew, as his running mate.

Nixon called Mrs. Douglas "the pink lady" although she had no Communist connections.

Political parties customarily nominate for Vice-President a person hand-picked by the Presidential candidate. This practice has come under sharp criticism.

Foreign affairs dominated Nixon's first term. Chapter 25 discussed the major events in detail: withdrawal from Vietnam, détente with both the People's Republic of China and the Soviet Union, and the efforts to bring peace between Israel and the Arab states. Henry H. Kissinger, first as a Presidential adviser and then as Secretary of State, played a key role in these events. But President Nixon had appointed him and supported his work. Hence, he deserves credit for his administration's diplomatic successes.

Because of the success and popularity of Nixon's foreign policy,

713

Robert Pryor

The Boston Globe

EQUAL·JUSTICE·UNDER·LAW·EXCEPT

EXECUTIVE PRIVILEGE

THE ADMINISTRATION OF PRESIDENT FORD

I believe that truth is the glue that holds government together

G.R.F.

How has each cartoonist interpreted an event in the Watergate affair and its aftermath?

715

'NEW BOOK'

most observers gave the Democrats little chance of winning the Presidency in the 1972 election. Their candidate, Senator George McGovern, was not well known and seemed too liberal for many voters. The polls consistently showed Nixon well ahead. In November, Nixon carried every state except Massachusetts, winning 60 percent of the total votes cast. It was this campaign, however, that involved the Watergate break-in and led to the resignation of President Nixon two years later.

Separate from the regular Republican campaign organization, President Nixon had organized the Committee for the Re-Election of the President (CRP). Almost a year before the election, members of the CRP had begun to plan an "intelligence campaign" aimed at the Democrats. On May 27, 1972, men hired by this group tapped the telephones of two officials of the Democratic National Committee. This committee had its offices in the Watergate apartment complex in Washington, D.C. Telephone messages recorded from the tapped wire were passed on to John Mitchell, Nixon's Attorney General and eventual campaign manager.

Then on June 17, 1972, the police arrested five men in the offices of the Democratic National Committee. Evidence linked these men to the CRP which had paid them through a former CIA agent named E. Howard Hunt. In a trial before Judge John J. Sirica in January 1973, Hunt and four of the burglars pleaded guilty. Hunt told reporters that no higher-ups were involved. But they were. Eventually, John Mitchell; two of Nixon's appointed Presidential assistants, H.R. Haldeman and John Erlichman; President Nixon himself; and others would be shown to have known about the break-in and to have been involved in attempts to cover it up.

But the term Watergate came to mean far more than the break-in of Democratic party headquarters. During the two years after the break-in, reporters and public officials used the term to describe a series of illegal or immoral acts involving President Nixon and his associates. Among many others, they included:

—the burglary of the office of a psychiatrist who had treated Dr. Daniel Ellsberg, the man who had released files of secret papers about Vietnam;

—illegal donations to the CRP by a number of large corporations, sometimes in return for favors from the administration;

—attempts by President Nixon to have the Internal Revenue Service investigate tax returns of people who opposed his policies;

—refusal by President Nixon to release voluntarily to a grand jury, the special prosecutor for Watergate matters, the Senate Committee on Campaign Activities, or the House Judiciary Committee tape recordings containing evidence about Watergate;

—revelations that President Nixon had made false claims on his income tax returns and owed $432,000 in back taxes.

Information about these issues and many others came to light over a period of two years. Three institutions inside the government—the courts, the Senate, and the House—and two groups outside—the media and the voters—were involved. Together they demonstrated the way in which a pluralistic democracy operates under a constitution.

The courts were involved by indicting major figures such as Mitchell, Haldeman, and Ehrlichman, and by bringing some of the people who took part in Watergate to trial. In the process, Judge John J. Sirica demanded that President Nixon release the tapes which figured in cases before his court. Finally, in July 1974 the Supreme Court by a vote of 8 to 0 ordered Nixon to turn the tapes over to Judge Sirica. This decision forced Nixon to release transcripts of conversations with H.R. Haldeman which showed that Nixon knew about and tried to cover up the break-in. Moreover, the tapes indicated that Nixon had withheld information about his role in the cover-up from the public and from his own attorneys.

The Senate played an important role by appointing in February 1973 a Select Committee on Presidential Campaign Activities headed by Senator Sam Ervin of North Carolina. For several months, the televised hearings of this committee exposed many of the illegal activities of the CRP. As the hearings continued, Nixon's popularity with voters fell steadily.

In May 1973, the Senate passed a resolution urging Nixon to appoint a special prosecutor for the Watergate affair. Leon Jaworski, who succeeded Archibald Cox in that office, pressed the fight for the tapes. He finally asked the Supreme Court to accept the case directly. The 8 to 0 verdict resulted. By its resolution, the Senate, a branch of the legislature, forced the President, the head of the executive branch, to take action against itself.

In October 1973, the House of Representatives ordered the House Judiciary Committee to begin impeachment proceedings against President Nixon. The members of this committee, chaired by Peter W. Rodino of New Jersey, finally recommended on July 27, 1974 that the House impeach Nixon for obstruction of justice in the Watergate case. The televised hearings of this committee had a profound effect on public opinion.

Throughout the entire Watergate affair, the media kept the public fully informed. The work of two young reporters for the *Washington Post*, Carl Bernstein and Bob Woodward, kept Watergate in the public eye. They were joined by a host of newspaper, magazine, television, and radio newspeople who investigated each new incident. Slowly editorial opinion turned against President Nixon. By reporting the facts as they saw them, media people played a vital role in informing citizens.

Finally, the voters played a key role in Watergate. Nixon and Spiro Agnew had won an overwhelming victory in November 1972. But

▶ The grand jury named President Nixon as an unindicted co-conspirator since they believed that a President cannot be tried while in office. In September 1974 President Ford pardoned former President Nixon. Do you think that Nixon should have been tried after leaving office, or had he already suffered enough? Why?

Nixon first appointed Harvard law professor, Archibald Cox. Cox demanded that Nixon release some of the tape recordings. Instead, Nixon ordered Attorney General Elliot Richardson to fire Cox. Richardson and his deputy resigned rather than do so. Cox's successor, Jaworski, pursued the tapes with as much vigor as Cox.

After Nixon resigned, the House accepted the report of the committee. The case did not go to the Senate for trial since Nixon was no longer President. Observers agreed, however, that Nixon would have been convicted if the case had come to trial in the Senate.

in October 1973, Agnew resigned from the Vice-Presidency after pleading no contest to a charge of income tax evasion. In his place, Nixon nominated Gerald R. Ford, for many years a Republican leader in the House of Representatives. Ford had not been involved in Watergate in any way. Agnew's resignation and the steady flow of news about Watergate-related events disturbed voters deeply. Nixon's popularity fell steadily. By summer of 1974, only about one fourth of the electorate approved of the way he handled his responsibilities. Letters from voters flowed into Washington and to editors of newspapers. These letters supported the work of the senators, representatives, and special prosecutor as they tried to untangle the Watergate issue. The voters demonstrated the influence they can have in a pluralistic political system where power is distributed to many people and institutions.

The nation seemed relieved when Nixon finally resigned in August 1974. Gerald R. Ford, the first person to become President who had not been elected to either the Presidency or the Vice-Presidency, took office on August 9. Ford acted immediately to bring the nation together and to heal the wounds of the past few years. He consulted with leaders of both parties in Congress as he made his first decisions. These actions showed that he wanted to share power with others and that he rejected the closed decision-making procedure of Nixon. He assured everyone that Henry Kissinger would remain as Secretary of State and that the nation's foreign policy would not change. He also promised to protect civil liberties, a clear rejection of the break-ins and secret tapings which had led to Nixon's downfall. He agreed to hold press conferences frequently in an attempt to win more support from the media. He proposed conditional amnesty for men who had evaded the draft during the war in Vietnam. He asked Congress for a new Cost of Living Council to advise him about his most pressing domestic problem—inflation and a stagnant economy. And he nominated a liberal Republican, Nelson A. Rockefeller, former governor of New York, as Vice-President. Most people in both parties seemed to approve heartily. And the public, represented by the media and in the polls, responded favorably to these new directions.

INDEX

Italicized page numbers refer to tables, charts, graphs, or illustrations.

B

balance of power: changes in (1920-1930's), 612; impact on World War II, 650-651

Balch, Emily, on immigrants' experiences (1800's), 407-409, 412

bankruptcy, 108

"Bank War," 210-211

Barnett, Ida Wells, on violence against blacks (post-Civil War), 390-391

Baruch, Bernard, on impact of World War I, 521-523

Battle of Bunker Hill, 95, 136

Battle of Tippecanoe (1811), 212

Baurmeister, on George Washington, 142, 145-146

Bayard, William, on Erie Canal, 172

Benét, Stephen Vincent, on John Brown, 314

Bessemer process, 339, 430-431

Beveridge, Albert J., on annexation of Philippines, 544-545

Beverley, Robert, on slavery and servitude, 40-41

Bill of Rights, 116-117, 153

birth rate: decline in (after 1850), 421; and urban growth (1900-1910), 500

"Black Codes," 324

black leaders, approaches of, 392-395, 398, 668-671

"black power," 677-679

blacks: attitudes toward (post-Civil War), 323; in Civil War, 320; in colonial society, 41-44, 68, 69; contributions of, 689; crimes against (post-Civil War), 390-391; during Depression, 592-593; discrimination against, 682, 684; disfranchisement of, 385, 388-390; employment of (post-World War II), 688-689; and FDR, 610; on integration, 680-681; during Jackson period, 208; migration of, (1910-1920), 667; militancy, 676-682; 710; and Muslim religious organizations, 689; opportunities of (1700's), 188; political advances of, 688; political party affiliation of (1920's), 582; population distribution of (1900-1930), 399-400; in public of-

fice (1960's), 671; impact of racism on, 403-404; separatism, 670-671, 689-690; in southern economy, 380, 382-383; status of (1900), 666-667, (post 1954), 676; in World War I, 668; *See also* black leaders; slaves

Blair, Lewis H., on economic development and race relations, 380, 382-383

"Bleeding Kansas," 286-287

Boston, Massachusetts: as reform center, 230-231; textile industry in, 180

Boston Manufacturing Company, 180-181

Boston Massacre (1770), 91, 93

Boston Tea Party, 80, 82

Boylston, Zabdiel, 59

Braddock, General Edward, 72, 124

Brazil, 23

Brown, Senator Albert G., on slavery, 251-252

Brown, John: and abolitionists, 302-304; antislavery action by, 287, 289; early life of, 291-294; evidence on, 308-309; execution of, 310-311; family of, 295-296; at Harper's Ferry, 304-307; in Kansas, 296-297, 301-302; and slave education, 295; speech of, 309-310; views of, 311-315

Brown vs. the Board of Education (1954), 672

Bryan, William Jennings, 402

Byrd, William II (1674-1744): background of, 53-54; life described, 54-55, 58

Bull Run (Virginia), Civil War battles at, 318, 319

Burgoyne, General John, 96

business: democratization of, 201; failures (1870-1930), 333

C

Cabaza de Vaca, on Texas Indians, 6-7

Cabral, Pedro, 23

Calhoun, John C., 284; and anti-tariff position, 208, 209-210; on national unity, 169, 171

California: acquisition of, 280; and slavery issue, 282, 284-285

Callender, Guy S., on U.S. economy (1800's), 177-178

Calvin, John, 22

Canadians, immigration to U.S., 424

Canning, George, 165

capital, definition of, 346

capital resources, and economic growth, 346-347

Carey Act (1895), 476

Caribbean, U.S. control of, 554-556

Carmichael, Stokely, on "black power," 677-679

Carnegie, Andrew, on economic growth, 334, 336, 338-339

Carnegie Company, strike against (1892), 435, 438

caste system, in South, 383

Catholic University, 391

cattle industry, development of, 473-475

Century of Dishonor, A (Jackson), 472

Chavez, Cesar, 683

checks and balances, in Constitution, 112-113, 115

Chesnut, Mary Boykin, on slavery, 252-253

Chicago, race riot in (1919), 400

Chicanos, 683-684; *See also* Mexican-Americans

child labor, laws regulating, 414

child-rearing, during 1920's, 563-566, 584

children, of immigrants, 409, 414

China, U.S. policy towards, 556

Chinese, immigration to U.S., 424

Chinese Exclusion Act, 424

Christian Indians, 19-20

Christianity, 3; and imperialism, 537-538

churches: and abolition movement, 231; development of new, 232-233

citizens, constitutional rights of, 116-117, 120-121

city(ies): "bosses" in, 487-488, 490-492; government in (1850-1900), 480-481; growth of (1800-1910), 259, 459-460, 497, *498;* impact of industrial growth on, 498-499; population of (1840-1860), *264;* (1900-1920), 479; problems of (1870-1930), 478, 479; slaves in (1850's), 245, 247; and violence, 464-

465; *See also* municipal government; urbanization

"Civil Disobedience" (Thoreau), 232

civil rights: definition of, 395; and Japanese-Americans, 618-624; legislation, 608, 709; of slaves, 253; Supreme Court rulings on, 671-672; tactics, 383

Civil Rights Act (1866), 324

Civil Rights Act (1964), 688, 708

Civil War, 316-321; black soldiers in, 320; Confederate surrender in, 321; impact of, 378-379; military events in, 319-321; North-South strength in, 318

Clay, Henry, 211, 284

Clark, George Rogers, 97

Clark, Victor S., on growth of textile industry, 180-181

Clark, William, 162

Clinton, Sir William, 96

Cleveland, Grover, political philosophy of, 512-514

Coercive Acts (1774), 93

Coke, Reverend Thomas, 146

Cold War: criticism of, 653-654; and Cuban missile crisis, 654-656, 658-659; in 1970's, 659-661, 663-664; policy objectives in, 654

collective bargaining, 442

college students, during 1960's, 710-711

colonies: black-white relations in, 41-44; and British authority, 75-76, 77-80, 82; commerce with Europe, 49-50; community life in (1700's), 69-70; development of, 26-27; economy of (1700's), 71, 72; establishment of, *47t;* and European conflicts (1700's), 72, 73; growth and development of, 44-51; political ties between, 49; population of (1700's), 52, 68, *69t;* relations among (1700's), 50, 51, 70; social structure in, 51; success of, 28; voluntary organizations in, 64, 65, 66

colonization, 24-26

Columbus, Christopher, 23

Committee for the Re-Election of the President (CREEP), 716

Committee of Industrial Organization, 452, 607, 611

Committees of Correspondence, 93, 99

Common Sense (Paine), 86-87

communication: pattern of (1820), 561; urban, 500

community life: in colonies (1700's) 69-70; of southern blacks, 400

Compromise of 1850, 284-285

"Compromise of 1877," 327

Confederate States of America, 316

Congress: and civil rights legislation (1960's), 688; and New Deal legislation, *606, 609,* 610; problems of first, 122; radicals in (during Civil War), 319; and Reconstruction policy (1867-1872), 325-326

conservation movement, roots of, 270-271

Constitution: amendment procedure for, 115-116; amendments to, 325; checks and balances in, 112-113, 115; citizen's rights in, 116-117, 120-121; creation of, 105; and distribution of power, 106-107; ratification of, 105-106, 116-117, 152; separation of powers in, 107-111; sources of, 106; *See also* Articles of Confederation

consumer goods, family expenditures on (1888-1918), *333*

Continental Congress, 93, 94, 99, 101, 102-104

Cooper, James Fenimore, 277

Cornell, Ezekiel, 143

Cornwallis, General, 136

Coronado, Francisco Vásquez de, on Plains Indians, 470

corruption, in government (1900-1910), 487

cotton gin, impact on slavery, 225

Cotton Kingdom, 256

Coughlin, Father Charles E., 608

Cox, Archibald, 717

crime rate, in 1800's, 465

criminal justice; in Constitution, 120-121; and English-Indian relations, 10

criminals, as indentured labor, 37

Crisis, The, 392

Crockett, Davy, 268

Cuban missile crisis, 654-656, 658-659

culture: of Africans, 32, 33-34; of Indians and Europeans compared, 3-4; of Virginia Indians, 8

Cumberland Gap, 268

D

Darling, John, 268

data: evaluation of, 192; for historical investigation, 189

Davis, Jefferson, 312-313, 316

Dawes Act (1887), 472

death, Indian attitude toward, 6

death rate, decline in (1900-1950), 348-349

Debs, Eugene, 452

Declaration of Independence, 87, 89-90, 94

Deerslayer, The (Cooper), 277

Democratic Convention (1924), issues in, 581

Democratic party: blacks in, 688; first national convention of, 211; and slavery issue, 288, 289

democracy, meanings of, 188

Demonstration Cities Act (1966), 709

Depression, 584; blacks during, 592-593; economy during, 603, 606; family during, 598-603; illustrative material on, 586-591; relief projects during, 598; unemployment during, *587,* 596-598; violence during, 593

détente, in Soviet-American relations, 663-664

de Tocqueville, Alexis, on American political life, 204

developing countries, outlook for, 694

Dewey, John, on impact of World War I, 524-525

Dias, Bartholomeu, 22-23

dictionary, American, 173-174

disfranchisement, of blacks, 385, 388-390; *See also* voting rights

Dix, Dorothea, and mental patient care, 219-220

Douglas, Stephen A., and Kansas-Nebraska Act, 285-286

Douglass, Frederick, 284; in abolitionist movement, 229; on John Brown, 302-303; newspaper of, 230; philosophy of, 229-230

Dred Scott decision, 287

Du Bois, William Edward Burghardt, career of, 392; on Booker T. Washington's philosophy, 395, 398

dust storms, of 1930's, 477

trial workers, 440; *See also* children; women

Farm Bureau Federation, 377

farmers: conditions of (1800's), 362-364; during Depression, 593-594; and finances, 374-376; in Great Plains, 454-455; grievances of, 374-377; political affiliation of, 376-377, 582; in southern social structure (pre-Civil War), 254-255; and transportation (1800's), 183; western settlement of, 475-476; *See also* agriculture; farms; rural life

farms: relationship with industry of, 370; technology (1870-1930), *371;* value of (1820-1930), *372; See also* agriculture; farmers; rural life

federal courts: creation of, 153-154; constitutional powers of, 115

Federal Deposit Insurance Corporation, establishment of (during Depression), 607

Federal Emergency Relief Administration, 608

Federal Farm Loan Act, 377

federal government: inactivity in (1865-1933), 525-529; role of, 515-519; impact of World War I on, 519, 521; *See also* federal legislation

federal legislation (1860-1930), 529, *530-533;* on corruption in government, 532-533; on industry (1887-1920), *530;* on money and banking (1863-1913), *531;* on public lands (late 1800's), 454-455

Federalists, 105, 155, 157, 158-159

Ferdinand of Aragon, 23

fertilizer, use of (1820-1930), *371*

Fifteenth Amendment, 325, 326

Fitzhugh, George, on slavery, 250-251

Florida, acquisition of, 165, 167

food: Indian, 16, 18; of slaves, 245, 247

Forbes, John, 73, 125

Ford, Gerald R., 712, 718

Fordney-McCumber Tariff (1922), 580

foreign policy, 535, 552-553; toward China (since 1940's), 659-661, 663; in Latin America, 536-537; and Monroe Doctrine, 165-166; in Pacific, 556-557; and Soviet Union, 663-664

forests, treatment of, 268

Fort Sumter, attack on, 317

Fourteenth Amendment, 325, 326

Franco-American Treaty of Alliance (1778), 161

Franco-British relations, and U.S., 160-161, 162, 164

Franklin, Benjamin, 64, 65, 66-67

Free Soil party, 288-289

French: and colonization, 24; in Revolutionary War, 96, 97, 142-143

French and Indian War, 72, 73, 74, 124-131

French Revolution, 157, 160

frontier: cattle, 473-475; description of (1860-1890), 469-470; farmers' last, 475-476; and land exploitation, 269-270; mining, 472-473

Fugitive Slave Law, 285

Fulton, Robert, 177

Fundamentalism, 584

funding, federal (1865-1933), 528-529

G

Gallaudet, Thomas Hopkins, 233

Gama, Vasco da, 23

Garibaldi, Giuseppe, 497

Garrison, William Lloyd: in abolitionist movement, 235; and anti-slavery newspaper, 248; on John Brown, 311-312

Garvey, Marcus, philosophy of, 670-671

Gates, General Horatio, 96

generalizations, in historical investigation, 192

generation gap, among immigrants, 409

Gibbons vs. Ogden (1824), 184

Gompers, Samuel, and American Federation of Labor, 452

government: attitudes toward unions, 451; corruption in (1900-1910), 487; and economic growth, 347; in English colonies, 46, 47, 49; European compared to Indian, 3; and industrial growth, 351-352; in Northwest Territory, 102; of Virginia Indians, 8; *See also* federal government; municipal government

"Grandfather clause," and black voting rights, 385, 388-390

Granger laws, 374

Grant, Ulysses S., 319-320, 326

Grapes of Wrath, The (Steinbeck), 598

Great Awakening, 70

"Great Compromise," 107

Great Depression, *see* Depression

Grimke, Angelina: on slave treatment, 227-228; on women's and black rights, 224-225

gross national product (GNP), during Depression, *591;* growth of (1869-1929), 331

Houston, Sam, and Texas annexation, 277

Howe, Samuel Gridley, 233

Howe, General William, 96

Hudson, Henry, 24

Huguenots, 24

Hull House, 493

human resources, and economic growth, 347-349

Humphreys, David, 147

hunters, tales about, 268

hypotheses: development of, 190, 191-192; in historical investigation, 189-190; implications of, 192-194, 196-198

H

Haldeman, H.R., 716-717

Hamilton, Alexander, 143-144, 153-155

Harding, Warren G., 581

Harper's Ferry (Virginia), John Brown's raid on, 304-307

Harrison, William Henry, 212

Harvard College, 59

Hawaii, annexation of, 539-541

Hawley-Smoot Tariff (1930), 580

Hawthorne, Nathaniel, 277

Hay-Bunau-Varilla Treaty, 556

Haymarket Affair, 451-452

Hay-Pauncefote Treaty (1901), 555

Head Start, 708

health, improvement of (1860-1950), 348-349

Heriot, Thomas, on Virginia Indians, 7-8

high schools, in 1920's, 566-570

historical investigation, steps in, 189-190

history: immigration in, 405; national politics in, 533-534; perspective in, 691

Homestead Act (1862), 454-455

Hoover, Herbert, 605

Hopkins, Harry, 608

House of Burgesses, 46

House of Representatives, and Presidential election (1824), 187

House of the Seven Gables, The (Hawthorne), 277

housing patterns: during Depression, 596-598; and technological development, 501; urban (late 1800's), 460

I

immigrants: adjustment of, 425-426; Americanization of, 416-420; characteristics of, 424; children of, 409; in colonial population (1700's), 68, 69; contributions of, 428; experiences of (1800's), 406-409, 412; impact on American life, 421-428; Jewish, 416-418; mutual aid organizations of (1800's), 408-409; and police brutality (1895), 466; and public education, 414-415; in steel strike of 1919, 442-443; in urban population (1900-1910), 500; in West, 475; *See also* European immigrants; Slavic immigrants

immigration: causes of, 422; to colonies (1700's), 52; cultural impact of, 416-418; and "nativism," 426-427; restriction of, 424, 427; sources of, 422, *423,* 424; to U.S. (1815-1920), 405; *See also* immigrants

impeachment, constitutional procedure for, 112-113; proceedings against Nixon, 717

imperialism, American, 536-537; and annexation of Philippines, 541-542; ideology of, 537-541; *See also* territorial expansion

impressment, 162

indentured labor, 36, 37

Indians: and Christianity, 19; in colonial development, 27; culture of, 1, 2-3, 6; discrimination against, 682-683; of

Great Plains, 470-472; grievances with English of, 10-11; during Jacksonian period, 208; of Northwest, 102; treatment of captives by, 15-16, 17-18

industrialization: role of business leaders in, 339, 346-347; role of government in, 351-352; impact of, 276, 330, 692; meanings of, 429; outlook for, 694; and urban growth, 498-488; *See also* industry

industrial workers of world, 452

industry: developments in (1880's), 446-447, 448; federal regulation of (1887-1920), *530;* growth of (1920's), 578; immigrants in, 426; iron and steel, 430-431, 435, 438; monopoly in, 447, 448; and railroads, 276; sit-down strikes in (1937), 611; workers in, 332, 438-441; working conditions in (1919), 431-435; *See also* industrialization

infant mortality, decline in (1900-1940), 348

integration, 672-674, 680-681

international politics, U.S. role in (1815-1875), 552; *See also* foreign policy

Interstate Commerce Act (1887), 374

Intolerable Acts, 93

Isabella of Castile, 23

J

Jackson, Andrew, 164; career of, 205; and reconstruction policy, 324; on strong executive, 208; and tariff issue, 210; *See also* Jacksonian period

Jackson, Helen Hunt, 472

Jacksonian period: "bank war" during, 210-211; democratization during, 188; descriptions of, 190, 191-192, 194, 196-198; equality during, 205, 208; impact of, 204-205, 208-212; reform movements during, 232; social structure in, 194, 196; tariff issue during, 208, 209-210; two-party system during, 211-212; *See also* Jackson, Andrew

Jackson, "Stonewall," 318

Jamestown, Virginia, slaves in, 29

Japan, U.S. policy toward, 556-557

Japanese, immigration to U.S., 424

Japanese-Americans, civil rights of, 618-624; military accomplishments of, 621

Jaworski, Leon, 717

Jay's Treaty, 160-161

Jefferson, Thomas, 53, 150; and Declaration of Independence, 87, 89-90; and exploration, 162; as President, 158-159

Jewish culture, impact of immigration on, 416-418

Jews, adjustment to American society of, 425

Jim Crow Laws, 384, 400

John Brown's Body (Benét), 314

Johnson, Andrew, impeachment of, 326

Johnson, Lyndon B.: civil rights legislation under, 709; second term of, 706, 708-712; and Vietnam war, 709-710

Journal of Times, 82-84

judicial branch, constitutional powers of, 110-111; *See also* Supreme Court

Judiciary Act (1789), 153

Jungle, The (Sinclair), 528

K

Kansas-Nebraska Act (1854), 285-287

Kennan, George, on impact of World War II, 650-651

Kennedy, John F., on Cuban missile crisis, 655-656, 658-659

Kennedy, Robert, 711

Khrushchev, Premier, on Cuban missile crisis, 658

Kingdom of Prester John, 22-23

King, Jr., Martin Luther, assassination of, 711; philosophy of, 674-675

King Philip's War, 9, 11, 13-14

Kissinger, Henry, on Cold War policy, 651, 653-654; as Secretary of State, 712-713, 718

Knight, Madam Sarah Kemble, on black-white relations, 43-44

Knights of Labor, 451-452

"Know-Nothing Party," 289

Knox, Henry, 151, 153

Ku Klux Klan, 384, 584

L

labor force: farm (1870-1930), *371;* women in (1920's), 582

labor-saving machinery, attitudes toward (1862), 340-341

labor unions: blacks in, 685; government attitudes toward, 451; growth of, *450,* 451, 607; in iron and steel industry (late 1800's), 435, 438; in West (late 1800's), 466-469

Lafayette, Marquis de, 151

land ownership: and cattle industry, 474; in colonial development, 27; and exploitation, 269-270; and Indian-white relations, 3, 10-11, 13, 470-472; during Jacksonian period, 190, 208; laws (1787-1832), *193t;* problems of (late 1800's), 453; in West, 477-478

language, impact on immigrant experience (1800's), 407, 409

Last of the Mohicans, The (Cooper), 277

Latin America, 165; Monroe Doctrine in, 553-556

Laurens, Henry, 139, 142-143

laws: on colonial commerce, 50, 51; on slavery, 36-37

League of Nations, 535, 559-560

Leaves of Grass (Whitman), 277

Lee, Henry, 147, 151

Lee, Robert E., 306, 319, 320-321

legislative branch, constitutional powers of, 107-109

Lewis and Clark expedition (1803-1806), 279

Liberal party, 288

Liberator, 235, 248

Liliuokalani, Queen, 539

Lincoln, Abraham: Civil War aims of, 317; and Congress, 319, 320; death of, 321; election of (1860) 316; and Emancipation Proclamation, 320; on John Brown, 313; and reconstruction policy, 323-324; re-election of (1864), 321; on slavery, 316, 317

Lincoln, Benjamin, 152

literacy test, and black voting rights, 385

Literary Test Act (1917), 427

literature, slavery in, 257, 258

litter, 700

Little Rock, Arkansas, integration of schools in, 672-674

localism, in communication (1870), 561

London Exhibition of 1851, 275

"long drive," 473, 475

Long, Senator Huey, 608

Los Angeles, California, transportation problems of (1911), 481, 484-486

Louisiana Purchase, 161-162, 167, 187

lower classes, and municipal politics, 504-505

lumber production, growth of (1829-1859), *264*

Lybrook, John, 268

lynchings, in South (late 1800's), 392

Lynd, Robert and Helen, American life study of (1920's), 562-571, 575-577

M

McCarthy, Senator Eugene, 711

McCulloch vs. Maryland (1819), 183-184

Mackenzie, Captain Robert, 135

McKinley, President, on annexation of Philippines, 542, 544

McNary-Haugen Bill (1924), 582

McWhorter, Reverend Alexander, 142

Macon's Bill Number 2 (1810), 163

Madison, James, 53, 151; and bill of rights, 116; on federalism, 155; and national debt policy, 154

Mahan, Alfred Thayer, on role of sea power, 539

Malcolm X, 689

Man and Nature (Marsh), 273-274

manifest destiny, 279

Mann, Horace, and free public education, 233

Mantoacs, 8

manufacturers, in southern social structure (pre-Civil War), 255

manufacturing, persons employed in (1840-1860), *262*

Marbury vs. Madison (1803), 183

market economy, expansion of (1840's and 1850's), 259

marriage, in Indian society, 7

Marshall, John, impact on Supreme Court, 183-184

Marsh, George Perkins, on ecological balance, 272-273

Mason, George, 134

Mason, Senator William E., on annexation of Philippines, 545-546

Massachusetts Bay Colony, 19, 47, 49

mass media, impact on national politics (1865-1933), 527

Mather, Cotton: background on, 59; and black cultural society, 43; on smallpox epidemic, 61-64

Mayflower Compact, 46

Meade, George, 320

mechanization, of farming, 372-373

Medicare, 708

Melville, Herman, 277

mercantilism, 51

merchants, in southern social structure (pre-Civil War), 255

Metropolitan Development Act (1966) 709

Mexican-Americans, 424, 473, 683; See also Spanish-speaking Americans

Mexicans, immigration to U.S., 424

Mexican War, 280, 282

Mexico, and Texas annexation, 277, 279-280

"Middle Passage," in slave trade, 35

Middletown: child-rearing in, 563-566; education in, 567-570; technology in, 571, 575-577

migration, within states (1850), 261; See also immigration

miners, and settlement of West, 466-469, 472-473

mining industry, and land policy, 477

Missouri Compromise, 187

Mitchell, John, 716-717

Moby Dick (Melville), 277

monopoly, definition of, 447

Monroe Doctrine: beginning of, 165-166; in Latin America (1800's), 553-556; and "Roosevelt Corollary," 555

Monroe, James, and "Era of Good Feelings," 182

Montgomery, Alabama, bus boycott in, 674

mores, defined, 435

More, Sir Thomas, and utopian community, 214

Morgan, J.P., 334

Mormon church, establishment of (1830), 232-233

motion pictures, impact on American life of, 576-577

Mott, Mayor Frank K., on urban political reform, 493-497

Mott, Lucretia, and women's rights movement, 221, 224

mountain people, in southern social structure (pre-Civil War), 255

municipal government, 502, 504-505; "boss" in, 487-488, 490-502; commission form of, 493-496; prescriptions for, 493-497; and urban growth (1810-1900), 501-502; See also city(ies)

music, in African culture, 33-34

mutual aid organizations, of immigrants (1800's), 408-409

Myrdal, Gunnar, 682

N

Napoleon, and Louisiana Purchase, 161

Narragansett Indians, 9, 15-16, 17-18

National Association for the Advancement of Colored People (NAACP), 392, 667

national bank, establishment of, 154-155

national growth, 259-260; data on (1840-1860), 261, 262, 264

National Labor Relations Act, 609-610

National Organization for Women (NOW), 684

national politics, characterized (1920's), 579-582; factors in (1876-1920), 508; impact of war on, 521-525; in history, 533-534; issues in (1872-1920), 529; sectionalism in (1800's), 185; traditional accounts of, 507; See also elections; federal government; Presidential election

National Recovery Administration, 607

national security, and Monroe Doctrine, 553

nationalism, artistic expression of, 174, 176; and colonization, 22; factors in, 172-173; growth of, (1800's), 537; and transportation, 169, 171

political parties, beginnings of, 155, 157;
and slavery, 288-289; strength of
(1865-1933), 526-527; *See also* Democratic party; Republican party; two-
party system
Polk, James, and territorial expansion,
279-280
Pontiac Conspiracy, 91
population, age of (1880-1950) 421-422;
of colonies (1700's), 52, 68, *69t;* distribution of (1840-1860), *261;* and economy (pre-Civil War), 275; farm labor
force in, 353, *371;* growth, 700-701,
703; growth and mobility of (1800-
1850), 259, 274; outlook for, 694; total
compared to urban (1860-1930), *331;*
trends in (1800-1850), 354; urban, *264,*
479; urban and rural compared (1860-
1920), 497; *See also* school population;
urban population; world population
Populist party, 402-403
Portugal, and colonization, 22-23
postal system, in colonies (1700's), 70
Powderly, Terence V., 451
praying Indians, 15, 18
Presidency, of Andrew Jackson compared
to John Quincy Adams, 204-205; during 1920's, 581
President, constitutional powers of, 110,
113; role of (1865-1933), 525-526
Presidential candidates, selection of
(1800's), *199t,* 200-201
Presidential election, bank issue in
(1832), 211; and Civil War issue in
(1864), 321; and political unity (1824),
187; Reconstruction issue in (1868),
326; territorial issues in (1844), 279;
voting in (1824-1844), *202t;* (1800),
158; (1836 & 1840), 212; (1860), 316;
(1876), 327; (1876-1920), 508, *509-512;*
(1892), 376-377; (1920-1928), 579, *580,*
581-582; (1932), 605-606; (1936), 610;
(1964), 708; (1968), 711-712
Presidential succession, constitutional
procedure for, 113
Prince Henry the Navigator, 22
prisoners of war, English treatment of,
37; Indian treatment of, 15-16, 17-18
Proclamation of 1763, 91
professionalism, in municipal government (1920's), 504, 505

progressive movement, 479
prohibition, 580-581
*Proposals Relating to the Education of
Youth in Pennsylvania* (Franklin), 66
public education, criticism of, 413-416;
establishment of, 66-67; during Jacksonian period, 192; segregation in, 384
public lands, controversy concerning,
455-456, 458-459; disposal of (by 1904),
477; federal laws on (late 1800's), 454-
455
public opinion, on national issues (1865-
1933), 527; in Spanish-American War,
554-555
public transportation, segregation in, 384
Puerto Ricans, 683-684
Puritans, in Massachusetts Bay Colony,
46, 47, 49, 59, 61-64

Q

Quakers, and antislavery society, 234
Quarles, Benjamin, on African culture,
32, 33; on slave trade, 34-36
Quartering Act, 82
Quebec Act, 93
quota system, 427

R

race relations, changes in (1890-1911),
384; impact of Civil War on, 378; *See
also* racism
race riots, in Chicago (1919), 400; in
South (late 1800's), 392; *See also*
lynchings
racism, effects of, 400-404; and imperialism, 540, 541; in national election
(1920's), 581, 582; during 1920's, 584;
in North, 400; in South, 385, 388-390,
667; and two-party system (in South),
400-403; *See also* race relations
Radical Republicans, and Reconstruction
policy, 325-326
radio, impact on American life of, 577
railroads, and cattle industry, 473-474,
475; and economic growth, 349; farmer's views on, 374; growth of (pre-Civil

War), 276; unionism of, 451; in West, 475

Raleigh, Sir Walter, 7

ranching, 475

Randolph, A. Philip, 685

Randolph, Edmund, 153

Reconstruction, 322-327; and congressional policy, 325-326; evaluation of, 327; and Presidential policy, 323-324

recreation, 701-702; problems of, 322-323

recycling, 697

Red scare, during 1920's, 584

Reed, Joseph, 137, 138

reform movements, center of, 230-231; church in, 231; pre-Civil War, 213, 233; women in religion, in colonies (1700's), 70; and English-Indian relations, 10; European compared to Indian, 2-3; impact of immigration on, 416-418; in Spanish-Indian relations, 23-24; of Virginia Indians, 8.

religion, *see* Christianity; religious freedom

religious freedom, and colonization, 22, 25; in Constitution, 120; *See also* religion

Republican party, and Federalists, 155, 157, 158-159; during 1920's 579, *580*, 582; and Reconstruction issue, 326; and slavery issue, 289

Revolutionary War, *see* American Revolution

"Rights of the British Colonies Asserted and Proved, The," (Otis), 76, 77-78

Rochambeau, 136

Rockefeller, John D., on economic growth, 335-336; and oil industry, 334

Rockefeller, Nelson A., 718

Rodino, Peter W., 717

Rolfe, John, and tobacco growing, 46

"Roosevelt Corollary," to Monroe Doctrine, 555

Roosevelt, Franklin D., election of, (1932), 605-606; and civil rights policy, 685, 688; re-election of (1946), 610; Supreme Court appointments of, 611

Roosevelt, Theodore, Latin American policies of, 555-556; on role of federal government, 515-517

Root-Takahira Agreement (1908), 557

Rough Riders, 555

Rowlandson, Mrs. Mary, as Indian captive, 15-16, 17-18

Royal African Company, 37

Rural Electrification Administration, 610

rural life, impact of city on, 364-365, 367-370

Rush, Benjamin, 137

S

Sagamore (sachem), 15

Sanborn, F.B., on John Brown, 304

San Francisco, California, sewer system in (late 1800's), 460-461

Scarlet Letter, The (Hawthorne), 277

Schecter vs. U.S. (1935), 609

school population, growth of (1870-1920), 348

scientists, and land policy, 477-478; and urban problems, 478

Scopes, John, T., 584

sea power, in World War I, 557-558

sectionalism, a growth of (1800's), 184-185; and slavery, 187; and tariff issue, 208, 209-210

segregation, in South (early 1900's), 384; in Washington, D.C., 391

"Selling of Joseph, The" (Sewall), 42

Seneca Falls Convention, on women's rights, 221, 224

"separate but equal" doctrine, 384

separation of powers, in Constitution, 107-111

serfdom, 382

Seven Years' War (1756), 73

Seventeenth Amendment, 533

Sewall, Judge Samuel, 42

Seward, William, 284, 285

sewer systems, 700; during late 1800's, 460-462, 464

"Share-Our-Wealth" movement, 608

Shays, Daniel, 104

Shays's Rebellion, 104-105, 147, 151

Sherman, General William T., 321

shipbuilding, in colonies, 50

Siemans Gas Furnace, 338

Sinclair, Upton, 528

Sirica, Judge John J., 716-717

sit-down strikes, in industry (1937), 611

Slater, Samuel, 275

slavery, 1; arguments for, 248, 250-253; and California statehood, 282, 284-285; colonists' views on, 36, 40-41; and cotton gin, 225; economic impact of, 256-257; and Emancipation Proclamation, 320; laws on, 36-37; and Missouri Compromise, 187; pamphlet against, 42; and political parties, 288-289; protest against (1688), 39; psychological effects of, 257-258; and sectionalism, 187; southern attitudes toward (post-Civil War), 323; in southern life of, 237-242; in territories, 285-287; and Texas annexation, 277, 279, 280; theory and practice compared, 253-254; George Washington's view on, 146; *See also* slaves; slave trade

slaves, citizenship of, 287; in Constitution, 107-108, 115; life of, 143-145; revolt of (1831), 248; treatment of, 227-228; *See also* slavery; slave trade

slave trade, in Africa, 26; beginning of, 29; description of, 34-36; during 1700's, 68, 69, 72; *See also* slavery; slaves

Slavic immigrants, organization of, 408-409; *See also* immigrants

smallpox epidemic, in Massachusetts Bay colony, 59, 61-64

Smith, Joseph, and Mormon church, 232-233

Social Darwinism, 514, 537

Social Security Act (1935), 610

social structure, in colonies, 51; during Jacksonian period, 194, 196; in South, 254-256

Sons of Liberty, 91, 309

South, agriculture in, 256; anti-abolition laws in, 235; antislavery in, 258; black population in (1900-1930), 399-400; blacks in economy of, 380, 382-383; caste system in, 380, 382-383; and Civil War, 317, 379; economy of, 177-178, 379-380; "Jim Crow" laws in, 384; political power of (1860-1900), 404; racial violence in, 390-392; racism in, 385, 388-390; secession of, 316-317; and sectionalism, 184-185; segregation in, 384, 667; slavery in, 237-242; social structure in, 194, 196, 254-256; urban population in (1850-1900), 498

South Carolina Exposition and Protest, The, (Calhoun), 208, 209

Southern Christian Leadership Conference, 689

Southwest, economy of (1800's), 177-178

Spain, and colonization, 23-24; and U.S. acquisition of Florida, 165

Spanish-American War, 535, 554-555

Spanish-Indian relations, 23-24

Spanish-speaking Americans, discrimination against, 683-684

Sparks, William Andrew Jackson, on public land acquisition, 455-456, 458

"spoils system," 205

"squatting," in Northwest, 101

Stamp Act, 80, 91, 99, 131, 134

Stanton, Elizabeth Cady, and women's rights movement, 221, 224

starvation, during Depression, 595-596

states, under Articles of Confederation, 104-105; authority of (mid-1780's), 104-105; constitutional powers of, 111, 115; formation of, *476*, 477; migration within, 1850, *261;* Supreme Court decisions on, 183-184

statistics, on economy (post-Civil War), *331, 333;* immigration, 422, 423, 424; on national politics (1865-1933), 529; on Presidential elections (1869-1920), *509-512*

steamboat, and U.S. economy, 177

steel industry, impact of Andrew Carnegie on, 334; collective action in, 440-441; employee benefits in (1900), 438-439; strikes in, 442, 445-446; *See also* steelworkers

steelworkers, community life of (1900), 438-441; conditions of (1919), 431-435; *See also* steel industry

Steinbeck, John, 598

Stephens, Uriah, 451

stereotyping, of immigrants, 406

Stevens, Thaddeus, 319

stock market, growth in (1920's), 578-579

Stowe, Harriet Beecher, 285

strip mining, 704

Strong, Reverend Josiah, ideology of, 537-538

Students for Democratic Society, (SDS), 711

suburbanization, during 1920's, 579

Sugar Act (1764), 76, 77-80, 91

Sumner, Senator Charles, 287

Supreme Court, and civil rights decision, 384, 671-672, 688; constitutional powers of, 110-111; and Dred Scott decision (1857), 287; and New Deal, 609, 610-611; strength of (1800's), 183-184

Sutter's Fort, gold discovery at, 472

taboos, in Indian society, 7

Taft-Katsura Agreement, 557

Taft, William Howard, 548-549

Tallmadge, James, 187

Tammany Hall, 487-488, 490-492

tariff, during Jacksonian period, 208, 209-210; legislation (1861-1931), *532*

tax, on liquor, 155

Teapot Dome scandal, 581

technology, advances in (1859-1918), *351;* and agricultural production, 359; and economic growth, 349, 351-352; farm (1870-1930), *371;* of Indians, 3, 8; during 1900's, 693; pre-Civil War, 275-276; and resources development, 346; and urban growth, 500-501; and urban problems (1920's), 579

Tennessee Valley Authority, 607

Tenure of Office Act, 326

Terkel, Studs, on depression living, 592-598

Terrell, Mary Church, on segregation, 391

territorial expansion, and economic growth, 346; during 1840's, 259; in Presidential election (1844), 279; in Texas, 277, 279-280; See also imperialism

Texas, annexation of, 277, 279-280; Indians of, 6-7

textile industry, growth of (1800's), 180-181; labor systems in, 276

Third World, definition of, 654

Thirteenth Amendment, 325

Thoreau, Henry David, 232, 272-273, 277

Timber-Culture Law, 456

tobacco, and colonial commerce, 50, 51; and land exploitation, 264

Townsend Movement, 608

Townsend Acts, 80

treason, constitutional provision for, 117

Treaty of Ghent, 164

Treaty of Guadalupe-Hidalgo (1848), 280

Treaty of Paris (1763), 74, 97, 98

trade unions, during Jacksonian period, 190, 191

transcendentalism, and nature, 272-273; and reform movements, 231-232

transportation, and economic growth, 349; during 1800's, 182-183; impact on farmers (1800's), 364; in Los Angeles (1911), 481, 484-486; and nationalism, 169, 171; urban, 460, 500; See also railroads

Trumball, John, 174, 176

Tubman, Harriet, and underground railroad, 236

Turner, Nat, and slave revolt (1831), 248

Tweed Ring, 327

Twelfth Amendment, 158

twentieth century, trends in, 693

two-party system, evolution of, 288; during Jacksonian period, 211-212; impact of racism on (in South), 400-403

U-boats, in World War I, 557-558

Uncle Tom's Cabin (Stowe), 285

underground railroad, 235-236

Underwood Tariff (1913), 580

unemployment, during Depression, *587,* 596-598

unions, *see* labor unions

United Farm Workers, 683

United States Steel Corporation, 334, 439, 440

University of Pennsylvania, 67

Up From Slavery (Washington), 394-395

urbanization, of North and South compared (1860-1900), 404; and political organizations, 502; problems of 453, 460-462, 464, 579; and technological development, 500-501. *See also* city(ies), urban population

Urban Mass Transportation Act (1964), 708

urban population, sources of (1900-1910), 500

Utopia (More), 214

utopian communities, 214, 216-218

V

Van Buren, Martin, 212

Vaughan, Alden, on Christian Indians, 19; on King Philip's War, 13-14

veto, constitutional procedure for, 113

Vietnam war, 709-710

vigilantes, in frontier towns, 477

violence, against blacks, 390-391, 685; and cities, 464-465; during Depression, 593, 594; in frontier settlements, 464; in labor disputes, 466-469; during Philippine insurrection, 550-552; police, 465-466; *See also* lynchings; police brutality; race riots

Virginia (colony), economy of (1700's), 53; government in, 45-46; Indians, 8; plantation life in, 54-55, 58

"Virginia Plan," 107

Volstead Act, 580, 581

voluntary organizations, in colonies, 64, 65, 66

voting, in Presidential elections (1824-1844), *202t;* qualifications (1800-1840), 202, *203t; See also* disfranchisement; voting rights

voting rights, during Jacksonian period, 191-192; in states (1780's), 104; *See also* voting

Voting Rights Act (1965), 688

W

Wagner Act, 609-610

Walden (Thoreau), 277

Walker, Charles, on steelworker experience (1919), 431-435

Wallace, George, 711

Wallace, Henry A., 607

Wampanoag Indians, 9, 10, 11, 13-14

war, causes of, 9-10; in Constitution, 108; among Europeans (1700's), 72, 73; between Indians and Europeans, 9, 11, 13-14; of Indian tribes, 7; and national politics, 521-525

War for Independence, *see* American Revolution

War of 1812, 163-164, 167, 185

War on Poverty, 708

Warehouse Act, 377

Warren, Governor Francis E., on public land acquisition, 458-459

Washington, Booker T., 392, 393-395, 667

Washington, D.C., segregation in, 391

Washington, George, 53, 72, 73, 106; on British policies (1765-1775), 131, 134-136; cabinet appointments of, 153; and constitutional convention, 150, 151; election of, 123-124; financial program under, 153-155; and French and Indian War, 124-131; as gentleman farmer (1783-1789), 145-147, 150-152; on government, 151; and leadership style, 124; as Revolutionary War general, 136-139, 142-145; on Shays's Rebellion, 147, 151

wastefulness, and Americans, 269-270

water pollution, 698

Watergate, 716-718

waterways, federal expenditures for (1822-1830), *179t*

Watson, Tom, 402-403

wealth, American attitudes toward, 197-198

Wealth Tax Act, 610

Webster, Daniel, 284

Webster, Noah, 173-174

Weiser, Conrad, on George Washington, 126

Weld, Theodore Dwight, and American Anti-Slavery Society, 226-227; on slave treatment, 227-228

West, Indians in, 470-472; labor disputes in (late 1800's), 466-469; land policy in, 265, 268-270, 477-478; public land acquisition in, 455-456, 458-459; settlement of, 101, 102-104, 475-476; *See also* Northwest

Whigs, national convention of (1840), 212; program of, 212; and slavery issue, 288, 289

Whiskey Rebellion, 133

whites, and racism, 385, 388-391, 400, 403

Whitman, Walt, 277

Whitney, Eli, 225

Willett, Captain Thomas, 11

Wilmington, North Carolina, race riots in, 392

Wilmot Proviso, 282

Wilson, James, on British authority in colonies, 84-85

Wilson, Woodrow, 535; and Fourteen Points, 559-560; on role of federal government, 517-519

Winthrop, Governor John, 47

Wiroans, 8

witchcraft trials, in Salem, Massachusetts, 59

"Wobblies," 452

women, discrimination against, 684, and immigration, 414, 416-418; in labor force (1920's), 582; legal status of (1800's), 220-221; in political life (1800's), 204; in reform movements, 219-225; and voting rights, 533; *See also* women's rights

women's rights, and birth rate, 421; and blacks, 224-225; during Jacksonian period, 208; movement, 221, 224; during 1700's, 188; *See also* women

work, American attitudes toward, 349; and industrialization, 429; pre-Civil War, 276

Works Progress Administration (WPA), 598, 608

world population, outlook for, 694; trends in (late 1800's), 693

World War I, blacks in, 668; and farm prices, 377; industrial workers during, 441, 443; and role of federal government, 519, 521; U.S. involvement in, 535, 557-560

World War II, and balance of power of, 650-651

writ of habeas corpus, 117

Y

Young, Brigham, and Mormon church, 233

Z

Zimmermann Note, 557

ART ACKNOWLEDGMENTS

Chapter 1: p. 4 (left) New York Public Library; (top right) Library of Congress; (bottom right) Brown Brothers. p. 5 British Museum. p. 12 (top) New York Historical Society; (bottom) Brown Brothers. p. 17 American Museum of Natural History.

Chapter 2: p. 30 (top) New York Public Library; (bottom) New York Public Library. p. 31 (top) New York Public Library; (bottom left) Brown Brothers; (bottom right) Institut de France Academie des Sciences. p. 40 (left) Michael Abramson, Black Star; (right) Eve Arnold, Magnum Photos. p. 44 Constantine Manos, Magnum Photos.

Chapter 3: p. 56 (top left) Shostal Associates; (top right) Shostal Associates; (bottom) Shostal Associates. p. 57 (top) Shostal Associates; (bottom) Herbert Lanks, Monkmeyer. p. 60 (top left) Joan Menschenfreund; (top right) Joan Menschenfreund; (bottom) Joan Menschenfreund. p. 61 Joan Menschenfreund. p. 65 Ken Wittenberg.

Chapter 4: p. 77 Ernest Haas, Magnum photos. p. 81 (top) Wide World Photos; (bottom) The Metropolitan Museum of Art, gift of Mrs. Russell Sage. p. 88 (top) Library of Congress; (bottom left) Huntington Hartford Collection; (bottom right) Library of Congress.

Chapter 5: p. 118 (top left) State Historical Society of Wisconsin; (top right) Brown County Historical Society; (bottom) The Smithsonian Institution. p. 119 (top left) Minnesota Historical Society; (top right) Brown Brothers; (bottom) Collection of the Boatman's National Bank of St. Louis.

Chapter 6: p. 128 (top left) Culver Pictures; (top right) Culver Pictures; (bottom) Library of Congress. p. 129 (top) Culver Pictures; (bottom) New York Public Library. p. 132 (top left) courtesy, Kenneth M. Newman, The Old Print Shop, New York City; (top right) Culver Pictures; (bottom) New York Public Library. p. 133 (top) The Metropolitan Museum of Art, bequest of William Nelson; (bottom) Library of Congress. p. 140 (top) courtesy, Janice E. Chabas; (bottom) engraving by J. Rogers from J. McNevin, © National Geographic Society. p. 141 (top) New York Historical Society; (bottom) U.S. Capitol Historical Society, © National Geographic Society. p. 148 Library of Congress. p. 149 (top) Library of Congress; (bottom) Library of Congress. p. 156 (top left) courtesy, The John Carter Brown Library; (top right) U.P.I.; (bottom) New York Public Library.

Chapter 7: p. 170 (top) National Academy of Design. H.R. & W. Photo by Russell Dian; (bottom) Chicago Historical Society. p. 171 Maryland Historical Society. p. 175 (top) National Geographic Photographer, courtesy U.S. Capitol Historical Society; (bottom) Wadsworth Atheneum, Hartford, Connecticut. p. 186 (top left) courtesy of the New York Historical Society, New York City; (top right) courtesy of Alton Ketchum. Drawing by Gordon Gray; (bottom) Historical Society of Pennsylvania.

Chapter 8: p. 191 (left) Danny Lyon, Magnum Photos; (right) Burk Uzzle, Magnum Photos. p. 195 H.R. & W. Photo by Russell Dian. p. 206 (top) New York Historical Society; (bottom left) Chicago Historical Society; (bottom right) Library of Congress. p. 207 (top) New York Public Library, originally published in *Harpers Weekly*, March 12, 1881; (bottom left) The Hermitage, Nashville, Tennessee; (bottom right) Culver Pictures.

Chapter 9: p. 215 (top left) Burk Uzzle, Magnum Photos; (top right) Cary S. Wolinsky, Stock, Boston; (bottom) Owen Franken, Stock, Boston. p. 222 (top left) Elliott Erwitt, Magnum Photos; (top right) Mimi Forsyth, Monkmeyer; (bottom left) Daniel S. Baliotti; (bottom right) Mimi Forsyth, Monkmeyer. p. 223 (top left) U.P.I.; (top right) American Airlines; (bottom) Hinton, Monkmeyer. p. 234 Owen Franken, Stock, Boston.

Chapter 10: p. 238 (top left) Isaac Delgado Museum of Art, Collection of W.E. Groves; (top right) J.B. Speed Art Museum; (bottom) Library of Congress. p. 239 (top left) Bettmann Archive; (top right) Brown Brothers; (bottom) Preston Player Collection, Knox College. p. 240 (top left) New York Public Library; (top right) New York Public Library; (middle left) Culver Pictures; (middle right) Valentine Museum; (bottom) Brown Brothers. p. 241 (top left) Virginia State

Library; (top right) Brown Brothers. p. 242 (top) New York Historical Society; (bottom left) Virginia State Library; (bottom right) *New York Times.* p. 246 (top left) Owen Franken, Stock, Boston; (top right) Owen Franken, Stock, Boston; (bottom) Owen Franken, Stock, Boston. p. 249 New York Public Library.

Chapter 11: p. 263 (top) Shostal Associates; (bottom) Culver Pictures. p. 266 (top left) New York Public Library; (top right) Ray Atkeson, DPI; (bottom) J. Alex Langley, DPI. p. 267 (top left) John Bintiff, DPI; (top right) Ken Wittenberg; (bottom) National Park Service Photo by Fred E. Mang, Jr. p. 271 D. Corson, Shostal Associates.

Chapter 12: p. 283 (top) New York Historical Society; (bottom left) Culver Pictures; (bottom right) Culver Pictures. p. 298 (top left) Metropolitan Museum of Art; (top right) New York Public Library; (bottom) Brown Brothers. p. 299 (top) Virginia State Library; (bottom) Kansas Department of Economic Development. p. 300 (top left) New York Public Library; (top right) Brown Brothers; (bottom) Culver Pictures.

Chapter 13: p. 337 (top left) Brown Brothers; (top right) Brown Brothers; (bottom) Solomon D. Butcher Collection, Nebraska State Historical Society. p. 350 (top left) Hugh Rogers, Monkmeyer; (top right) Mimi Forsyth, Monkmeyer; (bottom left) Mimi Forsyth, Monkmeyer; (bottom right) Mimi Forsyth, Monkmeyer.

Chapter 14: p. 355 (left) U.P.I.; (right) Rod Heinrichs/Grant Heilman. p. 360 (top) Library of Congress; (bottom) Minnesota Historical Society. p. 361 (top) Museum of the City of New York; (bottom left) New York Public Library; (bottom right) Museum of the City of New York. p. 366 (top) F.P.G.; (bottom) Bella C. Landauer Collection, New York Historical Society; p. 367 (top) Culver Pictures; (bottom left) Culver Pictures; (bottom right) Culver Pictures.

Chapter 15: p. 381 (top) Culver Pictures; (bottom left) Culver Pictures; (bottom right) Culver Pictures. p. 386 (left) Collection of Selma and John Appel; (right) Collection of Selma and John Appel. p. 387 (top) Collection of Selma and John Appel; (bottom left) Collection of Selma and John Appel; (bottom right) Collection of Selma and John Appel. p. 396 (top left) Culver Pictures; (top right) Culver Pictures; (bottom) Nebraska State Historical Society. p. 397 (top) The National Archives; (bottom left) Brown Brothers; (bottom right) Culver Pictures. p. 401 Culver Pictures.

Chapter 16: p. 410 (top) from William P. Shriver, *Immigrant Forces;* (bottom) from Peter Roberts, *Anthracite Coal Communities.* p. 411 (top) from Peter Roberts, *Anthracite Coal Communities;* (middle) from Peter Roberts, *Anthracite Coal Communities;* (bottom) from William P. Shriver, *Immigrant Forces.*

Chapter 17: p. 432 U.S. Steel. p. 436 (top left) Carnegie Library of Pittsburgh; (top right) Carnegie Library of Pittsburgh; (bottom) Carnegie Library of Pittsburgh. p. 437 (top) Lewis Hine Photo, James Oppenheimer Papers, Ms. Division, New York Public Library; (bottom left) Carnegie Library of Pittsburgh; (bottom right) Lewis Hine Photo, James Oppenheimer Papers, Ms. Division, New York Public Library. p. 444 Bettmann Archive. p. 447 Shostal Associates.

Chapter 18: p. 457 (top) Stephen Sallay Photos; (bottom) Stephen Sallay Photos. p. 463 Burk Uzzle, Magnum Photos.

Chapter 19: p. 482 (top) Automobile Association Manufacturers Association; (middle) Nebraska State Historical Society; (bottom) Culver Pictures. p. 483 (top left) New York Public Library; (top right) Culver Pictures; (bottom) Culver Pictures. p. 489 (top) New York Public Library; (middle left) Library of Congress; (middle right) New York Public Library; (bottom) New York Public Library. p. 503 Declan Haun, Time-Life Picture Agency.

Chapter 20: p. 520 (top left) Collection of The New Jersey Historical Society, courtesy of American Heritage Publishing Co.; (top right) Library of Congress; (bottom) Collection of the New Jersey Historical Society, Courtesy of American Heritage Publishing Co.

Chapter 21: p. 538 (left) Collection of Selma and John Appel; (middle) Collection of Selma and John Appel; (right) Collection of Selma and John Appel. p. 543 (top) Collection of Selma and John Appel; (bottom left) Collection of Selma and John Appel; (bottom right) Collection of Selma and John Appel. p. 547 (top left) Collection of Selma and John Appel; (top right) Collection of Selma and John Appel; (bottom) The Granger Collection.

Chapter 22: p. 572 (top) Department of Manuscripts and University Archives, Cornell University, Ithaca, New York; (middle) Department of Manuscripts and University Archives, Cornell University, Ithaca, New York; (bottom) Department of Manuscripts and University Archives, Cornell University, Ithaca, New York. p. 573 (top) The Bettmann Archive; (middle) Minnesota Historical Society; (bottom) Minnesota Historical Society. p. 574 (top) Minnesota Historical Society; (middle) Culver Pictures; (bottom) Culver Pictures.

Chapter 23: p. 586 (top left) Wide World Photos; (top right) *The Detroit News;* (bottom) The Photography Collection, University of Washington Library. p. 587 (top) Franklin D. Roosevelt Library; (bottom) The Library of Congress. p. 588 (top) The Library of Congress; (bottom left) The National Archives; (bottom right) The Library of Congress. p. 589 (top) Franklin D. Roosevelt Library; (bottom) Lewis W. Hine Photo, George Eastman House. p. 591 Keystone Photo, Office of War Information. p. 595 U.P.I. p. 600 Culver Pictures. p. 604 (top left) *N.Y. American,* Print from the Collection of the Franklin D. Roosevelt Library; (top right) *New Orleans Times-Picayune,* Print from the Collection of the Franklin D. Roosevelt Library; (bottom left) *N.Y. Herald Tribune,* Print from the Collection of the Franklin D. Roosevelt Library; (bottom right) *Philadelphia Record,* Print from the Collection of the Franklin D. Roosevelt Collection. p. 605 (left) Culver Pictures; (right) *The Washington News,* Print from the Collection of the Franklin D. Roosevelt Library.

Chapter 24: p. 614 (top left) H.R. & W. Photo by Russell Dian; (bottom) H.R. & W. Photo by Russell Dian. p. 615 (left) H.R. & W. Photo by Russell Dian; (right) H.R. & W. Photo by Russell Dian. p. 624 (top) Wide World Photos; (middle) U.S. Army Photograph; (bottom) U.S. Army Photograph. p. 626 (left) Culver Pictures; (right) The Library of Congress. p. 627 Culver Pictures.

Chapter 25: p. 652 (top left) Pierre in *Aux Ecoutes,* Paris; (top right) Die Selt, *Berlin Tarantel,* Press, Berlin; (bottom) *Algemeen Handelsblad,* Amsterdam. p. 657 (top left) Jimmy Scott, *The Topaze,* Santiago, Chile; (top right) Green in the *Providence Journal;* (bottom) Pratt in the *Sacramento Bee.* p. 662 (top) Wide World Photos; (bottom) Bill Stanton, Magnum Photos.

Chapter 26: p. 668 Elliot Erwitt, Magnum Photos. p. 674 U.P.I. p. 678 Will Scott, Shostal Associates. p. 686 (top) Gerhard Gscheidle, Magnum Photos; (bottom) Daniel S. Brody, Editorial Photocolor Archives. p. 687 (top) Daniel S. Brody, Stock, Boston; (bottom) Stock, Boston.

Chapter 27: p. 695 (top) Hiroji Kubota, Magnum Photos; (bottom left) Mimi Forsyth, Monkmeyer; (bottom right) Bill Anderson, Monkmeyer. p. 706 (top left) Burt Glinn, Magnum Photos; (top right) Owen Franken, Stock, Boston; (bottom) Danny Lyon, Magnum Photos. p. 714 Robert Pryor, *New York Times.* p. 715 (top) Szep, *The Boston Globe;* (middle) Auth in *The Philadelphia Inquirer;* (bottom) © 1974 Herblock.